INNOCENT ABROAD

INNOCENT ABROAD

BELGIUM AT THE PARIS PEACE

CONFERENCE OF 1919

BY SALLY MARKS

THE UNIVERSITY OF NORTH CAROLINA PRESS

CHAPEL HILL

Library of Congress Cataloging in Publication Data

Marks, Sally.

Innocent abroad.

Bibliography: p.

Includes index.

1.   European War, 1914–1918—Belgium.   2.   European
War, 1914–1918—Peace.   3.   Paris.   Peace Conference,
1919.   4.   Belgium—Foreign relations—1914–1951.

I.   Title.

D651.B3M36   940.3'493   80-13698

ISBN 0-8078-1451-2

To my mother

and

to the memory of my father

CONTENTS

PREFACE

Few of the countries whose representatives ceremoniously put their signatures to the peace treaty with Germany in the Hall of Mirrors at Versailles on 28 June 1919 were satisfied with it. In fact, dissatisfaction ran rampant not only in Germany but also among the victors, large and small, for a variety of reasons, some more valid than others. Among the dissatisfied was Belgium. At first glance this seems surprising, for one might expect, as Belgian leaders did expect, that Belgium would occupy a privileged position at the Paris Peace Conference. After all, it was the German violation of Belgium that, more than anything else, escalated the 1914 hostilities into a world war. Allied oratory and propaganda had to a high degree focused on "brave little Belgium," and disagreement over her future had been a consistent impediment to a compromise peace. Moreover, the sine qua non of every Allied statement of war aims was the restoration of Belgium.

Belgium was restored in the sense of liberation but not in the broader sense. This was a major cause of dissatisfaction both at the popular level and within the government. Though Belgium gained important concessions on reparations, she had been promised much more by both Germany and the Allies. Another grievance was that she had almost no voice in the peace settlement despite wartime promises of participation. Because invasion of Belgium constituted not only aggression but also violation of international law and because Belgium was the only established European small power with direct interest in the German settlement, her leaders had assumed that her position at the peace conference would be different from that of the other small powers, but by and large it was not. Despite her constant protests, Belgium remained excluded from the decision-making process even on German questions, where the great powers took it for granted that she, alone among the small nations, would contribute substantially to enforcement of their decisions.

Belgium was also dissatisfied because she gained so little from the Versailles treaty. Her expectations had been much larger. Because she

possessed an articulate foreign minister, an abnormal and temporary
national consensus of opinion, a special moral position in regard to the
war, and a strong legal case on some of her claims, Belgian hopes were
high; yet they were soon sharply disappointed. In the territorial respect,
her European acquisitions were miniscule, far less than those of any
other Continental victor except Portugal. There was the added problem
that so few Belgian questions were actually decided by the Versailles
treaty. Moreover, those that were settled showed a disconcerting tendency to come unsettled, returning to complicate not only the difficult relationships within the Western Entente but also its increasingly
problematic relationship to Germany. Among the questions not decided at all were Belgium's future status and her security. The post-
Versailles controversy about these two related issues constituted in a
broader sense one of the crucial debates over the nature of the Western
Entente and its relationship to Germany and over whether there was to
be a west European security system.

It is surprising that Belgium's role at the peace conference and in
broader aspects of the peace settlement has not hitherto been studied
in depth. Several books have examined the activities of various small
powers at Paris in 1919, but Belgium, whom the other small nations
there recognized to be *primus inter pares*, has received scant attention
despite her prominence in wartime oratory, propaganda, and peace
conditions; her undeniably strategic location; and her importance in
prewar trade. In addition to Jonathan Helmreich's recent survey of
Belgian diplomacy from 1830 to 1966, *Belgium and Europe: A Study in
Small Power Diplomacy* (1976), and a number of general histories, there
exist four studies of interwar Belgian diplomacy. Of these, only Baron
Pierre van Zuylen's *Les Mains libres: politique extérieure de la Belgique,
1914–1940* (1950), and Fernand van Langenhove's *La Belgique en quête
de sécurité, 1920–1940* (1969), are based upon access to Belgian Foreign
Ministry papers; but van Langenhove's brief summary largely excludes
the peace conference and van Zuylen was a career diplomatist whose
career much influenced his views. Jane K. Miller's *Belgian Foreign Policy
between Two Wars, 1919–1940* (1951), and Omer de Raeymaeker's *België's internationaal belied, 1919–1939* (1945), are both careful works
written before the Belgian and great-power archives for the era were
opened or the Dutch diplomatic documents became available. Thus

none of these early studies of interwar Belgian diplomacy could examine fully either Belgium's unhappy experiences at the Paris conference of 1919 or her place in the Europe that emerged from the peace settlement. This needs to be done. To omit Belgium is to leave a gap in our comprehension of the postwar power structure, particularly within the Western Entente and in its relations to Germany. Indeed, even the most particular-appearing Belgian problems, such as revision of the 1839 treaties or the fate of Luxemburg, prove to have much broader implications. Thus there are many questions to be posed.

Why, for example, did the small nation that had occupied such a distinctive position in regard to the war and that, as a consequence of this position and the outspoken nature of her foreign minister, had become the de facto leader of the smaller states at Paris fare so poorly in the peace settlement? The answers to this question are diverse and require examination not only of Belgium's diplomacy but also of the policies of the great powers toward that small nation which was of such vital significance to two of them. There are additional questions as well. Why were so many of the decisions made at Paris on Belgian questions the subject of repeated efforts at revision by the great powers? Further, one must not only explore the underlying implications of the Allied debate over Belgian security but also ask why and how this weak little nation, which was so excluded at Paris, suddenly and quickly emerged as the only small-power member of the Western Entente as it grappled with enforcement or nonenforcement of the Versailles treaty. Moreover, did Belgium's prominent but junior role in the Entente matter, and where, in brief, did this little nation fit into the increasingly unstable diplomacy of the early postwar years? Once again, one cannot confine oneself to a study of small-power diplomacy, for the answers involve the attitudes of Britain and France toward Belgium, each other, and Germany.

In my search for the answers to these questions, I have incurred many debts of gratitude over the years. In very summary form, this work constituted the opening chapters of a dissertation on British policy toward Belgium, 1918–23, at the University of London. I am grateful to William N. Medlicott for insisting that I work upon Belgium as well as for many kindnesses in the years since, and to James Joll and

G. A. Grün for giving me the kind of direction I wanted. The libraries of the University of London, the London School of Economics, the Royal Institute of International Affairs, the Anglo-Belgian Club, and the Foreign Office contributed much to my early labors. Needless to say, the British Library was indispensable, both in its printed materials and in its manuscript collections. I am grateful to the India Office Library for access to the Curzon Papers and to the Beaverbrook Library, which granted me early access to the Lloyd George and Bonar Law Papers, now at the House of Lords Record Office. I owe a special vote of thanks to the staff of the Public Record Office in Chancery Lane, in Portugal Street, and at Kew, who all remained unfailingly cheerful in response to my endless requests for more documents.

I am particularly grateful to the late Elizabeth Wiskemann, Hester Marsden-Smedley, and Lady Phipps, who all, in their distinctive ways, did much to help me. Mrs. Ivan Snell and Henry Villiers, daughter and grandson of Sir Francis Villiers; T. F. Lindsay, assistant editor of the *Daily Telegraph*; and the late Hilda Sykes, secretary to the Belgian ambassador, all patiently answered my questions in person or by mail. The University Libraries at Birmingham and Cambridge, along with Churchill College, Cambridge, kindly permitted access to their important collections of private papers, and the Scottish Record Office promptly provided photocopies from the Lothian Papers.

In Brussels, the Royal Library's helpfulness and efficiency always exceeded the call of duty. The College of Europe in Brugge also kindly permitted access to its library. At the Belgian Foreign Ministry Archives, the late Pierre Desneux, H. de Jonghe, M. Dernelle, Mvr. Matton, and Mlle. Marie-Paule Bourdon patiently endured my repeated visits and endless inquiries. At the Archives Générales du Royaume, Carlos Wyffels, Mme. Desmed-Thielmanns, and Mme. Scufflaire did the same. In addition, I must thank the families of Pierre Forthomme, Jules van den Heuvel, Paul Hymans, Henri Jaspar, Pierre Orts, Vicomte Prosper Poullet, and Baron Edouard Rolin-Jaequemyns for allowing access to their papers. Henri Jaspar's son and daughter, M. Jacques Henri-Jaspar and Mme. Marcel Roberte-Jaspar, both granted interviews, and Mme. Roberte-Jaspar generously permitted me to read her father's private letters.

Many other Belgians have contributed to this work by according interviews, answering written inquiries, or assisting with arrangements and access to individuals or archives. At the Belgian Embassy in London Baron de Gerlache de Gomery and Mlle. Fernande van Haelewyck were particularly helpful. In Belgium, my thanks to Henri Bernard of the Royal Military School, Baron van der Bruggen of the Catholic University of Leuven, M. K. Ceule of the Foreign Ministry, Emmanuel Coppieters of the Royal Institute of International Relations, Baron Drion du Chapois, M. N. Erkens of the Foreign Ministry, His Excellency the late Camille Huysmans, de Heer Herman Liebaers, Grand Marshal of the Court, Comte Jacques-Henri Pirenne, Omer de Raeymaeker of Leuven, M. Georges Sion of *La Revue générale belge*, His Excellency M. Paul Struye, M. William Ugeux of the Belgian Institute of Information and Documentation, M. A. Vanbergen and his enthusiastic young assistant at the Belgian National Railway Society, Herman van der Wee of Leuven, and M. Charles d'Ydewalle. Among Belgian historians, I am particularly grateful to Vicomte Terlinden for sharing his memories of the peace conference with me and to Jacques Willequet of the Free University of Brussels and the Foreign Ministry for much generosity and kindness in the days when I was a graduate student and ever since. Among my Belgian friends, I wish to thank Ir. and Mevr. Luc Devogel for introducing me to the Flemish viewpoint and for many kindnesses. No expression of appreciation can repay my debt of gratitude to Comte and Comtesse Michel d'Ursel and to the entire family. I would, however, particularly like to thank young Comtesse Bénédicte and Comte Ghislain for generously initiating me in the mysteries of Dutch abbreviations.

Among Dutch historians, I must thank Ger van Roon of the Free University of Amsterdam for troubling to call the published Dutch diplomatic documents to my attention. I have also profited from long discussions of the Luxemburg question with Christian Calmes of the Grand Duchy. In Paris, the Bibliothèque Nationale was a source of useful material. At the Foreign Ministry Archive, Mme. Enjalran and her archivists, Mme. Guyot, Mlle. Katharine Laurent, and M. Jacques Pilot, were all patient, generous, and helpful, as were several members of the international community of scholars pursuing researches there. The staff of the Archives Nationales kindly cut red tape in affording me rapid access to reparations and Rhineland files. At the Château de

Vincennes, I am grateful to Général Porret, Chef du Service historique, and to the staff of the Archives historiques not only for very prompt service but also for access to the files of the French military attachés in Brussels and London.

In Washington, at the National Archives, Marion M. Johnson and her amiable assistants were unfailingly good-humored, helpful, and patient. Similarly, the staff of the Manuscripts Room at the Library of Congress speeded my labors. I am grateful to the archivists of the House Collection, Sterling Memorial Library, Yale University, not only for access to the collection but also for prompt replies to telephone inquiries, and to the Houghton Library, Harvard University, for access to the Dresel Papers. At the Hoover Institution on War, Revolution, and Peace, Agnes Peterson, Adorjan I. de Galffy, Grace Hawes, and Ronald Bulatoff all treated me royally and enabled me to accomplish much in a short time.

A research fellowship from the American Council of Learned Societies, although primarily devoted to continuing study of the broader topic of the Western Entente, afforded an opportunity to plug some gaps in my research and the rare luxury of time to think. In addition, research in the wider context of the Western Entente has undoubtedly contributed something to this work. Rhode Island College has provided sabbaticals and released time for research that have helped to move this study toward completion, and the Faculty Research Fund has twice assisted with expenses. At the Adams Library, Linda Catino, Barbara Cohen, Frank Notarianni, Beth Perry, Louise Sherby, and Sally Wilson have all far exceeded the call of duty in graciously putting up with me and solving my problems. I am also grateful for much-needed access to the Rockefeller Library at Brown University and to the excellent Reference Service and Business Department at the Providence Public Library for such patience and tenacity in response to my bizarre inquiries.

Paul Helmreich kindly answered my questions about the Treaty of Sèvres; the late Allan Nevins patiently clarified some oddities concerning the Whitlock Papers; and Don Smythe, S.J., drew my attention to important material on Luxemburg in the Pershing Papers. Gerhard L. Weinberg has repeatedly been kindness itself. Among my friends and colleagues in the profession working on the postwar period, I am particularly grateful to Manfred J. Enssle,

Carole Fink, and Stephen A. Schuker for long conversations, sympathetic support, helpful suggestions, and countless instances of generous assistance.

At The University of North Carolina Press, everybody I have encountered has been prompt, professional, and friendly. I am also particularly grateful to the two preliminary readers of my manuscript. The second reader has already been heartily thanked in person, but to my unknown first reader, I must convey my heartfelt gratitude for the most thought-provoking critique I have ever seen. I only hope that I have thought enough.

The long quotation in Chapter 4 from volume 2 of S. W. Roskill's *Hankey, Man of Secrets*, is reprinted by permission of Captain Roskill, Collins Publishers, London, and the United States Naval Institute, Annapolis, Maryland. Quotations from Crown-copyright records at the Public Record Office appear by permission of the controller of H. M. Stationery Office. Part of the material concerning Luxemburg in Chapters 1, 5, and 8 appeared originally in the *Revue belge d'histoire contemporaine* in 1970 as an article entitled "The Luxemburg Question at the Paris Peace Conference and After." This material is reproduced by kind permission of Jan Craeybeckx, Director of the *Revue*.

Finally, a note on usage: for Belgian place names where there exists an English form different from either French or Flemish versions, the English form is used. For the rest, the local language is followed, although, at the first citation of Flemish place names, the French version is also provided because it is generally better known to English-language readers. When a river traverses both Dutch- and French-speaking areas, the French form is used, as it is more common in English. Prefixes are included with or omitted from the names of individuals according to national usage. Hence de Gaiffier, van Karnebeek, and Margerie. In the bibliography and index, however, names are not alphabetized according to prefixes.

ABBREVIATIONS

A	Série A, Conférence de la Paix, 1914–31 (Archive, France, Ministère des Affaires Etrangères, Paris)
AA	Auswärtiges Amt
ACNP	Files of American Commission to Negotiate Peace (National Archives, Washington, D.C.)
AGR	Archives Générales du Royaume, Brussels
AJ⁵	Délégation française à la Commission des Réparations (Archives Nationales, Paris)
AJ⁹	Haute Commission interalliée des Territoires Rhénans; Haut Commissariat français dans les provinces du Rhin (Archives Nationales, Paris)
Alle	Allemagne
AN	Archives Nationales, Paris
B–	Classement B files (Archive, Ministère des Affaires Etrangères, Brussels)
Belg.	Belgique
BL	British Library, London
BMAE	Belgique, Ministère des Affaires Etrangères, archive, Brussels
B Micro	Belgium, Political Correspondence, General and Bound (microfilm, Library, National Archives, Washington, D.C.)
BUL	Birmingham University Library
C.A.	Conference of Ambassadors
CAB	Cabinet files (Public Record Office, London)
CC	Churchill College, Cambridge, archive
C.I.D.	Committee of Imperial Defence
CPC	Correspondance politique et commerciale (Archive, Ministère des Affaires Etrangères, Paris)
CUL	Cambridge University Library

DB	Délégation Belge files (BMAE)
DBFP	Great Britain, Foreign Office, *Documents on British Foreign Policy, 1919–1939.* All citations to 1st ser. unless otherwise specified.
DD	France, *Documents diplomatiques*
DDB	Belgique, *Documents diplomatiques belges, 1920–1940,* 5 vols.
DuB	Nederland, *Bescheiden betreffende de buitenlandse politiek van Nederland, 1848–1919: Derde Periode, 1899–1919,* 8 vols. in 10
DuD	Nederland, *Documenten betreffende de buitenlandse politiek van Nederland, 1919–1945: Periode A, 1919–1930*
FMAE	France, Ministère des Affaires Etrangères, archive, Paris
F.O.	Foreign Office files (Public Record Office, London)
FR	France
FRUS	United States, Department of State, *Papers Relating to the Foreign Relations of the United States*
FRUS PPC	FRUS, *The Paris Peace Conference, 1919,* 13 vols.
GB	Grande-Bretagne
GFM	German Foreign Ministry (microprint, Foreign Office Library, London)
Guerre	Sous-Série Guerre, FMAE
HI	Hoover Institution on War, Revolution, and Peace, Stanford, Calif.
HL	House of Lords Record Office, London
Ind	Classement Indépendance, Neutralité, Défense militaire de la Belgique, Garantie des Puissances, BMAE
Inquiry	Records of the Inquiry (National Archives, Washington, D.C.)
IOL	India Office Library, London
LC	Library of Congress, Washington, D.C.
Lux	Luxembourg
NA	National Archives, Washington, D.C.
NS	Nouvelle Série, FMAE

PB	Pays-Bas
P.I.D.	Political Intelligence Department, Foreign Office
PRO	Public Record Office, London
RC	Reparation Commission
Revision	Belgique, Ministère des Affaires Etrangères, *Documents diplomatiques relatifs à la revision des traités de 1839*
R.G.P.	Nederland, Rijks Geschiedkundige Publicatiën, Grote Serie (DuB and DuD)
SD	United States, Department of State decimal file, NA
SML	Sterling Memorial Library, Yale University, New Haven, Conn.
SRO	Scottish Record Office, Edinburgh
Vin	France, Service Historique de l'Armée, Château de Vincennes, Vincennes
W.O.	Great Britain, War Office
Y	Série Y, Internationale, 1918–40, FMAE
Z	Série Z, Europe, 1918–29, FMAE

INNOCENT ABROAD

NORTH SEA

Rhine Riv
Ro

Hollandsche Diep

East Scheldt

Moerdij

WALCHEREN

West Scheldt

Flushing

SOUTH
BEVELAND

Hansweert

Wielingen

Blankenberge

FLEMISH

Zeebrugge

Terneuzen

ZEELAND

Ostend

Brugge

Zelzate

Ant

Nieuwpoort

De Panne

Ghent

River

Dunkerque

River

Brussels

Ijzer

Ieper

Scheldt

BELGIUM

FRANCE

Legend
Railways ▩▩▩▩▩▩▩▩
Canals ··········
Enclave ◉

echt

Meuse (Maas) River

Cleves

Rhine River

Wesel

NETHERLANDS

reda

Tilbury

NORTH
BRABANT

Baarle-Hertog

•Geldern

GERMANY

NORTH

LIMBURG

Roermond

Mönchen-
Gladbach

Düsseldorf

RUHR

LOWER

Cologne

LIMBURG

Maastricht

en

Aachen

MORESNET

Liège

Eupen

EUPEN

RHINELAND

Verviers

Monschau

River

Malmedy

MALMÉDY

St·Vith

Gerolstein

Bastogne•

LUXEM-
BURG

River

Trier

Sedan

Moselle

Luxemburg

Longwy

SAAR

Adjoining Territories

ONE

PRELUDE

HISTORICAL ORIGINS

When the diplomatists, professors, and politicians converged on Paris to make peace after World War I, the spotlight naturally focused upon the ranking representatives of the five great victor powers. It quickly became evident, however, that first in prominence among the twenty-two other states present was a small country that had never even declared war on Germany. Belgium, soon to be the reluctant and unofficial spokesman of the smaller nations, had throughout the war been staunchly with the Allied and Associated Powers but never of them. At the firm insistence of her king, she had stood squarely upon her unique legal status, had conducted her own military operations on Belgian soil only, and had formulated her own strictly limited official war aims separated from the broader pronouncement of the Allied leaders.

Along with the crucial importance of her geographic location and the outspoken nature of her foreign minister, it was the special legal status of Belgium and the resulting legal, moral, and military character of the war in that country which pushed Belgium into prominence at the Paris Peace Conference. The whole western world was familiar with the tale of the famous "scrap of paper" and with the carefully nurtured picture of King Albert fighting grimly on with the remnants of his tattered army in "the little corner never conquered." Thanks to German actions and announcements regarding the scrap of paper, the Belgian wartime public stance was not only famous but morally and legally impeccable. As Anglo-Saxon publicists turned the war in part into a crusade for the rights of small nations, the *roi-chevalier* in Flanders field became the shining symbol of that crusade.

Although the tale of the scrap of paper was widely publicized, few outside the chancelleries of Europe were aware of the contents of this document or, more accurately, set of documents, or of the substantial Belgian dissatisfaction with them. The treaties of 1839 had in some respects served Belgium well, and some of her strongest claims at the peace conference were based upon them. But one of her most important war aims, beyond the obvious one of liberation, was extensive revision of the 1839 treaties. As Belgian diplomatists repeatedly pointed out, these treaties had been imposed upon Belgium by the great powers, notably Britain, in response to assumptions and conditions that were no longer valid. In Belgian eyes, the German attack in 1914 had been the last dramatic proof that the treaties were obsolete and unworkable. Thus, Belgium turned to Britain and France, the two remaining powers among those who had created her, with a demand that they undo their work of 1815, 1831, and 1839, and devise a more satisfactory arrangement.

The status of Belgium derived in part from the work of the Congress of Vienna, which, as the Belgians hopefully noted, was now widely condemned by prominent idealists on both sides of the Atlantic. The Final Act of Vienna of 9 June 1815 had merged the two Low Countries into a United Kingdom of the Netherlands to which was attached the newly created Grand Duchy of Luxemburg as a personal possession of King William I. This arrangement arose from the desire of the victorious coalition to build a strong military barrier against France, as also did the transfer to Rhenish Prussia of several Dutch and Belgian border districts.

The new enlarged Dutch kingdom lasted only until the Belgian revolution of August 1830, in which all parts of pre–World War I Belgium, Luxemburg, and the province of Limburg participated. The revolution led to a series of military encounters between the Dutch and the Belgians. As France seemed eager to help the Belgians, and other states, especially Britain, suspected ulterior motives behind the altruism of the newly installed Louis Philippe, great-power intervention came rapidly. Intense diplomatic activity in London in 1831 among representatives of the great powers quickly produced draft treaties generous to the Belgian rebels, but, as the fortunes of war favored the Dutch while British suspicions of France grew, the treaties were revised to the advantage of Holland. The militarily helpless Belgians reluctantly accepted the new drafts but the Dutch did not, and so from 1830 until 1839 both Limburg and Luxemburg remained in all respects part of the precarious new Belgian state. When in 1839 the second set of treaties was reimposed upon Belgium after eventual Dutch acceptance, there were loud cries from the detached territories, especially Luxemburg, and all the considerable prestige of the first king of the Belgians was required to induce his bitter subjects to accept what they could not fight. Luxemburg became their Alsace-Lorraine and after 1871 they often referred to it as such.

The treaties of 19 April 1839,[1] which Belgium accepted so reluctantly, consisted of three related documents, all heavily influenced by British and Continental fear of revived French imperialism. On the unfounded assumption that Belgium would inevitably become a French satellite, she was deliberately made small, weak, and defenseless; and as much of the 1815 barrier as possible was preserved. The three treaties achieving this effect—one between Belgium and Holland; a second between Belgium and the five powers of France, Great Britain, Prussia, Russia, and Austria; and a third between Holland and the five powers—were closely interrelated and formed one integral whole.

By the territorial terms of these treaties, much of Luxemburg, including most of the French-speaking districts, was incorporated into Belgium, but the remaining smaller portion reverted to its former status as a personal possession of the Dutch king, thus detaching from Belgium and returning to the anti-French Netherlands (and in effect to Prussia, which had a garrison there) the strong fortified position of Luxemburg City. Belgium retained western Limburg, which became the Belgian province of that name, but both north and south Limburg reverted to King William I of the Netherlands as a personal possession eventually incorporated into Holland as the province of Limburg in 1867. Dutch retention of lower Limburg, a narrow tongue of land at some points only five miles wide, which dipped southward for thirty-five miles between the Prussian Rhineland and Belgium, reduced the Belgo-Prussian border to a mere fifty miles but also rendered Belgium defenseless against any invasion from the east, for the Netherlands continued to control the right bank of the Meuse (Maas) River throughout the province of Limburg and both banks at the key point of Maastricht. Dutch possession of southern Limburg and the truncated Grand Duchy of Luxemburg, both of which were members of the German Confedera-

1. For texts, see Great Britain, Foreign Office, *British and Foreign State Papers*, 27:990–1002.

tion, was equally disadvantageous to Belgium from the economic point of view, as Belgian use of the Meuse and traffic to Germany were obstructed, whereas Luxemburg was soon to form the natural rail route from Antwerp to Strasbourg, Switzerland, and Italy.

In Belgian eyes, Dutch retention after 1839 of Flemish Zeeland (Zealand Flandres or Zeeuws-Vlaanderen, also known as Dutch Flanders) was equally unsatisfactory from both the military and the economic points of view. This sparsely settled district, which France had annexed in 1795, consisted of the territory south of the Scheldt River and north of the eventual Belgian border. It comprised the southernmost portion of the Dutch province of Zeeland, entirely cut off from the remainder of the province and the rest of the Netherlands by the Scheldt. Although Flemish Zeeland had taken no part in the Belgian revolution and at no time thereafter had formed part of the new kingdom, Belgian leaders tried unsuccessfully to obtain it for economic and military reasons. If Holland held both banks of the Scheldt, Antwerp would have no commercial access to the sea except through forty miles of indisputably Dutch waters, Ghent would suffer a similar handicap, and either Belgian or other, presumably British, naval relief to Antwerp in wartime would be rendered impossible. However, the powers decreed that Flemish Zeeland remain Dutch. Although the Belgians complained that their country had been multilated at all three corners of the triangle that they deemed to form their national territory, and although they particularly resented the fact that all three decisions redounded to the benefit of the Dutch against whom they had rebelled, they were powerless to reverse these rulings.

Because what remained to Belgium was clearly indefensible against attack and because Britain feared that she might be tempted to participate in future French efforts at aggrandizement, a condition of perpetual neutrality was imposed upon her. As a consequence, Belgium became the only country aside from Switzerland then in a state of permanent, formally recognized neutrality. She was further obligated to uphold and defend this neutrality against all comers. To render this obligation feasible, the five major powers committed themselves individually and collectively to the maintenance of the independence, territorial integrity, and neutrality of Belgium, a commitment that the North German Confederation (and thus, by universally accepted implication, the German Empire) formally assumed from Prussia in July 1870.[2] In Britain there was debate for some years about whether the wording of the treaties made the guarantees both individual and collective, that is, whether if one guarantor violated the guarantee, it lapsed altogether, or whether the other guarantors remained committed to the defense of Belgium against the delinquent. During the diplomatic crisis accompanying the Franco-Prussian War of 1870, however, common sense asserted itself, along with British national interest, and it was recognized that unless the guarantee was individual as well as collective, it would be worthless and Belgium could easily cease to exist. Britain not only signed confirmatory treaties in August 1870 with France and the North German Confederation to defend Belgium against attack from either power but also declared in Parliament that the British government rejected the notion that Britain was not bound to maintain and actively uphold the existing status of Belgium.[3] It was upon this interpretation that the British government acted in August 1914, after some hesitation,[4] in response to the German invasion of Belgium, as also did the French government, whose interpretation of the guarantee, so vital to French security, had never been in dispute.

The framers of the 1839 treaties recognized that the Dutch, possessing both banks of the Scheldt River, could easily revive the past and destroy both Antwerp and the Belgian economy by closing the Scheldt to navigation, as they had done between 1609 and 1792 and again in 1830, unless they were formally prevented from doing so. The Belgo-Dutch treaty therefore consisted largely of restrictions imposed by the great powers to prevent such an occurrence. While Antwerp was confined to a limited role as a purely commercial port and Belgian warships were forbidden the Scheldt, articles 108 through 117 of the Final Act of Vienna of 1815, requiring free commercial transit on international rivers, were carefully invoked. The Netherlands was authorized to levy

2. Forthomme to Johannesburg *Star*, 10 Apr. 1918 (quoting Bismarck letter of 22 July 1870), BMAE Ind/1918; Charles de Visscher, *Belgium's Case*, p. 83.

3. Great Britain, Foreign Office, *British and Foreign State Papers*, 60:10–17; Fernand van Langenhove, *Le Dossier diplomatique de la question belge*, pp. 4–6; van der Essen note, 12 Sept. 1917, BMAE Ind/1917.

4. Keith Robbins, *Sir Edward Grey*, p. 297; Asquith to George V, 30 July 1914, Crewe to George V, 2 Aug. 1914, PRO, CAB 41/35.

tolls on ships using the Scheldt but restricted in their amount. Most technical matters concerning commercial use of the Scheldt, such as dredging and pilotage, were to be administered by a joint Belgo-Dutch commission, and the Dutch were committed to maintenance of the channel in their part of the river. Similar arrangements were made for the Ghent-Terneuzen canal, as this waterway, designed to give Ghent access to the Scheldt and thus to the sea, inevitably crossed the Dutch territory of Flemish Zeeland en route to the great river.

These economic arrangements proved in practice to be as displeasing to Belgium as the territorial decisions.[5] While Belgian politicians continued to eye Flemish Zeeland, Limburg, and Luxemburg—refusing to recognize the thoroughly Dutch character of Flemish Zeeland, the gradual dissipation of active pro-Belgian sentiment in southern Limburg, and the growing enjoyment of semiindependence in Luxemburg—Belgian administrators, with considerably more justification, developed an increasing sense of frustration over the Scheldt regime. The Dutch, seeing no reason to develop Antwerp at the expense of Rotterdam, engaged in delay and obstruction. They made no effort to maintain the Scheldt channel and would only permit the Belgian government to do so in Dutch waters under crippling restrictions and upon condition, contrary to the Belgo-Dutch treaty, that Belgium pay the costs. The Dutch also adhered rigorously to the literal wording of the treaty regarding maintenance of the channel and argued that they had no obligation either to improve it or to countenance Belgian improvements, although the advent of larger steamships made a deeper channel imperative. In fact, Dutch rhetoric was more rigorous than Dutch practice and some improvements were permitted at Belgian expense, but the systems of pilotage, lighting, and buoyage remained obsolete and there were endless difficulties and delays over dredging. After long negotia-

5. For the history of Belgium, 1839–1914, there are three recent surveys: Georges-H. Dumont, *Histoire de la Belgique*; Frank E. Huggett, *Modern Belgium*; and Vernon Mallinson, *Belgium*. More detailed recent studies include Jonathan C. Helmreich, *Belgium and Europe*; E. H. Kossmann, *The Low Countries, 1780–1940*; and the long introductory chapter of Michael F. Palo, "The Diplomacy of Belgian War Aims during the First World War." Of the numerous earlier studies, the most useful are Henri Pirenne, *Histoire de Belgique*; Jan-Albert Goris, ed., *Belgium*; Amry Vandenbosch, *Dutch Foreign Policy since 1815*; and the British Admiralty Naval Intelligence Division Handbooks, *A Manual of Belgium and the Adjoining Territories, Belgium, Luxemburg*, and *Netherlands*.

tion, in 1863 Belgium succeeded, with the financial assistance of maritime nations using the Scheldt, in purchasing the Dutch right to levy tolls, which the Belgian government had been paying itself in order to foster the development of Antwerp. But ugly and frequent squabbles continued about all technical matters, none of which could be improved without Dutch consent. Similar difficulties developed over the Ghent-Terneuzen canal, and although technical agreements on specific problems regarding the two waterways were achieved from time to time, the situation remained fundamentally unsatisfactory to Belgium. Excessive Dutch customs delays for river and canal traffic on the Meuse at Maastricht, to the extent that traversing the five Dutch miles of the canal always required at least three days and sometimes a month, along with Dutch obstruction of a projected Rhine-Meuse canal, only intensified Belgian feeling.

The only important aspect of the 1839 treaties that was not a major issue in Belgium before World War I was the neutrality clause and its accompanying guarantee. This arrangement did seem to be working satisfactorily. It not only saved Belgium a good deal of military expense but also brought her unscathed through both the Luxemburg crisis of 1867, which generated Europe's third state in a condition of internationally recognized neutrality, and the Franco-Prussian War of 1870. But the distinctive international status of Belgium had a profound effect upon the mentality of the Belgian people. Although the new nation developed a competent diplomatic service, the political leadership in Brussels and the population in general remained almost entirely outside the mainstream of European international politics. One purpose of the compulsory neutrality and concomitant great-power guarantee had been to isolate and even more to insulate a recognized danger point, the crossroads of Europe that historically had so often been a battleground, and to insure that the major powers would not again do battle over it. In one sense, until 1914 this arrangement succeeded only too well. Although over the years Belgium became a great commercial artery, the guarantee turned the crossroads of Europe into an unfrequented country lane so far as European diplomacy was concerned. Belgium, isolated and protected, remained outside the tensions and quarrels of the Continent; as time passed, her population became increasingly indifferent to them and her interests became parochial. And as neutrality and the great-power guarantee seemed to have proved their effectiveness after 1870, both people and government tended to assume that they would always remain effective.

In the years after 1839, Belgium created her institutions and industrialized her country, primarily Wallonia. She proudly sailed through the tumultuous years of 1848 and 1849 without major upheaval and continued serenely on her course. After the crises of 1867 over Luxemburg and of 1870 over the Franco-Prussian War appeared to have demonstrated the efficacy of the great-power guarantee, her attention turned inward and industrial growth continued. In the late nineteenth century, the Liberal and Catholic parties disputed both power and religious instruction in the schools while the non-Marxist and intensely pragmatic Belgian Socialist party, formally created out of Flemish and Bruxellois components in 1877, gathered strength, itself entered the entrepreneurial system to provide directly for the needs of the working class, and began to press for both social and political reforms, notably universal manhood suffrage and later the end of plural voting. In the meantime, though French-speaking Walloons dominated both government and society, the Flemish consciousness and desire for equality developed, along with a belated industrialization in Flanders.

As the century drew toward a close, the Belgian people and their leaders continued to focus upon these domestic concerns while Belgian businessmen, actively encouraged and supported by King Léopold II, moved out into the world and began to invest heavily abroad. As Antwerp prospered greatly despite continuing restriction, becoming one of the major ports of the world, Belgium itself became the world's fifth ranking trading nation, competing actively on world markets with the great powers. Belgian firms constructed the railways of China, the tramways of Kiev, and the Paris Métro. They invested in Russian oil, dominated Russia's glass industry, built Egyptian suburbs, and made fortunes all over the world. With these developments and the discovery of important new coalfields in Flemish-speaking areas, Belgian national wealth rapidly increased by two-thirds. In these halcyon years, Belgian diplomacy concerned itself almost entirely with the ever-expanding Belgian commercial interests and remained largely aloof from the diplomatic concerns of power politics.

One almost inevitable concomitant of a long period of peace and prosperity, together with Belgium's enforced neutrality, was a progressive lowering of the quality of the Belgian army. Though it was deemed to be of good caliber in 1839, its state of preparedness and level of competence declined as the century wore on and there was no need for its use. As Belgium was both neutral and guaranteed, the public saw little need for expensive appropriations to maintain the country's defenses, despite Belgium's 1839 treaty commitment to defend her neutrality. Ambitious young men of outstanding quality were rarely attracted to service in an army that was unlikely ever to fight. The national lack of enthusiasm for matters military culminated in 1902 in a decision to entrust the army largely to volunteers. As they did not enroll in sufficient numbers, the old system of conscription by lot, all too susceptible to the purchase of substitutes, continued in reduced degree.

In the first years of the twentieth century, economic expansion continued apace, fueled in part by such intensive German investment in the country that Belgium came to be viewed in some quarters as a German economic satellite, but otherwise Belgium became a less placid place to be. The long painful crisis over the Congo, set off by attacks in Britain against Léopold II's undoubted malpractices there, culminated in the Parliament's decision to wrench the colony away from Léopold, and so Belgium became a reluctant colonial power on 15 November 1908. Though France and Germany recognized Belgium's acquisition at once, Britain hesitated in deference to E. D. Morel's loudly expressed conviction that the Congo should be transferred to Germany and thus prolonged a deterioration in Anglo-Belgian relations already in progress for some years as a consequence of the Congo question. Only in 1913, when it had become clear beyond doubt that the Belgian government's reform of Léopold's abuses in the Congo was both thorough and permanent, did Britain concede formal recognition of Belgium's immensely valuable colony.

More importantly, relations with Britain and the entire European power balance concerning Belgium were affected by the Entente Cordiale of 1904. Hitherto, Belgians had viewed Britain as the primary barrier to any possible French designs on their country, and they now wondered whether this barrier had been removed. Furthermore, though the population in general saw no reason to distrust Germany, the possibility arose that, because Britain could henceforth probably be expected to support France in any Franco-German war, Germany would now have much less reason to avoid violation of Belgium in the course of such a war. Indeed, the Schlieffen Plan, drawn up between 1904 and 1906, proceeded on this premise, calling for a massive invasion of Belgium as the most effective military route into France. Although Belgian leaders were not privy to German military planning, the logic of the situation was obvious. When Léopold II visited Wilhelm II on 28 January 1904 and the irrepressible kaiser informed him not only that a Franco-German war was probably imminent but also that Belgium must join on Germany's side, the old king took alarm.[6] The Entente Cordiale in April and the kaiser's conduct in the Moroccan crisis of 1905 only deepened his alarm and that of the government.

The British had also considered the logic of the situation and in 1906 initiated military talks with the Belgian government. The Barnardiston-Ducarne conversations between the British military attaché in Brussels and the chief of the Belgian General Staff have been the subject of considerable controversy, particularly because, after the seizure of Belgian Foreign Ministry files during World War I, the Germans tried to utilize the captured dossiers to prove that Belgium had violated her own neutrality by these talks. Though Maj. Gen. G. E. V. Ducarne did provide Lt. Col. Nathaniel W. Barnardiston with information concerning Belgian defensive plans, he stressed on government orders that the talks were nonbinding, that British troops could not in any circumstances enter Belgium until after a German violation of her neutrality, and that Belgium would defend herself against attack from any direction. Wartime German propagandists found little to work with beyond a file folder on which a Belgian official had erroneously scribbled "Conventions anglo-belges." Of this the Germans made the most but there were in fact no conventions, only conversations. When the British made new overtures in 1912, they succeeded only in horrifying the Belgian government by a hint, later disavowed, that they might, if need be, land troops without Belgian invitation.[7]

6. Palo, "Belgian War Aims," p. 72.

7. Emile Waxweiler, *La Belgique neutre et loyale*, pp. 175–84. The file folder is in BMAE Ind/15.

The increasing signs that Belgium might actually have to defend herself lent urgency to the task of repairing the country's enfeebled military defenses. As the population at large, quite unaware of the dangers that threatened, remained intensely allergic to both military expenditure and military service, this was excruciatingly difficult to accomplish. Nonetheless, strengthening of the network of fortifications around Antwerp, long considered the national redoubt, began in 1906. There ensued a protracted struggle to pass a new military bill, providing for conscription of one son from each family for a fifteen-month term of service. Léopold thankfully signed it into law on his deathbed in December 1909. His successor, Albert I, had been fully advised by his uncle of the dangers ahead and continued on the same course. As a consequence, the cabinet of Count Charles de Broqueville finally achieved another military reform in the summer of 1913, providing for sharply increased military expenditures and for general conscription on terms of fifteen months for infantry and twenty-four months for cavalry with a thirteen-year reserve obligation.[8] Though these latter reforms had not taken full effect by August of 1914, the royal and governmental efforts over the previous decade did contribute to a Belgian resistance in 1914 that considerably exceeded what any of the major powers had thought possible. The wisdom of the course chosen was confirmed to Albert during a state visit to Berlin in November 1913 when the kaiser, in another burst of probably calculated indiscretion, confided Germany's intent to march on France, apparently in hopes of obtaining Belgian cooperation. Albert not only informed his government but also arranged that a discreet report of the conversation be passed to President Raymond Poincaré of France.[9]

While the storm clouds gathered around a Belgian citizenry largely oblivious to the impending danger, the Belgian government clung firmly and almost obsessively to its prescribed neutrality. Although some Foreign Ministry officials argued that a minor German violation of the southern portion of Belgian Luxemburg en route to France need not entail a full-scale defense, this view never received official sanction and

8. Villiers to Grey, 30 Jan. 1914, no. 10 (Annual Report, 1913), PRO, F.O. 371/1908.
9. Baron Napoléon Eugène Beyens, *Deux années à Berlin*, 2:39–50; Baron Napoléon Eugène Beyens, "Albert Ier chez Guillaume II," pp. 824–30.

the Schlieffen Plan rendered it nothing more than a historical curiosity. In general, the Belgian government announced frequently to its great-power neighbors that it would defend the country against violation from any direction, a declaration that the British and French took more seriously than the Germans did. Further, in their determination to remain outside any coming conflict if humanly possible, Belgian diplomatists made it amply clear that they would not welcome friendly assistance until actual invasion had occurred and they themselves had requested aid from guarantor powers, an attitude that was punctiliously maintained until after German border crossings had been confirmed on 4 August 1914.

Until that shattering event, neutrality and its great-power guarantee had been Belgium's anchor, her only real protection as a small country with three mighty neighbors, and certainly her only hope of passing unscathed through the storms ahead. Not surprisingly, while reinforcing Belgium's military strength as rapidly as the political climate would allow, Belgian leaders clung tenaciously, almost fanatically, to the only safety they had or could ever have under the terms of the 1839 treaties, hoping against hope not only through the tensions of the last prewar decade but also through the July crisis of 1914. On 4 August 1914, the German army destroyed their illusions, at least in regard to their eastern neighbor. That Germany's march had permanently destroyed the prewar Belgium and the prewar Europe as well was not immediately clear either to Belgium or to most of her defenders.

THE WARTIME DILEMMA

August 1914 was self-evidently a tragic time for Belgium but, in a strange sense, it was also a period of great exhilaration. Suddenly this quiet, undramatic little country was the center of the world's attention and commanded front-page headlines everywhere. As the Belgian army's stubborn resistance astonished the Germans and damaged their timetable, with General Gérard Leman holding out at surprising length and in heroic style in the fortified positions at Liège, the press of the western world was filled with a chorus of tributes to "brave little Belgium" and "gallant little Belgium." The leaders of the Entente were equally lavish in praise, the French in particular assuring Belgian representatives that they would never forget France's debt of gratitude,[10] while both British and French statesmen frequently declared publicly that their nations would fight on until Belgium was not only fully restored in her independence and territorial integrity but also fully indemnified for her ordeal and the damage it entailed.[11] As the war turned into a struggle between two power blocs for supremacy and then survival, Allied leaders needed a cause to rally public opinion to the war effort. For want of anything else of high moral tone, Belgium became the cause, along with the sanctity of treaties and the rights of small nations, again symbolized by Belgium and her warrior-king in Flanders field. As a consequence, in the early months of the war an extraordinary amount of rhetoric was concentrated upon Belgium.

Unfortunately, those responsible for the conduct of Belgian foreign policy became addicted to this heady diet of praise and glory. They reveled in the national heroism and expected appreciation at regular intervals. After November 1914, when what then remained of the Belgian army's front settled into relative quiescence, the tide of war shifted elsewhere and there were other battles, occasional victories, and other tragic, heroic defenses for Allied orators to celebrate. Naturally, British and French oratory gradually began to dwell less lengthily on "gallant little Belgium." Officials at the Belgian Foreign Ministry noticed this tendency and fretted, less in terms of a deteriorating Belgian bargaining position for a peace settlement ahead as the war lengthened and encompassed more countries than out of national amourpropre. If a French cabinet minister was so careless as to make a speech on the Allied war effort without mentioning Belgium's contribution, a prompt inquiry would be dispatched to the Quai d'Orsay. As a consequence, British and French leaders became practised at inserting brief

10. For example, Guillaume to Davignon, 27 Sept. 1914, no. 9603 / 2976, BMAE FR/ 1914; de Gaiffier to Beyens, 12 Oct. 1916, no. 7457/2913, FR/1916; de Gaiffier to Hymans, n.d. [early Sept. 1917], no. 5334/2433, FR/1917/I.

11. For example, Asquith on 9 Nov. 1914: "We shall never sheathe the sword, which we have not lightly drawn, until Belgium recovers in full measure all, and more than all, which she has sacrificed." Paul Guinn, *British Strategy and Politics, 1914 to 1918,* p. 122.

tributes to Belgian gallantry in every speech but, as the war wore on, these became merely routine and pro forma, a fact that Belgian leaders rarely recognized.

Unfortunately as well, Belgian officials and cabinet ministers tended to believe Allied promises implicitly. When the British and French said that they would never forget, the Belgian leaders took such statements as a commitment. As novices in the harsh world of major-power rivalries, they did not understand that in international politics, "never" can be an extraordinarily brief time indeed. When Allied cabinet members declared that Belgium must be reimbursed to the last farthing, Belgian officials assumed that they meant what they said, which they probably did in 1914. However, after four years of bloodshed, devastation, economic exhaustion, and skyrocketing debts, British and French perspectives altered considerably, and Belgian leaders never fully recognized this shift. They also tended to confuse the lavish Allied oratory directed toward them with formal written commitments. Indeed, in August and September of 1917, during one of the intermittent Belgian efforts to plan for the peace settlement to come, they carefully collected every declaration that had been made by British and French leaders about Belgium's future since the war had begun. Although the sheer quantity was impressive, most of the statements were oratorical rhetoric, and they constituted a pathetic armory to take into the diplomatic power struggle that lay ahead at the end of the war.[12]

Even in the early weeks of Belgium's ordeal, officials at her Foreign Ministry did not fail to contemplate a future peace settlement. Indeed, the first planning document was prepared on 15 September 1914[13] while the Belgian government was still at Antwerp, where it had moved when Brussels became indefensible. Though this document considered the possibility of a German victory, which would probably mean the destruction of Belgium, or a negotiated peace that would bring Belgium no new benefits, it focused on the prospect of an Allied victory and on what Belgium might hope to gain. While clearly delineating most of

12. De Broqueville to de Gaiffier et al., 24 Aug. 1917, no. 1609, de Gaiffier to de Broqueville, n.d. [early Sept. 1917], no. 5334/2433, BMAE FR/1917/I; Hymans to de Broqueville, 5 Sept. 1917, no. 8034/1313, BMAE GB/1917/II. The report from London ran to sixty-six typed pages.

13. De Bassompierre memo, 15 Sept. 1914, BMAE B–1.

Belgium's primary concerns, the Direction Politique of the ministry, which wrote the memorandum, tended to be cautious. It took full reparation for granted and displayed a frank interest in Luxemburg. The memorandum endorsed annexation of the Walloon canton of Malmédy but warned against excessive demands on Germany. Even though a senior Dutch diplomatist in London had indicated that the Netherlands might be willing to cede Limburg and Flemish Zeeland in return for German territory, and French diplomatists were already encouraging such ideas,[14] the Direction Politique advised caution in regard to any claims on Holland, for her future role in the war was as yet unclear and good relations were important. In some eventualities, perhaps the problems of the Scheldt and Limburg could be solved to Belgian satisfaction by compensating Holland with German territory. If not, the risk of serious damage to Belgo-Dutch relations had to be considered before any decisions were made.

This document was only the first of many and merely the opening phase of a long debate. On the whole, the Belgian government had little time for such debate in the first months of the war. It was too distracted by the pressures of coping with the national defense and the growing number of refugees, dealing with Allied assistance and Allied orders, some of which were incompatible with Belgian defense plans and capabilities, and of moving first to Antwerp and then to Le Havre. In addition, there were two immediate problems to occupy the harried professional diplomatists. One was to define the status of the Belgian Congo and the other was to fix the legal status of Belgium itself in regard to the war.

The Belgian government made an immediate unsuccessful effort to preserve the neutrality of the entire Congo basin under the provisions of the Treaty of Berlin of 1885, and then to maintain the neutrality of the Belgian Congo alone. But the great powers showed little inclination to neutralize the entire basin, which would have required the agreement of Germany, France, and Britain, and Britain and France wished to use the facilities of the Belgian Congo to their own military ends. Further, in late August and early September 1914 forces from German East Africa committed a series of minor but clearly hostile acts. In the

14. Palo, "Belgian War Aims," pp. 255–56.

circumstances, the effort to hold the Congo aloof from the fray was abandoned,[15] and, as the war progressed, the Congo became increasingly involved, playing a role of some consequence in the East African campaigns of 1916.

The question of Belgium's exact legal status in relation to the war was more difficult to define. Was she a belligerent or was she not? Belgium had not declared war on any power but she indubitably was fighting with all her strength, if only in self defense and in fulfillment of her distinctive treaty obligation to defend her neutrality. The German ultimatum of 2 August 1914 indicated clearly that rejection of German demands would cause Belgium to become an enemy of the Reich and thus constituted a conditional declaration of war. Stressing that Belgium had committed no hostile acts, the Foreign Ministry contemplated the situation at their temporary Antwerp quarters. While they did so, Austria-Hungary formally declared war on Belgium on 28 August. By mid-September the Belgian government, anxious not only to limit Belgium's role and to preserve the benefits potentially accruing to her under her special status but also to gain the rights arising from legal belligerency, concluded that Belgium was indeed a belligerent but in no way a member of the Entente alliance. With this last view, the Allies fully agreed. Belgium was neither asked to participate in nor informed in advance about the Anglo-French-Russian Declaration of London on 5 September 1914, pledging not to conclude a separate peace. Belgian inquiries brought the response that Belgium's special status precluded participation, a view that Allied governments maintained whenever the question of Belgian adherence was later considered.[16] In the circumstances, questions remained about whether Belgium's neutrality and the treaty system of 1839 remained in legal force. As the implications for Belgium's future were so profound, debate on this question continued within the Belgian government without any definitive view being reached in the early months of the war.

15. Davignon to Lalaing, 7 Aug. 1914, tel. 32, BMAE B–1; J. Helmreich, *Belgium and Europe*, pp. 178–82.

16. German government to Belgian government, 2 Aug. 1914, BMAE B–1; Davignon to Havenith, 14 Sept. 1914, no. 19, BMAE Ind/14; A. Johnstone to Grey, 28 Aug. 1914, no. 140, F.O. 371/1910; Davignon to Guillaume, 12 Sept. 1914, no. 69, BMAE GB/1914; Beyens note, 13 Dec. 1915, BMAE FR/1915/II.

By November 1914, the battered remnants of the Belgian army were entrenched behind the flooded banks of the IJzer (Yser) River. King Albert, who had taken personal command of the army on 4 August, as was his constitutional prerogative, set up his headquarters in a modest villa at the seaside resort of De Panne (La Panne) in "the little corner never conquered." At French invitation, the Belgian government established itself at Le Havre, with the Foreign Ministry located in the suburb of Sainte-Adresse. The prewar Catholic ministry remained in office with de Broqueville continuing as head of the cabinet[17] and directing the War Ministry as well, while Viscount Julien Davignon continued as foreign minister. In the first days of the war, Paul Hymans, head of the Liberal party, and Emile Vandervelde, the Socialist leader, had been made ministers of state and thus participants in crown councils. In January 1916 both entered the cabinet, along with another prominent Liberal.[18] Both opposition parties wholeheartedly supported the war effort from the first days of August 1914 and continued to do so throughout the war. Both the newly exiled government and the population in occupied Belgium were strengthened in their resolution by numerous reports of German atrocities, some of which were later confirmed by British and American investigations.[19] Once again, Belgium commanded the world's headlines and Allied sympathies.

Once Belgium's military situation had stabilized in the autumn of 1914, King Albert found himself faced with Anglo-French proposals to break up the Belgian army and to scatter Belgian brigades among Brit-

17. Belgian and Dutch usage, unlike that of France, retains the prefixes "de" and "van" except in the most informal of circumstances. In this work, the various national usages are followed in the text and notes but not in the bibliography and index, where names are not alphabetized under prefixes. Until the Armistice, the official title of the leader of the Belgian government was *chef de cabinet*.

18. Klobukowski to Briand, 11 Jan. 1916, no. 23, FMAE CPC Guerre Belg./419. Crown councils, convoked by the king on important occasions, consisted of all cabinet members plus all ministers of state, who were either former cabinet members or other distinguished Belgians named by the king.

19. Whitlock to Lansing, 12 Sept. 1917, HI Hugh Gibson Papers/4; Dept. of Information Intelligence Bureau memo, 4 Jan. 1918, Cabinet Paper G.T. 3209, CAB 24/38; Brig. Gen. John H. Morgan, *Assize of Arms*, pp. 145–46, 270–71; Trevor Wilson, "Lord Bryce's Investigation into Alleged German Atrocities in Belgium, 1914–15," pp. 369–83. For an eyewitness account of the sack of Leuven (Louvain), see Hugh Gibson, *A Journal from Our Legation in Belgium*, pp. 155–72.

ish and French divisions. The king wisely refused, taking the consistent view that the Belgian army would remain intact under his command, fighting on Belgian soil only for Belgium's strictly limited war aims.[20] Though these war aims had not yet been defined, king and cabinet were agreed that Belgium desired no involvement in broader Allied war aims involving the Balkans, the Middle East, Asia, and other areas of little concern to the occupied kingdom. Still, Albert faced continual Allied high-handedness regarding use of the Belgian army and Allied campaigns on Belgian soil. His consent, which he did not always give, was generally assumed and he was informed, but rarely consulted, at the last minute.[21] On the diplomatic front, the Foreign Ministry encountered similar difficulties, and much of its wartime activity was dedicated to attempting to find out what was being decided by the Allies. One inter-Allied conference after another took place without the Belgians being permitted to participate. Some of these concerned matters of no interest to Belgium but others did not, and information about the conferences and other key events was always difficult to obtain, mainly because Britain and France were too preoccupied with a war for survival to take time for courtesy notifications to their smaller associate. Belgian leaders were not pleased to learn of Italian entry into the war and a variety of other important events from the press.[22] Under the circumstances, they began to fear that the great powers might make peace at the end of the war without consulting them and that Belgium's future might be settled without her gaining any voice in the decisions. All agreed that Belgium must ensure her participation in the eventual peace negotiations.

After Italy adhered to the 1914 Declaration of London in December 1915, the Belgian cabinet considered whether Belgium should do the same, but such a step seemed an unsatisfactory solution from both Belgian and Allied points of view.[23] Instead, on 20 December 1915 the

20. Albert I of Belgium, *The War Diaries of Albert I, King of the Belgians*, pp. 25–26.

21. Ibid., pp. 132, 136–38, 155, 167–68, 209, 215.

22. BMAE FR/1915/II passim; Génie to Guerre, 15 Jan. 1917, no. 369, Vin 6N/127; Génie to Guere, 4 Aug. 1917, no. 457, Vin 7N/1160.

23. Beyens note, 13 Dec. 1915, BMAE FR/1915/II; Beyens to Hymans, 27 Dec. 1915, no. 1084, BMAE GB/1915; Beyens to Hymans, 31 Dec. 1915, no. 1103, BMAE B–280.

cabinet directed Baron Napoléon Eugène Beyens, a career diplomatist who had succeeded the ailing Davignon as foreign minister in July 1915,[24] to seek a special Allied commitment to Belgian participation that would at the same time safeguard Belgium's separate neutral position and the benefits it might bring. Beyens immediately visited Paris but before an approach could be made to London, the British took the initiative on 23 December. They were fully aware of the Belgian concern and deemed a declaration by the powers advisable to counter signs of defeatism in certain sectors of the Belgian population undergoing the hardships of occupation and to bolster King Albert's uncertain willingness to continue the struggle. The fact that the British had made and to a degree were still making difficulties about American efforts to feed the Belgian population, arguing that if Britain and America did not, the Germans in time would be forced to do so themselves, thus straining their resources, probably contributed to the British decision that a placatory declaration was advisable.[25]

The British offer was promptly accepted and the Belgian Foreign Ministry quickly drafted a declaration. The British and French governments approved it largely as it stood, deleting only a reference to Belgium's "just claims" at French request. When consulted, the Russian government was hesitant, fearing a similar request from Serbia, but was soon persuaded that Belgium constituted a special case. Italy and Japan declined to participate as they were not among Belgium's guarantors, but they approved the declaration and took formal note of it when it was officially made.

As a consequence, on 14 February 1916 in the Declaration of Sainte-

24. Beyens was acting foreign minister until the death of Davignon in March 1916. Hymans to Grey, 7 Aug. 1915, no. 3513, F.O. 371/2293; Préfecture, Nice, to FMAE, 12 Mar. 1916, FMAE CPC Guerre Belg./420.

25. Herbert Clark Hoover, *The Memoirs of Herbert Hoover*, 1:152–53, 162–63, 179; Joan Hoff Wilson, *Herbert Hoover, Forgotten Progressive*, p. 45; Hymans to Beyens, 24 Dec. 1915, no. 8043/1226, BMAE GB/1915; Frances Stevenson [Lloyd George], *Lloyd George*, pp. 14, 15; P. Cambon to Briand, 7 Feb. 1916, tel. 141, FMAE Paul Cambon Papers/2; David W. Southern, "The Ordeal of Brand Whitlock, Minister to Belgium, 1914–1922," p. 116. The negotiations that ensued may be traced in the following files: BMAE: GB/1915, 1916, FR/1915/II, 1916, B–280, B–348; PRO, CAB 37/140–42, F.O. 371/2636; FMAE P. Cambon Papers/2, CPC Guerre: Afrique, Congo Belge/1553, Guerre: Dossier Général/68, Guerre Belg./420.

Adresse, the diplomatic representatives of Britain, France, and Russia formally pledged to Beyens that "the Allied guarantor powers declare that, when the moment comes, the Belgian government will be called to participate in the peace negotiations and that they will not put an end to the hostilities unless Belgium is reestablished in its political and economic independence and largely indemnified for the damages which she has undergone. They will lend their aid to Belgium to assure her commercial and financial rehabilitation." At Albert's insistence, on 29 April 1916 the declaration was extended to the Congo, with the three powers promising formally to support Belgium's retention of the colony intact and a special indemnity for the wartime damages it suffered.[26] As American representatives had proposed that perhaps the Congo could be sold to Germany, with the proceeds being used to restore Belgium,[27] the king's precaution was a wise one. The two declarations together perhaps constituted Belgian diplomacy's most substantial wartime achievement, although the first declaration had been offered before it was formally requested and thus could not be entirely attributed to Belgian diplomatic efforts. Belgian representatives had, however, conveyed Belgian dissatisfaction and fear and had made what little they could of discouragement in occupied Belgium. Certainly, the declarations constituted one of the few formal commitments Belgium gained in the course of the war and represented one of the few Belgian desires that was not countered by an unattractive quid pro quo or dilatory tactics. Yet after the war at the peace conference, the declarations of Sainte-Adresse proved to be much less than they had seemed.

Though the Belgian government could agree within itself and with the king on the desirability of the Allied declarations, it could reach consensus on little else. By this time the cabinet, despite internal disputes about specific war aims and how to achieve them, was wholeheartedly committed to the Allies, whereas Albert was not. The king was deeply pessimistic and convinced that the war would end in a

26. For texts of both, see Paul Hymans, *Mémoires*, 2:904–5. It should be noted that the Hymans *Mémoires* consist to a large degree of contemporary documents.

27. It was Colonel House who proposed sale of the Congo. Albert, *Diaries*, pp. 89–90. There had been an earlier, less categoric Anglo-French guarantee of Belgian retention of the Congo. Villiers to Davignon, 19 Sept. 1914, BMAE GB/1914; William Roger Louis, *Great Britain and Germany's Lost Colonies, 1914–1919*, p. 69.

stalemate and a negotiated peace.[28] This assessment, together with his profound concern for the suffering of the Belgian soldiers in the trenches and civilians under occupation and a determination to spare the nation the horrors of physical devastation if at all possible, led him to be extremely cautious about committing his troops to offensives that he deemed hopeless and inclined him toward abortive efforts to negotiate with the Germans from time to time.[29] As rumors of these moves reached the Allies, they redounded to the disadvantage of the Belgian government, which, on the whole, did not share the king's inclinations.

Albert was equally conservative in his approach to war aims. In part, he had little faith in an Allied victory, the only outcome affording any scope for Belgian claims, and in part his instincts dictated caution. The cabinet wanted to plan for an Allied victory but was sharply divided most of the time about how to proceed. Part of the trouble was that at Le Havre the government did not have a great deal to do. As a consequence, cabinet members and senior government officials squabbled and politicked and intrigued. At the same time, they planned toward the day of liberation, engaging in bitter disputes over both Belgian goals and the appropriate tactics toward them. Because the government was in exile and retained only a few slender links with occupied Belgium, only the most primitive soundings of public opinion, generally the views of prominent citizens remaining in the country, were possible. On the question of territorial claims, the Belgian leaders encountered an awkward conflict of British and French attitudes. The French government pressed the Belgian leaders to put claims forward and complained sharply when they did not. When Belgian diplomatists were finally instructed to raise obvious Belgian interests, the British invariably replied that all discussion was premature. Thus, Belgium revealed her goals and gained little or nothing in return. She began to find herself caught, as she so often was to be in the postwar years, between the conflicting approaches of her two senior partners to virtually all European problems.

28. This theme runs through his *Diaries*. See also Jacques Willequet, "Guerre et neutralité," pp. 69–81.

29. See Fritz Fischer, *Griff nach der Weltmacht*, pp. 262–74; Albert, *Diaries*, pp. 109–13, 123–24, 126–28, 143, 184, 198, 218–19.

The entire Belgian government was united in its determination that Belgium should be fully restored in its independence, territorial integrity, and economic prosperity. There was universal interest in Luxemburg but less consensus about what form of closer relationship to seek or how to achieve it. For the rest, there was no agreement at all. The first wartime foreign minister, Davignon, was very cautious, and Beyens, who was considered to be the king's man, pursued the same wary course. But de Broqueville was more venturesome until 1917, while Jules Renkin, minister of colonies, and Count Henry Carton de Wiart, minister of justice, favored "la grande Belgique" and, along with de Broqueville, intrigued to this end. Senior Colonial Ministry officials, notably Pierre Orts, and Foreign Ministry officials, including Baron Albert de Bassompierre, advocated an aggressive policy. In the diplomatic service, the leading exponent of forthright and far-reaching claims was Baron (Paul) Guillaume, Belgian minister at Paris, who was recalled on grounds of insubordination in August 1916 after he vigorously denounced the foreign minister's cautious policy not only to Beyens himself but also to Albert, Poincaré, various French political leaders, and Belgian journalists.[30] On the other hand, Hymans, who became minister to London in February 1915; Vandervelde; and several other cabinet ministers, Prosper Poullet among them, were voices of moderation through most of the war.

One of the most difficult and earnestly debated questions was that of the future international status of Belgium. Should Belgium seek an end to obligatory neutrality and, if so, when and how? Those who opposed early overtures in this direction, notably Albert and his first two wartime foreign ministers, pointed out that considerable benefits, including full reimbursement of war costs, might be obtained as a consequence of Belgium's special legal position.[31] Throughout the war, Belgium remained, with the possible exception of Luxemburg, the only country whose violation was not only an act of aggression but also a crime against clearly established international law. As the war broadened to

30. Albert to Davignon, 2 June 1915, BMAE DB/32/I; Guillaume to Beyens, 24 Dec. 1915, no. 13737/3059, BMAE FR/1915/II; Margerie to Briand, 21 Aug. 1916, FMAE CPC Guerre Belg./421; DuB, R.G.P. 109, pp. 631–33.

31. Albert, *Diaries*, pp. 32–36; Emile Cammaerts, *Albert of Belgium, Defender of Right*, pp. 264–66; van der Elst memo, May 1915, BMAE Ind/1915/I.

include more countries, more bloodshed, and more costs, this distinction appeared to be an advantage worth conserving (and indeed it did yield Belgium an important if partially illusory concession at the peace conference). Under the circumstances, there was no further question whether Belgian neutrality had been destroyed in 1914. The treaties of 1839 were assumed to remain in effect, as Britain and France clearly assumed as well, and Belgium prepared to make the most of them.

The question still remained, however, whether Belgium should seek an end to her special restricted status after the war was won. Pressures to this end built up in the cabinet and the Foreign Ministry until the king could no longer contain them. Adherents to the argument that the guarantee under the 1839 treaties had failed grew steadily in number. To the extent that the great-power guarantee had been designed to prevent Belgium from becoming an object of attack and a battleground, this argument was sound. But in another sense, the guarantee had worked perfectly: two guarantors had rushed to Belgium's aid and a third had done so on paper. True, Belgium was under occupation, but the war was not over and the three powers had pledged to fight until Belgium was liberated. Those advocating the end of obligatory neutrality rarely mentioned this aspect of the matter. Instead, they stressed that compulsory neutrality was a humiliating limitation on Belgian sovereignty and argued that Belgium's behavior through eighty-five years of nationhood and her meticulous, wholehearted fulfillment of her obligations in 1914 had earned her the right to full sovereignty and equality in the family of nations.[32]

As the consensus swung toward a postwar release from the obligation and guarantee of 1839, debate centered on a question that had been discussed since the first days of the war: what regime should replace that of 1839? The merits of voluntary neutrality, an Anglo-French guarantee (preferably without Belgian obligation), or alliance with Britain and France were weighed. Though any system involving a future German guarantee was generally deemed unthinkable, the other proposals all had their adherents. Proponents of "la grande Belgique," who consciously or unconsciously dreamed of elevating Belgium to a power of the second rank, found voluntary neutrality unattractively timid. An

32. For example, de Gaiffier note, 10 Mar. 1915, BMAE Ind/1915/I.

Anglo-French guarantee with possible Russian and Italian adherence, although desirable of itself, would probably involve conditions, including perhaps minimum levels for the Belgian army. Alliances, as the king pointed out, would mean satellite status. While Beyens opted against postwar maintenance of obligatory neutrality in August 1915 and the cabinet reached unanimity on this view by the end of the year, a decision that the enlarged cabinet formally confirmed in February 1916, Belgian diplomatists were cautioned not to discuss the country's future status, as no decision had yet been taken. As far as could be ascertained, the decision to abandon conventional neutrality conformed to the wishes of occupied Belgium,[33] but there was no further consensus either within Belgium or in exile about the future. Meanwhile, debate on what one official called "this agonizing problem"[34] continued. The difficulty was how to achieve both full sovereignty and security without becoming the satellite of one power or a group of powers. As there was no real solution, Belgian officials did not find one.

In the end, with considerable naiveté the Belgian leaders tried to have their cake and eat it, too. Worried by an excess of pressing offers from France toward sweeping economic and military arrangements amounting to potential French domination, Beyens approached London. On 7 July 1916 he gave Sir Edward Grey, the British foreign secretary, a memorandum formally announcing Belgium's desire to end her special status after the war, rejecting alliances, and proposing instead an Allied guarantee without Belgian signature. The memorandum closed with a proposed Belgian commitment to defend herself as in 1914 on the basis of general conscription. Shortly thereafter, however, this counterpart was awkwardly withdrawn after cabinet objections on the grounds that the powers might interfere in Belgian military policies and that it was unnecessary in view of the Belgian military law of 1913. The British were not impressed by this tenuous argument, knowing that the 1913 law could easily be repealed, and proposed a military agreement

---

33. Albert, *Diaries*, pp. 34–36, 117–18; Poullet note, 26 May 1915, Beyens note, Aug. 1915, Beyens to Renkin, 20 Jan. 1916, Beyens to Albert, Feb. 1916, Capelle note, 22 Mar. 1916, BMAE Ind/1915–16; Beyens to Guillaume et al., 7 Dec. 1915, no. 2427, BMAE FR/1915/II; de Broqueville to Hymans, Feb. 1915, BMAE B–280; Belgian questionnaire, late 1916, BMAE B–377.

34. Van der Elst note, 29 Apr. 1915, BMAE Ind/1915/I.

tantamount to an alliance, which Belgium rejected. What Belgian diplomacy spent the postwar years trying to achieve was declined in 1916
with little thought, primarily because, after long years of neutrality, the
Belgian leadership retained an instinctive aversion to alliances. Though
Beyen's memorandum was handed unofficially to the French in late
July 1916 and submitted officially to the Italian and Russian governments in the autumn, it brought no further substantive response. In this
question as in others, the Belgian leaders had succeeded only in revealing their hand. Meanwhile the cabinet, much to Albert's relief, decided
firmly against alliances.[35]

Little else had been decided, however, and the debate continued. It
soon became entangled in growing tension between Albert and Beyens
on one side and, on the other, those members of the cabinet favoring
more aggressive policies. Finally in August 1917, Beyens was forced
out after a long series of battles over several aspects of Belgian foreign policy, and de Broqueville took over the Foreign Ministry himself,
relinquishing the War Ministry to a general. De Broqueville had been
consistently cautious regarding Belgium's future international status, if
not about territorial questions.[36] However, after the failure of General
Nivelle's spring offensive, he was seriously compromised in the summer and early autumn of 1917 by the Coppée-von der Lancken peace
maneuvers. He lingered on at the Foreign Ministry only because of
disagreement over a successor, but Hymans took that portfolio in January 1918 and when the last wartime Belgian cabinet was constituted
in May 1918, de Broqueville was excluded altogether.[37] Through the
political maneuvering, solution of the impossible problem did not progress, although the Beyens memorandum of July 1916 was disavowed.
As the war neared its conclusion, Hymans informed the Allies in September 1918 that Belgium renounced permanent neutrality and the

35. Beyens memo, 7 July 1916, Hymans to Beyens, 18 July 1916, Beyens to de
Gaiffier et al., 13 Sept. 1916, BMAE Ind/1915–16; BMAE circular, 13 Sept. 1916,
BMAE B–280.
36. Albert, *Diaries*, pp. 96–97; Klobukowski to Ribot, 14 July 1917, no. 113, FMAE
CPC Guerre Belg./424.
37. Clinchant to Pichon, 28 Nov. 1917, tel. 173, J. Cambon note, 20 Nov. 1917,
FMAE note, 26 Nov. 1917, FMAE CPC Guerre Belg./425; Klobukowski to Pichon, 1
Jan. 1918, no. 2, FMAE CPC Guerre Belg./426; Klobukowski to Pichon, 26 May 1918,
tel. 71, FMAE CPC Guerre Belg./427.

concomitant guarantee but reserved the right to seek "additional guarantees." Allied inquiries as to their nature brought no response, partly because he cautiously wanted a clearer view of the future organization of Europe before committing himself,[38] but primarily because the Belgian leadership had found no way to reconcile full sovereignty, genuine security, and real independence.

Other Belgian war aims proved equally thorny. On the territorial front, the chief difficulty was that the districts that Belgium most desired belonged not to the Central Powers but to Allies and neutrals. The Belgian leaders were fully aware of this difficulty and very cautious in most respects in the early stages of the war. As time passed, the more ambitious members of the cabinet and of the Foreign Ministry, recognizing that the peace settlement would entail far-reaching territorial revision, foresaw a possibly unique opportunity to overturn the decisions of 1839 and, in the eyes of a few, those of 1648. The ensuing battles, which centered more on tactics than on goals, contributed much to the departure of Beyens, who had consistently advocated caution about claims on friends and neighbors. His successors gradually lost sight of the difficulty and came to believe that there must be some way, if only Belgium were sufficiently forthright and aggressive, to obtain the desired territories from Holland and Luxemburg, and in Africa from Portugal.

Aside from the question of full reparation for damage done and for the cost of the war to Belgium, which was so fully agreed that it did not warrant much discussion, the paramount Belgian war aim after the abolition of compulsory neutrality was the return of Luxemburg to Belgium. The king, the cabinet, and the Foreign Ministry unanimously thought it necessary and important to right the wrong of 1839, as they viewed it. At first, this appeared an easily achievable goal but, as the war progressed, the situation became increasingly complex, and debate over how to pursue the claim became acrimonious. It was complicated by the awkward fact that a Belgium who was making the most of her position as a state whose independence, territorial integrity, and neu-

---

38. Hymans to Moncheur, 18 Sept. 1918, no. 927, Moncheur to Hymans, 23 Sept., 22 Oct. 1918, nos. 7510/1703, 8349/1914, BMAE GB/1918/II; Hymans to de Gaiffier, 4 Oct. 1918, no. 2140, BMAE FR/1918/II.

trality were specially guaranteed by the powers could hardly violate a neighboring state that was similarly guaranteed.

The guarantee of Luxemburg was collective but not individual, and thus did not commit guarantors to defend the Grand Duchy if another guarantor attacked it. Further, Luxemburg, unlike Belgium, was neither obligated nor permitted to defend her compulsory perpetual neutrality, and her army was limited to the tiny force necessary to maintain domestic order. These conditions were imposed by the Treaty of London of 11 May 1867, which resolved a dangerous Franco-Prussian clash arising from a proposal of the Dutch king to sell Luxemburg to France. At the same time, the Prussian garrison was removed and the fortress dismantled. Gradually, the Grand Duchy gained increasing autonomy from Holland and in 1890, when Queen Wilhelmina ascended the Dutch throne, Luxemburg passed, by the terms of the Nassau family compact of 1783, to the male heir of an older German Nassau branch and became an independent state. Meanwhile, Luxemburg had entered the Zollverein in 1842 and had prospered greatly without developing any popular enthusiasm for Germans. As a consequence of the Franco-Prussian war, administrative control of the main Luxemburg rail company, the Société Guillaume-Luxembourg, originally awarded to a French concern in 1857, was transferred by force majeure to the Prussian state railways in 1872 with the express proviso that the rail lines not be used for any military purpose, a commitment violated on 1 August 1914.[39]

39. For the history of Luxemburg to 1914, see Grand-Duché de Luxembourg, *Le Luxembourg: Livre de Centenaire*; Grand Duchy of Luxembourg, Grey Book, *Luxembourg and the German Invasion, Before and After*; Great Britain, Foreign Office, *Handbooks Prepared under the Direction of the Historical Section of the Foreign Office*, no. 27, *Luxemburg and Limburg*; Admiralty, *A Manual of Belgium*; Admiralty, *Luxemburg*; Henri Bernard, *Terre commune*; Paul Weber, *Histoire du Grand-Duché de Luxembourg*; Xavier Prum, *The Problem of Luxemburg*; Whitlock to Lansing, 1 Nov. 1918, no. 637, LC Whitlock Papers/38; Steefel memo, 10 Apr. 1919, Inquiry/552. For the 1914 invasion, see Luigi Albertini, *The Origins of the War of 1914*, 3:681–82; van den Steen to Davignon, 2 Aug. 1914, no. 449/139, BMAE B–1; Francis Gribble, "The Luxemburg Railways," pp. 178–79. The Nassau family compact specified that the succession could pass to a female if the male line was entirely extinct. The first Luxembourgeois grand duke's only brother had made a morganatic marriage to Alexander Pushkin's daughter. Marie Adelaide had five sisters and no brothers. The Luxembourgeois Chamber confirmed her succession in 1907 and she inherited in 1912. Joseph Meyers, *Deux Maisons souveraines, 1890–1955*, pp. 31–34.

Luxemburg was occupied by the German army on 2 August 1914. The cabinet under Paul Eyschen protested vigorously in all directions to no avail and prevailed upon Grand Duchess Marie Adelaide to telegraph the kaiser, but a lightly armed gendarmerie of three hundred men could not possibly put up an effective resistance and none was attempted. The rigors of German occupation only intensified the already active Luxembourgeois dislike of Germany.[40] The young grand duchess, however, acted as if there were no war. Whether at her own decision, under the influence of her entourage, or on ministerial advice, Marie Adelaide showed much more cordiality to the conqueror than was strictly necessary. Because she appeared as the war progressed to be governing personally against the will of her Parliament in other matters, she was held responsible for her actions in this matter as well, and her conspicuously pro-German stance rendered her so intensely unpopular that there was serious doubt whether her reign could long survive the German occupation.[41]

During the war the Belgian government, though entirely cut off from Luxemburg, did what little it could to help, usually at Luxembourgeois request. It tried unsuccessfully to arrange for supply of the Grand Duchy by the American-organized Commission for the Relief of Belgium in the face of British and often French objections, tried equally in vain to protect Luxemburg from Allied bombings, and took other, similar steps on behalf of the occupied Grand Duchy.[42] But throughout, Belgian eyes were on the future status of Luxemburg and the potential opportunity to undo the separation of 1839. Both the Belgians and the French, with no dissent from Britain, quickly concluded that Luxemburg must be removed from the German economic orbit and that Marie

40. Albertini, *Origins*, 3:682; Edith O'Shaughessy, *Marie Adelaide*, pp. 125–26; Maurice W. R. van Vollenhoven, *Memoires, beschouwingen, belevenissen, reizen en anecdoten*, p. 411; Klobukowski to Delcassé, 21 July 1915, no. 929, FMAE CPC Guerre Lux/599; Eyschen to Davignon, 2 Aug. 1914, tel., BMAE B–1.

41. O'Shaughessy, *Marie Adelaide*, pp. 134–61. This biographer, who is hagiographic, consistently blames Marie Adelaide's actions on her advisors.

42. Guillaume to Delcassé, 19 Aug. 1915, FMAE CPC Guerre Belg./416; Fleuriau to Briand, 10 Aug. 1916, tel. 1025, Margerie to Fleuriau, 8 Aug. 1916, tel. 2543–44, Briand to Fleuriau, 17 Aug. 1916, tel. 2631, FMAE CPC Guerre Lux/600; de Gaiffier to Hymans, 1 Apr. 1918, no. 2144/901, BMAE FR/1918/I.

Adelaide would be repudiated by her subjects. They assumed that the dynasty would fall as well. Indeed, the French frequently assured the Belgians that the dynasty would not be permitted to remain.[43] As Luxemburg, a mere 999 landlocked square miles, was too small to stand entirely alone, the question was obvious: to which neighbor would Luxemburg adhere and in what fashion? Belgian leaders, quite oblivious to the degree to which the Luxembourgeois had come to enjoy independence and genuinely assuming that their cousins were as eager for reunion as they, contemplated how this could best be accomplished.

Virtually every Belgian planning document on Luxemburg during World War I carried two conditions: (1) provided that the Nassau dynasty was ended (or that Luxemburg ceased to be independent), and (2) provided that the Luxembourgeois themselves were willing to join Belgium. But both provisos were largely pro forma because Belgian leaders, fortified by repeated French assurances, universally assumed that the dynasty would go and that the Luxembourgeois were willing. As to the modalities of reunion, there were three possibilities: (1) Belgian annexation of the Grand Duchy, the course strongly favored by most of the proponents of "la grande Belgique"; (2) a personal union, with Albert becoming grand duke and Luxemburg otherwise retaining its own institutions; or (3) an economic union. Although most Luxembourgeois strongly favored the maintenance of national independence, there was a good deal of sentiment within the Grand Duchy during the war in favor of the second or third Belgian solution. There was also sentiment in support of a French tie, although not as much as Parisian adherents of French annexation claimed.[44]

French wartime policy in regard to Luxemburg fluctuated somewhat

43. Guillaume to Davignon, 7 Apr. 1915, no. 3267/802, Davignon note, 22 June 1915, BMAE FR/1915/I; Davignon to Hymans, 14 June 1915, no. 6266, BMAE GB/1915. See also Christian Calmes, *1914–1919: Le Luxembourg au centre de l'annexionnisme belge.* Though this last is the most detailed study available, limitations of viewpoint and research restrict its utility.

44. Report of Luxembourgeois group to Bertie, 21 Aug. 1916, BMAE GB/1916; Mollard to Briand, 7 Sept. 1916, FMAE CPC Guerre Lux/600; Guillaume to Beyens, 22 Mar. 1916, no. 2488/876, BMAE FR/1916; J. Cambon note, 22 Jan. 1917, Vin 6N/75; Rumbold to Balfour, 27 Nov. 1917, no. 850, F.O. 371/2973; Robertson to Balfour, 3 Oct. 1918, no. 212, F.O. 371/3256.

with changes of ministries and disagreements among officials at the Quai d'Orsay. President Poincaré was a consistent proponent of a Belgian Luxemburg, as was Jules Cambon at the Foreign Ministry, whereas Pierre de Margerie wavered. On the other hand, Philippe Berthelot, whose influence there varied with changes of ministers, thought in terms of French annexation; and some cabinet ministers were more communicative than others. Nonetheless, the broad outline of French policy, with some variations, seems clear. France would accept Belgian acquisition of most or all of Luxemburg under one form or another provided that Belgium entered into military and economic alliance with France. Though few wartime French Foreign Ministry files survive, those still extant, together with the voluminous Belgian files, convey the distinct impression that the Quai d'Orsay assumed early in the war that Belgium would become a French satellite after the war.[45] If France was to have Belgium, Belgium could have Luxemburg. After Belgian resistance to the economic and military conditions could not be overcome, French enthusiasm for a Belgian solution to the Luxemburg question diminished markedly.

Though Belgian attention was fixed on Luxemburg from September 1914, in the early months of 1915 both Poincaré and various French diplomatists encouraged and heightened Belgian interest, informing willing listeners that Luxemburg's independence could not survive the war, assuring them that Luxemburg should return to Belgium, and displaying charts of French schemes for the postwar settlement that allotted Luxemburg to Belgium.[46] Then a certain reserve set in, causing a Belgian demarche in June 1915 to French Foreign Minister Théophile Delcassé, who said nothing. A similar demarche in London established only that Britain had made no commitments on the subject to France. Soon thereafter came the first of repeated French complaints about Belgian indecision and unwillingness to accept Luxemburg, together with increasing evidence through the remainder of the year and early 1916 of French interest in the Grand Duchy. French industrial and

45. For example, J. Cambon note, 22 Jan. 1917, Vin 6N/75.
46. Direction Politique notes, 15 Sept. 1914, 25 Jan. 1915, BMAE B–1; Guillaume to Davignon, 10 Mar., 7 Apr., 22 June 1915, nos. 2459/609, 3267/802, 5371/1389, BMAE FR/1915/I; Hymans to Davignon, 3 June 1915, no. 1910/515, BMAE GB/1915; de Gaiffier to de Broqueville, n.d. [Sept. 1917], no. 5334/2433, BMAE FR/1917/I.

military circles were particularly interested in the southern, more strategic and more economically valuable part of the country.[47]

As a consequence, in May 1916, Belgium made another effort in Allied capitals but without result. Soon thereafter the unofficial French tone became more favorable to Belgium, probably because talks on French-Belgian economic relations were scheduled for early September. After these had demonstrated Belgian hostility to both a customs union and a political-military alliance with France, the Quai d'Orsay in the person of Berthelot refused to discuss Luxemburg at all, although Aristide Briand, then prime minister and foreign minister, told Vandervelde over lunch that France would not claim Luxemburg and assured him that Berthelot stood alone. At the same time, however, Briand pressed for close economic relations.[48]

While Beyens cautiously pursued the Luxemburg question with little success through traditional diplomatic means, revealing his country's aspirations clearly to Belgium's potential French rivals, de Broqueville was independently taking another tack. His agents in both a propaganda campaign and such efforts as were possible to influence Luxembourgeois opinion were Pierre Nothomb, unofficial secretary to Carton de Wiart and the ultimate exponent of "la grande Belgique," and the infintely more subtle Gaston Barbanson, administrator of Luxemburg's largest steel company, who was temporarily assigned to a Belgian economic bureau in Paris. Both were of Luxembourgeois origin. Nothomb was openly annexationist, a romantic, almost medievally minded Belgian nationalist who, whether authorized or not, conducted clumsy propaganda campaigns toward a greater Belgium; the more cautious Barbanson doubted the wisdom of annexing Luxemburg unless Belgium could gain from the Allies a satisfactory economic regime wherein Luxembourgeois steel would not swamp that of Belgium. In time he came to favor a personal union. Although Nothomb had had Foreign

47. Davignon to Guillaume, 18, 23 June 1915, nos. 938, 959, Guillaume to Davignon, 29 June 1915, tel. 105, BMAE FR/1915/I; Hymans to Davignon, 5 July 1915, no. 2521/614, BMAE GB/1915; Guillaume to Beyens, 20 Jan., 22 Mar. 1916, nos. 508/203, 2488/876, BMAE FR/1916; Beyens to Albert, 6 Feb. 1916, BMAE B–280.
48. Lahure note, 22 Apr. 1916, FMAE CPC NS Belg./36; Beyens to Hymans, 20 May 1916, no. 460, BMAE GB/1916; Guillaume to Beyens, 21 June 1916, no. 4817/1723, de Gaiffier to Beyens, 5, 18 Oct. 1916, nos. 7271/2822, 7656/3020, BMAE FR/1916.

Ministry authorization for limited activities in Switzerland and Italy since October 1915, de Broqueville assigned the two men directly to the Luxemburg question in April 1916, apparently without Beyens's consent. He did so in response to Nothomb's ardent desire, Beyens's caution, and a growing Parisian propaganda campaign for French acquisition of the Grand Duchy.[49] This last was directed by Armand Mollard, French minister to Luxemburg, now in Paris, and centered on the sizable Luxembourgeois refugee colony in the French capital. In 1917, Mollard succeeded in organizing a series of committees, of which the Comité Mollard and the Comité Franco-Luxembourgeois were the most important, to issue propaganda and influence French parliamentary opinion toward a French solution of the Luxemburg question. Mollard's efforts were both skillful and effective, unlike those of Nothomb, whose inept activities only aroused Luxembourgeois fears and redounded to French benefit.[50]

In the spring of 1917, the Parisian propaganda campaign became so intense that Beyens, in accord with the cabinet, felt that counteraction must be taken. Accordingly, Baron Edmond de Gaiffier d'Hestroy, who had replaced Baron Guillaume at Paris in September 1916 partly as a result of intense disagreement between Guillaume and Beyens over the Luxemburg question, was instructed to see Alexandre Ribot, then French prime minister. In a meeting on 9 June 1917, de Gaiffier extracted a promise that Ribot would discourage any French parliamentary campaigns toward annexation and an assurance that France had not claimed Luxemburg in correspondence with London. Ribot stated unconditionally that France would not ask for annexation of Luxemburg. He declined to make an official declaration but took note of the Belgian claim and authorized de Gaiffier to send him an official letter taking formal written note of the interview. Though Beyens was pleased, he also recognized the lacunae in Ribot's statement.[51]

Thereafter, Belgian policy regarding Luxemburg became more cir-

49. Jacques Willequet, "Gaston Barbanson, promoteur d'une 'Grande Belgique' en 1914–1918," pp. 335–75; Palo, "Belgian War Aims," pp. 322–23, 335–36.

50. De Gaiffier to Beyens, 13, 23, 25 Apr. 1917, nos. 2264/1246, 2463/1341, 2499/1355, BMAE FR/1917/I.

51. De Gaiffier to Beyens, 9 June 1917, no. 3426/1703, BMAE FR/1917/I; Beyens to Hymans, 16 June 1917, BMAE GB/1917/I.

cumspect, aside from Nothomb's efforts. Beyens was soon gone from the Foreign Ministry and de Broqueville, who replaced him, gave the matter little further attention, as he became disheartened by the unsatisfactory progress of the war and appears to have become embroiled in peace feelers. Also, after America entered the war and President Woodrow Wilson put increasing emphasis upon "self-determination of nations," Belgian diplomatists found it advisable to speak not of annexation but of "rapprochement," a term they continued to use at the peace conference. The Belgian Foreign Ministry considered another approach to Paris late in 1917, but Jules Cambon advised delay. A few days later he was removed from his post as secretary-general at the Quai d'Orsay and Belgium lost one of its strongest French supporters on the Luxemburg question.[52]

After Hymans took over the Belgian Foreign Ministry, a new approach was made in February 1918 to Stephen Pichon, the last wartime French foreign minister, who adhered narrowly to Ribot's declaration and could not be moved beyond it. Meanwhile the propaganda campaigns in Paris continued and gathered strength. In late October 1918, Hymans sent a carefully worded note to Britain, France, and the United States enunciating Belgian interest in Luxemburg, and also saw Pichon in Paris. Pichon flatly declined to go beyond Ribot's declaration, refused additional assurances, and, while making no objection to Belgian participation in the forthcoming Allied military occupation of Luxemburg, also made no promises concerning either the occupation or French support to Belgium regarding the ultimate fate of the Grand Duchy.[53] Thus, as the war ended, all Belgium's efforts had gained no British or American commitment and nothing from France beyond Ribot's narrow 1917 declaration.

Early in the war, when France was being more generous than later on over Luxemburg, she also proposed that Belgium acquire a good deal of German territory, notably the "Walloon cantons" and part of the

52. Hymans to de Gaiffier, 16 Feb., 17 Mar. 1918, nos. 360, 604, de Gaiffier to Hymans, 5 Feb. 1918, no. 766/346, BMAE FR/1918/I; de Cartier to Hymans, 23 Jan. 1918, tel. 23, BMAE Ind/1918.

53. De Gaiffier to Hymans, 11 Feb. 1918, no. 901/408, Hymans to de Gaiffier, 17 Mar. 1918, no. 604, FR/1918/I; Belgian note to U.K., U.S., France, Italy, 22 Oct. 1918, BMAE Ind/1918; Hymans to Albert, 24 Oct. 1918, BMAE FR/1918/II.

Rhineland, although the French often suggested as well that even an enlarged Belgium could not stand alone and should become part of a larger confederation whose components usually included Belgium, Luxemburg, and the Rhineland plus either France or Holland. As Belgium proved less docile than anticipated, French diplomatists had second thoughts and began to stress that Belgium should not absorb too many Germans who might combine with the Flemish against French interests. Belgian leaders entirely agreed that Belgium should not absorb large numbers of Germans, although chiefly out of fear of arousing German desires for revenge. They did contemplate the Walloon cantons, those small border districts annexed by Prussia in 1815, always vaguely defined, whose number varied from five to eleven according to who was doing the counting. The Belgian Foreign Ministry showed consistent interest in Malmédy, an area whose population was predominantly French-speaking, and took measures to ensure that captured Malmédians not be treated as prisoners of war. By the time of the Armistice, it was evident that Belgium would claim Malmédy and that no decision had been made about the remainder of the Walloon cantons, but that Belgium would not favor any large-scale annexation of German territory.[54]

Because French diplomatists, especially in 1915, talked both of Belgian annexation of the northern Rhineland (with France taking the remainder) and of an independent neutralized buffer state, the Belgian Foreign Ministry contemplated the Rhenish problem. There was no serious consideration of annexation, but the idea of an independent buffer state between Germany and Belgium was enormously attractive, provided that the Rhenish state were truly independent. If it were French dominated and particularly if France dominated Luxemburg as well, Belgium would find herself almost encircled by France and her independence of action would be seriously threatened. By the end of the war, most senior Belgian officials had recognized that any Rhenish buffer state was almost bound to become a French satellite, although

54. De Broqueville note, 15 Apr. 1915, BMAE B–280; Direction Politique notes, 3 Mar., 17 Apr. 1915, BMAE B–348; Direction Politique note, 25 Jan. 1915, BMAE B–1; Direction Politique note, 12 July 1917, BMAE B–331; Guillaume to Davignon, 17 Sept. 1915, no. 9223/2898, BMAE FR/1914; Hymans to Davignon, 3 June 1915, no. 1910/

Hymans himself retained some illusions about the possibility of a genuinely independent Rhineland until the opening of the peace conference.[55] When he faced reality, he resisted French schemes to detach the
Rhineland from Germany.

Minor territorial acqusitions from Germany after a victorious war
appeared to be a relatively simple matter but, aside from Luxemburg,
Belgium's chief territorial interests in Europe centered on neutral Holland, and that was a much more delicate question. At the end of July
1914, the Dutch government had proposed to coordinate the defense
of lower Limburg with that of Liège, but Holland withdrew the proposal upon receipt of German assurances. Similarly, on 4 August 1914,
the Netherlands offered British warships the use of the Scheldt to
aid in the relief of Belgium, but rescinded the offer the next day on
grounds of British belligerency and closed the Scheldt to warships of all
belligerent nations. As a consequence, British leaders intimated to the
Dutch in the autumn of 1914 that Holland would lose Flemish Zeeland
to Belgium after the war was over.[56] Nonetheless, the Netherlands
welcomed a flood of six to seven hundred thousand Belgian refugees,
mostly after the fall of Antwerp. The majority of these soon returned
to Belgium, but about one hundred thousand stayed on, sharing the

515, BMAE GB/1915; Guillaume to Davignon, 7 Apr. 1915, no. 3267/802, BMAE
FR/1915/I; de Gaiffier to Beyens, 25 Sept. 1915, 21 Oct. 1916, nos. 7676/2703, 7714/
3050, BMAE FR/1916; de Gaiffier to de Bassompierre, 30 Aug. 1917, BMAE FR/1917/
I; de Broqueville to de Gaiffier, 24 Dec. 1917, no. 2632, BMAE FR/1917/II; de Gaiffier
to Davignon, 3 Mar. 1915, BMAE Ind/1915/I; de Gaiffier to Hymans, 12 Oct., 18 Nov.
1918, nos. 7256/2603, 8671/2944, BMAE FR/1918/II. The "Walloon cantons" were
generally considered to be Eupen, Malmédy, St. Vith, Kronenburg, Schleiden, and sometimes also Bitburg, removed from Luxemburg in 1815.

55. Hymans to Davignon, 2 Apr., 3 June 1915, nos. 1072/303, 1910/515, BMAE
GB/1915; Guillaume to Davignon, 22 June 1915, no. 5371/1389, BMAE FR/1915/I;
Guillaume to Davignon, 20 July 1915, no. 6115/1614, BMAE FR/1915/II; de Gaiffier
to Davignon, 3 Mar. 1915, Direction Politique to Beyens, 10 Apr. 1915, no. 6366,
BMAE Ind/1915/I; de Gaiffier to Beyens, 3 May 1915, BMAE Ind/1915–16; de Gaiffier
to Beyens, 25 Sept. 1916, no. 7676/2703, BMAE FR/1916; Lahure to Pila, 22 Apr.
1916, FMAE CPC NS Belg./36; de Gaiffier notes, 24 Nov. 1914, 4 Apr. 1915, de
Broqueville note, 15 Apr. 1915, BMAE B–280; de Gaiffier notes, 3 Mar., 15 Apr. 1915,
Hymans to Masson, 2 Jan. 1919, no. 11193, BMAE B–348.

56. DuB, R.G.P. 137, pp. 416–17, 425–28; Amry Vandenbosch, *The Neutrality of the
Netherlands during the World War*, pp. 318–21; DuB, R.G.P. 109, pp. 121–22, 156.

scant Dutch food ration throughout the war, despite a growing Dutch dislike for their Belgian guests, whom they considered frivolous.[57]

Through four painful years, the Dutch government struggled to maintain Holland's precarious neutrality and to avoid being sucked into the struggle. On the one hand were German threats and demands; on the other, British menaces and control of the seas, which interfered mightily with Holland's overseas trade. The Dutch position became excruciatingly difficult in the summer of 1917 when the British threatened to cut off food supplies and Germany threatened to end coal shipments.[58] Ultimately, the Dutch success in remaining neutral arose from British and German desires that she do so. Germany feared an extension of the front and valued the supplies arriving via Holland despite Allied restrictions, whereas Britain, along with France, recognized that a German conquest of the Netherlands would give the enemy free disposal of both Rotterdam and Antwerp.[59] While Dutch diplomatists bobbed and weaved between the conflicting demands of their great-power neighbors, Dutch policy was on balance perhaps somewhat pro-German. Some governmental and court circles were undoubtedly pro-German but, primarily, Dutch leaders feared Germany more, having recognized fairly early in the war that Britain did not intend to invade the Netherlands, whatever rumors the Germans floated. Further, a major and technically unneutral Dutch concession to Germany in the continually vexatious question of sand and gravel shipments across Holland to occupied Belgium was made in April 1918, a critical time on the western front, with the tacit consent of the Allied governments to prevent a German occupation of the Netherlands.[60] Although it is easy to find a number of Dutch deviations from strict neutrality,[61]

57. Adriaan J. Barnouw, *Holland under Queen Wilhelmina*, pp. 180, 183; Gillain to Hymans, 30 Dec. 1918, no. 62/66, BMAE B–383.

58. Vandenbosch, *Dutch Foreign Policy*, p. 115. DuB, R.G.P. 109 and 116, passim, indicate clearly the precariousness of the Dutch position.

59. The most detailed study of this question is Charles Albert Watson, "Britain's Dutch Policy, 1914–1918."

60. Townley to Balfour, 29 Apr. 1918, no. 64 Treaty, F.O. 372/1146; DuB, R.G.P. 116, pp. 490–91; DuB, R.G.P. 146, p. 284.

61. A sizable collection of documentary evidence of Dutch violations of neutrality, including photocopies of German orders for use of Dutch railways, may be found in FMAE Z/PB/32–33.

any judgment of Dutch policy must take into consideration the extreme difficulty of the position throughout.

At first, Belgian leaders fully appreciated this fact and were grateful for Dutch kindness to Belgian refugees. Preoccupied with Belgium's heroism, they never contemplated the fact that their country would undoubtedly have followed Holland's prudent policy if events had given her an opportunity to do so. Nonetheless, they did recognize that territorial claims upon Holland would be a very delicate matter, and planning documents were almost invariably predicated upon Dutch consent, which somehow was to be arranged, preferably by Britain, and compensation to the Netherlands, usually in the form of German border districts. The territories upon which some Belgian eyes soon fixed were of course Dutch Limburg and Flemish Zeeland. The Foreign Ministry also deeply desired improvements in the regime of the Scheldt, but those presumably could be achieved by negotiation, particularly with British and French assistance.

Both Davignon and Beyens carefully refrained from formal enunciation of any territorial claims on Holland, mindful of how both the image and the postwar bargaining position of "gallant little Belgium" could be harmed, along with Belgo-Dutch relations, by unwarranted claims upon the territory of a neutral and friendly neighbor. But Foreign Ministry officials, eager to seize what might be the only chance to undo the decisions of 1839, continued to debate the matter, although they concluded that annexationist claims would be inopportune during the war and perhaps should not be made at all.[62] As they considered acquisition of not only lower Limburg but also both banks of the Scheldt for military and economic reasons, they were urged on toward annexationism by French officials who, early in the war, tried to turn Belgian eyes northward in an effort to distract them from Luxemburg, a tactic France also attempted at the postwar peace conference.[63] During the

62. Direction Politique note, 10 Apr. 1915, de Gaiffier to Davignon, 3 Mar. 1915, Arendt note, May 1915, BMAE Ind/1915/I; Davignon to Fallon, 19 July 1915, no. 191, BMAE PB/1915; de Broqueville note, 15 Apr. 1915, BMAE B–280; Direction Politique note, 15 Apr. 1915, BMAE B–348; Direction Politique note, 25 Jan. 1915, BMAE B–1.

63. De Broqueville to Beyens, 13 Sept. 1915, Barbanson note, 26 Mar. 1917, BMAE B–280; Guillaume to Davignon, 20 July 1915, no. 6115/1614, BMAE FR/1915/II; Guillaume to Davignon, 7 Apr. 1915, no. 3267/802, BMAE FR/1915/I; Guillaume to

war, French support of and encouragement to Belgian claims on Flemish Zeeland and lower Limburg was constant. Through 1916, the British, although vague about territorial matters, reserving them as always for postwar discussion, held out some hope that there could be a postwar alleviation of the Scheldt regime in return for a great-power guarantee of Holland against Germany or of her East Indian colony against Japan.[64] Though the Belgian Foreign Ministry was perfectly frank about the need to improve the Scheldt regime, it continued to avoid claims on Dutch territory, despite French encouragement and despite a possibly misleading indirect diplomatic report in August 1916 that the Dutch government might be prepared to cede Flemish Zeeland and Dutch Limburg in return for territorial compensations elsewhere.[65]

If the Belgian government was extremely circumspect during the war in regard to its northern neighbor, the Belgian press was not. Unlike the newspapers of other belligerents, the wartime Belgian press was under no governmental restriction whatever because none of it was on Belgian territory. It was a press in exile, scattered in France, Britain, and the Netherlands. The Belgian government was thus unable to exercise even normal peacetime influence, let alone wartime censorship. In early 1916 an intense campaign toward annexation of Dutch territory built up in the exile press, partly in response to earlier suggestions in Allied newspapers. Though the Belgian government had not sanctioned this chorus and Beyens was much displeased, it is entirely possible that certain ministers (notably de Broqueville, Carton de Wiart, and Jules Renkin) had privately encouraged it, as the king suspected. In addition, Nothomb was doing his awkward best to drum up popular sentiment for the reacquisition of Limburg. The Belgian cabinet had in fact taken no decision in favor of annexationism and Beyens disavowed the newspaper campaign several times to the Dutch, but to little avail as the press activity did not cease.[66]

Davignon, 25 Nov. 1914, no. 12351/3264, BMAE FR/1914; de Gaiffier to Beyens, 28 Sept. 1916, no. 7128/2731, BMAE FR/1916.

64. Grey to Villiers, 10 July 1915, no. 58, F.O. 371/2637; de Bassompierre note, 18 Sept. 1916, BMAE Ind/1915–16; Hymans to Beyens, 1, 14 Sept. 1916, nos. 9034/1220, 9500/1288, BMAE GB/1916.

65. Palo, "Belgian War Aims," p. 432.

66. Albert, *Diaries*, p. 95; Beyens to de Buisseret, 9 Sept. 1916, BMAE Ind/1915–16;

In due course the Dutch press became extremely agitated, claiming that the Belgian campaign indicated that British and French promises to respect Dutch neutrality were being violated. As a consequence, when Beyens arrived in London in July of 1916 to discuss the Scheldt regime and other matters, he encountered heavy pressure for an immediate joint Anglo-French-Belgian declaration. He had no choice but to agree on the spot, and thus a joint declaration was issued repudiating the newspaper campaign. Because the Dutch press continued to sound alarms and became as irresponsible as the Belgian press, Beyens not only confirmed the statement in writing at Dutch request but also strengthened it to state that the Belgian government strongly disapproved of all intrigues aimed against Dutch territorial integrity. As the Dutch requested permission to publish his statement, he gave that as well.[67]

Under the circumstances, it was impossible for the Belgian government to pursue the questions of Limburg and Zeeland, on which, in any event, no decisions had been taken. While Dutch opinion became alarmed again in 1917, there was considerably less cause this time,[68] although the interest of the more ardent Belgian annexationists in both areas had never abated. Meanwhile, official Belgian efforts focused on the fluvial regime of the Scheldt, which did not involve territorial transfer. A note pointing out the deficiencies of the Scheldt regime and the need to remedy them but not advocating any particular solution had been sent to Grey in May 1916 and also handed to the French, who favored revision to Belgium's benefit. Grey, though sympathetic, was more cautious, pointing to Britain's delicate situation vis-à-vis Holland, but he did not rule out postwar negotiations.[69]

When Beyens visited Grey in July 1916, he presented another note favoring negotiated revision of the 1839 regime, ruling out annexation,

---

DuB, R.G.P. 137, pp. 381, 398–99; Beyens to Fallon, 29 Jan., 7 July 1916, nos. 138, 881, BMAE PB/1916; BMAE archives note, n.d., BMAE B–280.

67. Beyens to de Buisseret, 9 Sept. 1916, BMAE Ind/1915–16; DuB, R.G.P. 109, pp. 580–81; Beyens to Hymans, 13 Dec. 1916, no. 1253, BMAE GB/1916.

68. De Broqueville to Klobukowski, 24 Nov. 1917, no. 623, BMAE FR/1917/II; DuB, R.G.P. 146, pp. 990–92, 997–99.

69. Grey to Villiers, 5 May 1916, F.O. 371/2637; Beyens to Hymans, 10 May 1916, no. 419, Hymans to Beyens, 27 May 1916, no. 5194/635, BMAE GB/1916; Barbanson note, 26 Mar. 1917, BMAE B–280.

and urging cosovereignty over the western Scheldt, which would solve many of Belgium's problems. As he had cleared neither this nor his other note on neutrality with the cabinet, he encountered difficulty on his return to Le Havre. Meanwhile, Grey listened politely and, as usual, made no commitments. He indicated that British recognition of Dutch neutrality in August 1914 implied recognition of Dutch sovereignty on the Scheldt. He was not encouraging but willing to consider a negotiated arrangement during the peace conference.[70] Hymans tried again in September, pointing out the anomalies of the existing regime. Grey acknowledged that it was unjust, said that nothing could be done during the war, but again held out hope that after the war a revision could be gained against a guarantee of the Dutch East Indies. He insisted that the peace conference would be the the proper place to raise the question. Beyens made another approach to the British just before he left office. Hymans was sent to see Arthur James Balfour, then foreign secretary, bearing a historical memorandum on the Scheldt and an acknowledgment that, if Holland maintained her neutrality, no alteration of the frontier was possible, but asking for revision of the fluvial regime. Like Grey, Balfour recognized that the existing situation was unfair and promised to study the matter but made no commitments.[71]

As long as he was minister in London, Hymans remained very moderate on the question of claims against Holland and consistently opposed annexationist designs on Dutch territory.[72] After he became foreign minister in January 1918, however, he gradually fell under the influence of the more annexationist-minded senior officials at the ministry, notably Albert de Bassompierre, who now headed the Direction Politique, and Pierre Orts, who had moved from the Colonial Ministry to the Foreign Ministry in 1917 and who became acting secretary-general in 1918. Orts specialized in questions involving Africa and Holland, and pursued territorial aims in both areas. In time and particularly as victory became assured in the summer of 1918, Hymans at least

70. Grey to Villiers, 10 July 1916, no. 58, F.O. 371/2637; Beyens to de Buisseret, 9 Sept. 1915, BMAE Ind/1915–16.
71. Hymans to Beyens, 14 Sept. 1916, no. 9500/1288, BMAE GB/1916; Hymans to Beyens, 2 July 1917, no. 5995/1001, BMAE GB/1917/I; Balfour to Villiers, 2 July 1917, no. 53, F.O. 371/2896.
72. For example, Hymans to Beyens, 19 June 1916, no. 6060/752, BMAE GB/1916.

partially absorbed the Direction Politique view that the peace conference would be the one and perhaps the only chance ever to "right the
wrongs" of 1839. Faced with the unhappy facts of Dutch neutrality and
Belgian declarations disavowing annexationist aims, he fell back on a
tactic he had recommended regarding the fluvial regime during his
years in London.[73] He proposed to point out the numerous difficulties
of the existing frontiers without formulating claims and to hope that the
British would both recommend solutions and bring their influence to
bear upon the Netherlands to achieve them. As a consequence, Belgium never made any formal claims upon Dutch territory, but the general pattern of Belgian policy as the war drew to a close understandably
gave rise to Dutch alarm.[74]

If claims upon neutral Holland and occupied Luxemburg were delicate, designs on the African possessions of Allied Portugal were even
more awkward. Indeed, the Congo's role in the African campaigns,
once its neutrality had been abandoned, was the subject of endless dissension, both Belgian and British. At Le Havre, the colonial minister,
Renkin, favored conquering a new African empire without delay, but
cooler heads prevailed and the cabinet decided that Belgian troops
would act only in concert with the British.[75] The latter, however, could
not decide whether they wanted Belgian aid. The difficulty from the
British point of view was that troops from the Congo were badly
needed for operations against German East Africa, as Belgium had
considerably more troops available to this end than any other power,
but Britain wished to keep all the conquered territory for herself. As a
consequence, the Foreign Office, which favored Belgian assistance to
shorten the campaign and reduce British casualties, haggled with the
Colonial Office, which objected that Belgium would probably wish to
keep some of the territory it conquered. Thus, Belgian assistance in the
defense of Abercorn in northern Rhodesia was first rejected but then
requested and provided when it became essential. The British were

73. Hymans to Beyens, 21 Jan. 1916, no. 712/81, BMAE B–348; Hymans to Beyens,
22 Jan. 1916, BMAE GB/1916.
74. Hymans instructions to Carton de Wiart mission to Italy, June 1918, BMAE Ind/
1918; DuB, R.G.P. 117, pp. 691–92, 698–701; de Gaiffier to Hymans, 28 Sept. 1918,
no. 6941/2463, Hymans to de Gaiffier, 4 Oct. 1918, no. 2140, BMAE FR/1918/II.
75. Albert, *Diaries*, pp. 90–91.

also forced to ask for Belgian help in protecting the Uganda frontier when the sparse British troops were needed elsewhere. Belgian forces also assisted the French in French Equatorial Africa and participated throughout the French campaigns in the Cameroons.[76]

After the War Office took charge of the British African campaigns, the British finally faced the fact that they needed the substantial Belgian force in the Congo (which, like the African armies of other powers, consisted of European officers and native troops), and the campaigns in German East Africa were consequently coordinated by local commanders with the consent of both Brussels and London. In April and May of 1916, Belgian forces overran Ruanda and Urundi, the northernmost provinces of German East Africa. Then they seized the Ujiji district, took control of the vital German central railway, reached Lake Victoria in the north, and finally marched hundreds of miles southward to occupy the key administrative center of Tabora on 19 September 1916. The Belgian campaign had been supported by British matériel and porters, both paid for by Belgium, and had met with little resistance aside from a few sharp encounters as German forces fled southward. Because the Belgians were delayed by difficult terrain, abnormally heavy rain, and floods, they did not succeed in trapping the German army. The Belgians of course extolled their glorious military feat, while the British, who wanted the territory conquered by the Belgian forces for themselves, consistently argued then and thereafter that the Belgian contribution had been minimal, made possible only by British assistance, lack of German resistance, and British campaigns elsewhere in German East Africa that tied up German forces. Nonetheless, by September 1916, Belgian forces were in effective control of most of northern and much of western German East Africa and held the central railway from Kigoma to Tabora.[77]

In fact, aside from frontier rectifications, the Belgian government had no desire to keep any of the conquered territory, whereas the British wanted it very much. Ruanda and Urundi were temperate high-

76. Louis, *Germany's Lost Colonies*, pp. 63–64; cabinet memo, Aug. 1915, CAB 37/133; Orts to Council of Ten, 30 Jan. 1919, AGR Orts Papers/433; Murray memo, 8 Oct. 1915, CAB 42/4.

77. Subcommittee of C.I.D. meeting, 12 Nov. 1915, CAB 42/5; William Roger Louis, *Ruanda-Urundi, 1884–1919*, pp. 215–16, 218–23.

lands, deemed (in the invariable parlance of the day) eminently suitable for white settlement. Further, the British considered the eastern portion of this area to be the best route for the Cape-to-Cairo railway, which they still hoped to build now that the impediment of German East Africa was being removed. Accordingly, the British loftily announced as the Belgian invasion began in April 1916 that they would take over provisional administration of all conquered territories until the peace conference determined a final settlement. This the Belgians firmly rejected, as they intended to use their considerable conquests as pawns to obtain what they really wanted, a broadening of the Belgian Congo's embarrassingly short Atlantic coastline. Belgian interest centered on Cabinda, a Portuguese enclave just north of the Congo border, and the northernmost portion of Portuguese Angola to the south, a territory of little intrinsic value but whose possession would gain Belgium control of both banks of the mouth of the Congo River. The Belgian plan was to retain control of most of the territory she controlled in German East Africa until Britain, by concessions elsewhere, persuaded Portugal to cede the desired territories to Belgium.[78] Meanwhile the Belgians did offer on 8 September 1916, when it had become clear that they would reach Tabora before the British, to evacuate it. They did not need it for their purposes, it was expensive to administer and a logistic problem, and a potentially dangerous situation could develop if the native population should rebel or the Germans return. In short, the British could take over the Tabora district if they would accept indefinite Belgian occupation of the other East African territories she had conquered, which Belgian officials considered more than enough for eventual trading purposes.[79]

As the British had no troops available, they were slow to reply. Instead, they inquired about Belgian territorial goals in Africa. On 10 October, Renkin replied with the utmost frankness that Belgium

78. Beyens to Villiers, 26 Apr. 1916, Hymans to Beyens, 27 May 1916, no. 5194/635, BMAE GB/1916; Davignon to Hymans, 23 May 1915, no. 431, BMAE GB/1915; Direction Politique notes, 15 Sept. 1914, 25 Jan. 1915, BMAE B–1; de Broqueville to Hymans, Feb. 1915, BMAE B–280.

79. Louis, *Ruanda-Urundi*, pp. 225–26; Louis, *Germany's Lost Colonies*, p. 67; BMAE note, 20 Dec. 1916, Orts Papers/433. This note implies that the Belgians expected their offer to be rejected, as Britain lacked the necessary troops.

wanted to gain as much as possible in return for her military effort in
Africa, and he openly revealed Belgian plans to trade her East African
holdings for Portuguese territories in the west. He asked for an indemnity for Belgian losses and administrative costs, along with various
lesser postwar concessions in Africa, and strongly implied that Belgium
would not cooperate in further campaigns unless her terms were met.
The British, who had their own designs on Portuguese territory at
Delagoa Bay in Mozambique, reacted sharply to this blatant ploy, rejecting the Belgian proposals, refusing to discuss the final territorial
settlement before the peace negotiations, remarking that the Belgian
notes caused them "embarrassment," and at the same time accepting
the Belgian offer of Tabora. This British note arrived on 10 November
just as the Belgian cabinet was deciding to rescind the 8 September
offer. After some hesitation, the Belgians decided to try to hold Tabora.
The British held firm: they wished to occupy Tabora and they wanted
Belgian assistance in further campaigns. After further complex and
unpleasant negotiations, the Belgians conceded on 14 December 1916.
They evacuated Tabora and about one-third of their conquests in February 1917.[80] They also participated in the Mahenge campaign in southern German East Africa and came to the rescue of the British at Tabora
when the Germans threatened in May 1917. Thereafter, Belgian leaders wisely resisted French pressure to transfer their African troops to
the western front.[81]

Belgium had retained her valuable pawn but she had gained no British commitments and she could not achieve her ultimate goal without
British assistance, particularly because Portugal had entered the war
partly in order to protect her colonial holdings.[82] In this matter, as in
regard to Luxemburg and the Scheldt, Belgium had revealed her hand
most fully to the power that was most likely to thwart her. The East
African negotiation was a rare occasion when Belgian leaders, led this

80. BMAE note, 20 Dec. 1916, Louwers note, Dec. 1920, Orts Papers/433; Villiers to
Grey, 10 Oct. 1916, no. 166, Grey to Villiers, 8 Nov. 1916, no. 90, CAB 37/157.
  81. Robertson to cabinet, 12 July 1917, CAB 24/19; Orts to Council of Ten, 30 Jan.
1919, Orts Papers/433; Hymans, *Mémoires*, 1:339; Génie to Guerre, 6 June 1917, no.
428, Vin 7N/1160; Briand to Klobukowski, 13 Feb. 1917, no. 70, Klobukowski to
Briand, 19 Feb. 1917, tel. 27, FMAE CPC Guerre Belg./423.
  82. Louis, *Germany's Lost Colonies*, p. 73.

time by Renkin, attempted some hardheaded Realpolitik, mainly because it was almost the only time when they actually had something
with which to dicker, but they did so with considerable ineptitude,
revealing all and gaining nothing. They acted out of well-founded fears
that they would be left out of the colonial settlement and emerge
empty-handed, but the British had only to take a lofty moral stance, at
which they were so practised, and to indicate outrage. As the Belgians
could not really afford to hold Tabora indefinitely, the British gained
their goal easily at no cost in cash or commitments. In addition, Belgian
haggling over money and men and threats not to cooperate further
could be unfavorably compared to what Britain had poured forth at
Ieper (Ypres) and elsewhere in Flanders fields.

In East Africa the Belgians had used their pawn clumsily. The only
other domain under the general rubric of war aims where Belgium had
even the smallest weapon to use in dealing with Britain and France was
in the economic sphere. In the years just before World War I, the
Belgian economy had oriented itself increasingly toward Germany.
Though most Belgian leaders had no intention whatever of returning to
the German economic orbit after the war, they concluded that the
threat of doing so would be their most effective weapon to induce
concessions from Britain and France.[83] Certainly they had no other.
Although they gained no concessions, they did generate a certain
amount of alarm, particularly in Britain. The Belgians also tried to play
the British and French off against each other, and in regard to France,
whose embrace often seemed too enthusiastic, they played the Flemish
card to escape excessive entanglement. None of the Belgian government leaders wanted a full-scale Franco-Belgian customs union, but
Flemish opinion, which was traditionally hostile to France, provided a
convenient excuse, as did the isolation of the government in exile from
the business community.[84]

Indeed, the difficulty of consulting business leaders in occupied Belgium, despite occasional limited soundings for the Foreign Ministry by
Baron Léon Capelle, who had remained in Brussels, was one reason

83. De Gaiffier to Beyens, 21 Oct. 1916, no. 7714/3050, BMAE FR/1916.
84. Génie memo, 14 Feb. 1916, no. 264, Klobukowski to Briand, 21 Feb. 1916,
FMAE CPC NS Belg./36.

why Belgian economic policy evolved slowly in the early years of the war. Another was that the business community wished to know the future international status of Belgium before advising, and the decision to abandon permanent neutrality was reached slowly. In fact, one of the arguments for its retention, both by businessmen and by officials, was that it favored commerce and Belgian prosperity. In August 1915, however, Beyens argued forthrightly to the cabinet that Belgian commercial success arose from lower prices and superior quality, not from conventional neutrality.[85] By the time he made this argument, the Belgian cabinet was close to a decision to abandon neutrality and being forced to consider its postwar economic orientation by the obvious strings attached to French offers of Luxemburg early in 1915.

In economic matters as in political questions, the Belgian goal was to achieve genuine independence and to avoid becoming the satellite of any one power. There was widespread recognition that Belgium had fallen under excessive German economic influence before the war and that, whatever else happened, this orientation must be replaced by new markets elsewhere.[86] Belgium's economic pattern was similar to that of Britain. She imported raw materials and food while exporting technical skills and manufactured goods from her highly developed industries. Accordingly, Belgium had long been a free-trade country. Because Britain also pursued a free-trade policy, whereas France was strictly protectionist, in one sense logic dictated a turn in the British direction. Yet the Belgians began to explore the economic possibilities with France first, partly because the French raised the subject in connection with Luxemburg, and partly because France's postwar territorial aims in Europe, combined with her existing economic laws, could pose a serious threat to Belgian recovery and prosperity.

Before World War I, the Belgians were complaining bitterly about the French tariff of 1910, which seriously hampered Belgian exports to France.[87] In those years, Belgium enjoyed a booming trade from Antwerp into Alsace-Lorraine. If France annexed those provinces, as she

85. Capelle notes, 13 Nov. 1915, 22 Mar. 1916, Beyens to cabinet, Aug. 1915, BMAE Ind/1915–16.

86. Homberg note, 3 June 1915, FMAE CPC NS Belg./36.

87. FMAE note, 18 July 1914, FMAE CPC NS Belg./36.

frankly confided her intention to do, the French tariff would seriously affect that lucrative market. If France took Luxemburg, as she hinted she would do if Belgium did not—and sometimes suggested she might do in any event—she could not only shut off that lesser market but, more importantly, through control of the main Luxembourgeois rail lines, also hamper Belgian access to Strasbourg, Switzerland, and Italy. If France dominated the Rhineland as well, Belgium would find herself encircled economically as well as politically, with all of her major Continental markets seriously impeded. Beyond the French tariff lay a second problem, that of the *surtaxe d'entrepôt*. This measure, codified in 1892 for the benefit of the French channel ports, levied a special flat-rate duty on all overseas goods entering Franch via a non-French port.[88] Antwerp had already suffered from this measure, but it would suffer far more severely if the surtax were imposed on the flourishing trade to Alsace-Lorraine and possibly in Luxemburg as well. Under the circumstances, it behooved the Belgian leadership at Le Havre, planning in enforced idleness, to sound the French and see what concessions they were prepared to make.

The Belgians raised the question of their economic future with French representatives at Le Havre in June of 1915, hinting that they might have to turn toward Britain to replace the prewar German market if France did not make concessions. French experts studied the question in detail during the remainder of the year, but serious negotiation did not begin until 1916.[89] Much of it occurred in the context of the Allied Economic Conference held in Paris in June of that year, which foresaw a virtual Allied economic wall against Germany. Although its recommendations were not in fact maintained after the war when the American government declined to continue the wartime arrangements, during the war and for some time after it the French proceeded on the assumption of a rigid trade barrier against Germany. During the war, the Belgians, who had been permitted to participate in

---

88. Bernard Auffray, *Pierre de Margerie (1861–1942) et la vie diplomatique de son temps*, pp. 378–79. The *surtaxe* was reinforced by an April 1916 law. Max Suetens, *Histoire de la politique commerciale de la Belgique depuis 1830 jusqu'à nos jours*, p. 195.

89. Homberg note, 3 June 1915, Lahure to Pila, 20 Dec. 1915, 22 Apr. 1916, FMAE CPC NS Belg./36.

this Allied conference if in few others, had little reason to anticipate otherwise than that their traditional market might be closed.[90]

Some casual Franco-Belgian discussions occurred early in 1916, in which de Broqueville mentioned the possibility that if Allied cooperation failed, Germany might again dominate a devastated Belgium after the war. Meanwhile, French economic experts prepared studies proposing to offer Belgium Luxemburg and the Rhineland north of the Moselle River in return for sweeping economic arrangements that would effectively grant France control of both Belgium and her new acquisitions. The experts urged immediate negotiations on the theory that Belgium would be more amenable during the war than after it.[91] This advice was accepted and cabinet level talks were conducted by French Minister of Commerce Etienne Clémentel at Le Havre and Paris with de Broqueville and Belgian Minister of Finance Alois van de Vijvere in May, August, September, and October of 1916. Clémentel argued for a full customs union, at which the Belgian ministers demurred, preferring special tariff arrangements on particular goods. From the first, they were alarmed by French political conditions but afraid to reject the French proposal outright for fear of protest from the Belgian business community. Thus the talks continued through the summer and fall of 1916. Though Clémentel pursued his vision of a customs union, offering to call it by another name, no conclusion was reached.[92]

These early talks revealed the basic problems, which were never resolved. Belgium came to the negotiations seeking much but with very little to offer in return. As their tariff was already very low, there were few concessions the Belgian leaders could make to gain what they wanted. They could and did offer to lower the Belgian barrier against French wine, but Clémentel refused concessions to Belgian textiles, let alone the broader concessions that Belgium wanted, without a full customs union with political and military strings attached. In response,

90. FRUS, 1916, Supplement, pp. 974–81.

91. Génie report, 14 Feb. 1916, no. 264, Lahure note, 22 Apr. 1916, FMAE CPC NS Belg./36.

92. Suetens, *Politique commerciale*, p. 167; comptes-rendus, 18 Aug. 1916, FMAE CPC NS Belg./36, 6 Sept. 1916, 5, 9, 17 Oct. 1917, FMAE CPC NS Belg./37; Beyens to Hymans, 23 June, 9 Sept. 1916, AGR Hymans Papers/182.

van de Vijvere made a speech about Belgian independence,[93] and that in fact was the heart of the problem.

The Franco-Belgian negotiations continued through the remainder of 1916 and much of 1917.[94] The Belgians consistently rejected a customs union under any name, stressing the importance of independence and noting that although they wanted access to the French market, high tariffs on food imports were out of the question. Clémentel pressed on, despite the hesitations of some French industrialists and politicians about Belgian competition. To circumvent the problem of a customs union, various schemes were aired for Franco-Belgian consortia in specific industries and/or special frontier tariff zones, but no agreements were reached, as the Belgians continued to seek more than the French were prepared to concede. After Hymans returned to Le Havre, first in the newly created post of minister of economic affairs in October 1917, and then as foreign minister from January 1918 on, he showed markedly less enthusiasm for the Franco-Belgian economic negotiations,[95] and nothing was settled at the end of the war.

Meanwhile, as early as October 1916, the French, aware that the Belgians had already approached the British, asked them to press London for a postwar French-Belgian-British economic entente.[96] Hymans had in fact made the first Belgian overtures in London in the spring of 1916, both to the British and to Dominion representatives, seeking postwar reconstruction aid, preliminary talks before the Paris Conference, and inclusion of Belgium in the British system of imperial preference, which it had enjoyed from 1862 to 1897.[97] No talks took place before the Paris Conference, but at the end of June 1916, de Broqueville and Renkin discussed economic matters in London with several British leaders who were consistently sympathetic to the needs of Bel-

---

93. Compte-rendu, meeting of 6 Sept. 1916, FMAE CPC NS Belg./37.

94. The negotiations may be traced in FMAE CPC NS Belg./36–39.

95. De Gaiffier to Beyens, 25 Sept. 1916, no. 7035/2689, BMAE FR/1916; Klobukowski to Pichon, 12 Jan. 1918, no. 19, FMAE CPC NS Belg./38; Georges-Henri Soutou, "La Politique économique de la France à l'égard de la Belgique, 1914–1924," p. 260.

96. Compte-rendu, 9 Oct. 1916, FMAE CPC NS Belg./37.

97. Grey to Villiers, 6 Mar., 5 Apr. 1916, nos. 18, 25, Villiers to Grey, 14 Apr. 1916, no. 24, CAB 37/146; Hymans to Beyens, 6 May 1916, no. 4364/525, BMAE GB/1916; Suetens, *Politique commerciale*, p. 165.

gian reconstruction but otherwise studiously vague. In September, Sir Walter Runciman, president of the Board of Trade, proposed an Anglo-French-Belgian economic entente to Hymans. This initiative, which would have solved many of Belgium's problems and which was also what the French desired, was cut short by the fall of H. H. Asquith's cabinet in early December 1916.[98] As the Belgians were by then finding French economic demands onerous, they turned to the new British government for support. The new foreign secretary, Arthur James Balfour, was strongly in favor of aiding Belgian reconstruction, and in June 1917 the British set up a committee, which the French eyed warily, to study Belgian economic problems.[99] But repeated Belgian overtures yielded nothing concrete, partly because the British remained innately cautious about commitments, partly because an intense debate was in progress about postwar British trade policy, and partly because David Lloyd George, the new prime minister, thought that Britain's needs should come first. Although the Foreign Office continued to be sympathetic to the needs of Belgian reconstruction, the Treasury rejected all proposals, noting that concessions to Belgium would generate a renewal of Serbian demands, and argued that all should await the end of the war.[100] The Treasury prevailed and, aside from Lloyd George's formal commitment to the political, territorial, and economic restoration of Belgium "and such reparation as can be made for the devastation of its towns and provinces" in his speech on war aims on 5 January 1918, and a vague speech by Balfour in April, which implied that Britain would move to counteract French economic influence in Belgium, no decisions were taken.[101] Hymans renewed talks with the Brit-

98. Grey to Villiers, 27 June 1916, no. 51, CAB 37/150; Hymans to Beyens, 27 June, 16, 27 Sept. 1916, nos. 6361/795, 9580/1306, 9941/1359, BMAE GB/1916; Suetens, *Politique commerciale*, p. 166.

99. Hymans to Beyens, 1 Feb. 1917, no. 1038/149, BMAE GB/1917/I; Imperial War Cabinet minutes, 22 Mar. 1917, CAB 23/43; Klobukowski to Pichon, 10 Jan. 1918, no. 2, Bertie to Ribot, 24 June 1917, Ribot to Clémentel, 4 July 1917, no. 1360, FMAE CPC NS Belg./38; de Gaiffier to Hymans, 22 Apr. 1918, no. 2671/1121, BMAE FR/1918/I.

100. De Broqueville to Lloyd George, 7 Mar. 1917, Hymans to Beyens, 22 Feb., 27 Mar., 30 Apr. 1917, nos. 1693/269, 2795/456, 3860/638, BMAE GB/1917/I; Treasury to F.O., 12 Nov. 1917, no. 35958, Villiers to Balfour, 20 Dec. 1917, no. 303, F.O. 371/2898; Imperial War Cabinet minutes, 22 Mar. 1917, CAB 23/43.

101. Cd. 9005, p. 232; de Gaiffier to Hymans, 22 Apr. 1918, no. 2671/1121, BMAE FR/1918/I.

ish although not the French in 1918, but achieved no commitments. Thus, at war's end, an increasingly devastated Belgium had no concrete commitments from any power to aid in her reconstruction, much less in regard to her future economic orientation.

In economic matters, as in virtually everything else, Belgian diplomacy emerged from the four war years empty-handed. In later years, Belgian critics charged Belgian leaders with insufficient wartime planning for the future.[102] The difficulty was in fact not lack of planning but rather lack of accomplishment. The Belgian leaders had considered virtually every question except reparations in great detail and over time had reached a considerable degree of consensus on most of them. They had raised these questions repeatedly with the French and certainly more often than the British wished, but they had gained very few commitments. After American entry into the war, a special mission had been sent to the United States in an effort to enlist aid for Belgian reconstruction and to discover Woodrow Wilson's views on peace terms. The only concrete result was the seventh of Wilson's Fourteen Points of 8 January 1918: "Belgium, the whole world will agree, must be evacuated and restored, without any attempt to limit the sovereignty which she enjoys in common with all other free nations."[103] Though Belgian leaders were delighted with this statement, at least part of which would have undoubtedly been included without their special mission, it partook of the oratorical vagueness of virtually all other commitments to Belgium, including Lloyd George's own pledge of a few days before and the Declaration of Sainte-Adresse as well.

There were many reasons why the Belgians failed to gain specific commitments from the major powers. One was their acute inexperience in international politics. Various British and French leaders would from time to time make carefully qualified oral promises, usually starting with "I give you my word of honor that . . . " The Belgian officials would note the nuances but would reassure themselves by saying to each other that they could not doubt the pledged word of honor of a British (or French) cabinet minister. Most strikingly, the Belgian cabi-

---

102. See especially Baron Pierre van Zuylen, *Les Mains libres*, p. 78.
103. Moncheur to de Broqueville, 14 Aug. 1917, BMAE Ind/1917; Beyens note, 20 May 1917, BMAE B–348; Thomas Woodrow Wilson, *War and Peace*, 1:160.

net gave little attention to the most vital problem of all, that of reparation, partly because it was virtually the only point on which all Belgians
agreed, but primarily because they had been assured over and over in
1914 and thereafter by British and French leaders that Germany would
be required to pay for every penny of the damage done. The Belgian
cabinet and Foreign Ministry believed these assurances absolutely and
were content.

No doubt British and French leaders meant what they said in 1914,
but the Belgian leadership never realized how much had changed in the
course of a long and bitter war. They recognized that their country was
less the object of attention, praise, and promises late in the war than
early on, and they fretted over this, but they never fully realized that
their claims would meet with sharp competition after the war, not only
from other small-power belligerents, for whom special concessions to
Belgium might constitute a useful precedent, but also from the great
powers themselves. During the war, most of the Belgian leaders seemed
to assume that British and French resources were boundless. It never
occurred to them that after four years of astronomical expenditure in
men and money, and considerable economic damage not only to France
but also in a different sense to Britain as well, these two powers might
put their own recovery first and regard with a jaundiced eye the only
small power with large reparation claims on Germany's finite resources.
Though the Belgian Foreign Ministry followed the nuances of French
policy regarding Luxemburg with care, otherwise it rarely paid sufficient attention to shifting attitudes, although some of them were detected by Belgian diplomatic representatives. However, none of the
Belgian officials ever noticed the growing British irritation with the
Belgian refugees in England or the mounting British dismay over the
amount of British blood shed in Flanders. Proud of having done their
own duty, they did not realize that the British were less pleased at
having done theirs and had developed a certain unspoken tendency
to blame Belgium for Britain's involvement in the carnage. Similarly,
whereas Britain was hostile to the Netherlands in the autumn of 1914,
by 1918 she was positively grateful for Dutch neutrality. This fact never
occurred to Belgian leaders. They were making common cause with
their great Allies and Holland was not. Without sufficient thought, they

expected British diplomatic support in postwar negotiations with the Netherlands.

From time to time, the French, when urging Belgian diplomatists onward toward forthright claims, would complain that the Belgians expected the French to arrange everything for them and did not do enough for themselves. In a sense, this complaint had some validity in regard to both Britain and France, but Belgium had little choice. Betwixt the delicacy of some of her desires and the feebleness and isolation of her position, there was little she could accomplish on her own. Dependent on the Allies for food, funds, such scant information as they received, liberation, compensation, and concrete postwar gains, Belgian leaders could only make their interests known, once they had decided what they were, and hope. In this respect, they soon found themselves caught between conflicting French and British concepts of how to proceed. The French, in hopes of dominating postwar Belgium, urged Belgian leaders to stake out large and precise claims, even on Dutch territory. The British, on the other hand, wished to defer all decisions until the peace conference and consistently declined substantive commitments in the interim. As Belgian leaders recognized French aims, they sought British support but gained none.

Certain circumstances peculiar to Belgium complicated policy formulation. The squabbling and intrigue in the enforced idleness of Le Havre did not facilitate a reasoned approach, nor did the extreme propaganda campaigns of ardent Belgian annexationists. King Albert's status as hero, together with his dissent from much of his cabinet, his deep distrust of the British, and his inclination to negotiate with the Germans, all complicated matters, especially in the first three years of the war. Further, the last wartime ministry, that of Gérard Cooreman, took office in May 1918 on the express condition that it resign at the end of the fighting. Finally, the complete isolation of the government from the country during the war and the divisions that developed between those under occupation and those in exile dictated that decisions on some questions be postponed until public opinion could be consulted.

Nonetheless, despite all difficulties, the Belgian leaders reached a fairly clear consensus on what they wanted, if not always on how to obtain it. As Beyens remarked in September 1916, it was one thing to draw up a program of Belgian ambitions, another to execute it.[104] One reason that Belgian attempts at execution accomplished so little is that their aims contained contradictions. Belgium wanted full independence and sovereignty, yet she also wanted special protection. Security and prosperity were paramount concerns, but Belgium was unprepared to be anybody's satellite, either economically or militarily. Special concessions were sought in both spheres without adequate recognition that a price would have to be paid, particularly because the attempt to balance between Britain and France, the only possible hope of maintaining a degree of independent action, was frustrated both during the war and afterwards by British policy. Similarly, Belgian leaders devoutly desired good relations with Holland, but some of them harbored designs on Dutch territory, for both economic and security reasons. They seem, Beyens aside, to have given little thought either to the effect on Belgo-Dutch relations or to the question whether even maximum annexationist programs could afford genuine security against great powers, but their concentration upon some sort of Allied guarantee against future German invasion implies the evident answer.

The other fundamental problem was of course that in international politics one generally has to give something in order to get something, whereas the Belgians had much to get (in their eyes, at least) and precious little to give. Except in East Africa, where Orts and Renkin played Belgium's one good card badly, they were virtually empty-handed. Occasionally the cabinet would try to obtain something substantial without counterpart, as in the summer of 1916 when it forced Beyens to withdraw the offer to maintain a conscript army in return for an Anglo-French guarantee. In general, however, the Foreign Ministry, when debating concessions to be sought, would ask itself what Belgium could offer in return. The answers were always pathetically slender, not out of any particular reluctance to bargain—provided that "real" independence was not jeopardized—but because there was almost nothing at hand. Belgium's needs were enormous and her assets were tragically few. In short, Belgian diplomatists had little to work with and, as a consequence, achieved little. Belgium was essentially a mendicant, dependent upon the good will of other powers. Excluded from

104. Beyens to de Buisseret, 9 Sept. 1916, BMAE Ind/1915–16.

Allied conferences and decision making, isolated from the more crucial military fronts in the later stages of the war, caught between French pressure and British delay, the Belgian leaders could only hope with excessive optimism that their early heroism, of which they were so proud, would be generously rewarded by the great powers.

When it became evident in the late summer of 1918 that the end of the war was in sight, and planning for the peace settlement ahead began in earnest, the Belgian Foreign Ministry could catalogue few substantial commitments. True, Britain, France, and Russia had promised to fight on until Belgium was liberated, and two of these guarantor powers were fulfilling their promise. There had been endless speeches guaranteeing that Germany would pay both for the widening damage and Belgian war costs but, as Belgian leaders did not fully realize, oratory did not equate with formal written commitments. The most solid gains, such as they were, had been the Declaration of Sainte-Adresse and Ribot's carefully worded statement on Luxemburg, the latter never confirmed in writing. Both of these proved to be less than they seemed. Finally there were Lloyd George's and Wilson's commitments to "restoration" of Belgium, a term susceptible of many interpretations. These pronouncements, all vague and largely rhetorical, amounted to very little. No really solid commitments had been obtained on any key point in the Belgian program except liberation. Despite four years of continual effort, the Belgian Foreign Ministry had to start virtually from the beginning in its preparations for the peace negotiations ahead, with few assets in hand beyond a limited reservoir of good will. In their optimistic faith in the benevolence of the great powers and their absolute conviction of the justice of their cause, Belgian leaders failed to recognize that the record of the four years past did not bode well for the future.

LAST BATTLES AND FIRST SKIRMISHES

As the armies on the western front waged the last battles of the war in the summer and autumn of 1918, the first skirmishes of the coming diplomatic fray began. Unfortunately, the inexperienced Belgian leaders had little comprehension that the diplomatic equivalent of war

lay ahead. Nonetheless, as it became evident in the late summer that
the tide of battle had really turned and that the end of the war might be
in sight, Hymans and his aides moved to formalize some of Belgium's
claims to the Allies. They did so in optimism and faith, startlingly unaware of the inadequacies of the Belgian diplomatic armory for what
they hoped to achieve.

The Foreign Ministry was not only excessively convinced of the rectitude of Belgium's position but also overly trusting to the power of
rectitude. Certainly, in regard to both the events of 1914 and publicly
enunciated war aims, the Belgian position was impeccable, for whatever
that might be worth in the power politics of the peace settlement
ahead. Over Anglo-French objections, the Belgian government had
insisted upon enunciating its own official war aims. At a July 1917
Allied conference in Paris, de Broqueville had served notice that Belgium desired revision of the 1839 treaties but was careful not to explain
how sweeping a revision he had in mind. In its replies to Woodrow
Wilson on 10 January 1917 and to the pope on 24 December 1917, the
Belgian government had confined its statement of war aims to the
integrity of Belgian European and colonial territory; full political, economic, and military independence; reparations for the damage incurred
and for war costs; and some undefined securities and guarantees against
future aggression.[105] Aside from the last item, these aims had for the
most part been at least tacitly and often explicitly accepted by the Allies
before the end of the war. But Belgium's other war aims, especially the
territorial ones, remained highly controversial and largely unsecured by
Allied promises. Unfortunately, the Foreign Ministry was equally convinced of the rectitude of these goals and confident that they could be
accomplished with relative ease. All the wartime British refusals of any
commitment on territorial questions and all the French evasions on
Luxemburg had failed to warn them of serious difficulties ahead.

One reason for the lack of realism was excessive Belgian faith in
Allied pronouncements and promises, formal and informal. The resto-

105. David Hunter Miller, *My Diary at the Conference of Paris with Documents*, 4:426;
Belgian reply to papal note, 24 Dec. 1917, Hymans Papers/184; FRUS, 1917, Supplement I, pp. 8–9; R. Graham memo, 29 Dec. 1916, CAB 1/22; Beyens to Hymans, 1 Jan.
1917, tel. 2, BMAE GB/1917/I; de Gaiffier to Beyens, 3 Jan. 1917, no. 43/28, BMAE
FR/1917/I; Génie to Guerre, 17 Jan. 1917, no. 373, Vin 7N/1160.

ration of Belgium figured first in every formal Allied statement of war aims as the sine qua non of any peace settlement. Although this was accomplished in the sense of liberation, Belgian officials had meanwhile somehow translated "restoration" into territorial reward for heroism. Armed with numerous British declarations that Germany would pay in full, they did not take alarm at Lloyd George's carefully limited commitment to "such reparation as can be made for the devastation" in his 5 January 1918 declaration of war aims. Wilson's Fourteen Points were perhaps more important, as they became the official basis for negotiations, and certainly more satisfactory, especially after it was established that Point Seven concerning Belgium committed the United States not only to the abolition of compulsory Belgian neutrality but also to full reparations, including war costs. On this last point, the Belgians were particularly confident, because there was a German promise as well. On 4 August 1914, the German chancellor, Theobald von Bethmann-Hollweg, had acknowledged to the Reichstag that Germany had wronged Belgium and had declared that upon the cessation of hostilities Belgium would be restored.[106] Although Belgium had lost faith in German promises, it appeared to most Belgian leaders that Germany would probably be fair game after the war and would be given no choice but to fulfill this particular promise. While at the end of the hostilities, the Belgian Foreign Ministry contemplated methods of German payment and declined a common reparations policy with France, it did not take sufficient account of the fact that France, Britain, and Italy, each more powerful than Belgium, were all equally determined to be restored at the expense of Germany.[107]

With equal innocence, the Belgian leadership tended to rest upon the considerable apparent strength of Belgium's moral and legal status. As they knew that territorial claims at the expense of neighbors could only damage this unique position, they were careful never to make such claims explicitly. Instead, they stressed that, aside from Serbia, Belgium was the only smaller state to fight the war from start to finish. Whereas Serbia's role in the onset of the war remained rather murky, Belgium's

106. Cd. 9005, p. 232; Edward M. House, *The Intimate Papers of Colonel House*, 4:204; Wilson, *War and Peace*, 1:160, 511; J. R. H. O'Regan, *The German War of 1914*, pp. 49–50.
107. Direction F note, 12 Dec. 1918, BMAE B–366/I.

position in this respect was impeccably pure. Of all the Allies, she could be said to have had no option at any time during the long 1914 crisis or thereafter. Her only choice had been between surrender in violation of her treaty obligations or fighting in self-defense. The particular legal heinousness of the German invasion in violation of the 1839 treaties appeared in Belgian eyes to have strengthened the Belgian position, as had the dogged Belgian resistance of 1914, especially after Allied propaganda had made capital out of both. In their inexperience, Belgian leaders put considerable faith in Allied propaganda.

In addition to Belgium's special legal position in regard to the war and the various Allied pronouncements, including the ambiguous Declaration of Sainte-Adresse, Belgian officials thought that certain other factors would help their cause. They counted too heavily upon the undeniable strategic importance of Belgium to both Britain and France, the similarity of her military interests in Europe to those of France, and the importance of her economic reconstruction to the trade revival so desired by the British. Influenced by the historical tutelary relationship to the great powers, along with Anglo-French wartime assistance and oratory, Hymans and his staff could not bring themselves to face the fact that France would put French interests first and refuse to give way in the Luxemburg question until its strategic interests were met by a Franco-Belgian military accord. Similarly, it never occurred to them, although it certainly did to Lloyd George, that Belgian economic revival would only generate competition for Britain's declining industries. In the same vein, Belgian leaders assumed without much thought that the deliberate German spoliation of the Belgian economy both during the war and during the retreat to eliminate future Belgian competition, which had evoked so much Allied sympathy, would strengthen the Belgian case, an assumption that proved sound only in regard to the United States. In addition, the Belgians overestimated the value of King Albert's personal friendship with Lord Curzon, a member of the British War Cabinet who was to take charge of the Foreign Office in London during the peace conference in Paris.

With this collection of assets, some of them not very substantial, the Belgian leaders tended to be overly optimistic. Like Wilson, they forgot how quickly idealism evaporates in the aftermath of war and, self-confident of their own rectitude, they did not fully realize that such idealism as remained to their account would largely vanish at the first mention, however indirect, of claims on Holland. Moreover, it did not occur to them that ordinary people in Allied countries who had talked so much about "brave little Belgium" would resume normal peacetime lives, putting Belgium out of mind. Also like Wilson, they were novices in international diplomacy. Belgium's unusual status during her relatively brief career as a modern state had left both government and people strangely insular, and though the horizons of both had been broadened somewhat by the war, few members of the Belgian cabinet were equipped to function effectively in the tumultuous Paris scene. Although Belgium possessed a few outstanding career diplomatists, like Baron de Gaiffier, they were relegated to secondary roles at the peace conference, as Belgium's political leaders, like those of most other countries, took the vital negotiations upon themselves. Their performance soon indicated that war and exile had not fully erased the effects of the historical fact that although Belgium had long been considered the crossroads of Europe, the Belgians themselves had been primarily bystanders there, watching the traffic.

In addition, Belgian leaders only partially recognized how much the situation had changed to Belgium's detriment since the beginning of the war. Their transcendent experience was still very important to them but no longer to others, who by now were rather bored with it. Whereas in 1914 there had been only two small states fighting conspicuously beside the great powers, by the end of the war there were twenty-two smaller nations at least technically involved in the fray. Belgian claims would have to compete with those of twenty-six other victor nations, most of them more powerful than she. With so many countries involved in so unwieldy a conference, it was almost inevitable that the five great states would arrogate all power of decision to themselves and form an inner council where the peace would be written. Under these circumstances, the Allied promise at Sainte-Adresse of Belgian participation in the peace negotiations had little value.

As Hymans and his staff were quite unaware that Belgian participation in the peace conference was to be more nominal than actual, they began to plan for it in the latter part of 1918. Though it is not surprising that they were cautious about enunciating territorial aims to the Allies, it is curious that these were not worked out in more precise detail

within the Foreign Ministry, especially in regard to Europe. Of the so-
called Walloon cantons, Belgium clearly intended to claim Malmédy,
which contained many French-speaking Walloons, a large German military base, and a number of railroads running straight to the Belgian
frontier; but even as the peace conference opened, the Belgian government had not decided whether to seek the more northerly and much
more Germanic district of Eupen, also transferred to Prussia in 1815.
Similarly, the debate over Dutch territory continued, with the army
advocating Belgian acquisition of both banks of the Scheldt so that a
secure military base could be established in Flanders and supplied via
Antwerp. Though most Foreign Ministry officials and Hymans himself
continued to cherish hopes that some arrangement could be reached
to acquire Flemish Zeeland and southern Limburg in return for compensation to Holland from Germany or possibly German overseas colonies, they did not bother to consider which border districts might be
suitable for transfer until they were asked and they never, even at the
peace conference itself, came to any real decision about what German
territory should be offered to the Dutch. In this as in other questions,
the Belgians blithely expected the great powers to arrange matters for
them. Aside from Malmédy, the only European territorial claim about
which the Belgians were forthright and decided before the peace conference opened was a largely noncontroversial one, the tiny sliver known
as neutral Moresnet, accidentally assigned to nobody in 1815 and awkwardly administered jointly by Belgian and German local officials. In
regard to Luxemburg, the tactic was to seek "rapprochement" by free
consent and, until February 1919, a good many Belgian officials retained hopes of annexation. Similarly, Belgian territorial aims in Africa
had not changed and were fully known to British officials, who were
also reminded in 1918 that Belgium wished to move into the British
economic orbit.[108]

As most of Belgium's territorial desiderata presented such dangerous
problems, Hymans not surprisingly began his diplomatic efforts in the
autumn of 1918 by formalizing Belgium's desire for revision of the

108. Arthur Herchen, *Manuel d'histoire nationale*, p. 254; Fallon to Hymans, 15 Nov.
1918, tel. 774, BMAE PB/1918; Gillain to Hymans, 1 Dec. 1918, BMAE B-280;
Robert Devleeshouwer, "L'Opinion publique et les revendications territoriales belges à
la fin de la première guerre mondiale, 1918–1919," p. 233.

1839 treaties, a claim that could be interpreted in a variety of ways. In his eyes, the 1839 treaties had formed one integral whole and, because a key feature of this structure had been smashed by the German invasion, the treaties should be revised in their entirety. Such revision would include not only abolition of perpetual neutrality and the great-power guarantee but also, Hymans hoped, some sort of union with Luxemburg; either the return of Dutch Limburg or a joint defense arrangement there; the cession of Flemish Zeeland if possible; and, as a minimum demand, thoroughgoing revision of the regime of the Scheldt and of the other Belgo-Dutch waterways, including reconsideration of the status of Antwerp as a nonmilitary port. In Belgian eyes, if not in British, the impossibility of relieving Antwerp by sea had been a large and fatal factor in its fall to the Germans. Although the territorial aspects of this program had been intimated during the war to the French and more obliquely to the British, it was clearly inadvisable to present them formally, especially to Wilsonian America.[109]

Accordingly, on 18 September 1918, Hymans ordered the Belgian diplomatic representatives, Baron Moncheur in London, Baron de Gaiffier in Paris, Baron de Cartier de Marchienne in Washington, and Count van den Steen de Jehay in Rome, to lay before the Allied foreign ministers a memorandum stating that Belgium renounced both obligatory neutrality and the existing system of guarantees and that she expected to enter the League of Nations in a state of full political, military, and economic independence. Though the memorandum made no mention of territorial aims, it added that the Belgian government "intends, moreover, to claim additional guarantees. . . . The circumstances in which the peace is concluded will guide it in its claims." Both Balfour and Berthelot pressed for precise details about these additional guarantees but, on instructions, the Belgian diplomatists refused to be drawn, indicating only that such matters would depend upon the future condition and frontier arrangements of Europe. Despite the hesitations of Cambon and of the Foreign Office, France quickly and Britain eventually consented to the suppression of Belgian neutrality. So did the

109. Hymans note, n.d., Hymans Papers/184; Orts to Cooreman, 23 Oct. 1918, BMAE note to Allies, 29 Oct. 1918, Hymans Papers/161; F.O. memo, 14 Mar. 1918, G–203, CAB 24/5; de Cartier to de Broqueville, 3 Sept. 1917, no. 2418, NA B Micro/21.

United States and Italy. Thereafter, Belgian policy was fixed upon total revision of the 1839 treaties, with all that could imply.[110]

Long before, the Belgian wartime efforts had led to some considera- tion of Belgian desiderata in Allied capitals. The French had consis- tently encouraged territorial claims on Holland and Germany. They had also endorsed revision of the Scheldt regime and treaty revision in general. On 5 February 1918, Pichon had adhered to Ribot's 1917 declaration on Luxemburg but had refused to go beyond it. The British Foreign Office, on the other hand, had consistently discouraged claims on Holland, not even endorsing revision of the Scheldt regime, and had privately concluded that Belgium should be fully indemnified, should incorporate Luxemburg, and should join Britain and France in a treaty of permanent alliance. Balfour had long urged that Britain plan for the wholesale reequipping of Belgium, but he had been overruled by Lloyd George.[111]

The Belgian leaders were as yet not fully aware of these conflicting views, but they noted, without full comprehension of the import, that most of the commitments hitherto gained were vague and oratorical, and that admission to Allied conferences remained difficult to obtain. They knew, too, that because Jules Cambon's power had faded and Margerie was seriously ill, the dominant figure at the Quai d'Orsay was Philippe Berthelot, who earlier in the war had been forthright about the need to "resume the policy of Louis XIV." Hymans recognized as well the extreme British edginess about any proposal involving Hol-

110. De Cartier to Hymans, 14 Nov. 1918, no. 636, B Micro/22; Hymans, *Mémoires*, 1:180–83; Moncheur to Hymans, 23 Sept., 22 Oct. 1918, de Gaiffier to Hymans, 20 Sept. 1918, BMAE Ind/1918/II; Balfour to Villiers, 24 Sept. 1918, no. 120; Cecil to Moncheur, 31 Oct. 1918, F.O. 371/3164; Lansing to de Cartier, 13 Nov. 1918, Hymans Papers/184. The French reply was somewhat delayed by an inadvertently unfortunate wording, which the Belgians successfully protested. Pichon to de Gaiffier, 30 Sept. 1918, BMAE DB/30/I; Hymans to de Gaiffier, 1 Oct. 1918, tel. 275, Hymans to de Gaiffier, 4 Oct. 1918, no. 2140, de Gaiffier to Hymans, 2 Oct. 1918, no. 7017/2490, BMAE FR/1918/II.

111. Hymans, *Mémoires*, 1:192–93; F.O. memo, 9 May 1921, F.O. 371/6970; Hano- taux notes, 11 Nov. 1917, 11 Nov. 1918, Préliminaires de paix avec l'Allemagne, n.d., FMAE A/67; E. Babelon, "La Condition politique du Grand-Duché de Luxembourg," 12 Nov. 1918, FMAE Z/Lux/11; David Lloyd George, *Memoirs of the Peace Conference*, 1:11–12; FRUS, *The Lansing Papers, 1914–1920*, 2:29.

land, although he did not face up to the reasons or the implications.[112] Accordingly, as 1918 wore on, Belgian diplomatic activity intensified.

This new intensity of diplomatic maneuver was matched in other countries, for by the autumn of 1918 victory was in sight and all the Allies were planning in earnest for the peace ahead. In Britain and Belgium, the major effort centered in their respective foreign ministries and is relatively easy to trace; in France and America the planning agencies were outside the normal government structure, thus making reconstruction of official thinking more difficult. Further, the American Inquiry gained considerable influence in the eventual American delegation to the peace conference, whereas that of the French Comité d'Etudes was much more tenuous. Despite these complications, some indications exist. The American attitude perhaps seemed friendlier to Belgium than it actually was, for the United States was only mildly interested in Belgium, despite the influence and the wartime efforts of the American minister to Belgium, Brand Whitlock, and of Herbert Hoover, chairman of the Commission for the Relief of Belgium. Secretary of State Robert Lansing had concluded that Belgium should gain full sovereignty; accordingly he endorsed the Belgian request for the end of permanent neutrality, but he was doubtful about Luxemburg. Wilson himself was committed only by the Fourteen Points. In an effort to discover American views, on 3 November Hymans saw Colonel Edward M. House, then Wilson's personal representative in Europe, who was to become Belgium's most effective advocate at the peace conference. House assured him of the sympathy of America, and on 24 December, Hymans had his first meeting with Wilson, who was pleasant but vague. It was noticed, however, that the president's trip to Belgium, the only small country that he consented to visit, was postponed repeatedly.[113]

112. Hymans, *Mémoires*, 1:185–86, 190; Stamfordham to Bonar Law, 2 July 1917, HL Bonar Law Papers 82/2/4; Auffray, *Pierre de Margerie*, pp. 347–50; de Gaiffier to Hymans, 16 Nov. 1918, no. 8647/2931, BMAE FR/1918/II.

113. Chamberlain memo, n.d., NA Inquiry/93; Robert Lansing, *The Peace Negotiations*, p. 196; Charles T. Thompson, *The Peace Conference Day by Day*, pp. 50–51, 82–83; Hymans, *Mémoires*, 1:224; Hymans memo, 24 Dec. 1918, Hymans Papers/160; House, *Intimate Papers*, 4:252; House to Wilson, 9 Dec. 1918, tel. 19, LC Wilson Papers 5B/1;

The Belgian leaders rested content with fragmentary indications of American thinking but were more active in trying to discover French and British intentions. Hymans had hitherto avoided talks with the French but, with an armistice nearing, went to Paris at King Albert's suggestion on 23 and 24 October for discussions with Pichon, Clemenceau, Jules Cambon, and Poincaré. From these meetings he concluded that the French would support the end of neutrality and revision of the Scheldt regime but probably not the transfer of lower Limburg. Although French planning documents of this era allocated both Limburg and Luxemburg to Belgium, the French leaders were extremely cautious in discussing Luxemburg. They showed no willingness to restrain the parliamentary and press campaign of the Comité Franco-Luxembourgeois and indicated that assignment of occupation troops in the Grand Duchy was a military matter. The French leaders all used virtually identical language, refusing to discuss the eventual disposition of Luxemburg and consistently adhering to the narrowest possible interpretation of Ribot's pledge. Poincaré did, however, casually express his desire for the closest intimacy between France and Belgium and mentioned the possibility of a military alliance, leading Hymans to conclude accurately that such might be the price of French acceptance of a Belgian solution to the Luxemburg question.[114] Despite these discouraging indications, Hymans continued to hope that a way could be found to gain Luxemburg without the military alliance if Britain and America would support Belgium on this issue.

Belgian efforts to ascertain British attitudes were less successful, mainly because British policy was still developing. Unlike the French, the British had deferred all decisions until the end of the war. In mid-1918, however, in unfulfilled hopes of dominating British activities at the peace conference, the Foreign Office organized a careful study by

---

Whitlock to Lansing, 12 Dec. 1918, LC Lansing Papers/40; Close to Hymans, 20 Dec. 1918, Wilson Papers 5B/3; House to Whitlock, 20 Dec. 1918, Whitlock Papers/38 (LC); Wilson to Whitlock, 10 Jan. 1919, Wilson Papers 5B/7; Wilson to Whitlock, 7 Feb. 1919, Wilson Papers 5B/14; Wilson to House, 3 Mar. 1919, tel., Wilson Papers 5B/18; Wilson to Lansing, 5 June 1919, Wilson Papers 5B/42.

114. Hymans, *Mémoires*, 1:184–209; Hymans to Cooreman, 22 Oct. 1918, Hymans Papers/161; Hymans to Albert, 20 Oct. 1918, BMAE DB/32/I; French planning document, 19 Dec. 1918, FMAE A/162; Hanotaux note, 11 Nov. 1918, FMAE A/67.

many experts of the problems likely to require resolution.[115] This effort resulted in a sheaf of memoranda and many comments thereon, from which a point of view gradually evolved.

The Foreign Office decided that transfer to Belgium of the Dutch provinces of Flemish Zeeland and Limburg would be reasonable but impossible. On the German border, their experts endorsed cession of Malmédy, considered neutral Moresnet without coming to any conclusion, and did not contemplate Eupen at all. Provided that the inhabitants of Luxemburg were willing, the Foreign Office recommended support for the Belgian solution. It was thought unlikely that France was interested in Luxemburg but, even if she were, the prior Belgian claim was preferred and Belgian participation in the occupation of the Grand Duchy was approved. Concerning colonies, one memorandum flatly stated that Belgium "should not be permitted" to retain any part of German East Africa, although a minor frontier rectification might be possible.[116]

Even after the British government had officially committed itself to an end to compulsory Belgian neutrality, the Foreign Office displayed a cautious reserve on this point, which is perhaps significant, considering how often in later years the British tried to obtain Belgian reversion to an undefined neutrality. It was even more cautious regarding the new guarantees hinted at by Belgium and clearly hoped that this problem could be passed to the League of Nations if it materialized. Then and thereafter, the British, influenced by their costly experience in the great war, preferred not to face this problem and to refer it to the League for quiet interment. The Foreign Office did recognize that the Scheldt regime needed revision and strongly favored both internationalization of the river and technical arrangements more satisfactory to Belgium. After extended consideration, it concluded that Belgian warships should be permitted access to Antwerp in both peace and war under a short-term treaty subject to revision if the international situa-

---

115. Baron Hardinge of Penshurst, *Old Diplomacy*, p. 229.
116. Villiers to Balfour, 8 Dec. 1918, no. 415, F.O. 371/3164; F.O. memos, 3, 11 Dec. 1918, Peace Conference paper P.C. 28, 69, F.O. 371/4554; Headlam-Morley memo, 12 Dec. 1918, P.C. 112, F.O. 371/4344; Balfour to Imperial War Cabinet, 30 Dec. 1918, G.T. 6584, CAB 24/72.

tion changed. There was considerable fear in the Foreign Office, the Department of Overseas Trade, and the Treasury that Belgium would quickly return to the German economic orbit, a fear that the Belgians had encouraged. Hence the Foreign Office urged that Belgium be granted generous financial credits and participation in the system of imperial preference.[117]

These were only Foreign Office views, however, most of them as yet not considered by other departments, the prime minister and his secretariat, or the cabinet. The Admiralty soon vetoed the opening of the Scheldt to Belgian warships, and the cabinet later decided against Belgian participation in imperial preference.[118] Other Foreign Office views were to be similarly modified at Paris. Although the policy was not yet clearly formulated in their own minds, much less on paper, both the prime minister and the Foreign Office were already beginning to think in terms of reviving Germany as a barrier to potential French domination of the Continent. Given their assumptions of Belgian subordination to France, this attitude had implications unattractive to Belgium, as became evident with the passage of time. Their equally unexpressed irritation at having been obliged to uphold the guarantee of Belgium through four costly, bloody years and their implicit gratitude for Dutch neutrality constituted similar obstacles to the realization of Belgian aspirations.

The Belgians, unaware that Foreign Office thinking had crystallized, launched a concerted diplomatic drive to muster British support and gain French concessions. King Albert was a major weapon in the Belgian diplomatic armory, and during the last months of the war and the hiatus before the peace conference he was used frequently to emphasize Belgian interests and intentions. He was especially deployed in the British direction. Although Albert was consistently reluctant to leave Belgian soil during the war, in June 1918 he visited London incognito to congratulate the king and queen on their silver wedding anniversary,

---

117. P.I.D. memo, 4 Nov. 1918, G.T. 6213, CAB 24/69; P.I.D. memo, n.d., P.C. 55, F.O. 371/4553; W.O. memo, 2 Jan. 1919, F.O. 374/20; F.O. memo, 11 Dec. 1918, P.C. 77, F.O. 371/4355; Wellesley to Cecil, 26 Aug. 1918, F.O. 371/3165; Cecil memo, 26 Oct. 1918, BL Cecil Papers/51094; W.C. 491B, 26 Oct. 1918, CAB 23/14.

118. Admiralty memo, 23 Dec. 1918, F.O. 371/3164; War Cabinet paper W.C. 565, 9 May 1919, CAB 23/10.

and he returned in July to visit Curzon and talk with British leaders. In October he sent Curzon a letter lavishly praising the recent work of the British air force in Flanders.[119] Armistice Day found him in Paris for talks with the French and with Curzon, and that same week he entertained Curzon at the castle of Loppem (Lophem) near Brugge (Bruges), where he was otherwise preoccupied with constitutional reform and cabinet reconstruction. On this occasion he urged upon Curzon the transfer of Flemish Zeeland, a diplomatic feeler undoubtedly requested by the Belgian Foreign Ministry. Albert went to Paris early in December for a state visit and talks with Clemenceau but carefully informed Lord Derby, the British ambassador, of all that passed, while Hymans similarly reported to Sir Francis Villiers, the British minister in Brussels. The Belgians used the visit to France to request Anglo-French-Belgian talks at Paris before the peace conference, especially regarding revision of the 1839 treaties.[120]

Before this objective could be pursued, Belgian diplomatists found themselves faced with a more immediate objective, that of gaining participation in the armistice talks. In early October, Belgium had asked to send a delegate to the meetings of military representatives at Versailles and had, despite British opposition, gained admission when questions affecting her were under discussion. However, she failed to attain admission to the Supreme War Council, partly because Albert had declined to participate in the unified command under Marshal Ferdinand Foch.[121] At his interview with Hymans on 24 October, Clemenceau indicated that Germany had requested an armistice and intimated that Belgium would be invited to participate in a discussion

119. Curzon to Lloyd George, 5 June 1918, HL Lloyd George Papers F/11/9/14; Curzon to Balfour, 6 July 1918, BL Balfour Papers/49734; W.C. 489B, 22 Oct. 1918, CAB 34/14.

120. Marchioness Curzon of Kedleston, *Reminiscences*, p. 94; Charles d'Ydewalle, *Albert, King of the Belgians*, p. 124; Curzon memo, 19 Nov. 1918, CAB 21/1; Curzon to Balfour, 8 Dec. 1918, F.O. 800/199; Defrance to Pichon, 18 Nov. 1918, tel., FMAE Z/Belg./56; Hymans, *Mémoires*, 1:297–99; Cambon to Lloyd George, 6 Dec. 1918, Lloyd George Papers F/50/3/66; Derby to Balfour, 6 Dec. 1918, tel. 1706, Villiers to Balfour, 7 Dec. 1918, no. 79, F.O. 371/3164.

121. International Conference paper I.C. 81, 9 Oct. 1918, CAB 28/5; Maj.-Gen. Sir Charles Edward Callwell, *Field Marshal Sir Henry Wilson*, 2:135; de Gaiffier to Hymans, 10 Oct. 1918, tel. 137 bis, Hymans to de Gaiffier, 5 Dec. 1918, no. 2550, BMAE FR/1918/II.

of terms. On 28 October, however, Jules Cambon casually remarked to de Gaiffier that such a meeting would take place at Versailles the next day and added that it was a pity that Belgium could not attend as she was not a belligerent. De Gaiffier angrily retorted that Belgium had become a belligerent when the first shot was fired and at once notified Hymans, who protested energetically to the British and French ministers at Sainte-Adresse. As a result, Belgium gained admittance to subsequent meetings, although the summons came so late that Hymans and the Belgian chief of staff found that much had been settled without them. Though Belgium did not succeed in incorporating all her terms in the armistice conditions, they contained nothing objectionable to her.[122]

Both before and after the Armistice, the Belgian campaign for a commitment on Luxemburg continued. Belgian armistice conditions included the full evacuation of Luxemburg and, at the request of the grand ducal government, Belgian leaders arranged, despite French objections, for the American Commission for the Relief of Belgium to extend its supply operations to Luxemburg immediately after the German evacuation.[123] On 22 October, Hymans addressed to the powers another note, never answered, claiming a reunion of Belgium and Luxemburg if the Luxembourgeois were willing, and in conjunction with the Belgian military authorities, he made a persistent effort to achieve Belgian participation in the military occupation of the Grand Duchy.

122. Hymans to Albert, 24 Oct. 1918, tel. 144, BMAE FR/1918/II; de Gaiffier to Hymans, 29 Oct. 1918, Hymans to de Gaiffier, 30 Oct. 1918, BMAE Ind/1918/II; I.C. 83, 29 Oct. 1918, I.C. 88, 1 Nov. 1918, CAB 28/5; James Brown Scott, ed., *Official Statements of War Aims and Peace Proposals, December 1916 to November 1918*, p. 477. The chief Belgian gains in the Armistice conditions were requirements for the German evacuation of Luxemburg and the immediate return of the reserves of the National Bank of Belgium, which had been removed to Germany in violation of international law. Belgian concerns about potentially unfavorable interpretations of Wilson's Point Three (free trade), which might allow German dumping in Belgium during the reconstruction period, and Point Five (colonies) were given short shrift, although House was reassuring about access to raw materials, and the official interpretation of the Fourteen Points indicated that existing colonies of victor states were not at issue. FRUS, 1918, Supplement I, 1:448, 456; House, *Intimate Papers*, 4:175–76, 194–95; Hymans, *Mémoires*, 1:220–28.

123. Hymans to de Gaiffier, 12 Oct. 1918, no. 2216, BMAE GB/1918/II; Peltzer to Hymans, 6 Nov. 1918, tel. 204, BMAE DB/32/I; de Cartier to Hoover and Lansing, 2 Nov. 1918, BMAE DB/32/II; Pichon to Jusserand et al., 30 Oct. 1918, tel. 2918, Pichon to Allizé, 30 Oct. 1918, tel. 667, Vin 6N/291.

The British consented and the French officially made no objection to this latter request, but Foch raised such an unending stream of difficulties that, despite the technical consent of the French government to limited participation, Belgian troops were not permitted to enter Luxemburg. An appeal to Balfour evoked astonishment and sympathy but no assistance.[124]

Even more alarming indications of French intentions appeared soon after the Armistice. Brussels was initially in the French military zone and at first no other Allied forces were allowed there, while French troops paraded through the city with much ceremony and monotonous regularity. French generals and diplomatists openly proclaimed to their British and American counterparts the French intention of displacing the British entirely in Belgium and of making it a French sphere of influence.[125] Belgian dismay deepened when they learned that at London on 1 December 1918, Marshal Foch proposed a confederation of France, Belgium, Luxemburg, and the Rhenish provinces.[126]

Although amply warned by their minister in Brussels, the British failed to react to the French campaign, but the Belgians did, making every effort to court the British government. A conspicuously large number of Britons were invited to the royal entry into Brussels on 22 November and to the palace luncheon after the ceremony.[127] To insure further that Britain did not misconstrue Belgian intentions, a royal review of British troops in Brussels to counter the incessant French parading was arranged at Belgian initiative on 5 January 1919, and Albert took advantage of this opportunity to summon Derby, ask for a meeting of Hymans with Lloyd George and Balfour, and say

124. BMAE note to Allies, 22 Oct. 1918, BMAE DB/32/I; Hymans, *Mémoires*, 1:199, 344–45; Imperial War Cabinet paper I.W.C. 48, 31 Dec. 1918, CAB 23/42; Jean Jules Henri Mordacq, *Le Ministère Clemenceau*, 3:19–20; Joseph Brand Whitlock, *The Letters and Journal of Brand Whitlock*, 2:538; Pichon to de Gaiffier, 21 Nov. 1918, BMAE B–1–1519; Moncheur to Hymans, 17 Dec. 1918, no. 9908/2274, BMAE GB/1918/II.

125. Defrance to Pichon, 26 Nov. 1918, tel. 184, Vin 6N/128; Whitlock to Lansing, 24 Jan. 1919, 811.20/3, NA ACNP/437; Villiers to Curzon, 7 Aug. 1920 (Annual Report, 1919), no. 571, F.O. 371/3651; Whitlock, *Letters*, 2:543; Whitlock to House, 10 Dec. 1918, SML House Papers 20/24; Defrance to Pichon, 26 Nov. 1918, tel. 184, FMAE Z/Belg./56.

126. Hankey Diary, 4 Dec. 1918, CC Hankey Papers 1/5; Callwell, *Sir Henry Wilson*, 2:153; Lloyd George, *Memoirs*, 1:78–79; Foch note, 28 Nov. 1918, FMAE A/162.

127. Callwell, *Sir Henry Wilson*, 2:151–52.

bluntly, "Why should we have to do all our conversations with the French when it is with England that we wish to make arrangements?"[128]

In an effort to facilitate such conversations, the Belgian government also embarked upon a long campaign to raise the respective British and Belgian legations to the rank of embassy. But Balfour opposed the multiplication of embassies on principle. Consequently, Britain declined a useful opportunity to reinforce its influence and only acceded to the Belgian request in July 1919 after France, the United States, Italy, and Spain had elevated their legations, thus forcing the British hand.[129] In another vain move to emphasize the identity of Belgian and British interests and institutions, the Belgian government abandoned the traditional title of *chef de cabinet* when the first post-Armistice cabinet was formed and, on the recommendation of Hymans, deliberately replaced it by that of prime minister.[130]

Meanwhile there had been the delirious joy of liberation. This had occurred gradually through the later part of November, for at the time of the Armistice three-fourths of Belgium remained under German occupation and the battle lines ran through the eastern part of the city of Ghent.[131] However, on 22 November, Albert made his triumphal entry into Brussels, bringing to the Parliament a moving account of his stewardship of the Army of the IJzer. In the dramatic royal address from the throne, he paid homage both to the Belgian army and to the Belgian citizenry who had suffered within the country, urged national unity in the urgent task of reconstruction, and graciously thanked both the Allies and the Dutch for their aid. To heal the divisions that the Germans had tried to exacerbate, Albert promised equal manhood

128. Villiers to Curzon, 7 Aug. 1920 (Annual Report, 1919), no. 571, F.O. 371/3651; Derby to Balfour, 6 Jan. 1919, Balfour Papers/49744. Derby was visiting Villiers, who was his uncle. Albert's statement was made in his slightly erratic English.

129. Villiers to Russell, 2 Jan. 1919, F.O. 800/152; Balfour to Curzon, 22 Jan. 1919, F.O. 800/215; Balfour to Curzon, 7 July 1919, Balfour Papers/49734; W.C. 594, 16 July 1919, CAB 23/11; de Gaiffier to Hymans, 4 June 1919, no. 4718/1899, BMAE FR/1919. After diplomatic relations were resumed in 1920 and throughout the era of the Weimar Republic, Germany refused to elevate its Brussels legation to an embassy, initially pleading poverty. The Dutch also did not elevate their legation, but that gave no offense because the Netherlands had no embassies anywhere until after World War II.

130. Hymans, *Mémoires*, 1:259.

131. Marc Ferro, *The Great War, 1914–1918*, p. 222; Belgian army maps, Dec. 1918, BMAE B-383.

suffrage, full language equality, and a Flemish university at Ghent. In a passage drafted by Hymans, the king declared that Belgium would be freed from her neutral status, stated that the treaties must be revised, asked for new guarantees, and appealed to the Allies for aid in the reconstruction of the country. He added: "Belgium, reestablished in all her rights, will regulate her own destinies in full sovereignty according to her needs and her aspirations. In her new statute she must find the guarantees which will shelter her from future aggressions. She will assume the position which is appropriate to her dignity and to her rank in the international order founded on justice which is about to begin."[132] It was with this illusion, and this contradictory policy, that Belgium leapt largely unarmed into the bitter power struggle that lay ahead.

In the interim, the habitual optimism of the Belgian Foreign Ministry had been reinforced by two events that occurred at the time of the Armistice. The first of these was the arrival of Kaiser Wilhelm II in Holland on 10 November 1918. Although suspicions at the time by the victors and later on by Dutch historians that the kaiser had come at Dutch invitation were almost certainly unfounded, the Netherlands suffered an extremely hostile press in Britain until mid-December and in France until mid-January.[133] Belgian leaders, not realizing that the furor over the kaiser was bound to dissipate with the passage of time, thought that the Dutch government's grant of political asylum to the German emperor, whom the Allies planned to try for the crime of invading Belgium and Luxemburg,[134] could only lend support to Belgian ambitions on Dutch territory.

More importantly, on 12 November the Dutch government authorized the transit of approximately 120,000 retreating German soldiers

132. Whitlock to House, 18 Nov. 1918, House Papers 20/24; Belgique, Parlement, Annales parlementaires de Belgique, Chambre des Représentants, *Compte rendu analytique des discussions des chambres législatives de Belgique: Chambre des représentants,* 22 Nov. 1918, pp. 1–6; Hymans, *Mémoires,* 1:254–55, 284–85.

133. Van Vollenhoven, *Memoires,* pp. 404–5; de Villegas to Hymans, n.d. [late Nov. 1918], no. 10273–223/87, BMAE PB/1918/II; DuB, R.G.P. 117, pp. 728–877 passim; DuB, R.G.P. 146, pp. 1138–39. For an example of assumptions by Dutch historians, see C. Smit, *Diplomatieke geschiedenis van Nederland,* pp. 332–33.

134. France, Ministère de la Guerre, *Examen de la responsabilité pénale de l'empereur Guillaume II,* p. 11.

across Limburg. Though the Dutch authorities confiscated all visible arms, they permitted the passage of everything else, thus depriving Belgium of prisoners, equipment and livestock, much of which had been seized in Belgium.[135] Although the Belgians were possibly well rid of the Germans, they could have used some of them for emergency repairs to the devastated Belgian railroads, and they certainly needed the equipment and livestock. It was also technically possible that the German troops might return to fight another day if hostilities resumed. Though the Dutch foreign minister informed the Allied and Belgian ministers on 13 November of the Dutch decision, he later blotted the Dutch copybook further by claiming publicly and inaccurately that German transit was accorded in the interests of Belgium and after agreement of the British, French and Belgian ministers.[136]

The Belgian government wasted no time in claiming to the British and French that the Dutch had permitted the passage because they were incapable of preventing it; Holland apparently could not defend lower Limburg, and the precedent of the German transit was dangerous to Belgium's future defense. The Belgian government also proceeded to move its military base at Calais to Antwerp via the Scheldt, merely notifying the Netherlands afterwards of the fait accompli. During the diplomatic flurry over the German passage through Limburg, Berthelot suggested that Belgium take the initiative to propose an Allied military occupation of Dutch Limburg and Foch was asked to prepare plans. Orts, in charge of the Belgian Foreign Ministry in the absence of Hymans at Brugge with the king, favored immediate and unilateral Belgian action, ostensibly to facilitate the march to the Rhine but actually to occupy lower Limburg. When consulted, Hymans and Albert deemed an occupation of Dutch territory inadvisable. Hymans wished to stand

135. Estimates of the number of German troops ranged from the official Dutch figures of 69,000 to an estimate of 200,000 by local residents. The Belgian consul in Maastricht, who investigated with great thoroughness and caution, deemed 120,000, the judgment of the Dutch lieutenant commanding on the spot, a reliable figure. De Villegas to Hymans, 14 Dec. 1918, no. 248/212, BMAE PB/1918/II; Gillain note, 15 Feb. 1919, Orts Papers/431. See also van Karnebeek to Fallon, 16 Jan. 1919, no. 81219, BMAE PB/1919. In addition, the Dutch permitted some evacuation via the Roermond railway in northern Limburg. DuB, R.G.P. 117, pp. 730–31, 738–39.

136. DuB, R.G.P. 146, pp. 909, 1118; DuB, R.G.P. 117, pp. 749, 752–54, 757–58, 768.

with Britain on this issue and so merely had Moncheur seek British views on Berthelot's proposal. The Foreign Office clearly opposed any occupation and so, it developed, did Pichon. Thus the French, pretending to the British that the idea had originated in Belgium, complained of Belgian timidity but quickly dropped the matter. Curiously, Hymans reverted to it in December, proposing not only that the Allied armies in the Rhineland be supplied across Limburg (which would benefit Antwerp) but also that the Allies occupy the province. Britain and France agreed to the first proposal and all three powers so notified the Dutch, citing the German transit as sufficient reason. But Britain rejected any belated occupation of Dutch Limburg to Belgian benefit and, as a consequence, France, partly with an eye to Wilson, did the same.[137]

Although Britain had successfully blocked any occupation of Limburg, the Belgian, British, French, and Italian governments all registered strong formal protests on 23 November against the German troop transit as an infringement of Dutch neutrality, and the American government complained unofficially.[138] The British and the Belgians also remarked that the Dutch could not now object to the transit of military supplies up the Scheldt for Allied forces in the Rhineland. Although use of the Scheldt would facilitate supply of the British and Belgian armies, it would also contribute to the revival of Antwerp. At the same time the Belgians accepted a proposal for resumption of the prewar Scheldt regime, but indicated that such would be temporary and served notice of Belgium's desire for treaty revision. Hymans also seized this moment to ask the Allies formally for renegotiation of the

137. The British files (F.O. 371/3164 and 371/3256) shed little light on the proposals to occupy Limburg. The surviving Quai d'Orsay files (Z/PB/32) are extremely fragmentary, and the duplicate telegrams at Vincennes (4N/72 and 6N/290) are far from complete. The Belgian files on the subject (FR/1918/II, GB/1918/II, PB/1918/II, Ind/1918, B–297, B–383, B–348, DB/31) are voluminous but contain lacunae. Some of the gaps undoubtedly arise from the oddities of the Belgian filing system, but others clearly result from the fact that Orts resorted to private letters and also kept no copies of some important communications. See also Hymans to Orts, 20 Nov. 1918, tel., BMAE B–1–1519. The Dutch government was prepared to use force if the Germans violated the conditions of the transit, which they did not. DuB, R.G.P. 146, p. 1118; Fallon to Hymans, 23 Nov. 1918, tel. 784, BMAE PB/1918/II.

138. Pichon to Allizé, 22 Nov. 1918, tel. 778, FMAE Z/PB/32; Fallon to Hymans, 2 Dec. 1918, no. 17745/3249, Garrett to van Karnebeek, 27 Nov. 1918, Fallon to Hymans, 5 Dec. 1918, no. 178/3268, BMAE DB/31.

treaties. He further requested that they refrain from making any statement to Holland which might prejudice possible solutions and that
they concert in advance with Belgium on any communication to the
Dutch about Limburg, Flemish Zeeland, the Scheldt, and the Meuse.
The Americans replied that they intended making no communications
on these subjects and the French agreed to all that Belgium asked. As
the British suggested that treaty revision be raised at the peace conference and assented to the other requests, Hymans pressed on to urge
a tripartite meeting on treaty revision before the peace conference
convened.[139]

Both the presence of the kaiser in Holland and the German troop
transit through Limburg made officials at the Belgian Foreign Ministry
overconfident. They did not realize that tempers would cool over the
kaiser or that the British and American protests over Limburg were
purely pro forma. Although they knew that the Dutch government was
moving effectively to strengthen its popularity in Flemish Zeeland, a
long-neglected area, and to suppress pro-Belgian sentiment in Limburg,
it did not occur to them that the Dutch could or would take measures
to influence Allied opinion. In fact, the Dutch had a variety of assets
available. Alarmed not only by Allied press and governmental criticism
about both the kaiser and the Limburg passage but also by a misleading
press report that Hymans had implied to the Belgian Chamber of Representatives on 2 December that treaty revision might encompass territorial claims at Dutch expense,[140] they wasted no time in deploying
these assets with immense skill, which seemed to be bred into their
bones by centuries of experience in European statecraft.

The Dutch government then in power was in fact new and inexperi-

139. Hymans, *Mémoires*, 1:266–75; Moncheur to Balfour, 14 Nov. 1918, Balfour
to Moncheur, 20 Nov. 1918, F.O. 371 / 3164; de Cartier to Lansing, 15 Nov. 1918,
185.1131/1, ACNP / 301; Hymans to de Cartier, 13, 15, 20, 23 Nov. 1918, tels. 336,
339, 351, 357, B. Micro/22; de Cartier to Hymans, 17 Nov. 1918, tel. 538, Polk to
de Cartier, 17 Dec. 1918, Hymans to de Cartier, 25 Dec. 1918, no. 10839, B Micro/23;
Hymans to de Gaiffier, 1 Dec. 1918, no. 2537, BMAE GB/1918/II.

140. Fallon to Hymans, 17 Dec. 1918, no. 18471/3423, Gillain to Hymans, 20 Dec.
1918, no. 6178, BMAE B–383; Fallon to Hymans, 13 Dec. 1918, no. 18320/3388, de
Villegas to Hymans, 17 Dec. 1918, tel. 56, BMAE PB/1918/II; Moncheur to Hymans,
11, 14, 16 Dec. 1918, nos. 9724/2224, 9836/2252, 9852/2259, BMAE GB/1918/II;
DuB, R.G.P. 117, pp. 923–24.

enced, but it had an instinctive sophistication and appreciation of how to proceed that few members of the Belgian cabinet possessed. In September 1918, the first Catholic-dominated cabinet in Dutch history took office. Much of its electoral strength; three members of the cabinet including the minister-president of the council, Jonkheer C. J. M. Ruys de Beerenbrouck; and the party leader came from Catholic Limburg, a circumstance whose significance the Belgians failed to consider. The new foreign minister, Jonkheer Herman van Karnebeek, was, unlike his immediate predecessors and successors, not a career diplomatist. Although he had had little prior diplomatic experience and was excessively voluble at first, he learned extremely quickly and soon developed a sinuosity and finesse possessed by none of the Belgian leaders except perhaps de Broqueville. While careful to observe the diplomatic niceties with Brussels, sending felicitations on the occasion of liberation and a royal mission headed by Ruys de Beerenbrouck to the same end in January,[141] van Karnebeek moved with much skill to marshall both Holland's resources and her diplomatic and financial experts to meet the Belgian challenge.

Despite the shower of sympathetic attention given to Belgium during the war and again at the moment of liberation, the Netherlands held a much stronger diplomatic position, a fact to which the Belgian Foreign Ministry remained oblivious. By the end of the war, the British were certainly more grateful for Dutch neutrality than for Belgian resistance and thankful that the Scheldt had remained closed as a result of that neutrality. As British leaders began instinctively soon after the war to consider reviving Germany as a barrier to France, their attitude redounded to the benefit of the somewhat pro-German Dutch at the expense of the allegedly pro-French Belgians. In addition, Belgium was in the unfortunate position of having nothing to give and much to seek. To make matters worse, many of her desires, if gained, could come only at the expense of British and French reparations or could lead only to economic competition with Britain and France, who were seriously

141. Fallon to Hymans, 10, 13 Sept. 1918, tel. 588, no. 13464/2482, BMAE PB/1918/II; DuB, R.G.P. 146, 1118–19, 1143–45; Townley to Balfour, 25 Oct. 1918, no. 230, F.O. 371/3254. The leader of the Dutch Catholic party, Monsignor Nolens, was a deputy but not a member of the cabinet. Queen Wilhelmina preferred that her foreign ministers be professional diplomatists.

concerned about their own iron and steel industries. The Netherlands, on the other hand, had much to give and nothing whatever to seek. Indeed, in the later stages of negotiations, her greatest diplomatic challenge was to find graceful forms of refusal. She also possessed the enormous advantage that her economy was far more complementary than competitive with those of Britain and France. Furthermore, that economy was intact. At the end of World War I, the Netherlands was one of the few countries of Europe with ample capital, livestock, agricultural machinery, and seed to export to devastated areas. Beyond these important diplomatic assets lay the vital raw materials of the Dutch East Indies. The Dutch cabinet quickly made use of these economic weapons, along with Holland's most experienced diplomatic and financial leaders, to alter Allied attitudes to Dutch benefit.

At the time of the Armistice, Allied economic talks were in progress in London and the British had already requested a Dutch representative to discuss credit. On 13 November, the Dutch cabinet authorized a credit of 150 million florins ($60 million) and assigned a senior financier to negotiate in London. The resultant agreement between the Allied powers and the Netherlands, signed on 15 November, revealed Holland's strong position. Dutch rights to receive essential German coal and other minerals were protected and Holland was, in essence, permitted to ship livestock to Germany, provided that twice as many cows and three times as many horses were sent to Belgium and northern France. Indeed, by the spring of 1919 the demand for Dutch cows had become so great that Dutch leaders encountered great difficulty in meeting it.[142]

Because the French government and press remained hostile to Holland far longer than their British counterparts, further steps were taken to influence French official and unofficial opinion. The Dutch legation in Paris under the aged Ridder de Stuers was reinforced by the tempo-

---

142. DuB, R.G.P. 117, pp. 710, 737–38, 758, 1027; DuB, R.G.P. 146, pp. 914–18; Dutch Orange Book, *Mededeelingen van den Minister van Buitenlandsche Zaken aan de Staten-Generaal: Juni 1919–April 1920* [cited hereafter as Dutch Orange Book, 1919–20], p. 21. The Dutch were competing with the Swiss in the supply of cows and capital. The Belgians were not a party to the Allied agreement but did receive Dutch cows, originally as aid and then in exchange for Belgian coal. Devleeshouwer, "L'Opinion publique," p. 216; Dutch Orange Book, 1919–20, pp. 25–26.

rary assignment of a former Foreign Ministry official and banker, along with other very senior economic advisors. These financiers used their excellent connections at the Bank of France and elsewhere in French financial circles to gain interviews with Jean Herbette, editor of *Le Temps*, and also repeatedly with Berthelot; Louis Loucheur, minister of industrial reconstitution and member of the French peace conference delegation; and Georges Mandel, influential *chef de cabinet* of premier Georges Clemenceau. They also saw Colonel House, but primarily they made a conscious and successful effort to influence the attitudes of key French leaders.[143]

In addition, on 23 December the Dutch cabinet authorized a special mission to Paris to offer aid in the economic reconstruction of northern France. The resultant commission, led by Joost van Vollenhoven, a director of the Dutch National Bank, arrived in Paris in early February and received much attention from Poincaré, Pichon, and Clémentel. The mission dangled Franco-Dutch economic rapprochement, closer banking ties, twenty-five thousand cows, agricultural machinery, and the help of Dutch engineers before the French leaders, along with a credit of $10 million to pay for this aid. After the mission left, it was replaced by a semipermanent Economic Bureau attached in March 1919 to the Dutch legation to pursue the negotiations. Meanwhile, van Vollenhoven and his successors had made it abundantly clear that the price of Dutch aid was French abandonment of support to Belgian territorial aspirations at the expense of Holland. Although France was in no position to abandon Belgium altogether, she carefully held her support to a level that would not accomplish anything against Anglo-American opposition and, when territorial transfer was officially excluded in early June 1919, the Dutch loan was approved within a few days for French purchases of goods in both Holland and the Dutch East Indies. Long before that, however, the prompt Dutch campaign, starting in November 1918, began to yield fruits. On 31 December, Clemenceau, despite the obvious French strategic interest, deplored to de Gaiffier the Belgian "appetite for aggrandizement" in Limburg. Although de Gaiffier had finally become aware of the presence of two of

143. DuB, R.G.P. 117, pp. 755–57, 785–86, 791, 793, 834–35, 842, 847–48, 850–51, 860–64, 955–59, 965–66.

the more eminent Dutch representatives and had reported it, neither he nor the Belgian Foreign Ministry pondered the reasons for their arrival, naively swallowing instead the half-truth of a letter of invitation from Queen Wilhelmina to Wilson.[144]

Although the Netherlands as a neutral had no official delegation at the Paris Peace Conference, it had the unofficial equivalent. In addition to the several high-ranking financial diplomatists, by early December Jonkheer John Loudon, a former minister to Washington and van Karnebeek's immediate wartime predecessor as foreign minister, was in Paris, assigned to see Wilson and to influence the American delegation against Belgian claims. Once the peace conference had opened, van Karnebeek sent Jonkheer Reneke de Marees van Swinderin, another former minister to Washington and former foreign minister who was now Dutch minister in London, to Paris for several extended visits to play the same role with the British delegation.[145] Both men had dozens of valuable diplomatic contacts and great skill. They proceeded with much geniality and delicacy, appreciating that harried statesmen are often best dealt with briefly or left alone, a fact that Hymans, who tended to pester, did not recognize. The indirect influence of Loudon and van Swinderin, along with that of the financiers, on French policy, was soon felt, and the fact that the Netherlands did not have an official seat at the peace conference faded into insignificance. Beyond all that, van Karnebeek was able to make good use of the Dutch Catholic party's ties to the Vatican, working against Belgian annexationism through the Dutch bishops, his own representative at the Holy See, and the papal nuncio in Brussels. He was also able to capitalize on the hostility to territorial aggrandizement of Cardinal Mercier, primate of all Belgium and a national war hero, who advised Albert against annexation of Dutch territory both on principle and because he did not want to strengthen the Flemish element, for whom he had a profound contempt.[146]

144. Dutch Orange Book, 1919–20, pp. 23–40; DuB, R.G.P. 117, pp. 823, 925, 946–47, 951, 953–59, 965–66, 984–85, 1018; DuB, R.G.P., 146, pp. 1142–43, 1185–86; de Gaiffier to Hymans, 31 Dec. 1918, no. 9600/3303, BMAE B–383.

145. Vandenbosch, *Dutch Foreign Policy*, p. 36; DuB, R.G.P. 117, pp. 792, 856–58, 944.

146. DuB, R.G.P. 117, pp. 944, 975–76, 1021–22, 1031.

Both before and during the peace conference, the Belgian government remained serenely unaware of this multifaceted and high-powered Dutch counter-campaign. But the Belgian Foreign Ministry reacted sharply at the start of October 1918 when it learned that the Dutch government had renewed a long-standing request to hold the conference in the peace palace at The Hague. In April 1915, the Belgian cabinet had unanimously decided, in reaction to very informal Allied assurances, that the peace conference should be held in Brussels. By the end of the war, however, the idea of bringing Germany to poetic justice in the Belgian capital had lost support almost everywhere and evoked little enthusiasm from anybody except Lord Northcliffe, the British press baron, and the Belgian citizenry. The post-Armistice Belgian cabinet was lukewarm and the king strongly opposed, for he realized that after four years of occupation Brussels should not undertake the strain of such a conference. Hymans, too, was dubious but dutifully submitted the proposal several times, especially after the Dutch revived their request, noting each time the lack of any response. Despite a French warning, he seemed unaware that such futile efforts only depleted the limited reservoir of good will that was one of Belgium's few assets, without gaining anything in return. The Belgian bid failed partly from lack of support but primarily because Clemenceau, who was determined that the resulting treaty be signed in the Hall of Mirrors at Versailles, had no intention of yielding the presiding chair to Albert.[147] The Belgian government was not dismayed, but public opinion was.

As it became evident that Belgium was not to receive the advantage of being host at the peace conference, Belgian diplomatic activity to

147. Albert, *Diaries*, pp. 34–36; Davignon note, 4 Nov. 1914, BMAE FR/1914; Davignon to Guillaume et al., 4 May 1915, no. 698, BMAE FR/1915/I; Hymans to Davignon, 24 May 1915, no. 1731/475, BMAE GB/1915; Hymans to Allied ministers, 30 Oct. 1918, Hymans to de Gaiffier, 4, 12 Oct. 1918, no. 2141, tel. 289, de Gaiffier to Hymans, 19 Oct., 11 Nov. 1918, nos. 8021/2680, 8553/2888, BMAE FR/1918/II; Moncheur to Hymans, 14, 30 Oct. 1918, nos. 8108/1847, 8595/1972, BMAE GB/1918 / II; Hymans, *Mémoires*, 1:185, 199–200, 204, 450; Robert Fenaux, *Paul Hymans*, p. 107 n; Stephen Bonsal, *Suitors and Suppliants*, p. 12; Whitlock, *Letters*, 2:519; Western & General Report no. 93, CAB 24/149; W.C. 501, 13 Nov. 1918, CAB 23/8; Hymans to Whitlock, 30 Oct. 1918, de Bassompierre memo, 11 Nov. 1918, Hymans to de Cartier, 12 Nov. 1918, tel. 334, B Micro/22; Whitlock to House, 8 Nov. 1918, House Papers 20/24; House to Whitlock, 15 Nov. 1918, Whitlock Papers/38 (LC).

obtain prior agreement on both Luxemburg and the 1839 treaties intensified. On 9 November at Loppem, Albert took the matter of Luxemburg up with Poincaré, who agreed that a Belgian solution would be best for the Grand Duchy. On 20 November, de Gaiffier extracted from Clemenceau a categorical statement that France had no designs on Luxemburg. This success was followed on 16 December and 16 January by promises from Pichon and Poincaré that France would support Belgium's efforts to obtain the Grand Duchy. But other reports implied otherwise. When Hymans was in Paris on 23 December, Clemenceau was both vague and discouraging, and Belgian efforts to participate in the military occupation of Luxemburg still met with no success.[148]

In these circumstances, the Belgian Foreign Ministry turned to the British. On 16 November 1918, de Bassompierre visited the Foreign Office for talks with his British counterparts. He pointed out that Serbia, Italy, Rumania, France, and even neutral Denmark would receive new territories and indicated that Belgium should share in this largesse. He particularly stressed Luxemburg and argued, in regard to the Scheldt and the Meuse, that if the powers had the right to give Holland territory in 1839, they equally had the right to take it away now. This session was followed by similar conversations between Sir Francis Villiers, the British minister in Brussels, and Pierre Orts, now acting secretary-general, and by several requests for a tripartite meeting in Paris and for a visit to Brussels by a senior British official. The Belgians were, they claimed, too busy resisting constant French pressure to make another visit to London. When the British agreed to the tripartite meeting in Paris, the request for a visit to Brussels was withdrawn.[149]

In due course the Paris meeting was arranged and the French wired for Hymans to come at once to Paris for talks with Clemenceau, Balfour, and Lloyd George about the 1839 treaties. Hymans rushed to

148. Albert to Hymans, 9 Nov. 1918, BMAE B–1–1519; de Gaiffier to Hymans, 20 Nov. 1918, no. 8746/2971, BMAE FR/1918/II; de Gaiffier to Hymans, 18 Nov. 1918, no. 8675/1944, BMAE DB/31; de Gaiffier to Hymans, 23 Nov. 1918, no. 8831/3007, BMAE DB/32/II; F.O. memo, 9 May 1921, F.O. 371/6970; de Gaiffier to Hymans, 24 Dec. 1918, BMAE Ind/1918; Alexandre Ribot, *Journal d'Alexandre Ribot et correspondances inédites, 1914–1922*, p. 257.

149. De Bassompierre memo, 16 Nov. 1918, BMAE DB/30/I; Moncheur to Akers-Douglas, 25 Nov. 1918, Villiers to Balfour, 8, 11, 19 Dec. 1918, no. 415, tels. 82, 90, Moncheur notes, 7, 11 Dec. 1918, Balfour to Moncheur, 14 Dec. 1918, Villiers to

Paris for meetings on 22 December, only to discover that Lloyd George and Balfour had decided not to come after all. On 23 December, Hymans had a long talk with Clemenceau, who urged him to be more aggressive, and then went to the British embassy, where he saw Derby and proposed continuing on to London at once. Upon being told that Balfour could not receive him, he saw Wilson and then returned to Brussels, inquiring again through Villiers urgently and repeatedly when and where he could see Balfour. He offered once more to go to London and suggested alternatively that a British official come to Brussels. As Balfour was about to leave for a holiday at Cannes before the rigors of the peace conference and nobody could be spared to visit Brussels, no meeting took place until Balfour arrived in Paris during the first week in January. On that occasion, which was chiefly social, Hymans brought a letter from Albert stressing Belgium's need of British diplomatic assistance. The meeting was very friendly and Balfour seemed willing to support Belgian claims in Luxemburg, although he was reserved about Holland. He recognized that Belgium had valid complaints about the 1839 treaties but did not hide his view that territorial concessions from Holland would be extremely difficult to obtain. Hymans concluded that no British help could be expected in this matter.[150] However, he did not change his strategy of laying out the problem with all its implications and trusting to the great powers, especially Britain, to impose the desired solution. Whether he considered that there was no alternative strategy, as Belgium could not openly claim Dutch territory, or deemed that a futile quest must be indirectly pursued in response to pressures from within the cabinet and the country, or was blinded by his usual optimistic faith in eventual British support to his "just" cause is not clear.

Hardinge, 11, 12 Dec. 1918, F.O. 371/3164; Balfour to Curzon, 9 Dec. 1918, F.O. 800/199.

150. Hymans note, Dec. 1918, BMAE B–383; Moncheur to Hymans, 29 Dec. 1918, no. 10187/2341, BMAE GB/1918/II; Defrance to Hymans, 18 Dec. 1918, Hymans memo, n.d., Hymans Papers/160; Villiers to Balfour, 24 Dec. 1918, tel. 96, Balfour to Villiers, 27 Dec. 1918, no. 178, 2 Jan. 1919, tel. 3, Derby to Balfour, 24 Dec. 1918, tel. 1859, F.O. 371/3164; Villiers to Hymans, 3 Jan. 1919, BMAE GB/1919/I; Hymans, *Mémoires*, 1:299. Why Lloyd George and Balfour canceled the 22 December meeting at the last minute is not entirely clear. The French summons to Hymans had been made in good faith. Clemenceau to P. Cambon, 15 Dec. 1918, tel., FMAE Clemenceau Papers/1.

While Hymans pursued British support with insufficient thought to the implications of his lack of success, officials at the Belgian Foreign Ministry continued to plan for the peace conference ahead. They prepared enormous dossiers that, while displaying a suitable reserve about claims on Holland and Luxemburg, made Belgian territorial concerns clear. As the Belgian cabinet, in response to British discouragement, after considerable debate finally rejected any open claim on Dutch territory, Hymans's tactic of reciting the facts and hinting was adopted. The Foreign Ministry does not appear to have considered that, in the absence of appreciable great-power support, this tactic could accomplish nothing except much damage to Belgium's moral position. Like Hymans, the ministry was unrealistic about Belgium's role in the forthcoming conference. With undue faith in the Declaration of Sainte-Adresse, both Hymans and his staff expected Belgium to have not only a place at the peace conference but also a real voice, particularly in decisions concerning Germany. With equal optimism and belief in Allied promises, they took full reparation largely for granted, although Belgian diplomatists continued to indicate, as they had done throughout the war, that the almost total destruction of their country dictated a substantial Belgian priority on German payments. They also argued that, because the German invasion had been not only an act of aggression but also a crime against international law, a deliberate violation of a formal treaty that Germany was obliged to uphold and defend, Belgium's crushing war debt, arising directly from that act, should be transferred to Germany. That, too, had been promised by the Allies, including the United States.[151]

While the Foreign Ministry planned for the negotiations in Paris, it enjoyed unusual freedom from the pressures of public opinion, as the Belgian delegation continued to do throughout the peace conference itself. Belgium, a country known for its deep linguistic, political, and class divisions, was for once extraordinarily unified. The German occupation had accomplished this, along with the exhiliration of libera-

151. DuB, R.G.P. 117, pp. 876–77; de Gaiffier to Hymans, 21 Dec. 1918, no. 9390/3225, BMAE FR/1918/II; Delacroix to Hymans, 5 Dec. 1918, Direction F note, 12 Dec. 1918, Delacroix note, 10 Jan. 1919, Delacroix to van den Ven, 10 Jan. 1919, no. 437, BMAE B–366/I.

tion, and briefly most of the people remembered that first of all they were Belgians. King Albert's call for national unity through the gargantuan task of reconstruction was heeded and the old quarrels were temporarily buried. Further, German wartime efforts to capitalize on Flemish discontent had boomeranged to the temporary benefit of Belgian national unity. Although a few Flemish activists had collaborated with German schemes to divide the country in two, most Flemings had not, declaring that they would claim their rights from the Belgian government after liberation but would not accept them from the hated conqueror. Though the German efforts probably sowed some seeds for future trouble, in the short run they had the reverse effect.[152] At the war's end, most of the Flemish, temporarily satisfied by the reforms promised by the king, were carefully demonstrating what good Belgians they were.

In addition, the Belgian people, who were to a large degree preoccupied with the extreme difficulty of their daily life, were not given a great deal of information about diplomatic questions, either before or during the peace conference. What news they did receive tended to be reassuring, and they, like their leaders, largely put their faith in Belgium's great-power protectors. Annexationist sentiment was widespread, particularly concerning the lost brethren in Luxemburg, and most of the press favored territorial increase but, on the whole, both press and people were calm, interested in moderate annexation but not unduly excited about it. In general, the Flemish and the Socialists were less enthusiastic about territorial aggrandizement than the other elements, but both groups were divided and contained interest groups and individuals favoring territorial expansion. Besides, acquisition of Luxemburg, the "Walloon cantons," and sometimes Limburg was often considered not annexationism but rather redressal of past injustice.[153]

152. De Gaiffier to de Broqueville, 9 Nov. 1917, no. 6633/2972, BMAE FR/1917/II; Hymans to Moncheur, 22 Jan. 1918, tel. 19, BMAE GB/1918/I; Fallon to Hymans, 24 Sept. 1918, no. 14048/2583, BMAE PB/1918/II; Allizé to Delcassé, 14 July 1915, no. 903, FMAE CPC Guerre Belg./416; Allizé to Briand, 26 Sept. 1916, no. 1483, FMAE CPC Guerre Belg./421; Allizé to Briand, 15 Mar. 1917, no. 280, FMAE CPC Guerre Belg./424; Auffray, *Pierre de Margerie*, p. 369.
153. *Gazet van Antwerpen*, 14 Feb. 1919, p. 1, 15 Feb. 1919, p. 1; *De Standaard*, 13 Feb. 1919, p. 1; Rouquerel to Clemenceau, 17 Jan. 1919, no. 17S, Vin 7N/1160;

Exceptions to the generally calm tone were the strongly annexationist *Vingtième Siècle*; *La Nation belge*, which was French financed; and the Comité de Politique Nationale (CPN), founded at the end of 1918 by Pierre Nothomb to agitate for "la grande Belgique." Just after the Armistice, Nothomb had been unofficially attached to the Foreign Ministry for propaganda work, a circumstance that caused Hymans later embarrassment and regret.[154] At first the CPN attracted a moderate amount of support and a number of distinguished Belgians, including some prominent Socialists, but its crude and blatant campaign, particularly its enormous posters portraying a greater Belgium considerably exceeding the government's maximum hopes, quickly caused it to lose much of its membership. Whereas Nothomb and his closest adherents dreamed of reviving medieval Lotharingia in modern form, most Belgians were not so unrealistic and went stolidly about the daily struggle to survive, largely ignorant of events in Paris.[155]

---

de Cartier to Hymans, 2 Dec. 1918, no. 23/23 (citing Associated Press report, Brussels, 26 Nov. 1918), BMAE B-383; *L'Indépendance belge*, 14 Feb. 1919, p. 2; BMAE Archives notes, n.d. [both 1919], BMAE B-348. See also Devleeshouwer, "L'Opinion publique."

154. Paul Struye, "Pierre Nothomb, homme politique," p. 72; Devleeshouwer, "L'Opinion publique," p. 232; Hymans, *Mémoires*, 1:301. It is not clear why Hymans took Nothomb into the ministry. Possibly he wanted him, despite his poor record; possibly he faced pressure from de Broqueville, Renkin, and Carton de Wiart, of whom the first two were members of the new cabinet; possibly he thought he could restrain Nothomb in an official position. The fact that Nothomb was a much-beloved figure in Belgium, came of a distinguished founding family, and possessed enormous charm, acknowledged by even his bitterest enemies, may also have been a factor. Why nothing was done in later months to restrain Nothomb and the CPN is equally unclear. In addition to some of the factors noted above, Belgium's tradition of free speech, the fact that Nothomb's nongovernmental activities as head of the CPN were not illegal, the eminence of his early supporters, and the extended absence of Hymans and all his senior aides in Paris may have contributed to Nothomb's remarkably free hand. It is conceivable but unlikely that Hymans actually welcomed such inept propaganda, of which he seems to have been little informed. The Hymans Papers shed no light and those of de Broqueville and Nothomb are temporarily closed at the time of writing. Nothomb was not a member of the Belgian delegation to the peace conference and had almost no contact with it.

155. Struye, "Pierre Nothomb," pp. 72-74; Jean Stengers, "Belgium," in Hans Rogger and Eugen Weber, eds., *The European Right*, p. 147; Devleeshouwer, "L'Opinion publique," pp. 232-34. For a photograph of inflammatory CPN propaganda, see DuB, R.G.P. 117, pp. 976-77. The Dutch investigated the question of the CPN's financing. They concluded that no government funds were involved but strongly suspected that large sums of money were being passed by Sir William Lever, an important British concessionaire in the Congo, through the editor of *Le Soir* (Brussels) to Renkin for the

One reason why the country was so abnormally unified and also, in general, moderately in favor of annexation was that each territorial acquisition would, in one respect or another, benefit every section of the country. Although some Socialists were, out of their own political interests, reluctant to annex intensely Catholic areas and some Walloons cautious about adding too many Flemings, who might become a dominant majority dedicated to ending Wallonia's favored position, on the whole national economic and security interests took precedence. In such a small country, these were truly national, not regional. Acquiring some of the so-called Walloon cantons, which were not of great economic value except to certain nearby local Walloon industries, might add a German ethnic element that perhaps would combine with the Flemish, but it would also lengthen the distance from Liège to the frontier, thus better assuring the defense of southern Belgium. Although Luxemburg, whose official languages were French and German but whose people spoke their own Germanic dialect comprehensible to neighboring Walloon-speaking Belgians, would bolster Wallonia, its railways were vital to Antwerp's commerce. Similarly, acquisition of lower Limburg not only was advocated by the Antwerp shipping interests and the Brussels Chamber of Commerce, but was endorsed by almost everybody, as it would benefit not only Liège and Namur's commercial traffic but also the entire nation's security against renewed German attack. While the Antwerp shipping interests and the Brussels Chamber of Commerce also urged that Flemish Zeeland become Belgian, so did most others.[156] Antwerp and Ghent were industrial Wallonia's only important outlets to the sea and thus to world trade. Both were dependent upon the Scheldt and, as matters stood, upon Dutch concessions. In addition, after 1914 the entire nation understood the importance of free transit of the Scheldt for the relief of Belgium from abroad in the event of another attack.

Because the devastation and misery were universal, the country was equally united on the need for immediate and generous reparations.

CPN. Renkin was known to be a strong supporter of the CPN. DuD, R.G.P. 156, pp. 4–7, 18–19.

156. Moncheur to Hymans, 12 Dec. 1918, no. 9791/2234, BMAE GB/1918/II; de Cartier to Hymans, 2 Dec. 1918, no. 23/23, BMAE B–383; BMAE Archives note, n.d. [1919], BMAE B–280.

Although only a small portion of Flanders was heavily battle-scarred, the Germans had, in brief, picked the entire country clean, dismantling factories, transferring livestock to Germany, and tearing up railway tracks all over the country with Teutonic thoroughness. As a consequence, misery, unemployment, and hunger were widespread in all parts of the country. Despite American efforts, food remained painfully scarce and, after four years of undernourishment, the chief Belgian preoccupation remained the task of finding something to eat. As the industrial and agricultural structures were almost completely destroyed, there was nothing to work with and thus no work. Unemployment exceeded 80 percent of the labor force, even though the army was not demobilized at first. Housing and clothing were as scarce as jobs. The flood of returning refugees, internees, and prisoners brought reunion but multiplied the problems, particularly because the rail network was so utterly devastated. The ordinary citizen's attention was continually distracted from world diplomatic events not only by the abnormal effort involved in daily life but also by such immediate excitements as the feat of Belgian army engineers in reconstructing, with German prisoner labor, a single track across the seventy miles from Brugge to Brussels and the triumphant arrival of the first train in Brussels on 3 December after a precarious fourteen-hour journey.[157]

In addition to the struggle to exist, which consumed so much of the depleted energy of the Belgian people, there were political distractions as well. There was the novelty of an extraconstitutional revision of the Constitution to end plural voting and bring about equal universal manhood suffrage more rapidly than the legal amendment process would permit. The Socialists pressed, with a good deal of Liberal support, for a series of important reforms, many of which were enacted in 1919. As measures to restrict the sale of alcoholic beverages sharply (the Vandervelde law to combat working-class alcoholism), institute a progressive income tax, impose death duties, and provide funds for working-class housing were debated and became law,[158] public attention was diverted to the domestic political scene.

157. Moncheur to Hymans (with *Times* clippings), 12, 24, 27 Dec. 1918, nos. 9759/2229, 10101/2322, 10128/2326, BMAE GB/1918/II.
158. Mallinson, *Belgium*, p. 99; P.I.D. memo Belg./004, 2 May 1919, G.T. 7253, CAB 24/79.

In addition, in the aftermath of liberation, there was a somewhat surprising new cabinet, in whose construction the king had a large hand. The first post-Armistice cabinet, the "ministry of Loppem" created at the king's temporary residence near Brugge, was announced at the time of Albert's "Joyeuse Rentrée" into Brussels on 22 November and took office the next day. It was carefully balanced between those who had remained in occupied Belgium and those who had been in exile, although the Flemish element was slightly weakened. The three-party national coalition continued but with added minority representation, so that the cabinet comprised six Catholics, three Liberals, and three Socialists. To everyone's astonishment, the king chose as prime minister Léon Delacroix, a somewhat naive and perennially optimistic political novice, whose chief claims to office were his residence in occupied Brussels and his close friendship with Emile Francqui, the powerful financier who had organized and directed the Belgian aspect of the international effort to feed wartime Belgium. Hymans remained at his post; de Broqueville rejoined the cabinet and Carton de Wiart left it. Both Vandervelde and Renkin remained cabinet ministers but were given new assignments, Vandervelde at Justice and Renkin at Railroads, Posts, Telegraphs, and Telephones; Louis Franck, a Liberal who had remained within the country, inherited the Colonial Ministry.[159]

Because the new cabinet was a Ministry of National Union representing all three major parties, and Belgium was conveniently expected to receive three seats at the Paris Peace Conference, it was decided without serious discussion that there should be a plenipotentiary from each party. This decision preserved national unity and largely eliminated politically motivated criticism from the sidelines, but it created problems within the delegation. As Hymans was foreign minister, he naturally took the Liberal seat and became first plenipotentiary. He chose the former barrister, cabinet minister, and diplomatist Jules van den Heuvel as the Catholic representative, and Vandervelde chose himself as the Socialist delegate, much to the annoyance of Hymans.[160]

159. Jacques Willequet, *Albert Ier, roi des Belges*, pp. 173–77; Charles d'Ydewalle, *D'Albert I à Léopold III*, pp. 9–15; Hymans, *Mémoires*, 1:239–59; Carl-Henrick Höjer, *Le Régime parlementaire belge de 1918 à 1940*, pp. 81–98.

160. Defrance to Pichon, 17 Dec. 1918, tel. 244, FMAE A/38; Hymans, *Mémoires*, 1:296.

Vandervelde, who returned Hymans's dislike in full measure, remains in some respects as enigmatic a figure as de Broqueville and for the same reason: his actions so rarely coincided with his words. Both at the peace conference and in later years when he was foreign minister, Vandervelde tended in the main to be a pragmatic Belgian nationalist, but in addition he was leader not only of Belgium's Socialist party but also of the Second International. Thus his words tended to follow socialist doctrine, whereas his actions usually supported Hymans's foreign policy. In general, Vandervelde, who was consistently voluble with representatives of other countries, would blame all policies unattractive to the Dutch, the British, or the international socialist community on Hymans and assure his listeners either that he had not been consulted or that he had dissented vigorously. Both at the peace conference and later on, he took credit for any signs of Belgian restraint and no responsibility for more aggressive moves. As a consequence, Hymans gained a reputation as an extreme annexationist and a French disciple, while Vandervelde posed as the apostle of moderation. In his memoirs, Vandervelde claimed that he had threatened to resign from the delegation if annexationist claims on Holland were put, and he told Dutch representatives at the time that he had threatened to make a public protest. Yet, as the Dutch noted, he had participated in the cabinet deliberations that had set Hymans's course and he lent his presence and support when Hymans put the Belgian case to the conference, hinting at territorial transfer. Indeed, Vandervelde rallied to the delegation on all important occasions and at all moments of crisis. So far as can be ascertained, he did not engage even in much private dissent on any issue of consequence.[161]

For the rest, Vandervelde went his own way much of the time at Paris. Conscious that he was the only socialist plenipotentiary at the conference, he devoted himself to work on the Labor Charter, in the drafting of which he played a major role, and contributed only intermittently to the work of the Belgian delegation. In deference to established socialist doctrine, he declared himself opposed to any territorial

---

161. Emile Vandervelde, *Souvenirs d'un militant socialiste*, p. 286; DuB, R.G.P. 117, pp. 876–77, 937–38; DuD, R.G.P. 156, pp. 4–7. Vandervelde's papers disappeared during World War II.

aggrandizement for Belgium, which appeared to undercut his own delegation. Nonetheless, he hastened to add that the return of Eupen and
Malmédy to Belgium would be not annexation but disannexation.[162] In
his mind, as in that of most Belgians, the return of Luxemburg was
similarly not really an annexation, and his opposition to transfer of
Dutch territory was more apparent than real. On reparations from
Germany, Vandervelde stood squarely with the delegation, ignoring
appeals from socialist brethren across the Rhine.

Though more retiring than Vandervelde and much less politically
influential, Jules van den Heuvel was probably more important to
the work of the Belgian delegation at Paris. He concentrated chiefly
on reparations and, aided by excellent assistants, including Georges
Theunis, did valuable work on this complicated problem. Yet for the
broader range of work of the delegation he was probably both too old
and too traditionalist in his orientation. He was an outstanding jurist
and tended to assume that a solid legal case would suffice to gain the
desired end.[163] Although he had had some diplomatic experience, his
intense Catholicism had led him during his tenure as the Belgian representative to the Holy See to become closely identified with the Vatican's views, a circumstance unlikely to endear him to the Big Three of
the peace conference.

Paul Hymans dominated his delegation as he later came in a sense to
dominate the interwar foreign policy of Belgium. Small, dapper, and
suave, he was very much a representative of the haute bourgeoisie of
Brussels. He was both intelligent and intellectual and both idealistic
and in some respects realistic. Hymans had an exceptionally clear and
logical mind, and was an outstanding administrator as well as an excellent jurist. Universally acknowledged in Belgium as a brilliant parlia-
mentarian, he was, like most foreign ministers, a nationalist but, beyond
that, also unquestionably a dedicated patriot. In his intense devotion to
Belgium's cause, he sometimes refused to face up to facts that he had
invariably seen. During his wartime assignment in London, he had
developed a deep admiration for most things British. Hymans was

162. Geneviève Tabouis, *The Life of Jules Cambon*, pp. 323–24; Hymans, *Mémoires*,
1:334; Lucien Colson, *Malmédy et les territoires rétrocédés*, p. 8.
163. Interview with Vicomte Terlinden (Brussels, 5 Sept. 1967).

widely and correctly regarded in Belgium as extremely Anglophile in both personal proclivities and policy, although the British persisted without reason in assuming him to be pro-French. Though usually coldly realistic about the French, he was consistently overly optimistic about British support, and one reason that much of his policy failed was that it rested on his faith, in the teeth of the evidence, that Britain would come to recognize the justice of Belgium's cause and accomplish his goals for him.

On 1 January 1918, Hymans became foreign minister for the first time, and thus, when the peace conference opened, he lacked experience in this crucial post. Yet he ran the ministry well and was much admired by most of his subordinates there. He planned policy systematically and encountered little difficulty in carrying the cabinet with him. In addition, Hymans possessed an extraordinary shrewdness in scenting the future direction of policies in neighboring countries affecting Belgium, although he often rejected his own sound instincts where Britain was concerned. With his suave elegance and total command of the diplomatic niceties, he appeared on the surface to be the very model of a foreign minister.

Yet Paul Hymans conspicuously lacked several essential aspects of the diplomatist's skills particularly necessary for the personal negotiations he was about to undertake. He was neither tactful nor agreeable, and at Paris he succeeded in irritating or offending or enraging many of the people he needed to charm, especially most of the ranking members of the British delegation. Hymans was probably too honest (except occasionally in domestic politics) and undoubtedly too frank to be a first-class diplomatist. His personality was prickly and a trifle chilly, and he tolerated neither fools nor fuzzy thinking with any grace. In his earnestness, he seems to have lacked both imagination and humor, and he certainly had no capacity at all to see matters from the viewpoint of any other nation. In himself, he summed up Belgium's insulated, parochial diplomatic history, and though he had many talents, they were not those most needed for effective competition in the tumultuous Paris scene.

Furthermore, Hymans was extraordinarily sensitive to any slight, not to himself but to Belgium, of whose sovereignty and dignity he was intensely conscious, and as the slights multiplied he protested, sometimes with great eloquence, usually sharply, and occasionally explosively. He wisely refused a Serbian request to create and lead a bloc of small nations,[164] but by his outspoken and repeated challenges to the great powers, he did in fact become the spokesman of the lesser states. He refused to accept the undeniable fact that Wilson, Lloyd George, and Clemenceau had constituted themselves a tribunal before which the delegates of other states were to plead. Belgium would not beg: such was beneath her dignity, and every time Hymans was condescendingly treated as a humble supplicant, he flared, doing his cause much harm. In the course of the conference, he became widely disliked by members of the key delegations. He also bored the Big Three. With his legal and parliamentary background, he tended to think that a solid juridical case or a brilliant display of oratory would win the day, a tendency reinforced by van den Heuvel. These characteristics, coupled with his earnestness and his almost compulsive desire for precision and clarity, led him to make excessively long, overly detailed speeches through which the Big Three suffered.[165]

It is extremely difficult to establish to what degree Hymans had become a genuine convert to annexationism and "la grande Belgique."[166] To some extent he was clearly under the influence of Orts and de Bassompierre, both key members of the Belgian delegation, whose territorial ambitions were never in doubt. Yet the Dutch minister in Brussels thought that in large part Hymans was reacting, with an eye to the electoral future of the Liberal party, to political pressures in the press, Parliament, and cabinet. Certainly in some respects his policy in large matters and small was too responsive to popular demand. He did not know how to lead opinion and made little effort to do so either before or during the conference. The Dutch minister reported as well a Belgian view that Hymans had decided to adopt the semblance of

164. Hymans, *Mémoires*, 1:327.

165. The conclusions in these paragraphs have been largely confirmed by interviews in Brussels with a variety of Belgians who either knew Hymans or are students of the period. For the best analysis of Hymans, see d'Ydewalle, *D'Albert I*, pp. 34–37. Jacques Willequet has suggested that the mentality of Hymans was too logical to harmonize with that of the British leaders. For a different assessment of Hymans, see J. Helmreich, *Belgium and Europe*, pp. 208–9.

166. The copious Hymans Papers, which consist largely of official correspondence and memoranda, shed no light on this point.

annexationism, asking for much in hopes of gaining a little.[167] There is no doubt that his initial presentation of the Belgian case was a maximum bargaining position, prepared with an eye to future concessions. It is clear that Hymans was realistic enough to abandon hope of annexing Luxemburg early on, pursuing economic union instead, and it is questionable whether he seriously expected to gain Dutch territory. Yet it is also likely that, under the pressures of an exceptionally long difficult conference, he lost perspective and became a trifle frantic. In his earnestly fervent patriotism, he came to believe to some degree that he *must* succeed in Belgium's one great opportunity to right at least some of the wrongs of 1839 and that he *would* succeed if only he tried harder. Thus, not facing up to the slimness of his chances in most respects, he bothered the British and was quite unaware of the great-power attitude, as expressed by an American delegate, that "these small nations with intense national feelings bore me."[168] Further, his insistence on Belgium's sovereign equality and his indignant view that Belgium would not beg before the great powers, though heartfelt assertions of national dignity, were not only highly undiplomatic but also, because Belgium was indeed begging daily for attention, territory, money, and guarantees, rather pathetic and, in the eyes of some, preposterous. Finally, his belief in a new world order founded on justice, in which Belgium would assume a role befitting her dignity and heroism, was naive. The Dutch, infinitely more experienced in dealing with the great powers, knew better that money, influence, and sharp bargaining were what usually succeeded. But Belgium had no money, little influence, and nothing with which to bargain. At any rate, Paul Hymans did not think in such terms. With dogged determination, he pursued justice as he saw it.

Belgium was perhaps unfortunate not only in her own delegation but also in those of the great powers. The American president was an unknown quantity to the entire delegation and Belgium was largely unknown to him. His outlook on Belgium was generally sympathetic in a vague, inactive way, partly because Belgium was a convenient symbol

---

167. DuB, R.G.P. 117, pp. 901–3; DuD, R.G.P. 156, pp. 4–7, 18–19.
168. George Louis Beer to his diary, 14 Feb. 1919, as cited by William Roger Louis, "The United States and the African Peace Settlement of 1919," p. 430.

of his crusade and partly through his friendship with Brand Whitlock, the influential American minister in Brussels. By the Fourteen Points, Wilson was committed to the evacuation and restoration of Belgium and to the end of compulsory neutrality. Beyond that his interest perhaps did not extend. The hostility to Belgian claims of Robert Lansing, the legalistic American secretary of state, was evident throughout but lacked influence on Wilson or anyone else until the later stages of the conference, when he thwarted Belgian hopes for sweeping revision of the 1839 treaties. The Belgians discovered that Colonel House was both their best friend at the conference and their best route to Wilson and they exploited this advantage to good effect. Indeed, without the sympathetic support of House, Belgium would have gained very little, especially in the financial sense, at Paris. Belgian diplomatists also quickly realized that the other two American plenipotentiaries were of no importance but, trusting to House, they apparently failed to cultivate Professor Charles Homer Haskins, the Harvard medievalist assigned by the American delegation to all west European questions and consequently to the Belgian Commission. Although Haskins was moderately sympathetic to Belgium, this oversight probably contributed to the awkwardness of the commission's eventual compromises.

In many respects, the British delegation was more important to Belgium and more difficult to deal with. Its leader, David Lloyd George, was steadfast in his goals but disconcertingly mercurial in his tactics, as he ignored his foreign secretary, Foreign Office, and experts, relying instead on his own intuition and that of members of his private secretariat, notably Philip Kerr. With dazzling diplomatic skill, Lloyd George gained most of Britain's desiderata in the opening weeks of the conference and then joined Wilson on the pedestal, where together they posed as impartial arbiters of the world's destinies. But the reparations question was not settled and it was evident that France and Belgium would be the chief obstacles to substantial payments for Britain. Because a clash with France would be injudicious, Lloyd George, whose own public pronouncements on the restoration of Belgium had been cautious, tried to erode the Belgian position. Before the conference convened, he began making his oft-repeated remark, accurate but irrelevant, that Belgium's military casualties had been fewer than those of Canada (or Australia or New Zealand). In vain was he informed that

Belgium had been engulfed before she could raise a large army and that much of the army she did have was quickly imprisoned by the Germans or interned by the Dutch. Lloyd George continued to make the comparison, often adding that Belgium had not done her share. Part of his dislike of anything Belgian seems to have arisen from personal prejudices, of which he had many, but his hostility to Belgian aspirations was heightened by a desire, which had begun to manifest itself before Belgian problems were considered by the Big Four in April 1919, for a rapprochement with both Germany and Holland, as Britain began instinctively to work her way back to her traditionally preferred position as the pivot in the European balance of power. Because he shared with much of his Foreign Office the erroneous assumption that Belgium had been, was, and would remain a French satellite, blindly following a French policy unattractive to Britain, his gradual shift could only operate to further Belgian disadvantage. In fact, the Belgians disagreed sharply with France on many major issues, feared French policy greatly, and said so frequently, but their protestations went unheeded.

One of the few who occasionally listened was the second British delegate. Arthur James Balfour, the elderly foreign secretary, was one of the more objective men at Paris and, within the limits of his own traditionalist views and his country's policy assumptions, he seems to have weighed problems on their merits. Upon occasion he made significant and energetic efforts on Belgium's behalf, being defeated only by his prime minister or the prime minister's secretary. Balfour relied heavily on his two senior Foreign Office officials, Lord Hardinge and Sir Eyre Crowe. Consequently, Belgian diplomatists cultivated both men with erratic success. Crowe, who was nominally charged with west European questions, was the more sympathetic, but Hardinge, who found Hymans exasperating, was the more senior of the two. The Belgian delegation realized that the other British plenipotentiaries were of little importance and regretted that Curzon remained in London, where he had almost no influence on policy.

Though the Belgians feared neglect and indifference from the British, they anticipated the reverse from the French, and their fears were well founded. Georges Clemenceau, who dominated the French delegation as he had dominated France since 1917, was perhaps more friendly and less aggressive toward Belgium than some other French politicians, but he shared the prevailing disdainful French view that Belgium should be an obedient French tool, submissively following French direction and expecting little in return. Because his overriding concern was French security and Belgium was an essential factor in French defensive plans, Clemenceau tended to back any Belgian claims not in competition with those of France, but, when French interests were involved, he was inflexible, partly in response to parliamentary pressure, and Belgian efforts, unsupported by the Anglo-Saxon powers, proved unavailing.

Belgian diplomatists were caught in the middle between Britain and France and remained in this uncomfortable position for years to come. At the peace conference, the divergence between French and British policy on Belgian issues took the form of French efforts to deflect Belgium from Luxemburg and to encourage some of her claims on Holland, while Britain conversely discouraged Belgian interest in Dutch concessions and tried to mollify her with occasional support regarding Luxemburg. Neither policy succeeded, as the Belgians tenaciously pursued both goals, but British annoyance about Holland may possibly explain the ultimate refusal of Lloyd George to back the Luxemburg claim, whereas Clemenceau's irritation over the stubbornness of the Belgian stance regarding the Grand Duchy may have helped to dissipate French diplomatic support for Belgium vis-à-vis Holland, although the financial factor clearly came into play as well. In addition, Clemenceau's anger at the independent Belgian position on the Rhineland may well have contributed both to the exclusion of Belgium from the Rhineland negotiations, despite promises to the contrary, and to the decline of French support on other issues.

The only member of the French delegation sympathetic to Belgian claims was Jules Cambon, but he was no longer secretary-general at the Quai d'Orsay and had little influence. Stephen Pichon, the foreign minister, was little more than Clemenceau's messenger, and Louis Klotz, the finance minister, was widely regarded, above all by Clemenceau, as a nonentity. André Tardieu was both more influential and more involved in Belgian issues, as he served as the French expert on all west European territorial questions, but he had been selected for his sympathy with Clemenceau's views. The feud between Clemenceau and President Raymond Poincaré was a complicating factor that the Belgian delegation was occasionally able to exploit. Poincaré tended to favor the Belgian claims and sometimes intervened on their behalf, but he did not have the final power of decision. Then, too, Ferdinand Foch, generalissimo of the Allied armies, was present in Paris much of the time and, though his influence was probably less than it appeared to be, his oft-proclaimed advocacy of a confederation of France, Belgium, Luxemburg, and the Rhineland or a fifty-year Rhineland occupation terrified the Belgians.[169]

There were nominally five great powers at the peace conference, but Italy and Japan played little part in western questions and the Belgian diplomatists wasted little time on their delegations. Both countries were represented on the Belgian Commission; it soon became evident that the Italian delegation would support Belgian claims regularly and formally, but not aggressively, in hopes of establishing precedents for their own more grandiose territorial ambitions, whereas the Japanese, who had no genuine interest in any Belgian question, would attend meetings conscientiously, would vote with any majority, and would abstain in the absence of one. Though the Japanese delegation had many opportunities to cast deciding votes between Latin and Anglo-Saxon blocs in the Belgian Commission and elsewhere, in European matters it declined most of them.

However, as the year turned into 1919, the hostility of Lloyd George and Hardinge, the helpfulness and concern of House, the polite indifference of the Japanese, and the inflexible dedication to French security of Clemenceau and his cohorts all lay in the future, largely unanticipated by Hymans and his staff. In the last months of 1918, they had systematically prepared their dossiers and made Belgium's desires known to the great powers, assuming that such would suffice. With his lack of awareness of what kind of power struggle and competition for influence lay ahead, Hymans thought that his preparations for the conference were complete when he finally managed to see Balfour, if not Lloyd George, during the first week of January. But a few days before the conference began, a new problem, symptomatic of the administrative disorganization among the great powers in Paris, presented itself. On 15 January, Belgium received her formal invitation to the peace

169. Lloyd George, *Memoirs*, 1:78–79; Hymans memo, 14 Apr. 1919, Hymans Papers/ 150.

conference, specifying that she was to have only two plenipotentiaries. There had been no previous official statement about the number of seats, but the unofficial indications had consistently been three, and so three plenipotentiaries had long since been chosen and notified to the French government. Not only would reduction to two create an awkward domestic problem, forcing the elimination of one political party from the delegation, but national pride would be severely wounded, particularly because Brazil, whose contribution to the war had been slight, had been awarded three seats in deference to Wilson's concern for pan-American relations. The reduction of Belgian representation was the doing of Lloyd George. The French, the Italians, the Foreign Office itself, and especially the Americans favored three seats for Belgium. Furious Belgian protests followed, and at a meeting at the Quai d'Orsay on 17 January 1919, the representatives of the great powers decided, despite continuing objections from Lloyd George and Balfour, that Serbia and Belgium would each be granted three seats.[170]

This good news awaited Hymans when he and his delegation of fifty-six[171] arrived that evening in Paris at their assigned headquarters, the Hôtel Lotti, to prepare for the first plenary session of the peace conference the next day. They were unduly optimistic and certainly naive in thinking that their battles were largely behind them when in fact they were just beginning and the prospects of success were very uncertain at best. Armed with little more than their faith, both in the good will of

170. Defrance to Pichon, 17 Dec. 1918, tel. 244, FMAE A/38; *De Standaard*, 19 Jan. 1919, p. 2, 21 Jan. 1919, p. 1; *Gazet van Antwerpen*, 17 Jan. 1919, p. 1, 19 Jan. 1919, p. 1, 20–21 Jan. 1919, p. 1; Pichon to de Gaiffier, 15 Jan. 1919, BMAE DB/1; Hymans, *Mémoires*, 1:209–10; Whitlock, *Letters*, 2:546–47; de Gaiffier to Lloyd George, 16 Jan. 1919, War Cabinet, Paris, W.C.P. 8, CAB 29/7; I.C. 111, 17 Jan. 1919, CAB 28/6; F.O. MS, 5 Jan. 1919, Wilson Papers, 5B/6; Miller & Scott observations, 12 Jan. 1919, Wilson Papers 5B/8; Whitlock to ACNP, 16 Jan. 1919, tel. 5, de Gaiffier to Clemenceau, 16 Jan. 1919, minutes, 17 Jan. 1919, 183.5/4,5,7, ACNP/171; Lansing Desk Diary, 17 Jan. 1919, Lansing Papers. The Belgian Foreign Ministry knew that originally the peace conference was to be confined to countries that had participated in the combat but that Brazil had protested, pointing out that she had provided ships to the Entente and that a Brazilian plenipotentiary was in mid-Atlantic en route to Paris, which embarrassing situation had caused the rules to be stretched. De Gaiffier to Hymans, 18 Nov. 1918, no. 8893/3040, BMAE B–366/I.

171. Delegation list, Orts Papers/430. This total does not include clerical staff or those, like Baron de Cartier, who were assigned temporarily to the delegation.

the Allied great powers and in the rectitude of their own cause, the Belgian delegation set forth hopefully into modern Belgium's first extended and intensive diplomatic fray, unguided by any relevant previous national experience or any diplomatists accustomed to the brutal realities of high-level international politics.

THE BATTLE OF THE SEINE

TWO

SEEKING A VOICE

A VOICE ON THE COMMISSIONS

The members of the Belgian delegation had innocently assumed that the Declaration of Sainte-Adresse and their three seats at the conference table would insure that Belgium's voice would be heard. They soon learned otherwise, for it quickly became evident that three seats at plenary sessions were quite meaningless, because decisions were made elsewhere. Within a week of the formal opening of the conference, events obliged them to recognize that the battle for representation and influence had barely begun. The first plenary session in the Salle de la Paix at the Quai d'Orsay on 18 January 1919 consisted of little more than oratory and ceremony. The only action of significance was Wilson's nomination of Clemenceau to be president of the peace conference. He was elected by acclamation and thus the presiding chair passed from Poincaré, who had formally opened the conference on behalf of the host country, to the firm-minded first French plenipotentiary, who had no thought of submitting great-power decisions to any democratic vote.[1] This became evident when the second plenary session on 25 January revealed in part how the conference was to be organized. It was immediately obvious that Hymans's successful fight for three Belgian plenipotentiaries had solved nothing except an awkward problem in domestic politics, and so, with his customary energy and forthrightness, he returned to the fray. At this juncture, the idealist in Hymans was dominant over the realist and, though he won the battle, he inevitably lost the war, for the great powers had no intention of delegating or diluting their own authority.

Their intentions became evident on 25 January when Clemenceau announced from the presiding chair to the plenipotentiaries assembled the creation of five commissions to investigate various issues of the conference. His scheme, which represented a compromise between

1. Philippe Erlanger, *Clemenceau*, p. 568; Alexandre Zévaès, *Clemenceau*, pp. 270–71.

French and American planning,[2] provided that each of the five "Powers with General Interests" (the official euphemism for the Big Five) would have three seats on every commission, whereas the remaining twenty-two "Powers with Special Interests" would collectively choose five representatives to each body. Hymans protested at once, followed by the chief delegates of Serbia, Greece, and Rumania. Hymans heatedly argued that Belgium should have two representatives on the League of Nations and International Labor Commissions, one on the Commission on Ports, Waterways, and Railways, one on the Commission on the Responsibility for the War and Sanctions, and two on the Commission on Reparation. He defended the need for fuller representation of the small states in general and inquired sharply into the basis for such startling discrimination. When he persisted, Clemenceau informed him bluntly that the millions of dead soldiers of the great powers gave them the right to dominate the conference and intimated that, if the lesser states would not accept the announced arrangements, the great powers would proceed without them. He closed the session with his customary abruptness, leaving behind a tense and disgruntled atmosphere.[3]

Although Hymans later realized that his protest had gained him nothing except the ill will of the representatives of the powers upon whom Belgium's fate depended,[4] at the time he followed up his public stand with a written protest.[5] He continued his struggle when the smaller states were summoned on 27 January to a meeting chaired by Jules Cambon, at which they were to choose their delegates to the commissions. By agreement, Hymans served as spokesman for the caucus of small powers and expressed their views at length to Cambon, who could only promise to pass them on to the Big Five. The smaller nations then settled down to selecting representatives. Serbia gracefully yielded her place on the Labor Commission to Belgium, thus giving her two seats on that body. There was no dispute about membership on either

2. U.S. plenipotentiaries to Wilson, 8 Jan. 1919, Wilson Papers 5B/7; FMAE memo, 5 Jan. 1919, FMAE A/57; Pichon to Jusserand et al., 27 Nov. 1918, tel. 6325–34, FMAE Pichon Papers/6.

3. D. H. Miller, *Diary*, 4:64–83. Nobody was so tactless as to inquire into Japan's casualty rate.

4. Hymans, *Mémoires*, 1:328.

5. I.C. 121, 27 Jan. 1919, CAB 28/6.

the Labor Commission or the War Crimes Commission, upon which Belgium also obtained a seat, but the competition for places in the League of Nations Commission and the Ports, Waterways, and Railways Commission necessitated a formal vote. Belgium, however, headed the poll on both occasions and so gained a seat on each.[6]

The complaints of the small powers evoked little response except from House and to a lesser extent from Clemenceau, but in time more small-power seats were added to the League of Nations and Reparation Commissions, although not to the other commissions.[7] In the meantime, Cambon summoned the small powers again on 3 March to choose their five representatives on two additional commissions for economic and financial questions. The small powers rebelled and chose ten members for each body, including Belgium on both. They informed Cambon that if the Supreme Council was adamant about a limit of five, they themselves would select the five.[8] As the Supreme Council was indeed adamant, they met again on 6 March to make their choices. On this occasion, the Latin American states voted en bloc out of annoyance at European domination of the places. As a result, four Latin American states plus Portugal were chosen for the Financial Commission, and three Latin American and two Asian nations were elected to the Economics Commission. Six indignant European states, including Belgium, abstained in the further voting for supplementary lists of four powers for each commission to be submitted to the Supreme Council in a final effort to gain more seats.[9] When the Supreme Council received these startling results, together with a formal protest from the European states, it decided to set aside the election and accordingly chose six European states to have one seat each on the Financial Commission and seven states, five of them European, to sit on the Economic Commission. France had nominated Belgium to the latter in the surprising hope that she could be induced to vote with the semiprotectionist French-

6. Hymans to BMAE, 27 Jan. 1919, tel. 30, BMAE DB/1; D. H. Miller, *Diary*, 4:93–97.
7. I.C. 131, 3 Feb. 1919, CAB 28/6; Charles Seymour, *Letters from the Paris Peace Conference*, p. 130; D. H. Miller, *Diary*, 5:381.
8. Meeting, Powers with Special Interests, 3 Mar. 1919, F.O. 374/20.
9. Meeting, Powers with Special Interests, 6 Mar. 1919, F.O. 374/20.

Italian combination against the free-trade Anglo-American bloc.[10] As French leaders declined to accept the fact that the British and Americans would not cooperate in French plans for postwar economic organization, they were equally slow to recognize that Belgian national interests would dictate Belgian economic policy. In any event, as Belgium was included in both the Economics and Financial Commissions, she had gained a seat on every major commission, as well as a number of minor ones, and had two seats in both the Labor Commission and the Commission on Reparation, whose membership was decreed by the Supreme Council of the great powers without reference to any democratic process.[11] The remarkable representation of Belgium on the commissions owed something to Hymans's outspoken protests, but more perhaps to Belgium's unique position in relation to the war, which made it impossible to exclude her from commissions dealing with war crimes and reparations; her location, which had made her expert in problems of international waterways; and her highly industrialized society and prewar commercial strength, which made her an appropriate choice for commissions concerning economics, finance, and labor.

Belgium's prominent role in the commissions did much for the national amour-propre but very little for her foreign policy. Hymans had fought for representation in the commissions in the belief that they would have the power of decision, but they did not, and Hymans was mistaken about the nature of power. As he discovered in time, the promise of Sainte-Adresse that Belgium would be permitted to participate in the peace conference had clearly been fulfilled but not in any meaningful sense. The commissions did a great deal of valuable work but only made recommendations. Decisions were made by the Supreme Council consisting of the Big Four (or occasionally Five or Three) and then referred for final drafting to various great-power committees, on which neither Belgium nor any other small state had representation. As a consequence, the Belgian delegation had no share in drafting any of the clauses concerning Belgium. More importantly, it had little or no

10. Supreme War Council paper S.W.C. 386, 387, 8, 10 Mar. 1919, CAB 28/6; de Gaiffier to Hymans, 13 Mar. 1919, no. 1953/780, BMAE FR/1919.
    11. I.C. 117, 23 Jan. 1919, CAB 28/6.

voice in these decisions. The great states had the power that Belgium so conspicuously lacked, and accordingly they had the power of decision. This fact was not at first clear to the Belgian delegation, and so initially it was much gratified by Belgium's conspicuous representation on the commissions, thinking that Belgium's special status had been universally acknowledged and that her membership on so many commissions would ensure her participation in decision making.

The Belgian members of the various commissions tended to be hardworking, competent, and prominent. Vandervelde was a major figure in the Labor Commission, and the technical knowledge of Paul Segers became indispensable to the Commission on Ports, Waterways, and Railways, although in the end the problem of the Scheldt was handled elsewhere.[12] Indeed, everything of real importance was decided elsewhere. Hymans himself sat on the League of Nations Commission, where he was his usual energetic and aggressive self, much to the annoyance of the representatives of the great powers, who clearly felt that the smaller states should be seen but not heard. With his precise mind, he was useful in clearing up drafting ambiguities and in sorting out the muddled arguments of fuzzy-minded orators. However, he talked so much that he was eventually relegated to a "clarification committee" composed of the most loquacious delegates, who were thus kept occupied while the others got on to business without their interruptions.[13]

In the League of Nations Commission, Hymans annoyed the French by his refusal to support some of their plans and infuriated the British delegate, Lord Robert Cecil, by his dogged insistence upon representation for the smaller states on the Council of the League of Nations, where originally only the five great powers were to sit. When, after considerable Belgian pressure, Cecil argued that two seats for all the small states would be ample, Hymans shouted at him, "What you propose is a revival of the Holy Alliance of unhallowed memory!" Wilson placated him and, after he had protested further, agreed to four Council seats for the smaller powers. In this and in the award to Belgium of one of

12. W.C.P. 704, 26 Mar. 1919, CAB 29/14.

13. Thompson, *Peace Conference*, pp. 185–86; House Diary, 8 Feb. 1919, 15:40, House Papers.

the Council seats from the start, Hymans undoubtedly gained a signal victory, but he engendered considerable irritation in the process.[14]

Though four seats on the League Council for all the small states proved inadequate in time and the small-power representation was enlarged four times until it ultimately reached eleven, four seats at the outset was a great deal more satisfactory than none at all. At least the principle of small-power participation had been established. Again, Hymans had been the spokesman of the small states, and this time he had accomplished something, although how much of importance is questionable. Moreover, his victory came at the cost of some erosion of great-power good will toward his country's cause in other, more vital, matters. Because Belgium held her seat in the League Council until 1926, when a system of rotation was established for the small powers, a Belgian representative, usually Hymans himself, had a voice on the Council's decisions in the first crucial years of the League and enjoyed a prominence there that exceeded Belgium's actual power. By the time that Belgium relinquished her seat in 1926, it had become clear that matters of real importance were not decided in the League Council. Like other small nations who clung to the League, although perhaps to a lesser degree, Belgium had been mistaken about the nature of power and where it was located.

During the peace conference itself, in the commission to draw up the League Covenant, Hymans irritated and bored almost everybody by his persistent pleading for Brussels as the site of the League of Nations, a quest doomed to failure from the outset, because no great power was enthusiastic about Brussels and Wilson's preference for Geneva was widely known. Yet Hymans fought on for a hopeless cause, writing memoranda and raising the question at every opportunity.[15] It is doubt-

14. D. H. Miller, *Diary*, 5:39–41, 45–47, 97–101; Stephen Bonsal, *Unfinished Business*, pp. 26, 52–54, 162–63, 166. Other Belgian efforts to obtain compulsory arbitration of disputes and to broaden the application of sanctions, although backed by France, were defeated by Anglo-American opposition, as both governments, especially the British, sought to evade binding commitments. George W. Egerton, *Great Britain and the Creation of the League of Nations*, pp. 133–35.

15. Hymans to de Cartier, 26 Feb. 1919, tel. 7, BMAE DB/5; Bonsal, *Unfinished Business*, pp. 26–27, 145, 147, 168–69; D. H. Miller, *Diary*, 1:182, 278, 5:104, 8:264–65; David Hunter Miller, *The Drafting of the Covenant*, 2:365–66; Hymans to Lloyd George, 17 Mar. 1919, Lloyd George Papers F/49/4/4; de Cartier to Hymans, 4 Mar.

ful whether he really personally cared and he certainly realized later that Brussels would have been a poor choice. But he was well aware of the intensity of parliamentary and public opinion in Belgium on this point.[16] He over-responded to this pressure, probably with an eye to the next Belgian election and the fortunes of the Liberal party, but to the detriment of Belgium's other claims. Furthermore, the city of Brussels, stronghold of the Liberal party, was campaigning actively for the honor and had offered the elegant eighteenth-century Egmont Palace as a gift to the League if Brussels were to be its seat. In addition, the Dutch were pressing for the selection of their peace palace at The Hague.[17] Though the Netherlands had no more chance of success than Belgium, the outside possibility that The Hague might become a compromise choice undoubtedly spurred Hymans on, for such a selection would have been much resented by Brussels. Hymans's persistence may also have owed something to the likelihood that Britain would be blamed for the inevitable blow to Belgium's pride. Although Wilson's wishes were the decisive factor, the French let it be widely known that they had no objection to Brussels but that the British had.[18] Given French dominance of Belgium's leading weekly magazine and of at least one of the largest daily newspapers of Brussels,[19] and the avowed French intention of displacing the British in Belgium, Hymans may well have thought it advisable to seek British support for a cause he knew to be hopeless. However, he did so ad nauseam and to no effect. Though

---

1919, B. Micro/23; Hymans to Wilson, 26 Mar. 1919, no. 348, Wilson 5B/23; House Diary, 31 Mar., 11 Apr. 1919, 15:125–26, 150, House Papers; Hymans note, 29 Mar. 1919, BMAE DB/30/III.

16. Hymans, *Mémoires*, 1:305, 402; Cecil to Balfour, 26 Apr. 1919, F.O. 608/217; Bonsal, *Unfinished Business*, p. 169; *La Nation belge*, 2 May 1919, p. 1; Whitlock to ACNP, 17 Apr. 1919, tel. 12, Wilson Papers 5B/29; Whitlock to ACNP, 18 Apr. 1919, no. 11, 855.00/8, ACNP/448.

17. A. Max to Wilson, 11 Mar. 1919, no. B1598, BMAE DB/5; DuB, R.G.P. 117, pp. 938–39, 977–81, 1039–43; DuD, R.G.P. 156, p. 247. Dutch persistence eventually paid off in the establishment of the Permanent Court of International Justice at The Hague.

18. Villiers to Curzon, 8 Apr. 1919, no. 117, F.O. 371/3645; de Gaiffier to Hymans, 24 Mar. 1919, Hymans Papers/196; Whitlock to House, 2 May 1919, House Papers 20/24.

19. For some years after World War I, *Pourquoi pas?* and *La Nation belge* were French financed and served as instruments of French propaganda. Information derived from interviews in Brussels, Sept. 1967. See also DuD, R.G.P. 156, pp. 4–7.

France and three smaller nations voted with Belgium, Cecil and Wilson were both outspoken and Geneva won easily.[20]

While Hymans was boring the British about Brussels in the League of Nations Commission, Jules van den Heuvel was struggling with a far greater problem in the Commission of Reparation. But it soon became evident that the key decisions about reparations were political, not technical, and would be taken by the Big Five alone. Accordingly, Hymans early began to canvass for diplomatic assistance, although he was not optimistic. French support was probable if French interests were unaffected, but a price tag would be attached; and British lack of interest in Belgian problems was clear to him as early as 22 January. Hymans complained repeatedly of British indifference and quickly recognized that no support would be forthcoming on either reparations or any issue involving Holland. The open hostility of Lloyd George was evident to both Hymans and other members of the delegation, although it had to be observed from afar because no member of the Belgian delegation was able to gain access to Lloyd George at all during the first ten weeks of the conference. Hymans repeatedly sought interviews with Lloyd George, who replied through his private secretary that he knew from Balfour what Hymans had to say and there was no need for a meeting. Hymans persisted in a letter "from one first delegate to another first delegate," adding that he had other questions to discuss, but received no reply. Although Hymans, who seemed oblivious to the pressures upon members of the Big Four, complained to Villiers during a trip to Brussels about Lloyd George's manners, that accomplished nothing.[21]

20. Minutes, League of Nations Commission, 10 Apr. 1919, BMAE DB/5. In view of Swiss slowness to approve the Geneva location and American failure to approve the Versailles treaty, France revived the question of Brussels as the site for the League in November 1919 and continued to press the matter, particularly in regard to the first Assembly meeting scheduled for November 1920, at the fifth Council meeting in May 1920 at Rome. However, the Swiss approved the Geneva site in May, and Wilson's call for the first Assembly, issued in July 1920, specified Geneva. That settled the issue, which the French had probably raised in hopes of placating Belgium on other questions. Warren Kuehl, "Getting the League Started, 1919–20" (paper read at American Historical Association annual meeting, New York, 28 Dec. 1979).

21. Hymans, *Mémoires*, 1:353, 355–57, 378 n; Hymans to Balfour, 26 Mar. 1919, F.O. 608/2 pt. 1; Vicomte Terlinden, "Lloyd George à la conférence de la paix," pp. 4–5;

If Lloyd George was unavailable, other Britons had to be sought out, and Hymans went in search of them, complaining that they were hard to find and that he had many talks with French and American representatives but almost none with the British.[22] Although this charge was exaggerated in regard to other issues, it is true that the Belgians had considerable difficulty in achieving any meetings with British diplomats to discuss reparations or the Rhineland and it is certainly true that they gained no support on either question from the British delegation, largely because of the attitude of its chief. Belgian charges as to Lloyd George's hostility to Belgium in general and to Belgian reparations in particular were amply justified. In addition to his growing dislike of Hymans, his antipathy to all things Belgian, and his emphatic desire to increase British reparations at the expense of Belgium, Lloyd George appears to have had a general anti-Catholic bias, which also influenced his attitude toward France and Poland.[23]

A VOICE IN THE RHENISH SETTLEMENT?

British hostility and indifference also contributed to Belgium's exclusion from discussions of the future of the Rhineland, particularly as the French also wished to bar the Belgians from debates on this question. The Rhineland bordered upon Belgium and so was of immediate concern to her. Further, she had participated in the occupation from the outset. The Allied troops had marched en masse "elbow to elbow"[24] eastward through northern France and Belgium in the latter part of November 1918, circumventing lower Limburg, as they progressed toward the Rhineland. The Belgian government was pleased that their army marched through the "Walloon cantons," but as the Belgian army was on the northern end of the Allied line, it was assigned the northern-

---

interview with Vicomte Terlinden; van den Heuvel notes, 31 Mar. 1919, AGR van den Heuvel Papers/46; Villiers to Curzon, 4 Apr. 1919, IOL Curzon Papers F112/214b.

22. Hardinge to Balfour, 26 Mar. 1919, F.O. 608/2 pt. 1.

23. Hymans, *Mémoires*, 1:378 n; Wallace to Colby, 19 Nov. 1920, NA SD 741.51/6. Cecil also remarked that the seat of the League must not be a Catholic country. Villiers to Curzon, 4 Apr. 1919, Curzon Papers F112/214b.

24. Paul Tirard, *La France sur le Rhin*, p. 5.

most occupation zone, whereas the Walloon cantons fell to the British and French zones. Initially, the Belgian zone extended only from the Rhineland's northern border with Holland southward along upper Dutch Limburg to Mönchen-Gladbach. Its administrative headquarters were at Aachen in a sector occupied by the French, an arrangement that caused much inconvenience and confusion. After all possibility of Dutch territorial transfer had been ruled out and after the British and Americans had begun to demobilize their armies, zonal boundaries were rearranged in August 1919 and the Belgian zone was enlarged to run the length of Dutch Limburg (west of the British army at Cologne, a French enclave below it, and the American army at Coblenz) southward through Malmédy to Gerolstein just above the Luxemburg border. Lieutenant-General Augustin Michel's headquarters remained at Aachen but now alone, as the French had withdrawn, and the Belgian zone remained without a bridgehead.[25]

Belgian government policy from the first stressed the importance of a benevolent occupation in hopes of developing cultural and economic ties, although Belgium had no political aims in the Rhineland aside from some of the Walloon cantons. Accordingly, the troops were ordered to treat the Rhenish well and to avoid incidents. Nonetheless, persistent reports indicated that the Belgian occupation was the most severe of any and the Belgian forces the most detested of all the occupiers. There seem to have been three reasons for this. Initially, General Michel conscientiously obeyed all of Foch's directives concerning administrative measures until he discovered that the British and Americans were ignoring many of them. Thereafter he obtained permission from Brussels to ease his policy. Secondly, the Belgian army, unlike those of the other three occupying powers, contained scarcely a single soldier whose family had not suffered at the hands of the Germans and, despite orders, some took revenge. Finally, the Belgian army was par-

---

25. Boseret to Gillain, 30 Nov. 1918, Hymans to Masson, 9 Jan. 1919, no. 263, BMAE B–348; Masson to Hymans, 6 Feb. 1919, no. 124/13PC, BMAE B–10.442; Cd. 9212, pp. 12–13; Tirard, *La France sur le Rhin*, frontispiece maps. Later the zonal boundaries were rearranged again, with the Belgian zone reduced so that the zonal boundary fell just below Aachen. British army map, July 1921, F.O. 371/7521. The Belgian zone gained a bridgehead as a result of the March 1921 sanctions.

ticularly loathed by the Germans because Belgium was a small power and thus held in contempt. In German eyes, the presence of British, French, and American armies on German soil was a humiliating indignity but at least these were great powers, whereas the Belgian occupation was an outrage. No amount of orders from Brussels could dissolve this attitude.[26]

While the Belgian government in Brussels fretted about conditions in its zone and renewed orders for benevolence, the Belgian delegation in Paris struggled unsuccessfully to obtain a voice in deliberations about the future of the Rhineland. On no other subject except reparations did it protest so repeatedly and vehemently about lack of consultation. Aside from an interest generated by economic ties, Belgian concerns were several. The delegation wished to be consulted about disposition of the area and also to avoid any settlement generating deep resentment in Germany, who might retaliate against her weaker neighbor. Above all, however, it wished to prevent any extended French domination of the Rhineland, because that might imply French economic, military, and political encirclement of Belgium. The Belgian government favored demilitarization and neutralization of the area but opposed any long-term Allied occupation. If there were to be an extended occupation after the treaty went into effect, however, Belgium wished to participate in order to reduce the area of French influence. Hymans inclined toward establishing an autonomous, self-governing Rhenish state attached to a larger Germany, which appeared to be what the inhabitants also desired. On the whole, the Catholic Rhenish would have been glad to be rid of the Protestant Prussian officials who governed them, but they wished to remain in Germany. Along with one or two of his staff, Hymans personally would have liked a truly independent buffer state between Belgium and Germany, but de Gaiffier frequently reminded him that true independence was out of the question; France would

26. Boseret to Gillain, 30 Nov. 1918, Hymans to Masson, 9 Jan. 1919, no. 263, Michel to Gillain, n.d. [late Jan. 1919], no. 30422, Gillain to Masson, 8 Feb. 1919, no. 6990, Peltzer to Hymans, 11 Mar. 1919, no. 2345/363, van Wernelle note, 10 June 1919, BMAE B–348; French Mission, Luxemburg, to Guerre, 25 Jan. 1919, tel. 487, Vin 5N/188; compte-rendu, French army meeting, Luxemburg, 22 May 1919, AN AJ⁹/3776.

dominate the buffer state under one form or another and thus would encircle Belgium on three sides.[27] Except for specific claims to the small border districts of Malmédy, Moresnet, and possibly Eupen, the Belgian government had no thought of annexing any part of the Rhineland, as it desired neither a larger German minority nor a basis for German revisionism. A few ardent Belgian nationalists, including some junior army officers in the Rhineland and the aggressive Comité de Politique Nationale, favored annexation in vain romantic hopes of recreating the old medieval Middle Kingdom under the Belgian monarchy, but they gained no support from the Belgian delegation.[28]

In France, annexationist sentiment was more pronounced and, during the war, more official. In 1917, the French government had considered annexing part of the Rhineland.[29] This idea had been dropped by the end of the war and, in November 1918, Clemenceau endorsed Foch's arguments against annexation but in favor of the Rhine as the western frontier of Germany. The left bank would be demilitarized, neutralized, and organized into one or more autonomous states in a customs union with other western states. Finally, the area would be placed under long-term Allied military occupation. Because Clemenceau had recognized both the drawbacks of annexation, notably the presence of protesting Germanic members in the French Chamber of Deputies, and the fact that Belgium would not be as docile as earlier anticipated, there was no more French talk of Belgian domination of the northern, more economically valuable half of the Rhineland, although Nothomb's CPN continued to agitate for and scheme toward two buffer states until the end of 1923. Before and during the peace conference, French officials declined to discuss the Rhineland at all with their Belgian counterparts until 24 February 1919, when Tardieu misleadingly informed Hymans and de Gaiffier that the conference had decided upon a neutral, de-

27. Hymans, *Mémoires*, 1:385–86; Hymans note, 14 Apr. 1919, BMAE B–10.440; van Wernelle note, 10 June 1919, BMAE B–348; de Gaiffier to Hymans, 26 Feb., 11 Mar. 1919, nos. 1506/580, 1989/753, BMAE FR/1919.

28. G. Grahame to Curzon, 9 Feb. 1921, no. 135, F.O. 371/6041; G. Grahame to Curzon, 18, 27 Dec. 1920, nos. 906, 918, F.O. 371/5460; Curzon memo, 30 Apr. 1919, F.O. 800/151.

29. Georges Maurice Paléologue, *An Ambassador's Memoirs*, 3:192.

militarized, and autonomous Rhenish state. As the Belgians expressed only surprise, Tardieu gave them no further information.[30]

Meanwhile, before the peace conference began, French views were put before House and Wilson, who did not at first object, and were argued in a further memo from Foch to the plenipotentiaries of the great powers. However, British resistance was immediate,[31] and with the passage of time, Clemenceau recognized that Wilson would not countenance detachment of the Rhineland from Germany unless the inhabitants desired it, which most of them clearly did not. Nonetheless, through March and April of 1919, Clemenceau fought for the Rhine frontier against the combined opposition of Lloyd George and Wilson. As they remained adamant, he gradually retreated, over the protestations of Foch, from the military line of the Rhine, the Rhenish Republic, and the original claim of six Allied bridgeheads across the Rhine. In return for a promise on 14 March of an Anglo-American guarantee of France, he proposed on 17 March to accept the agreed fifty-kilometer demilitarized zone east of the Rhine, five bridgeheads, demilitarization of the left bank, a permanent commission of inspection, and thirty-year Allied military occupation of the left bank and the bridgeheads. But Anglo-American resistance to an extended military occupation remained firm and, on 22 April, again over the protests of Foch, he had to accept the compromise solution of four bridgeheads[32] and a phased occupation of three zones for five, ten, and fifteen years.[33]

The Belgian delegation was obliged to observe this extended struggle

30. André Tardieu, *The Truth about the Treaty*, p. 145; Foch note, 28 Nov. 1918, FMAE A/162; Foch note, 10 Jan. 1919, Pichon Papers/7; Nothomb to Hymans, 29 July 1919, BMAE B–10.440; de Gaiffier to Hymans, 12 Oct. 1919, no. 7556/2603, BMAE FR 1918/II; de Gaiffier to Hymans, 25 Feb., 11 Mar. 1919, nos. 1471/564, 1898/753, BMAE FR/1919.

31. Tardieu, *Truth*, pp. 170–71; Foch memo, 10 Jan. 1919, no. 580, FMAE A/162; House to Wilson, 23 Feb. 1919, tel. 3, Wilson Papers 5B/17.

32. In addition to the three zonal bridgeheads, there was a small one at Kehl opposite Strasbourg. FRUS PPC, 13:160.

33. French memo, 25 Feb. 1919, FMAE A/162; Foch note, 31 Mar. 1919, Pichon Papers/7; Commandant René Michel Lhopital, ed., *Foch, l'armistice et la paix*, pp. 194–213; Tardieu, *Truth*, pp. 172–90; FRUS PPC, 5:113–18, 244–48, 11:512–13; Paul Mantoux, *Les Délibérations du conseil des quartre*, 1:50–51. For a detailed account of the struggle over the Rhineland, see Keith L. Nelson, *Victors Divided*, chaps. 4 and 5.

from afar and largely in a state of ignorance about what was being debated.[34] Early on, French representatives canvassed for Belgian support but discovered no enthusiasm for the line of the Rhine and outright antipathy to extended military occupation.[35] In view of these attitudes, the French saw no reason to campaign for Belgian inclusion in the Rhineland discussions. The Belgians turned to the British, whose views on the Rhineland they largely shared, but the British were indifferent. Lloyd George wished to avoid all Belgians, especially Hymans, whereas Balfour, who was more cordial, was convinced that France had no ulterior motives in the Rhineland.[36] Under the circumstances, Belgium gained nothing more than promises of participation.

These promises were numerous but never fulfilled. The Belgian delegation did not rest content with its isolation on an issue of direct concern and made energetic efforts to gain admission to the debates. When Hymans presented the Belgian position before the Council of Ten on 11 February 1919, he confined his excessively long address to direct Belgian claims against Germany and indirect claims against Holland but carefully reserved Belgium's right to participate when the conference took up the Rhineland question. However, by the time it did so, the Big Four was coming into being, and this was an inner council into which no small state could penetrate.[37] It seems incongruous that Italy and, on occasion, Japan, neither of whom had any direct interest in the Rhineland, were entitled to participate in debate of this vital question, whereas Belgium, who was not only directly concerned and had a sizable military force in the Rhineland but also expected to participate in both the continuing military occupation and its administration, was consistently excluded. Yet Italy and Japan were classed as "Powers with General Interests" and thus automatically entitled to participate in everything, whereas Belgium was merely a "Power with Special Interests," even if one of those special interests was indubitably the Rhineland. In part, it was too much trouble to summon Belgium for Rhineland discussions, especially because no great power particularly desired her pres-

34. Hymans, *Mémoires*, 1:387.
35. Ibid., 1:351.
36. Balfour to Curzon, 1 Mar. 1919, tel., Balfour Papers/49734.
37. Hymans, *Mémoires*, 1:385.

ence, and in part it was too inconvenient, for the agenda of the Big Four was astonishingly erratic, darting from topic to topic, and discussions of the Rhineland were often sandwiched between debates of no concern to Belgium. There was the further problem that admission of Belgium to Rhineland debates would have set a precedent, causing other small states to clamor for admission on problems of interest to them. Primarily, however, it was taken for granted that small states should be treated like small children and that great issues should be settled by great powers. Indeed, the creation of the Council of Four doomed Belgium's last hope of participation.

Before this became apparent, Hymans raised the question at every opportunity to French and British representatives, but without effect.[38] In this matter as in others, he does not appear to have approached the American delegation. The old instinct to turn to the guarantor powers remained strong. On 31 March, Hymans was suddenly summoned before the Four on no notice to discuss the German boundary and happened by chance to be present when Foch made one of his several impassioned pleas for the Rhine frontier. After Foch left, Hymans seized the moment to complain of lack of consultation on several issues, adding: "The same may be said of the question of the Rhine, for this concerns Belgium as much as any other Power. If the left bank of the Rhine is to be occupied, Belgium will have to take part. We would not like to hear it said, some fine day, that the great powers came to this or that decision without consulting us."[39]

The oral complaint was quickly followed by a written one, formally protesting meetings of the Four without Belgian participation on reparations, the western frontier of Germany, and the question of the left bank.[40] This accomplished nothing, however, and so stronger measures seemed to be necessary. The exclusion of Belgium from debate on so many questions of interest to her was one of several reasons why the Belgian delegation summoned King Albert to the rescue.

---

38. Hymans note, 28 Mar. 1919, Hymans to BMAE, 31 Mar. 1919, tel. 288, BMAE B–366/I; de Gaiffier to Hymans, 25 Feb. 1919, no. 1471/572, BMAE FR/1919.

39. Mantoux, *Les Délibérations*, 1:92–95; Hymans, *Mémoires*, 1:391; Hymans note, 1 Apr. 1919, BMAE B–366/I. According to Hymans's account, he stressed that Belgium had a right to know what its obligations in the Rhineland would be.

40. Hymans to Clemenceau, 31 Mar. 1919, BMAE DB/7/I.

Albert's arrival on 1 April was dramatic, as he was the only king to attend the peace conference and the first king ever to arrive in Paris by airplane.[41] The day of kings was largely past, but this king was very technologically minded and commanded headlines as a result of his spectacular arrival by air. He brought with him a memorandum he had drafted himself, insisting upon Belgian participation in discussion of the Rhineland, and remarked, "It was not proper that we were reduced to learning from the newspapers that four statesmen are deliberating together on questions which directly involve the destiny of Belgium." This comment probably derived from a recent report by Hymans that four men were negotiating the fate of the world in secret, sadly remarking that "the four soothsayers are inapproachable," and adding that he did not know what to do, along with another from de Gaiffier indicating that the peace terms, including the German frontier, were nearly completed although the Belgian delegation had been neither consulted nor informed.[42] Albert opposed a military occupation, arguing that it would be ineffectual because it was unlikely that the Allies could maintain it for thirty years until it was genuinely needed. If a sanction was required to enforce the financial clauses of the treaty, he thought that the threat of British naval blockade of German ports should suffice.[43] Albert's new inclination to lean on the British, whom he had previously much distrusted, probably derived both from Hymans's influence and from a desire to avoid future Belgian military action against Germany.

As not even Lloyd George could refuse to see the king of the Belgians, Albert talked with all the Allied leaders and gained formal assurances from Poincaré, Clemenceau, Lloyd George, Balfour, and Wilson that nothing would be definitively settled without Belgium. However, when he met formally with the Four on 4 April, he again opposed any extended military occupation of the Rhineland. Thereafter, Hymans

41. Hymans, *Mémoires*, 1:430–32, 439–44; Carlo Bronne, *Albert Ier, le roi sans terre*, p. 349; *Le Temps*, 3 Apr. 1919, p. 1; *L'Etoile belge*, 4 Apr. 1919, p. 1; *De Standaard*, 5 Apr. 1919, p. 1, 6 Apr. 1919, p. 1, 7 Apr. 1919, p. 1; van den Heuvel notes, 31 Mar. 1919, van den Heuvel Papers/46. King Nicolas of Montenegro, whose kingdom was rapidly ceasing to exist, was in Paris but not permitted to attend the conference.

42. Hymans, *Mémoires*, 1:388; Hymans note, 28 Mar. 1919, BMAE B–1–1519; de Gaiffier to Hymans, 29 Mar. 1919, no. 2495/985, BMAE FR/1919; Hymans to Orts, 26 Mar. 1919, BMAE B–366/I.

43. Hymans, *Mémoires*, 1:388.

remained excluded from meetings of the Four on the Rhenish question, as the French saw no point in adding to the number of their opponents and the other powers were indifferent to Belgian protestations.[44] Through all these weeks of argument, neither the British nor the Americans made any real effort to enlist Belgium against the French. Both assumed that the status of the Rhineland was a question for the great powers to decide and feared to set a dangerous precedent by consulting a small power about anything. In addition, Lloyd George disliked Hymans and considered him a French lackey.

As the struggle over military occupation reached its height in mid-April, there were two belated and halfhearted attempts to canvass for Belgian support, although neither the British nor the French went so far as to offer the promised participation in the debate. On 13 April, Foch and Gen. Maxime Weygand called upon Hymans to argue for a military occupation lasting thirty to fifty years. Unofficially, Hymans demurred, pointing out that Britain and America would not participate and the burden upon France and Belgium would thus be onerous, especially for a regime that would end just as an angry, revengeful Germany was regaining strength. He added that Belgian opinion opposed a peacetime military occupation, fearing that German desires for vengeance could lead to a new war. Later that evening, Lloyd George summoned Hymans, Vandervelde, and Delacroix, who was visiting the Belgian delegation, to his flat in the Rue Nitôt to give them a belated and fragmentary briefing on the peace terms. On the Rhineland, he said that there would be a demilitarized zone but no buffer state. He implied that agreement had been reached against an occupation after the peace treaty entered into force. Though this was untrue, it pleased the Belgian delegation. After consulting Delacroix, Hymans saw Foch again to say officially that Belgium did not favor a military frontier on the Rhine.[45]

A few days later, Hymans was stirred to new action by misleading press reports implying that various matters of concern to Belgium had been settled, including both a revision of its legal status and a Franco-Belgian occupation of the Rhineland. He addressed a stiff note to the

44. Ibid., 1:388–89; Mantoux, *Les Délibérations*, 1:144–45.
45. Hymans note, 14 Apr. 1919, Hymans Papers/150.

conference secretary, the French career diplomat Paul Dutasta, demanding that he be informed of dispositions concerning Belgium.[46] By this time, he had largely abandoned hope of participation in the decisions. On 23 April, the day after the Rhineland settlement was finally agreed upon, Hymans wrote a memo which indicated that he was aware of the rough shape of the probable compromise but not that it had actually been achieved. With incurable optimism, he declared, "I will be informed on this question very shortly." He added that Belgium must adhere to the agreement and participate in the occupation to prevent a dangerous unilateral French occupation and to maintain good relations with the Allies for the sake of other political and financial negotiations.[47]

Although the Belgian government opposed any peacetime occupation, it never considered refusing to participate. The risks, both in regard to French forces on Belgian frontiers and in regard to Anglo-American loans, would have been too great, and no Belgian cabinet minister wanted it said that Belgium was not doing its share, as Lloyd George continued to charge concerning Belgium's military effort in the past. The Belgian attitude was fortunate, because all the great powers took it for granted, to the extent of not bothering with notification, that Belgium would participate in the occupation and indeed would do so to a substantially greater degree than either Britain or America, who promised only to show their flags. Nonetheless, the Belgian delegation still had to mount a constant campaign to participate in the administrative planning for that occupation. As Belgian forces had occupied the northernmost Rhineland zone since shortly after the Armistice and as a Belgian representative served on the four-power civilian Inter-Allied Rhineland Commission created on 21 April 1919, Belgian participation in planning for the permanent occupation to follow should have been automatic, but it was not. At this stage, exclusion of Belgium derived more from habit and absentmindedness than from any deliberate intent. On 5 May, Lloyd George, who was worried that occupation costs would eat heavily into reparations receipts, raised the question of the size of the army of occupation. It was agreed that a committee composed of British, French, and American generals would consider the question.

46. Hymans to Dutasta, 19 Apr. 1919, no. 472, BMAE DB/1.
47. Hymans note, 23 Apr. 1919, BMAE Ind/1919/I.

However, on 8 May this task was turned over to the military representatives of the Supreme War Council at Versailles, along with the job of drafting a convention for the military occupation of the left bank. Belatedly, Belgian participation was invited for both tasks.[48]

When this committee reported, Pierrepont Noyes, the American member of the Inter-Allied Rhineland Commission, successfully protested that the scheme was too draconian, and so the Four reconsidered the matter on 29 May. Almost automatically, the job of revising the draft convention was referred to a new four-man committee consisting of senior British, French, American, and Italian civilians who, together with generals from those four states, would consider the total size of the occupying forces. Italy was of course not expected to participate in the Rhineland occupation at all; however, her status as a member of the Big Four dictated her automatic inclusion in the committee. When the Belgian delegation heard that meetings were in progress, it asked for representation. Because Belgium was expected to provide the second largest occupying force, she clearly could not be denied. Though the Belgian members had already missed the first two sessions, they participated thereafter. De Gaiffier, who was the civilian Belgian representative, bent his energies in support of Cecil's unsuccessful effort to reduce the occupying force below 150,000 men. He recognized that the burden would fall on France and Belgium and that the prior charge of occupation costs, of which France would probably get the lion's share, would delay rapid reparations needed for Belgian reconstruction. On several counts, it was in Belgium's interest to reduce the size of the French army in the Rhineland, but she did not succeed. After the peace treaty entered into effect, France provided 90,400 of the occupation troops; Belgium provided 19,700 and Britain 15,000. The American force shrank steadily until its withdrawal in 1923.[49]

48. Tirard, *La France sur le Rhin*, pp. 100–102; K. Nelson, *Victors Divided*, p. 102; FRUS PPC, 5:471, 515.

49. FRUS PPC, 6:108–14; de Gaiffier to Hymans, 3 June 1919, 5 June 1919, no. 4763/1919, BMAE DB/13/II; de Gaiffier to Hymans, 6 June 1919, no. 4773/1925, BMAE FR/1919; de Gaiffier to Hymans, 7 June 1919, BMAE Ind/1919/I; France, Ministère des Affaires Etrangères, DD, *Documents relatifs aux réparations*, 1:187; Maj. Gen. Henry T. Allen, *The Rhineland Occupation*, pp. 249, 294; Tirard to Leygues, 8 Jan. 1921, Jusserand to Briand, n.d. [26 Oct. 1921], tel. 967, Tirard to Poincaré, 19 Feb. 1922, tel. 39–41, Jusserand to Poincaré, 6 June 1922, tel. 662, AJ⁹/3112.

While negotiations in Paris toward arrangements for the peacetime occupation were still in progress, the first abortive Rhenish Republic proclaimed itself on 1 June 1919 under the leadership of Dr. Hans Adam Dorten. The reactions of General Michel, the Foreign and War Ministries in Brussels, and the Belgian delegation at Paris to this separatist outbreak and the events immediately preceding it reveal clearly the extent of Belgian ignorance and confusion as a consequence of exclusion not only from the more substantive deliberations at the peace conference but also from Foch's unified command organizations then administering the occupied territories. Although Michel had at first thought that a good deal of separatist sentiment existed in the Rhineland, by mid-May he had concluded that separatism was dead, an opinion affording much amusement to the French officers then organizing Dorten's republic.[50]

When French representatives informed Michel late on 28 May that the Rhenish Republic would be proclaimed the next day at Aachen, he took steps to maintain order, banned pending instructions any publication of the German government's denunciation of the new republic as treason, and sought instructions from both Brussels and Foch. On the twenty-ninth he declared to the separatists that he must support the existing officials from Berlin until he received orders on this political question and must forbid proclamation of the Rhenish Republic in the Belgian zone. As a consequence, the separatist outbreak was postponed. On Hymans's instructions, the Belgian government endorsed these decisions while Foch ordered a benevolent neutrality toward the separatists.[51]

50. Masson to Hymans, 24 Dec. 1918, no. 424/13, Michel to Gillain, 11 Dec. 1918, no. 166, BMAE B–348; Michel to Gillain, 23 Jan. 1919, no. 2542, BMAE B–331; compte-rendu, French army meeting, Luxemburg, 22 May 1919, AJ⁹/3776. The French officers took Michel's accurate assessment as proof of his incompetence.

51. Foch to Michel, 29 May 1919, tel. 2737, Maglinse to Hymans, 1 June 1919, Maglinse to Masson, 29 May 1919, no. 149, Michel to Gillain, 29 May 1919, BMAE B–348; Michel to Foch, 29 May 1919, tel. 556, Vin 5N/64; Michel to Tirard, 29 May 1919, tel. 43, Vin 6N/118; Fayolle to Foch, 2 June 1919, tel. 4097, AJ⁹/3776. Michel's terse telegrams, both to Foch and to Brussels, are susceptible to more than one interpretation, but his detailed report, written late on 29 May, makes his position clear. However, he may have received an earlier notice from Mangin that a separatist outbreak was imminent. If so, he did not report it. Clemenceau to Mangin, 31 May 1919, Vin 6N/73; K. Nelson, *Victors Divided*, p. 111.

Meanwhile, in Brussels the War Ministry was seeking instructions from the Foreign Ministry. Because virtually all senior Foreign Ministry officials were in Paris, Baron Roger de Borchgrave, Hymans's acting *chef de cabinet* in Brussels for the duration of the peace conference, had to refer the matter there. As the Belgians in Brussels and Paris had no indication that the Rhenish movement was not spontaneous, de Borchgrave, along with de Gaiffier and Jacques Davignon in Paris, thought that it could only benefit Belgian security, although they worried that France might dominate the infant republic. Hymans, however, was more cautious. He replied only that he would consult the powers and that in the interim Michel's attitude of reserve should be maintained.[52] When Foch's orders to all four Allied commanders decreeing benevolent neutrality arrived at Brussels and at the Belgian delegation, Hymans's staff and apparently Hymans as well took this to be an expression of Allied policy, with which they wished to be in accord. Given the complexities of communication both at the peace conference and between the Belgian delegation and Michel, the Rhenish Republic collapsed from lack of support before Hymans managed to see any of the great-power representatives and while the orders to Michel against endorsement of the separatists still stood. As a consequence, the Rhenish Republic was not proclaimed at Aachen (or anywhere else in the Rhineland except in the French zone).[53]

In this matter, the Belgian government was extremely fortunate that it did not stumble through sheer ignorance into a policy contrary to that of the Allies in its effort to march with them, for in fact the Rhenish Republic was not endorsed by any of the great powers, including France. As the powers probably would not have believed that Belgian actions came out of confusion caused by exclusion from Foch's headquarters and peace conference debates on the Rhineland, the error might have

52. De Borchgrave to Hymans, 30 May 1919, Davignon to Hymans, 2 June 1919, Hymans to de Borchgrave, 30 May 1919, BMAE B–10.440; de Gaiffier to Hymans, 2 June 1919, no. 4640/1866, BMAE FR/1919. During the absence of Hymans and all senior officials in Paris, Moncheur, a former secretary-general, was brought over from London to run the ministry. He does not appear to have expressed any views on the subject of the Rhenish Republic.

53. Davignon to de Borchgrave, 2 June 1919, de Borchgrave to Masson, 4 June 1919, no. 4642, BMAE B–10.440; Fayolle to Foch, 2 June 1919, tel. 4135, AJ⁹/3776; van Wernelle memo, 10 June 1919, BMAE B–348.

proved costly. Further, within two weeks, Michel acquired German documents indicating that French officers in the Rhineland had assured the leaders of the Rhenish Republic that they would induce Belgium to renounce Eupen and Malmédy. These documents also revealed to the Belgians, apparently for the first time, that General Charles Mangin of the French army of occupation had largely organized the movement. Michel assumed that Mangin had done so on instructions. In reality, Foch had blessed the Rhenish Republic, and possibly Poincaré as well, but Clemenceau, who was minister of war as well as premier, had not been consulted. When he discovered on 31 May what was afoot, he erupted in fury. He had been assuring Wilson and Lloyd George throughout the Rhineland negotiations that France had no annexationist aims, and his credibility was considerably damaged by the ill-timed Rhenish outbreak. Mangin was soon relieved in disgrace.[54]

The episode of the Rhenish Republic complicated the Paris negotiations on the future status of the Rhineland, which continued unabated. Though the special committee to devise a Rhineland convention reached agreement on 6 June upon a scheme that put a civilian commission over the military authority, it was not initially accepted. Foch protested without cease but to little effect, insisting upon a continuing state of siege in occupied territory, a permanent military frontier on the Rhine, and military dominance over Allied civilian authorities on the left Bank. More importantly, Lloyd George, who had always opposed any peacetime occupation, was impelled to reconsider his consent by German objections, opposition from his own cabinet, and possibly the episode of the Rhenish Republic. On 2 June, Lloyd George presented to Wilson and Clemenceau the unanimous opposition of the British Empire delegation and the British cabinet to any large-scale or long-term occupation. The British wanted a minimal occupation lasting no more than two years. Otherwise they would neither sign the treaty nor participate in the occupation. As Wilson, Lloyd George, and Clemenceau argued this question for two weeks in the presence of Italian and Japanese

54. Michel note, 16 June 1919, BMAE B–10.440; Clemenceau to Mangin, 31 May 1919, Vin 6N/73; Nothomb to Hymans, 29 July 1919, BMAE B–348; K. Nelson, *Victors Divided,* p. 113; Jacques Chastenet, *Clemenceau,* p. 223; Erlanger, *Clemenceau,* pp. 590–91; de Gaiffier to Hymans, 13 Oct. 1919, no. 9286/3895, BMAE FR/1919.

representatives and occasional British and French experts, they gave no thought to seeking Belgian views, although the issue obviously concerned Belgium far more directly than either Italy or Japan. The Belgian delegation had always agreed with the British that extended and extensive occupation was undesirable, but no member of the British delegation sought Belgian support or even informed Hymans of the struggle in progress. After all, great powers should settle great matters and the annoying Hymans was to be avoided. Finally, on 13 June the great powers began to reach some agreement, and so Wilson, Clemenceau, Lloyd George, and the Italian foreign minister, Baron Sidney Sonnino, in the presence of Baron Makino of Japan, initialed a convention on the Rhineland establishing an Inter-Allied Rhineland High Commission to be composed of British, French, American, and Belgian civilian representatives and setting forth the terms of the occupation. Further, on 16 June, Wilson, Lloyd George, and Clemenceau, with Sonnino and Makino in attendance, signed a declaration on the Rhineland that raised the possibility of its evacuation before the fifteen years had lapsed in the event of complete German fulfillment of the treaty or satisfactory guarantees of fulfillment. It also promised to reduce the occupation costs to be levied upon Germany once German disarmament to treaty levels was complete. Thus were Lloyd George's objections met.[55]

When this latter declaration was signed, Lloyd George remarked that "some similar arrangement would have to be made with Belgium," and Col. Sir Maurice Hankey, who served as secretary to the Four, was instructed to prepare a copy for Belgian signature. In this manner, the Allies proposed to honor their promises to Albert that nothing would be definitively settled without Belgian participation. In short, Belgium would be permitted to adhere to basic documents after they had been signed by the great powers. On this occasion, however, Hankey's machinelike efficiency evidently failed, for the Belgian delegation only learned of the Rhineland Declaration when it appeared in *Le Temps* on 4 August. De Gaiffier was thunderstruck, as he had seen Louis Loucheur,

55. De Gaiffier to Hymans, 7, 12 June 1919, nos. 5012/1943, 5151/2013, **BMAE** FR/1919; FRUS PPC, 3:384–88, 6:141–45, 327–29, 342–43, 386–88, 377–81, 395–96, 473, 522.

who served as the French Rhineland expert, repeatedly during June and July without hearing a word about the Rhineland Declaration. In this fashion, France chose to punish the Belgian failure to accept French policy dictation on the Rhineland question. Hymans ordered a protest more severe than usual, but as the declaration had already been published without Belgian signature, the damage to Belgian pride had been done. On 8 August, Dutasta belatedly sent the declaration, along with the final text of the Rhineland Convention of 13 June, officially to the Belgian delegation, but his curt one-sentence note did not invite Belgium to adhere to either document. The Belgian protest had in fact accomplished nothing. On 1 August, the Supreme Council had approved Foch's plans for the continuing occupation under a French commander, but not until 11 September did Pichon think to instruct his ambassador in Brussels to inform the Belgian government, adding that he assumed that Belgium would wish to adhere and to take the necessary measures. Belgium had no choice but to do so, while asking for more information at the same time, as she did not wish to leave districts along the Belgian border in French control.[56]

A VOICE IN TREATY EXECUTION

The Belgian struggle to participate in the Rhineland settlement and in planning the occupation in which Belgium was to play a prominent part was largely typical of the Belgian experience both during the debates of the peace conference and in regard to the agencies established to supervise the peace. Though the Belgian delegation achieved a high degree of representation on committees of the conference, there were curious lacunae. Belgium was not a full member of the Armistice Commission, which was located for months at Spa on Belgian soil, although she had intermittent representation on some of its subsidiary agencies. At the peace conference, there were no Belgian members on committees deal-

56. FRUS PPC, 6:473; *Le Temps*, 4 Aug. 1919; de Gaiffier to Hymans, 1 Sept. 1919, no. 7729/3244, Hymans to Rolin-Jaequemyns, 20 Aug. 1919, no. 295, BMAE DB/13/II; Dutasta to Rolin-Jaequemyns, 8 Aug. 1919, BMAE B–366/I; Pichon to Margerie, 11 Sept. 1919, tel. 1578–79, Jaunez to Pichon, 17 Sept. 1919, no. 629, Pichon to Margerie, 27 Oct. 1919, no. 761, FMAE A/171.

ing with prisoners of war or German colonies, although Belgian troops remained in possession of much of German East Africa. She was neither represented on nor consulted by the two committees concerned with the Allied response to the German observations on the peace treaty, and Hymans was only allowed to read part of the reply just before it was given to Germany. Similarly, Belgium was not a member of the committees charged with organizing the League of Nations and the International Labor Organization, despite the prominence of Hymans and Vandervelde in the peace conference commissions that created the two agencies. Only by protest did she gain a seat on the commission charged with organizing war crimes trials, although clearly her interest in this issue was immediate.[57]

As the Belgian delegation soon recognized that major decisions were not taken in the committees, they were more concerned about gaining participation in discussion of key issues and in the organizations created to administer the peace treaty after it entered into force. During the conference, Hymans followed up his initial claim before the Council of Ten for participation with a written request to join in sessions on peace terms of interest to Belgium. This elicited a formal written assurance from Dutasta that the Supreme Coucil had decided that Belgium could join in deliberations on the western frontier of Germany and that Hymans could expect an invitation. However, when he was summoned on no notice on 31 March for debate on this topic, discussion turned to other matters. As he had an acrid exchange with Lloyd George, he was not invited again despite his repeated requests.[58]

By this time, all members of the Belgian delegation were seizing every opportunity to complain that the peace treaty was being written without them. Although they received periodic promises of consultation, none in fact materialized. The Declaration of Sainte-Adresse had specifically promised that Belgium would participate in the peace negotiations but, on key issues, this participation proved to be nominal at best. The British feared that Belgian attendance at meetings of the Four would set a dangerous precedent affecting other small states and, despite

57. Committee lists, FRUS PPC, 3:91–153, 9:114–15, 99; Hymans note, 15 June 1919, BMAE B–366/I.
58. Dutasta to Hymans, n.d., BMAE DB/13/II; Mantoux, *Les Délibérations*, 1:95–97.

House's efforts, would not recognize any distinction between Belgium and other small powers that had not participated fully in the war; the French mistrusted Belgian independence on several issues; and the powers in general felt, as Hymans noted, "that it would be impertinent for the small states to claim to participate in the debates of the mighty."[59] Though Hymans noted this fact, he did not accept it and continued to protest to no avail, again not facing the realities of power. Given all the circumstances of the peace conference, it is not surprising that Belgian participation was minimal, but the Belgian government, in its innocence of great-power politics, had taken the Declaration of Sainte-Adresse as a promise. One of the many reasons for Belgian dissatisfaction with the Versailles treaty was that Belgium was so little consulted about it.

By the middle of April, Hymans had at last accepted the inevitable and was merely asking to be informed of what had been settled. His letters indicate that his chief source of information was the press and that he was considerably annoyed that he had no information on a number of key questions, such as the Rhineland, reparations, revision of the 1839 treaties, and penalties to be imposed upon the kaiser for violations of Belgian neutrality. After the small powers were told on 16 April that they would receive the treaty terms only on the eve of their presentation to the German delegation, Hymans sought and gained permission from Clemenceau to ask Dutasta for the treaty clauses concerning Belgium. The request was promptly dispatched but brought no reply. He was in fact allowed to read the treaty at the end of April but not given a copy. As late as 1 May, six days before presentation of the Versailles treaty to Germany, the Belgian delegation found itself in the humiliating position of having to ask the Four for the text of treaty clauses that would require submission to the king of the Belgians. In a similar vein, the Belgian delegation managed to see the Austrian treaty before some of the other small powers did, but only at the same time as the Austrians.[60]

59. Hymans, *Mémoires*, 1:337, 524–26; de Gaiffier to Hymans, 29 Mar. 1919, no. 2495/985, BMAE FR/1919; Hymans to Clemenceau, 3 Apr. 1919, BMAE DB/7/I; FRUS PPC, 4:194–95; House Diary, 1 May 1919, 16:182–83, House Papers. Quotation from Hymans, *Mémoires*, 1:337.

60. Hymans note, 19 Apr. 1919, BMAE B–1–1519; Hymans to Dutasta, 19 Apr. 1919, no. 472, BMAE DB/1; FRUS PPC, 5:406; Hymans note, 8 May 1919, Rolin-

Aside from the Rhineland, the issue on which the Belgians most determinedly sought participation was that of reparations. Here their interest was immediate, their need was acute, and their fear of gaining little in the face of Anglo-French appetites was very real. They had finally recognized that, given British, French, and Italian claims, the Belgian right to full reparation was not as automatic as it had seemed. As soon as they realized that representation on the peace conference Commission on Reparation was of no avail because the key decisions would be taken by the Four, they mounted a major campaign to join the debates.[61] As with the Rhineland, they were unsuccessful. However, their efforts aroused the interest of House, who intervened to block Lloyd George's schemes to gain more reparations for Britain at the expense of Belgium, the only small power with a substantial claim against Germany, which was the only Central Power likely to be able to pay any appreciable amount of reparations.

The extended crisis over Belgian reparations claims also had the side effect of assuring Belgium a place on the permanent Reparation Commission established by the Versailles treaty to oversee its reparation clauses. Britain, France, Italy, and the United States were to have seats on this vital commission. After the Belgian delegation threatened to leave the peace conference out of dissatisfaction with the reparations clauses of the treaty, the fifth seat went to Belgium except on naval questions, when Japan replaced her, and east European questions, when Serbia or variously what became known as the Little Entente held the fifth vote.[62]

The Belgian vote on most German questions in the Reparation Commission soon assumed unanticipated significance. The Allies had intended that the American member be chairman of the commission, as American reparation claims were miniscule and she was the least-interested party. Further, to avoid deadlock, there would always be five

---

Jaequemyns to Hymans, 21 July 1919, BMAE B–366/I. Although the Belgian delegation was not fully aware of this fact, part of the trouble was that some portions of the German treaty, including a section of Article 232 concerning the Belgian war debt, were not completed until 3 May, after which the treaty was rushed to the printers.

61. Hymans to Clemenceau, 3 Apr. 1919, BMAE DB/7/I; Hymans, *Mémoires*, 1:425–26.

62. FRUS PPC, 13:461; Lamont to Wilson, 29 Apr. 1919, Wilson Papers 5B/32.

states voting and an abstention would count as a negative vote. When the United States withdrew and the number was thus reduced to four, France claimed not only the presiding chair but also the casting vote accorded to the chairmen of other commissions. Although this second vote was never used on a German question, its existence in reserve strengthened France's position and meant that, with the vote of only one other member, she could control the commission. As France and Britain were generally at odds, and Italy usually swung toward the stronger side, the Belgian vote could often determine the stronger side and settle the issue.[63] This fact was well appreciated by France and by Germany but ignored by Britain, who mounted a sustained drive to destroy Belgium's hard-won reparations rights, thereby assuring that Belgium would indeed vote with France. Thus, many of the key votes on German questions were three to one. Quite aside from the significance that the Belgian vote acquired with the passage of time, the inclusion of Belgium on the Reparation Commission from the outset was an important but perhaps fateful victory for her. Although it undoubtedly contributed to assuring Belgian participation in crucial postwar conferences and thus prevented what otherwise would surely have been a rapid and successful Anglo-French assault on Belgian priority of payment, Belgium's role in great-power reparations diplomacy led her eventually into the Ruhr, which exacerbated further her strained relationship with Britain, upon whom she wished to depend.

The Belgian seat in the Inter-Allied Rhineland High Commission, which fell to her as a consequence of her continuing share in the semi-permanent military occupation, was also of importance. The United States withdrew from active participation in the work of the high commission long before she withdrew her troops from the Rhineland. Because the number of voting commissioners was thus reduced to three and because Britain and France were usually in disagreement, the Belgian vote could often be decisive, a fact better appreciated by the French than by the British. As a consequence, in 1923, France and Belgium had no difficulty in passing Rhineland ordinances related to

63. Polk to Lansing, 27 Oct. 1919, tel. 4855, Wilson Papers 4/5021; Lord Salter, *Memoirs of a Public Servant*, p. 157; G. M. Gathorne-Hardy, *A Short History of International Affairs, 1920 to 1938*, p. 41; Robert Blake, *The Unknown Prime Minister*, p. 409; Harold Nicolson, *Curzon*, pp. 218–19.

the Ruhr occupation. During the eight months of German passive resistance in 1923, Belgium voted consistently with France; otherwise she generally occupied the middle ground, seeking compromise solutions. But in the Rhineland High Commission, as in the Reparation Commission, Belgian efforts to mediate between her great allies were usually regarded by the British as proof of subservience to France.

It was partly because the British persisted in assuming in 1919 and thereafter, despite considerable evidence to the contrary, that Belgium was a French satellite in all respects that Belgium had such difficulty in gaining participation in other peace-keeping agencies. Though she did obtain membership on a variety of specialized commissions, representation in the two generalized agencies to oversee the administration of the peace, the Conference of Ambassadors and the Supreme Council itself, required protracted effort. The Conference of Ambassadors, sitting at Paris, was designed to take charge of all the miscellaneous unfinished business arising from the peace treaties. As a number of these issues concerned Belgium, she mounted a long campaign to become a member. This effort began in October 1919 before the Conference of Ambassadors came into being and before the Belgians had any clear information about the purpose of the organization, and lasted until the spring of 1920. As at the peace conference, the first applications met with no response, but Hymans persisted. There was in fact no serious objection to the inclusion of Belgium in the Conference of Ambassadors for discussion of matters affecting her but, at British insistence, this decision was interpreted to mean that Belgium would participate only when the other members saw fit.[64] In practice, de Gaiffier was usually permitted to attend discussion of German questions whenever anybody remembered to invite him. The same pattern of limited participation developed over Belgian membership in the Inter-Allied Military Committee at Versailles.[65]

64. Rolin-Jaequemyns to Dutasta, 31 Oct. 1919, no. 1370, Rolin-Jaequemyns to Clemenceau, 13 Nov. 1919, BMAE FR/1919; Rolin-Jaequemyns to Clemenceau, 23 Nov. 1919, no. 1426, 180.033/5, ACNP/31; DBFP, 9:217n; Hymans to de Gaiffier, 26 Jan. 1920, no. 589, de Gaiffier to Hymans, 9 Feb. 1920, no. 1412/688, BMAE FR/1920/I; de Gaiffier to Millerand, 27 Jan. 1920, FMAE A/57; C.A. 3, 2 Feb. 1920, CAB 29/42; C.A. 16, 4 May 1920, CAB 29/43.

65. De Gaiffier to Hymans, 18 Nov. 1919, no. 10604/4432, de Gaiffier to Foch, 17 Jan. 1920, Hymans Papers/177.

The Conference of Ambassadors and the Military Committee had no more power, however, than the specialized commissions of the peace conference, and the crucial decisions were taken by the Supreme Council, intermittent meetings of the great powers that in practice extended the Big Four of the peace conference despite rapidly diminishing American participation. The Belgian effort to join these sessions was protracted. When de Gaiffier deduced from French press reports of an Anglo-French meeting at London in December 1919 that the Supreme Council would continue on an occasional, traveling basis, the Belgian government sought participation in the next session.[66] It did not succeed, as the great powers met alone in Paris in January 1920 in conjunction with ratification of the Versailles treaty, but it gained intermittent representation at the long February–March 1920 London conference for sessions devoted to German and economic questions, although not those on other issues. Thereafter the agenda became very diversified, devoting much time to Near Eastern and Polish questions, and the Belgians often had to mount an extended campaign to gain admission to any part of the proceedings.[67] Usually the British objected and the French supported the Belgians. Whatever the agenda, the Belgian government tried to gain admission on the well-founded assumption that the question of German reparations was bound to arise. When it invariably did, the Belgian delegation proved indispensable in papering over the yawning gap between French and British views. Though Belgian compromise solutions tended to give France the form and Britain the substance, the British continued to raise difficulties about Belgian attendance and it was years before Belgium's right to be present was securely established. In the end, however, the seat on the Reparation Commission and the eventual role in the Supreme Council were the chief Belgian gains from Hymans's protests about lack of consultation. Given the weakness of Belgium's power base, these were considerable achievements and certainly more than any other small power obtained.

The continuing British objections were based partly on the persistent

66. De Gaiffier to Hymans, 15, 16 Dec. 1919, nos. 11690/5052, 11736/5081, BMAE FR/1919. See also *procès-verbaux*, Anglo-French meetings, 13 Dec. 1919, FMAE Y/16.
67. For instance, de Gaiffier to Millerand, 13 Apr. 1920, no. 4172, FMAE Y/17; Hankey Diary, 28 Dec. 1920, Hankey Papers 1/5.

false assumption that Belgium was a French satellite and partly on the fact that Belgium had no pretensions to great-power status. From the Armistice through the peace conference to the years of trying to enforce the Versailles treaty, the difficulty that Belgium encountered in making her voice heard arose from the fact that she was a small power and indeed the only established small power with a direct interest in much of the German settlement. In brief, among the lesser states, Belgium was a special case but was not recognized as such by the great powers at the peace conference or for some time thereafter. At Paris, the other small powers recognized Belgium's special status by electing her without fail to peace conference commissions, but the great powers could not admit that any small state should join in their deliberations. Thus, at the peace conference, the Declaration of Sainte-Adresse was fulfilled only in the technical sense that Belgium signed the Versailles treaty. However, as time passed, so many difficulties arose over reparations and the Rhineland, where the Belgian military contingent was second only to the French, that, by dint of determined effort, Belgium finally gained fairly consistent access to the inner council of the great powers. This belated success provided her with a voice in the implementation of the peace settlement, a settlement in which she had had little say even on the key questions, both territorial and financial, affecting her future. It also pitched Belgium into a fairly major role, despite her small size and lack of experience, as she participated with Britain and France in the unhappy effort to enforce an unstable peace.

The ultimate inclusion of Belgium in the Supreme Council was deeply satisfying to her national amour-propre but, when the peace conference ended, that achievement lay in the future. In 1919, when the Versailles treaty terms became public, Belgian opinion took the view that the delegation had succeeded in minor matters but had failed in what was most important. Extensive representation on the conference commissions and the prominence of Vandervelde in drafting the Labor Charter satisfied national pride but did not yield concrete benefits to Belgium. Hymans's failure to gain Brussels as the seat of the League of Nations was considered important by Belgian opinion, whereas his success in securing small-power representation on the League Council was generally dismissed as trivial, although dispassionate observers thought otherwise. Belgian opinion was dissatisfied with the delegation's achievements, notably on reparations, and dismayed that several issues of vital interest to Belgium remained unresolved. When the treaty terms were revealed, Belgians on the whole were intensely relieved that they had gained a seat on the Reparation Commission, a share in the Rhineland occupation, and token representation on the military control commissions to be sent into Germany. At the same time, their chagrin at not having been consulted in these matters, particularly the Rhineland settlement, was profound. They did not realize that Belgium had gained a significant share in the enforcement of the peace and, thanks to her location and her unique wartime history, had briefly become almost a power of the second rank despite her lack of the usual qualifications for such a role.

THREE

THE ANNEXATIONIST

ATTEMPT

BELGIAN TERRITORIAL DESIRES
IN EUROPE

The chief Belgian aim at the Paris Peace Conference was revision of the 1839 treaties. This simple-sounding but complex claim involved not only the end of compulsory neutrality and revision of the Scheldt regime but also territorial cession by Germany and possibly the Netherlands. In practice, the territorial questions were addressed first, as they had to be settled before the treaty could be presented to Germany. As to the rest, Germany could be and was obliged to accept in advance any future revision of the nonterritorial aspects of the 1839 treaties.[1]

From the Belgian point of view, the most acute territorial deficiencies of the 1839 treaties arose from Dutch possession of Flemish Zeeland and lower Limburg. If Belgium could gain Flemish Zeeland, she would hold the south bank of the Scheldt and probably half of its main channel. Thus, many economic and military problems concerning use of that river would be resolved. In addition, the vital Ghent-Terneuzen canal would then be entirely in Belgian hands. Belgian interest in lower Limburg was similarly both military and economic. The overriding concern was military but Belgium also wished to build a canal across Limburg to the Rhine.[2] Though there was no sign of postwar pro-Belgian sentiment in Flemish Zeeland, which had never been part of modern Belgium, there was briefly just after the Armistice noticeable support for annexation to Belgium in lower Limburg, which until 1795 had been under the joint sovereignty of the United Provinces of the Nether-

1. Article 31, Versailles treaty, FRUS PPC, 13:135.
2. Comert memo, 22 Feb. 1919, FMAE A/133.

137

lands and the Prince-Bishops of Liège, and which also had been part of Belgium from 1830 to 1839.[3]

Belgian territorial aspirations at the expense of Holland were highly logical but quite impossible. Even van Karnebeek, the Dutch foreign minister, acknowledged privately that what Hymans wanted was exactly what Belgium needed, but he added that Belgium still did not have any just claim on Holland, as "needs are not rights and create no obligation for third parties."[4] Therein lay the difficulty, especially because both Britain and America saw no reason to force a neutral power to cede territory against her will.[5] Though Belgium anticipated territorial compensation to Holland from Germany that would have given Holland greater economic benefit, more coherent boundaries, and a solution to a long-standing problem, one could not reasonably expect the ruling Dutch Catholic party to relinquish its electoral base in Limburg. As Hymans, who was himself partly guided by domestic political considerations, was quite unable to envisage anybody else's political necessities, he kept attempting the impossible.

Hymans had an intensely logical mind and, with reason, he considered the existing boundaries irrational. Flemish Zeeland was entirely cut off from the rest of the Netherlands by the Scheldt. It was a sparsely populated,[6] predominantly agricultural area that had been badly neglected by the Dutch government. Rail, tram and road communications to Belgium, all built at Belgian initiative and with Belgian capital, were excellent, but there was no form of land transportation at all between Flemish Zeeland and the rest of Holland and until 1916 no route of any variety between eastern and western parts of the region except through

3. De Villegas to Hymans, 1, 11, 17 Dec. 1918, tel. 43, no. 243/212, tel. 56, BMAE PB/1918; de Villegas to Hymans, 7 Mar. 1919, no. 54/51, BMAE DB/31; FMAE memo, n.d. [June 1919?], FMAE A/133; Laroche to Neilson, 5 Aug. 1919, FMAE A/134; BMAE note, n.d. Hymans Papers/164.

4. DuD, R.G.P. 156, p. 125.

5. DuB, R.G.P. 117, pp. 960–62, 923–24, 986–89; Balfour memo, 24 Feb. 1919, F.O. 608/4.

6. The Belgian estimate was 58,000, that of the Dutch press 80,000. The official Dutch figure was 73,000, although the Dutch minister-president used the figure of 60,000, adding that half the population was Roman Catholic. BMAE note, 20 Dec. 1918, BMAE B–383; Moncheur to Hymans, 14 Feb. 1919, no. 1182/309, BMAE GB/1919/I; Townley to Balfour, 20 Feb. 1919, no. 44, F.O. 608/4.

Belgian territory. This last situation arose partly from neglect and partly from the fact that an arm of the Scheldt dipped southward, virtually cutting Flemish Zeeland in two. By water, there were small ferries to Flushing and Hansweert on Walcheren and South Beveland islands, adequate for travelers and mail but not for commercial traffic and affording no direct access to any important Dutch population center; to Belgium, there was the large modern Ghent-Terneuzen canal. Not surprisingly, all of Flemish Zeeland's economic ties were to Belgium, its markets were there, and its only real town, Terneuzen, owed its prosperity to the canal. In addition, Belgians owned a large percentage of the property in the area, both in land and in dwellings.[7]

Obviously it was in the interests of the inhabitants of Flemish Zeeland to turn to Belgium. But human beings are not entirely economic creatures. There were many complaints of Dutch neglect before and during the war and some sentiment for joining Belgium. However, World War I abruptly severed the Belgian tie for more than four years, creating considerable hardship for the inhabitants. The Dutch government did not respond to Flemish Zeeland's wartime economic misery and isolation but it did react to the 1916 Belgian press campaign toward annexation. Queen Wilhelmina toured the area in that year and again in March 1919. In 1916 the Dutch government launched a massive and expensive program to fulfill old promises of public works and improved communications. The money flowed freely until the Belgian threat was over. Thus by 1919, sentiment for attachment to Belgium had dissipated, even though it continued to be economically sensible. As Belgian leaders recognized, the determining factor was religious. Flemish Zeeland was half Catholic and half Protestant. The Protestants thought that Belgium contained too many Catholics, whereas the Catholics thought it contained too many Freemasons. The Belgian government well knew that Flemish Zeeland preferred to languish as it was and that Belgium could not win any referendum there.[8]

Belgian commercial and shipping interests coveted Flemish Zeeland

7. Goffart to Beyens, 13 Oct. 1916, no. 8974, BMAE PB/1916; de Gaiffier to Hymans, 25 Feb. 1919, no. 1471/564, BMAE FR/1919; Fallon to Hymans, 7 Sept. 1918, no. 13099/2430, BMAE PB/1918/II; maps, Orts Papers/429.

8. Fallon to Hymans, 7 Sept. 1918, no. 13099/2430, BMAE PB/1918/II; Goffart to Beyens, 13 Oct. 1916, no. 8974/218, BMAE PB/1916; BMAE historical note, 4 Sept.

for obvious reasons. Of Belgium's eight commercial ports of any significance at all, three, including the two largest ports of Antwerp and Ghent, had access to the sea only through Dutch territory and/or Dutch waters. Transfer of Flemish Zeeland would put an end to that problem. Accordingly, the port cities, including Brussels, strongly urged acquisition of the territory, as did more southerly Walloon cities dependent upon Antwerp and Ghent for export outlets. In addition, the Belgian army pressed the government to obtain the territory, both for naval use of the Scheldt to afford wartime relief of the national redoubt at Antwerp and to provide a suitable location for a military base as far from Germany as possible.[9]

The Belgian army also provided the strongest pressure toward annexation of part of Dutch Limburg. Although Antwerp, Liège, and Namur all had strong economic interest in acquisition of this area in terms of rivers and canals (built and as yet unbuilt), the overriding concern in the aftermath of the war was national security against another German attack. Though Belgium probably would have been willing to accept all of Dutch Limburg and perhaps the western portion of North Brabant, which it had held until 1839, had these territories been offered, it made no attempt to obtain them. In practice, Belgian interest centered exclusively on lower Limburg from Roermond southward, and when Belgian officials spoke of "Limburg," they in fact meant only this narrow strip of land dipping down between Belgium and Germany, which made defense of Belgium extremely difficult by denying the Belgian army the natural line of the Meuse River and creating a dangerous gap in the Belgian defenses. Because the Dutch army was small and lightly armed, and also widely considered at the time to be politically unreliable, there was genuine doubt whether the Netherlands had the capacity to put up

---

1919, Orts Papers/429; Townley to Balfour, 20 Feb. 1919, no. 44, F.O. 608/4; Gillain to Hymans, 30 Dec. 1918, no. 62/66, BMAE B–383; de Ligne to Vandervelde, 7 July 1926, no. 1341/608, BMAE PB/1922–26; DuB, R.G.P. 146, pp. 1155–56, 933–34; de Gaiffier to Hymans, 25 Feb. 1919, no. 1471/564, BMAE FR/1919.

9. Admiralty, *Belgium*, p. 392; Gillain to Hymans, 1 Dec. 1919, Masson to Hymans, 4 Jan. 1919, BMAE B–280. The third port dependent on Dutch territory was Zelzate (Selzaete) on the Ghent-Terneuzen canal just below the Dutch-Belgian border. The other five ports were Ostend, Zeebrugge, Brugge, Brussels, and Nieuwpoort, only three of them on Belgium's forty-two miles of coastline. Of these, Ostend was the largest (and Belgium's third port) but not capable of handling large quantities of heavy cargo.

any serious resistance and, on the part of the Belgian army, real doubt whether it had the will to do so. As Belgian generals, with an eye to the war just past, wished a better defensive line in general and more effective protection for Liège in particular, it is not surprising that they sought lower Limburg.[10]

Further, this area had long-standing and close historical, cultural, religious, economic, and familial ties with Belgium. Unlike Flemish Zeeland, lower Limburg was not entirely cut off from the rest of Holland. Rail travel from Maastricht to Rotterdam without traversing Belgian territory was possible, if rather complicated. But lower Limburg was largely isolated from the rest of the country and its residents tended to speak of "the Dutch" as if they were foreigners. Like the inhabitants of Flemish Zeeland, they depended on Belgium for much of their prosperity and had suffered a certain amount of governmental neglect in the past. As its shipping routes by water led much more directly to Belgian cities than to Dutch ones, the area stagnated after 1839 until the Dutch government became interested in the coal basins and appropriated them as state property, a move considered by some of the local inhabitants to be foreign exploitation. All in all, Maastricht and its environs retained close ties to Belgium. The economic link was only reinforced by the fact that so many families were separated by the frontier between Dutch and Belgian Limburg. During the war, Maastricht, where many Belgians took refuge, remained the most intensely pro-Belgian of Dutch cities.[11]

At the end of the war, the Dutch government moved energetically against sentiment in lower Limburg for reunion with Belgium. Within a

10. Gillain to Masson, 19 Jan. 1919, no. 6723, BMAE B–331; Gallet notes, n.d. 1919, B–280. The Dutch estimated the population of the entire Dutch province of Limburg at 400,000, of which 85 percent was Roman Catholic; the Belgian estimate was 300,000, of which about 200,000 lived in lower Limburg. DuB, R.G.P. 145, pp. 634–35; BMAE note, 20 Dec. 1918, BMAE B–383.

11. Belgian army maps, BMAE B–383, Orts Papers/429; Townley to Balfour, 17 Nov. 1918, no. 258, F.O. 371/3256; FMAE memo, n.d., FMAE A/133; *Daily Telegraph* articles, 11 Feb., 6 Mar. 1919, BMAE GB/1919/I; de Villegas to Hymans, 29 Nov. 1918, no. 233/209, BMAE PB/1918/II. It should be noted that in this small and complex area, one can easily drive in and out of four countries (Germany, Holland, Belgium, and Luxemburg) within two hours. Many border families, of which the aristocratic d'Ansembourgs are one, have branches in all four countries.

month, its campaign began to take effect and, though some pro-Belgian sentiment remained, it was no longer expressed openly. Patriotic demonstrations were organized and the queen toured the area at the start of March 1919. Nothomb's CPN, which was active in lower Limburg, was no match for the Dutch authorities, and its crude posters only simplified the Dutch task. By the time that the peace conference addressed itself to the territorial question in late February 1919, Belgian officials acknowledged that the Dutch campaign had been effective and doubted that Belgium could win a popular referendum in lower Limburg.[12]

Nonetheless, Hymans still hoped that Holland could be persuaded to surrender Flemish Zeeland and lower Limburg in exchange for territorial compensation from Germany, notably East Friesland, Gelderland, and Cleves, plus perhaps the town of Wesel and the old County of Bentheim. These predominantly agricultural districts were similar in area and greater in population than those coveted by Belgium. Belgian investigations during the peace conference indicated that these territories were all pronouncedly Dutch in character, particularly Cleves, the most economically valuable region, where Dutch financial interests were extensive. In most of this border area, the local dialect was similar to Dutch and there were many family ties. Further, the Gelderland coal basin would provide the Netherlands with more coal than she would lose in Limburg and the region in general was more thriving than the towns of lower Limburg. In addition, possession of East Friesland would not only give Holland the port of Emden but also solve the long-standing problem of the Ems estuary, whose channel lay entirely within German waters, to the considerable detriment of Dutch ports, notably Delfzijl. As Belgian diplomatists hopefully noted, statements in the Dutch Parliament and press indicated Dutch interest in frontier rectifications on the Ems, although not at the price of transferring any territory to Belgium. But the Dutch cabinet, though desirous of negotiating a better arrangement for the Ems estuary directly with Germany, resolutely

12. De Villegas to Hymans, 1, 11, 17 Dec. 1918, tel. 43, no. 243/212, tel. 56, Fallon to Hymans, 9, 13, 30 Dec. 1918, nos. 18095/3332, 18320/3388, 19170/3589, BMAE PB/1918/II; Gillain to Hymans, 20 Dec. 1918, no. 6176, BMAE B–383; Fallon to Hymans, 4 Mar. 1919, no. 2238/449, BMAE PB/1919; Garrett to Lansing, 10 Mar. 1919, no. 2603, SD 763.72/12998; de Gaiffier to Hymans, 25 Feb. 1919, no. 1471/564, BMAE FR/1919; D. H. Miller, *Diary*, 5:10–11.

opposed accepting any territory and creating a German motive for revenge. As to the inhabitants of the districts concerned, Belgian investigators noted that they tended to be hostile to Berlin and probably would be willing to join Holland if they were given food and relieved of German financial obligations but, regrettably, their first preference was for a Rhenish republic.[13]

Despite the obvious obstacles to more coherent boundaries, the Belgian delegation remained optimistic, hoping that Dutch unneutral conduct during and after the war might incline the Allies to insist upon territorial transfer. In addition to wartime German use of Dutch railways and intermittent shipment of excessive amounts of sand and gravel across Holland, there was the large-scale German troop transit across Limburg, which the Belgian government took much more seriously than any other, and another crossing of German troops, together with Belgian stallions stolen near Brugge, by rail via Tilbury at the end of the war.[14] After the Armistice and until mid-March 1919, there were repeated difficulties with the Dutch government over shipments of Allied supplies and troops to the Rhineland through Holland, release of Belgian and British troops interned in Holland, and transit for Allied troops and former prisoners of war returning from Germany. Given the extremely battered condition of the Belgian and northern French rail systems, the Dutch attitude was a serious barrier to efficient transport and occasioned numerous protests. Finally, Dutch willingness to grant political asylum to Kaiser Wilhelm and the German crown prince had undoubtedly angered the Allies.[15]

13. Dorff report n.d., de Bunswyk report, 1 Mar. 1919, Fallon to Hymans, 25 Feb. 1919, no. 2003/392, BMAE DB/30/IX; de Bunswyk notes, Mar. 1919, BMAE B–348; *Daily Telegraph*, 6 Mar. 1919, BMAE GB/1919/I; Townley to Balfour, 20 Feb. 1919, no. 44, Villiers to Curzon, 8 Mar. 1919, no. 86, F.O. 608/4; DuB, R.G.P. 117, pp. 1036–37; DuB, R.G.P. 145, pp. 645–48; Belgian army questionnaire, 28 Feb. 1919, no. 5152, BMAE B–10.442.

14. Fallon to Hymans, 5 Jan. 1919, no. 198/27, 15, 18 Feb. 1919, nos. 1684/319, 1768/335, BMAE PB/1919; de Gaiffier to Pichon, 17 July 1919, FMAE A/133.

15. R. Graham to Curzon, 19 Aug. 1920, no. 655 (Annual Report, 1919), F.O. 371/3848; Fallon to Hymans, 16 Nov. 1918, tel. 778, van Karnebeek to Fallon, 12 Nov. 1918, no. 71481, BMAE PB/1918/II; Hymans to de Gaiffier, 22 Mar. 1919, no. 2551, de Gaiffier to Hymans, 27 Mar. 1919, no. 2428/9623, BMAE FR/1919; DuB, R.G.P. 117, pp. 957–58; Garrett to Lansing, 16 Feb., 3 Mar. 1919, tels. 5864, 5964, SD

Nevertheless, Belgian hopes were quickly dashed by British and French hostility to the idea of Dutch territorial transfer. The British agreed that Belgium's frontiers were most unsatisfactory but thought that nothing could be done, as the Netherlands was both neutral and unwilling to make any new arrangements. Accordingly, British representatives displayed the greatest reserve on this subject. Similarly, Clemenceau opposed transfer of lower Limburg despite the military implications and was not prepared to help Belgium to the extent of offending Holland, jeopardizing Dutch loans and supplies, or permitting any appreciable number of Flemings to be added to Belgium. Though the Americans were somewhat more sympathetic, the Belgians realized that any openly annexationist campaign would irritate Wilson. Accordingly, they never formally requested Dutch territorial transfer but contented themselves with hinting at its desirability and striving to ensure that such a possibility was not definitively excluded. In the end, this tactic backfired and the Belgian government only gained the worst of both worlds.

German territory was another matter. Belgian representatives made no secret of their desire to annex Moresnet and Malmédy. The claim to Moresnet met with no resistance, as it was clearly desirable to resolve a long-standing little problem. In 1815 this tiny piece of territory, originally part of Limburg, was divided between Prussia and the United Netherlands, but drafting ambiguities made demarcation of the frontier impossible and left 1.21 square miles in neither country. As both sides wanted the zinc and lead mines there, neither gave way and a provisional agreement in 1816 providing a special status for neutral Moresnet and a joint administration by local Dutch and Prussian officials became permanent, the Dutch role reverting to Belgium after 1830. An attempt in 1886 to divide the territory between Germany and Belgium failed. By that time, the mines had been worked out but the Société de la Vieille Montagne continued as a metallurgical establishment doing preliminary work on ores from Eupen for shipment to Belgium. The war brought German occupation but no change in the economic pattern. Before World War I, the inhabitants, fewer than five thousand in number, had

763.7211/7295, 7310; W.C. 537, 26 Feb. 1919, CAB 23/9; Townley to Curzon, 2 Mar. 1919, no. 55, F.O. 371/3849.

repeatedly sought union with Belgium, and they renewed their appeals immediately after the Armistice. Although the area was not of great economic value, it had industrial ties to Belgium and was heavily forested. Because the Germans had cut Belgian timber indiscriminately during the war and many years would be required for the forests to recover, Belgian industry wanted to acquire neutral Moresnet's wood for its own immediate use.[16]

The Belgian claim to Malmédy was similarly noncontroversial. About half a dozen "Walloon cantons" had been transferred to Prussia in 1815 but, after some debate, the Belgian government decided not to claim them all, as too many German-speaking inhabitants would be involved. However, Malmédy, a district of 314 square miles with a population of 36,916, which included the old Belgian canton of St. Vith, was 80 percent Walloon and had close commercial ties with Belgium. It had been pure Walloon until shortly before World War I, when Germany's insistence on school instruction in the German language had begun to bear fruit with the young. Malmédy had also served as a main point of concentration for the German attack in 1914. During World War I and again early in 1919, the French-speaking inhabitants petitioned in number for attachment to Belgium.[17]

The canton of Eupen, also transferred to Prussia in 1815, presented a greater problem to both the Belgian government and the peace conference. This district, which now included Prussian Moresnet (1.31 square miles), was linguistically mixed, with a Mosan patois derived from Flemish and German similar to the dialect of Belgian Luxemburg,

16. Marion I. Newbigin, *Aftermath*, pp. 23–24; Whitlock to Lansing, 7 Nov. 1918, no. 636, 855.014/2, ACNP/449; FRUS PPC, 13:139–40; Margerie to Pichon, 1 July 1919, no. 305, FMAE Z/Belg./66; Timmerhans to Albert, n.d. [late Nov. 1918], tel., Hymans to Arscholt, 26 Dec. 1918, Grinard to Albert, 24 June 1919, BMAE B–10.794; Terlinden note, 7 Jan. 1919, de Broqueville note, 15 Jan. 1919, Crahay note, 3 Feb. 1919, BMAE B–10.997.

17. Newbigin, *Aftermath*, pp. 24–25; Oman note, 12 Dec. 1918, P.C. 112, F.O. 371/4355; Hymans note, 22 Feb. 1919, Hymans Papers/151; anon. note re Goffart trip to Malmédy, n.d. [early Mar. 1919], Malmédian petition to Clemenceau, 26 Mar. 1919, de Bassompierre to Hymans, 12 Feb. 1919, no. 1384, Hymans to Balfour, 10 Feb. 1919, BMAE DB/30/XIV/I; Hymans to Villiers, 9 Feb. 1919, no. 1316, BMAE GB/1919/I; Sarah Wambaugh, *Plebiscites since the World War*, 1:518–20; Jaspar notes, n.d., AGR Jaspar Papers/169.

but it was far more Germanic in character than Malmédy. Although only 68 square miles in area, it contained a population of 27,024, some of whom were employed in Aachen nine miles to the north. Though its zinc mines and wool industry were economically valuable and the forests of both Eupen proper and Prussian Moresnet were badly needed to replace the crippling losses to Belgian forests during the war, Hymans was reluctant to incorporate so many Germans in Belgium. Although some of the inhabitants petitioned for attachment to Belgium, they were obviously a minority. However, the Société de la Vieille Montagne stressed the economic necessity of incorporation, as it depended upon Eupen's zinc and its concession included seven of the nine communes of the canton. More importantly, the Belgian military authorities insisted that both Malmédy and Eupen be annexed to gain a superior defensive line against Germany. The generals prevailed and, after much hesitation, the Belgian delegation decided at the end of February 1919 to ask for Eupen as well as Malmédy and Moresnet. Thereafter, the claim to both Eupen and Malmédy was always carefully termed "dis-annexation."[18]

AT THE PEACE CONFERENCE:
THE FIRST PHASE

When the peace conference opened, however, the Belgian delegation left the question of Eupen open. On 17 January, they sent to the great powers a lengthy memorandum formally requesting revision of the 1839 treaties. This document was written with an eye to future bargaining and, in most respects, represented maximum Belgian claims. On territorial questions, it hinted at Dutch cession of both Flemish Zeeland and lower Limburg with territorial compensation from Germany. In particular, it noted the problem of the defense of lower Limburg, point-

18. FRUS PPC, 13:139–40; Wambaugh, *Plebiscites*, 1:518–20; Hymans, *Mémoires*, 1: 465; Eupen petition to Albert, 23 Jan. 1919, Timmerhans memo, 17 Feb. 1919, BMAE DB/30/XIV/I; Hymans note, 22 Feb. 1919, BMAE DB/13/I; Dutasta to Hankey, 28 Feb. 1919, F.O. 608/5; Xhaflaire to de Radzitsky, 3 May 1919, de Sincay to Hymans, 21 Feb. 1919, Orts to de Sincay, 27 Feb. 1919, no. 1834, BMAE B–331.

ing out Dutch military incapacity there, but took care not to offer a solution. The memorandum openly claimed Malmédy and Moresnet and, in a veiled reference to Eupen, expressed a desire to recover territory ceded to Prussia in 1815.[19]

Hymans pursued the same line when Belgium received her day in the limelight before the Council of Ten. As the great powers had arrogated all power of decision to themselves, the smaller states had to be granted some appearance of activity to placate their domestic opinion, and so each was given an opportunity to come before the Ten, which consisted of the prime ministers and foreign ministers of the five great powers, to recite documents already submitted in great detail. When the three Belgian plenipotentiaries made their appearance on 11 February, Hymans did exactly that, adhering to the 17 January memorandum in most respects. In addition to specific claims to neutral Moresnet and Malmédy and an ambiguous reference to the "Walloon cantons" taken by Prussia in 1815, he asked for "free disposal" of the Scheldt, "absolute sovereignty" over the western Scheldt as far as the sea in both peace and war, and sovereignty also over the Ghent-Terneuzen canal and the port (but not the town) of Terneuzen. Aside from the waterways, he made no claims to Dutch territory but, in the course of a three-hour speech, made the drawbacks of the existing frontiers abundantly clear. When Wilson inquired how he proposed to persuade the Dutch to cede territory, Hymans replied that he was presenting a problem, not a solution. When he was asked about compensation to Holland, Hymans said Belgium had nothing to offer; perhaps economic or colonial concessions would be possible, but Holland would probably prefer German territory. Rather vaguely, he mentioned Gelderland, East Friesland, and Bentheim. This vagueness was not assumed; it was only eight days later that he urgently ordered investigation of German districts suitable for cession to the Netherlands.[20] Once again, Hymans had assumed that the great powers would make the necessary arrangements.

19. Van Zuylen, *Les Mains libres*, p. 29; D. H. Miller, *Diary*, 4:436–67.

20. I.C. 138, 11 Feb. 1919, CAB 28/6; DuB, R.G.P. 117, pp. 38–39; DB to BMAE, 19 Feb. 1919, tel. 140, BMAE DB/30/IX. The Belgian press was given only an extremely brief communiqué about Hymans's presentation to the Council of Ten and relied largely on the foreign press for information. *Gazet van Antwerpen*, 14 Feb. 1919, p. 1, 15 Feb. 1919, p. 1; *De Standaard*, 13 Feb. 1919, p. 1, 14 Feb. 1919, p. 1.

To a degree, the great powers did take charge, as they certainly intended to make the decisions. The next day, at Balfour's initiative, the Ten approved a resolution to establish a commission of two representatives of each of the five great powers to deal with the Belgian territorial claims and suggestions, including the possibility of compensating Holland with German territory if Flemish Zeeland and southern Limburg were ceded to Belgium. Thus was born the Belgian Commission, later rechristened the Belgian and Danish Commission when the problem of Schleswig was assigned to it on 21 February.[21] Belgium had no representation on this commission and was not privy to its deliberations. In its excessive optimism, the Belgian delegation did not cultivate many of the commission members aside from the French.

Also the next day, 12 February, the European press carried an inaccurate Havas telegram declaring that Hymans in his appearance before the Ten had claimed both Flemish Zeeland and lower Limburg. This misleading report did the Belgian cause a good deal more harm than Hymans's long speech had done, for it led to much confusion and widespread belief that Belgium had in fact made major territorial claims on the Netherlands. In Holland itself, public opinion immediately became both agitated and very bitter, charging Belgium with ingratitude for Dutch hospitality to refugees during the war, and the hitherto popular Belgian minister found himself entirely isolated. Not surprisingly, the Dutch government made a formal declaration on 14 February in the Second Chamber emphatically rejecting any territorial cession,[22] and Dutch diplomatic agents began a whirlwind of activity.

In Brussels, the Dutch minister-resident, Maurice van Vollenhoven,[23]

21. I.C. 140, 13 Feb. 1919, CAB 28/6; D. H. Miller, *Diary*, 10:3.

22. DuB, R.G.P. 117, pp. 929–30; Townley to Balfour, 20 Feb. 1919, no. 44, F.O. 608/4; Fallon to Hymans, 13 Feb. 1919, no. 1580/305, BMAE PB/1919; H. T. Colenbrander, *Nederland en België: Proeve*, p. 156.

23. During the war, the Dutch minister to Brussels, Jonkheer H. van Weede, was sent to Le Havre; van Vollenhoven remained in Brussels with the title of minister-resident. After the war, van Weede, who was in ill health, retired. Although too junior for the post, van Vollenhoven remained in Brussels because no successor could be found. Brussels was considered the most difficult Dutch diplomatic post in the best of times, and both van Swinderin and Loudon declined the job. Van Swinderin preferred to remain in London, and Loudon wanted Paris, which he gained after de Stuers died in early May 1919. Finally in September 1919, C. G. W. F. van Vredenburch was transferred from Stockholm to

twice saw Orts, who claimed to have no information beyond the fact that French press reports were inaccurate. He also saw two of the Socialist cabinet ministers, Joseph Wauters and Vandervelde, who both assured him that the Havas report was inaccurate and that Hymans had not claimed Dutch territory. Another visit to Orts confirmed this, but nonetheless the Dutch government formally requested information about Hymans's speech. The Belgian reply stated only that Belgium had proposed renegotiation of the 1839 treaties and had asked that Holland participate, a statement not calculated to reassure the Dutch.[24]

Meanwhile in London, van Swinderin had wasted no time in seeing Curzon, who on 12 February tried to reassure him by pointing out that Hymans, like everybody else at the peace conference, had started with maximum demands and would soon cut them down. Despite reports that both Curzon and the Conference of Ten were annoyed with Belgium, which had lost much sympathy by its attitude, he sent Curzon a letter saying that Holland would sacrifice no territory or population and followed this, on instructions, with a formal declaration of the same purport. Then, at van Karnebeek's request, he rushed to Paris to say the same on 24 February to Balfour, who replied that it was not the business of the peace conference to interfere with the territory of neutrals. Though some of the Dutch contingent already in Paris had been felled by influenza, its healthy members were equally active.[25]

Despite the sharp Dutch reaction, the Belgian Commission convened on 25 February with André Tardieu presiding. The other French delegate was Jules Laroche of the Quai d'Orsay. Hymans promptly sought the support of both men regarding Flemish Zeeland and lower Limburg, but they opposed transfer of Flemish Zeeland while hinting that renunciation of Luxemburg might be the price of French support on the Limburg question. The British representatives were Crowe, who, as the Dutch noted, was more favorable to Belgium than other senior British

Brussels. Van Vollenhoven went to Madrid. DuB, R.G.P. 117, pp. 972–73, 1019–21; Dutch Orange Book, 1919–20, p. 2.

24. DuB, R.G.P. 117, pp. 934, 937–38, 943, 959–60; Orts note, 14 Feb. 1919, BMAE PB/1919.

25. DuB, R.G.P. 117, pp. 930, 940–41, 960–62, 964; Curzon to Townley, 12, 19 Feb. 1919, nos. 47, 55, F.O. 608/4; Balfour memo, 24 Feb. 1919, SRO Lothian Papers GD/40/17/65.

officials but who rarely showed much enthusiasm for Belgian claims, and the more sympathetic but less influential J. W. Headlam-Morley of the Foreign Office. The chief American representative was Charles Homer Haskins of Harvard, who inclined, on the whole, to generous treatment for Belgium.[26]

When the Belgian Commission met on 25 February, it quickly decided that its terms of reference lacked clarity, and so the next day Tardieu came before the Ten with a series of questions. Despite Balfour's attempt to rule out any consideration of Dutch territorial cession, the commission retained the right to investigate this possibility, although it was not empowered to conduct on-the-spot inquiries or to collect Belgian and Dutch testimony.[27] With this decision and an authorization to examine other aspects of treaty revision, the commission on 6 March quickly approved a report drafted by Tardieu, which recommended that the 1839 treaties be thoroughly revised by Belgium, Holland, and the five great powers and that Holland be invited to put her views before the Supreme Council. On 10 March, the Ten unanimously approved the report.[28]

THE PEACE CONFERENCE:
THE DECISION-MAKING PHASE

Armed with the decision of the Council of Ten and with detailed documentation provided by the official Revendications Belges (Belgian claims) submitted at the end of February, the Belgian Commission began work on specific issues. The statement of the Belgian case in the Revendications Belges was massive, consisting of five thick dossiers supported by a volume of maps and covering every aspect of treaty revision except that of compensation to the Netherlands, which the Belgian government was just belatedly beginning to explore. Aside from that oversight, the Belgian delegation had come to realize that

26. D. H. Miller, *Diary*, 1:486–87, 10:3–5; de Gaiffier to Hymans, 25 Feb. 1919, no. 1471/564, BMAE FR/1919; DuB, R.G.P. 117, pp. 974–75.

27. FRUS PPC, 4:141–44.

28. D. H. Miller, *Diary*, 10:37, 177; FRUS PPC, 4:270–71.

imposing substantiation would be required to overcome Wilsonian distaste for annexations, British and French reluctance to offend Holland, Dutch hostility, and British indifference. Although Belgian diplomatists still did not seem to recognize that no amount of documentation could overcome all these obstacles, they did know that they faced a difficult task. Van Swinderin had jubilantly made public Balfour's remark that Holland should not be asked to surrender territory, and it had reached Hymans's ears. He complained at once that British hesitation was encouraging Dutch obstruction. As Balfour did not take kindly to Hymans's lecture on the proper conduct of diplomacy, the two men parted coldly. Fortunately for his relations with the British delegation, Hymans did not know that Lord Hardinge had told van Swinderin that the Belgian claims were "preposterous" and that nothing should come of them or that van Swinderin considered the British entirely won over, aside from Crowe.[29]

In the interim, the Belgian Commission had applied itself to specific territorial questions. Despite the strong Dutch stand, it examined the question of territorial compensation to Holland. Although it lacked any quantity of information about the territories concerned from Belgian sources or any other, the commission deemed some districts more suitable for transfer than others. It was inclined to rule out East Friesland and Emden but hoped that improved arrangements on the Ems estuary could compensate the Netherlands for concessions to Belgium on the Scheldt. The commission came to no conclusion about the Bentheim district but thought the Cleves-Gelderland-Wesel area suitable for cession if the Dutch and the local inhabitants agreed. Because this scheme could probably not be arranged with the Netherlands before the German treaty was completed, it pointed out that a conditional treaty clause affording German consent to such a future arrangement would be necessary.[30]

At the same time, the commission considered Belgium's German borderlands. It agreed with little debate that neutral Moresnet and Malmédy should go to Belgium, although Headlam-Morley insisted

29. Revendications Belges, F.O. 608/2 pt. 2; Hymans, *Mémoires*, 1:293, 295, 371–73, 378–79; Balfour memo, 8 Mar. 1919, Balfour Papers/49750; de Gaiffier to Hymans, 3 Mar. 1919, no. 1641/635, BMAE FR/1919; DuB, R.G.P. 117, pp. 974–75, 977–81.

30. Belgian Commission report, 9 Mar. 1919, F.O. 608/4.

that the inhabitants of Malmédy should be given a right of protest. But in regard to Eupen, openly requested in the Revendications Belges, there was considerable disagreement. The French backed the Belgian claim, as they invariably did when their own interests were unaffected, and the Italians agreed, in hopes of establishing precedents for their own copious claims elsewhere. The British and the Americans opposed the transfer, however, because too many Germans would be incorporated into Belgium. The Japanese, as usual, announced their willingness to support any majority and otherwise said nothing until one emerged. After several days of impasse over Eupen, on 12 March the British and American members accepted transfer of the canton, provided that the inhabitants were given a right of protest.[31]

The Belgian Commission submitted its report on 19 March. It pointed out the possibility of compensation to Holland and advocated outright incorporation of neutral Moresnet along with cession of Eupen and Malmédy, subject to protest, but ignored the one remaining problem concerning the so-called Walloon cantons. Because of the difficult terrain, the railway from Eupen to Malmédy swung eastward in a wide arc and, as matters now stood, would pass through about fifteen miles of German territory. Although this railway was linked to other lines, its primary purpose was communication between the two towns. However, the British noticed the problem and Crowe arranged for the Central Committee on Territorial Questions to write in a treaty clause giving the boundary commission that would delimit the precise frontier unusual latitude and charging it to consider economic factors and means of communication in arriving at the final boundary. This committee also strengthened the wording in favor of Belgium, particularly in regard to Prussian Moresnet as compensation for Belgian forests destroyed in the war, and inserted a clause specifying advance German acceptance of any necessary boundary change with Holland, subject to the possibility of protest or plebiscite.[32]

The Belgians, who had been given very little information about how

---

31. W.C.P. 660, 662, 8, 12 Mar. 1919, CAB 29/13; Belgian Commission report, 9 Mar. 1919, F.O. 608/4; D. H. Miller, *Diary*, 10:118–19; Sir James W. Headlam-Morley, *A Memoir of the Paris Peace Conference, 1919*, p. 164.

32. Headlam-Morley to Crowe, 15 Mar. 1919, Territorial Committee report, n.d., W.C.P. 417, F.O. 608/4.

rapidly matters were progressing, also raised the question of the Eupen-Malmédy railway, asking for transfer of part of the canton or circle of Monschau (Montjoie). The issue was discussed in the Belgian Commission on 5 April. The Japanese representative for once strongly endorsed the Belgian request but the British and Americans were much opposed, although the British began to waver when they discovered that only forty-five hundred people were involved.[33] In the end, however, the question went to the Big Four, who considered the proposed Belgian clauses on 16 April with Hymans present. He asked for modification of the frontier to incoporate the railway, but the Four decided to leave the matter to the Boundary Commission. They further deleted the clause providing for German territorial transfer to Holland, as the British thought that it would be impossible to arrange and Wilson opposed territorial transfer to and from neutrals on principle.[34] Thus, territorial compensation to Holland from Germany was ruled out and, by implication, so was any Dutch territorial concession to Belgium. This latter implication was confirmed when the long-deferred meetings with Dutch representatives on revision of the 1839 treaties took place in late May and early June and, in their wake, the great powers decided on 4 June that territorial transfer by Holland should be excluded from future negotiations.[35]

As a result, Belgian territorial gains in Europe were confined to Eupen, Malmédy, neutral Moresnet, and Prussian Moresnet, thus finally reuniting all three slivers of Moresnet. As all of the territories involved were tiny, Belgium gained less than any other European Continental victor except Portugal, less even than neutral Denmark. Furthermore, in Eupen and Malmédy, the cession was subject to a proviso for local protest and the final award was to be made thereafter by the League of Nations. The question of the Eupen-Malmédy railway was left unresolved.[36] There was, however, one additional benefit to Belgium. On

33. De Gaiffier to Hymans, 29 Mar. 1919, no. 2495/985, BMAE FR/1919; Rolin-Jaequemyns to Crowe, 1 Apr. 1919, no. 377, F.O. 608/4; D. H. Miller, *Diary*, 10:161–63.

34. I.C. 171B, 16 Apr. 1919, CAB 29/37; Hymans note, 23 Apr. 1919, BMAE PB/1919.

35. FRUS PPC, 4:729–47, 779–801.

36. Articles 32–34, Versailles treaty, FRUS PPC, 13:139–40.

3 May 1919, John Maynard Keynes of the British delegation pointed out to the Four that, except in Alsace-Lorraine, German state properties in ceded territories were to be paid for by the recipient nations in the form of reparations credit to Germany, and he inquired about Belgium. The Four decided for political reasons not to exact payment from Belgium, despite Lloyd George's grumbling, and amended the treaty accordingly. Belgium was not, however, granted Alsace-Lorraine's exemption from assuming a portion of the German Empire's state debts as of 1 August 1914 and eventually had to pay 640,609 gold marks in respect to Eupen and Malmédy.[37]

Nevertheless, there remained one further debate over the mechanics of the cession of Eupen and Malmédy to Belgium. The draft treaty presented to the German delegation on 7 May specified that for six months after the treaty came into force, the Belgian government would maintain open registers in both districts for those inhabitants who wished to record their protests. When the German delegation submitted its reply to the draft treaty on 29 May, it not only protested the cession of Eupen and Malmédy but also took particular exception to the absence of a plebiscite in these districts. Accordingly, the matter was referred to the Belgian and Danish Commission. In the debate that followed, the Belgian delegation was neither consulted nor informed. At the instance of Haskins and Headlam-Morley, the commission proposed that there should be a secret plebiscite conducted by the League of Nations. On 14 June, however, the Four decided not to change the original treaty clause, but they also let stand the draft reply to the German delegation prepared by the Belgian Commission on the assumption that the clause would be revised. As a consequence, the reply sent to the Germans on 16 June specified that "in every case the transfer will only take place as the result of a decision of the inhabitants themselves taken under conditions which will ensure complete freedom to vote" and "the Treaty makes provision for consulting the population under the auspices of the League of Nations."[38] This wording provided some partial basis for later German protests about the open registers administered by the Belgian government in accordance with Article 34 of the treaty.

37. I.C. 180D, 3 May 1919, CAB 29/37; FRUS PPC, 13:535–36.
38. Germany, Peace Delegation, *Comments by the German Delegation on the Conditions of Peace*, pp. 27–28; Wambaugh, *Plebiscites*, 1:522–23; Haskins to Wilson, 2 June 1919,

THE BRITISH IN MALMÉDY

As the Belgian delegation to the peace conference was unaware of the discrepancy between the treaty and the reply to Germany and assumed that final agreement had been reached on Eupen and Malmédy before the treaty was presented to the Germans, Hymans proposed on 10 May that both districts be incorporated in the Belgian zone of military occupation in the Rhineland in order to facilitate steps toward the ultimate transfer of sovereignty.[39] As matters now stood, Malmédy lay in the British zone of occupation, whereas Eupen was controlled by French troops. One factor lending urgency to the Belgian request was a long history of difficulty with the British military commander at Malmédy, who was so correct in his neutrality that he consistently favored the pro-German minority there and suppressed all demonstrations of sympathy for Belgium.

Difficulties with Brig. Gen. Henry Hyslop commanding at Malmédy had evoked Belgian protests as early as 9 February. Hymans complained that the general was threatening the leader and members of the pro-Belgian movement with prison, preventing the sale of Belgian newspapers, and living at the home of the Landrath. On 20 February, a new Belgian protest reported that Hyslop was engaging in threats, arrests, and expulsions and had forbidden all French-language newspapers, the Belgian flag, and trips to Belgium without German consent, which was generally refused. The British defended Hyslop and took no action,[40] so the complaints continued. Although a few of the charges proved to be exaggerated and the arrival of a Belgian military mission in Malmédy in April for liaison duties alleviated the situation somewhat, the Belgians continued to protest both the continuing suppression of Belgian newspapers in the canton and a general lack of cooperation.[41] The

---

Wilson Papers 8A/54; Headlam-Morley, *Memoir*, pp. 156–57, 164–65; Council of Four paper C.F. 69, 14 June 1919, CAB 29/39; Cmd. 258, pp. 7–8. I am grateful to Manfred J. Enssle for bringing this matter to my attention. Headlam-Morley, *Memoir*, p. 157, indicates a further emendation by the Four on 16 June, but no record of the decision survives. See also FRUS PPC, 5:454.

39. Hymans to DB, 10 May 1919, tel. 244, BMAE DB/30/XIV/I.

40. Hymans to Villiers, 9 Feb. 1919, no. 1316, de Bassompierre to Villiers, 20 Feb. 1919, Villiers to Hymans, 4 Mar. 1919, BMAE GB/1919/I.

41. Anon. note re Goffart trip to Malmédy, n.d., BMAE DB/30/XIV/I; Orts to

Foreign Office continued to deny all charges even after three members of the Belgian Parliament visited Malmédy late in May and reported that (1) most of the population favored Belgian annexation, even many of the German minority who wished to escape German war debts; (2) the German authorities were investing the funds of local savings banks in German war loans; and (3) they were shipping large quantities of livestock and merchandise to Germany. As the livestock consisted entirely of Belgian cows seized during the retreat and Belgium had been virtually stripped of livestock by the Germans, Belgian opinion was particularly indignant about the precious cows. After leisurely investigation, the British army virtuously announced on 14 July that the shipment of cows had been stopped at the end of May and that the regime in Malmédy was not unduly harsh.[42]

The Belgians thought otherwise, at least so far as non-Germans were concerned. They were particularly offended by an incident on 21 July, the Belgian national day. The Belgian military mission in Malmédy celebrated the occasion by raising the Belgian flag, but General Hyslop ordered it hauled down so as not to offend the German minority. Moncheur hinted to the Foreign Office that his government wanted Hyslop recalled, and *La Nation belge* inquired why British troops still remained in control of territory awarded to Belgium a month after the Versailles treaty had been signed.[43]

By this time, both British and Belgian diplomatists were asking the same question. The Belgian government had first formally requested transfer of both Eupen and Malmédy to Belgian command on 15 May. Though Foch was willing, Gen. Sir William Robertson, commander of the British army of occupation at Cologne, insisted upon continuing British use of the large military camp at Elsenborn in Malmédy until autumn and claimed that transfer of the rest of Malmédy was a political question that he must submit to the British government. On 8 June,

Ramaix, 24 Apr. 1919, no. 511, BMAE GB/1919/I; Ramaix to Curzon, 28 Apr. 1919, no. 2808, F.O. 371/3644A; Curzon minute, 30 Apr. 1919, F.O. 800/152.

42. F.O. to Maskens, 3 June 1919, Villiers to Curzon, 1 June 1919, no. 190, Director of Military Intelligence to F.O., 14 July 1919, no. 0140/2007, F.O. 371/3644A; Delacroix to Hymans, 31 May 1919, no. 3071, BMAE DB/30/XIV/I.

43. DBFP, 5:93–94, 135–36; Hymans to Moncheur, 25 July 1919, tel., BMAE GB/1919/II; *La Nation belge*, 24 July 1919, FMAE Z/Belg./66.

Foch recommended that the matter be submitted to the peace conference, but on 17 June the French government authorized the transfer of Eupen.[44]

Hymans immediately saw Crowe in Paris to tell him that the French had evacuated Eupen and to ask that Robertson be ordered to do the same in Malmédy. Crowe made no commitment but soon decided that this should be done. Thus, on 24 June the British army asked Foch to transfer the zone to Belgium except for continuing British use of the Elsenborn barracks. Unfortunately, nobody thought to inform the Belgians of this decision.[45]

Nothing happened. Hymans twice renewed his request and the British army again asked for transfer of the zone, but again nobody told the Belgians and Foch took no action, evidently enjoying the invidious comparisons being made between French promptness and apparent British dilatoriness. In early July the Belgian request was renewed every few days. On 14 July, Moncheur sent a stiff note listing all the previous demarches and pointing out that there had been no response to any of them. By this time, Curzon was arguing that if Belgium occupied the area, the "referendum" there would be biased, but his staff pointed out that the Versailles treaty specified that Belgium was to administer the protest registers.[46]

After the flag incident on 21 July, which brought another Belgian request for evacuation, British officials began to realize what was afoot and that invidious comparisons were in fact being made. In addition, Hymans had written personally to Lord Birkenhead, the lord chancellor, asking him to intervene, and had told Moncheur that if this move did not bring fast results, he would ask for the immediate recall of Hyslop. Meanwhile, Moncheur was to suggest that such recall would be appreciated. Belatedly, the Foreign Office told Moncheur on 26 July that Foch had twice been asked, and was being asked again, to arrange

44. Foch to Gillain, 22 May 1919, Gillain to Foch, 3 June 1919, no. 154/10, Foch to de Gaiffier, 8 June 1919, Hymans memo, 17 June 1919, BMAE DB/30/XIV/II.

45. Hymans note, 17 June 1919, no. 836, BMAE DB/13/I; Crowe minute, 18 June 1919, Thwaites to Weygand, 24 June 1919, F.O. 608/5.

46. Hymans to Crowe, 28 June 1919, Villiers to Curzon, 7 July 1919, no. 248, Twiss to Weygand, 12 July 1919, F.O. 608/5; DBFP, 5:19–21; Moncheur to Hymans, 10 July 1919, tel. 161, BMAE GB/1919/II; Moncheur note, 14 July 1919, F.O. 371/3644A.

British evacuation of all of Malmédy except Elsenborn. The Belgian army had badly wanted the camp in order to avoid expensive construction of a new training camp in Belgium and had mounted a long campaign to obtain at least partial use of Elsenborn. By this time, however, it had been overriden by the Belgian government, which was prepared to do without Elsenborn for the time being in order to achieve the departure of Hyslop and his troops from the rest of Malmédy.[47]

At the beginning of August, Curzon urged Balfour, then in Paris, to resolve the situation, and Balfour became alarmed at the acrimony arising from both the flag episode and the prolongation of British occupation. He took the view that Britain should accommodate Belgium in small matters as she was disappointing her on so many major issues. As always when Balfour became interested in a problem, he acted decisively. His efforts were reinforced by an appeal to the Quai d'Orsay from the Belgian government, which was now finally aware that Foch was the stumbling block. As a result, Foch gave the requisite order to Robertson on 5 August and, when execution seemed slow, the Quai d'Orsay intervened directly with Foch. Thus, the district finally passed under Belgian military control on 12 August, and the British evacuated Elsenborn on 20 August after completion of British artillery maneuvers there.[48]

GERMAN RESISTANCE

Once the British had left Malmédy, the Belgians could concentrate on the remaining problems of the Eupen-Malmédy railway and the German effort to prevent the transfer of both districts. Germany had protested nearly every clause of the Versailles treaty and the Belgian territorial

47. DBFP, 5:93–94, 135–36; Curzon to Moncheur, 29 July 1919, F.O. 608/5; Masson to Hymans, 27 May 1919, no. A517/63C, BMAE DB/30/XIV/I; Gillain to Foch, 3 June 1919, no. 154/20, BMAE DB/30/XIV/II; Hymans to Birkenhead, 20 July 1919, Hymans to Moncheur, 24 July 1919, BMAE GB/1919/II; Hymans to Moncheur, 25 July 1919, tel., BMAE B–10.121; Maglinsen to Hymans, 29 July 1919, no. 210/1, BMAE B–10.792.

48. Hymans note, 2 Aug. 1919, BMAE GB/1919/II; DBFP, 5:93–94, 135–36; de Gaiffier to Pichon, 5 Aug. 1919, no. 6977–P8, FMAE to Foch, 11 Aug. 1919, Foch to FMAE, 13 Aug. 1919, no. 3858, FMAE Z/Belg./66.

clauses were no exception. The German government argued that Eupen was exclusively German, claimed that Malmédy was predominantly German, and even devoted a lengthy, inaccurate paragraph to protesting the award of neutral Moresnet to Belgium.[49] Though the Belgian government was not consulted about the Allied response to any of these assertions, the powers did in fact hold firm, aside from their oversight in leaving the misleading wording about the form of voting at Eupen-Malmédy in their reply to the German delegation. Thus, the Versailles treaty was signed on 28 June 1919 without any changes in the various Belgian clauses.[50]

The Germans also protested with more justification and at greater length against the mechanism established to register local dissent in Eupen and Malmédy. Article 34 of the Versailles treaty specified:

> During the six months after the coming into force of this Treaty, registers will be opened by the Belgian authorities at Eupen and Malmédy in which the inhabitants of the above territory will be entitled to record in writing a desire to see the whole or part of it remain under German sovereignty.
>
> The results of this public expression of opinion will be communicated by the Belgian Government to the League of Nations, and Belgium undertakes to accept the decision of the League.[51]

Both before and after the treaty was signed, the German government persisted in terming this arrangement a plebiscite and then complaining that it was not a fair plebiscite, carefully ignoring the fact that it was never intended to be a plebiscite in the first place. The oddity of the arrangement, together with the wording of the 16 June reply to the German delegation, lent some color to the German charges even though the Belgian authorities meticulously fulfilled the terms of the treaty. The more meticulous the Belgians were, however, the more the Germans protested.

The difficulty started on 1 August 1919 in Eupen. As Germany had already ratified the treaty, Belgian officials began, in their capacity as occupying power, to take over the civil administration to facilitate the

---

49. FRUS PPC, 6:824–25.
50. C.F. 69, 14 June 1919, CAB 29/39; Cmd. 258, pp. 3, 7, 8.
51. FRUS PPC, 13:140.

forthcoming transfer of sovereignty. Germany promptly complained that Belgium had no rights whatever in Eupen until the treaty came into force. A few days later the Germans protested even more heatedly that the Belgian authorities had assured local railway workers that they could retain their jobs when the railway system came under Belgian administration. They further argued that no changes whatever should take place "until the decision of the people as to the final lot of the Eupen and Malmédy circles."[52] In a tart reply based upon a Belgian draft, the powers informed Germany that Belgium had certain rights as occupying power, would enjoy full sovereignty in both districts from the day the treaty entered into effect, and was certainly entitled in the interim to take steps to ease the hardships of transfer for the local citizenry.[53]

Then Germany repeatedly demanded a plebiscite in Eupen and Malmédy, but to no avail.[54] When Belgium officially gained sovereignty on 10 January 1920 and the Belgian high commissioner, Lt. Gen. Herman Baltia, promptly opened the protest registers, Germany began to dispute the mechanics of their administration and to demand League of Nations supervision. In particular, the Germans complained that the registers were not open a sufficient number of hours per week and that those availing themselves of the opportunity to protest had their identity cards stamped. Again Germany sought a plebiscite and was refused. For the rest, the Belgian government pointed out that it was even opening the registers on Sundays after church for the convenience of those who could not meet the weekday hours and that identity cards were stamped not only to prevent individuals from voting more than once but also at the request of German officials who wished to have evidence of their loyalty to show to the German government. Indeed, departing German

52. DBFP, 1:797, 801–4. Quotation from p. 803.

53. Dutasta to Rolin-Jaequemyns, 22 Aug. 1919, no. 1252, Clemenceau to von Lersner, 26 Sept. 1919, BMAE DB/30/XIV/II; Hymans circular letter, 14 Feb. 1920, BMAE FR/1920/I.

54. Heads of Delegations paper H.D. 86, 88, 7, 10 Nov. 1919, CAB 29/74; von Lersner to Clemenceau, 29 Dec. 1919, no. 67, F.O. 371/3644B; DBFP, 12:38–39. Because the inhabitants remained German citizens until the final decision of the League Council, the constitution and laws of Belgium did not enter immediately into effect. Hence the provisional regime of the royal high commissioner. Hymans circular letter, 14 Feb. 1920, BMAE FR/1920/I.

officials and railway workers had to show proof of protest to obtain new jobs in Germany.[55]

When the registers closed on 23 July 1920, it became obvious that protest had been minimal. In Eupen, where there were 13,975 eligible voters (those of both sexes over twenty-one and resident there by 1 August 1914), there were 218 protests, 121 of them from German officials. In Malmédy, out of 19,751 eligible voters, there were 62 protests, of which 4 were withdrawn. Of the remaining 58, 40-odd came from German officials, some of whom admitted that they had voted on orders from Berlin. In both districts, especially Malmédy, a good many of the protests came from teachers who had been imported from elsewhere in Germany in April 1914 as part of the Germanization program and who had been required to sign a special loyalty oath.[56] When the Belgian government transmitted these lopsided results to the League in August, Germany responded by appealing in September to the League Council, complaining about the manner in which the "plebiscite" had been carried out, claiming that the results did not represent the wishes of the population, and asking the League to void the results of the "plebiscite" run by Belgium and call a new one.[57]

The League Council appointed a committee chaired by its Brazilian member to examine the Belgian report and registers and also the German charges. As the German evidence in support of charges of Belgian

55. Villiers to Curzon, 20 Jan. 1920, no. 33, Derby to Curzon, 15 Apr. 1920, no. 1149, F.O. 371/3644B; C.A. 46, 29 May 1920, CAB 29/46; Wambaugh, *Plebiscites*, 1:524–30, 2:542–43; Xhaflaire to Baltia, 30 Apr. 1920, BMAE B–11.443. The registers were open from 9:00 to 12:00 A.M. and from 2:00 to 4:00 P.M. Monday through Saturday, and from 9:00 to 12:00 A.M. on Sundays and holidays.

56. Villiers to Curzon, 27 July 1920, F.O. 371/3644B; Margerie to Millerand, 24 July 1920, tel. 465, FMAE Z/Belg./67; Hymans, *Mémoires*, 1:466; Capitaine-Commandant A-E-M Dendal, "Le Rattachement d'Eupen et de Malmédy à la Belgique," p. 87; Wambaugh, *Plebiscites*, 1:531–32. There are slight discrepancies in the figures reported by various sources, perhaps because local officials in the two districts kept records by different methods. The original records from the districts show 208 valid protests from Eupen and 68 from Malmédy. In its official report to the League of Nations, the Belgian government listed a combined total of 271 protests (62 from Malmédy and 209 from Eupen), of which 201 were from German government employees or their wives. Eupen report, 24 July 1920, Malmédy report, n.d., BMAE B–11.443; League of Nations, *Official Journal*, 1920, 1:2, no. 7, p. 407.

57. FRUS PPC, 13:141; League Council Document H. 3, 13 Sept. 1920, F.O. 371/5456.

intimidation consisted mostly of a quantity of anonymous letters allegedly from inhabitants of Eupen and Malmédy but neither notarized nor
validated in any way, the charges were dismissed, and on 20 September
1920 the Council officially recognized transfer of both districts to Belgium.[58] Thus the *Kreise* of Eupen and Malmédy passed definitively to
Belgium, becoming the cantons of Eupen, Malmédy, and St. Vith in the
arrondissement of Verviers in the province of Liège.[59] In response to the
Council decision, Germany refused to recognize the validity of the
transfer, arguing that the League Council, to which it had itself appealed,
had no jurisdiction. Germany made a series of attempts to bring the
matter before the League Assembly late in 1920 and again in 1921, but
the Council held firm and the Assembly took no action.[60] In conjunction with the first attempt, German cabinet ministers made a series of
denunciatory speeches in the Reichstag and in the Rhineland, especially
in the Belgian zone, so inflammatory as to occasion a joint Allied note
of protest on 6 December 1920 threatening to ban future tours of the
occupied territories unless German high officials ceased such attacks. In
addition, the American commissioner, Ellis L. Dresel, made separate unofficial representations. Although these incidents were part of a broader
German campaign against the Rhineland occupation, the rhetoric about
Eupen and Malmédy was particularly inflamed.[61] On the heels of the
second attempt to lay the question before the League Assembly, the
German government, which still did not recognize Belgian acquisition
of the two districts, insisted that Belgium should arrange at the August

58. League of Nations, *Official Journal*, 1920, 1:2, no. 7, pp. 394, 406, 408, 409.
Belgian reports consistently indicated little hostility to incorporation in Belgium in either
canton. Xhaflaire to de Radzitsky, 23 Apr. 1919, BMAE B–331; Moncheur to de Gaiffier,
28 June 1919, no. 5318, BMAE FR/1919; Coppejans to Delobbe, 6 June 1919, no.
9862, BMAE B–348.

59. Admiralty, *Belgium*, p. 126. On 18 May 1940, Hitler reincorporated all three
districts in the Third Reich. After World War II, they reverted to Belgium.

60. Drummond to Curzon, 20 Oct. 1920, League Council Document 84, F.O. 371/
5456; League of Nations, *Official Journal*, 1920, 1:2, no. 8, pp. 5–6, 85; Drummond to
League Council, 7 Feb. 1921, League Council Document 138, F.O. 371/6962; Gérard to
Leygues, 21 Nov. 1920, no. 36, FMAE A/169.

61. Jaspar to Rolin-Jaequemyns, 25 Nov. 1920, tel. 83, Jaspar to Moncheur, 30 Nov.
1920, tel. 266, Moncheur to Jaspar, 3 Dec. 1920, tel. 234, BMAE GB/1920; DBFP,
10:338–42; K. Nelson, *Victors Divided*, p. 207; della Faille to Delacroix, 19 Nov. 1920,
no. 7879/2965, 4, 9 Dec. 1920, nos. 8287/3116, 8390/3141, BMAE Alle/1920/III;
Laurent to Leygues, 6, 7 Dec. 1920, tels. 2241, 2249–50, FMAE A/170.

1921 Supreme Council meeting in Paris for the end of the Allied sanctions taken in March in connection with reparation and disarmament disputes.[62] As the military sanctions were not raised, Germany continued to withhold recognition but could do nothing about Belgian possession, de facto and de jure, of Eupen and Malmédy.

As all the sound and fury had not undone the transfer of the two districts, all that remained as a bone of contention was the border delimitation. The seven-man Belgo-German Boundary Commission commenced work promptly at Liège after the Versailles treaty went into effect but immediately encountered sharp disagreement between the Belgian and German representatives over the railway that zigzagged three times across the cantonal boundaries into Monschau and back en route from Eupen to Malmédy. Both Britain and France supported the Belgian claim to the entire railway, although the British thought that Belgium should compensate Germany elsewhere, as Belgium was prepared to do. The commission initially agreed with the French view, particularly because most of the territory in question consisted of largely uninhabited forests, but German opposition was so intense that the entire commission went to Malmédy to inspect the problem on the spot and appointed its Italian and British members to study the question in detail. When they reported that Germany could easily build another line if she saw any need for it, the commission without further ado awarded the railway on 27 March 1920 to Belgium by a unanimous vote, with Germany abstaining. Although Belgium had indicated willingness to provide compensation, the commission did not require it.[63]

The first German response beyond the protest of the German representative at Liège was an official press release stating that the German government refused to recognize the decision. Neither this statement nor any subsequent German one made any mention of the fact that Article 35 of the Versailles treaty specified that "decisions will be taken by a majority and will be binding upon the parties concerned."[64] Then a

62. Della Faille to Jaspar, 12 July 1921, no. 5441/1996, BMAE Alle/1921/IV.

63. Margerie to Millerand, 18 Feb. 1920, no. 141, FMAE to Margerie, 26 Feb. 1920, no. 164, Margerie to FMAE, 29 Mar. 1920, tel. 190, FMAE Z/Belg./66; DBFP, 9:112–14, 271–72; *La Libre belgique*, 31 Mar. 1920, p. 2.

64. Margerie to Millerand, 3 Apr. 1920, no. 404, FMAE Z/Belg./66; FRUS PPC, 13:142.

general strike, protesting both the administration of the registers and cession of the railway, broke out in Eupen. The Belgian government briskly suppressed the strike and soon thereafter submitted considerable evidence to the League of Nations that German authorities, industrialists, and unions had organized its outbreak. Meanwhile, on 16 April, the German government filed a seven-page protest arguing that Belgian willingness to provide compensation elsewhere proved that Belgium recognized that she had no legal claim to the railway. Asserting that the Boundary Commission had exceeded its powers, the German government flatly refused to accept the decision, demanded its retraction, and threatened recourse to an international arbitration tribunal. The next day disorders and hostile attacks against Belgian forces at Aachen became so severe that the Rhineland High Commission banned public meetings for a month. Shortly thereafter the German press began to carry highly distorted accounts of the amount of territory claimed by Belgium. As the press reports listed much territory already awarded to Belgium, including Elsenborn, the effect was to suggest that Belgium was claiming vast areas instead of a few small slivers of largely uninhabited territory.[65]

On 1 May the Conference of Ambassadors considered the problem. Though de Gaiffier was not permitted to attend, he had submitted a note defending the commission's authority and decision, pointing out that the territory in question was largely deserted and uncultivated, and noting that a strict ethnic line would require three double customs barriers within 36 kilometers (22.5 miles), a patent impossibility from both the local and international point of view. The Ambassadors decided to refer the matter to the Technical Geographic Committee. However, Derby, who was thoroughly confused about the whole matter, insisted that Belgian representatives not participate in future sessions and argued that a strict reading of the Versailles treaty would award the railway to Germany. On the latter point, he was sharply corrected from London.[66]

The Technical Geographic Committee unanimously upheld the pro-

---

65. Wambaugh, *Plebiscites*, 1:529–30, 534; Gerardin to FMAE, 15 Apr. 1920, tel. 44, Margerie to Millerand, 16 Apr. 1920, no. 448, Briere to FMAE, 23 Apr. 1920, tel. 58, FMAE Z/Belg./66; DBFP, 9:454–55.
66. C.A. 35, CAB 29/45; DBFP, 9:497–98.

priety of the Boundary Commission's decision and the accuracy of Belgium's statement of the facts. Thus on 29 May the Ambassadors, despite Derby's hesitations, approved the decision of the Boundary Commission, while at the same time deciding to ask Belgium to specify what concessions it would give in exchange. On 5 June, de Gaiffier reported that Belgium was prepared to cede the vastly more valuable area in northwest Eupen containing the Aachen waterworks, exclude the town of Monschau (Montjoie) from Belgium, establish the only two villages west of the railway as German enclaves, and make special arrangements for local inhabitants in German territory who needed to use the railway. The Belgians had known for a year that the Germans were particularly concerned about the Aachen waterworks and had long planned to trade it for the railway, if need be. But when they had offered the transaction to the German member of the Boundary Commission, he had rejected it outright even though the commission's estimated value of the scrubby heath to go to Belgium was only 150,000 francs, whereas that of the waterworks, exclusive of the land involved, was 20 million francs. Though Derby made difficulties about the Belgian proposal, the rest of the Ambassadors thought it satisfactory, approved it in principle, and asked for written details.[67]

On 11 June the Ambassadors considered the written Belgian proposal. Derby wanted it referred to the Boundary Commission and the Belgians themselves were concerned about the proposed German enclave at Roetgen, which consisted of only a few houses but controlled the sources of the Vesdre River, on which the wool-washing industry of Eupen and Verviers depended. The five great-power members of the Boundary Commission, after merely consulting the Belgian and German members, unanimously recommended a slight adjustment at Roetgen approved by the Belgian member and full acceptance of the Belgian proposal. On 22 July 1920, with de Gaiffier not present, the

---

67. Technical Geographic Committee, 20 May 1920, no. 12, de Gaiffier to Hymans, 20, 26 May 1920, nos. 5432/2848, 5600/2975, de Gaiffier to J. Cambon, 8 June 1920, no. 6024, BMAE FR/1920/I; C.A. 47 (VI), 29 May 1920, FMAE Z/Belg./66; DBFP, 9:521–22; C.A. 47, 5 June 1920, CAB 29/46; de Borchgrave to Hymans, 31 May 1919, BMAE B–348; Derby to Curzon, 27 May 1920, Curzon Papers F112/197; Derby to Curzon, 5 June 1920, Curzon Papers F112/198.

Conference of Ambassadors unanimously accepted these recommendations as a supposedly definitive decision and instructed the Boundary Commission to finish its job, whether the German member participated or not.[68]

The German delegation to the peace conference was informed of the decision on 29 July 1920. On 28 October it replied with an exceptionally long note and a memorandum of about seventy printed pages. The German government again insisted that the Boundary Commission had exceeded its mandate, acted against the Versailles treaty, and ignored the wishes and economic interests of the inhabitants. Germany flatly rejected the decision, demanding that either it should retain the railway or the matter should go to arbitration. The German government did offer Belgium a small, entirely uninhabited slice of Monschau on which to build a new railway, remarking that this was a "great concession." The internal Foreign Office reaction was that "the compromise proposed by the Germans appears reasonable and just."[69]

And so the matter dragged on. Part of the trouble was that in the face of absolute German refusal, the only way to enforce the treaty was by force and no power was prepared to do that. Belgium could not, Britain would not, and France, after a unilateral expedition at Frankfurt in April of 1920, was not prepared to take action again without British consent, particularly on a matter not of direct interest to France. As Britain became increasingly alarmed at apparent French preponderance on the Continent and more sympathetic to Germany in small matters and large, the use of force was obviously out of the question. The only alternative seemed to be to bribe Germany into acceptance by granting more concessions at Belgium's expense.

Thus at the end of 1920 the Boundary Commission began to consider giving Germany more of northwest Eupen. The early months of 1921 were enlivened by a 306-page German protest and a series of German notes simultaneously insisting that the Boundary Commission had no authority and demanding that it transfer much more territory, including

68. C.A. 49, 11 June 1920, CAB 29/46; C.A. 64, 22 July 1920, CAB 29/48; Derby to Curzon, 6, 9 June 1920, Curzon Papers F112/198.
69. C.A. to German Delegation, 29 July 1920, FMAE Z/Belg./67; Sthamer to Curzon, 15 Nov. 1920, A. 2009, F.O. 371/4809.

the key Belgian rail center at Herbesthal, to Germany. After long debate, Germany was conceded most but not all of what she asked, including five hundred Belgian inhabitants, while the less valuable district to go to Belgium had now been reduced so that it contained only twenty Germans. This decision on 21 April 1921 brought a predictable German rejection and a new insistence upon arbitration, complete with a proposal for the president of Switzerland to appoint a three-man panel. The Ambassadors maintained their decision but did nothing about it beyond the ritual notification to Germany, because nobody knew what to do.[70]

By this time the Belgians, in full awareness that the Germans intended to stall indefinitely, began to press for a final solution by the end of 1921. The Ambassadors were not eager to fix a deadline, as then they would be forced to face the problem, and Belgium alone lacked sufficient power to enforce her will and her rights. As a consequence, the problem dragged on throughout 1922 and was finally resolved by a Belgo-German protocol signed at Aachen on 6 November 1922 and approved by the Conference of Ambassadors on 14 March 1923. By this agreement, Belgium gained essentially extraterritorial rights on the tracks of the Eupen-Malmédy railway without transfer of any of the surrounding territory. Accordingly, Germany did not acquire the Aachen waterworks. Though the protocol was not in fact ratified until 1931,[71] after Germany had lost her last weapon with which to negotiate a return of the cantons, the 1922 settlement for all practical purposes completed the transfer of Eupen and Malmédy to Belgium and appeared definite. Briefly and misleadingly, the question of the two border cantons seemed to be laid to rest.

In actuality, the German government had not laid the issue to rest and in later years revived it as the diplomatic headache known as the Eupen-Malmédy question. Originally there was no connection between

70. G.F.A. Whitlock to F.O., 20 Dec. 1920, no. 95, F.O. 371/4809; C.A. 105, 9 Feb. 1921, CAB 29/53; C.A. 117, 27 Apr. 1921, CAB 29/54; C.A. 128, 3 June 1921, CAB 29/55.

71. C.A. 136, 5 Aug. 1921, CAB 29/57; A. Vanbergen, Société Nationale des Chemins de Fer Belges (Brussels), to author, 11 Oct. 1967; C.A. 209, 14 Mar. 1923, F.O. 893/20. The Aachen waterworks were ceded to Germany after World War II when the frontier and the rail regime were renegotiated. Vanbergen interview, Brussels, 9 Jan. 1968.

the two districts, which were quite different in character, but Germany sought the return of them both and so they became hyphenated. What Hymans feared had happened; Belgium had incorporated too many Germans and had generated a German desire for revisionism at Belgium's expense. Though the number of true ethnic Germans who lost German citizenship was not large, it was sufficient to cause continuing difficulty.

Probably the main concern was Eupen. Certainly Germany had no real interest in neutral Moresnet. After the ritual protest in Germany's reply to the treaty, it was never mentioned again. German efforts concentrated always on Eupen and Malmédy. Although there were few signs of any serious dissatisfaction about Belgian sovereignty in either district, some of the departed German officials banded together to form an association in Berlin, housed in a government building, which issued a steady stream of propaganda and kept the Reichstag conscious of the injustice of what had been done to a few Germans and of the need to reclaim the lost territories.[72] Thus, when Gustav Stresemann decided in 1925 to commence territorial revisionism in the west at the expense of Germany's weakest neighbor, he found both an issue and an instrument ready at hand.

Whether Stresemann would have adopted this tactic if Belgium had confined its territorial acquisitions to predominantly French-speaking Moresnet and Malmédy is impossible to say. There is no doubt, however, that without the tiny but densely populated and Germanic district of Eupen for the Reichstag to agitate about, his maneuver would have been more difficult to launch. Although Stresemann's ploy failed in the end, it put the Belgian government through a good deal of internal division, fear, and misery while, at the same time, making the solution of other unfinished business with Germany more complex. Probably Hymans's initial judgment that he should not ask for Eupen, for fear of creating a German grudge against Belgium, was sound. His decision to add Eupen to the list of Belgian claims was made only at the end of February 1919 and shows every sign of having been made hastily, without any careful assessment of the advantages and drawbacks. He was

72. Kerchove to Hymans, 20 Feb., 19 May 1920, nos. 646/260, 3045/1181, BMAE Alle/1920/I.

clearly responding to pressure from the Belgian army and the Vieille Montagne in Moresnet and no doubt keeping an eye on Belgian opinion with electoral considerations in mind. Probably, as well, he was aware by then that he might fail to gain any Dutch territory and fearful of returning home too nearly empty-handed. Even with Eupen, Belgian territorial gains in Europe were very modest, almost the least of any Continental victor. But in his determination to have something to show for his labors, Hymans made the mistake that he had wished to avoid and that both Holland and Denmark so carefully did avoid: giving a powerful neighbor a reason to seek revenge.

FOUR

THE STRUGGLE

FOR REPARATIONS

THE DAMAGE DONE

Aside from territorial expansion and treaty revision, Belgium's chief concern at the peace conference was financial. Reparation for damage done, including immediate payments to make possible the reconstruction of a totally devastated economy, was so vital to Belgium that this issue nearly caused her to reject the Versailles treaty. From start to finish, the entire country and all three political parties were united in their insistence upon the urgency of their nation's needs. The battle over Belgian reparations claims was long and bitter and, as with so many other Belgian issues, her gains at Paris remained a bone of contention for many years thereafter.

The Belgian reparations claims were extraordinarily diverse, arising from her special legal position under the 1839 treaties, the extent and duration of the German occupation, and the total destruction of her economy. There were even claims against Austria, which, although a signatory of the 1839 treaties, had participated with Germany in the fighting in Belgium in mid-August of 1914 without declaring war until 28 August. Thus, Belgium claimed a variety of historic coins, armor, archives, and works of art removed by the Austrians during the wars of the French Revolution. Though Belgium was awarded these items by the Treaty of Saint-Germain, Austria succeeded on appeal in 1921 in retaining the two chief items, the treasure of the Order of the Golden Fleece and a Rubens triptych, on the argument that their removal had been a normal exercise of her eighteenth-century sovereignty over the area.[1]

There was no such complication about Belgian claims against Ger-

1. Hymans to Clemenceau, 13 May 1919, van den Heuvel to Clemenceau, 20 May 1919, no. 569, BMAE DB/7/II; FRUS PPC, 13:525–26.

many for works of art. Most of the pieces had been seized during the occupation and the remainder, historic claims for the return of seizures a century before, were justified as recompense for artistic destruction in the course of the fighting, as at Ieper.[2] Equally clear-cut was a demand for books, maps, manuscripts, and incunabula to replace those destroyed in the sack of Leuven (Louvain) in 1914. In much the same category was a Belgian claim for return of government archives, especially those of the Foreign Ministry, removed to Berlin during the war.[3] Though these claims were of considerable importance to national pride and, at Leuven, of symbolic and scholarly significance, they were not the heart of the matter.

Much more urgent was the economic reconstruction of the country. Many of Belgium's claims were based upon the fact that no other industrial country had been so thoroughly despoiled. Though the people of Serbia and Poland had suffered as much as, if not more than, the Belgians, both countries were predominantly agricultural and had relatively little industrial plant to be destroyed. The heavy industry of northern France was utterly devastated but this region, although of vital economic importance, constituted only a small portion of the country and the rest was untouched. Thus, France did not suffer Belgium's horrendous unemployment rate, and most of her rail network was in working order.

In Belgium, almost nothing survived except, by great good fortune, most of the coal mines. The German authorities had planned to flood them, as in France, and started to do so in the last two weeks of the war. But at the request of Emile Francqui, the Spanish and Dutch ministers in Brussels protested sharply. The Germans hesitated and postponed the flooding. Probably more importantly, Hoover prevailed upon Wilson to request via Switzerland late in the Armistice negotiations that the Belgian mines be spared.[4] As a consequence, most of them sur-

2. Hymans and van den Heuvel to Clemenceau, 24 Apr. 1919, van den Heuvel Papers/47; Hymans and van den Heuvel to Clemenceau, 22 Apr. 1919, no. 478, van den Heuvel Papers/48.

3. Hymans and van den Heuvel to Clemenceau, 24 Apr. 1919, no. 909, Hymans Papers/150.

4. Van Vollenhoven, *Memoires*, pp. 356–60; Defrance to Pichon, 3 Nov. 1918, tel. 148, Vin 6N/128; Hoover to Wilson, 2 Nov. 1918, HI Hoover Papers/4; Francis William O'Brien, ed., *The Hoover-Wilson Wartime Correspondence*, p. 279.

vived, but in poor condition. In the best of times, production was insufficient for Belgian needs, but now, thanks to German overuse, lack of tools, a severe shortage of pit ponies, lack of maintenance, and acute malnutrition among the few remaining miners, production had dropped by 1918 to 40 percent of prewar levels and did not begin to revive until May 1919.[5] The port of Antwerp was also intact, but it too had lacked maintenance and had lost much equipment. Further, wartime silting in the Scheldt, together with several years without dredging, made the river unusuable by large oceangoing ships. The absence of Belgian exports hurt the port as well. It revived slowly and by late 1920 had not reached its prewar level of activity. The coastal ports and Ghent took longer to recover, as they had been severely damaged.[6]

The rest of the Belgian economy was, on the whole, in much worse condition. Some of the damage was done during the German retreat, when the German army removed everything that was removable, but more arose from a deliberate German policy in 1917 and 1918 to destroy Belgian economic potential for the future. Thus whole factories were dismantled and transported to Germany and entire industries that could compete with German counterparts were wiped out. As a consequence, the Belgian spinning industry was demolished. Because the Germans were very thorough, they generally removed all machines and spare parts and even iron and copper roofs. Often nothing remained of a factory but the four walls with shattered windows and the concrete blocks on which the machines had stood. Sometimes not even this much remained, as the Germans, after removing all of value, had frequently blown up the buildings. It was Germany's policy to requisition what it wanted and to destroy what it did not want.[7]

5. Fernand Baudhuin, *Histoire économique de la Belgique, 1914–1939,* 1:68, 94–95; Belgique, Ministère de l'Industrie, du Travail, et du Ravitaillement, *La Situation des industries en Belgique en février 1919 après les dévastations allemandes,* p. 9; Hoover to Wilson, 21 Oct. 1918, Hoover Papers/4; encl. (*Times,* 27 Dec. 1918) to Moncheur to Hymans, no. 10128/2326, 27 Dec. 1918, BMAE GB/1918/II.

6. Fernand Baudhuin, "La Restauration—Deux ans après l'armistice," p. 6; Admiralty memo, 23 Nov. 1918, G.T. 6365, CAB 24/70; de Ramaix to Hymans, 19 Apr. 1919, no. 2669/847, BMAE GB/1919/I; Moncheur to Hymans, 17 July 1919, no. 4567/1476, BMAE GB/1919/II.

7. Encls. (*Times,* 12, 27 Dec. 1918) to Moncheur to Hymans, 12, 27 Dec. 1918, nos. 9759/2229, 10128/2326, BMAE GB/1918/II; O'Brien, *Wartime Correspondence,* pp.

As a result, Belgian industrial statistics in 1918 and 1919 were horrifying. The coke, iron, and steel industries were particularly hard hit. In 1913, Belgium had sixty blast furnaces, of which nine survived the war intact, the remainder being damaged, often heavily, or destroyed. Coke production in 1918 was about one-seventh of the prewar level and steel production less than one-tenth. Lead production in 1918 was one-fifth of the 1912 level and zinc production only one-twentieth. Figures for 1919 tended to be worse as a consequence of German destruction during the retreat. In January 1919, the steel industry, quarrying operations, zinc works, and textile and paper factories were entirely halted and all remained so until May, although the steel industry's lack of cast iron prevented it from starting its revival until midsummer. The chemical industry was almost as severely afflicted, as were cement production and glassworks. The situation was compounded by German thoroughness in removing stocks of industrial goods, primary materials, semifinished products, and spare parts down to the smallest screw. Most of these industries managed to reach their prewar levels of production in 1925 but few before then.[8]

All in all, 85 percent of Belgium's industrial production was paralyzed after the Armistice and so remained long thereafter. In April 1919, while unemployment had finally dropped below the million mark, three-quarters of the work force, 900,000 out of 1,200,000, remained unemployed. Though other countries had suffered, few could present figures that stark. Under the circumstances, there was no way to restore the economic structure of the country without a massive infusion of construction materials, production machinery, and spare parts. To their dismay, Belgian leaders discovered that the British were far more willing to sell manufactured goods than machines that could be used for

276–77; Imperial War Cabinet, 19th meeting, 20 June 1918, CAB 23/43; Sûreté Militaire Belge note, 18 Apr. 1919, Deuxième Bureau report, 10 Sept. 1918, Vin 6N/127; Samuel G. Shartle, *Spa, Versailles, Munich*, pp. 35, 64.

8. Belgique, Ministère de l'Industrie, *La Situation*, pp. 9–12; Fernand Baudhuin, *L'Industrie wallonne avant et après la guerre*, pp. 30–36; Baudhuin, "La Restauration," pp. 3–4; Baudhuin, *Histoire économique*, 1:68–71, 94–95; Derek H. Aldcroft, *From Versailles to Wall Street, 1919–1929*, pp. 108–9. Most statistics compare economic data with those of 1913, which had been an unusually poor year for Belgian industry. Fernand Baudhuin, "La Balance économique de la Belgique avant et après la guerre," p. 9.

Belgian manufacture. Although enormously grateful for American relief efforts, Belgian businessmen and politicians of every persuasion pleaded for tools, machinery, and raw materials so that they could begin to help themselves and put the citizenry back to work.[9]

Industrial reconstruction was slowed not only by Allied reluctance to provide credits and goods to this end but also by the devastation of the transportation network. Worse, at the time of the Armistice, what remained of the Belgian rail system was under five different administrations, two French, one British, and two Belgian (military and civilian). At French request, the Belgians put an end to this administrative nightmare by taking full charge of their own battered railway network,[10] but repairing the damage was less easy. The Germans had torn up great quantities of trackage to obtain steel and, during the 1918 retreat, had completely destroyed all remaining railways to the Armistice lines, while locomotives hauled heavily laden cars eastward into Germany. About a third of the main lines were completely destroyed or heavily damaged, and well over half of the local lines lost their rails and rolling stock. In addition, 350 railway bridges were destroyed. Of almost 3,500 locomotives, 81 survived. Such rolling stock as still existed was in dangerously poor condition after more than four years without maintenance. The telephone system also sustained much damage and suffered a shortage of wire for reconstruction.[11]

Rebuilding the industrial and communications base of the country was severely hampered by an acute shortage of timber. Wood was desperately needed in the coal fields, to rebuild the railways, and in several industries, but the Germans had destroyed Belgian forests indiscriminately, both for military use and to prevent later Belgian economic revival. The entire Belgian portion of the vast forest of Hertogenwald had disappeared altogether and, not surprisingly, the Belgian government sought the German portion of the forest in Eupen as compensation. All in all, Belgian officials estimated that at least a ten-year supply

9. Francqui note, 4 Apr. 1919, Hymans Papers/150; Mantoux, *Les Délibérations*, 1:140; Jaspar to Theunis, 8 Apr. 1919, Jaspar Papers/199; Whitlock to House, 28 Nov. 1919, House Papers 20/24.

10. De Gaiffier to Hymans, 31 Dec. 1918, tel. 235, BMAE FR/1918/II.

11. De Ramaix to Hymans, 19 Apr. 1919, no. 2669/847, BMAE GB/1919/I; Bryce Lyon, *Henri Pirenne*, p. 277; Baudhuin, *Histoire économique*, 1:65–67.

of wood had vanished beyond recall and noted sadly that trees grow slowly.[12]

Agriculture was equally shattered but able to revive more quickly. Only about 5 percent of the farmland had been severely damaged. More serious was the lack of farm machinery and animals, fertilizer, and seed. When spring came in 1919, Belgian farmers had no plows, no horses to draw them, no fertilizer, and very little seed to plant. They did manage somehow in the end to plant 92 percent of the normal acreage, but crop yields were extremely low in 1919 and not much better in 1920 on soil that had not been fertilized for five years.[13] The losses of livestock were harder to replace. Intermittently during the war, the Germans engaged in large-scale seizure and removal of Belgian farm animals. As the 1918 retreat began, Germany attempted to transfer as much Belgian livestock and poultry as possible across the frontier. This policy continued before, during, and after the Armistice, in contravention of the Armistice terms, and Allied protests did not stop the removals.[14] Food stocks, sheep and cows, agricultural implements, seed, chickens, and pigs continued to cross the border ahead of the Allied armies. As a consequence, Belgium lost two-thirds of her horses, including about 40 percent of her farm horses, and over half her cattle, along with nearly half of her pigs. In addition, thirty-five thousand sheep and goats, along with 2 million fowl, had disappeared across the frontier. Aside from one special breed of Belgian horses, all of which had been taken to Germany, none of the livestock or poultry was identifiable. Hoover estimated that it would require several years to breed enough draft horses for Belgian commerce alone and to restore the dairy herds sufficiently to supply milk for Belgian children. In fact, the livestock herds reached their 1913 levels only after 1930.[15] Despite these emergency conditions, the Versailles treaty confined Belgium to an immediate levy on Germany of only 10 percent of her livestock losses, together with a right to submit later claims to the Reparation

12. Fallon to Hymans, 15 Oct. 1918, no. 15074/2778, BMAE PB/1918/II.

13. Baudhuin, *Histoire économique*, 1:96.

14. Shartle, *Spa*, pp. 23, 30, 54; W.C. 26, 3 Jan. 1917, CAB 23/1; Hoover to Wilson, 21 Oct. 1918, Hoover Papers/4.

15. Hoover to Wilson, 29 Apr. 1919, Hoover Papers/2; Baudhuin, *Histoire économique*, 1:171, 97; Lyon, *Pirenne*, p. 277.

Commission established by the treaty. Even the modest 10 percent restitution was achieved only at American insistence over British opposition. Although the Germans had retained two-thirds of their prewar herds, to say nothing of what they had acquired from both eastern and western neighbors, the British worried about the repercussions of restitutions on German economic life.[16]

Given the agricultural circumstances, food was both scarce and expensive in Belgium through the entire period of the peace conference. Milk and butter were unobtainable and Belgian babies were kept alive, as during the war, by American condensed milk provided by the Commission for the Relief of Belgium (CRB). In addition to milk, the CRB shipped massive amounts of bread, beans, rice, meat and fats, and clothing to Belgium and several other countries, thus saving many lives while disposing of the American agricultural surplus. To supplement this aid, the Belgian government ordered two million pairs of boots and shoes in the United States immediately after the Armistice, plus more than six million yards of khaki material, to replace the battered clogs and tattered clothing of the citizenry. Although these purchases and American aid prevented death from starvation or exposure, still food and clothing remained scarce and expensive, as did housing: between fifty and a hundred thousand dwellings had been destroyed. As Hoover pointed out, Belgium had imported 70 percent of her food before the war, unlike more agricultural areas such as Poland and Serbia, and, as she had not suffered the staggering loss of lives of those two countries, there were proportionately more mouths to feed.[17]

Prices rose correspondingly. Though most countries suffered inflation as a consequence of the war, that of Belgium was the most severe of western Europe. Almost immediately, the cost of living rose 300 percent. Then it rose again.[18] In March 1919, Whitlock remarked,

16. Tibbault to van den Heuvel, n.d., draft clause 6, Annex 4, n.d., Tibbault interview with Caziot, 2 May 1919, Tibbault interview with Strauss, 2 May 1919, BMAE DB/36; Nudant to Guerre, 12 Jan. 1919, tel. 281/N, Vin 6N/118.

17. Hoover to Wilson, 29 Apr. 1919, Hoover Papers/2; Hoover to Wilson, 21 Oct. 1918, Hoover Papers/4; Strauss to Bliss, 3 Jan. 1919, Hoover to Bliss, 17 May 1919, Hoover to Supreme Economic Council, 22 June 1919, HI Bliss Papers; Baudhuin, *Histoire économique*, 1:64; Lyon, *Pirenne*, p. 277; Mallinson, *Belgium*, p. 94; Moncheur to Hymans, 24 Dec. 1918, no. 10101/2322, BMAE GB/1919/II.

18. Hymans note, 11 May 1919, Hymans Papers/150; meeting of the Four, 29 Apr.

"Living conditions have been very hard here since our return. The Germans left nothing in the country, and prices have been higher than they would be at the North Pole if two National Political Conventions were suddenly to be held there."[19] He was not exaggerating. In January 1919 the price index in Brussels was 639 percent of the 1914 level. It dropped somewhat thereafter but as late as April 1920 it stood at 461 percent. The price of food averaged out at 470 percent of the 1914 level, whereas in France it stood at a mere 273 percent.[20]

The inflationary spiral was fueled in part by Belgium's parlous budgetary situation, which consisted primarily of deficits, both in 1919 and for half a dozen years thereafter. In view of the urgency of reconstituting the economic structure of the country and getting the population back to work, the Belgian government, living on Allied loans, paid for most of the reconstruction itself, putting its faith in reimbursement from the promised German reparations. Until the country was at least partially reconstructed and certainly through the peace conference, the Belgian government also paid out between $600,000 and $800,000 each month to keep the unemployed alive. In addition, the wartime German forced levies on the towns were repaid to them. In this period, tax receipts were minimal, despite unpopular new taxes, because so few people were working. In 1919, government expenditures were nearly seven times tax receipts and in 1920 five times receipts. On the average between 1919 and 1926, one-third of all government spending was at deficit, primarily for reconstruction. This situation contributed to the progressive decline of the Belgian franc, which only aggravated price inflation, and to severe financial crisis when the day of reckoning came in 1926.[21]

In the circumstances prevailing in 1919, the Belgian government had no option but to continue borrowing from the Allies, as it had done during the war. Virtually the entire war effort had been financed by

1919, 185.119/336, ACNP/325; Herman van der Wee and K. Tavernier, *La Banque Nationale de Belgique et l'histoire monétaire entre les deux guerres mondiales*, p. 75.

19. Whitlock to Albert Ruddock, 8 Mar. 1919, Whitlock Papers/39 (LC).

20. Baudhuin, *Histoire économique*, 1:97–98; Baudhuin, "La Restauration," pp. 4–5.

21. De Ramaix to Hymans, 19 Apr. 1919, no. 2669/847, BMAE GB/1919/I; Aldcroft, *From Versailles*, p. 148; Margerie to Pichon, 31 Mar. 1919, tel. 153, Vin 6N/128; Baudhuin, "La Balance," pp. 39–40; Baudhuin, *Histoire économique*, 1:105–6; Fernand Baudhuin, "La Richesse de la Belgique dix ans après la déclaration de guerre," pp. 6–7.

massive British, French, and American governmental loans. Because almost the entire country had been under occupation, the government in exile, and the reserves of the National Bank removed to Berlin in violation of the laws of warfare, Belgium had been the only country with no choice but to finance all its military and governmental costs by borrowing. In view of its special legal position in regard to the war, Belgium believed that Germany should assume these costs, as Wilson had promised. Also, after Germany had conquered Belgium, she had not only requisitioned all available food stocks but had further refused to feed the inhabitants; America had provided food, but Belgium had been obliged to borrow from the United States to cover her share in the cost of the CRB's operations. In addition, Germany had imposed forced war contributions upon the Belgian state and various cities to a total of 3 milliard (U.S. billion) Belgian francs ($537.5 million). After the Armistice the Belgian government continued to borrow to pay off the forced levies, finance the government, feed the people, cover other emergency expenses, and commence the costly economic reconstruction. Alas, these post-Armistice loans, initially obtained from Allied governments, could not be charged to Germany's account, although they arose from German actions. In fact, the large Allied and American post-Armistice loans were technically conditional upon repayment out of the first monies received by Belgium from Germany, even though these early reparation payments were obviously needed for reconstruction.[22]

There was one additional category of financial cost that the Belgian government hoped and expected the German government would be required to assume, particularly as Belgium at first appeared to have American support. The wartime occupiers had forced the citizenry to

22. Mantoux, *Les Délibérations*, 1:139–40; Hymans to House, 24 May 1919, Hymans Papers/150; Hymans, *Mémoires*, 1:225; Baudhuin, "La Richesse," pp. 8–10; Baudhuin, *Histoire économique*, 1:106; Baudhuin, "La Balance," pp. 45–48; Delacroix note, 24 Dec. 1918, BMAE B–366/I; Margerie to Pichon, 31 Mar. 1919, tel. 153, Defrance to Pichon, 24 Dec. 1918, tel. 270, Vin 6N/128; de Ramaix to Hymans, 19 Apr. 1919, no. 2669/847, BMAE GB/1919/I. The Brussels Bourse was not reopened for some time after the Armistice out of fear that the franc would plunge alarmingly. Thus, the Belgian franc was not listed on international exchanges until late January 1919, when its value was 5.66 to the dollar. A British or French milliard is the equivalent of a German or American billion. Milliard is a more exact term, however, because the word "billion" has different meanings in Britain and America.

exchange their Belgian currency for German money at the disadvantageous rate of 1.25 Belgian francs for 1 paper mark. In the course of the war the paper mark fell to half its prewar value on free markets. In the last days of the war, the Cooreman cabinet, thinking that the people should not be made to suffer further deprivation and perhaps fearing dangerous unrest if any additional burdens were imposed in a politically volatile climate, made plans to redeem the marks at the rate at which the people had been forced to buy them. Neither the government in exile nor the National Bank of Belgium had any reliable figures on the number of marks in circulation and both assumed that the prewar state of affairs, whereby holders of paper marks were entitled to automatic reimbursement in gold marks from the Reichsbank, would continue to prevail. Both thought it urgent to end circulation of the marks and to restore the national currency within Belgium. Thus the Bank readily cooperated and the Cooreman cabinet promulgated the necessary decrees. Unfortunately, these decrees were made public before the Armistice, when the Belgian government controlled no more than a quarter of the country and could not close its frontiers. Thus marks flooded into Belgium from Germany, Luxemburg, and especially Holland during and immediately after the liberation. As a consequence, the new Delacroix cabinet inherited the entire complicated mark redemption scheme and the National Bank inherited over 6 milliard increasingly valueless paper marks, having paid out over 7.5 milliard Belgian francs (about $1,340 million) for them. The Bank thought that conversion into gold marks would be a mere formality but discovered otherwise when Germany flatly refused a Belgian government request to convert them. Thus 6 milliard dirty, tattered German paper marks continued to sit in the coffers of the Belgian National Bank and became a continuing problem. The French also had 2 milliard German marks to redeem, chiefly in Alsace-Lorraine, but had no American support because their mark redemption operation involved territory to be annexed from Germany. Guided by the Belgian experience, France did not hasten to withdraw the marks. Initially, redemption was promised at a generous rate but, as the paper mark fell, the French government postponed the operation and reconsidered the exchange rate, thus adding to Alsace-Lorraine's grievances. Meanwhile, the Belgian government had taken well-intentioned but overly precipitous action, leaving it with marks whose value declined almost daily. Belgium had made several fruitless efforts during periodic Armistice renegotiations to impose conversion into gold upon Germany. Thus, reimbursement of the marks became an important Belgian goal at the peace conference, although not one that was achieved.[23]

Aside from mark conversion and post-Armistice loans, neither of which was ultimately chargeable to Germany, it is difficult to obtain an accurate total for allowable Belgian claims. Estimates of material loss varied from 7 or 8 percent of the national assets to over 60 percent. Like most other countries, the Belgian government probably inflated the totals somewhat.[24] How much the claims were exaggerated is difficult to say, as the figures were estimates, subject to worldwide postwar price inflation and the erratic course of the Belgian franc, for work to be carried out over a number of years. The formal Belgian claim submitted in early 1921 for material damages (excluding restitutions and war costs) was $2.22 milliard plus $0.5 milliard for pensions and various allocations. The Belgian war debt amounted to about $1.5 milliard. Both John Maynard Keynes and the Belgian authority, Fernand Baudhuin, charged that the Belgian claims were considerably exaggerated; on the other hand, the very precise Belgian reparation expert, Gaston Furst, writing in retirement in 1927, estimated the Belgian material restoration costs (including a modest sum for pensions) to have been $2.57 milliard, which would indicate only slight exaggeration and very accurate original estimates.[25]

23. Delacroix note, 10 Jan. 1919, DB to BMAE, 25 Jan. 1919, tel. 15, DB to Delacroix, 1 Feb. 1919, tel. 56, Hymans note, 7 May 1919, BMAE B–366/I; Lasteyrie to Guerre, 27 Nov. 1918, no. 37/N, Vin 6N/118; Derby to Curzon, 25 Nov. 1919, Curzon Papers F112/196; van der Wee and Tavernier, *La Banque Nationale*, pp. 37–42. This last work contains a judicious account of the entire marks problem upon the basis of extensive research at the Belgian National Bank and the Foreign Ministry archives.

24. Baudhuin, *Histoire économique*, 1:73–76. John Maynard Keynes was probably correct when he said in *The Economic Consequences of the Peace* (p. 123) that Belgian claims were exaggerated. Baudhuin agrees (*Histoire économique*, 1:74). However, Keynes displays a mixture of ignorance and contempt when he declares that the land ("Belgium's chief wealth") was intact and that industrial reconstruction would not amount to much (p. 122) and when he attributes possession of paper marks by Belgian citizens to an "instinct of individual self-preservation unusually well developed" and to a desire for profit (pp. 122–23). Keynes's estimates are consistently lower than anybody else's.

25. Baudhuin, *Histoire économique*, 1:73–76; Keynes, *Economic Consequences*, pp. 123–

In any event, there was no way to know the exact cost in 1919, but there was no doubt about the extent of the damage. The devastation had already been documented beyond dispute through the work of the CRB, surveys by the United States Army Corps of Engineers, and inspection tours both by the American Chamber of Commerce and British journalists, not to mention the Belgian government's survey in progress. It was the original intent of the American government to verify damages in all Allied countries before the peace treaty was completed, and a team was sent into Belgium before the peace conference began. In February 1919 this effort was abandoned, but not before Belgium had been systematically surveyed. As a consequence, it remained at the time of the peace conference the only country whose damages had been thoroughly and independently documented.[26] Given this fact, most Belgians took it for granted that the substantial Belgian reparation claims would be fulfilled without question. After all, Wilson's Fourteen Points, the official basis of the Armistice, specified that Belgium was to be "restored." Before the peace conference, Wilson had endorsed German assumption of Belgian war costs and, at the conference, the American delegation showed open sympathy for Belgium's plight, endorsed full restitution as a principle, and agreed that Belgium required some priority of payment to facilitate economic reconstruction.[27] The French could not oppose Belgian claims without undercutting their own, and throughout the war, British politicians had told cheering crowds that Belgium would be recompensed to the last far-

25; Gaston A. Furst, *De Versailles aux experts*, pp. 14–15, 130, 321. Furst was using the formal Belgian claims to the Reparation Commission in early 1921 and Reparation Commission data. His figures are based on the exchange rate of the Belgian franc in the spring of 1921 when it had sunk to about 13 to the dollar. Although Belgian estimates from December 1918 on in Belgian francs did not vary appreciably from the final figures submitted in 1921, their dollar value was higher because the franc was worth more earlier on. Delacroix figures, 24 Dec. 1918, BMAE B–366/I.

26. ACNP to Davis, 13 Feb. 1919, tel. 111, Wilson Papers 5B/16; D. H. Miller, *Diary*, 1:10–11; *Times*, 27 Dec. 1918, p. 4; Arthur Walworth, *America's Moment*, p. 85; Whitlock to Hymans, 20 Jan. 1919, DB to BMAE, 29 Jan. 1919, tel. 23, van den Ven to Hymans, 1 Mar. 1919, BMAE B–366/I.

27. Jusserand to FMAE, n.d. [3 or 4 Nov. 1918], tel. 1586, FMAE A/90; Inquiry/971; Polk to Lansing, 6 Dec. 1918, tel. 6, Wilson Papers 5B/1; Wilson to Albert, 20 Feb. 1919, Wilson Papers 5B/17.

thing.[28] Under the circumstances, Belgian optimism, both within the country and within the delegation at Paris, was high.

This optimism was, however, naive. Despite Wilson's opposition to indemnities, both the British and the French governments were determined to recover a substantial portion of their war costs from Germany one way or another and both were soon aware that the amount their electorates expected to receive far exceeded what Germany could pay. Under the circumstances, the easiest way to gain more for themselves was at the expense of the only small state with large reparation claims on Germany. Although the French did not dare to assault the Belgian claims openly, for fear of undercutting their own, the British, frankly worried about the effect of a Belgian revival upon the shaky British economy, had no such scruples. They raised so many difficulties that intense American intervention, particularly from House, was required to preserve Belgian rights at all. House, who had a high regard for his own diplomatic skills, remarked in May 1919 to Whitlock, "From the beginning of the Conference I have made Belgium and her desires my especial care . . . and have urged liberal treatment for Belgium at every turn of the negotiations."[29] In regard to reparations, House's statement was entirely accurate, and Belgium would not have fared well without him. Unlike the European great powers, the United States did not have any appreciable claims on Germany, and so House could view the matter disinterestedly. He made great efforts on Belgium's behalf and emerged as the hero of the Belgian view on reparations. As the entire Belgian nation deemed full reparation its unquestioned right and was much dissatisfied with what Belgium actually obtained, Belgian gratitude to House was not as great as it should have been. Without his efforts, Belgium would probably have emerged nearly empty-handed.

House's assistance was particularly necessary to achieve Belgium's two primary reparations claims, which were generally known as privilege and priority. Privilege meant relieving Belgium of her war costs,

28. Villiers to Curzon, 7 Aug. 1920 (Annual Report, 1919) and minutes, F.O. 371/3651.
29. House to Whitlock, 14 May 1919, House Papers 20/24. Hoover also strongly supported Belgian reparation claims but had less influence on the decision-making process. Francis William O'Brien, *Two Peacemakers in Paris*, p. 65.

including government expenses and the cost of provisioning the country, whereas priority meant some arrangement whereby Belgium would receive the first German reparation payments to facilitate economic reconstruction of the only formally constituted country that Germany had entirely ravaged. Both were eventually achieved despite stiff British opposition.

THE STRUGGLE FOR PRIVILEGE AND PRIORITY

At the peace conference, the whole question of reparation for damage done to civilians, as defined under the pre-Armistice agreement sent to Germany on 6 November 1918, was initially referred to the conference's Commission on Reparation of Damages. This body was charged with determining what sum the Central Powers were liable for, how much of it they could actually pay, and the modalities of payment. As the financial experts comprising the commission and their technical assistants tackled these issues, they soon became embroiled in heated debate about such questions as whether war costs, not only of Belgium but of other countries as well, should be charged to Germany's account; whether pensions to the wounded and to war widows should be considered civilian damages, as the British insisted; whether there should be a time limit for payment and a fixed sum included in the treaty; if so, how long and large they should be, as opinions of what Germany could actually pay and how long she would pay varied widely; and finally, the fascinating game of apportionment or trying to decide what percentage of the eventual figure should go to each reparations-hungry victor. Disagreement was intense between delegations and sometimes within them.[30] Though all these questions were of great technical complexity, they were also fraught with enormous political significance, as they would determine how much money each country could expect to receive. Although the experts knew that German resources were finite,

---

30. In the British delegation, Keynes and Lord Cunliffe resigned the same day, the one complaining that the burden on Germany was much too heavy, the other that it was much too light. Frances Lloyd-George, *The Years That Are Past*, p. 156.

no politician at the mercy of parliamentary majorities representing a population expecting to be paid in full wanted to acknowledge that fact. Given the political implications of the technical questions, the peace conference Commission on Reparation was unable to make many decisions of much consequence, and almost all major questions on reparation were referred to the Big Four, who settled them or found ways to postpone them or produced formulas sufficiently confusing to mislead electorates into wishful thinking. On the whole, the Big Four preferred not to face reparation questions it could postpone, as the effect on present relations with allies and future national budgets was profound. Thus certain key issues, including how much Germany should pay and how the payments should be apportioned among the victors, were not settled by the Versailles treaty. Though willing to do battle for their own shares of the spoils, the Big Four were particularly reluctant to face the claims on Germany of smaller states, of which Belgium's was much the largest.[31]

In the Commission on Reparation, the first struggle was over war costs. Many countries, including Britain, had hoped to add their war costs to Germany's account, but Wilson's opposition was so intense that all countries except Belgium dropped these claims by mid-March. The Belgians held out, however, pointing to the Fourteen Points and the Declaration of Sainte-Adresse. The American experts acknowledged that Belgium was a special case, in view of the illegality of the German invasion, and that Wilson was committed to German payment of Belgian war costs, although Wilson himself showed increasing signs as the peace conference progressed of having forgotten his own commitment. The tenacious Belgian effort was further based upon the evident impossibility of paying debts totaling the entirety of her government's expenditures during four and a half wartime years in which there had been no revenues at all; upon the strength of her particular legal claim; upon the impossibility of deriving large sums from pensions, because the country had been engulfed before it could raise a large army; and upon the obvious sympathy of the American delegation. The Belgian

---

31. The most convenient compendium on the reparation question at the Paris Peace Conference is Philip Mason Burnett, *Reparation at the Paris Peace Conference from the Standpoint of the American Delegation.*

diplomatists felt confident that the Americans were prepared to make an exception to their general rule for Belgium. Thus, in the Commission on Reparation, van den Heuvel held out for war costs to Belgium and to Belgium alone.[32]

Although the battle for privilege on war costs was the more bitter of the two primary reparations struggles Belgium had to fight, that for priority was the more protracted, particularly because neither Lloyd George nor Clemenceau cared to contemplate a long wait for reparations while Belgium's needs were met. The Belgians soon realized that their hopes rested with the American delegation, which could afford to be more altruistic, as its own reparation claims were minimal. Accordingly, in mid-February the Belgian leadership made a major effort to obtain Wilson's support. King Albert wrote him a long, carefully drafted letter in English, stressing Belgium's plight and the world's conscience and asking for special consideration in regard to both reconstruction aid and reparations. Delacroix brought it in person when he came to Paris to see Wilson and House on 14 February just before Wilson's departure for the United States. The American president was sympathetic but noncommittal.[33] However, House's interest was aroused and, in Wilson's absence, he took action. When Hymans came on 26 February to plead for preferential consideration, House promised to take the matter up with the British and the French. He asked for an estimate of what Belgium required for urgent needs, requesting that Hymans otherwise leave the matter entirely to him.[34] While Hymans

32. Thomas A. Bailey, *Woodrow Wilson and the Lost Peace*, p. 239; Belgian memo to great powers, 27 Mar. 1919, BMAE DB/7/III; Lansing Desk Diary, 16 Feb. 1919, Lansing Papers; Hymans and van den Heuvel to Clemenceau, 18 Apr. 1919, 184.611/233, ACNP/260; Lansing to Wilson, 15 Feb. 1919, Wilson 5B/16; D. H. Miller, *Diary*, 3:102–3, 5:127–28, 199–201; W.C. 536, 25 Feb. 1919, CAB 23/9; minutes, 7th, 8th meetings, RC, 15, 17 Feb. 1919, van den Heuvel Papers/47.

33. Albert to Wilson, n.d. [13 Feb.? 1919], van den Heuvel note, 14 Feb. 1919, Hymans Papers/150. The correspondence printed in O'Brien, *Two Peacemakers*, pp. 65–66, 70–71, implies that Wilson had no time to see Delacroix, who was sent to Lansing instead. Though Delacroix did see Lansing, he also saw Wilson before the president sailed to America. Lansing Desk Diary, 16 Feb. 1919, Lansing Papers; Hymans to de Cartier, 15 Feb. 1919, tel. 5, BMAE B–366/I; Wilson to Albert, 20 Feb. 1919, Wilson Papers 5B/17.

34. Hymans note, 27 Feb. 1919, BMAE B–366/I; Hymans, *Mémoires*, 1:397; House Diary, 26 Feb. 1919, 15:71, House Papers.

was consulting Brussels about how much to request, House returned
the next day and announced that he had already acted on his own, had
seen Balfour, and had gained his agreement. He would see Klotz on the
morrow to say that he and Balfour agreed that Belgium should have a
priority of $500 million. House told Hymans firmly not to argue about
the amount: the offer was $500 million or nothing. The Belgians were
delighted and Klotz was willing, but Lloyd George was not. In the
Commission on Reparation the British representatives refused to discuss priority at all, and Hymans heard repeated rumors that Lloyd
George was saying that Belgium did not need anything, as she had
enriched herself during the war.[35]

This sort of rumor, coupled with the inaccessibility of Lloyd George,
the difficulty of gaining a hearing before the Four, and the lack of action
on Belgian priority, indicating that House's campaign had stalled, led
Hymans to seize the moment when he was suddenly called before the
Four for discussion of the Belgo-German frontier on 31 March to raise
the matter of reparations. Lloyd George immediately complained that
this topic was not in the order of the day and announced bluntly that he
had other things to do. Hymans pointed out that his previous efforts to
see the British prime minister had been unavailing and countered that
this was his first chance since the start of the conference to speak to
Lloyd George.[36]

In the course of a session lasting three and a half hours, there were
further sharp exchanges between an irritable Lloyd George and a nervous Hymans. At one point, when Lloyd George's tone particularly
annoyed him, Hymans announced flatly that he spoke in the name of a
sovereign state and declared that this was the first plenipotentiary of
Belgium addressing the first plenipotentiary of Great Britain. He added
that he would maintain the attitude of equal to equal throughout and
demanded Belgian participation in Big Four discussions when questions

35. Hymans note, 27 Feb. 1919, BMAE B–366/I; Hymans, *Mémoires*, 1:397–98, 420;
W.C. 536, 25 Feb. 1919, CAB 23/9; Orts to Hymans, 1 Mar. 1919, Hymans Papers/150;
House Diary, 28 Feb., 11, 18 Mar. 1919, 15:73, 91–92, 102–3, House Papers; House to
Wilson, 1, 7 Mar. 1919, tels. 13, 2, House Papers 49/12.

36. Hymans note, 26 Mar. 1919, BMAE B–366/I; Mantoux, *Les Délibérations*, 1:95;
Hymans, *Mémoires*, 1:433–39; van den Heuvel memo, 31 Mar. 1919, van den Heuvel
Papers/46. Lloyd George had been in London at the time of Hymans's appearance before
the Council of Ten on 11 February.

of interest to Belgium, especially reparations and the Rhineland, were under consideration.[37] Although Wilson and Orlando were generally sympathetic and Clemenceau devoted his efforts to calming tempers, the demand for equality on specific issues was not well received, particularly by Lloyd George. The tension increased when Hymans raised the question of priority and spoke of the suffering of Belgium. Lloyd George announced that Hymans's account of Belgian suffering and devastation was greatly exaggerated and burst forth with the statement that nobody considered the wartime suffering of Britain. Hymans angered him further by making a pointed comparison of the condition of the two countries and by declaring that he could not accept the doubt Lloyd George had cast upon his word. When a little later he was so ill-advised as to charge Lloyd George with lack of diplomatic support to Belgium during the peace conference, Lloyd George erupted with a recitation of the number of British and Australian soldiers buried in Flanders and told Hymans that his argument was "discreditable." Hymans expressed gratitude for the wartime aid but pointed out that he was talking about the peace conference, adding that Belgium had made some wartime efforts, too. Lloyd George interrupted with a disdainful gesture that enraged Hymans, who declared that Belgium had done everything possible and had suffered four years of occupation. If his words were "discreditable," those of Lloyd George were also. Despite Clemenceau's efforts, the meeting continued in this vein, and at the end, Hymans had virtually to force Lloyd George to the barest gesture of a handshake.[38]

After this confrontation, Hymans returned to the Hôtel Lotti to find a telegram announcing King Albert's impending visit to Paris. Such a visit had been under separate and simultaneous consideration in Paris and Brussels for several days, as Belgian concern had mounted over the unsatisfactory situation in general and the lack of progress on the reparations question in particular. House's proposal had not taken concrete

37. Mantoux, *Les Délibérations*, 1:96–97; Hymans, *Mémoires*, 1:433–39; van den Heuvel memo, 31 Mar. 1919, van den Heuvel Papers/46; Hymans memo, 1 Apr. 1919, BMAE Ind/1919/I.

38. Mantoux, *Les Délibérations*, 1:96–97; Hymans, *Mémoires*, 1:433–39; van den Heuvel memo, 31 Mar. 1919, van den Heuvel Papers/46; Hymans memo, 1 Apr. 1919, BMAE Ind/1919/I; Villiers to Curzon, 10 Apr. 1919, F.O. 800/152.

shape and a series of Belgian demarches to gain a larger priority of $2 milliard had met with no response from anybody. As Lloyd George was the chief obstacle and access to him was so difficult, Hymans had requested royal intervention even before his stormy session with the Four. Nobody could refuse to see the king of the Belgians and so, after a briefing from Hymans, Albert made the rounds alone, reporting in detail afterwards to his foreign minister.[39]

The visits to Clemenceau and Poincaré on 2 April did not proceed pleasantly. Poincaré was hostile to Belgian priority, and Clemenceau complained at length about Hymans, adding sharply, "Remember, Your Majesty, that there has been only one great King in the past five hundred years!"[40] The Americans and British were more tactful. Wilson and House were particularly friendly and promised full support to Belgian priority. Lloyd George and Balfour stressed their sympathy but were vague about concrete issues. It was Lloyd George who suggested and Balfour who arranged that Albert meet with the Four. The Belgian contingent decided the invitation should be accepted provided that the meeting was a participation, not an audition, and provided that Hymans attended. These terms were readily agreed upon, although Balfour informed Lloyd George, "It is understood that M. Hymans, like other good children, shall be *seen* and not *heard*."[41]

Albert's two-hour meeting with the Four on 4 April was informal, without secretary or official *procès-verbal*. According to extant accounts, Lloyd George was pleasant and attentive throughout, although determined to avoid any decisions on reparations priority. Albert started with this question, stressing the acute economic and financial plight of his country. He provided an array of statistics, pointing out that tracing stolen machinery was an impossibly slow process and that using German labor to reconstruct the country was out of the question with

39. Hymans, *Mémoires*, 1:428–32, 439–44; Delacroix to Hymans, 21 Mar. 1919, tel. 130, Hymans Papers/150; Hymans to House, 24 Mar. 1919, Maskens to Hymans, 27 Mar. 1919, no. 2128, BMAE DB/7/I; Villiers to Curzon, 31 Mar. 1919, tel. 67, Curzon to G. Grahame, 29 Mar. 1919, no. 585, F.O. 371/3645; Tardieu, *Truth*, pp. 248–49.

40. Hymans, *Mémoires*, 1:442, 450, 2:826.

41. Hymans, *Mémoires*, 1:441–42; House Diary, 3 Apr. 1919, 15:131–32, House Papers; I.C. 170D, 3 Apr. 1919, CAB 29/37; Mantoux, *Les Délibérations*, 1:126, 131; Balfour to Lloyd George, 3 Apr. 1919, Lloyd George Papers F/3/H/20.

so many Belgians unemployed. Lloyd George, who seemed ignorant of Belgium's devastation, took copious notes and appeared to be impressed. However, House, who sat in for the ailing Wilson, remarked in his diary, "I tried to get Lloyd George down to the matter of priority but it was impossible. That was too near accomplishment. I can easily see how the time has been wasted in the Council of Four. They did not come to grips with the King about anything. It was all talk and a promise to look into matters later."[42]

Noting the ambiguity, Albert immediately sent Lloyd George a letter in English, together with a note on Belgium's economic condition prepared by Emile Francqui, who was not only a leading Belgian financier but also chairman of the Belgian committee that coordinated the CRB's efforts.[43] But Francqui's graphic statistics had no effect on Lloyd George. The next day he was again intransigent and on 7 April in a meeting of the Four, he argued against any special treatment for Belgium, cleverly trying to sow dissension by suggesting that Belgian priority would be unfair to France. House was disgusted at British and, to a lesser degree, French indifference to Belgium's economic condition. He quietly instructed the American experts to hold firm and, if Britain and France would not accept Belgian priority, to file a minority report that he would provide to the Belgians and to the press.[44]

The Belgian delegation knew nothing of this, nor of the progress of reparations negotiations, for they were neither consulted nor informed until they received in mid-April a list of categories of damages approved by the Four. Hymans and van den Heuvel immediately protested that this list applicable to all states did not cover Belgium's special needs and particularly insisted upon war costs, wartime food costs, the expenses of the government in exile, and the price of redeeming the marks. When this brought no immediate response, Hy-

---

42. House Diary, 4 Apr. 1919, 15:134, House Papers; I.C. 170F, 4 Apr. 1919, CAB 29/37; Hymans, *Mémoires*, 1:444–47; Mantoux, *Les Délibérations*, 1:139–42; van den Heuvel notes, 4 Apr. 1919, van den Heuvel Papers/46.

43. Albert to Lloyd George, 4 Apr. 1919, Lloyd George Papers F/49/4/1; Francqui note, 4 Apr. 1919, Hymans Papers/150.

44. I.C. 170I, 5 Apr. 1919, I.C. 170K, 7 Apr. 1919, CAB 29/37; House Diary, 5 Apr. 1919, 15:138, House Papers.

mans saw Tardieu, who was studiously vague about the content of the proposed financial clauses. Finally on 23 April, Louis Loucheur, the French reparation expert, called together representatives of Belgium, Serbia, Portugal, and Brazil to tell them what the reparation clauses contained. There was no mention of art treasures or manuscripts or state documents. More importantly, the proposed clauses did not provide for Belgian priority or privilege, nor for redemption of the marks, nor for completing payments within ten years, as Belgium had particularly requested.[45]

The Belgians erupted in protest. Hymans saw Loucheur again and visited the British delegation. Albert summoned Whitlock, and two letters were promptly dispatched to Clemenceau, with copies to the British and American delegations, reiterating Belgium's claims in full. Meanwhile, the Three (in the absence of Italy) considered the situation twice on 25 and 28 April, noting that all the smaller states were protesting but that Belgium deserved separate consideration. After steadfastly refusing for months to distinguish Belgium from the other small states, they finally decided to do so on this one issue, and on 28 April they agreed that they must hear the Belgian claims. This decision owed something to the merits of the case, something to House, and something to the arrival of Delacroix in Paris.[46]

While the struggle over priority and related matters was thus approaching a climax, the British and French had been successfully evading the question of privilege. Van den Heuvel had made the Belgian stand clear in the Commission on Reparation, arguing that Belgium alone should be indemnified for war costs, and had received American support. But nothing could be settled until the Big Three ruled, which they seemed unwilling to do. Finally, Belgium's diplomatic activity over priority and the paper marks, together with strong pressure from the

45. Hymans and van den Heuvel to Clemenceau, 18 Apr. 1919, Hymans note, 23 Apr. 1919, BMAE DB/7/I; Hymans note, 23 Apr. 1919, Hymans Papers/150.

46. Hymans note, 23 Apr. 1919, Hymans Papers/150; Whitlock to ACNP, 23 Apr. 1919, tel. 15, 855.50/10, ACNP/449; Cecil to Balfour, 26 Apr. 1919, F.O. 608/217; Hymans and van den Heuvel to Clemenceau, 24 Apr. 1919, no. 5685, BMAE FR/1919; Hymans and van den Heuvel to Clemenceau, 24 Apr. 1919, van den Heuvel Papers/47; Lamont to Hymans, 25 Apr. 1919, 185.119/325, ACNP/325; I.C. 176D, 177A, 25, 28 Apr. 1919, CAB 29/37; Hymans, *Mémoires*, 1:403–4; House Diary, 1 May 1919, 16:182–83, House Papers.

American experts and the inescapable fact that Belgium's legal case for war costs was sufficiently strong to create an awkward problem for two reparations-hungry powers and another hostile to indemnities, led to the reluctant decision by the Three on 28 April to face up to all the Belgian claims on the following day.[47]

On 29 April, the three Belgian plenipotentiaries arrived in united defiance, bearing a letter drafted in conjunction with Delacroix that demanded reimbursement of the marks and reiterated the 24 April requests for priority, privilege, exemption from the requirement to repay post-Armistice loans at once from the first German receipts, a ten-year payment period for Belgium's share of German reparations, and replacement of literary and artistic losses. This letter further threatened, if their demands were not met, to lay the matter before the Belgian Parliament.[48] To the Three, they repeated the request for priority of payment at excessive length and finally gained Lloyd George's consent. When they raised the matter of privilege, however, they encountered his intense opposition, Clemenceau's opinion that "it would have been preferable if the Belgian point of view had been expressed not in the form of a protest but in the form of an appeal," and Wilson's reluctance to make an exception for one state. Vandervelde emphatically defended the Belgian claim, pointing out that even Bethmann-Hollweg had admitted that Germany should compensate Belgium. In the course of a heated and turbulent session, the Three conceded wartime food costs but nothing else. In the face of Lloyd George's evident anger, Hymans declared that his government might withdraw the delegation and refuse to accept the treaty. Wilson begged the Belgians not to leave but, forgetting or pretending to forget previous promises, said he could not make an exception for Belgian war costs. With shaking hands, Hymans said that the matter must be taken to the Belgian Parliament. Lloyd George immediately remarked that, if the Belgians did not plan to attend the forthcoming plenary session to present the treaty to Germany, all claims on behalf of Belgium would be dropped from the treaty and she would be left to settle with Germany however she could.

47. Lloyd George, *Memoirs,* 1:324; RC meetings, 15, 17 Feb. 1919, van den Heuvel Papers/47; Lamont to Wilson, 25 Apr. 1919, McCormick to Wilson, 24 Apr. 1919, Wilson Papers 5B/31; I.C. 177A, 28 Apr. 1919, CAB 29/37.
48. Belgian note, 29 Apr. 1919, van den Heuvel Papers/48.

Clemenceau joined in the pressure but the Belgians did not flinch and the meeting broke up into confused groups.[49]

The Belgian threat was superbly timed. Italy had just left the conference and Japan was threatening to do so. The additional defection of Belgium, a state that had figured so prominently in Allied propaganda and wartime promises, might well have tipped the balance of an already uncertain public opinion. As the Allied leaders faced this fact, they agreed to entertain Belgian proposals for an arrangement whereby Germany would reimburse the Allied governments for Belgian pre-Armistice debts contracted as a consequence of the violation of the 1839 treaties, thus effectively relieving Belgium of war costs. With House's assistance, an arrangement to this end was quickly achieved.[50]

Even the official minutes of the 29 April meeting reveal acute tension, despite their staid tone, and Hymans reported to Delacroix that "the discussion was painful."[51] In addition, there exists an unofficial satiric account prepared by Keynes, who was present as a Treasury expert, and endorsed by Hankey, the official secretary. Although perhaps exaggerated on some points and probably containing a few admixtures of material from other meetings, the Keynes account sheds a good deal of light on both the Big Three and the Belgian delegation:

Council of Three
29th April 1919

(*What actually happened*)
The question before the Council was whether Belgium should have priority in Indemnity payments and should receive from Germany the 'costs of the war'.

Three Belgian Delegates addressed the Council, each in a set speech.

M. Hymans read a number of letters to which nobody paid

---

49. Hymans, *Mémoires*, 1:404–7; I.C. 177D, 29 Apr. 1919, CAB 29/37; Louis Loucheur, *Carnets secrets, 1918–1932*, p. 76; Hymans to Delacroix, 29 Apr. 1919, BMAE B–366–I.

50. I.C. 177D, 29 Apr. 1919, CAB 29/37; Hymans, *Mémoires*, 1:406; House Diary, 1 May 1919, 16:182–83, House Papers; Hymans to Delacroix, 29 Apr. 1919, BMAE B–366/I.

51. Hymans to Delacroix, 29 Apr. 1919, BMAE B–366/I.

attention. M. Clemenceau slept. President Wilson read the paper. Mr. Lloyd George kept up a running fire of comments, to the effect that M. Hymans was in his best form, was a poseur of the old type, and was attempting blackmail.

M. Van den Heuvel delivered his oration in a falsetto voice which attracted the attention of the British Prime Minister, who compared it to a number of other voices, human and animal, that he remembered to have heard—the comparison being in each case to the disadvantage of M. Van den Heuvel. Mr. Lloyd George remarked that M. Van den Heuvel was obviously enjoying himself immensely. M. Clemenceau slept. President Wilson read the paper.

M. Vandervelde very nearly lost the chance of speaking at all as M. Clemenceau at this stage of the proceedings woke up and was inclined to interrupt. M. Vandervelde insisted however on delivering the speech which he had prepared. M. Clemenceau went to sleep again. President Wilson read the paper. Mr. Lloyd George remarked that this fellow was really very good: but that he talked a good deal more about Belgium's right than about Belgium's fight. The Belgians, in point of fact, never fought at all. They refused to fight. And now they were trying to bully. Mr. Lloyd George would not endure being bullied. How many dead had Belgium in comparison with Australia?

The Belgian Delegates having delivered their speeches, M. Clemenceau was woken up. President Wilson put down his paper, and remembering the Fourteen Points reminded the Assembly that his conscience could not allow Belgium to claim the costs of the war.

The Belgian Delegates thereupon left the room with the subordinate representatives of the Allies, to see if there was really anything doing in the way of business.

The interval was fortunately filled up by the arrival of a telegram giving the text of Signor Orlando's speech in Rome. This speech was translated to the Council. President Wilson made two comments, one on a passage referring to the efforts made by Orlando to arrive at an arrangement with President Wilson. The President's comment was 'You bet he did'. His second remark, referring to one of the more rhetorical passages in Signor Orlando's speech was brief and to the point. (Textually 'Rats'.)

At this stage the Belgian Delegates returned, but were unable to obtain a hearing on account of the exclusive attention devoted to the news from Rome. They consequently withdrew, and repudiated all the agreements which had been informally reached in discussion in the interval.

Signor Orlando's speech having been translated, M. Clemenceau enquired whether the Belgians had run away. He said he would kill M. Hymans for his bad manners and his bad diplomacy, and exhorted everybody else to do the same.

M. Hymans returned and made a further speech to the effect that Belgium adhered to her demands. M. Clemenceau muttered 'kill him'. Mr. Lloyd George winked to himself. President Wilson read the paper.

The meeting now broke up into two parts; one part, including the Belgians and the subordinate representatives of the Allies, attempted to come to terms. The other part, including the Council of Three, listened to the anecdotes which Mr. Lloyd George had to relate about the behaviour of Belgian troops at Nieuport in 1917.

It was then discovered that the French Delegates were attempting to fix up with the Belgians an arrangement that would be considerably to the advantage of the French. Mr. Lloyd George was warned and immediately protested. This woke up everybody. There was a general mêlée in the middle of the room, where explanations and protests, avowals and disavowals, were tossed about in noisy confusion. Nothing of what was said could be clearly distinguished above the storm except the cries of M. Clemenceau who wailed continuously, 'Kill them, kill them'. Suddenly Mr. Lloyd George emerged from the tumult and flounced out of the room in a passion, winking to himself.

The upshot of it all was that M. Klotz realised that he had been detected and, with instinctive and hereditary compliancy, hoped Mr. Lloyd George was not really very angry. President Wilson once more took up the paper. M. Clemenceau composed himself to sleep.

It was agreed that Belgium should be released from the debt which she would in any event never have paid to the Allies; and that the Allies should require Germany to pay that debt. But nobody ever supposed for a moment that any addition had been made or had ever been contemplated to the total German Indemnity, and it was understood among the interested parties that whatever advantage Belgium derived from this arrangement (if any) should be deducted subsequently by reducing the percentage of her reparation allotment. The Belgians were apparently satisfied.[52]

In his final paragraph, Keynes was somewhat confused, as he often was about reparations. To begin with, he scrambled two separate concessions, that concerning a privileged position on war debts and that concerning priority of payment. His charge that Belgium in any case would never have paid her war debts to the Allies cannot be documented. What Belgium would have done had she not already received repeated assurances, including the official interpretation of the Fourteen Points, that she would not have to pay these debts cannot be known. One can only say that because the United States did not ratify the Versailles treaty, Belgium ultimately had to pay her American pre-Armistice debt. She came to terms in 1925, ahead of any other nation except Britain, and paid faithfully until the Hoover Moratorium on governmental debts in July 1931. Further, in the 1921 London Schedule of Payments the Belgian war debt was in fact added to the German bill, although to the more ephemeral portion of it. The remainder of Keynes's penultimate sentence concerns the mechanism for priority of payment, although he apparently confused priority with privilege. Keynes clearly did not understand that the purpose of priority was not to increase Belgium's share of the receipts but to insure that she obtained the first monies received from Germany in order to facilitate her economic reconstruction.

BELGIAN REACTIONS

Keynes notwithstanding, the Belgian battle for privilege had been won. So had the battle for priority. During the stormy session of 29 April, most of the dispute had focused on privilege, for Lloyd George and

---

52. Stephen Roskill, *Hankey, Man of Secrets*, 2:84–87. Compare to FRUS PPC, 5:344–51; and Mantoux, *Les Délibérations*, 1:411–20. The original of Keynes's account, together with a cover letter dated 2 May 1919, may be found in Hankey Papers 8/15.

Wilson had already reluctantly concluded that priority of payment must be conceded. When the Belgian delegation threatened to leave the peace conference, the long-proposed priority of $500 million, ranking immediately after occupation costs, was hastily arranged. That appeared to settle matters, as the Belgian plenipotentiaries promised to support the arrangement and did so unanimously, advising their government that nothing more could be obtained.[53] However, the Belgian cabinet, armed with the support of all three parties and a unanimous resolution of the Belgian Senate to appeal to the Allied parliaments, voted on 30 April with Albert presiding to reject the treaty unless Belgium was reimbursed for the German marks within three years, in view of the imperative economic needs of the country.[54] A stream of telegrams from Delacroix ordered the delegation to maintain the refusal and announced the immediate departure of several ministers for Paris.[55]

When Hymans reported his government's decision, the Four offered a carrot while Lloyd George tried to wield the stick. The Four agreed on 30 April to a Belgian seat on the permanent Reparation Commission, but when the experts met the next day to work out a formula for Belgian priority, Keynes reported that Lloyd George was very irritated by the Belgian claims. He had said that Belgium had made fewer sacrifices than Australia and, if she persisted, he would make a public comparison of achievements. Hymans refused to be intimidated.[56]

Actually, Hymans had advised the Belgian ministers to concede. By now half the Belgian cabinet was in Paris exhorting him to hold firm, but in a series of hasty meetings on 1 and 2 May, Hymans convinced them that nothing more could be gained and that only a dangerous isolation could arise from further protests. It was finally agreed that the delegation would make one last effort to obtain a more formal liberation from war costs and a guarantee that Belgium would not be obliged to consume her first German reparations payments to repay Allied post-Armistice loans. Hymans told Delacroix flatly that the three pleni-

53. Hymans, *Mémoires,* 1:406–7; Hymans to BMAE, 29 Apr. 1919, tel. 378, Hymans Papers/150; Hymans to Delacroix, 29 Apr. 1919, BMAE B–366/I.
54. Delacroix to DB, 29 Apr. 1919, tel., Delacroix to Hymans, 30 Apr. 1919, tel., Hymans Papers/150.
55. Delacroix to DB, 29 Apr. 1919, tel., Delacroix to Hymans, 30 Apr. 1919, tel. 206, 2 tels., Hymans Papers/150; Delacroix to DB, 1 May 1919, tel. 211, BMAE DB/7/II.
56. Hymans to Clemenceau, 30 Apr. 1919, no. 944, Hymans note, 8 May 1919,

potentiaries could not accept responsibility for rejecting the treaty and would all resign their positions if the cabinet persisted in its refusal. As Hymans and Vandervelde led two of Belgium's three parties in the coalition cabinet, Delacroix was quickly convinced.[57]

When the Three met on 2 May, however, the Belgian refusal still stood, although slightly tempered by new requests for artistic and literary restitution, return of state archives, relief on post-Armistice loans, and, after the priority of $500 million, 15 percent of German payments until Belgian claims in certain categories were fulfilled.[58] This last proposal arose from Belgian concern that no agreement whatever had been made on the future division of German reparations and a well-grounded fear that, when the Allies finally cut up the pie, the Belgian slice would be small. As the Three examined these claims, Loucheur and Wilson urged that, after her priority, Belgium be granted 15 percent of German reparations until her share—whatever that might be—was fulfilled. Lloyd George vehemently disagreed. He insisted that there be no special terms for Belgium, particularly because she was a near neighbor and close competitor of Scotland, which was heavily in debt. Despite further Franco-American pressure, he would not yield. The debate became so confused that even Hankey lost its thread, but apparently the Allies only tentatively agreed that Belgium need not repay her post-Armistice loans at once.[59]

Lloyd George's hostility had no effect on Hymans and his colleagues, who were now under intense pressure from Belgian opinion. During the first week of May, the Belgian press exhibited unanimous rage all across the political spectrum from the Francophile *La Nation belge* to the Socialist *Le Peuple*, and across the linguistic divide as well. Though short on information, the newspapers were full of indignation, sure that Belgium was being deprived. The blame was assigned according to the predilections of the newspaper in question but otherwise agreement was total. The leading evening newspaper, *Le Soir*, recited the Declara-

Hymans Papers/150; I.C. 177E, 30 Apr. 1919, CAB 29/37; Hymans, *Mémoires*, 1:409; Whitlock, *Letters*, 2:560.

57. Hymans to Delacroix, 1 May 1919, tel. 382, Hymans note, 8 May 1919, Hymans Papers/150; Delacroix to Jaspar, 2 May 1919, tel. 385, BMAE DB/7/II.

58. Hymans and van den Heuvel to Clemenceau, 1 May 1919, no. 551, Hymans to House and Lamont, 2 May 1919, Hymans Papers/150.

59. I.C. 179C, 2 May 1919, CAB 29/37.

tion of Sainte-Adresse, the Fourteen Points, British government promises, and numerous quotations from the British parliamentary debates
of August 1914. The dominant morning newspaper, *L'Indépendance
belge*, cited leading articles in London's *Times*, *Daily Chronicle*, and *Daily
News* in support of Belgium, quoted Vandervelde's remarks in defense
of Belgian reparation claims, and printed three columns of speeches,
telegrams, and reports of demonstrations all over Belgium against signing the treaty.[60] In the Flemish-language press, the *Gazet van Antwerpen* complained equally about the importance of returning Belgian
livestock and industrial equipment, the need to redeem the German
marks, and the lack of definite information. Perhaps *De Standaard* of
Brussels expressed the national emotion most graphically, if a trifle
inelegantly. Under the headline, "Belgium Deserted and Humiliated by
Its Allies," it complained:

> It is simply awful how we are treated by our Allies. During four
> years, with an extraordinary rivalry they have wreathed Belgium,
> our king, our leaders, our statesmen, in the most beautiful pane-
> gyrics and made our heads dizzy with the most glittering promises
> for the future.
>
> We won't even get excited that Geneva was chosen over Brussels
> for the League of Nations. Even what is happening with Luxem-
> burg—where France has come to spoil the meal which was ready
> for us—is still not the most serious thing, although it is important
> for our economic development, for our military security, and for
> our independent policy that Luxemburg be joined not to France
> but to Belgium. The most serious thing is that our Allies appear to
> leave Belgium to her misery after she had been owed a debt from
> the origin of their conflict with the Germans and had been struck
> even in the very sources of her prosperity.
>
> We can't bear it that the possibility to work, and by work to
> revert to our earlier status, has been removed.[61]

60. *Le Peuple*, 3 May 1919, p. 1; *La Nation belge*, 3 May 1919, p. 1, 4 May 1919, p. 1, 5
May 1919, p. 1; *Le Soir*, 1 May 1919, p. 1, 5 May 1919, p. 1; *L'Indépendance belge*, 3 May
1919, p. 1, 5 May 1919, p. 1, 6 May 1919, p. 2, 7 May 1919, p. 1.
61. *Gazet van Antwerpen*, 5–6 May 1919, p. 1; *De Standaard*, 3 May 1919, p. 1 Unfortunately, *Het Laaste Nieuws* could not be obtained at the Bibliothèque Royale for
consultation.

The next day, *De Standaard* carried the headline: "A Death Penalty—12 Milliard Owed. Is it worthwhile to sign? What if Belgium becomes a nullity?"[62]

As usual, Whitlock caught the Belgian mood superbly. He sadly wrote to House: "In all the years of the war, I have never seen Belgium quite so depressed and discouraged. For four years Belgium lived on hope, feeling that her claims for priorities in indemnities would be readily granted by the Allies, and now the newspapers are filled with alarming statements to the effect that these hopes will be disappointed."[63] As Whitlock knew, the unanimity and the emotion arose largely from fear. The king, the bankers, the businessmen, and the Socialist leaders all agreed that the country faced ruination if its industries were not soon restored. The king repeatedly insisted that, though new housing was urgent in the devastated regions, economic reconstruction was even more critical and could not be accomplished without the priorities Belgium sought. Although the Belgian leadership was undoubtedly orchestrating a campaign, it was also genuine in its alarm over the economic situation. Subsequent events were to show that Belgian fears were not groundless but rather based upon hard economic and budgetary realities. After World War I, Belgian taxes multiplied to eight times their prewar level (and eight times the postwar German level as well) to pay for the reconstruction, but still the budget deficits were so severe and the borrowing so heavy as to cause virtual collapse of the Belgian franc in 1926. Yet all this effort did not fully restore the situation. Belgium never did regain her prewar prosperity, her lost markets, or her former position in world trade, and the net effect of the war and the peace settlement was to leave Belgium permanently weaker economically. In May 1919 the details of that unhappy story could not yet be determined, but the broad outlines were clear to both government and people. Indignant demonstrations took place in Antwerp, Brussels, and Ghent, chiefly over the reparations settlement.

62. *De Standaard*, 3 May 1919, p. 1. The figure of 12 milliard was arrived at by adding up Belgium's prewar debt, her war debt, and a low estimate of the German marks and then substracting the Belgian priority, all of which reveals a good deal of confusion.

63. Whitlock to House, 2 May 1919, House Papers 20/24.

Whitlock reported that the intense pressure of Belgian opinion might well force the retirement of the delegation from Paris.[64]

As the agitation of Belgian opinion became known at the peace conference, Lloyd George's threat to leave Belgium to settle on her own became meaningless. On 3 May, the experts drew up a settlement that provided for return of the artistic and literary works and state archives, specified repayment of Belgium's pre-Armistice loans by Germany, left Belgium free to dispose of the marks as she saw fit, and pledged a priority of 2.5 milliard French francs ($500 million), which Georges Theunis shrewdly insisted be valued in gold.[65] Despite the intensity of Belgian opinion, the experts gave no serious consideration to authorizing mark redemption as a category of reparations because that would create a precedent applicable in a number of other countries. Later in the day, the Three reviewed the proposal, limiting the priority to cash and excluding German payments in goods. As early German payments were primarily made in goods, Belgian priority was effectively deferred to the benefit of France and Britain, especially France. The Three also agreed that German liability would cover Belgian pre-Armistice debts but not post-Armistice loans, for which Belgium would remain responsible without any relief provisions. As a consequence, much of the hard-won priority would be legally committed to repayment of the Allies. There was much debate about whether the Belgian war debt should have some sort of priority of German payment, as Britain was eager for prompt reimbursement of her share, but the Three decided only to create a special German bond issue to cover this category of Allied claims. Lloyd George complained throughout the meeting about preference to Belgium, maintaining that "Belgium was in an extremely favourable position. . . . In fact, the whole priority of Belgium was absolutely indefensible." Though he was forced to concede on privilege and priority, he succeeded in preventing allocation of any percentage of subsequent German payments to Belgium.[66]

64. Ibid.; Whitlock to ACNP, 2 May 1919, tel. 21, 185.119/366. ACNP/326; Admiralty, *Belgium*, p. 544; Devleeshouwer, "L'Opinion publique," p. 237.

65. Hymans note, 8 May 1919, 3 May 1919 formula, Hymans Papers/150; d'Ydewalle, *D'Albert I*, p. 75.

66. I.C. 180D, 3 May 1919, CAB 29/37. In fact, no special bonds to cover the Belgian war debt were ever issued. The Belgian debt was tacked on to the putative 132

With these decisions, the Versailles treaty was rushed to the printer to be hastily prepared for presentation to the German delegation four days later, and Hymans entrained for Brussels, summoned to a crown council on 4 May. Because the Allies would still have first claim on Belgium's priority for payment of post-Armistice loans, Vandervelde and van den Heuvel remained in Paris, authorizing Hymans to speak for them.[67] On Hymans's recommendation, the crown council, consisting of all ministers of state whether in office or not, unanimously authorized signature of the Versailles treaty. This decision was taken, however, on the assumption that the 2.5 milliard franc priority would come to Belgium in full, but continuing negotiations in Paris indicated otherwise. Neither the British nor the Americans would relinquish their rights to early repayment of post-Armistice debts, and the effect of their stand would be to reduce the Belgian priority to 1.5 milliard francs. As the Belgian government insisted upon the entire 2.5 milliard, van den Heuvel negotiated intensively with the American experts, but to no avail. Although they assured him that the United States did not wish to impede Belgian recovery, they categorically refused to make any written commitments in respect to the post-Armistice loans. Clearly, when her own financial interests were directly involved, the United States proved to be no more altruistic than the European Allies. As the experts advised reliance on American sympathy and good will and warned that further resistance would endanger Belgian credit, Vandervelde and van den Heuvel announced on their own initiative on 5 May that Belgium would accept the Versailles treaty.[68]

Consequently, the Belgian plenipotentiaries attended the plenary session of 7 May when the treaty was presented to the German delegation. Its leader, Count Ulrich von Brockdorff-Rantzau, in an otherwise defiant speech, three times reiterated Germany's willingness to

milliard gold mark total of the London Schedule of Payments of 5 May 1921. For text, see RC, *Official Documents*, 1:4–9.

67. Thompson, *Peace Conference*, p. 354; Delacroix to Hymans, 3 May 1919, tel. 220, Delacroix to DB, 3 May 1919, tel., van den Heuvel and Vandervelde to Delacroix, 4 May 1919, tel. 404, Hymans Papers/150.

68. Hymans, *Mémoires*, 1:409–10; Hymans to DB, 5 May 1919, tels. 230, 233, van den Heuvel to Clemenceau, 5 May 1919, van den Heuvel Papers/48; van den Heuvel to Hymans, 5 May 1919, tel. 409, Hymans to DB, 5 May 1919, tel. 235, Vandervelde and van den Heuvel to Hymans, 6 May 1919, tel. 418, BMAE DB/7/II.

redress the wrong done to Belgium. Similarly, when the massive German observations on the Versailles treaty arrived on 29 May, they accepted reparations for Belgium, unlike most other matters, without argument.[69] Though the lack of German protest was reassuring, the Belgian delegation was still trying to protect the priority from further Allied inroads. An American draft of the priority agreement late in May proposed to deduct from the 2.5 milliard francs the value of all goods shipped to Belgium since the Armistice, including even restitution of Belgian property removed to Germany. The Belgian experts did long and ultimately successful battle against such further devices to reduce the cash available for Belgian economic reconstruction.[70]

In its later stages, this struggle merged with the final Belgian battle over priority and privilege. Although the Allied leaders had made certain promises, they had committed none of them to paper. On 5 June, Hymans sent House a polite reminder, together with a proposed Belgian draft. As the text of the Versailles treaty already committed Germany to assumption of the pre-Armistice Belgian debt, the question of privilege was easily resolved by a letter to Hymans on 16 June from Clemenceau, Wilson, and Lloyd George, promising to recommend to their respective governments acceptance of German bonds to the amount of the Belgian wartime debt.[71]

The formal arrangement for priority took longer to achieve, thanks to assorted Allied attempts at further inroads and Anglo-French foot dragging. Finally, Hymans appealed directly to Wilson and, as a consequence, the Big Four signed an agreement on Belgian priority on 24 June 1919 and initialed an annex demonstrating how it would operate.[72] The agreement accorded Belgium the promised priority of

69. FRUS PPC, 3:417; Germany, Peace Delegation, *Comments*, p. 54.

70. Bemelmans to Jaspar, 21, 22 May 1919, Jaspar Papers/233; Belgian note, 21 May 1919, Hymans to House, 24 May 1919, Hymans Papers/150; van den Heuvel to Delacroix and Hymans, 11 June 1919, tel. 534, van den Heuvel Papers/48; van den Ven to Delacroix, 19 June 1919, tel. 538, Delacroix to van den Ven, 16 June 1919, tel. 322, BMAE DB/7/II.

71. Hymans to House, 5 June 1919, House Papers/10; FRUS PPC, 13:425, 851.

72. House to Hymans, 6 June 1919, Hymans to DB, 13 June 1919, tel. 319, BMAE DB/7/II; C.F. 87/1, 23 June 1919, CAB 29/39; Hymans to Wilson, 23 June 1919, Wilson to Hymans, 24 June 1919, Wilson Papers 5B/48; W.C.P. 1060, 24 June 1919, CAB 29/17. For texts of the two documents, see FRUS PPC, 13:849–50.

2.5 milliard gold French francs. This priority of payment ranked immediately after Allied occupation costs and the expense of provisioning Germany, both prior charges upon Germany embodied in the Versailles treaty and both very substantial items that delayed the payment of reparations per se. The priority was to be in the form of cash paid by Germany and/or the proceeds from the sale of securities transferred by Germany to the new permanent Reparation Commission. After 1 May 1921, by which time the total German liability was to be established, the value of deliveries of goods (reparation in kind) would also be included, but until that date other powers would retain unimpaired claims to German coal and timber shipments and the like. Although restitutions were specifically excluded from the priority arrangement, nothing whatever was said about the post-Armistice Belgian debt, thus leaving intact Allied rights to draw upon Belgian priority for its repayment. Finally, the agreement and its annex made clear the Allied intent that the priority arrangement would have no effect upon the as yet undetermined Belgian percentage of the future total German reparations liability. The intent of the priority was to provide Belgium with more than her percentage share in the first years, with the clear understanding that, after the priority was extinguished, Belgium would "repay" it by taking a share below her established percentage in later years, so that at the eventual completion of German payments, she would have received her assigned percentage and no more.

This concession, like so many of the wartime promises to Belgium, proved in its execution to be a great deal less than it appeared initially. The priority arrangement was made in good faith but upon false premises. Allied leaders at the peace conference blithely assumed that Germany would pay promptly and in full, and they took it for granted that the Belgian priority would be extinguished within two years at the most. As Germany paid neither promptly nor in full, reparations quickly dwindled to a trickle, particularly cash payments. In the circumstances, Britain and France, sometimes abetted by Italy, mounted repeated campaigns to erode Belgian priority so that they could obtain some much-needed cash for themselves. By great tenacity, the Belgian government did eventually obtain the full $500 million, but not before the end of 1925. Thus the priority did not effectively serve the goal for which it was designed, that of affording Belgium a certain amount of early financial relief to facilitate economic reconstruction, and Belgium's postwar economic problems correspondingly worsened. Fortunately for the survival of the Belgian government, the Belgian people had no crystal ball in 1919 and, like the Allied leaders, assumed that Germany would pay their priority promptly. Though the priority was sadly inadequate to cover Belgium's needs, it at least appeared certain in 1919, and it was largely on the assumption that it would be rapidly forthcoming that the Belgian government borrowed so heavily. But instead of aiding Belgium appreciably, the priority became a bone of constant Allied contention, contributing considerably to the complex shifting of relationships among Britain, France, Italy, Belgium, and Germany. It embittered relationships within the Western Entente and complicated further its already intricate efforts to enforce or revise the reparations clauses of the Versailles treaty, which soon became the issue on which the power struggle over the postwar settlement was primarily joined.

Even though neither worked out as planned, priority and privilege were among Belgium's major gains at the peace conference, but neither was received with any noticeable enthusiasm in Belgium: both were deemed to be Belgium's unquestioned entitlement but not her full entitlement. What had been gained was much less than had been promised, and vital matters, including Germany's total obligation and Belgium's share of it, remained unresolved. After many disappointments, Belgians were becoming suspicious and skeptical, fearing that, after the priority was exhausted, they would be left to pay their own bills at whatever cost to the country's future. In commenting on the generally bitter Belgian reaction, a British Foreign Office official remarked:

> Politicians in this country, from Cabinet Ministers to Party hacks, could and did raise cheap cheers at public meetings by promising Belgium payment to the uttermost farthing; and there is no doubt the great mass of Belgians did really believe that we should not sheathe the sword until Belgium had received reparation in full. . . . The Belgian leaders possibly foresaw that these promises could not be kept; but it is hardly surprising that the masses were and are disappointed.[73]

73. G. Villiers minute, 6 Oct. 1920, on Sir F. Villiers to Curzon, 7 Aug. 1920, no. 571 (Annual Report, 1919), F.O. 371/3651.

Unfortunately, Belgian leaders had not foreseen in the slightest that Allied promises could not be kept. Faith in the guarantor great powers—their good will and their bounteous resources—remained strong, and the Belgian leaders all believed the promises as implicitly as the Belgian people, until their diplomatic baptism by fire at the peace conference tore away their innocent illusions and left some of them bitter. King Albert, always less trusting in the great powers, was more philosophic. He said, "What would you have? They did what they could."[74]

74. Cammaerts, *Albert of Belgium*, p. 347.

FIVE

THE QUEST

FOR LUXEMBURG

THE SITUATION IN THE GRAND DUCHY

When the final version of the Versailles treaty was signed on 28 June 1919, two issues of great concern to Belgium remained unresolved. The Belgian delegation had long accepted that renegotiation of the 1839 treaties would be deferred until after more pressing questions were decided, but they were dismayed that the status of Luxemburg also remained unsettled. The decision about the 1839 treaties resulted from extended examination by an expert commission and careful consideration by the Four, culminating in establishment of a procedure for further progress. Quite the reverse was true of the Luxemburg question, which never received any coherent or systematic attention at all.

The mishandling of the Luxemburg question arose both from a series of British errors and from French determination to defer the issue. Unlike the other great powers, France was intensely interested in Luxemburg and thus hoped to avoid settlement of the problem until she could deal alone with an isolated Belgium in a thoroughly disadvantageous position, without the intervention of Britain or America on Belgium's behalf. As she succeeded, the Versailles treaty disposed of the Luxemburg question in essentially the same way as the revision of the 1839 treaties. The peace treaty merely required that Germany renounce all ties with the Grand Duchy and accept in advance any future arrangements made by the Allies.[1]

Hymans brought the problem of Luxemburg before the peace conference in the course of his exposition of Belgian claims on 11 February. Although all other questions arising from the 1839 treaties were

1. Versailles treaty, Article 40.

206

referred to the Belgian Commission for study, Balfour argued successfully on 12 February that the future of Luxemburg was a political question that did not require expert study in a commission. Thus what
became the Big Four retained exclusive control of the Luxemburg
problem.[2] As a consequence, the question of the Grand Duchy was
divorced not only from Belgian issues but also from the problems of
the Rhineland, the Saar Basin, and the other west German borderlands
to which it had a direct relationship. The French clearly appreciated
this relationship and in time much of the British delegation came to
recognize it as well. But Lloyd George and his immediate entourage
remained oblivious to the connection, partly as a consequence of Balfour's early error in withholding the Luxemburg question from an expert commission, and thus they overlooked an important diplomatic
opportunity.

Some expert analysis of Luxemburg's tangled past and confused present would undoubtedly have been a good idea. The great powers dealt
with the question intermittently and offhandedly in their spare time.
Except for Clemenceau, the Four were in almost total ignorance of
events and opinions in the Grand Duchy, despite Belgian efforts to
inform them. The Big Four were in wholehearted agreement on only
one point: the international status of Luxemburg must be revised. By
this, they meant the legal status whereby the Grand Duchy had become
a German satellite.

With this view the people of Luxemburg fully concurred. Though
sentiment was divided on many other matters, the wartime occupation
had only intensified the already active Luxembourgeois dislike of Germany and had generated a nearly unanimous desire to depart from the
German economic orbit. Events during the occupation had also given
rise to acute popular dissatisfaction with the young and intensely pious
grand duchess, who did not share the open hostility of her subjects
to the conqueror. She was of German descent, and her mother and
five younger sisters spent much of the war in Bavaria, sending the

2. Hymans, *Mémoires*, 1:369; I.C. 140, 12 Feb. 1919, CAB 28/6. Why Balfour took this
view is not entirely clear. Probably he was trying to block assignment of the question to
the Belgian Commission, whose chairman was French.

kaiser frequent telegrams of support, which the French intercepted.[3]
Although Marie Adelaide remained in Luxemburg, she did not maintain a neutral stance. She protested throughout the war against nursing
of Belgian civilians by the Luxemburg Red Cross and greeted the German occupation with open enthusiasm. In September 1914, the kaiser
arrived on almost no notice and, instead of retiring to her country
home at Berg, Marie Adelaide gave him a banquet and drank to the
"glorious German army." In 1915, she telegraphed him, saying, "My
sisters pray daily for the victory of the German army." Later she became
godmother of Crown Prince Wilhelm's child. Throughout the war, she
retained a German priest as her religious advisor and welcomed, especially in the last year of the war, extended visits from the kaiser,
Chancellor Georg von Hertling, and a variety of German generals.
From 1915 on, her attempt to govern personally in defiance of parliamentary majorities only increased her unpopularity. An election campaign in Luxemburg in the summer of 1918 revealed that Marie Adelaide had signed two secret treaties, one to supply food to Germany and
another giving Germany jurisdiction over her subjects. These treaties
may possibly have been inescapable and might have been forgiven,
despite the acute shortage of food in the Grand Duchy. However, the
final straw in the eyes of Marie Adelaide's subjects was the announcement on 25 August 1918 of the betrothal of her younger sister, the
eighteen-year-old Antonia, to the fifty-year-old widower Crown Prince
Rupprecht of Bavaria, who had commanded the German Fourth Army
in Flanders in 1914. This engagement was neither the mésalliance nor
the purely political arrangement that it appeared to be, but the Luxemburgers, like Allied observers, leapt to the obvious conclusion. Marie
Adelaide's approval of the engagement largely destroyed what little
popular support she still enjoyed.[4]

3. The file of telegrams may be found in FMAE CPC Guerre Lux/599. Marie Adelaide's
messages were more circumspect.

4. De Cartier to Lansing, 13 Nov. 1918, Whitlock to Lansing, 1 Nov. 1918, no. 637,
Whitlock Papers/38 (LC); Steefel memo, 1 Apr. 1918, Inquiry/552; Whitlock to House,
28 Nov. 1918, House Papers 20/24; *Washington Post*, 8 Jan. 1919, BMAE DB/ 32/I;
Moncheur to Hymans, 6 Sept. 1918, no. 7076/1602, BMAE GB/1918/II; de Gaiffier to
Hymans, 13 Nov. 1918, no. 8592/2904, BMAE FR/1918/II; Mollard to Pichon, 24
Dec. 1917, FMAE CPC Guerre Lux/600. Rupprecht was in fact devoted to Antonia. He
released her from the engagement when the Bavarian monarchy fell at the time of the

At the end of the war, events moved swiftly and confusedly in the Grand Duchy. On 10 November 1918, there were riots in Luxemburg City followed by demands for Marie Adelaide's abdication. She responded by announcing that she would withdraw from affairs of state until a popular referendum could be held.[5] The situation stabilized somewhat when the American Third Army arrived on 21 November. Over Belgian protests, Foch had assigned the Grand Duchy to the American zone of occupation, but then he chose to make the capital city his own military headquarters and the generalissimo, who had never before accepted a guard of honor, suddenly required an entire regiment, together with an extensive staff of officers, all of whom arrived on 22 November. The French regiment, the 109th of the Line, was supposedly assigned to the marshal's personal protection, although he was almost never there. The American forces were largely displaced from the city, and most of them were soon reassigned elsewhere. Nonetheless, the American commander General John Pershing refused Foch's immediate request that two French divisions be incorporated in the American army of occupation in Luxemburg, and so the French military presence in the Grand Duchy within the American zone remained without technical legal sanction.[6]

On 17 December, the French government declared that the French state railways had taken over administration of the Grand Duchy's most important rail lines, those of the Société Guillaume-Luxembourg, which had been run since 1872 by the Alsace-Lorraine network of the German state railways. Two days later, Luxemburg denounced its rail convention with Germany and announced its withdrawal from the Zollverein as of 31 December 1918.[7] Late in December there was an abor-

Armistice, but she married him on 7 April 1921. They had six children and, by all accounts, were an exceptionally happy couple.

5. Herchen, *Manuel*, p. 254; Fallon to Hymans, 15 Nov. 1918, tel. 774, BMAE PB/1918/II.

6. Shartle, *Spa*, p. 30; Whitlock to Lansing, 15 Dec. 1918, tel. 164, 850A.0146/3, ACNP/443; Manton memo, 24 Dec. 1918, 850A.001, ACNP/442; Menschaert memo, 30 Nov. 1918, Gillain to Hymans, 6 Dec. 1918, no. 6114, de Ligne to Hymans, 9 Dec. 1918, no. 21/15, BMAE B-1-1519; de Gaiffier to Hymans, 18 Dec. 1918, no. 9287/3178, BMAE DB/32/II; Pershing Diary, 30 Nov.–2 Dec. 1918, LC Pershing Papers/4–5; Hymans *Mémoires*, 1:344–45; K. Nelson, *Victors Divided*, pp. 32–33.

7. Pierre Majerus, *Le Luxembourg indépendant*, pp. 70–71, 74–75.

tive rebellion in the Grand Duchy, and a republican revolution broke out in earnest in Luxemburg City on 9 January 1919. Against his orders from Foch and to the later fury of Clemenceau, the romantic and chivalrous local French commander intervened on behalf of the royal family and especially Princess Charlotte, younger sister of Marie Adelaide. As a consequence, the tumult was suppressed on 12 January and the cabinet regained a precarious control. Marie Adelaide abdicated on 13 January amid continuing unrest and went into exile on 28 January. After unsuccessfully attempting both the convent life in Italy and medical studies in Munich, she died at the family home in Bavaria in January 1924 at the age of twenty-nine.[8] Meanwhile, in Luxemburg itself, Princess Charlotte took the oath of office as grand duchess on 15 January 1919. Out of the turmoil emerged her enormous popularity, a coalition government led by Emile Reuter, an understanding that a plebiscite would be held on the future form of government, and a national attitude best expressed by the Luxembourgeois anthem, which declares, "We wish to remain what we are." In February, the Chamber unanimously voted to retain the independence and sovereignty of the Grand Duchy.[9]

8. Marie Adelaide's decision to abdicate was taken on 9 January in response partly to the outbreak that day and partly to word from Paris that she must go. Her letter of abdication was signed on 9 January at the Château Berg, given to the cabinet on the thirteenth, and notified to the Chamber on the fourteenth. De Gaiffier to Hymans, 31 Dec. 1918, no. 9585/3290, BMAE FR/1918/II; Gilbert Trausch, "Les Relations franco-belges à propos de la question luxembourgeoise (1914–1922)," p. 286; O'Shaughessy, *Marie Adelaide*, pp. 176–91. This last work, a rather colored biography, also provides an account of her remaining years. After a French army investigation (with Luxembourgeois government cooperation), which concluded that General de la Tour had made an honest error and should not be penalized but that the republic would have succeeded if the French army had not intervened at the request of the Luxemburg government, Clemenceau unceremoniously sacked him. Roques report, 8 Feb. 1919, Clemenceau to Gen. Lacombe de la Tour, 23 Feb. 1919, Vin 6N/198.

9. The course of events in Luxemburg during this period can be pieced together from the following sources: Weber, *Histoire*, p. 102; Herchen, *Manuel*, p. 254; Majerus, *Le Luxembourg*, pp. 70–75; Mordacq, *Le Ministère Clemenceau*, 3:87–88, 93–94, 131; Hymans, *Mémoires*, 1:345–46; Western & General Report no. 102, 15 Jan. 1919, CAB 24/150; Pichon to Derby, 17 Jan. 1919, Lothian Papers GD/40/17/69; Reuter to Balfour, 22 Jan. 1919, Villiers to F.O., 12 Jan. 1919, tel. 10, F.O. 371/3638; Brown to C/S AEF, 12 Jan. 1919, tel. A-317, Wilson Papers 5B/8; Roques reports, early Feb. 1919, 8 Feb. 1919, Vin 6N/198; Picard to Clemenceau, 24 Jan. 1919, Pichon Papers/7. The

What had occurred was the one possibility that no Belgian official and, as well as can be determined from the few surviving dossiers, no French official had contemplated at all.[10] Marie Adelaide had departed but the dynasty had survived. Further, Charlotte's popularity was both beyond doubt and growing daily. To Clemenceau, this made no difference. Throughout the peace conference he continued to mutter that the "Boche dynasty" must go. But the Belgian government reassessed its position when it became clear that there was no popular sentiment in Luxemburg for Belgian annexation and very little for a dynastic union. As it became evident that Charlotte, whose pro-Allied attitude only reinforced her popularity, enjoyed a genuinely secure position in the affections of her subjects, Belgium abandoned two of the three options under consideration during the war and pursued the third: economic union with the Grand Duchy. In mid-November 1918, Belgium had sent the Prince de Ligne as chargé d'affaires accredited only to the government, not to the Grand Duchess Marie Adelaide. On instructions, from February to September 1919, he conveyed repeated assurances to the Luxembourgeois cabinet and Chamber on behalf of the Belgian king and government that the independence of Luxemburg would be respected and that Albert was not a candidate for the Luxembourgeois throne. Although these declarations were widely disbelieved in Luxemburg, the assurances, on the part of the king and most government officials, were a perfectly genuine recognition of reality.[11]

---

entire refrain of the Luxemburg national anthem, "De Feîerwon [The Train]," written in 1859, is very pointed:

Come ye from Prussia, Belgium, France
To view our land with friendly glance.
And learn how here, on every side,
No discontent does abide!
We wish to remain what we are.

Admiralty, *Luxemburg*, p. 69.

10. Willequet, "Gaston Barbanson," p. 1185.

11. De Gaiffier to Hymans, 13 Nov. 1918, no. 8592/2904, BMAE FR/1918/II; Prum, *Problem*, p. 41; Weber, *Histoire*, p. 104; Whitlock to Colby, 1 Aug. 1920, Whitlock Papers/42 (LC); Whitlock to House, 10 Dec. 1918, House Papers 20/24; de Cartier to Hymans, 13 Dec. 1918, tel. 591, B Micro/23; *Le Soir*, 4 May 1919, p. 1; Mordacq, *Le Ministère Clemenceau*, 3:19–20; Whitlock, *Letters*, 2:538; F.O. memo, 9 May 1921, F.O. 371/6970; *Gazet van Antwerpen*, 8 May 1919, p. 1; Moncheur to Hymans, 18 Sept. 1919,

It was self-evident, however, that a nation of 999 square miles (smaller than the state of Rhode Island) and about 250,000 inhabitants could not stand entirely alone. As Luxemburg clearly wished to abandon her previous dependence on Germany, she would have to turn to one or both of her other neighbors. Already her economy was suffering severely from the loss of Ruhr coal and her traditional German markets. Luxemburg soon approached both Belgium and France and promptly became a bone of bitter contention between them. This struggle arose from a variety of factors, not least from the French desire to dominate Belgium and the Belgian determination to escape such domination. Moreover, Luxemburg, although tiny, was of enormous strategic and considerable economic importance. The year 1914 had proved, as 1940 would prove again, that a disarmed Luxemburg afforded a convenient invasion route from Germany into France. August 1914 had also demonstrated that the Belgian provinces of Luxembourg and Namur were indefensible against a hostile great power entrenched in the Grand Duchy. In addition, the Luxemburg railways constituted short but vital segments of some of western Europe's most important main rail lines, including not only those from Dutch and Belgian North Sea and riparian ports to Alsace-Lorraine, Switzerland, and Italy, but also three lines from Germany to the Paris basin, variously via the Ruhr and Aachen through eastern Belgium and Luxemburg to Metz and westward, via Saarbrücken, or via the Ruhr, Coblenz, and Trier, also to Metz. Though the military significance of these lines is obvious, they were also indispensable in the exchange of Ruhr coke and Lorraine ore.[12] Finally, Luxemburg possessed an economic significance of its own. Its steel industry was large, efficient, undamaged, and of international importance. As most of the steel production was exported, a new outlet was urgently required, along with a reliable supply of coke.[13]

---

no. 5753/1966, Hymans to Moncheur, 22 Sept. 1919, no. 1331, BMAE GB/1919/II; Devleeshouwer, "L'Opinion publique," pp. 226–27, 229; Orts to de Ligne, 21 Apr. 1919, no. 6071, BMAE B–1–1519; de Ligne to Hymans, 29 Apr. 1919, no. 773/253, BMAE B-10.121.

12. Admiralty, *Luxemburg*, pp. 73, 291–92; Jean de Clerq, *Les Petites Souverainetés d'Europe*, p. 133; Paul Simon, "Le Problème ferroviaire luxembourgeois," pp. 3–4. Another line from the Ruhr and Aachen passed through Belgium and Luxemburg en route to France.

13. Camille Wagner, *La Sidérurgie luxembourgeoise sous les régimes du Zollverein et de*

The Belgian steel industry was at first dubious about embracing such formidable competition, especially when Belgian steel plants had been shattered by the war and faced a struggle to regain their former productivity and markets, but appeals to patriotism and the higher national interest were effective. In addition, Belgian concerns dependent upon cast iron were eager to tap Luxemburg's ample supply. For the rest, the country was united in its desire for and expectation of union in some form with Luxemburg. In particular, the Flemish were as hostile to French domination of the Grand Duchy as were French-speaking Walloons along the border, where cultural and familial ties had always been strong.[14]

In France the steel industry and its national organization, the Comité des Forges, were also wary of Luxembourgeois competition and at first favored maintenance of protective tariffs against it. France's evident strategic interest changed the minds of some, but not all. Also, a few major French firms, including both Schneider and Wendel, scented an opportunity to take control of the Luxemburg steel industry. First, aided by French government pressure to induce Luxembourgeois cooperation and some private Belgian financial participation, they gained control of two German steel companies in the Grand Duchy. Then, with governmental encouragement, these firms quietly bought up shares in Luxemburg's largest steel concern, the Société des Aciéries Réunies de Burbach-Eich-Dudelange, or ARBED, and at the same time prevailed upon the French government to decree ruinously high tariffs to bring the Luxembourgeois competition to its knees and under French control. Aside from industrial circles and the government ministries most closely connected with them, French interest in Luxemburg appears to have been confined to the army and to Paris. The sizable Luxembourgeois colony in the French capital was divided in its sentiments, but the most active element was the Comité Franco-Luxembourgeois, many of whose members were naturalized French citizens. Its determined efforts toward a French solution to the Luxemburg question had gained it many friends in the French Parliament and fi-

l'union économique belgo-luxembourgeoise, pp. 26–27, 31–33.

14. Ibid., p. 49; Rouquerel to Clemenceau, 17 Jan. 1919, no. 17/S, Vin 7N/1160; Devleeshouwer, "L'Opinion publique," p. 225.

nancial support from the Paris Municipal Council. The rest of France showed very little interest in the fate of Luxemburg.[15]

Foch, however, remained intensely concerned about the Grand Duchy and his headquarters remained in Luxemburg City. Because the Belgian government had not yet realized that British indifference would render genuine independence without neutrality impossible, and because it viewed French domination or acquisition of Luxemburg as a threat to Belgian independence, particularly if France also dominated the Rhineland, as both Foch and some French officials indicated a desire to do, the French military presence in Luxemburg gave rise to great concern in Brussels. Foch's pronouncements and the activity of his regiment only deepened the concern.[16] Not surprisingly, the Belgian government renewed its efforts to participate in the military occupation of the Grand Duchy. These efforts had, in fact, never been abandoned. All through the upheavals in Luxemburg itself, the Belgian government pursued the matter with the French authorities.

In anticipation that consent would be forthcoming, the Belgian army sent a regiment containing numerous Luxemburgers and Belgians of Luxembourgeois origin to Arlon under command of a general who came of a Luxembourgeois family and spoke the local dialect, but the regiment never succeeded in moving into the Grand Duchy. Clemenceau, while appearing to agree that Belgium should participate in the occupation, insisted that military matters were the province of Foch, who raised an unending stream of difficulties. First he pretended to have no instructions and not to have received Pichon's letter authorizing Belgian entry; then he enumerated a variety of military complexities

15. Bertie to Grey, 6 July 1915, F.O. 371/2637; Weber, *Histoire*, p. 105; Jacques Bariéty, *Les Relations franco-allemandes après la première guerre mondiale*, pp. 148–49; Nemry to Hymans, 9 Apr., 12 June 1919, BMAE B–10.121; Wagner, *La Sidérurgie*, pp. 36–37, 48; de Ligne to Hymans, 26 Feb. 1919, BMAE DB/32/II; de Gaiffier to Hymans, 10 July, 27 Oct. 1919, nos. 6161/2483, 9945/4153, BMAE FR/1919; de Rulle to Gunther, 26 June 1919, 850.A00/33, ACNP/442; de Gaiffier to Beyens, 24 May 1917, no. 3056/1553, BMAE FR/1917/I; Hymans to Albert, 30 Oct. 1918, BMAE FR/1918/II.

16. De Gaiffier to Hymans, 13 Nov. 1918, no. 5892/2904, BMAE FR/1918/II; Prum, *Problem*, p. 41; Weber, *Histoire*, p. 104; Whitlock to Colby, 1 Aug. 1920, Whitlock Papers/42 (LC); Whitlock to House, 10 Dec. 1918, House Papers 20/24; de Cartier to Hymans, 13 Dec. 1918, tel. 591, B Micro/23; Mordacq, *Le Ministère Clemenceau*, 3:19–20; Whitlock, *Letters*, 2:538; F.O. memo, 9 May 1921, F.O. 371/6970.

concerning troop dispositions, transport, and lines of communication, none of which withstood close examination. Next he argued that no changes could be made until the Allied armies had taken the line of the Rhine. This excuse continued to serve for some time after the Rhineland occupation had been completed.[17] In December 1918, Foch's representatives announced that he alone was responsible in Luxemburg and would give all orders there, remarking that the marshal wished the Grand Duchy to be treated as a French province.[18] As Belgium persisted, Foch began to blame Pershing for the delay, and the French government suddenly decided that it required formal British and American consent to Belgian participation in the occupation. The two governments gave their blessing but Pershing did not. He opposed the admixture of armies on principle and his constant difficulties with Foch only increased his opposition. He was not hostile to Belgium, but he preferred to see the situation simplified, not complicated. By mid-January, Foch's actions in Luxemburg led Pershing to threaten repeatedly to withdraw the few remaining American troops. Eventually, Foch promised to withdraw his own forces instead, but did not.[19]

In January 1919, Foch finally authorized the transfer of one Belgian battalion to the border village of Wiltz in northwest Luxemburg, an offer that Hymans declined as worthless and insulting. Foch then created difficulties over the fact that Albert had rejected incorporation of the Belgian army in the unified command, so that it was not under his

17. Manton memo, 24 Dec. 1918, 850A.00/1, ACNP/442; Hymans, *Mémoires*, 1: 344–45, 347; de Gaiffier to Hymans, 22, 29 Nov., 4 Dec. 1918, no. 8796/2990, tel. 181, no. 9018/3088, BMAE FR/1918/II; Fallon to Hymans, 7 Dec. 1918, tel. 797, BMAE PB/1918; Menschaert memo, 30 Nov. 1918, Menschaert to Foch, 21 Dec. 1918, no. 3, Weygand to Menschaert, 22 Dec. 1918, no. 9692, BMAE B-1-1519; de Gaiffier to Hymans, 18 Dec. 1918, no. 9287/3178, BMAE DB/32/II.

18. Gillain to Hymans, 6 Dec. 1918, no. 6114, BMAE B-1-1519; Whitlock to Lansing, 15 Dec. 1918, tel. 164, 850A.0146/3, ACNP/443.

19. Hymans to de Ligne, 31 Dec. 1918, no. 11185, Menschaert reports, 6, 14 Jan. 1919, Hymans to de Ligne, 9 Jan. 1919, no. 17, Tinant to Gillain, 10 Jan. 1919, tel., Menschaert to Weygand, 10 Jan. 1919, no. 63/B, Tinant memo, n.d. [12 Jan.? 1919], BMAE B-1-1519; de Gaiffier to Hymans, 18 Dec. 1918, tel. 218, BMAE FR/1918/II; de Gaiffier to Hymans, 7 Jan. 1919, no. 96/33, BMAE FR/1919; de Bassompierre to Hymans, 27 Dec. 1919, Tinant note, 18 Jan. 1919, BMAE DB/32/I; Pershing Diary, 12, 20, 23, 26 Jan. 1919, Pershing Papers/4–5; K. Nelson, *Victors Divided*, pp. 42–43; I.W.C. 48, 31 Dec. 1918, CAB 23/42.

orders, a circumstance he had never forgiven. The fact that the American army also remained technically outside his command was not mentioned. He also argued that, from the military point of view, Belgium would find Luxemburg an "elephant" and a real danger. Finally, he claimed that Belgium was incapable of defending Luxemburg, although against whom in 1919 is not clear. In his obsession with French security against renewed German invasion, Foch was determined to hold Luxemburg for France and to reject, on one pretext or another, any Belgian presence in the Grand Duchy as potentially dangerous to French safety. He in fact strongly opposed any enlargement of Belgium's territory or sphere of influence unless Belgium committed itself to a large military establishment and guaranteed Britain and France a free hand for any military activity they wished on Belgian territory.[20] In the circumstances, the French troops remained in Luxemburg and the Belgian army never arrived.

Gradually, the French forces in the Grand Duchy began to capitalize on their position for propaganda purposes. At first they were circumspect, but by December 1918, the campaign had become overt. To Belgian disgust, French troops en route to Luxemburg made large detours to parade through Brussels. Once in Luxemburg, they distributed French flags and false rumors that Belgium planned to annex the Grand Duchy. There were parades, concerts, and dramatic soirées at which the French, American, and Luxembourgeois anthems were played, but never the Brabançonne unless a member of the audience had the courage to request it. To reinforce the obvious, Foch summoned the Luxembourgeois cabinet ministers and lectured them, saying, "Little countries, if they want to survive, must depend upon powerful countries."[21]

At Christmas, the French imposed rigid controls on travel between Belgium and Luxemburg, requiring that all passports carry visas from the French command in Luxemburg, despite the fact that it was supposedly only Foch's staff headquarters within the American zone. The

20. De Bassompierre to Hymans, 27 Dec. 1918, Tinant to de Bassompierre, 16 Jan. 1919, tel., BMAE DB/32/I; de Gaiffier to Hymans, 16 Dec. 1918, 22 Jan. 1919, nos. 9235/3160, 487/191, BMAE DB/32/II; de Gaiffier to Hymans, 15 Jan. 1919, no. 259/104, BMAE B-1-1519; Foch note, 22 Dec. 1918, Vin 6N/70.

21. Whitlock, *Letters*, 2:534; de Ligne to Hymans, 9 Dec. 1918, no. 21/15, BMAE B-1-1519; de Ligne to Hymans, 17 Dec. 1918, no. 48/33, BMAE DB/32/II.

procedure was cumbersome, requiring all Belgians to apply to Brussels and the Belgian authorities to submit humiliating requests to the French commander. Next, Mollard, the French minister to Luxemburg, who was still in Paris, announced tendentiously in the Luxemburg press that France had taken over supply of Luxemburg, although the Belgian authorities and the Commission for the Relief of Belgium were in fact supplying Luxemburg and continued to do so for some time, as the French government was unable to supply northern France, let alone Luxemburg. Variously, Belgium was charged with trying to buy annexation by its supply efforts. In time, France began to provide coal and food, while also continuing the campaign of lavish parties and balls, complete with French pastry and chocolates. In addition, to reassure the pious Luxemburgers, who were suspicious of French anticlericalism, the devout Foch attended mass frequently and ceremoniously and required his officers to do the same. To garner support from the monarchists, he was conspicuously gallant to both grand duchesses. Tricolors, parades, and frequent visits from French dignitaries further curried pro-French sentiment.[22]

This was reinforced by French postal, press, and telegraphic censorship, control of three newspapers, and attempts to buy others at generous prices. The French utilized their position to run a press campaign against Belgium and to print false reports that Belgium had forbidden French supply of the Grand Duchy. They also charged that Belgium would not buy Luxemburg's agricultural produce and had nothing to offer Luxemburg. Consistently but mendaciously, the French posed as protectors of the dynasty against Belgian determination to destroy it. At the same time, communication between Belgium and the Grand Duchy was made as difficult as possible. In February 1919, telegraphic communication between Luxemburg and Belgium required fifteen days and de Ligne was obliged to route his telegrams via The Hague. Even so, they were often delayed. Rail service from the nearby Belgian cities of Liège and Verviers to Luxemburg was infrequent and took about

22. De Ligne to Hymans, 23 Dec. 1918, no. 81/52, de Gaiffier to Hymans, 6 Jan. 1919, no. 89/29, BMAE B-1-1519; de Ligne to Hymans, 30 Dec. 1918, no. 103/64; BMAE DB/32/II; Griffith report, n.d. [late Jan. 1919], anon. report, n.d. [end Jan. 1919], 185.1132/2, 9, ACNP/302; Hymans, *Mémoires*, 1:345–48; Bernard, *Terre commune*, pp. 682–87; de Ligne to Orts, 2 Apr. 1919, BMAE B-10.121.

thirteen hours, despite the absence of any technical problems. Thus the slightest errand required two nights and three days.[23]

Under the circumstances, it was impossible for the Belgian government to compete for Luxembourgeois favor and, aside from trying to arrange loans, provisioning the Grand Duchy, and repeatedly denying false charges, it did not attempt to do so, concentrating instead upon the increasingly futile effort to gain a physical presence in Luxemburg. Nothomb's CPN, however, launched a strident counterattack in the Belgian press. Though the Belgian Foreign Ministry had initially approved the CPN's creation late in 1918, when there was still reason to think that the Luxembourgeois dynasty would be abolished, by now Hymans found its efforts an embarrassment and a handicap, particularly because he and his staff had accepted that annexation was not possible in the foreseeable future. The CPN, inspired by Nothomb's romantic fervor and absolute determination to right the wrongs of 1839, was openly and blatantly annexationist, and its clumsy efforts not only undermined the Belgian government but also irritated the Luxemburgers and led them to disbelieve de Ligne's repeated assurances that Belgium harbored no designs on Luxemburg's independence. Whereas other news from Brussels met with every impediment, the French promptly published reports of the CPN's pronouncements with devastating effect.[24]

In these circumstances, opinion in the Grand Duchy shifted. At the end of the war, Luxemburg turned to Belgium for assistance and awaited the arrival of Belgian troops. There were from the first a few who favored France, chiefly a small republican, socialist element that never gained a great deal of support and that waned as Charlotte established her popularity. For the same reason, enthusiasm for a personal union

23. Griffith report, n.d., 185.1131/2, ACNP/302; Orts to de Gaiffier, 12 Apr. 1919, no. 3155, BMAE DB/32/I; de Ligne to Hymans, 27 Feb. 1919, no. 378/142, Nothomb to Orts, 16 May 1919, tel. 264, BMAE DB/32/II; Prum to Hymans, 9 Feb. 1919, de Ligne to Hymans, 22 Feb. 1919, no. 294/127, BMAE B-1-1519; de Ligne to Orts, 2 Apr. 1919, BMAE B-10.121.

24. Hymans, *Mémoires*, 1:301, 380–82; anon. memo, n.d., 185.1132/9, ACNP/302; Whitlock to ACNP, 24 June 1919, tel. 47, Wilson Papers 5B/48; Weber, *Histoire*, p. 105; d'Ansembourg to Hymans, 22 Feb. 1919, BMAE B-1-1519; Banque Nationale de Belgique to BMAE, n.d. [10 Mar.? 1919], BMAE DB/32/I; Hymans note, 27 Mar. 1919, BMAE B-366/I.

with Belgium also declined. After Charlotte became grand duchess, Luxembourgeois opinion overwhelmingly supported independence and maintenance of the dynasty. Nonetheless the question of economic orientation remained, although it was increasingly obscured by confusion over the dynastic issue. The Germanophile clergy were ardent supporters of the dynasty and were led to believe that France would protect it but Belgium would overturn it. Not knowing that Clemenceau was as hostile to Charlotte as to Marie Adelaide, they exerted their enormous influence on behalf of France. The peasants initially favored Belgium, but they were pious, ill educated, dominated by the clergy, and allowed to read only Catholic newspapers. With time, their support shifted to France, particularly because the protected French market would be a convenient outlet for their produce. The Liberal party, some of the Catholic political groups, and the towns, aside from Luxemburg City, were initially strong supporters of a Belgian tie. For the rest, perceptions of economic interest were important. Those producing essentially domestic products favored France's protected market, whereas those manufacturing goods for international export preferred free-trade Belgium. Thus, while the clergy were probably decisive, the farmers were lured to France's side by false reports that Belgium would reject their produce, which in any event would have met stiffer price competition on the Belgian market. To lend credibility to the reports, France blocked the sale of Luxembourgeois livestock to Belgium. The viticulturalists, wine makers, and brewers, who hoped to replace Germany on the Belgian market, preferred Belgium throughout for evident economic reasons. Heavy industry was at first attracted to the Belgian free-trade policy, supply of coal, and need for iron ore, recognizing that France, after the reacquisition of Alsace-Lorraine, would be oversupplied with ore and no market for Luxemburg's exports of ore, semi-finished products, and steel. France's lack of coking coal to replace the traditional shipments from the Ruhr was an issue at first but less of one after the Versailles treaty assured Luxemburg shipments of German coal. Once that problem was resolved, some steel manufacturers, including Emile Mayrisch, director-general of ARBED, wanted to combine with the Lorraine and Briey industries to form an iron and steel cartel to dominate Europe and possibly the world export trade. Others, after considerable pressure from French steel interests and French tariffs, came to feel that they faced ruination if Luxemburg did not enter into economic union with France. As a consequence of these pressures, the Belgian position quickly eroded. Indeed, in February 1919 a commission of the Luxembourgeois Chamber assigned during the war to study the economic future of the country reversed an earlier endorsement of economic union with Belgium and unanimously with one abstention approved union with France, while adding that a three-way arrangement would be ideal. In short, all Anglo-American evidence indicates that in 1918 the Luxemburgers heavily favored economic union with Belgium, but as the occupation became prolonged, the variegated French effort had an increasing influence upon opinion in the Grand Duchy.[25]

The attitudes of the Luxembourgeois prime minister are more difficult to assess. Emile Reuter became head of the government in October 1918 and so remained, except for the brief revolutionary upheavals, until 1925. In 1918 and 1919, he was in an extraordinarily awkward position and, of necessity, pursued a complex and indirect policy in his

25. Fallon to Hymans, 25 Nov. 1918, tel. 790, BMAE PB/1918/II; Orts to de Ligne, 27 Nov. 1918, 21 Apr. 1919, nos. 10105, 607, BMAE B-1-1519; Steefel memo, 10 Apr. 1918, Inquiry/552; Hymans to de Cartier, 10 Nov. 1918, tel. 332, B Micro/22; Whitlock to House, 1, 28 Nov. 1918, House Papers 20/24; Whitlock, *Letters*, 1:272; Prum, *Problem*, p. 12; Western & General Report no. 101, 8 Jan. 1919, CAB 24/150; Oppenheimer to Akers-Douglas, 30 Nov. 1918, F.O. 371/4355; Robertson to F.O., 2 Jan. 1919, no. 1766, tel. 18, F.O. 371/3636; Zeigler report, 17 Nov. 1918, Jacquimot to Lansing, n.d., Griffith reports, late Jan., 27 Jan., 14, 23 Apr. 1919, Gunther reports, n.d., 28 May 1919, 185.1132/2, 4, 7, 9, 23, 26, 28, 36, ACNP/302; Soutou, "La Politique économique," p. 264; Maurice Baumont, "La Belgique, la France, et le Luxembourg en 1919–1920," p. 175; Robertson to Balfour, 3 Oct. 1918, no. 212, F.O. 371/3256; encls. (*Times* articles, 19, 21 Apr. 1919) in de Ramaix to Hymans, 19, 21 Apr. 1919, nos. 2662/846, 2670/848, encl. (*Daily Telegraph* article, 8 Feb. 1919) in Moncheur to Hymans, 8 Feb. 1919, no. 1038/276, BMAE GB/1919/I; de Rulle to Gunther, 29 June 1919, 850A.00/33, ACNP/442; Admiralty, *Luxemburg*, p. 251; Wagner, *La Sidérurgie*, p. 47; Devleeshouwer, "L'Opinion publique," pp. 227–28; de Ligne to Hymans, 3 Apr. 1919, no. 628/205, BMAE DB/32/I. Probably American evidence, which reported both strong pro-Belgian sentiment initially and later heavy pressure from France and the clergy, is most reliable, as the United States was the only disinterested party with observers in Luxemburg, including an experienced diplomatist sent from The Hague. All Belgian evidence and some of the fragmentary surviving French evidence (for instance, Deuxième Bureau, Etat-Major reports, n.d. [late Dec. 1918], 6, 8, Jan. 1919, Vin 6N/74) also indicate substantial early support for Belgium.

efforts to preserve Luxemburg's independence. His task was complicated by the fact that, at Belgian request, the powers did not formally recognize Charlotte's accession pending clarification of the whole situation at the peace conference, and by the fact that Charlotte herself was engaged to Prince Felix of Bourbon-Parma, who had fought in the Austrian army, although, at his own insistence, only on the Russian front.[26] The Belgian decision not to recognize Charlotte at once was undoubtedly a mistake made without full appreciation of French intentions or realization that Belgian participation in the occupation would never be achieved and in the fear that if a Belgian minister were accredited to Charlotte, Mollard would arrive on the next train. After Charlotte's accession, Reuter sent virtually identical notes on successive days to the French, British, and Belgian governments, asking to put Luxemburg under the protection of each.[27] Silence was the only answer from all three. Reuter was certainly a wholehearted supporter of independence and the dynasty; there is fragmentary evidence to suggest that he favored a French tie, but, given the circumstances, it is far from conclusive. His country was under almost oppressively benevolent French military occupation, was dependent in his own eyes upon the French army to prevent further revolutionary outbreaks and threats to the dynasty, and was encountering growing French economic pressure, particularly upon ARBED.[28] After the Comité des Forges in general and Schneider in particular decided that they wished to take over ARBED, in whose administration and capital shares Belgians had long been dominant, his circumstances became increasingly difficult, particularly because the grand ducal economy was in urgent need of some

26. Hymans to Lansing, 21 Jan. 1919, no. 7, 850A.001/5, ACNP/443; de Gaiffier to Hymans, 21 Jan. 1919, no. 462/181, BMAE DB/32/II. The Belgian chargé, Prince Albert de Ligne, was accredited to the grand ducal government but not to Charlotte. Two of Felix's brothers, the Princes Sixtus and Xavier de Bourbon-Parma, had fought in the Belgian army. Willequet, *Albert Ier*, p. 145.

27. Reuter to French govt., 21 Jan. 1919, FMAE Z/Lux/12; Reuter to Balfour, 22 Jan. 1919, F.O. 371/3638; d'Ansembourg to Hymans, 23 Jan. 1919, BMAE B-1-1519.

28. Foch to Clemenceau, 10 Feb. 1919, no. 1062, Vin 6N/70; de Ligne to Hymans, 26 Feb. 1919, no. 313/138, BMAE DB/32/II; *Times*, 19 Apr. 1919, p. 9; Griffith to Haskins, 14 Apr. 1919, Griffith report, 23 Apr. 1919, no. 20, 185.1132/26, 28, ACNP/302; de Rulle to Gunther, 26 June 1919, 850A.00/33, ACNP/442.

new outlet to replace the abruptly ended German tie. Reuter was reputed to be an exceptionally honest man,[29] and it is possible that he did
not recognize French duplicity in maintaining that France would protect
the dynasty whereas Belgium would destroy it. On the other hand,
his path was not straightforward. As he frankly admitted, some of his
moves were designed to provoke a French declaration of interest in
Luxemburg. He appears to have hoped for a three-way economic union
as affording Luxemburg the greatest freedom of action and at least a
prospect of avoiding domination by one more powerful partner. Given
all the pressures upon him and given the abrupt, intermittent inter-
ventions by the Big Four of the peace conference into Luxemburg's
internal affairs, Reuter's delicate dance from side to side proves little.
He was probably trying to balance between Belgium and France to
preserve a degree of independence for the Grand Duchy just as Belgium was trying to balance between Britain and France to the same end.

It is equally difficult to assess Clemenceau's policy on the Luxemburg
question at the end of 1918 and as the peace conference progressed.
He and Pichon repeatedly promised that Belgium should have Luxemburg and repeatedly ordered Foch to arrange Belgian participation in
the occupation.[30] How genuine these orders were is impossible to say,
but Foch did not take them seriously. There is fragmentary French
evidence to suggest that at first Clemenceau's assurances, in which
Poincaré also joined, were genuine, as the Belgians believed. However,
their belief was founded in part upon the notion that one could not
doubt the word of honor of a French prime minister. If Clemenceau
initially favored a Belgian solution to the Luxemburg question, he soon
bowed to the pressures upon him. First there was Foch, preoccupied
with strategic dispositions for the next war against Germany, who had
full support from the General Staff in Paris. Then there was Berthelot
at the Quai d'Orsay, whose inclinations probably remained annexation-

29. De Gaiffier to Hymans, 3 Oct. 1919, tel. 136, BMAE FR/1918/II; Ziegler to
Nothomb, 22 Jan. 1919, BMAE B-10.121.

30. De Gaiffier to Hymans, 22 Nov., 15 Dec. 1918, no. 8796/2990, tel. 206, BMAE
FR/1918/II; Mordacq, *Le Ministère Clemenceau*, 3:19–20; de Gaiffier to Hymans, 16 Dec.
1918, no. 9235/3160, BMAE DB/32/II; de Gaiffier to Hymans, 26 Jan. 1919, BMAE
FR/1919; de Gaiffier to Hymans, 15 Jan. 1919, tel. 36, BMAE DB/32/I; de Gaiffier to
Hymans, 24 Dec. 1918, BMAE Ind/1918/III.

ist. Annexationist pressure came as well from Mollard and the Comité Franco-Luxembourgeois, which was extremely active both in the Grand Duchy and in Paris, and which had long bragged of its ties to Clemenceau's entourage, notably Georges Mandel. The Comité had great success in generating a powerful movement in the French National Assembly and the Paris press for French retention of the Grand Duchy. Beyond that, there were the pressures exerted by the Comité des Forges, representing the French steel industry.[31] Whatever his original intentions, Clemenceau, along with other senior officials, became increasingly reserved in statements to Belgian leaders. By January, French diplomatists were echoing Foch's opinions on the military dangers to Belgium of a Belgian attempt to dominate the mountainous and easily fortified Grand Duchy and suggesting with increasing frankness that the price of a Belgian solution to the Luxemburg question was French military conventions with both states.[32]

Clemenceau, who had lived through two German invasions of France and who was thus determined that there never be a third, probably sympathized with Foch's concern to guard one of the gates to France, although his relations with the generalissimo were increasingly strained. Undoubtedly, he did not wish to strain them further over the question of Luxemburg. He also came to detest Hymans and treated him with mounting rudeness and contempt. Before the peace conference began, Clemenceau stated that France had no designs on the Grand Duchy and asked de Gaiffier to trust him to arrange matters. As time passed, he began to term Belgian requests that he advise Luxemburg to turn to

31. Ribot, *Journal*, p. 257; Paul Cambon, *Correspondance, 1870–1924*, 3:296–97; Mordacq, *Le Ministère Clemenceau*, 3:19–20; de Gaiffier to Hymans, 8 Feb., 30 Nov., 1 Dec. 1918, nos. 838/382, 8746/2791, tel. 183, BMAE FR/1918/II; de Gaiffier to Hymans, 16, 22 Jan. 1919, nos. 293/116, 487/191, BMAE DB/32/II; de Gaiffier to Hymans, 16 Jan. 1919, tel. 40, BMAE B-10.121; Whitlock, *Letters*, 2:546; Prum, *Problem*, p. 12; Hymans, *Mémoires*, 1:189; de Gaiffier to Hymans, 15 Jan. 1919, tel. 36, BMAE DB/32/I; Hymans to Defrance, 10 Jan. 1919, de Gaiffier to Hymans, 18 Feb. 1919, no. 1270/484, BMAE FR/1919; de Broqueville to de Gaiffier, 14 Dec. 1917, no. 2541, BMAE FR/1917/II.

32. De Gaiffier to Hymans, 10 Jan. 1919 [misdated 6 Feb. 1919], no. 206/72, BMAE FR/1919. Domination of Luxemburg would not be a military danger to Belgium. The real French concern was with French security and with the possibility that Belgium might not fight to defend the Grand Duchy against German invasion.

Belgium "humiliating" and to declare abruptly that Belgium must not appear to inflict a defeat on France.[33] Self-evidently, if France were not in competition in Luxemburg, she could not be defeated there. Further, Belgian representatives could scarcely utter the name of Luxemburg at the Quai d'Orsay without counter-mention of either Franco-Belgian economic union or a military convention or both. It appears that, aside from the Comité Franco-Luxembourgeois and its French adherents, the Comité des Forges, Foch, and possibly Berthelot, few in France, including Clemenceau, had any profound interest in Luxemburg per se. It was viewed primarily as a means of pressure on Belgium. French policy had not fundamentally changed: Belgium could have Luxemburg if France could have Belgium. In that way, France would be secure on her northern and eastern frontiers and could throw the assets of both countries into the economic balance against Germany.

AT THE PEACE CONFERENCE

When the peace conference opened in mid-January 1919, the outlines of French policy were starting to become clear. Clemenceau and Pichon now clung firmly to the narrowest possible interpretation of Ribot's 1917 declaration that France would not claim Luxemburg; they never violated it technically but did nothing whatever to restrain Foch, the French press and Chamber, or the Comité Franco-Luxembourgeois. The French policy was one of delay,[34] and of trying to avoid a decision on Luxemburg at the peace conference, where Anglo-American pressure might be brought to bear in support of Belgium. If a settlement could be postponed until after the British and American delegations had left Paris, Belgium would be isolated and could be forced to terms. Once Belgium had fully accepted French military and economic domination, with all that implied, Luxemburg would be her consolation prize. In the interim, Berthelot was left free at the Quai d'Orsay to pursue a policy contrary to the promises made to Belgium, and Belgian overtures to French officials met with increasing reserve, although eco-

33. De Gaiffier to Hymans, 8 Apr. 1919, no. 2888/1126, BMAE B-1.
34. Trausch, "Les Relations franco-belges," p. 288.

nomic and military conventions were often mentioned. These proposals alarmed Belgian leaders as much as French plans for the Rhineland, particularly because the three schemes together amounted to a revival of Foch's plan for a confederation of France, Belgium, Luxemburg, and the Rhineland in which France would be entirely dominant and Belgium encircled. Hymans, who had asked the powers to take no decisions about Luxemburg without prior concert with Belgium, protested repeatedly to the British about French policy in the Grand Duchy, but to little avail. The British had decided to support Belgium on the Luxemburg question and intimated as much to Hymans, but his frequent plaints about French encirclement and his requests for British diplomatic intervention did not, at this stage, evoke any concrete assistance. A Belgian diplomat carefully commented to Villiers in January 1919 that, had France annexed Luxemburg thirty years before, Belgium would not have gone to war against Germany in 1914, but to no effect. In the interim, the French grip on the Grand Duchy tightened.[35]

On 6 February, Hymans saw Balfour and Hardinge in an effort to gain support against French tactics, stressing particularly the potential threat to Belgian economic and political independence. Both men agreed that France must not have Luxemburg.[36] Armed with this assurance, Hymans requested, in his presentation to the Ten on 11 February, not annexation of the Grand Duchy but a closer union. He asked "the Conference to facilitate a rapprochement between the two countries" to be achieved "by free consent." He opposed Lansing's suggestion of a plebiscite but wanted the powers to urge Luxemburg toward talks with Belgium regarding closer relations.[37] Although rejecting a plebiscite was awkward in view of Wilson's enthusiasm for self-determination, Hymans understandably resisted a vote to be held under French military occupation.

35. Pichon to Derby, 17 Jan. 1919, Lothian Papers GD/40/17/69; Villiers to Balfour, 8, 9, 10 Jan. 1919, tel. 4, no. 8, tel. 6, Moncheur to F.O., 18 Jan. 1919, no. 467, F.O. to Moncheur, 24 Jan. 1919, F.O. 371/3638; Hymans, *Mémoires*, 1:353, 356; P. Cambon, *Correspondance*, 3:296–97; F.O. memo, 9 May 1921, F.O. 371/6970; *Le Soir*, 4 May 1919, p. 1; Bernard, *Terre commune*, p. 690.

36. Hymans, *Mémoires*, 1:360; Balfour memo, 6 Feb. 1919, F.O. 800/215.

37. I.C. 138, 140, 11, 12 Feb. 1919, CAB 28/6; Kerr to Lloyd George, 12 Feb. 1919, Lloyd George Papers F/89/2/9; Lansing Desk Diary, 11 Feb. 1919, Lansing Papers.

After his speech, Hymans judged that the British and Italians supported his stand on Luxemburg, the Americans were hesitant, and the
French were embarrassed. He thought that Clemenceau wanted Luxemburg for France but did not dare to say so outright. He also sensed
Clemenceau's annoyance that a small state would dare to oppose him
so stubbornly.[38] British diplomatic support would clearly be needed
to move Clemenceau, and such support was to an extent forthcoming.
Balfour, recognizing Clemenceau's passive resistance, asked Lloyd
George to back Belgium to the hilt on the Luxemburg question and to
make this issue part of the broader Rhineland settlement, but Lloyd
George showed no interest. At the same time, Hardinge and Crowe
took the lead in blocking an early plebiscite in the Grand Duchy, as
announced by Reuter to the peace conference on 12 February. They
also recommended without effect that Britain insist to France upon
Luxemburg's economic union with Belgium.[39]

There matters stood on 21 February when Reuter requested economic negotiations with both France and Belgium. Hymans saw Pichon
and Tardieu, who echoed the thinking of Foch and manifestly regarded
the Luxemburg question in relation to both the Saar Basin and the
Rhineland. Pichon refused to decline Reuter's invitation but, at Belgian
insistence, finally agreed to make no reply. Hymans then turned to
Balfour, who was becoming increasingly concerned about the situation.
As yet he could see no device for effective British unilateral action.
He thought discussion with Pichon or in the conference would be useless but recommended to Lloyd George that, when Clemenceau had
recovered from the assassination attempt, "you or I should privately
sound him as to whether the country which has reacquired Alsace and
Lorraine, and is very likely to acquire the Saar coal-fields, might not
show a little generosity to its weaker neighbor, who has suffered so
much by the war and got so little out of it."[40] In this paragraph lay the
first hint that a Belgian solution to the Luxemburg problem might be a

38. Hymans memo, 11 Feb. 1919, BMAE Ind/1919/I; Hymans *Mémoires*, 1:378.
39. Reuter to Clemenceau, 12 Feb. 1919, BMAE DB/32/I; F.O. memo, 9 May 1921,
F.O. 371/6970.
40. D'Ansembourg to Hymans, 21 Feb. 1919, BMAE DB/32/I; de Gaiffier to Hymans,
25 Feb. 1919, no. 1471/564, Hymans note, 1 Mar. 1919, BMAE FR/1919; Balfour
memo, 25 Feb. 1919, Balfour Papers/49750.

possible quid pro quo for British support to France regarding the Saar Basin.

As Lloyd George made no reply and took no action, French propaganda in Luxemburg intensified and Crowe pointed out that a plebiscite held under French guns would be calamitous for Belgium and a threat to her independence. Late in February and early in March, Balfour and House discussed the matter repeatedly and decided to act on their own initiative. Together they tackled Clemenceau on 4 March. He blamed the situation in Luxemburg largely on Foch and disclaimed any designs there, promising to withdraw the French forces. However, he insisted that he could not refuse any Luxembourgeois request to join France and he strongly favored a plebiscite. When Hymans thanked Balfour on 8 March for his efforts, he pointed out that France would not hear of a plebiscite in Alsace-Lorraine and asked how Luxemburg differed. The others were skeptical as well. House recorded his doubts in his diary while the Foreign Office noted that Clemenceau had not promised to stop the propaganda campaign.[41]

As Luxemburg continued to plan for an early plebiscite in which voters would indicate their preference for the existing dynasty, another unspecified dynasty, or a republic, French propaganda continued unabated. Under the circumstances, Balfour was again willing to exert pressure for delay, although delay would not benefit Belgium, but he could see little else to do unless Lloyd George and Wilson would take advantage of the struggle over the Rhineland then in progress to make Luxemburg part of a general settlement with France. Other British officials scented the same opportunity. When Headlam-Morley, who was soon to become the British member of the Saar Commission, complained on 25 March that Britain was giving Belgium insufficient support and should back her to the utmost over Luxemburg, Crowe wrote: "I quite agree that we should stand by Belgium as regards the Luxemburg question, and I go so far as to suggest that our support of French claims in the Saar Valley and to a pro-French settlement of the

---

41. House to Wilson, 27 Feb. 1919, tel. 10, House Papers 49/12; House Diary, 27 Feb., 1, 2, 4, 6 Mar. 1919, 15:71–72, 75, 78–79, 81, House Papers; House to Wilson, 4 Mar. 1919, tel. 1, Wilson Papers 5B/18; Hymans memo, 8 Mar. 1919, BMAE DB/32/I; Balfour to Curzon, 14 Mar. 1919, no. 245, F.O. 371/3638.

Left-bank-of-the-Rhine question should distinctly be made conditional
on Luxemburg being given to Belgium." This recommendation, clearly
proposing Luxemburg as a quid pro quo for the Saar and possibly also
for the Rhineland, was emphatically endorsed by Hardinge and read by
Balfour but never sent to Headlam-Morley.[42]

The next day, Hymans saw Hardinge to report that Luxemburg had
asked to negotiate a military convention and diplomatic, economic, and
monetary union with Belgium, and also was seeking a loan. At the same
time, he complained of British inaccessibility and lack of sympathy on
other issues. Balfour was annoyed by this, especially because he himself
had recently had a chilly session with Hymans about Holland. Nevertheless, on 27 March he sent Lloyd George a new memorandum by
Crowe urging that British consent to French acquisition of the Saar coal
fields be made contingent upon a Belgian solution to the Luxemburg
question, himself adding a note saying that the matter was important. In
the next ten days, the British delegation took no action regarding Luxemburg in the crucial period when the Four began meeting as such and
the struggle over the Saar Basin was at its height. Wilson was reluctant
to detach the Saar from Germany, as its inhabitants were indisputably
German, but France insisted upon obtaining the coal mines in recompense for German destruction of French mines. No way had yet been
devised to give the French the Saar mines without the Saarlanders and,
in view of the Franco-American deadlock, British policy assumed crucial importance. It would have been easy to link the Saar and Luxemburg just then but Headlam-Morley, who was assigned to the Saar
Commission on 29 March, saw Lloyd George frequently without re-
ceiving any instructions about Luxemburg. Headlam-Morley supported
the French claim to the Saar, partly in hopes of strengthening Belgium's
claim to Luxemburg. Had he known of Crowe's thinking, he could
easily have made Luxemburg a condition of his support to France, but
the British were poorly coordinated, thanks largely to Lloyd George's
propensity to play a lone hand, whereas the French assigned Tardieu to
all west German problems and mounted a concerted effort.[43]

42. Garrett to ACNP, 22 Mar. 1919, tel. 223, Wilson Papers 5B/22; Headlam-Morley
memo, 25 Mar. 1919, F.O. 608/2 pt. 1; F.O. memo, 9 May 1921, F.O. 371/6970.

43. Hardinge to Balfour, 26 Mar. 1919, F.O. 608/2 pt. 1; F.O. memo, 9 May 1921,
F.O. 371/6970.

Lloyd George's failure to seize the moment, which probably arose either from his reluctance to read memoranda or from his stormy confrontation with Hymans about reparations on 31 March, was of greater importance than anybody then realized. Suddenly at the end of March, the Luxembourgeois cabinet, having already made the necessary arrangements for the dynastic plebiscite, proposed to hold an additional simultaneous plebiscite on the future economic orientation of the country and formally presented the matter to the Chamber on 2 April. Upon Belgian investigation of this startling development, it appeared that Pichon had informed grand ducal representatives through French deputies associated with the Comité Franco-Luxembourgeois that the peace conference could not and would not pronounce on the Luxemburg question and did not have the matter before it at all. He had apparently added that it was up to the people of Luxemburg to decide their future. Charged with these statements, Pichon admitted most of them, dodged the rest, and repeated Clemenceau's recent declaration that Belgium must not appear to win a victory over France. At about the same time, a senior Quai d'Orsay official advised the Luxemburgers to vote on the economic question as soon as possible. He added that the dynastic plebiscite (which France had no hope of winning) was less urgent and could be deferred. Because the Luxemburg cabinet acted on the misleading advice from Paris, France had essentially succeeded in arranging an economic plebiscite to be held under French guns. Although it could be and was deferred, under Luxemburg law the proposal could not be withdrawn.[44] Thus the French had gained another instrument of pressure on Belgium just at the moment when the British could most easily have blocked them.

These developments in the Grand Duchy lent added urgency to King Albert's trip to Paris. In part, his visit was a response to the entire coordinated French campaign involving the Saarland, the Rhineland, and Luxemburg. Though no Belgian was privy to great-power debates about the Saar Basin, Albert was justifiably concerned about Luxem-

---

44. Vannerus to Pichon, 27 Mar. 1919, FMAE Z/Lux/17; Garrett to ACNP, 5 Apr. 1919, tel. 250, Wilson Papers 5B/26; de Ligne to Hymans, 3, 12 Apr. 1919, nos. 628/205, 689, BMAE DB/32/I; de Ligne to Orts, 2 Apr. 1919, Ziegler to Nothomb, 12 Apr. 1919, BMAE B-10.121; de Gaiffer to Hymans, 8 Apr. 1919, no. 2839/1108, BMAE FR/1919.

burg and the Rhineland. At his meeting with the Four on 4 April, the session became stormy as soon as he raised the Luxemburg question. Lloyd George asked what language the inhabitants spoke. Clemenceau said French and Hymans corrected him, whereupon Clemenceau launched into a furious diatribe against the Belgian government in general and Hymans in particular, charging him with organizing a frantic propaganda campaign in the Grand Duchy, interfering with the wishes of the Luxemburgers, and trying to inflict a defeat on the French. At the same time, he claimed that his sole wish was "the disappearance of the German dynasty" and that France wanted nothing in Luxemburg, but he insisted vehemently on a plebiscite. Although he said that he would be happy to see Luxemburg become Belgian, the atmosphere became so heated during his denunciation of Belgian policy that Albert and even Hymans deemed it useless to try to reply. Albert took care, however, to see Hardinge later to tell him about the incident. He claimed that the position of the government and even the monarchy in Belgium would be precarious if Luxemburg went to France, and he asked that Balfour enlist Lloyd George's aid. Albert himself wrote to the prime minister, assuring him that Clemenceau's charges could be fully refuted by Belgian documents and asking for his sympathy. There is no evidence that Lloyd George ever replied.[45]

Nonetheless the Belgian delegation continued to rely on the British and on the consistently sympathetic House, who advised that Hymans see Balfour about an Anglo-American effort to safeguard Belgian interests. As Balfour was ill, on 7 April Hymans brought identical memoranda to House and Crowe, asking that Britain and the United States intervene to persuade the French to cease their pressures upon the Grand Duchy and to induce the Luxembourgeois to defer the economic plebiscite. The memoranda further requested that both countries ex-

45. Hymans, *Mémoires*, 1:444–47; Mantoux, *Les Délibérations,* 1:146–48; Hardinge to Balfour, 4 Apr. 1919, F.O. 608/2 pt. 1; Balfour to Curzon, 12 Apr. 1919, no. 481, F.O. 371/3638; Albert to Lloyd George, 4 Apr. 1919, Lloyd George Papers F/49/4/1; van den Heuvel notes, 4 Apr. 1919, van den Heuvel Papers/46; Raymond Poincaré, *A la recherche de la paix, 1919,* p. 336. Mantoux's account of the 4 April meeting differs from that of Hymans on matters of detail and, judging from the later remarks of Hymans, King Albert, and Clemenceau, suffers from an excess of discretion.

press in writing to Belgium their hopes that the forthcoming economic negotiations with Luxemburg would succeed. Hymans told Crowe that he had conclusive evidence that French pressure had forced the economic plebiscite. He asked for Anglo-American intervention "at once," adding that House was willing if Balfour were.[46] Crowe wrote on Hymans's memorandum:

> I would urge that we should at once
> (a) definitely intimate to M. Clemenceau that our acceptance of the Saar Valley solution now under discussion is conditional on France leaving Luxemburg to Belgium and
> (b) make the communication to Luxemburg together with the U.S., as suggested by M. Hymans, informing M. Clemenceau and S[r] Orlando that we are doing so.

Balfour added:

> I don't know exactly how the Saar valley negotiation now stands. But I think it would be most unjust, and in the long run most inexpedient, that France should get Alsace-Lorraine and the Saar coal—and Belgium *nothing*.

He forwarded these comments under cover of a sheet bearing the words: "Prime Minister. This is both important and pressing. A.J.B."[47]

After further pleas from Hymans, Crowe again urged Anglo-American intervention and drafted an appropriate letter endorsing Belgo-Luxembourgeois economic union. It was never sent and Lloyd George did not reply to Balfour's note. On 8 April, the day after Balfour had sent Crowe's memorandum to him, Lloyd George, responding to Headlam-Morley's urgings, supported France on the Saar question. The next day, Wilson, finding himself isolated, began to yield, and the matter was in essence settled. France therefore received the Saar coal fields without condition and the Saarland was placed under League of

46. House Diary, 6 Apr. 1919, 15:141, House Papers; Derby to Curzon, 7 Apr. 1919, no. 374, F.O. 371/3638; de Cartier memo, 6 Apr. 1919, Hymans to House, 7 Apr. 1919, BMAE DB/32/I.
47. Hymans to Crowe, 7 Apr. 1919, and minutes, F.O. 608/2 pt. 1; F.O. memo, 9 May 1921, F.O. 371/6970.

Nations administration. Lloyd George had either rejected Balfour's advice or, more probably, had failed to read his recommendations.[48]

The Belgian delegation continued its campaign, not knowing that the moment had passed. On 8 April, Clemenceau rejected a Belgian request that he advise Luxemburg to turn to Belgium, was unpleasant over what he termed a humiliating Belgian demarche, and once again said that Belgium must not have the appearance of a victory over France. Clemenceau undoubtedly was more concerned with reality than appearance and wished to capitalize upon France's dominant position in the Grand Duchy. Nonetheless, on 9 April, Hymans notified the powers that economic negotiations with Luxemburg were about to begin, thus providing the vehicle for the requested Anglo-American blessing. On 11 April, he saw Balfour and Philip Kerr, Lloyd George's private secretary, both of whom promised urgent action that did not materialize. Finally, when Delacroix, Vandervelde, and Hymans saw Lloyd George on the thirteenth about the treaty terms, they pressingly requested a British communication endorsing Belgo-Luxembourgeois rapprochement. Lloyd George said that he must first warn Clemenceau. It was agreed that Balfour would take the matter to the Four, as Tardieu had told the Belgian delegation that although Clemenceau could not himself urge Luxemburg toward Belgium, the peace conference could do so. Lloyd George promptly told the Four that the Belgian leaders had wished to discuss Luxemburg but he had refused, and Clemenceau, who was fully informed on the situation in Luxemburg and Belgian concern about it, maintained that he needed more information before dealing with the matter.[49]

As Hymans distrusted Balfour's initiative, he also saw House, who promised to try to get Wilson to raise the question at once, thus forcing Balfour's hand. In Belgian eyes, the situation was becoming urgent, for the Luxembourgeois Chamber was about to vote on the plebiscite bill. House did talk to Wilson and later took credit for what then transpired, but in fact Wilson did not raise the Luxemburg question when the Four

48. Hymans to Balfour, 9 Apr. 1919, no. 425, Hymans to Crowe, 9 Apr. 1919, F.O. 608/2 pt. 1; F.O. memo, 9 May 1921, F.O. 371/6970.

49. De Gaiffier to Hymans, 8 Apr. 1919, no. 2888/1126, BMAE FR/1919; Hymans memos, 5, 11, 14 Apr. 1919, BMAE B-1-1519; de Cartier memo, 7 Apr. 1919, BMAE DB/32/I; Mantoux, *Les Délibérations*, 1:238.

next met on 15 April. Balfour, substituting for Lloyd George, who was in London, did so. He started by pointing out the effect on world opinion if France gained Alsace-Lorraine, the Saar, and Luxemburg while Belgium obtained nothing. Clemenceau smoothly agreed but, pleading ignorance of opinion in the Grand Duchy, said he could not sign a letter endorsing Belgo-Luxembourgeois rapprochement, adding that such a letter without his signature would have a deplorable effect upon French opinion. The Four agreed only to request postponement of the plebiscite.[50]

Because Luxemburg still fell nominally within the American zone, the Allied request was relayed through American channels. On 17 April, however, Hymans pointed out to Crowe that the Luxembourgeois Chamber was voting that very day on the plebiscite bill and asked what was being done about it. This news caused considerable mystification in Paris, but investigation revealed that the instructions from the peace conference had not specified whether one plebiscite or both should be postponed. This fact, coupled with the incompetence of the American commander's interpreter, created sufficient confusion for Reuter to choose to assume that the dynastic vote could proceed. The Belgians thought it better to avoid interference in a clearly domestic matter, but Clemenceau's opposition to confirmation in power of what he invariably referred to as "the German dynasty" was well known to the British and American leaders. Thus, at Balfour's insistence, Wilson agreed to send instructions to defer both plebiscites.[51] The Belgian delegation was not consulted about this decision, which they did not favor, as their chief concern was the economic plebiscite to which their representations had been consistently confined, and they were unable even to obtain the text of the instructions sent to the American commander in Luxemburg. Nonetheless, the inhabitants of the Grand Duchy

50. Hymans memo, 14, 15 Apr. 1919, BMAE B-1-1519; Hymans to Balfour, 14 Apr. 1919, F.O. 608/2 pt. 1; Hymans to BMAE, 15 Apr. 1919, tel. 343, Balfour to Hymans, 15 Apr. 1919, BMAE DB/32/I; House Diary, 14, 15 Apr. 1919, 15:154, 161, House Papers.

51. Drummond to Clerk, 17 Apr. 1919, F.O. 800/329; Hymans to Balfour, 14 Apr. 1919, and Crowe minute, 18 Apr. 1919, F.O. 608/2 pt. 1; de Ligne to Hymans, 17 Apr. 1919, no. 689/232, BMAE B-1-1519; Orts to DB, 18 Apr. 1919, tel. 182, BMAE DB/32/I; Mantoux, *Les Délibérations*, 1:246–47; F.O. memo, 9 May 1921, F.O. 371/ 6970; Bliss to Close, 18 Apr. 1919, Close to Bliss, 19 Apr. 1919, Wilson Papers 5B/29.

blamed Belgium for postponement of the dynastic vote, assuming interference in their internal affairs and annexationist designs. Their suspicions seemed to be confirmed when the French quietly and inaccurately informed them that Belgium had insisted upon deferring both plebiscites, urged them to defy the Supreme Council and force the issue by voting, and added that France would not refuse Luxemburg if it offered itself. Although Luxemburg rejected the advice to hold the plebiscites at once, the Big Four intervention, contrary to Balfour's and House's intent, only redounded to French benefit.[52]

Hymans was encouraged, however, when on 16 April Poincaré told him that Luxemburg should go to Belgium and that Clemenceau now concurred with this view, having resolved earlier hesitations. Though Clemenceau confirmed this report three days later, it appears that he was primarily maneuvering to exclude Britain and America from the negotiations. On the surface, Clemenceau's resistance seemed to be evaporating, although he still insisted that the present wishes of the Luxemburgers must be decisive, and he reiterated, as always, that no defeat must be inflicted upon France, two provisos with sweeping implications for the final outcome. Still, Clemenceau made no objection to Belgo-Luxembourgeois negotiations. Technical talks toward an economic union finally began in Brussels on 24 April and proceeded smoothly in their early stages.[53]

Moreover, when at the end of April a British official noticed that nothing had been done about treaty clauses concerning Luxemburg and a committee was hastily appointed to draft some, de Gaiffier sat upon it and successfully blocked a French move to award control of the Guillaume-Luxembourg railway to France, a maneuver that the French had already unsuccessfully tried in the Commission on Ports, Waterways, and Railways. Hymans approved the resulting brief clauses, which, though of doubtful validity because Luxemburg was never invited to

52. De Ligne to Hymans, 22 Apr. 1919, tel. 46, BMAE B-1-1519; BMAE to DB, 22 Apr. 1919, tel. 186, Hymans memo, 25 Apr. 1919, Orts to Hymans, 25 Apr. 1919, BMAE DB/32/I; de Gaiffier to Hymans, 30 Apr., 10 May 1919, nos. 3582/1404, 3921/1532, BMAE B-10.121.
53. Hymans note, 16 Apr. 1919, BMAE B-1-1519; Hymans memo, 19 Apr. 1919, BMAE DB/32/II; BMAE to Albert, 18 Apr. 1919, BMAE B-10.121; Orts to Hymans, 25, 26 Apr. 1919, BMAE DB/32/I; Poincaré, *A la recherche*, p. 342.

adhere to the Versailles treaty, contained nothing offensive to Belgium, as Germany was merely required to renounce her past rights in Luxemburg and to accept in advance future Allied arrangements there. In addition, at Belgian insistence, Germany was obliged to concede to Luxemburg upon Allied request the economic advantages to which the victor powers were entitled, notably duty-free export to Germany for five years and a share in reparations coal.[54] Although Belgium sought these provisions to protect Luxemburg's economic interest, the net effect was to remove important obstacles to Franco-Luxembourgeois economic rapprochement. Under the circumstances, the French made no objection and tried to take credit for the benefits bestowed on Luxemburg.

These superficial Belgian successes, all more apparent than real, were countered, however, by increasing signs of renewed French pressure, both on Belgian diplomatists and in the Grand Duchy. The pro-French element in Luxemburg was blaming Belgian machinations for Big Four intervention, although Reuter insisted that this was untrue. However, he seized the moment to press for formal Belgian recognition of the dynasty. Though Hymans perhaps should have acceded to this request, there was not only Mollard's probable arrival to fear but also the technical consideration that a vote on the fate of the dynasty was pending in the Grand Duchy. Recognition of the dynasty would have done much to aid Belgium's cause, but in the circumstances it would have constituted interference in Luxemburg's internal affairs, a fact of which the French no doubt would have made much. At the time of Reuter's request, Tardieu suddenly renewed his demands for a Franco-Belgian economic union, which heightened Belgian fears and suspicions, particularly because the Flemish press was openly proclaiming its hostility to any such arrangement. While Clemenceau, in response to yet another Anglo-American demarche in favor of Belgo-Luxembourgeois economic union, insisted that he also favored a Belgian solution, French activity in the Grand Duchy became so open and intense that even the

54. De Gaiffier to Pichon, 29 Mar. 1919, no. 2478, FMAE Z/Lux/32; de Gaiffier to Hymans, 29 Mar. 1919, no. 2496/986, BMAE DB/10/II; de Gaiffier to Hymans, 29 Apr. 1919, no. 3552, Brunet note, 19 May 1919, BMAE DB/32/I; FRUS PPC, 5:309, 339;. D.H. Miller, *Diary*, 19:55; William M. Jordan, *Great Britain, France, and the German Problem, 1918–1939*, p. 184.

most Francophile of Brussels newspapers remarked on "a French annexationist manifestation."[55] When on 6 May Reuter suddenly, after a long silence, submitted Luxemburg's third request to be heard by the peace conference, Hymans officially supported the request, which was granted, although privately he was dismayed.[56]

Hymans would have been even more dismayed had he been present when the Four, in anticipation of the Luxembourgeois appearance, discussed the situation on 23 May. Clemenceau declared that Luxemburg wanted to vote on the economic question as soon as the peace treaty was signed and would probably vote for France unless openly told that France would refuse union, a step which he claimed that French opinion would not permit. Even more questionably, he added that a French refusal would only drive Luxemburg toward Germany, as she was hostile to Belgium. Clemenceau said that the Grand Duchy did not want political union with France, but he told the Four that he would accept union—whether political or economic he did not specify—if it were offered by Luxemburg. Nonetheless, he urged that the plebiscite again be deferred, ostensibly to ease relations with Belgium. Lloyd George, most of whose information on Luxemburg came from Clemenceau, argued that "it was a question primarily for the people of Luxemburg and no attempt ought to be made to manoeuvre them into political or economic union with Belgium, if they did not desire it." Clemenceau again asked to defer the plebiscite but Lloyd George, who seemed unaware that postponement would favor France, as Luxemburg remained under continuing benevolent French military occupation and French censorship, insisted that "the Powers should not meddle."[57] The next day, Pichon tried to use the threat of a Luxembourgeois vote for France to gain immediate economic talks with Belgium.[58]

55. P.I.D., F.O. memo, 2 May 1919, CAB 24/79; Derby to Curzon, 21 Apr. 1919, no. 445, F.O. 371/3758; BMAE to DB, 12 May 1919, tel. 250, BMAE to Orts, 15 May 1919, tel. 260, BMAE DB/32/II; de Gaiffier to Hymans, 8 May 1919, no. 3853/1505, BMAE FR/1919; *De Standaard*, 3 May 1919, p. 1; *La Nation belge*, 2 May 1919, p. 1.

56. Reuter to Clemenceau, 12 Feb. 1919, BMAE DB/32/I; I.C. 154, 5 Mar. 1919, CAB 28/6; Reuter to Wilson, 6 May 1919, Wilson Papers 5B/34; Hymans to Clemenceau, 18 May 1919, no. 640, Wilson Papers 5B/37; C.F. 13, 14 May 1919, CAB 29/38; Wilson to Reuter, 19 May 1919, Wilson Papers 5B/38.

57. FRUS PPC, 5:862–63.

58. Hymans note, 24 May 1919, BMAE B-10.121.

When the Luxembourgeois delegation appeared before the Four on 28 May,[59] Hymans was present by his own request. Possibly by pre-arrangement and certainly to induce a formal French indication of interest, Reuter proposed a three-way economic union of France, Belgium, and Luxemburg, and talked at length of the need for French participation. Clemenceau welcomed this proposal and announced that France would be pleased to participate in a tripartite union, asking that she join the Belgo-Luxembourgeois talks already in progress. He also gave his blessing to an early economic plebiscite. Hymans, who was perhaps more realistic than Reuter in recognizing that tripartite union would mean French domination of both countries, tried unsuccessfully to deflect Clemenceau from discussion in front of the Luxembourgeois delegates and then only remarked that the new proposal for negotiations *à trois* would require reflection. After the meeting, he protested sharply to Pichon, who said that there must be some misunderstanding. The next day, Clemenceau sought out Hymans after the plenary session of the peace conference and insisted that France had no interest in economic union with the Grand Duchy. He flatly denied that tripartite union had ever been mentioned or given French endorsement in the presence of the Luxemburgers. As Hymans became annoyed, Clemenceau referred him to Loucheur and began to make jokes to prevent further discussion.[60]

Loucheur, when Hymans saw him, was adamant, but Hymans threatened public disclosure of all that had occurred. As a result, he gained an agreed text stating that France was not interested in tripartite union. Clemenceau added a line declaring that he had never referred to the question and had only agreed to talk *à trois* if invited. The Luxem-

59. The official records of the meeting carry the date of 29 May in error. All other sources agree that it occurred on 28 May. Hymans, *Mémoires*, 2:525; Nicolas Welter, "Le Grand Duché de Luxembourg depuis la guerre," p. 309; C.F. 34, 39, 26, 29 May 1919, CAB 29/38; F.O. memo, 9 May 1921, F.O. 371/6970; Wilson to Reuter, 26 May 1919, Wilson Papers 5B/39; Hymans to Hankey, 29 May 1919, BMAE DB/32/II; Hymans memo, 29 May 1919, BMAE DB/32/I; Hymans to BMAE, 28 May 1919, tel. 493, BMAE B-10.121; Mantoux, *Les Délibérations*, 2:242, 244.

60. C.F. 39, 29 May [28 May] 1919, CAB 29/38; Hymans, *Mémoires*, 2:525–30; Nothomb to Hymans, 31 May 1919, Hymans to Pichon, 29 May 1919, no. 732, BMAE DB/32/II; Mantoux, *Les Délibérations*, 2:246–50. Hymans's version is confirmed by all extant accounts, including the official records.

bourgeois government pursued the matter, however, after Reuter had reported to the Chamber, which unanimously agreed that tripartite union was the most desirable choice. He twice proposed to Hymans that French negotiators join the Belgo-Luxembourgeois talks in progress. Hymans replied that France had decided not to pursue tripartite union and not to participate in the talks. De Gaiffier was sent to complain to Pichon, who agreed to tell Reuter that tripartite negotiations had been neither agreed on nor discussed, but Pichon apparently never did so. Reuter evidently expected the Belgians to break off the economic talks. When they did not, the Belgo-Luxembourgeois sessions began to drag on without progress, and meetings in Luxemburg were canceled on thin pretexts. At the same time, signs appeared that the Luxembourgeois were negotiating independently at Paris.[61]

In the interim, the Belgians had also faced up to economic talks with the French, who had adroitly arranged matters so that they dealt with each country separately. The Belgians might have been wiser to accept tripartite talks, although the results probably would have been similar. But Hymans had believed Loucheur's promise to reject tripartite union and to welcome the Grand Duchy's entry into the Belgian orbit if Belgium would agree to immediate talks without Luxemburg. Thus conversations began in Paris on 31 May with Clémentel and Loucheur representing France and Henri Jaspar, then minister of economic affairs, Orts, and de Gaiffier representing Belgium. Clémentel talked in terms of a customs arrangement and partly reciprocal concessions, as had been discussed during the war. He wanted a frontier free-trade zone, lower Belgian tariffs on French wine, an exchange of Belgian coal and coke for French ore, concessions to France at Antwerp in return for minimal alleviation of the *surtaxe d'entrepôt*, Belgian purchase of French potash in place of supplies from Germany, and a common defense against German products. Weighted as this list was in France's favor, Loucheur, who was very much in charge, brushed it aside, can-

61. Hymans, *Mémoires*, 2:530–31; Villiers to Curzon, 16 June 1919, no. 218, F.O. 371/3638; de Ligne to Hymans, 2 June 1919, no. 1090/333, d'Ansembourg to Hymans, 3 June 1919, BMAE DB/32/II; de Ligne to Hymans, 3 June 1919, no. 1103/337, BMAE to de Ligne, 5 June 1919, tel. 86 bis, Nemry to Hymans, 12 June 1919, d'Ansembourg to Hymans, 13 June 1919, de Ligne to Hymans, 23 June 1919, no. 1243/378, BMAE B-10.121; de Gaiffier to Hymans, 4 June 1919, no. 4716/1897, BMAE FR/1919.

celed some of Clémentel's concessions, and otherwise talked exclusively of a metallurgical cartel. He envisioned a French-Belgian-Luxembourgeois combination with British and later German participation to create a bloc against America's huge production, as there was no hope that the United States would join the organization.[62]

Loucheur's proposal was strikingly similar to the European Steel Cartel that eventuated in 1926. Given his efforts in 1921 to come to economic terms with Germany, there is no reason to doubt that he was in earnest in his 1919 proposal. Although he was probably motivated more by fear of Germany's economic, demographic, and military potential than by pan-European visions, his proposal did in many respects constitute a rational scheme for European reconstruction and one affording some hope of either harnessing or countering the German potential. For Belgium, inclusion of either Britain or Germany or both would resolve the problem of French domination. Though not inclined to make economic war on the United States, whose reconstruction aid she was still seeking, she could hardly afford to hold aloof from such a powerful bloc. Belgium had no real reason to believe in June 1919 that Britain would enter such a combination or that France really was prepared to admit the German foe, but Belgian diplomatists had an incurable tendency to believe the words of great-power cabinet ministers, which on this occasion were in fact straightforward,[63] and certainly the scheme, if realizable, was in Belgian interest. Accordingly, Belgium accepted the metallurgical cartel in due course, but negotiations eventually collapsed over more particular Belgo-French arrangements.

While the first round of negotiations was in progress in early June, Hymans informed the French of what he planned to say if questioned in the Belgian Chamber about Luxemburg. It was his intent to rest on the text of the statement devised at the end of May with Loucheur and Clemenceau, but Loucheur threatened to issue a formal denial and made it abundantly clear that France would disinterest herself in the

62. Hymans note, 31 May 1919, no. 756, de Gaiffier to Hymans, 1 June 1919, no. 4600/1845, BMAE FR/1919. In the 1920s, the United States did not in fact export much steel, but in 1919 it was too early to predict with certainty that the automotive revolution would consume America's huge production.

63. Soutou, "La Politique économique," pp. 263–65. Loucheur did approach Germany in June 1919.

Grand Duchy only if there were prior economic agreement on France's terms. In fact, he tried to impose an eight-day ultimatum on all his and Clémentel's conditions. Hymans was alarmed and agreed to revise his declaration to the Chamber but otherwise remained unyielding in the face of this obvious attempt to bludgeon Belgium. Further interviews with Pichon and Clemenceau elicited nothing except a remark which indicated to Hymans that Clemenceau had been thinking of a satellite Luxembourgeois republic on the French border and probably of eventual full incorporation.[64] Although the surviving French files are too fragmentary to establish with any certainty whether Hyman's deductions were accurate, there is no doubt that Clemenceau remained fixed in his determination to abolish the grand ducal dynasty.

Though the British had little information about the Franco-Belgian economic talks, Balfour was also worried about French plans and equally active. At the end of May, immediately after the Luxembourgeois session with the Four, he revived Crowe's memorandum of 7 April urging full support to Belgium regarding the Grand Duchy. He sent it again to Lloyd George with a note asking him to read it and stressing his view that the tripartite proposal was alarming. The paper was returned bearing only Kerr's initials. Crowe sent it to Lloyd George once more, with a note pointing to Balfour's request that the prime minister read it. The paper came back promptly without any indication that Lloyd George had seen it. Crowe then consulted Hardinge about how to put the memorandum before the prime minister, and the two of them debated with Balfour whether Kerr's initials might mean that Lloyd George had read the paper. After Balfour opined that he probably had not, Crowe sent it to Hankey on 10 June, saying that it was really important and asking if there was any way to lay it before Lloyd George. Hankey sent Crowe's original memorandum to Kerr and told him to give it to the prime minister, but Kerr returned it with a note saying that Lloyd George knew the problem and Balfour's views but thought that if Luxemburg wanted to join France, it was not up to Britain to stop her. On 15 June, Crowe resignedly wrote, "I gather from the above that Mr.

64. De Gaiffier to Hymans, 10, 21 June 1919, nos. 5069/1975, 5482/2962, BMAE FR/1919.

Kerr continues to withhold the papers from the Prime Minister. Put by."[65]

Headlam-Morley was equally concerned but also unable to achieve any action. On 12 June, he wrote to a friend:

> What distresses me is that after all we are going to let down Belgium about Luxemburg. This is, as far as I can understand, merely the result of the curious want of energy and initiative which all through has characterized the conduct of the more purely diplomatic side of the business. We do not seem to have taken any trouble to do what we could to help Belgium; we have not taken her into our confidence, not discussed things frankly, or explained, as we surely should have done, the reasons why in some cases we could not support her claims.[66]

Although he was unaware of the reason for British inaction, Headlam-Morley's assessment was sound and his prediction proved to be accurate. Nothing further was done about the Luxemburg problem before the German treaty was signed and the senior dignitaries disbanded.

The episode constituted a clear defeat for British diplomacy in that Britain failed to counteract the incessant French claim to be Belgium's only friend, failed to put Belgium in a position of gratitude to Britain, and failed to insure the independence of Belgium, which was, as always, a continuing British interest. Crowe's plan could easily have been achieved in April in view of France's need for British support to gain the Saar coal fields over Wilson's opposition, but the British were poorly coordinated and Headlam-Morley knew nothing of Crowe's ideas, whereas Tardieu, who had free access to Clemenceau, dealt with all west European territorial questions as one integrated problem. Lloyd George's well-known dislike of memoranda and his resulting dependence upon Clemenceau's interpretation of events undoubtedly played a part in the British failure, as did the actions of Kerr, who was expected to shield the prime minister, but not from his foreign secretary and second delegate to the peace conference. The Foreign Office representatives diagnosed the situation accurately and imaginatively

65. F.O. memo, Appendix III, 9 May 1921, F.O. 371/6970.
66. Headlam-Morley, *Memoir*, p. 144.

and strove steadily for an Anglo-Belgian success, but received no support from Lloyd George, who probably did not recognize the implications of the issue and, given his acute anti-Belgian bias, probably did not much care.[67]

What had occurred was a Belgian defeat by British default. The first error had been Balfour's. In refusing to assign the Luxemburg question to a committee, he probably hoped to keep it in his own hands to Belgian benefit and out of French control. However, he not only gave the French some faint technical excuse for their allegation to Luxembourgeois representatives that the question was not before the conference but, more importantly, unintentionally transferred the problem into Lloyd George's indifferent hands when the Big Four came into being. Lloyd George's ignorance of the question, his hostility to Hymans, and his disregard for all his experts did the rest. No amount of effort by Balfour and his assistants could compensate for this state of affairs, because the British delegation was having almost as much difficulty as the Belgian delegation in gaining access to the British prime minister.

There was also a degree of Belgian default. Hymans probably would have been wise to recognize Charlotte soon after the vote of the Luxembourgeois Chamber in February, despite the technical difficulty of the dynastic plebiscite and the fear of Mollard. Hymans knew then that annexation was out of the question for the present, although he appears to have retained some hopes for the long-term future. Mollard's presence in the Grand Duchy probably would not have done Belgium much more damage than that being accomplished by the French troops and, if Charlotte were recognized, France could no longer credibly have maintained that Belgium was trying to overturn the dynasty. For the rest, Belgium was largely helpless, given French control of Luxemburg and Belgian exclusion from the deliberations of the Big Four. Belgian policy on the Luxemburg question at the peace conference did not lack energy but, as in so many other matters, it lacked the requisite power to be effective. Beyond that, it lacked realism in its optimistic refusal to accept France's relentless determination to have her own way. From start to finish, Belgian diplomatists saw the implications

67. F.O. memo, Appendix III, 9 May 1921, F.O. 371/6970.

of French moves but refused to accept them. Thus they lived on unfounded hopes, trying too long to participate in the occupation, postponing the economic plebiscite to their own detriment, refusing to face the French terms because they threatened Belgium's independence, which they were determined to maintain. Part of the problem was that the years of protected status, together with deliverance in the great war, had given some Belgian leaders illusory notions about the disinterestedness and generosity of great powers. Although they had a good deal of distrust of France and comprehended what she aimed at, they could not quite believe that an Allied great power and guarantor would treat them in this fashion. And if she did, some other great power, especially Britain, whom Hymans admired so much, could surely arrange matters. Though this last expectation was optimistic, it was not entirely unreasonable, for Britain did in fact obtain the opportunity and Balfour did his utmost to capitalize on it.

The Belgians were not privy to the interior disarray of the British delegation and so they did not know what had gone wrong, but they were deeply disappointed that the Luxemburg question had not been settled. The absence of a solution contributed to Belgian dissatisfaction with the Versailles treaty both in government circles and in popular opinion. The Belgian leaders feared that they faced a long struggle over Luxemburg and that they would be left to fight the battle alone against France. Their fears proved well founded, but even at this late date they did not fully consider the implications. They continued to hope that some opportunity would present itself, because, after all, it must.

THE LINGERING PROBLEM

After the Versailles treaty was signed on 28 June 1919, the Luxemburg question remained quiescent until Clemenceau abruptly summoned Hymans to Paris on 25 August. Belgian negotiators had by then indicated that they would accept the proposed metallurgical cartel and a few of the other economic demands. As in the past, Belgium found that she had little to offer in return for what she sought and that France held the upper hand. The real stumbling block, however, was French insistence upon a preferential Belgian tariff that would have required

Belgium to raise her duties on goods from other countries, notably Britain.[68] Nonetheless, the French had obtained Belgian consent to the metallurgical cartel, which was what they wanted most, and other concessions as well; so matters appeared close to settlement. Thus, when Hymans arrived on 25 August, Clemenceau announced that he would advise Luxemburg to conclude an economic union with Belgium. Hymans's elation over this long-awaited announcement turned to alarm, however, when Clemenceau added that France would retain the Guillaume-Luxembourg railway and wanted a Franco-Belgian military convention.[69] Both proposals were equally unattractive to Belgium. Although she wanted some sort of defensive guarantee from the Allied powers, a unilateral military convention with France was viewed as yet another threat to Belgian independence. Similarly, economic union with Luxemburg would lose much of its significance if France continued to control the most vital rail lines in the Grand Duchy. Prewar imperialism had demonstrated that control of a vital railway could easily provide pretexts for control of a weak country. In any event, a continuing French presence in Luxemburg would inhibit any long-term prospect of "political union," as Hymans put it.[70] Further, French control of the rail rates could constrict Belgian through traffic southward and eastward to important markets. Finally, because the heavily traveled Guillaume-Luxembourg network was highly profitable, it was the one real economic attraction for Belgium in an economic union that she wanted for political reasons. Luxemburg's industry and agriculture would only compete with their Belgian counterparts, and France had already effectively penetrated the Grand Duchy's steel industry. As Hymans remarked bitterly to Margerie, France wanted to

68. Jacques Willequet, "Problèmes économiques franco-belges en 1919 et 1920," p. 307. One side effect of the economic negotiations, which failed in October, was a very partial lifting of the *surtaxe d'entrepôt* at Antwerp for the sake of Strasbourg, which was suffering acutely from the loss of the Antwerp traffic. Though this limited measure helped Antwerp somewhat, it was a concession made to Strasbourg, not to Belgium.

69. Hymans to de Gaiffier, 14 Aug. 1919, no. 6786/2966, BMAE FR/1919; Hymans, *Mémoires*, 2:532; file, BMAE DB/10/I; Clemenceau to Hymans, 3 Sept. 1919, BMAE DB/32/II. In Berthelot's account of the meeting, he noted that France remained very hostile to the grand duchess and should make this clear to Reuter before the plebiscite. Berthelot to Clemenceau, 25 Aug. 1919, Vin 6N/75.

70. Hymans to de Gaiffier, 22 Sept. 1919, no. 8351, BMAE FR/1919.

take all the pulp of the Luxembourgeois fruit and leave to Belgium the rind in the form of responsibility to redeem the Grand Duchy's supply of German marks.[71] Because by now Hyman's chief motive in pursuing economic union was to remove Luxemburg from the French orbit, he not surprisingly reacted sharply to Clemenceau's announcement that France would retain the Guillaume-Luxembourg network.

There had been difficulty over the Luxemburg railways ever since the Armistice. The standard-gauge rail lines were divided between two concessionary companies, both chartered in the Grand Duchy but neither of them ever administered by the Luxembourgeois. The less important of the two, the Société Prince-Henri, had its administrative seat in Brussels and Belgians heavily dominated its capital shares. This network, which had 193 kilometers (about 120 miles) of track and also ran the Grand Duchy's state tramways, made little profit, as its lines primarily handled local traffic. Though France had evident designs upon the Prince-Henri system, the main battle focused on the more important Société Guillaume-Luxembourg, whose headquarters were in Paris, whose administrators were French, and whose shares represented more French than Belgian capital. The Guillaume-Luxembourg network comprised only 206 kilometers (about 128 miles) of track, but its economic and strategic significance far outstripped its size, as it constituted vital segments in important north-south and east-west international routes. The French interest in the Luxemburg railways, beyond the obvious one of yet another form of pressure upon Belgium toward a military agreement and further economic concessions, was primarily strategic. However, the lines also served western Europe's largest iron and steel complexes in the Ruhr, southern Belgium, southern Luxemburg, Lorraine, and Longwy. In addition, they provided the most convenient routes for shipments of reparations coal from the Ruhr to Lorraine.[72]

71. Hymans note, 5 Oct. 1919, BMAE FR/1919.
72. Vanbergen interview; Admiralty, *A Manual of Belgium*, p. 197 n; Millerand to Colson, 16 Aug. 1919, FMAE Z/Lux/32; François Simon, "L'outillage national," in *Le Luxembourg: Livre du Centenaire*, pp. 207–8; P. Simon, "Le Probléme ferroviaire," pp. 3–4; Admiralty, *Luxemburg*, pp. 285–87; de Clercq, *Les Petites Souverainetés*, p. 133; Hymans to Moncheur, 12 Sept. 1919, BMAE GB/1919/II; Soutou, "La Politique économique," p. 264.

Belgium had an extremely strong legal claim to the main east-west line of the Guillaume-Luxembourg network from Wasserbillig to Kleinbettingen, arising from an 1869 agreement with the French government to transfer the line to Belgium on 1 January 1913. The prewar German administration had ignored the agreement, but the Belgian government renewed the claim to both France and Luxemburg immediately after the Armistice.[73] While Belgian diplomatists continued to press this claim, they also hoped for a broader Belgo-Luxembourgeois arrangement encompassing the entire Guillaume-Luxembourg network as an obvious corollary to the projected economic union. Reuter's representatives agreed with the Belgian view that economic union excluding the vital railway was illogical,[74] although, by this time, the overriding concern of the Luxemburgers was to end the continuing uncertainty over their future, a subject on which thus far they had been permitted singularly little voice.

After Clemenceau made his claim to the Guillaume-Luxembourg network, which was then under French military administration, Hymans consulted the Belgian Foreign Ministry, cabinet, and king, all of whom found the French terms unacceptable. As Clemenceau was advising Reuter to go ahead with the plebiscites, the Belgian Foreign Ministry also launched a new and extensive campaign to convince Luxembourgeois opinion that it favored the political referendum and that the Belgian dynasty was emphatically not a candidate for the grand ducal throne. But French propaganda had been effective and France, which still favored a republic in place of the dynasty, was widely viewed as the sole protector of Grand Duchess Charlotte. The Belgian Foreign Ministry would have preferred further postponement of the economic plebiscite, as the country remained under French military occupation, but concluded that Reuter was justified in his complaints that uncertainty was becoming economically ruinous. Accordingly, the Belgian government abandoned its efforts to delay the plebiscite further.[75]

73. Klobukowski memo, 2 Jan. 1919, de Gaiffier to Pichon, 20 Nov. 1918, no. 8737, Pichon to Margerie, 5 May 1919, no. 241, FMAE Z/Lux/32; Hymans to de Gaiffier, 17 Nov. 1918, no. 2487, Hymans to de Ligne, 11 Dec. 1918, no. 9, BMAE DB/32/I.
74. Moncheur to Hymans, 16 May 1919, BMAE DB/32/II; Hymans to Pichon, 12 Sept. 1919, BMAE GB/1919/II.
75. Berthelot to Clemenceau, 25 Aug. 1919, Vin 6N/75; Hymans, *Mémoires*, 2:531;

As the Grand Duchy made preparations for the plebiscite, Belgium and France reached total disagreement over the railway. When the Belgian cabinet unanimously rejected Clemenceau's terms, it also temporarily halted the economic negotiations, including those for the metals cartel. Clemenceau mendaciously replied that France had never dreamed that Belgium would claim the Guillaume-Luxembourg network, adding abruptly that further discussion was useless, for the French decision was final. The Belgians, with slightly more justification, were astonished by the French demands. After their two successes at the peace conference in preventing award of the network to France, the Belgian leaders had naively assumed that France had abandoned the claim, as it had never been raised during the long economic negotiations. They tried to find a compromise but with no success. The French insisted on having the Guillaume-Luxembourg network, indicated that they aimed to absorb the Prince-Henri company as well, demanded the several economic agreements, and required a Franco-Belgian military convention that would be fully reciprocal, pledging Belgium to the defense of France. They also threatened to prevent any Allied security guarantee of Belgium unless their desires were met. Only when these stiff terms had been accepted in full would France advise Luxemburg toward economic union with Belgium. In the interim, France asked for negotiations with Luxembourgeois representatives over the Guillaume-Luxembourg network.[76]

Though the French were genuinely concerned, and with reason, about the Luxemburg railways as an invasion route into France, they were even more concerned to achieve a military agreement with Belgium, which constituted a much more dangerous invasion route. Foch obviously distrusted both Belgium's ability and her willingness to defend herself or the Grand Duchy effectively, and the French were now

de Bassompierre memo, 9 Sept. 1919, BMAE DB/32/II; Moncheur to Hymans, 18 Sept. 1919, no. 5753/1866, BMAE GB/1919/II; DBFP, 5:513–15, 570, 572–73; Reuter to Clemenceau, 29 July 1919, 184.611/748, ACNP/266.

76. Hymans to Clemenceau, 28 Aug. 1919, Clemenceau to Hymans, 3 Sept. 1919, Berthelot note, 18 Sept. 1919, Reuter to Mollard, 19 Sept. 1919, FMAE Z/Lux/32; Hymans to Pichon, 12 Sept. 1919, de Gaiffier to Hymans, 14, 15 Sept. 1919, no. 8132/3413, tel. 201, Reuter to de Ligne, 20 Sept. 1919, BMAE FR/1919; de Gaiffier to Hymans, 23 Sept. 1919, no. 8534/3556, BMAE GB/1919/II.

much less impressed with Belgium's wartime effort than they had been in 1914. There was an implicit assumption, which Belgians noticed and resented, that they could not be counted on to stand up to Germany again. Beyond these concerns lay a clearly expressed French intent to control Luxemburg's steel industry and railways and to force both Belgium and Luxemburg to sweeping economic and military arrangements that France would easily dominate. If Belgium would accept virtual encirclement and satellite status to fulfill France's economic and security needs, she could have the dubious pleasure of dealing with the Grand Duchy's mounting debts and German marks.

It also appears probable that by now the French leaders, especially Clemenceau, were taking a certain pleasure in tormenting the earnest and rather trusting Belgians and in playing a classic cat-and-mouse game with Hymans. Clemenceau had considerable disdain for small nations in general and great dislike for Hymans in particular, but he summoned Hymans to Paris to impose his new terms in person on 25 August, instead of informing de Gaiffier or handing the chore over to Pichon. As Clemenceau was never noted for his courtesy, it is likely that he wished to relish the sight of Hymans's consternation. Until the end of the peace conference and the Anglo-American departure, France had been polite in its evasions and consistently gracious about small matters of no importance. Thus, Mollard had been held in Paris at Belgian request, as he was not needed in Luxemburg, where a French regiment and Foch's staff could do his work for him. Though Mollard remained in Paris, henceforth the French were hardly civil about matters of consequence connected to the Luxemburg question. They probably wanted the matter settled and resented the stubborn resistance of a small state to a great power's national interests. When relations became too strained, it was Pichon's role to be soothing and to make placatory promises, none of which were honored. For the rest, Clemenceau, Berthelot, and Loucheur became almost brutal in their blunt expressions of France's requirements.

Not surprisingly, the Belgian government consistently rejected the French terms. It was in fact prepared to concede on the metals cartel although not on the military convention, but diplomatic efforts focused on the railway. As the French raised strategic, economic, and even sentimental reasons for retaining it,[77] the Belgians offered military rights in wartime but to no avail. They also proposed a joint administration, but France offered only minority representation in a French-dominated administrative board, later substituting a larger Belgian voice in a consultative council with no authority. The Belgian authorities drew up plans to divide the railway, giving France the southern and eastern lines most vital to her, but abandoned the idea as it became obvious that France would reject it.[78]

Although the economic talks resumed and continued until late October, relations became so bitter over the French insistence on the railways that Hymans erupted to Loucheur, "In the final analysis, you want to take Luxemburg. Take it, since you are the stronger. But you will take it against us. Belgium will remember."[79] The French ambassador, Margerie, who privately thought that French policy over Luxemburg in general and the railways in particular was deplorable, had a painful interview with Hymans, who rehearsed the history of French duplicity and distrust, again refused a customs union alone with France or *à trois*, and declared, "I love France for both sentimental and political reasons. I am ready to negotiate accords with her to bring us together, but on one condition, that they do not endanger our independence. I love France but first of all I am Belgian."[80] A few days later he plaintively told Margerie, "I know that at Paris I am thought to be clumsy and stumbling. Maybe I don't know how to defend the rights of my country as one might wish, but I plead my cause to the best of my ability and I think, moreover, that I've proved moderate on many difficult occasions."[81] Alas, Hymans could not bring himself to accept that "rights,"

77. The sentimental argument was that the Guillaume-Luxembourg network was part of the heritage of Alsace-Lorraine and that the French National Assembly allegedly would not tolerate abandonment of any part of that precious patrimony. De Gaiffier to Hymans, 14 Sept. 1919, no. 8132/3413, BMAE FR/1919.

78. Hymans to de Gaiffier, 18, 22 Sept. 1919, BMAE Ind/1919/II; de Gaiffier to Hymans, 20, 23 Sept. 1919, nos. 8334/3506, 8534/3556, Hymans to de Gaiffier, 28 Sept. 1919, BMAE GB/1919/II; Pichon to de Gaiffier, 25 Dec. 1919, Berthelot to Hymans, 31 Dec. 1919, FMAE Z/Lux/33.

79. Hymans to de Gaiffier, 22 Sept. 1919, BMAE FR/1919.

80. Auffray, *Pierre de Margerie*, p. 375; Hymans note, 5 Oct. 191, BMAE FR/1919.

81. Margerie to Pichon, 9 Oct. 1919, tel. 649–54, Vin 6N/128.

even if better established than those of Belgium in Luxemburg, rarely suffice without power to enforce them.

Because Belgian independence was clearly in jeopardy, Hymans also repeatedly sought British support. The Foreign Office thought that France was treating Belgium unfairly but was reluctant to intervene. As Moncheur pressed the Belgian cause almost daily, Curzon agreed that the legal basis of the French claim, Article 67 of the Versailles treaty, which awarded the Alsace-Lorraine railways to France, was untenable and did not apply to Luxemburg. Finally he ordered a protest at Paris on this narrow point, but British officials there reported that France would be offended by such intervention. As Britain had no desire to offend France just when delicate negotiations over Syria were in progress, the protest was dropped. Thereafter, the Foreign Office gave Belgium much sympathy but no support.[82]

As the Franco-Belgian negotiations approached deadlock, the long-deferred Luxemburg plebiscites finally took place on 28 September 1919 with French troops still in occupation at Reuter's request, made officially on the basis that Luxemburg did not yet have a police force to keep order but probably in hopes of influencing the outcome. Whether Reuter really believed that France was the sole hope of saving the grand duchess, as his people did, is unclear, but he certainly preferred tripartite economic negotiations to bilateral ones. Although he announced repeatedly that the vote would not bind the government, Reuter made it equally clear that the real purpose of the plebiscite was to lead France to negotiate over economic union. The results were as anticipated. Of 125,775 registered voters, 90,485 voted on the dynastic question and 82,375 on the economic question. On the dynastic question, 1,113 votes were annulled, 66,811 were for Grand Duchess Charlotte, 1,286 for another grand duchess, 889 for another unspecified dynasty, and 16,885 for a republic. On the economic question, 8,609 votes were annulled, 60,135 were for economic union with France, and 22,242 were for economic union with Belgium.[83] Though this vote probably

82. Moncheur to Hymans, 20, 30 Sept. 1919, nos. 5810/1881, 5991/1943, de Gaiffier to Hymans, 26 Sept. 1919, no. 8635/3590, BMAE GB/1919/II; Gurney to Curzon, 26 Sept. 1919, no. 361, F.O. 371/3638; DBFP, 5:568, 573–74, 593.

83. Reuter to Clemenceau, 8 Sept. 1919, FMAE Z/Lux/17; Hymans to de Gaiffier, 27 Sept. 1919, no. 3924, BMAE GB/1919/II; DBFP, 5:603.

faithfully reflected Luxembourgeois opinion, despite the facts that over a third of the voters did not express any view on the economic question and that so many votes were annulled, it was an opinion shaped by more than ten months of French occupation, censorship, and misleading statements, and furthermore an opinion formed in total ignorance of events in Paris. If any Luxembourgeois cabinet minister had ever received accurate reports from non-Belgian sources of Clemenceau's oft-repeated declarations that the dynasty and Charlotte must go, the results would unquestionably have been reversed, but only the Belgians bothered to report French intentions, and they were not believed. American observers in Luxemburg had long foreseen the results of the plebiscites, not only noting French troops, propaganda, and economic measures, but also observing that the clergy, who had enormous influence over the newly enfranchised and poorly educated women voters, were campaigning strongly for France, which had misled them into believing that it would uphold the dynasty.[84] On the heels of the vote, Belgium terminated economic negotiations and, perhaps unnecessarily, withdrew the Prince de Ligne's special mission.[85]

As a consequence of this Belgian action, there was now no diplomatic representative of any power in Luxemburg. It had long been agreed that the powers would recognize Charlotte in concert and only after consultation with Belgium. However, the agreement disintegrated and Belgium's hand was forced on the recognition question by a diplomatic contretemps arising out of Charlotte's marriage on 6 November 1919. A week earlier, the Belgian Foreign Ministry, which was contemplating recognition and thinking that the wedding might afford a suitable occasion, inquired through Moncheur whether the British intended to recognize Charlotte at the time of the marriage. When Moncheur re-

84. Griffith to Haskins, 14 Apr. 1919, Garrett to Lansing, 28 May 1919, 185.1132/26, 36, ACNP/302; Gunther report, 10 May 1919, Wilson Papers 5B/36; de Gaiffier to Hymans, 10 May 1919, no. 3921/1532, BMAE B-10.121. The *Times* said much the same after the plebiscite, stressing the ignorance of the voters. The author of the article told Moncheur that it was originally more hostile in tone toward France but that the *Times* had been asked to soften the article in order not to worsen British-French relations over Syria. Paul Cambon also told Moncheur that, left to themselves, the Luxemburgers would have turned to Belgium. Moncheur to Hymans, 30 Sept., 1 Oct. 1919, nos 5991/1943, 6008/1951, BMAE GB/1919/II.

85. Hymans to Moncheur, 4 Oct. 1919, no. 8716, BMAE GB/1919/II.

ported, possibly in error, that the British had been asked to do so and were considering the matter, Hymans asked Villiers whether the king of England would be represented at the wedding. Without much thought, the British ordered their minister at The Hague, where relations with Luxemburg had traditionally been handled, to attend the wedding. He could not go, as he was to lunch with Queen Whilhelmina on the day, but suggested that Villiers might arrive in time by fast car from Brussels. Villiers could not, and no foreign representatives attended Charlotte's wedding (none, including the British, having been invited), but the hasty British exchanges with Luxemburg over the question clearly implied diplomatic recognition. The Luxembourgeois were delighted, while the French and Belgians were astonished at British unilateral action. When the Foreign Office sorted itself out, it was obliged to apologize profusely. Hymans thought he should go ahead with recognition, but Pichon and de Gaiffier counseled against it. Accordingly, he asked that Britain delay sending a diplomatic representative as long as possible, as a British minister would be followed by a French one, and the Belgians themselves wished to be first on the scene. In recognition of their gaffe, the British agreed to delay until 15 January 1920, but it was clear that Belgium would have no choice but to send a minister early in the new year.[86]

Under the circumstances, the Belgians hoped to resolve the Guillame-Luxembourg question and move on to negotiations on economic union before a French minister arrived in Luxemburg City. They were in a

86. Hymans to Moncheur, 30 Oct. 1919, tel. 241, Moncheur to Hymans, 1 Nov. 1919, tel. 209, BMAE GB/1919/II; Villiers to Curzon, 3 Nov., 5 Dec. 1919, no. 181, tel. 187, R. Graham to Curzon, 5, 8 Nov. 1919, nos. 1498, 1499, 1502, G. Grahame to Curzon, 5 Nov. 1919, no. 1154, Curzon to G. Grahame, 14 Nov. 1919, no. 1254, F.O. 371/3851; DBFP, 2:306–7, 5:907–10; FRUS PPC, 9:8, 147; Guillaume to Hymans, 13 Dec. 1919, no. 9454/2340, BMAE PB/1919; de Gaiffier to Hymans, 6 Nov. 1919, no. 10264/4295, BMAE FR/1919. The British files show no evidence that recognition had been requested or considered. The first document on the question is Villiers's report of Hymans's inquiry about royal representation at the wedding, and the British do not seem to have realized until after the event that recognition was involved. The Belgian government recognized Charlotte on 5 February 1920. The French government immediately followed suit. Hymans to de Cartier, 8 Feb. 1920, tel. 32, B Micro/24; Villiers to Curzon, 7 Feb. 1920, no. 75, F.O. 371/3638; Margerie to FMAE, 6 Feb. 1920, tel. 85, FMAE Z/Lux/12; Hymans to Moncheur, 7 Feb. 1920, no. 205, BMAE GB/1920.

fundamentally weak position, as France continued her military occupation and her administration of the railway, bolstered by her victory in the plebiscite. She capitalized on her position by negotiating to take formal control of the Guillaume-Luxembourg network. Belgium's only hope, which proved forlorn, was British support, and her only asset was French fear of alienating an essential ally astride the invasion route from Germany to France. Despite their shortage of diplomatic ammunition, the Belgians held firm in full awareness that the assorted French conditions taken together would lead to French economic domination of both Belgium and Luxemburg, encirclement of Belgium (particularly if any new French separatist schemes in the Rhineland reached fruition), and a serious threat to Belgian independence.[87] The French, who knew they held the high cards, were equally firm and refused all concessions.[88]

Hymans struggled doggedly to find a solution, despite the odds against him, but made no progress. Though there was little hope, he continued to hope anyway. Pichon made occasional promises but did not fulfill them, and Clemenceau and Berthelot did not waver on their stringent conditions for Belgo-Luxembourgeois economic union.[89] As a consequence, by the end of 1919, Franco-Belgian relations had deteriorated sharply. On the day that the Versailles treaty entered into effect, Margerie wrote that France could not hope to gain a military accord with Belgium unless she settled the Guillaume-Luxembourg problem, which was "a great cloud between us."[90] At about the same time, Hymans told Villiers that France and Belgium had reached "a clear and complete disagreement."[91] The British were kept fully in-

87. DBFP, 5:604–6, 621–22; Gurney to F.O., 10 Oct., 1919, no. 167, F.O. 371/3638; Hymans to de Gaiffier, 19 Dec. 1919, no. 6674, BMAE FR/1919; de Gaiffier to Hymans, 30 Jan. 1920, no. 1027/518, BMAE FR/1920/I; Kerchove to Jaspar, 8 Oct. 1919, no. 119, BMAE GB/1919/II; Margerie to FMAE, 7 Oct. 1919, tel. 657–58, FMAE Z/Belg./56.

88. De Gaiffier to Hymans, 18 Nov. 1919, no. 10600/4428, BMAE FR/1919.

89. Berthelot to de Gaiffier, 31 Dec. 1919, de Gaiffier to Hymans, 2 Jan. 1920, no. 5/2, BMAE FR/1920/I; Margerie to FMAE, 10 Jan. 1920, tel. 44–45, Vin 6N/128.

90. Margerie to FMAE, 10 Jan. 1920, tel. 42, FMAE Z/Lux/33.

91. G. Grahame to Curzon, 26 Feb. 1921, no. 188 (Annual Report, 1920), F.O. 371/6968.

formed of this state of affairs by Belgian diplomatists but made no effort to capitalize upon it. They were no longer interested in Luxemburg and, in a sense, no longer much interested in Belgium, which they placidly assumed to be a French satellite. Thus, Belgium was left to her own slender resources in her effort to avoid precisely that outcome to the Luxemburg question.

SIX

THE SEARCH

FOR SECURITY

AT THE PEACE CONFERENCE

The struggle to revise the 1839 treaties was even more protracted than that over Luxemburg and, from the Belgian point of view, even more unsatisfactory in its eventual outcome. When the peace conference opened, Belgium had gained the formal assent of Britain, France, and the United States to the suppression of compulsory neutrality and had served notice that she wished wholesale treaty revision but had not achieved any definite commitment on this latter point. Accordingly, the Belgian delegation addressed the question at once. Its lengthy memorandum to the powers on 17 January 1919 constituted a formal request for full revision of the 1839 treaties.

This memorandum made the Belgian concerns clear. In addition to the veiled hope of territorial transfer from Holland, which of itself would resolve some of the most acute problems, the Belgian claims focused primarily upon suppression of compulsory neutrality, permission to use Antwerp as a naval base, revision of the regime of the Scheldt and the Ghent-Terneuzen canal, and solution of the defensive problem of the Limburg gap. With an eye to future bargaining, some claims were expressed in maximum form, such as a request for sovereignty on the Scheldt and for transit rights by rail and canal across lower Limburg. The memorandum closed with a note on procedure urging that, after Anglo-French-Belgian agreement on principles and on compensation to be offered to Holland, the three powers should invite the Dutch to a conference for treaty revision. The four states should settle the terms of the new treaties, impose them on Germany and Austria, and inform Russia of what had been done.[1] This procedural approach

1. D. H. Miller, *Diary*, 4:436–67.

was derived not only from a need for maximum Allied support against the Dutch but also from the fact that Britain and France were the two remaining faithful guarantor powers; Germany and Austria had violated the 1839 treaties militarily and Russia's separate peace constituted a lesser lapse.

The long negotiations that ensued were complex and often hinged upon technical questions but had far-reaching implications. Not only did the course of events demonstrate once again Hymans's lack of realism about what the Dutch would accept and inability to comprehend their viewpoint, but it so embittered Belgo-Dutch relations as to preclude any serious consideration of a Benelux system until after World War II. During the long debates, the British generally backed the Dutch while the French supported the Belgians, thus exacerbating tensions in the Western Entente and contributing to the growing fragility and instability of the 1919 settlement. Beyond that, the complicated examination of defensive guarantees had profound implications for western Europe's security system or lack thereof.

None of these implications were evident to the Belgian delegation or anybody else, except perhaps the French, when the 17 January memorandum was submitted. For some months most diplomatists viewed revision of the 1839 treaties as little more than routine correction of an obsolete arrangement. Although even Hymans had anticipated Dutch hostility to territorial cession, he was surprised to discover that the British and French disliked his procedural proposals and desired American participation from the outset. He objected to inclusion of the United States because it had not been a signatory of the 1839 treaties and, legalistic to the core, held out for preliminary meetings *à trois* even though the Americans were clearly more sympathetic to Belgian aspirations than either the British or the French. Indeed, the American reaction to the 17 January Belgian memorandum was prophetic: "The new dispositions about to be made by reason of the destruction of the arrangements of 1831–1839 will have to find new safeguards for the independence of Belgium, which by its acts has deserved well of the Society of Nations. It may perhaps be suggested that Belgium has as much to fear from the friendship as from the enmity of its neighbours."[2]

---

2. Hymans to Pichon, 21 Jan. 1919, F.O. 608/3; Hymans, *Mémoires*, 1:351–54, 356;

The Belgians were unaware of this remark, but they knew they had the sympathy of House and Haskins. Besides, neither the British nor the French would talk formally without the Americans, so Hymans reluctantly decided to present the Belgian case to the five powers. During Belgium's day before the Ten on 11 February, he presented the claims of the 17 January memorandum in much detail and asked the powers to arrange negotiations with the Dutch. The next day, the Ten sent the questions of claims against Germany and of possible Dutch compensation from Germany to the Belgian Commission, on which Belgium had no representation; all problems concerning the Scheldt regime, the Ghent-Terneuzen canal, and communication eastward from Antwerp by canal went to the Commission on the International Control of Ports, Waterways, and Railways. In fact, this commission never dealt with any of the Belgian riparian questions. As it became evident that the Belgian Commission was moving to examine the entire question of treaty revision, Belgian representatives on the Commission on Ports successfully blocked any action there until it became clearly established that the Belgian Commission had the riparian problems in hand.[3]

The enlargement of the Belgian Commission's mandate to encompass all aspects of revision of the 1839 treaties occurred largely at French instigation. When Tardieu returned to the Ten on 26 February seeking clarification of the commission's terms of reference, he gained not only authorization to study the possibility of territorial compensation to Holland from Germany but also a decision that "the Belgian Committee should examine the question of the neutral status of Belgium as established by the Treaty of 1839, and make recommendations to the Council concerning modification of that status."[4] Within twenty-four hours, Tardieu had begun to interpret this decision as a mandate to explore all aspects of treaty revision. As British experts agreed that

Orts to Hymans, 14 Feb. 1919, BMAE Ind/1919/I; quotation from D. H. Miller, *Diary*, 4:494. F. L. Warrin of the American delegation later claimed credit for shifting Belgian tactics. (Warrin letter, 6 Sept. 1966, House Papers 30/97a.) Although his conversation with Hymans no doubt took place, it was probably less important than he thought and much less important than Anglo-French views.

3. I.C. 138, 140, 11, 12 Feb. 1919, CAB 28/6; W.C.P. 342, 18 Feb. 1919, CAB 29/10; W.C.P. 704, 26 Mar. 1919, CAB 29/14; Rolin-Jaequemyns to Dutasta, 26 Mar. 1919, no. 350, BMAE B-156/II.

4. Hymans to BMAE, 27 Feb. 1919, BMAE Ind/1919/I; FRUS PPC, 4:141–44.

the neutrality clause was the keystone of the 1839 treaty structure and that its removal would necessitate full-scale treaty revision, Tardieu proceeded unchecked. When he reported the Ten's decisions to the commission on 1 March, he interpreted them broadly to mean that it should make recommendations about methods and conditions of treaty revision in general.[5]

The commission worked very rapidly and on 6 March approved with only minor modification a draft report prepared by Tardieu. This report, which Tardieu presented to the Ten on 8 March, argued that revision of the treaties was "a matter of general interest." It concluded that the three treaties of 1839 comprised a single entity that should be fully renegotiated by Belgium, Holland, and the five "Powers with General Interests." The purpose of this revision should be to free Belgium from the limits imposed upon her sovereignty and "to remove the dangers and disadvantages" to her arising from the 1839 treaties. Though this phrase was unclear, the Belgians construed it to mean that there should be a new, more workable guarantee to replace that of 1839. As to procedure, the report recommended that the Ten ask the two faithful guarantor powers to invite Holland to present her views to the Supreme Council. Thus the question of treaty revision would be officially before the Supreme Council, which could then refer specific issues to the Belgian Commission and the Commission on Ports and Waterways.[6] Though in fact no question was ever sent to the Commission on Ports and Waterways, the report was unanimously adopted by the Ten on 8 March.[7] This decision provided the basis for Article 31 of the Versailles treaty requiring Germany to accept abrogation of the 1839 treaties and to consent in advance to whatever treaties might replace them. It also formed the basis for future Belgian demands for new security guarantees to reduce the dangers of her position.

Although the Belgian Parliament greeted the news that the Supreme Council had approved treaty revision with emotional demonstrations of joy, the Belgian delegation in Paris was increasingly concerned by un-

5. Tardieu to Crowe, 17 Feb. 1919, Headlam-Morley memo, 28 Feb. 1919, F.O. 608/2 pt. 1; D. H. Miller, *Diary*, 10:37.
6. FRUS PPC, 4:270–71.
7. Ibid.

mistakable signs of Dutch resistance and British encouragement of it. Loudon and van Swinderin continued to cultivate the American and British delegations to good effect, and already the Dutch had made their first effort to remove the question of treaty revision from Paris and from the aegis of the great powers, proposing direct Belgo-Dutch negotiations in which Belgium would stand without allies. Repeatedly, the Dutch had ruled out any territorial cession, even with compensation.[8] More importantly, Balfour had already told the Dutch that he did not believe they should be asked to cede any territory. After Dutch diplomatists had triumphantly repeated this remark, Hymans complained to Balfour that British hesitation was causing Dutch obstruction, but to no avail.[9] It did not occur to Hymans that Dutch reluctance to part with segments of the national domain was perfectly reasonable or that, given the British attitude, he should have abandoned territorial aims. Equally alarming to the Belgians were rumors that organized groups were striving for Anglo-Dutch rapprochement and reports that the South African delegates, Jan Christian Smuts and Louis Botha, were pressing the British government to cease all support to Belgium.[10]

Though there is no evidence in the existing British documentation to substantiate persistent rumors of Boer pressure on British leaders on behalf of Holland, it may well have been one factor contributing to the conspicuous British partiality to Holland, along with Lloyd George's evident anti-Belgian bias, and the absence of any clear-cut Belgian abandonment of desires for Dutch territory. Although Hymans was responding to considerable Belgian political pressure, he undoubtedly did his cause much harm by continuing to hint at the impossible. In addition, the British Admiralty, which tended to refight the last war just as everyone else did, strongly opposed any rights for Belgian or Allied warships on the Scheldt, arguing that occupation of Belgium by a major

---

8. Hymans, *Mémoires*, 1:383; Villiers to Curzon, 27 Mar. 1919, F.O. 371/3640; van Vollenhoven to Hymans, 26 Feb. 1919, Orts to Fallon, 28 Feb. 1919, no. 323, BMAE PB/1919; Whitlock to ACNP, 28 Feb. 1919, tel. 11A, 755.56/8, ACNP/424; de Gaiffier to Hymans, 10 Mar. 1919, no. 1841/721, BMAE DB/30/II.

9. Balfour memo, 24 Feb. 1919, Lothian Papers GD/40/17/65; Hymans, *Mémoires*, 1:378.

10. Hymans, *Mémoires*, 1:378n.

power would then render Antwerp a threat to Britain[11] (although such occupation would be facilitated by the impossibility of British relief efforts up the Scheldt). However, British hostility to Belgian claims extended to other matters where it was clearly in Britain's interest that Belgium be able to defend herself and to trivial technical matters regarding riparian administration. Increasingly, the British argued that Holland should not be asked to make any concessions at all.

Although the Netherlands showed signs of growing sympathy with Germany as 1919 progressed and the British were at first much irritated over the kaiser's refuge in Holland, these considerations had faded from British thinking before the 1839 treaty negotiations began in earnest. The British attitude was increasingly compounded of irritation with Hymans, fear of Belgian economic competition, gratitude for Dutch neutrality, and determination not to incur any obligation to defend Belgium again. British leaders largely put out of mind the facts that the independence of Belgium and small-power control of Antwerp were continuing vital British interests, and that Britain in any event would need to intervene against great-power attack on the Low Countries. Only the War Office kept these considerations firmly in mind, but it had no voice in the Belgian negotiations. As time passed and British policy swung gradually toward Germany and away from France, the shift was bound to favor Holland and work to the disadvantage of Belgium, whom the British blindly regarded as a French satellite. However, British resistance to almost all Belgian claims against Holland, even the most modest, was evident before this shift occurred.

It was because the Belgians recognized British resistance, Wilsonian hostility to annexations, and a certain French reserve as well, presumably arising from their financial negotiations with Holland, that they prepared the massive documentation of the Revendications Belges, hoping that the sheer weight of their evidence would carry them through to successful treaty revision. Armed with this reinforcement to the Supreme Council decision of 8 March, the Belgian Commission began work on specific issues. While the commission dealt with the question of the German border districts, steps were taken to arrange broader revision of the 1839 treaties in accordance with the procedural deci-

11. Fuller memo, 20 Feb. 1919, CAB 29/8; Seymour, *Letters,* p. 156.

sions of 8 March. Thus, on 13 March, Pichon and Balfour, speaking for the faithful guarantor powers, informed the Dutch minister in Paris of the Ten's decision and asked that the Dutch appear before the Supreme Council to express their views.[12]

A Dutch reply was slow to come despite British prodding at Belgian request;[13] the delegations busied themselves with other matters until a British clerk misaddressed an envelope to the Belgian delegation instead of the Belgian Commission. As a result, on 27 March, Hymans received a report of 20 February by the Naval Section of the British delegation opposing the opening of the Scheldt to Belgian warships because an enemy in occupation of Belgium would thus gain use of Antwerp and the river, thereby menacing the British coast. The report was a major blow to Hymans who, while recognizing Balfour's resistance to Dutch territorial transfer, had counted on British support to gain free Belgian naval use of the Scheldt in peace and war. As usual, he had been too hopeful about British assistance but, on this issue, the Belgian claims had been well received by the Ten, the Foreign Office, and the chief of the Imperial General Staff, and had recently been strongly endorsed by Admiral Sir David Beatty, commander of the Grand Fleet.[14]

Hymans took the document to Hardinge, who said, "That must have cost you dearly!" After Hymans proved that he had not bought the document, Hardinge read it and professed himself astonished. Hymans protested against the decision, asked why the Belgians had not been told, and complained of British indifference and lack of support on almost all issues. Hardinge heard him out and insisted that Britain was sympathetic, but he was visibly reserved about Belgian claims, especially those affecting Holland, and he gave no promises of support. He indicated that Britain had reason to be very cautious in matters concerning Holland and he encouraged Hymans to pursue the Luxemburg question.[15] Thereupon the Belgian delegation complained to Pichon

12. Pichon to de Stuers, 13 Mar. 1919, FMAE A/133; Balfour to de Stuers, 13 Mar. 1919, F.O. 608/3; DuB, R.G.P. 117, pp. 994–95.

13. Hymans to Balfour, 25 Mar. 1919, no. 347, Balfour to de Stuers, 2 Apr. 1919, F.O. 608/3.

14. Fuller memo, 20 Feb. 1919, CAB 29/8; Hymans, *Mémoires*, 1:421–24.

15. Hymans, *Mémoires*, 1:421–24; Hymans memo, 27 Mar. 1919, BMAE DB/31.

that four men were secretly negotiating the fate of the world and that Belgium was being told nothing, not even about revision of the 1839 treaties.[16]

When King Albert arrived in Paris a few days later, he pursued the Scheldt question. He told Hardinge he knew the Admiralty view but that "it is the same opinion as that which was held 100 years ago in England, and he felt that times had changed and a new policy was desirable. He had no desire for territorial gains in this direction; all he wanted was the free right of passage for Belgian ships in times of war as well as in times of peace."[17] Although this was a considerable modification of his earlier stand, Albert was a realist and Hymans, who had undoubtedly told Albert what to say, had been forced to face the unpalatable truth by the naval documents and his own interview with Hardinge. When Albert met with the Four on 4 April, he repeated the same argument and received support from both Clemenceau and Lloyd George, who said he disagreed with the Admiralty view.[18] With this endorsement, the Belgians faced more confidently the prospect of negotiations with the Dutch, which that very day had begun to appear likely.

On 4 April the Dutch minister in Paris notified Balfour and Pichon that Holland accepted their invitation to express Dutch views on treaty revision, provided that she dealt only with interested powers, not the peace conference in general. As the Dutch objected to any dealings with the Paris Peace Conference, including either a hearing by the Belgian Commission or a formal audition before the Supreme Council, it was agreed after some debate that because van Karnebeek apparently wished to attend in person, the foreign ministers of the great powers should meet with those of Holland and Belgium as soon as possible. It was understood, however, that this meeting would not occur at once because the Council of Five, consisting of the foreign ministers of the great powers, was too overburdened to consider anything not intended for inclusion in the text of the Versailles treaty.[19] As the Belgian dele-

16. Hymans memo, 28 Mar. 1919, BMAE B-1-1519; de Gaiffier to Hymans, 29 Mar. 1919, no. 2495/985, **BMAE FR**/1919.

17. Hardinge to Balfour, 4 Apr. 1919, F.O. 608/2 pt. 1.

18. Mantoux, *Les Délibérations*, 1:143–44; Hymans, *Mémoires*, 1:446.

19. *Revision*, p. 9; Crowe memo, 9 Apr. 1919, van Swinderin to Crowe, 10 Apr. 1919,

gation realized that negotiations with the Dutch could not be completed before the Versailles treaty was signed, it made an unsuccessful effort to insert a clause in the treaty committing Germany to compensate Holland for any Dutch territory ceded to Belgium. On 16 April, the Four deleted a clause to this effect from the report of the Belgian Commission, thus rendering improbable any transfer of territory from Holland to Belgium.[20]

As the meeting with the Dutch was deferred, the Belgians used the hiatus to seek support. Because they thought that French assistance could safely be expected and American sympathy was unlikely, as the friendly Haskins would be replaced by the hostile Lansing, they sought out the British. On this occasion, the Belgians were too optimistic about France and especially so about Britain. As the delay dragged on despite Dutch willingness to proceed, various members of the Belgian delegation made several overtures to British diplomatists, who were unfailingly sympathetic but unvaryingly vague. They tended to dodge issues and stress difficulties, indicating that Britain would give Belgium no support on any territorial issue nor in regard to the defense of lower Limburg. On questions concerning the Scheldt, the British seemed more amenable but made no promises. After naively and futilely asking how much pressure Balfour was prepared to put on the Netherlands to achieve results, the Belgian delegation concluded that Britain had little interest in the issues of treaty revision and would give small support.[21] Although this conclusion was sound, Hymans could not bring himself to face its implications. While these overtures were in progress, the Council of Five finally decided on 9 May that the meetings with the

---

Hankey to Dutasta, 18 Apr. 1919, F.O. 608/3; FRUS PPC, 4:588–89. The evidence is conflicting (DuB, R.G.P. 117, pp. 1014–15, 1054–55, R.G.P. 146, pp. 1179–80) on whether van Karnebeek really wanted to attend in person, but the Council of Five, on the strength of British talks with van Swinderin, thought he did. In refusing communication with the peace conference, where Holland was not represented on commissions and where the great powers would make the final decisions, van Karnebeek was responding to legal advice. H. T. Colenbrander, *Nederland en België: Adviezen*, pp. 10–11.

20. Hymans to Pichon, 11 Apr. 1919, no. 431, FMAE A/133; I.C. 171B, 16 Apr. 1919, CAB 29/37.

21. Crowe memo, 2 May 1919, F.O. 608/3; Hymans memo, 15 Apr. 1919, BMAE DB/30/II; de Grunne memo, 5 May 1919, de Gaiffier to Hymans, 6 May 1919, no. 3787/1482, BMAE DB/30/III; Akers-Douglas memo, 6 May 1919, F.O. 608/3.

Dutch, which became known as the Conference of Seven, would commence on 19 May. In response, the Belgian cabinet attempted to solidify the domestic front and soften the diplomatic front by unanimously endorsing a resolution giving Hymans complete latitude in negotiation but adding that Belgium would not accept any cession of territory without the full and free consent of Holland.[22]

The Dutch contingent in Paris used the delay to the same purpose but more effectively, observing that even Crowe, whom they considered the only Briton hostile to them, displayed a much more friendly attitude. The continuing concentration upon the American delegation had borne fruit, especially with Lansing. Although Tardieu was still urging the Belgians not to renounce either Flemish Zeeland or lower Limburg, the Dutch contingent was much relieved by the Belgian cabinet's announcement and noted a marked improvement in the tone of the Belgian press. At Paris itself, they considered the atmosphere greatly improved and were satisfied.[23]

THE CONFERENCE OF SEVEN

The Conference of Seven met three times, on 19 and 20 May and on 3 June. Hymans's opening address enraged the Dutch foreign minister, van Karnebeek, who thought that "Hymans proceeded by insinuation and allusions rather than by direct arguments."[24] He concluded that the atmosphere was very favorable for Holland and that the great powers found Belgium an embarrassment but did not feel they could abandon her completely while she clung to them so hopefully. Throughout the three sessions, van Karnebeek flatly ruled out any territorial transfer or joint military arrangements, tried to limit drastically the scope of treaty revision, refused to discuss specific issues, and attempted to delay organized negotiation in the expectation that great-power support to Belgium would decline after the end of the peace conference. He strongly

22. FRUS PPC, 4:685; Hymans, *Mémoires*, 2:485.
23. DuB, R.G.P. 117, pp. 1027–30, 1035–36, 1039–41, 1050–53; Fallon to Hymans, 2 May 1919, no. 3983/854, BMAE PB/1919; de Gaiffier to Hymans, 16 May 1919, no. 4099/1620, BMAE FR/1919.
24. DuB, R.G.P. 117, pp. 1063–64.

resisted Hymans's request for an international commission to revise the 1839 treaties, insisting that such narrow treaty revision as he was willing to contemplate could be achieved only through direct Belgo-Dutch negotiations without major-power intervention. He hinted strongly that only in this way could Belgium gain any concessions at all.[25] Hymans did not seriously consider bilateral negotiations because he thought that without great-power pressure on the Netherlands, Belgium would gain nothing. Bilateral negotiations might possibly have been productive, as Holland greatly feared major-power intervention, but on the other hand, the Dutch had only to delay until the great powers lost interest in order to escape concessions.

After the first two sessions of the Conference of Seven, Hymans provided the Dutch with a written statement of Belgian claims that focused primarily upon Belgian security requirements. In response, van Karnebeek called upon Hymans and found him extremely nervous. This first private encounter between the two foreign ministers, which proved to be their only conversation for some years, was not a success. Van Karnebeek viewed Hymans with a mixture of fear and contempt, although the fear ebbed as he discovered that Hymans had much less great-power support than he had anticipated. In addition to the issues dividing them, the two men were entirely different in personality, concepts, characteristics, and approaches to diplomacy. After the meeting with Hymans and before the third session of the Conference of Seven, van Karnebeek reported to his prime minister, "I shall see to it that I wriggle Friday to a satisfactory way out of the difficult position and arrange it so that the odium, if any, falls to Hymans."[26] Such tactics clearly did not enter into the thinking of Paul Hymans, which fact speaks well for his character but handicapped him in the devious art of diplomatic maneuver.

During their conversation, van Karnebeek insisted on bilateral negotiation without great-power involvement and argued that the existing situation in Limburg served to guarantee Belgium against danger. Armed with two pungently scornful Belgian military assessments of the

25. FRUS PPC, 4:729–47, 779–91; DuB, R.G.P. 117, pp. 1063–64.
26. Hymans to Pichon, 21 May 1919, no. 670, FMAE A/133; van Karnebeek to Hymans, 23 May 1919, BMAE DB/30/III; DuB, R.G.P. 117, pp. 172–73.

Dutch army and well aware that the Dutch had evacuated their forces from Limburg just before the German invasion of Belgium in 1914, Hymans was not impressed.[27] In the Conference of Seven, he insisted that a joint military arrangement was necessary. Though not pressing for territorial transfer, he stressed the defensive difficulties of the existing situation. He asked for an improved regime on the Scheldt and the Ghent-Terneuzen canal, a new canal at joint expense between Antwerp and Moerdijk on the Hollandsche Diep, and a large canal linking the Rhine, the Meuse, and the Scheldt. Although his primary emphasis was on security, Hymans wanted all aspects of the 1839 treaties renegotiated and fought to maintain major-power participation in treaty revision. The Belgian goal was to maintain the integral unity of all problems arising from the 1839 treaties and to ensure their examination in a commission including the major powers, without advance exclusion of territorial transfer.[28]

After the three sessions had demonstrated the total opposition of Dutch and Belgian views, the Council of Five met on 4 June without Dutch or Belgian participation to decide how extensive treaty revision should be and what procedures should be used. Aside from French experts, the foreign ministers met alone. Tardieu argued that territorial transfer should be excluded, which would please Holland (and also

27. Gillain to Hymans, 28 May 1919, BMAE Ind/1919/I; G.H.Q. E/M 2d Sect., Belgian army, 28 May 1919, G/S, Belgian army note, 24 July 1919, BMAE DB/13/I. Although based upon great pride in the Belgian army's role in the war, the Belgian military assessment of the Dutch army was essentially correct. The two armies had been equally feeble in 1910, but the Dutch army remained tiny, inadequately equipped, and untried. Its term of service was only eight months and in the process of being shortened further, its morale low, and its reliability considered doubtful even by Dutch leaders. On the other hand, the shattered Belgian army had been reorganized, retrained, and re-equipped in 1915. It was battle seasoned and regarded by French experts as highly competent. Kossman, *The Low Countries*, pp. 546, 558; Vandenbosch, *Dutch Foreign Policy*, pp. 15–16; DuB, R.G.P. 145, pp. 649–53; Dutch Orange Book, *Mededeelingen van den Minister van Buitenlandsche Zaken aan de Staten-Generaal: October 1922–September 1924*, pp. 9–10; Carton de Wiart to Hymans, 3 Oct. 1919, no. 7512/1886, Masson to Hymans, 17 Nov. 1919, no. 397/16PA, BMAE PB/1919; Masson to Hymans, 19 Feb. 1920, BMAE PB/1920; Albert, *Diaries*, p. 150; Génie to Guerre, 20 Feb. 1918, FMAE CPC Guerre Belg./423; Génie to Guerre, 13 Sept. 1917, no. 430, Vin 7N/1160; Rouquerel to Clemenceau, 17 July 1919, no. 3gh, Vin 6N/121.

28. FRUS PPC, 4:729–47, 779–91; Hymans to Balfour, 21 May 1919, no. 670, F.O. 800/216; Hymans note, 26 May 1919, BMAE Ind/1919/I.

fulfill the primary condition for the Dutch loan to France), but that the powers should participate, which would please Belgium. As France had a strong self-interest in Belgium's defense arrangements, the French delegates were otherwise the chief spokesmen for Belgian views. Balfour was substantially in agreement with Tardieu, although rather indecisive and reluctant to see direct major-power intervention for fear of doing anything the Dutch might consider coercive. Lansing, who was an old friend of van Swinderin and who, as an international lawyer, deemed existing treaties so sacrosanct that no alteration should be permitted at all, objected strongly and supported the Dutch on all points.[29]

There ensued a three-hour argument between Tardieu and Pichon on one hand, and Lansing on the other, while Balfour wavered between. The open hostility of Lansing to all the Belgian requests seems to have awakened in Balfour a sympathy for Belgium and, by the end of the long meeting, he stood fairly close to Tardieu's position. But Lansing remained immovable and eventually the Five decided to give Belgium the form and Holland the substance. They resolved that the five powers would participate in treaty revision and would establish a commission to this end. Taking the view that the interest of the great powers was limited to the neutrality and sovereignty of Belgium (without mention of security), they agreed that the commission would ask Belgium and Holland to submit joint proposals for a new regime governing the navigable waterways "in the spirit of the general principles adopted by the peace conference," a phrase that conveyed no meaning to anybody. Finally, the commission itself would study other measures of treaty revision, specifically excluding any transfer of territory or the imposition of any international servitudes upon Holland.[30] Neither then nor thereafter did anybody involved in treaty revision at any level pretend to know precisely what the term "international servitudes" meant. The phrase had been imposed by Lansing, who later triumphantly informed van Swinderin that he had discovered it in a file on an earlier Canadian-American fishing dispute. As Lansing implied and the Dutch fully

29. Balfour to Curzon, 4 June 1919, tel. 1013, F.O. 608/2 pt. 1; for minutes of meeting, see FRUS PPC, 4:792–801.
30. FRUS PPC, 4:795–801; *Revision*, p. 10; DuB, R.G.P. 117, pp. 1082–83.

appreciated, its ambiguity was an asset to Holland, which could and did claim that any proposal unattractive to her was an international servitude.[31]

The Dutch protested against the decision that the powers participate in the negotiations and were sufficiently alarmed to hint to Belgian officials that they might commit themselves to the defense of Limburg if Belgium would negotiate bilaterally, but their open jubilation and that of the Dutch press when they returned to The Hague revealed their satisfaction at gaining far better terms than they had anticipated. The Belgians were dismayed at the ruling of the Five, and, as they sought clarification, their dismay deepened. Although any consensus of opinion was conspicuously lacking, Crowe thought the ruling about international servitudes meant that the Dutch would not be expected to make any concessions going beyond the 1839 treaties, and even Tardieu wondered if the Belgians would do better to negotiate directly with the Dutch. The Belgians rejected this idea, knowing that alone they would be helpless against the Dutch, as they had little to offer in return for concessions that Holland obviously did not wish to make. Worse yet from the Belgian viewpoint, the Five apparently did not expect to consider the problem of Belgium's security. Hearing of Balfour's indecision at the 4 June meeting, Hymans recalled Lloyd George's endorsement of Belgian naval use of the Scheldt to Albert and supposed that Lloyd George had neglected to mention it to Balfour.[32] He concluded that "England does not want to offend Holland whom she desires to retain in her orbit" and decided that Belgium should not formulate any territorial demands but should maintain the integral unity of the problem

31. De Gaiffier to Hymans, 5 June 1919, de Bassompierre memo, 5 June 1919, Hymans memo, 7 June 1919, BMAE Ind/1919/I; Hymans, *Mémoires*, 2:485; DuB, R.G.P. 117, pp. 1093–94. Britain and America submitted North Atlantic fishing disputes to the Permanent Court of Arbitration, which in 1910 rejected America's claim of an international servitude. United States, Senate, Doc. no. 357, 61st Cong., 2d sess., *Treaties, Conventions, International Acts, Protocols and Agreements between the United States of America and Other Powers, 1776–1923,* 1:842–43; FRUS, 1910, pp. 544–69.

32. DuB, R.G.P. 117, p. 1085; Rolin-Jaequemyns memo, 7 June 1919, Hymans Papers/163; Townley to Curzon, 9 June 1919, no. 149, F.O. 371/3640; de Bassompierre memo, 5 June 1919, de Gaiffier to Hymans, 5 June 1919, Hymans note, 7 June 1919, BMAE Ind/1919/I.

and try to keep all aspects of treaty revision and all possible solutions before the commission to be established by the powers.[33]

Acting on this decision, Hymans notified Pichon on 14 June that Belgium accepted the invitation to participate in the commission with the proviso, pointing to the 8 March resolution of the Ten, that its procedure should not exclude examination and adoption of all measures necessary to abolish the risks and drawbacks of the 1839 treaties and to ensure Belgium free economic development and full security. On 17 June he saw Crowe and expressed Belgian concern over the 4 June decision. By now Hymans had abandoned any lingering hope of territorial transfer and his chief concern was that treaty revision might become an exercise in nothingness, as in the end it largely did. Crowe was very sympathetic, blaming Lansing for what had occurred, and said that after three hours of argument the others had, out of sheer exhaustion, let the unfortunate phrase "international servitudes" remain in the resolution. He admitted that a literal interpretation of this phrase would make treaty revision impossible. Crowe tried to cheer Hymans by offering hope that the restrictive obstacles could be circumvented in the commission, but that day he wrote, "We gave away the Belgians when we agreed to Mr. Lansing's demand that nothing should be considered which imposed any servitudes on Holland. The Belgians are not likely now to get anything at all."[34]

Though on this occasion Crowe's sympathy was genuine, in general British expressions of sympathy were designed to soothe and to escape commitment. Hymans was reluctant to face the fact that British declarations of concern cost them nothing and gained him nothing. He could not conquer his faith in the British, and their graceful phrases gave him unfounded hopes for something more concrete. Despite his legalistic nature, Hymans never fully accepted the fact that one specific written commitment was generally worth more than innumerable expressions of sympathy. In this he was probably influenced, like other Belgian leaders, by the 1914 experience.

33. Hymans memo, 7 June 1919, BMAE Ind/1919/I.
34. *Revision*, p. 10; Hymans memo, 17 June 1919, BMAE Ind/1919/I; Crowe minute, 17 June, on Townley to Curzon, 9 June 1919, no. 148, F.O. 608/3.

On 19 June the Dutch agreed to participate in the commission, although they reiterated that territorial transfer and the imposition of international servitudes must be excluded. They further insisted that the commission should not consider any measure on which Holland and Belgium were not in full agreement, a stipulation that would give the Dutch an effective veto over the commission's work. When the Five met on 25 June, it was agreed without discussion that this limitation was unacceptable, and the Dutch were so informed the next day. Pichon notified van Karnebeek that the five powers retained the right to participate in the discussion of all issues before the commission, which would be composed of two delegates and experts for each of the five powers plus Belgium and Holland. It would meet as soon as all the delegates arrived in Paris. The Dutch were asked to name their two members and told that the Belgian delegates would be Pierre Orts, acting secretary-general of the Foreign Ministry, and Paul Segers, minister of state, member of the Belgian Senate, and an expert on the problems of the Scheldt.[35] As Pichon's phraseology did not state that the great powers would serve as a court of final decision but rather that they would participate as necessary in discussions to resolve Belgo-Dutch differences, thus implying that nothing could be imposed upon the Netherlands against its will, van Karnebeek was content.[36]

Because Belgian parliamentary opinion was becoming aroused about treaty revision despite firm restraining efforts by Hymans, the Belgians urged that the Commission of Fourteen, as it came to be called, should start its labors at once. This pressure led to a decision that meetings would begin in Paris on 29 June 1919, despite Dutch preference for delay and transfer of the talks to The Hague.[37] As various powers named their delegates, it appeared to the Belgians that the commission would be composed largely of technicians concerned only with economic use of the waterways and that it thus might ignore the question of Belgian security. Accordingly, Orts saw Crowe on 26 July. Crowe's report of the interview was rather sharp in tone, possibly because he

35. *Revision*, pp. 10–11; FRUS PPC, 4:857–59.

36. DuB, R.G.P. 117, p. 1096; DuD, R.G.P. 156, pp. 9–10, 19–20.

37. DuD, R.G.P. 156, p. 19; Villiers to Curzon, 13 June 1919, no. 213, F.O. 371/3640; Hymans memo, 22 June 1919, BMAE Ind/1919/I; DBFP, 1:92.

was bested at every turn during the two-hour session. Orts pointed out that Holland wanted to confine discussion to commercial use of the navigable waterways and said he wanted to be sure that, when he raised the matter of security guarantees, the British delegates would not declare such questions outside the competence of the commission. Crowe was visibly embarrassed and said that the League of Nations would give all necessary security to Belgium. This was the first of many British attempts to dispose of the problem of Belgian security by transferring responsibility to the as yet unborn League. Crowe further argued that the commission could not be expected to resolve such important political problems, which should have been posed to the Five. Orts retorted that Hymans had done so at length and remarked that Britain and America did not seem to think the League gave France sufficient security, inasmuch as they had given her an additional guarantee. He reminded Crowe that the Belgian Commission of which Crowe had been a member had recommended treaty revision to suppress the dangers of the 1839 treaties and that this resolution had been approved by the Supreme Council. Orts added that he gathered that Britain felt Belgium had no need for guarantees similar to those given to France and ought to be satisfied with commercial improvements. If this were so, Belgium might withdraw from the commission.[38]

When talk turned to Limburg, Orts pointed out that, without Dutch military cooperation, Belgium would again be forced in the event of hostilities to abandon the line of the Meuse and make her first stand in the heart of the kingdom, a sacrifice she could not reasonably be expected to accept a second time. When Crowe mentioned the demilitarized Rhineland as a protection for Belgium, Orts again reminded him that France, although less exposed than Belgium, required an additional Anglo-American guarantee and accurately predicted that Limburg was where the Germans could most easily transverse the Rhineland and attack France through Belgium. When Crowe tried to escape this inexorable logic by complaining that the Belgians had not formulated precise proposals, Orts retorted that Belgium could hardly be expected to find alone the remedy for a situation for which she was in no way

38. Orts to Hymans, 26 July 1919, BMAE Ind/1919/I; Crowe memo, 26 July 1919, F.O. 608/3.

responsible. Belgium had appealed to the powers, and their intervention had only narrowed the range of possible results. As Crowe admitted that he saw no solution, Orts told him that Belgium chiefly
wanted two things: a Belgo-Dutch military convention for the common
defense of Limburg (and British aid in persuading the Dutch to such
an agreement) and an Anglo-American-French promise of aid against
German attack. Crowe was dubious about both and ended his account
of the session with the remark, "All this is clearly not very encouraging";
Orts, who tended to be more realistic than Hymans about lost battles,
reported: "This conversation no longer permits me to doubt the complete indifference of the British government toward the problem of
Belgian security. If it can, without too much trouble and without sub-
scribing to any precise commitment, give Belgium in this respect a
satisfaction that is more apparent than real, the British government will
not refuse it. But it will not bring any enthusiasm to it. We will not find
any effective assistance from this quarter." He added that Crowe had
said to him, "Why don't you simply conclude a military convention with
France?"[39]

As Crowe should have known, the last thing that Belgium desired
was a unilateral military accord with France. Belgian diplomatists had
said so repeatedly, but the British tendency to view Belgium as a French
satellite before the fact remained strong and contributed to partial
realization of this fact. In addition, the Belgian diplomatists, who were
looking at the question strictly from the point of view of their own
security, did not recognize the broader significance of their own proposals. Together, a Belgo-Dutch military convention and an Anglo-
American-French guarantee against German attack would have made
Belgium the focal point of a six-power military combination (including
Luxemburg) against Germany. Had such a potent bloc been achieved,
with or without American or Italian participation, there is little doubt
that the diplomatic and economic history of the 1920s would have been
vastly different. Whether such a combination against Germany would
have been desirable is arguable, but probably any clearly defined align-

39. Orts to Hymans, 26 July 1919, BMAE Ind/1919/I; Crowe memo, 26 July 1919,
F.O 608/3.

ment of powers would have been preferable to the acute instability that
ensued.

Such a combination was, however, impossible in the climate of late
1919 and 1920, and remained improbable for many years thereafter. In
the aftermath of World War I each country was, diplomatically speaking, refighting that war in the light of its own experience. Thus, France
and Belgium, motivated by fear, wanted every possible guarantee of
assistance against renewed German attack. Holland, whose good fortune it had been to escape involvement, was absolutely determined to
maintain her neutrality and to commit herself to nobody, in hopes that
this policy would protect her as well in the future as in the past. There
was from the outset no prospect that she would agree to participate
in any anti-German bloc or any Belgo-Dutch defense arrangement,
however limited. Hymans, who genuinely desired good relations with
Holland but who lacked any capacity to envision the Dutch point of
view, never understood why Holland's leaders so adamantly resisted his
eminently logical proposals to solve Belgium's security problem by
Dutch involvement or why Dutch opinion became so angry. He similarly failed to comprehend, as the French to a degree did as well, that
Britain's policy was motivated by determination not to be sucked into
another Continental war and thus to make no military commitments to
any of its recent allies beyond the Anglo-American guarantee to France,
which would enter into force only if the United States ratified it. Otherwise, despite their obvious vital interest in both Low Countries, the
British shied away from the potential cost in money and blood, taking
refuge in unsound perceptions of the future. With few exceptions, the
British leaders consistently underestimated the German potential for
resurgence and thus had no fear of Germany, though, in their over-
estimation of French capacity for sustained Continental predominance,
they did fear France. In the circumstances, they were delighted to rid
themselves of the old guarantee to Belgium, which effectively protected
France as well, and had no desire to replace it with another.

The question of a west European security pact against Germany was
in one form or another almost a constant feature of European diplomacy from the peace conference to Locarno. All the great powers including Germany recognized that formation of such a system depended

upon British willingness to participate. Because Belgium was one of the very few Continental countries that modern Britain had ever formally committed itself to defend, it is not surprising that an early phase of this continuing debate over creation of a west European bloc centered upon the question of British participation in a new guarantee to Belgium. Late in 1919, as the survival of the Anglo-American guarantee to France became increasingly doubtful, a convenient opportunity arose to re-examine the entire problem in the context of new Belgian security arrangements. For this reason and because Belgium's geographic lo-cation constituted one of the most strategically significant military passageways of western Europe, the long debates in the Commission of Fourteen revealed national attitudes of far broader significance than the questions of the Limburg gap and of new arrangements to replace Belgium's neutrality and concomitant great-power guarantee would at first glance indicate.

THE COMMISSION OF FOURTEEN

By mid-summer, the British and the French saw the implications of the Belgian security problem and reacted in diametrically opposed fash-ions. In this respect, the debates of the Commission of Fourteen devel-oped into a precursor in microcosm of the discordant history of the Western Entente. At the outset, however, the focus in the Commission of Fourteen was much narrower. It commenced work on 29 July with Jules Laroche of the Quai d'Orsay as chairman. The British members were Charles Tufton of the Foreign Office as vice-chairman and Brig. Gen. H. O. Mance, an expert on transportation problems. The Dutch delegates were van Swinderin and Professor Antonius A. H. Struycken, a legal advisor to the Foreign Ministry. At once, the Belgian delegates presented a written schema outlining their desires. These included re-vision of the arrangements for all navigable waterways, cancellation of compulsory neutrality, and provision of new security guarantees, as well as access to both the Scheldt and Antwerp for Belgian warships in peace and war. In addition, a joint Belgo-Dutch defense of Limburg was requested, despite the intense opposition of the chief of the Belgian

General Staff, whose contempt for the Dutch army was total. Territorial transfer was not mentioned, although the inconvenience of the existing boundaries was made obvious.[40]

The Belgian tactics were based upon Crowe's earlier advice that perhaps in the commission the obstacle created by exclusion of "international servitudes" could be circumvented if the phrase were never mentioned. Hymans was determined to involve the great powers in each aspect of treaty revision. He was well aware, as were the Dutch, that Belgian opinion was unanimous in believing that something had to be done to insure Belgium's defensibility and that use of her vital waterways should no longer depend upon Dutch good will. Van Karnebeek, on the other hand, was determined to remove negotiations over the waterways from the commission's aegis and from Paris. Concerned that Belgium would try to overturn the 4 June resolution, he had prevailed upon Lansing to remind the American members that territorial transfer and international servitudes must remain excluded. In addition, the Dutch delegates were armed with cabinet instructions that, if any attempt were made to retreat from the 4 June decisions, they should withdraw. They could endorse abandonment of Belgian neutrality and alteration of the status of Antwerp but had strict orders to reject territorial transfer, any plebiscite in Limburg, or wartime transit of the Belgian navy on the Scheldt. On riparian matters, they could consider slight enlargement of the competence of the joint Belgo-Dutch technical commission where the Netherlands already held effective veto power. After the initial Belgian presentation, these instructions were amplified in great detail and altered to reject any military cooperation, to press for abolition of Belgian neutrality in a form that would permanently end great-power intervention in Belgo-Dutch relations, to exclude possible cosovereignty on any of the mouths of the Scheldt, and to make alteration of the status of Antwerp (without wartime transit) dependent upon British wishes. Military questions should be referred to the League of Nations, and discussion in the commission, where support for Belgium was anticipated, was to be avoided. Similarly, discussion of the waterways should be avoided and reserved to bilateral negotiation at The Hague. In return for the Netherlands' "accom-

40. DBFP, 5:64–65, 95–101; Gillain to Hymans, 28 May 1919, BMAE Ind/1919/I.

modating spirit" about use of the Scheldt and willingness to examine Belgian proposals for canals across Dutch territory to the Rhine and northward from Antwerp to Moerdijk, the Dutch delegates were to require reciprocal concessions on Belgian waterways, notably between Maastricht and Liège.[41] As van Karnebeek knew he now held the upper hand in most respects, he prepared to drive a hard bargain.

Aside from a certain amount of time expended in organizational detail and in suppressing repeated Dutch objections, the first six meetings of the Fourteen were devoted to the Belgian arguments and the seventh to the Dutch rebuttal.[42] The Belgian case was presented in exhaustive detail and, though it made clear beyond any doubt the defenselessness of Belgium and the unsatisfactory nature of the existing waterways arrangements, it wearied the commission. It also angered the Dutch delegates, who considered withdrawing, although they were relieved that Belgium did not protest the 4 June decisions. The Dutch reply was, as Balfour reported, somewhat curt but admirably brief. It denied a few of the Belgian charges and ignored the rest. As instructed, the Dutch delegates flatly refused to consider any joint military arrangement for either the Scheldt or Limburg and tried unsuccessfully to remove all economic and fluvial questions from the commission and from Paris.[43]

The Dutch also tried another tactic. Although they thought they had emerged victorious from the early sessions of the Fourteen and that Belgium was losing support by making excessive claims, they were worried by CPN activity in Limburg.[44] Probably as a consequence, on 16 August the Dutch press printed what purported to be a letter signed by Hymans on 3 July urging discreet propaganda in Limburg toward its return to Belgium. Dutch opinion immediately became acutely inflamed. The Belgians were quickly able to prove that the document, which had been written on 20 May before territorial transfer was ruled

41. DuD, R.G.P. 156, pp. 18–19, 21–22, 59–60, 64–65, 97–100.

42. The *procès-verbaux* of all 1919 meetings of the Fourteen and its subcommittees may be found in DBFP, 5.

43. DBFP, 5:255, 260, 294; DuD, R.G.P. 156, pp. 101–2; Carton de Wiart to Hymans, 6 Aug. 1919, no. 6178/1515, BMAE FR/1919.

44. DuD, R.G.P. 156, pp. 127–28, 150; Carton de Wiart to Hymans, 6 Aug. 1919, no. 6178/1515, BMAE FR/1919.

out, had never been seen by Hymans, who was in Paris at the time. It was in fact a long memorandum by a minor official concerning visa procedures for residents of Limburg visiting Belgium or the Belgian Rhineland zone, which briefly mentioned measures to counter German anti-Belgian propaganda in lower Limburg. Before selected portions of this document were published, it had been edited to such a degree as to make Bismarck's famous rearrangement of the Ems telegram look like a child's effort. Five and a half paragraphs were deleted and a crucial phrase which specified that all propaganda should "be kept within respect for the established power" was suppressed.[45]

In response to immediate Dutch protest on 19 August, Hymans promptly provided the full text, noting the omissions and the misdating. On 22 August, van Karnebeek told the Dutch cabinet that three paragraphs had been deleted and that the date was erroneous. The cabinet decided that Holland had no responsibility to publish an accurate text. In fact, on 4 September it authorized a renewed protest, which was made at once.[46] Meanwhile, when faced by a flood of incontrovertible evidence and taxed by Laroche, van Swinderin privately admitted that "there must be some misunderstanding,"[47] but there was no retraction and the furor in the Dutch press continued unabated. It was fed by a series of minor episodes which led the Belgians to believe that the Dutch were deliberately trying to create a major incident to use as an excuse for breaking off negotiations. The Belgians refused to fall into what they considered to be a trap and told Villiers that they would send a civil reply to the latest Dutch protest about the Limburg letter and would restrain the Belgian press.[48] Hymans complained to the British

---

45. DuD, R.G.P. 156, p. 168; BMAE memo, 23 Aug. 1919, Hymans Papers/164; DBFP, 5:267–68, 273; Villiers to Curzon, 26 Aug. 1919, no. 316, F.O. 371/3641.

46. Van Vollenhoven to Hymans, 19 Aug. 1919, no. 8980, Hymans to van Vollenhoven, 20 Aug. 1919, no. 6944, Hymans Papers/164; DuD, R.G.P. 156, pp. 150–51, 167–68. The second Dutch protest was sent some days after van Vollenhoven had twice reported from Brussels that no member of the Belgian cabinet, including Hymans, knew anything about the instruction in question until the Dutch press published it. DuD, R.G.P. 156, pp. 156–59.

47. DBFP, 5:294, n. 2.

48. Gurney to Curzon, 10 Sept. 1919, no. 336, F.O. 371/3641; Hymans to van Vollenhoven, 11 Sept. 1919, Hymans Papers/164.

about Dutch propaganda among the Flemish but was careful not to mention it to the Dutch or in Parliament.[49]

As the meetings of the Fourteen continued and it appeared that the great powers would ask Holland to enter into joint defensive arrangements with Belgium for Limburg, the Dutch press revived earlier rumors of an impending raid by Belgian extremists on Limburg and threatened to publish a list of Belgian volunteers. Although the CPN was as usual issuing strident propaganda and thus considerably embarrassing the Belgian government, one British and one American investigation and two Belgian ones uncovered no evidence supporting the Dutch charges. The French ambassador said flatly that he disbelieved the rumors, and the Belgian press termed them ridiculous.[50] Nonetheless, the Dutch government imposed rigorous controls on Belgian travelers to Limburg, the furor continued in the Dutch press, and Dutch opinion had reached such a feverish pitch by October that the British minister to The Hague spoke of a rupture of diplomatic relations or even war.[51] Although evidence of the Dutch tactics was extensive, the British and French remained unperturbed and no protest was made to Holland.

Though these Dutch ploys did not succeed in terminating negotiations nor as yet in removing economic and fluvial questions from the aegis of the commission, the intransigence of the Dutch delegates yielded some concessions. After the Belgians and the Dutch had presented their respective views, the Dutch delegates retired to Holland,

49. DBFP, 5:625–26.

50. Hymans memo, 28 Sept. 1919, Hymans Papers/163; DBFP, 5:617–20, 626; Hymans, *Mémoires*, 1:380–82; Gunther to Lansing, 11 July 1919, tel. 6560, SD 755.56/4; DuD, R.G.P. 156, pp. 166, 236–37. As in the case of the truncated visa instructions, the furor was set off by the *Nieuw Rotterdamsche Courant*. Van Karnebeek had on 28 August received indirect word from the British military attaché at The Hague of a private meeting in Brussels (without any Belgian cabinet ministers present), which proposed, if the Dutch refused minimal Belgian demands regarding use of the Scheldt and construction of projected canals, that Limburg should be seized by force of arms. Van Karnebeek noted in his diary that neither he nor the chief of the Dutch General Staff took the report seriously. In the midst of the furor, the Dutch cabinet decided on 26 September not to send any troops to Limburg. DuD, R.G.P. 156, pp. 158, 200.

51. DBFP, 5:664; Paris *Herald*, 30 Oct. 1919, FMAE A/135; van Vollenhoven to Hymans, 28 Sept. 1919, Carton de Wiart to Hymans, 3 Oct. 1919, no. 7505/1879, BMAE PB/1919.

leaving behind the impression that they might not return.[52] The delegates of the five great powers constituted themselves a subcommittee and discussed both procedure and substantive issues without Dutch or Belgian participation. The powers ultimately decided that technical arrangements for the navigable waterways should be worked out directly between Dutch and Belgian negotiators. Thus the persistent Dutch refusal to entertain any other procedure was rewarded. The Belgians accepted their defeat in this respect with unusual grace, apparently aware that the Dutch were prepared to obstruct discussion in the commission indefinitely. Indeed, the Dutch delegates noted that relations had improved greatly and foresaw no further difficulties even on military questions.[53] On these, the great powers had decided that the broader issues involving Belgian security, such as access to the Scheldt for Belgian warships, removing the restrictions on Antwerp as a naval base, a possible guarantee of Belgium by the powers, and some joint arrangement for Limburg would be handled by the major powers and the full commission.

Thereafter the meetings became a prolonged wrangle between the French, who favored some of the defensive arrangements desired by the Belgians, and the British, who remained opposed to any Dutch concessions. Most of these battles took place in meetings of the five powers or in their military and naval subcommittee for, after the initial Belgian and Dutch expositions, the full commission met only three times more in 1919 and once in 1920. Throughout, the British refused to put any pressure on Holland and remained serenely confident that Dutch concessions were imminent, although evidence to support this view was lacking. Anglo-Belgian relations remained prickly throughout the negotiations.

When the powers briefly considered the economic aspects of the Scheldt regime before referring the problem to the Dutch and the Belgians, the British refused to contemplate any arrangements going beyond the 1839 treaties. They fought any limitation of the Dutch right to veto Belgian improvements in the river channel and objected to any proviso for arbitration of disputes because such would not favor Hol-

52. DBFP, 5:329–30, 314; DuD, R.G.P. 156, pp. 156–57.
53. DuD, R.G.P. 156, pp. 156–57, 182–83, 235.

land. They insisted that Holland be free to invoke her right of self-defense as an excuse to block Belgian construction work on the river whenever she chose. When discussion turned to a list of technical services on the Scheldt to be supervised by a joint commission, the British delegate successfully blocked inclusion of sanitary services on the ground that joint regulation would be an infringement of Dutch sovereignty. When a procedural difficulty developed, Tufton declared that the commission must do nothing that would go against the feelings of Holland.[54] As the Dutch had already made clear their preference for the existing arrangements, substantive treaty revision was clearly doomed, even in its fluvial aspects.

Thereafter the Belgians and the Dutch were left to work together to resolve technical problems concerning the waterways. The issues revolved around such matters as pilotage, lighting, buoys, construction work, sanitary services, telegraph arrangements, and, above all, dredging to maintain or deepen the channel. From the Belgian viewpoint, dredging was a particularly urgent problem, although Dutch regulations restricting the use of Belgian pilots were also a major issue. The Dutch, who understandably feared Antwerp as a competitor to Rotterdam, had before the war refused to dredge the channel (as they were required to do under the 1839 treaties) and had permitted Belgium to do so only under crippling restrictions that rendered maintenance difficult at all times and impossible in winter. During the war, the Scheldt had silted up so much that a thirty-foot channel was now only about seventeen feet deep. Indeed, plans for Wilson to leave Europe from Antwerp had been abandoned when it was discovered that the channel was now much too shallow for the *George Washington*, a fact that the Belgians took care to air.[55] Under the circumstances, Belgium was eager for a new technical regime. Although Holland had no desire to benefit Antwerp, her fear of major-power pressure on nontechnical matters under negotiation by the commission was so great that she hastened to be conciliatory on the riparian questions. Thus technical arrangements

54. DBFP, 5:278–82, 367–71, 387–91, 687–88, 696–99, 715.
55. DBFP, 5:95–101; minutes, meeting, ACNP Commissioners and Technical Advisors, 3 Sept. 1919, Wilson Papers 6A/11; House to Whitlock, 14 May 1919, Whitlock Papers/40 (LC).

that, from the Belgian point of view, were some improvement over the past were achieved with comparative ease. As the larger aspects of treaty revision eventually failed, these agreements were never put into effect. The sole concrete advance arising from these negotiations was a Belgo-Dutch agreement on 16 May 1920 dividing the Scheldt pilotage to end a competition harmful to both countries.[56]

While Belgian and Dutch experts worked on technical and riparian problems in the autumn of 1919, the great-power members of the Fourteen addressed themselves in subcommittee to military and naval matters. Again, the British representatives obstructed any substantial changes in existing arrangements to the benefit of Belgium. There was no real difficulty about permitting Antwerp to become a naval base, but access to it via the Scheldt was another matter. Both in the meetings of the five powers and in the military and naval subcommittee, the British adamantly opposed opening the Scheldt in wartime. In the Subcommittee on the Navigation of the Scheldt, Captain C. Fuller, RN, author of the Admiralty memorandum that had so fortuitously fallen into Hymans's hands in March, argued the Admiralty view in unchanging language, apparently unaware that both Lloyd George and Balfour had endorsed free transit of the Scheldt for Belgian warships. In peacetime, the British delegates argued, Belgian warships could travel up the Scheldt to Antwerp, provided that Holland retained the right to forbid this transit whenever she chose. At British insistence, the Belgians would be obliged to seek permission for each and every transit of a single ship. Belgian ability to send her fleet from Antwerp to the Atlantic upon the outbreak of war would also remain at the mercy of Dutch policy, as the concept of an automatic right of exit was rejected by the British experts as an objectionable infringement of Dutch sovereignty. According to Captain Fuller, it was British policy that small nations not be permitted sizable navies. He thought Belgium would be limited to two or three smallish ships that could just as well use Zeebrugge or

56. For text of the pilotage agreement, see Great Britain, Foreign Office, *British and Foreign State Papers*, 115:641. Texts of various draft Belgo-Dutch economic treaties may be found in Orts Papers/428. They include access for the Belgian navy to Antwerp (with a Dutch right to suspend the privilege temporarily on three days' notice), a mixed commission for technical questions, arrangements for the Ghent-Terneuzen canal, fishing regulations, and Dutch consent to Antwerp-Moerdijk and Rhine-Meuse-Scheldt canals.

Ostend. As all the British experts adamantly opposed any rights for the Belgian navy on the Scheldt, the Dutch made no concessions of substance, and the provision that Antwerp could become a naval base was thus rendered meaningless.[57]

The British delegates showed themselves similarly reluctant to contemplate anything more than vague phraseology concerning the Limburg gap and objected to a proposed statement that it was the duty of the great powers to obtain military guarantees for Belgium. Tufton, the senior British delegate, who was far more sympathetic toward Belgium than any other British official involved in the negotiations, argued that such a commitment might embroil Britain in a war against Holland, and he succeeded in changing the statement to read that the powers were interested in seeing that Belgium received guarantees. Though senior Foreign Office officials admitted privately to themselves that the danger of German attack across the Limburg gap was very real, they were not prepared to face the problem and so no instructions were sent to Paris. As the British did not want to defend Belgium again, they had no desire to render her defensible. Accordingly, British delegates argued that the danger was not pressing, because Germany would be unable to act for twenty or thirty years. Here as in so many other military questions in the interwar period, the British pursued their tradition of postponing problems as long as possible. At their insistence, a five-power declaration about the desirability of a Belgo-Dutch military arrangement for Limburg was diluted on the grounds that the statement might offend Holland. Similarly, a Franco-Italian proposal for a military accord between Holland and the four powers participating in the Rhineland occupation encountered sharp British resistance. This plan amounted to a west European and American security pact in ingenious form. The British rejected it for this reason, because they did not fully consider Britain to be a European Continental power, and because there was no prospect that Holland would accept it. Finally, a French proposal, with majority support, that the great-power representatives seek instructions from the Supreme Council so that they could speak authoritatively on behalf of the powers and force completion of new treaties was defeated by a British delegate who favored stalling, letting the Belgians

57. DBFP, 5:278–82, 367–73, 387–91, 687–88, 696–99, 715.

and Dutch squabble for a while, and optimistically awaiting Dutch concessions, of which there was in fact no sign.[58]

While the various subcommittees of the great powers were wrestling with military and naval problems, the Commission of Fourteen itself did not meet. Such broader negotiation as occurred was carried out by Laroche and Tufton with the Belgian delegates and also with the Dutch delegates on the intermittent occasions when they were in Paris. Finally, after a prolonged semantic struggle, Laroche achieved an agreed statement, which he read, speaking formally on behalf of the five powers, to a full meeting of the Commission of Fourteen on 16 September 1919:

> The delegates of the great powers consider that if one limits oneself purely and simply to suppressing in law a guarantee which the facts have demonstrated to be inoperative, one would, in restoring her liberty to Belgium, evidently end by giving her nothing which could fully replace the security which she found in perpetual neutrality. The instability of the general peace would thus be increased, and the Allied and Associated Powers, among which two are guarantors of the neutrality of Belgium, consider that they could not morally put their signature at the foot of a treaty of revision abolishing the neutrality of this country unless Belgium were to receive other guarantees which would in some way replace the old or rather would guard against the disadvantages which would result for her from the suppression pure and simple of perpetual neutrality.[59]

The Belgians, who were unaware of the struggles that lay behind this declaration, took it as a promise of new guarantees, which it was not. Thereafter diplomatic activity centered around the problem of Limburg and that of a guarantee for Belgium. The negotiations were conducted both through normal diplomatic channels and among the delegates remaining in Paris, as the commission and its subcommittees ceased to meet with any regularity. Solution of the Limburg problem largely depended upon the Dutch, who categorically refused to consider a joint military arrangement with Belgium and who pointed to their thor-

58. DuD, R.G.P. 156, pp. 191–93; Gurney to Curzon, 4 Oct. 1919, no. 167, F.O. 371/3641; DBFP, 5:277–78, 311, 329, 424–26, 458.
59. DBFP, 5:517–18.

oughly inflamed public opinion. The Belgians indicated that they would consider Dutch canalization of the middle Meuse, one of the few concessions open to them, in return for joint economic and military arrangements in Limburg, but to no avail. The British proposed that Holland commit herself to joining the League of Nations (thereby binding herself to resist aggression), declare that she would consider any violation of her territory a *casus belli*, and pledge herself to defend Limburg against invasion.[60] Though the Belgians did not consider this an adequate or realistic solution to a serious military problem, the Dutch agreed to join the League and at first accepted the other British proposals. As it became evident, however, that Belgium had little support from the powers and that no diplomatic pressure would be applied at The Hague, the Dutch went back on their commitment regarding the *casus belli* and eventually refused to participate in any statement that Belgian security was a matter of general concern or even that it should be put before the League.[61]

The Dutch had feared that their repeated refusal to surrender the kaiser might lead to Allied support of Belgium in the commission. They were both delighted and much more intransigent when it became apparent that such consequences would not arise. They told Laroche that Holland would not consider any military accord outside the framework of the League, with Belgium alone, or limited to Limburg. Further, they refused to discuss a military accord with anybody until Holland had entered the League. Part of the difficulty, as the British minister to The Hague remarked, was the personalities of the two foreign ministers. Van Karnebeek was obstinate, elusive, and uncompromising on large issues and small, whereas Hymans was tactless, forthright, irritatingly precise, and dogged. Both men were motivated by fear of Germany, but they reacted in opposite ways in response to their countries' different experiences in World War I. As the British instinctively dreaded the possibility of being dragged into another war in defense of Belgium, they increasingly resented Hymans's determination to assure

60. DuD, R.G.P. 156, pp. 235–37, 248, 329; DBFP, 5:545–46, 571–72; *Times*, 2 Sept. 1919, p. 9.

61. DuD, R.G.P. 156, pp. 306–7, 329; DBFP, 5:548–49, 607–8, 859–61, 873–74; Dutch draft, 24 Nov. 1919, BMAE DB/30/VI.

the security of the kingdom and so termed him difficult to deal with. That he was, but the problem he presented was even more important than he realized. Not surprisingly, as Hymans saw one promised protection after another dissolve into thin air, he became more dogged and thus more irritating to the British.[62]

Although the British recognized that Belgian alarm over the Limburg gap was militarily sound, they were unwilling to incur Dutch displeasure by trying to solve the problem and even more unwilling to commit themselves to France and Belgium, with all that such a commitment would imply for the European balance of power. Nobody at the Belgian Foreign Ministry seems to have understood that Britain was instinctively working her way back to her nineteenth-century position as the balance in the balance of power, a position she formally achieved at Locarno in 1925. The Americans, already tending toward withdrawal from formal diplomatic commitments in Europe, were reluctant to become involved at all and more reluctant to engage in major-power pressure on Holland, as proposed by Laroche. When Hymans complained that Belgium's wartime allies had a greater regard for neutral states than for Belgium, the British chargé d'affaires in Brussels said, "We and you together make a family, and one is often more attentive to strangers than to parents." To Hymans's rejoinder about "poor parents" came the reply, "Oh, you'll be the richest of us all in two or three years."[63] Though economic competition was indeed a factor, particularly in Lloyd George's thinking, the real stumbling block was British determination to avoid commitment to either side in the continuing Continental power struggle.

THE SECURITY QUESTION

As it became evident that nothing would be done about the Limburg gap or Belgian naval use of the Scheldt, the Belgians resigned them-

62. DBFP, 5:571, 619–20, 625–26, 664, 688–89; Tirman memo, 20 Sept. 1919, FMAE A/135; Crowe to F.O., 13 Oct. 1919, tel. 1434, F.O. 371/3642.
63. DBFP, 5:617; Bland to Carnegie, 16 Sept. 1919, F.O. 608/4; Wallace to Lansing, 27 Sept. 1919, tel. 4357, Wilson Papers 5B/51; quotations from Hymans memo, 7 Oct. 1919, BMAE GB/1919/II.

selves to separation of economic and defense problems. Thereafter, attention focused on the broader problem of Belgian security in general. To the weary delegates, the simplest solution seemed to be transfer of the problem to the Council of the League of Nations, which could be asked to find new guarantees for Belgium to replace those of the 1839 treaties. The British and the Dutch particularly favored this interment of the problem. The Belgians thought it unlikely that an effective and substantial guarantee could be gained from the larger body of the League if it could not be obtained from the five powers that presumably would dominate the Council, and they realized that their chance of success would be further reduced if Germany became a member of the League before the matter was settled. In addition, they pointed out that Belgium would be defenseless in the interim and that the powers were in fact proposing, contrary to their reading of Laroche's declaration on 16 September, to sign a treaty not containing any new security guarantees for Belgium. On 16 October, Segers told Crowe that Belgian public and parliamentary opinion would not accept the proposed treaty unless Britain and France continued the 1839 guarantee of the independence and territorial integrity (but *not* the neutrality) of Belgium until the League provided new guarantees.[64]

The resultant negotiations about an interim Anglo-French guarantee were long and involved. They were also rather confused at times, because the Belgians were simultaneously inquiring about the possibility of extending the Anglo-American guarantee of France to cover Belgium, with France added as a third guarantor, and, in addition, seeking British participation in the proposed Franco-Belgian talks toward a joint military convention. These three requests, all designed with the same end in view, were entirely distinct and Hymans pursued each one separately, but weary Foreign Office officials tended to confuse them, as Belgian diplomatists did also from time to time. Of the three, only the proposal for the interim Anglo-French guarantee was properly the business of the Fourteen, but it was dealt with outside the commission, which again ceased to function; negotiations were pursued in

64. Armour to ACNP, 18 Oct. 1919, tel. 72, 855.00/29, ACNP/449; DBFP, 5:671–76; DuD, R.G.P. 156, pp. 248, 255–56.

Paris, London, and Brussels without reference to delegates from other countries.

These negotiations were complicated by the development of extreme tension between Crowe and Orts. During a trip to Brussels, Orts saw the British chargé on 13 October and, in the course of the usual complaint about inadequate support from Belgium's allies, mentioned that he had found it difficult to talk with the British delegates, as he had few opportunities to meet them, and said that he hoped Crowe would grant him an interview when he returned to Paris. When he read the report of this meeting, Crowe, who tended to be factually unreliable when on the defensive, erupted in a lengthy screed, sharply impugning Orts's honesty and stating categorically that the British delegates had supported Belgium at every turn during the meetings of the Commission of Fourteen, which he claimed to have been in continuous session, thus affording regular and easy Belgian access to the British delegation. He appeared to be outraged by Belgian fears that the new treaty would not provide the promised security guarantees and expressed himself emphatically about "their impossible claims and uncompromising attitude." Although Belgian claims were impossible, given the Dutch and British attitudes, to expect any foreign minister willingly to compromise his country's security, perhaps irrevocably, is to expect beyond reason. Crowe's heated response caused considerable puzzlement in the Foreign Office, where Orts had been known and well liked during the war, but nonetheless it was circulated to the king and cabinet;[65] there it probably contributed to a hardening anti-Belgian attitude that ultimately settled the fate of the interim guarantee as well as of the other Belgian proposals.

When the Belgians first raised the matter of an interim guarantee, the French immediately announced their willingness to join the British in a temporary engagement of this nature. The initial Foreign Office reaction was also favorable, far more so than to either of the other Belgian security proposals, and Hardinge opined that the interim guarantee was both necessary and unlikely to encounter parliamentary opposition. He seemed particularly pleased when word arrived on 28 October that the

65. DBFP, 5:671–74; Crowe to Curzon, 21 Oct. 1919, no. 2001, F.O. 371/3642.

Belgian government had accepted the draft treaty with minor modifications. One of these, however, proved to be a new article specifying that Britain and France would maintain their guarantee of the inviolability of Belgian territory until permanent guarantees were arranged by the League Council.[66] After some consideration, Foreign Office experts concluded that the interim guarantee should be granted for a maximum of five years. On 10 November, Curzon, who had succeeded Balfour as foreign secretary in October, submitted this recommendation to the cabinet, saying that it would probably be unpopular and criticized in Parliament, but could be defended. He thought that any indefinite Anglo-French guarantee of Belgium against German aggression would be too heavy a responsibility to undertake.[67]

Curzon's comments were the first of many British remarks over a period of several years about the likelihood of public or parliamentary hostility to any commitment to Belgium. Though no treaty or convention with Belgium was ever brought before Parliament in these years, and thus no definitive assessment of political opinion is possible, the record of parliamentary debates, especially during question periods, reveals no trace of hostility to a Belgian tie. The more influential newspapers similarly displayed no alarm when the possibility of an arrangement with Belgium was discussed. The *Times* and the *Daily Telegraph* were emphatic supporters of Belgium's cause, and the *Manchester Guardian* was only slightly less partisan in its editorial stance. It seems likely that, given the cabinet's enormous majority in the House of Commons, British comments to Belgian officials about public and parliamentary opposition were no more than a convenient device to avoid action; comments of this sort to other Britishers may have constituted an effort to convince themselves that it would be difficult to take a step which they were instinctively loath to take because it was incompatible with the British tradition of disengagement from the Continent, because it would mean choosing a side, and because it might commit them to another war as painful as the last.

Before Curzon's memorandum was discussed in the cabinet, Belgian

66. Crowe to F.O., 17 Oct. 1919, no. 145, Villiers to Curzon, 18, 28 Oct. 1919, no. 378, tel. 178, F.O. 371/3642; DBFP, 5:754–55.
67. Tufton to Oliphant, 1 Nov. 1919, F.O. 371/3642; DBFP, 5:781–84.

diplomatists made a point of emphasizing their eagerness to have the Anglo-French interim guarantee. While reiterating their opinion that reference to the League of Nations would accomplish nothing, which was realistic but which it was ill-advised to announce, and complaining that all of the safeguards requested by Belgium had been eliminated from the draft treaty, they stated that their government would take no action on the proposed draft until the British government decided about the interim guarantee. When this statement elicited no reply, Belgian concern was conveyed through French channels. The British took refuge in the technicality that the Belgian government had never submitted a written request for the temporary guarantee. This deficiency was remedied without delay, and Hymans told Villiers that the latest draft treaty was unacceptable because it included neither a Dutch *casus belli* declaration nor an Anglo-French interim guarantee, both of which the Belgian government deemed essential.[68]

When a conference of cabinet ministers considered Curzon's memorandum on 18 November, it "inclined to the view" that a guarantee might be given if the United States would participate but, before making any decision, wished to know whether the United States was likely to ratify the Anglo-American guarantee of France, which would no longer bind Britain if it were defeated in the American Senate. Clearly, the cabinet members realized that any guarantee of Belgium would constitute a de facto guarantee of France as well. If the Anglo-American guarantee to France went into force, extension of it to Belgium would not constitute a significant additional commitment, but if it lapsed, the guarantee to Belgium would represent an important Continental obligation not to be undertaken lightly. An inquiry was duly dispatched to Lord Grey in Washington. In the interim, Foreign Office functionaries interpreted this action to mean that the guarantee of Belgium would not be given.[69]

Although Grey replied that Senate approval of the Franco-American

68. DBFP, 5:784–85, 795–97, 800, 857–59; DDB, 1:37–47; Pichon to P. Cambon, 14, 16 Nov. 1919, tels. 7741–74, 7798, Vin 6N/290; P. Cambon to Pichon, 15 Nov. 1919, tel. 735, P. Cambon Papers/2.

69. Conference of ministers, 18 Nov. 1919, CAB 23/18; DBFP, 5:823; Villiers to Curzon, 18, 19 Nov. 1919, tels. 185, 188, Smith memo, 27 Nov. 1919, F.O. 371/3642.

treaty was becoming increasingly unlikely,[70] his report had little effect on British thinking about the Belgian guarantee because the French, in an effort to achieve a new treaty acceptable to Belgium and also very useful to France, chose this moment, starting on 19 November, to point out to the British through every available diplomatic channel that the interim guarantee in no way represented a new or additional commitment: if it were not given, Belgium would probably reject the new treaty and, as a consequence, the old one with its indefinite guarantee would remain in force.[71] The French were careful not to mention that with it would remain the neutrality of Belgium, the guarantee by Germany, Austria, and Russia, and the old economic and fluvial regime, thereby eliminating any chance of improved Belgo-Dutch technical arrangements. It seems clear that the French motive was to persuade Britain to accept the interim guarantee, not to force Belgium back into her prewar status. France much wanted a military accord with Belgium, which would not be legally possible if the 1839 treaties remained in effect, and significantly, French reminders to the British began the day that the United States Senate rejected the Versailles treaty. Because the French undoubtedly realized that the Anglo-American guarantee of France was moribund, their efforts on behalf of Belgium were motivated partly by their desire to placate a neighbor disgruntled over Luxemburg but primarily by a need to regain some British protection for France through the device of a joint guarantee to Belgium.

It had not occurred to the British that the old guarantee might remain in force. There was rapid consultation of legal advisors, who confirmed the French view of the continuing validity of the 1839 treaties and who also noted the restrictions thus imposed upon Belgium.[72] Though the implications of this situation much confused the upper echelons of the Foreign Office, Hardinge remarked that it was British policy "to contract no new obligation towards Belgium which will mean the protection of the French frontier coterminous with Belgium."[73] The next day he added, "It must be to our advantage that the perpetual neutrality

70. DBFP, 5:581.

71. P. Cambon to Curzon, 19 Nov. 1919, F.O. 371/3642; DBFP, 5:826–27; Laroche to Tufton, 19 Nov. 1919, FMAE A/136.

72. Hurst to Hardinge, 20, 21 Nov. 1919, F.O. 371/3642.

73. DBFP, 5:852.

of Belgium should be abolished, since it removes from us the obligation of coming to her aid if it is infringed," and recommended that the interim guarantee be approved.[74] However, two demarches at the Foreign Office by the French ambassador, Paul Cambon, in support of the interim guarantee revealed that Curzon preferred maintenance of the 1839 system to all other solutions, arguing that compulsory Belgian neutrality was in Anglo-French interest and that if there were no neutrality, there should be no guarantee.[75] Although Curzon may have hoped to detach Belgium from her presumed subservience to France, his chief concern at the time and in later years was that Belgium pay a price for the guarantee against German attack. Without thinking through all the implications, he assumed that this price should be continuation of neutrality.

Though Foreign Office officials were pleased by word that the Dutch had rejected the latest draft treaty, there is no evidence that they had thought Britain's interest in the matter through, beyond a wish on the part of most to be rid of the existing obligation.[76] Then and thereafter they preferred a neutral Belgium because they assumed that otherwise Belgium would be a French satellite. Their aversion to Continental involvement was such that they did not consider obvious methods of preventing such a situation. Indeed, their overriding interest was in ending Britain's Continental commitments altogether. It was on this basis that Curzon proposed to the cabinet on 1 December that the indefinite 1839 guarantee be replaced by an interim guarantee without condition or Belgian obligation for "a short term of years."[77] When a conference of cabinet ministers met the next day, it authorized "making an arrangement with the Belgian government whereby Belgian integrity and independence would be guaranteed for a limited period by France and Great Britain, provided that Belgium undertook to maintain her neutrality."[78]

As the minutes of the 2 December conference are cryptic, it is not clear how the decision to make the interim guarantee contingent upon

74. Smith memo, 25 Nov. 1919, F.O. 371/3642.
75. P. Cambon to Pichon, 25, 27 Nov. 1919, tels. 742, 744, P. Cambon Papers/2.
76. DDB, 1:48–52; R. Graham to Curzon, 29 Nov. 1919, F.O. 371/3642.
77. DBFP, 5:876–77.
78. Conference of ministers, 2 Dec. 1919, CAB 23/37.

the continuation of Belgian neutrality was reached. At first, the issue was clearly a guarantee not involving Belgian neutrality. One cabinet member remarked that the duration of the commitment was unimportant because the guarantee, once given, would be difficult to withdraw. Another disagreed, pointing out that the territorial integrity of Belgium was a traditional and continuing British interest, that Britain would certainly have to intervene if Belgium were threatened even if there were no guarantee, "and that popular opinion, as in 1914, would be solid in support of a Government which intervened in Europe in order to fulfill its written pledges." At this point, however, it was suggested that "in return for guaranteeing the neutrality of Belgium, pending the establishment of the League of Nations, the British Government should demand from the Belgian Government a guarantee of Belgian neutrality."[79]

Nobody, including Curzon, noticed at the time the change from a guarantee until the League provided new ones to one "pending the establishment of the League of Nations," and it is not clear whether the shift from guaranteeing Belgian territorial integrity to guaranteeing Belgian neutrality and asking Belgium to do the same occurred by accident or design. In the confusion of discussion, it could easily have been an accident or the result of habitual patterns of thought. As late as 1922, the British government made an unsolicited written proposal to France to guarantee a Belgian neutrality that had gone to its de facto death two years before.[80] There could have been wishful thinking and a genuine desire to maintain Belgian neutrality temporarily or permanently. Certainly some British leaders preferred to see Belgium neutral, perhaps from a desire to establish a buffer zone between France and Germany or to redress the balance of power and restore in part the prewar status quo, perhaps from the hope of detaching Belgium from France. There was the official explanation that Britain needed to receive something in return for the guarantee, although just what Britain would gain from Belgian neutrality was never made clear,[81] especially as the British government also encouraged Belgium toward a military conven-

79. Ibid.
80. British Delegation, Cannes, to F.O., 9 Jan. 1922, tel. 13, F.O. 371/8249.
81. DBFP, 5:881–82.

tion with France. In addition, Belgian neutrality would mean greater French preponderance in the Rhineland, which Britain opposed.

There was a tendency in the Foreign Office to assume that as the old guarantee had been given in return for Belgian neutrality, the new one must be as well. It is also possible that the requirement of neutrality was inserted in the hope that Belgium would reject a guarantee with so high a price. Britain, having made an offer rejected by Belgium, could then feel free of any obligation to consider further the problem of Belgian security and, at the same time, be rid of an unwanted indirect guarantee of France. Certainly, any cursory examination of Belgian policy and public opinion would have yielded the conclusion that such a condition was unacceptable to Belgium, and Villiers reported in detail to this effect as soon as he learned of the British decision.[82] It is obvious that, as the first purpose of treaty revision was to abrogate the neutrality clause, reimposition of it was bound to be rejected by Belgium, but there is no evidence that either the Foreign Office or the government considered the matter with much care.

By early December 1919, it appeared that the sole remaining impediment to conclusion of new treaties to replace those of 1839 was the British condition for an interim guarantee. Substantial Belgo-Dutch agreement had been reached on the economic and technical fluvial clauses of the new treaty, and the Dutch had agreed to a somewhat diluted *casus belli* clause. Although unhappy about the situation, the Belgian delegates had largely abandoned serious efforts to alleviate the problems of the Limburg gap and Belgian use of the Scheldt by naval and commercial vessels in wartime. At this juncture, the Dutch gave every indication of readiness to conclude the treaty, and thus negotiation narrowed to the problem of the interim guarantee. As British officials recognized, the chief barrier to successful conclusion of new treaties was British insistence on Belgian reversion to neutrality. Although they were eager to escape from the old indefinite guarantee, they did not fully realize that a five-year guarantee without conditions was a small price to pay, as there was not the slightest prospect of hostilities arising during the next five years while British forces occupied Cologne. Thus, as they demonstrated repeatedly, the British could

82. Ibid., 5:883.

not bring themselves to take the small and largely meaningless step necessary to achieve the end they desired.[83]

The first indication to the Belgians of the British decision came on 3 December when Tufton saw Orts in Paris and gently broke the bad news. Overwhelmed by a sense of abandonment by the "faithful guarantor powers," Orts pointed out that if the League failed to act within five years' time, Belgium would have nothing. Tufton admitted that Britain was deliberately trying to avoid an indefinite guarantee in such circumstances. Orts replied that this decision revealed British lack of faith in a solution by the League Council, although it was Britain who had recommended submission of the question to the League and had largely imposed this course on Belgium. Orts was quite right: Britain was trying to dispose of the problem by consigning it to the diplomatic equivalent of the wastebasket. He added that it was impossible for Belgium to revert to her prewar enforced neutrality, for public and parliamentary opinion would not tolerate that and, furthermore, compulsory neutrality would force her to withdraw her troops from the Rhineland, to treat Germany exactly as she treated her wartime allies, and to refrain from participating in any future Allied actions against Germany.[84] Indeed, she would be unable to join the League of Nations.[85] In an inspired attempt at troublemaking, Laroche urged Orts to lay the problem of the British decision before the next plenary session of the Fourteen, a group of more than forty people of seven nationalities. Orts wisely refused in the hope that there might be more chance of modifying the British stand if it were not divulged. When he saw Laroche and Tufton together on 4 December, Laroche complicated matters further by proposing to drop both the neutrality requirement and the time limit but to maintain the guarantee only until the League

83. DuD, R.G.P. 156, p. 327; Berthelot to Benoist, 1 Dec. 1919, tel. 597–99, Berthelot to P. Cambon, 4 Dec. 1919, tel. 8372, Vin 5N/165; DBFP, 5:883–84, 886–89, 900–901, 904, 923; DDB, 1:59–63; Hymans to Maskens, 3 Dec. 1919, no. 1718, BMAE GB/1919/II; Guillaume to Hymans, 4 Dec. 1919, tel. 108, no. 9259/2271, BMAE PB/1919.

84. Berthelot to P. Cambon, 4 Dec. 1919, tel. 8379–86, Vin 5N/165; DDB l:56–59.

85. Whether in fact Belgium could have entered the League as a neutral is unclear. Switzerland was permitted to do so, but Luxemburg was not until she promised to amend the grand ducal constitution to delete reference to perpetual neutrality. DuD, R.G.P. 162, p. 234.

reached a decision, not until it provided new guarantees. The decision might of course be negative. Laroche added that before the League acted, Britain and France should take steps to ensure Belgian security, which he thought could best be provided by military accords with Britain and France, especially France.[86]

Throughout December, officials at the Quai d'Orsay and the Foreign Office devised a series of new drafts, none of which were acceptable to both Britain and Belgium. In the process, it became clear that there existed no consensus in the Foreign Office over what was really meant by Belgian neutrality. Each definition became more ambiguous than the one before, and apparently it did not necessarily mean full continuance of the 1839 system. Whatever Belgian neutrality meant, Curzon was determined to have it.[87] One explanation of British intransigence was provided by Hardinge, who remarked that Lloyd George "fancies that by keeping the French on tenterhooks as to the guarantee of that portion of their frontier we may be able to secure concessions from them elsewhere, e.g., in Syria or Palestine."[88] Clearly, the Belgian guarantee was being contemplated in its broader implications.

Because a British guarantee of Belgium was in France's interest, French diplomatists redoubled their efforts to find a formula that the Belgians could admit and the British would accept. As the Foreign Office finally realized that the Belgian government would not and could not sign any text including either "neutral" or "neutrality," euphemism was attempted, but without success. Curzon decided that if the original British proposal of 2 December was not acceptable, the matter would have to wait until he and Lloyd George visited Paris in January.[89] The Belgian response came in the form of a long speech by Hymans to the Belgian Chamber on 23 December. In a passage aimed directly at

86. DDB, 1:56–59.
87. Cambon to Pichon 5, 10 Dec. 1919, tels. 759, 771, P. Cambon Papers/2; Pichon to P. Cambon, 9 Dec. 1919, tel. 8527–28, Vin 5N/165; *procès-verbal*, London Conference, 11 Dec. 1919, FMAE Y/16; Crowe to Curzon, 4 Dec. 1919, tel. 1651, F.O. 371/3642; DBFP, 5:885–86, 889, 904; Crowe to Curzon, 11 Dec. 1919, tel. 1678, Hardinge to Curzon, 17 Dec. 1919, F.O. 371/3643.
88. Hardinge to R. Graham, 15 Dec. 1919, CUL Hardinge Papers/41.
89. DBFP, 5:930; Crowe to Curzon, 19 Dec. 1919, tel. 1706, F.O. to Crowe, 24 Dec. 1919, tel. 1525, F.O. 371/3643; P. Cambon to Pichon, 17 Dec. 1919, tels. 737, 778–79, P. Cambon Papers/2; Pichon to Margerie, 29 Dec. 1919, tel. 2353, Vin 5N/165.

Britain, he declared that Belgium could not revert to neutrality in any form and pointed out the implications of neutral status for Belgian participation in the Rhineland occupation, treaty execution, and the League of Nations.[90]

Once Christmas was past, Moncheur made a final effort in London, but his interviews with Cambon and Curzon yielded the discouraging information that the chief British opponents of the Belgian guarantee were Andrew Bonar Law, Balfour, and Lloyd George himself, that is to say, the leaders of both parties in the parliamentary coalition. When Moncheur saw Curzon on 31 December, he hinted that Belgium might prefer to do without a guarantee rather than accept such a humiliating limitation upon her sovereignty. Curzon "took his intimation to mean that the Belgian Government did not expect the matter to be pursued" and, when Villiers submitted yet another proposed phrasing on 1 January 1920, Hardinge did not bother to show it to Curzon because he assumed the issue to be dead.[91]

So it proved to be. The Belgian cabinet met on 5 January 1920 and unanimously accepted Hymans's recommendation that the request for a guarantee be withdrawn. In so doing, it abandoned hope that the great-power declaration of 16 September that something ought to re-place the perpetual neutrality arrangement would ever be fulfilled. Hymans argued that a five-year guarantee was largely worthless be-cause it covered only the period when the northern Rhineland zone would be occupied by Allied troops. He also pointed out that Belgium was unlikely to obtain more Allied support before the League Council than in the Fourteen, that the League might refuse to give any guar-antee at all or impose conditions limiting Belgian sovereignty, and that an inadequate guarantee might lull the country into a false sense of security. Hymans's judgment that the five-year guarantee was of so little value that it was not worth the price was undoubtedly sound. Probably he should have abandoned the effort earlier, but his dogged-ness, optimism about Britain, and underlying search for a more sub-stantial guarantee had driven him on. The cabinet unanimously decided

---

90. DDB, 1:78; Belgique, Parlement, Chambre des Représentants, *Compte rendu*, 23 Dec. 1919, p. 38.
91. DDB, 1:80–82, 85–86; DBFP, 5:947–48, 958.

that negotiations should be confined to revising the economic and
fluvial aspects of the 1839 treaties and to abrogating the neutrality
clause and that they should be concluded as soon as possible. When
Hymans informed the Allied ambassadors of this decision on 8 January,
Villiers was sympathetic, the Foreign Office was delighted, and Margerie
promptly said that Belgium must now conclude a military pact with
France.[92]

THE WIELINGEN DISPUTE

Laroche quickly prepared a new draft treaty that included only abrogation of the two great-power treaties of 1839 (that is, the neutrality
clause and the old guarantee), registration of a new Belgo-Dutch economic and fluvial treaty, and a Dutch *casus belli* declaration. The many
months of effort had come to no more than this. It appeared that treaty
revision might finally be accomplished but, from late January on, Belgian negotiators and British diplomatists began to see signs that the
Dutch were preparing to raise difficulties over both the *casus belli*
declaration and the ancient question of the Wielingen channel, which
had arisen in connection with the fluvial negotiations.[93] Of the three
mouths of the Scheldt, only the most southerly one, the Wielingen
channel, was of a satisfactory depth for use by large oceangoing vessels,
but it curved southward and flowed parallel to the Belgian coast. From
the Belgian-Dutch frontier down to Blankenberge, much of the channel
lay within the three-mile limit of Belgian territorial waters. The 1839

92. DDB, 1:91–94; Villiers to Curzon, 8 Jan. 1920, no. 5, F.O. 371/3643.
93. DDB, 1:96–98; Struycken note, 22 Jan. 1920, BMAE DB/30/VII; Guillaume to
Hymans, 24 Jan. 1920, no. 449/107, BMAE PB/1920; Orts to Hymans, 20, 22 Jan.
1920, Hymans to Moncheur, 17 Mar. 1920, BMAE Ind/1920/I; R. Graham to Curzon,
23 Jan. 1920, no. 92, Villiers to Curzon, 21 Feb. 1920, no. 106, F.O. 371/3852; Hymans
to de Gaiffier, 17 Mar. 1920, no. 1597, BMAE FR/1920/I; DuD, R.G.P. 156, pp.
461–62, 464–66. The Dutch argued that as the question of Belgium's security was not to
be referred to the League of Nations, the *casus belli* clause should appear only in the
commission report, not in the preamble of the treaty. On the Wielingen channel, the
Dutch cabinet decided on 9 January 1920 not to go beyond division on the *Thalweg* (or
possibly to arbitration) even if this meant breaking off negotiations. DuD, R.G.P. 156,
pp. 371–72, 390, 420–21, 448.

treaties had not specified the sovereignty over the Wielingen channel, nor had any of the agreements later concluded between Belgium and Holland. Since Belgium had come into being, Holland had never laid any formal claim to the channel and the question of sovereignty over it had never been resolved.[94]

In early 1920, after direct Belgo-Dutch negotiations, it was agreed that the question should remain in abeyance. Because the Dutch had reluctantly consented to make the *casus belli* declaration in the report of the Commission of Fourteen, although not in the treaty itself, the Belgian government approved the treaty drafts and Laroche called the Fourteen to meet for the first time since early October to approve the treaties. During this last meeting of the commission on 23 March 1920, Segers, speaking on behalf of Belgium, remarked by Belgo-Dutch prearrangement that two matters were being left unsettled with the position of each side reserved: the question of passage on the Scheldt for Belgian warships, which Belgium claimed, and that of the Wielingen channel, which Belgium considered to be largely within her territorial waters. To Belgian dismay, van Swinderin did not read the prearranged reply but substituted another, which he had read hastily to the Belgian delegates just as the meeting started. He declared categorically that no claim whatever concerning passage on the Scheldt by Belgian warships would be accepted, and he further, in the name of the Netherlands government, presented the first formal claim of exclusive and full Dutch sovereignty over the Wielingen channel in Belgian history. The gravity of the dispute was not at first evident, and Laroche hoped for another meeting within a few days to sign the treaty, particularly because the Belgian cabinet, after a stormy session, decided to go ahead with it. As both Holland and Belgium soon submitted detailed statements of their respective views on the Wielingen question, however, it became obvious that an acute impasse had developed.[95] After

94. Villiers to Curzon, 21 Feb. 1920, no. 106, F.O. 371/3852; Admiralty, *Netherlands*, p. 629.
95. Belgian cabinet meeting, 5 Mar. 1920, Jaspar Papers/247; de Bassompierre memos, 6, 8 Mar. 1920, BMAE DB/30/VII; R. Graham to Curzon, 16 Mar. 1920, no. 282, Villiers to Curzon, 20 Mar., 1 Apr. 1920, nos. 167, 195, Sargent to Tufton, 10 Apr. 1920, F.O. 371/3852; Hymans to Moncheur, 17 Mar. 1920, BMAE Ind/1920/I; de Bassom-

the Dutch reaffirmed their claim in a note on 3 May, the Belgian government decided to discontinue negotiations on the 1839 treaties until a solution safeguarding Belgian interests in the Wielingen channel was achieved.[96]

The Belgian claim to the Wielingen extended only to the part of the channel lying within the three-mile limit off the Belgian coast and rested chiefly upon international law regarding territorial waters. In addition, the Belgians pointed out that never since 1830 had Holland made any formal claim to the Wielingen and it had in fact four times during World War I explicitly declared the channel to be in Belgian waters. To this strong legal case the Belgians added the practical consideration that if Holland controlled the channel, wartime access to Zeebrugge, the only Belgian coastal port of military consequence, would be blocked. With Antwerp similarly closed, access to Belgium by sea would become impossible.[97] The Dutch response was a reaffirmation of the Dutch claim to the entirety of the channel and a defense based upon the argument that the Wielingen was a continuation of the Scheldt River. The Dutch also laid great emphasis on their historic rights to the channel, all of which predated the existence of Belgium and most of which rested upon treaties concluded in 1323, 1520, and 1562.[98] These historic rights were considerably undermined by the fact, bravely announced in the Amsterdam press by a Dutch scholar, that until the eighteenth century the term Wielingen applied variously

---

pierre memo, 27 Mar. 1920, BMAE PB/1920; DBFP, 12:10–33; Whitlock to Colby, 26 Mar., 16 Aug. 1920, tels. 54, 946, SD 755.56/9, 26. For copies of the two Dutch texts, see Orts Papers/428 or BMAE FR/1920/I. For a Dutch summary of the entire Wielingen controversy (with some notable omissions), see DuD, R.G.P. 156, pp. 612–18. The Dutch consistently took the view that the Belgian reaction to Holland's claim of sovereignty on the Wielingen was unwarranted and that the Belgian delegates should not have been surprised by the Dutch declaration.

96. De Bassompierre to Capelle, 8 May 1920, BMAE DB/30/VII; Hymans memo, 20 May 1920, Hymans Papers/165; Whitlock Journal, 26 May 1920, Whitlock Papers/5 (LC).

97. DBFP, 12:26–31, 42; Belgique, Parlement, Chambre des Représentants, *Compte rendu*, 26 May, 11 June 1920, pp. 496, 614; van Zuylen, *Les Mains libres*, pp. 96, 164–65.

98. DBFP, 12:31–32; H. de Hoon, *L'Escaut et son embouchure*, p. 27; Sima Adanya, *Le Régime international de l'Escaut*, p. 128; A. Jaumin and M. Jottard, *La Question de l'Escaut*, p. 82.

to part of the western Scheldt or to waters north of the present Belgian frontier, not to the channel now in dispute.[99]

No jurist outside Holland took the Dutch claim seriously. It was treated with contempt in the Foreign Office, where Crowe termed it "absurd and preposterous" and "bogus." The British scorn was based upon the Admiralty's emphatic view that any nation was entitled to a three-mile belt of territorial waters and upon British possession of a document written on 8 April 1919 by the Dutch Foreign Ministry for van Karnebeek. This report surveyed the history of the Wielingen down to 1880 and, without even considering the Dutch wartime statements about Belgian sovereignty, termed the Dutch argument "a claim to sovereign rights which is practically *based on nothing*." It recommended that the claim be dropped with the reservation that Dutch warships be granted a right of passage in return for a similar concession to Belgium on the Scheldt.[100]

Though the British, French, and Belgians all assumed that the Dutch had raised the Wielingen claim to escape the revised treaty, the Dutch were in fact astonished that Belgium broke off negotiations over the question and speculated that perhaps Belgium was seeking an excuse to reject the new treaty. As most of the Dutch diplomatists had by now lost their earlier ability to examine the Belgian viewpoint dispassionately, it did not occur to them that the much-heralded treaty revision had achieved nothing more than abrogation of Belgian neutrality (which had been agreed at the outset), loss of all guarantees, and modest improvement in fluvial arrangements. Loss of Belgium's territorial waters was clearly too high a price to pay for so little. As the Dutch noted, 90 percent of Belgian opinion supported Hymans on this issue; he might have lost office had he given way; and, as the waters in question were along the Flemish coast, few Flemings supported Holland. When

99. Hymans to de Gaiffier, 17 June 1920, no. 3565, BMAE FR/1920/I; Admiralty, *Netherlands*, p. 629. In June, the Dutch pointed out that a three-mile band of Belgian territorial waters would also block wartime access to Flushing. Although this was true, nobody took it seriously because Holland would still have Rotterdam, whereas if the Dutch claim held, Belgium would lose wartime use of all ports of any consequence except Ostend, which could handle only small vessels. DuD, R.G.P. 156, p. 645.

100. Moncheur to Curzon, 31 May 1920, Dutch Foreign Ministry paper P/00230, 8 Apr. 1919, F.O. 371/3643.

Franco-Belgian negotiations toward a military arrangement finally began in the spring of 1920, the Dutch Foreign Ministry became unduly alarmed, fearing that this signified a revival of French imperialism aimed at Holland, which it did not. Van Swinderin, who was probably the most able of the senior Dutch diplomatists, disagreed. He argued that Belgian policy was seven-eighths prompted by fear of renewed German attack and one-eighth by annexationist desires against Holland. He opined that Hymans had never been among Belgium's wholehearted annexationists and had long since abandoned this approach but that safeguarding Belgium was a matter of life and death to him. Van Swinderin added that Holland was on "very brittle ice" in the Wielingen question.[101]

The British minister at The Hague, Sir Ronald Graham, agreed that the Dutch claim was untenable but opposed Anglo-French protest for fear that the Dutch would remain adamant and the Allies would look as foolish as they had as a consequence of their attempts to obtain extradition of the kaiser. Nonetheless, the Foreign Office was at first willing to satisfy Belgium's request for diplomatic support.[102] Crowe, knowing the Admiralty's strong views about the three-mile limit, endorsed the Belgian argument that the question of sovereignty over its territorial waters could not be submitted to the arbitration proposed by Holland, and he also approved of the Belgian refusal to divide the channel, although he was unaware that the Belgian stand was based in part upon the complicating fact that the channel shifted its position from time to time.[103] The British did realize, however, that the new Belgo-Dutch treaty was endangered, particularly because Hymans announced to the Belgian Chamber on 26 May that negotiations had been broken off

101. DuD, R.G.P. 156, pp. 600–603, 633–34, 667–71, 674–76, quotation from p. 676. The Dutch also speculated that de Bassompierre (who replaced Orts briefly) or the Belgian delegation had lied to Hymans about events preceding and on 23 March. If so, the Dutch view that the Belgian delegation should not have been surprised by van Swinderin's declaration that day could well be justified.

102. De Ligne to Hymans, 27 May 1920, no. 3203/840, BMAE FR/1920/I; DBFP, 12: 46–48; R. Graham to F. O., 3, 5 June 1920, nos. 495, 502, F.O. 371/3643; Moncheur to Hymans, 31 May 1920, no. 2611/890, Hymans Papers/165.

103. DuD; R.G.P. 156, pp. 639–41; R. Graham to Crowe, 5 June 1920, no. 502, F.O. 371/3643; van Zuylen, *Les Mains libres*, pp. 164–65.

owing to the Dutch claim to the Wielingen and that, unless it were signed and ratified, the old commitment to defend Belgium would still bind Britain. Accordingly, Lord Derby in Paris was told on 7 June to ask the French to join in representations to the Dutch.[104]

The French had already proposed such a demarche to Hymans. They further proposed, possibly at Belgian instigation, to revive the question of Limburg's defense in conjunction with that of the Wielingen but, during discussions at the Boulogne Conference of 21 and 22 June 1920 and again at the Spa Conference in July, the British showed no enthusiasm for such a tactic and the French soon withdrew their proposal.[105] In the interim, the British had cautiously sounded Brussels about division of the channel or the creation of an international servitude in favor of Holland. Hymans had made extremely clear to Villiers the Belgian bitterness about international servitudes, and the suggestion was dropped.[106] There remained the proposed Anglo-French demarche at The Hague, on which agreement had been reached. On 21 July, after the French had prodded the British at Spa, Graham was told to proceed with his French colleague. Curzon informed Moncheur that the demarche would be made and Crowe warned van Swinderin that it was impending.[107] Although his wife was seriously ill, van Swinderin rushed to The Hague, whence he telegraphed asking that the protest be

104. DBFP, 12:51–52; Whitlock Journal, 26 May 1920, Whitlock Papers/5 (LC). For unknown reasons, Derby did not carry out his instructions until 18 June.

105. Margerie to FMAE, 8, 29 June 1920, tels. 347–50, 415–20, FMAE A/138; Margerie to Hymans, 14 June 1920, de Gaiffier to Hymans, 15, 19 June 1920, nos. 6386/336, 6497/3401, Hymans memos, 26, 29 June, 6 July 1920, Hymans Papers/165; Hymans to de Gaiffier, 17 July 1920, no. 4168, BMAE FR/1920/I. French and Belgian evidence does not clearly establish which country raised the question of Limburg first. It appears likely that Hymans, although very hesitant, first mentioned the matter to Margerie in response to parliamentary pressure, and that Millerand, over the objections of Laroche and Berthelot, had seized on the fact that France had recently obtained German documents indicating heavy Germany wartime use of the Limburg railways for military purposes as an excuse to reopen the Limburg question, because he preferred that the Belgo-Dutch treaty remain unsettled until after the Belgo-French military convention was concluded.

106. DDB, 1:382–83. Hymans was in fact willing to grant Holland a servitude on the Wielingen if Belgium obtained a corresponding servitude on the Scheldt, which the Dutch were unwilling to consider. DuD, R.G.P. 156, pp. 654; DuD, R.G.P. 162, p. 21.

107. Paléologue to Benoist, 12 July 1920, tel. 580, FMAE A/138; de Gaiffier to Hymans, 19 June 1920, BMAE Ind/1920/II; DBFP, 12:56–58.

postponed until his return. Graham was duly authorized to delay the demarche, which in fact was never made.[108]

On his return, van Swinderin proposed submission of the issue to a four-power commission of experts in which, he hinted, the Dutch would probably accept an unfavorable decision. The British, who were becoming increasingly loath to make the promised demarche, received this suggestion enthusiastically.[109] Further inquiry revealed, however, that the Dutch proposal was unofficial and would not be made officially. The Dutch would accept a commission if the suggestion originated elsewhere and provided that the Anglo-French protests were made to Brussels as well as to The Hague. The Foreign Office thought this response very promising but was much annoyed to learn that the Belgians, whose recent experience with commissions had been unhappy, would consider an expert commission only after the demarche was made to Holland and on the assurance that the British and French experts would be instructed not to consider the Dutch claims. Curzon, who thought time was needed to permit Dutch and Belgian opinion to cool, told the British chargé in Brussels that a demarche would gain nothing and that Dutch attitude was "not unconciliatory." Curzon argued rather speciously that in the unlikely event of a commission deciding against Belgium, she would be no worse off than at present. Thus he ordered the chargé to urge a commission of experts upon Belgium.[110]

Both the French and the Belgians resisted the British plan, but the question dragged on over the summer. Hymans resigned in August over unrelated questions and Delacroix, who replaced him as foreign minister, decided to attempt direct negotiations with van Karnebeek on all outstanding issues. In response, the Dutch made a genuine effort to be conciliatory and to settle the Belgo-Dutch treaty, but the gulf be-

108. Van Swinderin to Crowe, 22 July 1920, tel., F.O. 371/3643; DBFP, 12:58; Moncheur to Hymans, 30 July 1920, no. 3669/1276, Hymans Papers/165.
109. Benoist to Millerand, 29 July 1920, tel. 284, FMAE A/138; Millerand to Benoist, 29 July 1920, tel., FMAE A/133; de Bassompierre to Moncheur, 30 July 1920, Hymans Papers/165; DBFP, 12:59–61.
110. DBFP, 12:61–65; Villiers to Curzon, 6 Aug. 1920, no. 568, F.O. 371/3643; de Bassompierre to de Gaiffier, 6 Aug. 1920, no. 4496, BMAE to Villiers, 6 Aug. 1920, Moncheur to Hymans, 13 Aug. 1920, no. 3978/1413, Hymans Papers/165; DuD, R.G.P. 156; pp. 747–48.

tween the two countries' needs and views proved to be too wide. Van Karnebeek indicated willingness to accept some parts of the proposal, including Belgian sovereignty over the Wielingen channel, but only with a wartime servitude of passage for Dutch warships. He declined, however, to consider a joint defense of Limburg, thus ending the entire exchange, which, in Belgian eyes, was contingent upon resolving all issues at once.[111] While these direct negotiations were in progress in September and early October 1920, the Foreign Office took the view that the resignation of Hymans canceled the commitment to make a demarche at The Hague and that the two governments should resolve the problem directly without outside intervention. Although the French pressed for further great-power activity on behalf of Belgium, the British refused to intervene, partly because they thought the two countries preferred to negotiate alone together and partly because they were eager to wash their hands of the whole affair.[112]

By mid-October 1920, it was clear that Delacroix's overtures had come to naught, and his government resigned shortly thereafter. With its fall came an effective end to the two-year effort to revise the 1839 treaties, particularly as a brief attempt in 1921 to resolve matters came to nothing.[113] The new economic and fluvial arrangements were abandoned, as the old treaties remained in effect. Belgian neutrality died a

111. Fleuriau to Curzon, 17 Aug. 1920, F.O. 371/3643; DBFP, 12:65–66, 67–70; R. Graham to Curzon, 13 Oct. 1920, no. 770, F.O. 371/5457; Whitlock to Colby, 18 Sept. 1920, no. 956, 4, 20 Oct. 1920, Whitlock Papers/42 (LC); Whitlock to Colby, 10 Sept. 1920, tel. 116, 13 Sept., 2, 22 Oct. 1920, nos. 952, 995, 1005, SD 755.56/22, 24, 32, 33; Delacroix to Moncheur, 2 Oct. 1920, no. 1920, BMAE GB/1920/II. Delacroix was in part trying to save his collapsing government. For the course of the negotiations, which were dropped after an informal meeting in Brussels between Delacroix and the secretary-general of the Dutch Foreign Ministry, see DuD, R.G.P. 162, pp. 56–120 passim, and Delacroix memo, 2 Oct. 1920, BMAE Ind/1920/II. On the resignation of Hymans, see Henri Haag, "La Démission de Paul Hymans et la fin du second gouvernement Delacroix (juillet–novembre 1920)," pp. 393–414.

112. G. Grahame to Curzon, 22 Sept. 1920, no. 110, Curzon to G. Grahame, 28 Sept. 1920, no. 160, F.O. 371/5456; Derby to Curzon, 4 Oct. 1920, tel. 1160, F.O. 371/5457; DBFP, 12:69–75; British Embassy, Paris, to FMAE, 12 Oct. 1920, FMAE A/138; FMAE to Derby, 4 Oct. 1920, BMAE FR/1920/II; Moncheur to Delacroix, 6 Oct. 1920, no. 4743/1744, BMAE GB/1920.

113. Orts Papers/428 passim; DuD, R.G.P. 162, pp. 319–544 passim; R. Graham to Curzon, 31 Aug. 1921, no. 553, F.O. 371/6958; Whitlock, *Letters*, 2:705–6; Phillips to Colby, 7 Sept. 1921, no. 683, SD 755.56/42.

de facto death as Belgium joined the League, participated in the Rhineland occupation, and entered into a military accord with France. Under the circumstances, it was unclear whether the great-power guarantee remained in force. Increasingly, there was a tendency to assume that it did not. In short, the effort to revise the 1839 treaties removed the guarantees Belgium had enjoyed in the past and gave her nothing in return, not even a more viable riparian regime. Further, the damage done to Belgo-Dutch relations was not easily mended, for the Dutch fears and suspicions aroused in 1919 lingered on, as such fears often do, well after the basis for them no longer existed.

The subsequent history both of the Western Entente and of Belgo-Dutch relations suggests that substantial revision of the 1839 treaties had little prospect of success at any time during the years after World War I. It seems probable that prompt and firm Anglo-French pressure in 1920 would have induced Holland to withdraw the Wielingen claim, but it appears equally likely that some other obstacle would have arisen either before signature of the new treaty or as a barrier to parliamentary approval in the Netherlands. Understandably, Holland had little enthusiasm for treaty revision to Belgium's benefit, and there are no grounds for thinking that Dutch opposition could have been overcome without much more pressure than Britain and France, especially Britain, were willing to bring to bear. Once the Dutch discovered that British pressure, which they greatly feared, would not be forthcoming, the likelihood of achieving new treaties satisfactory to Belgium became virtually nonexistent. In addition, as the British fully realized, no amount of pressure would have induced the Dutch government to commit itself to any substantial military arrangement for the Limburg gap or to join any sort of occidental bloc.

Because Britain was equally averse to joining any western military system against Germany, the Belgian search for new guarantees to replace the old was doomed to failure. No matter how it was arranged, any new Anglo-French guarantee of Belgium was bound to constitute such a system, and so the British shied away. Although they did agree to a brief interim guarantee during the period of least danger, the price was prohibitive, as it also tended to be when the question arose in ensuing years of any British military commitment to Belgium and France. Five years of Belgian diplomatic effort had accomplished nothing. Belgium's geographic situation remained potentially as dangerous as ever, both to her and to the European peace, but there was now no British commitment at all. Undoubtedly, Hymans made a number of mistakes, but the larger problem was beyond his control. Because Britain did not wish to guarantee France, whom she regarded with increasing distrust, she was not prepared to guarantee Belgium. Though Belgian leaders told themselves that British interests would dictate intervention in any event against renewed German attack, they would have rested easier with a written commitment. The absence of this commitment and what its absence implied about British attitudes toward the Continent was a major factor in the fragility of the peace in the early 1920s. On 16 September 1919 the great powers had declared essentially that if the problem of Belgian security were not solved, "the instability of the general peace would be increased." In the end, Belgian security remained an unresolved problem, returning repeatedly to complicate further the increasingly precarious relationships within the Western Entente, and thus to contribute to the instability of the peace.

SEVEN

THE SECONDARY

SKIRMISHES

The pattern of indifferent Belgian success in achieving the kingdom's major goals at the Paris Peace Conference applied as well to lesser issues and for the same reason: lack of support from the major powers or, at best, division among them. As de Gaiffier sadly noted in early June 1919, "When France supports us, England disappears and conversely."[1] Although this was true, there were some questions on which none of the great powers had much sympathy with Belgian aspirations. Some of the secondary issues were matters of real substance; others were genuinely trivial. However, Belgian opinion tended to become most exercised over some of the least important issues, and Hymans responded to it, unwisely expending his limited diplomatic capital on minor questions where sometimes the Belgian case was weak.

DUTCH AND GERMAN QUESTIONS

The reluctant and divided support of the major powers for Belgium during the long effort to revise the 1839 treaties carried over as well to a variety of other issues concerning the Netherlands. Belgium never enjoyed much Allied support vis-à-vis Holland and, as time passed, such little sympathy as she had gained quickly dwindled. As early as January 1919, Belgium began to protest the Allied policy of supplying the armies of occupation in Germany through Rotterdam instead of Antwerp. Feeling ran high on the issue in Belgium, especially because the economic implications for the revival of Antwerp were profound.[2] The American delegation initially refused to reconsider, arguing that

1. De Gaiffier to Hymans, 6 June 1919, no. 4777/1929, BMAE FR/1919.
2. Whitlock to ACNP, 30 Jan. 1919, tel. 8, 811.20/4, ACNP/437; Moncheur to Hymans, 14 Mar. 1919, no. 1855/535, BMAE GB/1919/I; Maskens to F.O., 21 Mar.

the matter was purely one of military expedience, although Lansing said bluntly that "he would prefer to favor Holland"; the British similarly justified their policy on grounds of practical convenience.[3] Continued Belgian protests, however, along with technical factors, eventually swayed the American government. Concern to revive Belgium, hostility to Holland as the Dutch contractor involved at Rotterdam proved to be on the War Trade Board's enemy trade list, and pressure from the United States Treasury, worried both about repayment of the Belgian debt to the United States and about the Dutch exchange rate, led the American government in mid-March to establish a second base at Antwerp and to split its traffic.[4]

In May the French also agreed to shift a substantial percentage of their traffic to Antwerp but insisted on continuing some shipments through Rotterdam to counter Anglo-American competition to French interests there.[5] The British were more stubborn, even though the Dutch objected strenuously to the passage of troops and arms until mid-March 1919. Confident that Dutch objections could be overcome, the British continued to supply their Rhineland forces through Rotterdam, preferring the all-water route to the shorter Antwerp-Cologne route, which required transshipment by rail. In view of the urgency of restoring Antwerp to economic life, the Belgians persisted, and the issue lingered on, embittering relations and causing Anglo-Belgian conferences, pleas by Curzon on behalf of Belgium, and a special British commission to Belgium in the summer of 1919. Despite these efforts, supply of the British Army of the Rhine continued primarily through Rotterdam.[6]

1919, no. 2010, F.O. 371/3645; Defrance to Pichon, 11, 25 Jan. 1919, tels. 22, 63, Vin 6N/128; Fallon to Hymans, 30 Jan. 1919, no. 1268/217, BMAE B-348.

3. Meeting, U.S. Plenipotentiaries, 3 Feb. 1919, ACNP 184.00101/3; F.O. to Villiers, 14 Apr. 1919, no. 142, F.O. 371/3645.

4. Phillips to ACNP, 21 Feb. 1919, tel. 826, ACNP to Whitlock, 15 Mar. 1919, tel. 27, 811.20/7, ACNP/437.

5. De Gaiffier to Hymans, 13 May 1919, no 3996/1571, BMAE FR/1919.

6. DuB, R.G.P. 145, pp. 637, 663–64; Moncheur to Hymans, 14 Mar. 1919, no. 1855/535, BMAE GB/1919/I; Curzon to Maskens, 12 Apr. 1919, Moncheur to Curzon, 14 Apr. 1919, no. 2540, Curzon to W.O., 30 Apr. 1919, F.O. 371/3645; 3 May formula, Hymans Papers/150; Western & General Report no. 135, 3 Sept. 1919, CAB 24/50; Moncheur to Hymans, 18 Sept. 1919, no. 5752/1859, BMAE GB/1919/II.

Another issue where Belgian hopes of allied support vis-à-vis the Dutch proved to be even more ill founded was that of Baarle-Hertog (also known as Baerle-Duc). This small Belgian enclave, entirely surrounded by Dutch territory near Baarle-Nassau, was a long-standing problem that Hymans hoped to solve in conjunction with revision of the 1839 treaties. As the problem had been considerably exacerbated by World War I, the Belgian delegation raised the issue in the Revendications Belges at the end of February 1919 and again during the Conference of Seven in May. However, the first detailed exposition of the Belgian case was part of Belgium's massive presentation to the Commission of Fourteen and was enunciated in detail on 8 August 1919.[7]

Baarle-Hertog, a Belgian town with a population of about 1,400, was closely entangled with the Dutch commune of Baarle-Nassau and had been an enclave since the thirteenth century despite negotiations in the eighteenth century. Because the proposed bases of separation in 1831 envisaged a border with numerous enclaves on both sides, the treaty of June 1831 stipulated a Belgo-Dutch exchange of territory to suppress the enclaves. As bitterness mounted, however, the great powers had despaired of Belgo-Dutch negotiation and so the Treaty of 14 October 1831 summarily divided the enclaves. But the treaty failed to mention Baarle-Hertog, and thus the commissioners who actually delimited the frontier could not resolve the problem. Despite periodic unsuccessful Belgo-Dutch negotiations, particularly between 1875 and 1893, Baarle-Hertog remained a Belgian enclave surrounded by Dutch territory. In 1906, Holland imposed a customs frontier between the enclave and Belgium.[8]

During World War I, the situation in Baarle-Hertog, which was not occupied by Germany, caused considerable Belgo-Dutch tension. As the enclave became an active center of Belgian sentiment, the Dutch authorities imposed severe censorship on the Belgian mails there and

7. Revendications Belges, F.O. 608/2 pt. 2; FRUS PPC, 4:741; Hymans to Balfour, 21 May 1919, no. 670, F.O. 800/216; DBFP, 5:95–101, 161–63.
8. DBFP, 5:161–62, 249. Baarle-Hertog consisted of several noncontiguous segments of territory. The two communes were so entangled that often a house was in one country and its garden in another, and sometimes the frontier passed through the middle of a house. De Ligne to de Broqueville, 30 Oct. 1917, no. 13620/2333, BMAE PB/1917; Carbonnel to Pichon, 10 Feb. 1918, no. 55, FMAE CPC Guerre Belg./426.

limited free circulation on the highways. They further resisted establishment of Baarle-Hertog as a Belgian customs post and impeded action by the Belgian police to enforce Belgian laws against commerce with Germany. The most acute difficulties, however, arose over Belgian establishment in the spring of 1915 of a radio telegraph station that was of considerable military value to Belgium and the Allies. Although the Belgian authorities were within their legal rights in erecting the station on Belgian territory in the enclave, it was perhaps tactless of them to do so in wartime. After the Dutch noticed the station in October 1915, they never contested the Belgian right to build it, but their response undoubtedly constituted an excessively punctilious exercise in neutrality. First they tried to make contact with the wires linking the station to the post office and, failing that, forbade entry of coal, oil, and other supplies for the telegraph station. In forbidding coal and oil, which in any event the Belgians had already stockpiled in large quantity, the Dutch were firmly based in law, but they also banned import into the enclave of foil-wrapped chocolates, all alcoholic beverages, candles, and mustard (because it contained oil), on grounds that such items could conceivably be used for the telegraph, while at the same time they were exporting these products to Germany. Holland also surrounded the various segments of Baarle-Hertog in a network of barbed wire and seriously impeded provisioning of the population. After protests from the Belgian legation and the burgomaster of the enclave, the provisioning problem was solved by establishment of a mixed commission, but the barbed wire remained an impediment to daily life.[9]

The Belgians concluded their presentation of grievances concerning the enclave to the Fourteen with a statement that Dutch transfer of sovereignty over a corridor would be the best arrangement for Baarle-

9. Dutch Orange Book, *Recueil de diverses communications du Ministre des Affaires Etrangères aux Etats-Généraux par rapport à la neutralité des Pays-Bas et au respect du droit de gens*, pp. 168–70; Belgian mémoire, n.d., Orts Papers/429; Vandenbosch, *Neutrality*, pp. 175–76; Renault note, 26 Jan. 1916, FMAE CPC Guerre Belg./419; van Gilse to Fallon, 4 Feb. 1916, no. 9668, Fallon to Beyens, 15, 16, 18 Feb., 10 June 1916, nos. 1535/301, 1608/315, 1661/324, 5683/981, BMAE PB/1916; Carbonnel to Pichon, 10 Feb. 1918, no. 55, FMAE CPC Guerre Belg./426. The files do not answer the following questions: whether Belgium erected the station at Allied request; how Belgium managed to build it and stockpile supplies (probably from Breda) in wartime; why the Dutch did not notice it for about six months.

Hertog but, because that had already been excluded, Belgium hoped to find some other solution restoring the inhabitants of the enclave to their anterior rights. In response, Laroche declared that a transfer of sovereignty was excluded from the work of the Fourteen but could be arranged outside the commission by Belgo-Dutch negotiation. When van Swinderin presented the Dutch reply to all the Belgian charges on 20 August 1919, he claimed that Holland had maintained a perfect neutrality throughout the war, adding, "We refuse for this reason to listen to talk here of the question of sand and gravel,[10] of our exports to Germany, of the wireless telegraph station at Baarle-Hertog, of the passage of German troops through Limburg, etc." Nonetheless, he agreed to negotiate on the question of the enclave and assured the powers that Holland would not take advantage of the clause ruling out territorial transfer to oppose a reasonable solution.[11]

Under the circumstances, the question of Baarle-Hertog was referred to direct Belgo-Dutch negotiation outside the aegis of the Commission of Fourteen. The British remained hopeful that Holland would cede a corridor to Belgium but did nothing whatever to make that hope a reality. In the absence of major-power pressure, the Dutch showed no enthusiasm for concessions. Thus, by February 1920, Belgian hopes had dwindled to the negotiation of a customs regime for the enclave ensuring free transit of persons and goods. Negotiations to this end began on 9 March 1920. When, during the final session of the Commission of Fourteen on 23 March 1920, Laroche asked if anything had been done about the enclave, Segers indicated that no definitive solution had been reached but that a temporary clause had been agreed, pending further negotiation.[12] However, even this fell by the wayside during the crisis occasioned by the Wielingen dispute and, as a consequence, the anomaly of Baarle-Hertog remained unresolved.

10. The wartime transit of sand and gravel, probably for military purposes, from Germany across Holland to Belgium in large quantities did constitute a violation of Dutch neutrality, but some of the shipments were sanctioned by the Allies to ensure continuing Dutch neutrality.

11. DBFP, 5:163, 238, 249.

12. Bland to Carnegie, 16 Sept. 1919, F.O. 608/4; Hymans to de Ligne, 24 Feb. 1920, no. 334, de Ligne to Hymans, 12 Mar. 1920, no. 1546/428, BMAE PB/1920; DBFP, 12:13–14. An access corridor two or three miles long would have sufficed.

The Belgians argued that the Dutch record during World War I concerning Baarle-Hertog, sand and gravel, exports to Germany, troop passage, and similar matters dictated efforts to reinforce Belgian security against the consequences of German pressure on Holland in a future war.[13] Attitudes in the Netherlands during the course of 1919 lent some weight to the continuing Belgian concern. The Dutch remained consistent in their inclination toward Germany in both their opinion and their action. Publication of the peace terms in early May brought an almost unanimous condemnation in the Dutch press.[14] When the Versailles treaty was signed, Graham reported from The Hague:

> The signature was greeted with no manifestations of joy whatever. Not a flag was hung out. Not a glass of wine was drunk in its celebration. Not a smile of relief lighted a Dutch face. The press, no longer severely condemnatory as on the occasion of the first publication of the peace terms, is as gloomy as the Dutch sky which surely must have its effect on the national temper. Disappointment, uneasiness and, to a large extent, ill-will toward the Allies in general and Great Britain in particular prevail.[15]

The Dutch were in fact much less hostile to Britain than to France and Belgium, but relations were periodically strained over the question of the kaiser. Every time the subject of the kaiser's future arose in diplomatic conversation during 1919, the Dutch indicated that a request for extradition would not be well received. The great powers largely ignored these expressions but, in this issue as in others, time was on Holland's side. At the end of 1918, British crowds and British politicians had demanded the hanging of the kaiser. During April 1919, the Big Four repeatedly discussed his future trial, deciding that he would be charged with violation of the 1839 treaties, that Belgium would play the role of public prosecutor, and that she would seek his extradition from the Netherlands. The Belgian delegation was not pleased. On 16 April, Clemenceau reported that Belgium had declined both assignments on the ground that a monarchy could not take the

13. DBFP, 5:266.
14. Garrett to ACNP, 9 May 1919, tel. 277, Wilson Papers 5B/35.
15. DBFP, 5:14–15.

lead in prosecuting a monarch. Though Albert's views contributed to this decision, so did the pending Belgo-Dutch negotiations. The Big Four were undisturbed by the Belgian refusal, complacently assuming that Kaiser Wilhelm would nonetheless be tried on the charge of violating Belgian neutrality. In deference to Belgian sensibilities, however, the final text of Article 227 of the Versailles treaty merely arraigned Wilhelm II "for a supreme offense against international morality and the sanctity of treaties."[16] On 28 June 1919, the day that the treaty was signed, Clemenceau as president of the peace conference requested that the kaiser be turned over for trial. As van Karnebeek returned a chilly and noncommittal reply, Clemenceau waited until 15 January 1920, five days after the treaty entered into force, and tried again, charging Wilhelm with "cynical violation of the neutrality of Belgium and Luxemburg." In response the Dutch cabinet returned a categoric refusal and informally let the British know that the Netherlands was prepared for a severance of diplomatic relations, as had been threatened. On 14 February the Supreme Council sought Dutch reconsideration but in much weaker form. When van Karnebeek returned another refusal, Lloyd George, speaking for the London Supreme Council, was left to grumble about "proper internment," stressing Dutch exclusive responsibility for both custody and any future misadventures. By mid-1920 the continuing Dutch refusal to relinquish Wilhelm II came to be taken as a matter of course and in Britain as a matter of some relief; news reports of joint hunting expeditions by the kaiser and the Dutch prince consort evoked no British comment at all.[17]

Even more strikingly, although the Allies possessed massive evidence of German shipments of war materials for sale to and through Holland in violation of the Versailles treaty, the powers, with the very reluctant

16. France, Ministère de la Guerre, *Examen de la responsabilité*, p. 18, Robertson to Russell, 25 July 1919, F.O. 800/156; Mantoux, *Les Délibérations*, 1:185–92, 195–96, 238, 269; I.C. 172, 16 Apr. 1919, CAB 28/7; DuB, R.G.P. 117, pp. 1054–55; Hymans to de Gaiffier, 3 Feb. 1920, no. 663, BMAE FR/1920/I; Hymans, *Mémoires*, 1:479. Quotation from FRUS PPC, 13:371.

17. Dutch Orange Book, 1919–20, pp. 11–15; DuD, R.G.P. 156, 433 ff.; Pichon to Benoist, 17 Jan. 1920, tel. 42–45, Vin 6N/291; Hardinge, *Old Diplomacy*, pp. 247–48; DBFP, 9:627–30, 702; *Times*, 8 Dec. 1919, p. 13; R. Graham to Curzon, 19 Aug. 1920, no. 655, F.O. 371/3748. Quotations from Dutch Orange Book, 1919–20, pp. 12, 15.

assent of Britain, made only two mild protests, one to all the neutrals neighboring Germany and one directly to Germany and Holland, reminding them that this arms traffic constituted a treaty violation. Both were disregarded, the British government blocked further protests, and the shipments continued. Similarly, an Allied note in May 1920 asking that German war matériel abandoned in Holland in November 1918 be turned over to the Inter-Allied Military Control Commission was ignored by both Germany and the Netherlands. Finally, in mid-1921 the Dutch government accepted Allied controls over the sale of war materials, with proceeds to go to the Reparation Commission, but the German government ignored announcements to this effect for more than a year longer.[18]

Although the attitude of the Dutch government was perhaps not surprising, the lack of reaction from the victors was significant for treaty enforcement in general and the claims of Belgium in particular. Though the powers undoubtedly came to realize that it would be profitless and embarrassing to pursue the claim for the kaiser, the open violation of the military clauses of the Versailles treaty became an issue on which even the French largely abandoned all thought of serious protest. If the great powers were unwilling to enforce the treaty against Dutch violation of it, obviously Belgium could not alone enforce her claims against either Holland or the far greater power of Germany. Indeed, while pro forma allied protests to Holland over the kaiser continued in the first half of 1920, efforts to impose the will of the victors on Germany were soon largely abandoned except for acceptance of the treaty itself and a few issues of overriding concern to the security or financial well-being of the great powers. As early as the peace conference itself, the Belgian delegation found that both its claims and its legal rights were being brushed aside for the simple reason that the Big Four did not care to lay down the law to Germany. This attitude of the Four arose partly from indifference to Belgian concerns and partly from reluctance to issue ultimata to Germany that might have to be followed by force.

Many of the issues were minor but of a nature to wound Belgian

18. DBFP, 10:73, 109, 176–77, and passim; C.A. 22, 18 Mar. 1920, CAB 29/43; C.A. 39, 8 May 1920, CAB 29/45.

amour-propre and excite Belgian opinion, as in the instance of British failure to halt the removal of seized Belgian cows from Malmédy into unoccupied Germany. Under Article 19 of the Armistice agreement, Germany was required to return promptly the Belgian state documents she had removed during the war, notably much of the Archive of the Belgian Foreign Ministry. Instead of returning them, the German government began to publish these records in profusion. The Belgian delegation protested in vain and Foch recommended collective action, but the Council of Five decided to do nothing.[19] Another more extended Belgian campaign of protest against the German proposal to adopt the Belgian national colors met with a similarly hostile reception from the five foreign ministers. Though the new German tricolor of black, red, and gold was to be arranged differently from that of Belgium and was to be based on the brief historical precedent of the Frankfurt Parliament of 1848–49 to symbolize the proclaimed liberalism of the infant Weimar Republic, Belgium protested heatedly and repeatedly from December 1918 on that the new German colors would be confused with the long-standing Belgian flag and that such confusion would be invidious to Belgium. Although the French offered a little sympathy, Balfour and Lansing strongly opposed any action, so none was taken. Further Belgian protests through the summer of 1919, chiefly to the French, evoked only empty bureaucratic phraseology.[20]

A SHARE OF THE SPOILS

Sometimes the reason why Belgian claims encountered difficulty was that they clashed with the appetites of the great powers. Thus, Belgium fought an uphill battle to participate in the division of German merchant shipping and fishing boats. Although the great powers did initially have urgent need of the German ships to carry relief supplies to

19. FRUS PPC, 4:686–87, 757, 763; Harry R. Rudin, *Armistice, 1918*, pp. 429–30.

20. Moncheur to Hymans, 16 Dec. 1918, no. 9851/2258, BMAE GB/1918/II; FRUS PPC, 4:685–87; Lansing Desk Diary, 9 May 1919, Lansing Papers; Hymans to Maskens, 12 Aug. 1919, no. 1120, BMAE GB/1919/II; van der Elst to Hymans, 15 Apr., 23 Aug. 1919, nos. 3109/1229, 7497/3138-9, BMAE FR/1919; Hymans to Wilson, 17 May 1919, no. 698, Wilson Papers 5B/37.

Europe, their reluctance to award Belgium any share of the spoils continued well after the emergency was past. The Belgian claim was based upon the facts that all of her shipping had been put at Allied disposal in 1916, half of it had been sunk (a higher percentage of loss than any other nation) in cross-Channel service, and ships were badly needed to bring available stocks from the Congo to Europe. As Belgian opinion was agitated about exclusion from the booty, Hymans persisted, blaming the British forthrightly for great-power imperviousness to Belgium's needs and rights. As usual, he did so without consideration of the effect on his other claims. In the end his persistence yielded a share of the German river vessels as well as a modest amount of merchant shipping on reparation account.[21]

A similar struggle over the allocation of German colonies revealed not only the appetite of a far greater power than Belgium but also the remoteness of the Belgian delegation from the decision-making process. The bone of contention was German East Africa and especially the districts of Ruanda and Urundi, whose disposition had remained unsettled ever since the British had refused to discuss the matter in 1916. At the time of the peace conference, Belgian forces remained in occupation of about one-third of German East Africa, and the Belgian desire to trade part of what they held for Cabinda and the southern bank of the Congo in northern Angola remained unchanged.

As early as December 1918, the British Foreign Office had decided that Belgium should not "be permitted" to keep any part of German East Africa beyond a minor frontier rectification.[22] In part this decision had arisen from Britain's own desire to obtain the territory, and in part the dismissal of Belgium's colonial claim arose from a mistaken but widespread tendency to confuse the administration of the Congo by the prewar Belgian government with the earlier maladministration of it by

---

21. Hymans, *Mémoires*, 1:418; D. H. Miller, *Diary*, 1:154–55; Balfour to Hymans, 4 Apr. 1919, BMAE DB/7/I; DB to Ministère de Marine, 9 May 1919, tel. 433, BMAE DB/7/II; H.D. 17, Annex B, 27 June 1919, FMAE A/57; Derby to Pichon, 15 Dec. 1918, Vin 6N/70; Hymans note, 26 Mar. 1919, Hymans to Balfour, 26 Mar. 1919, no. 351, BMAE B-366/I; Margerie to Pichon, 31 Mar. 1919, tel. 154, Vin 6N/128; Villiers to Curzon, 4 Apr. 1919, Curzon Papers F112/214b; Maskens to Hymans, 28 June 1919, no. 4121/1331, BMAE GB/1919/I; FRUS PPC, 13:498, 858, 878, 914.

22. Percy memo, 3 Dec. 1918, P.C. 28, F.O. 371/4553.

King Léopold II. In fact, Belgian administration had promptly ended Léopold's improper practices and in its brief tenure before World War I had been on a par with the African administrations of other European powers and better than some. Nonetheless, there remained a certain belief among representatives of major powers that small states could not and should not administer large expanses of colonial territory and a certain tendency to impose upon the Belgian government the onus for the malodorous practices of its late unlamented monarch. In Britain, E. D. Morel, whose opinions had considerable influence on the general public and in the Labour party, still viewed Belgium in this light. At the peace conference, George Louis Beer, the American expert on colonial questions, did the same in pungent terms. Although Beer was unable to prevent award of additional territory to Belgium, he did succeed in blocking removal of the servitudes imposed upon the Congo by the 1885 and 1890 Acts of Berlin and Brussels, thus thwarting the Belgian effort to gain full sovereignty over the colony.[23]

In addition to full sovereignty in the Congo, Belgium wanted modest frontier rectifications, a financial indemnity for retrocession of its portion of German East Africa and improvements made there during the Belgian occupation, facilities in German East African ports that Britain would presumably keep, and especially a wider Congo seacoast than the existing forty kilometers (twenty-five miles) on the Atlantic. Because this last most important aim involved Portuguese territory, it could not be formally enunciated. Further, Belgium hoped to gain the territory outright, not as a mandate, but knew better than to enter into open opposition to Wilson's preferences. Thus when Belgium was summoned before the Ten on 30 January in response to Hymans's reminders that Belgium wished to participate in the colonial settlement, Orts, who spoke in the presence of all three Belgian plenipotentiaries, merely rehearsed the Belgian role in the African war and requested the right of "free disposition" of the territories that Belgium was provisionally administering.[24]

---

23. Louis, "The United States and the African Peace Settlement," pp. 429–32.

24. Franck to Hymans, 24 Dec. 1918, no. 167; *procès-verbal*, Council of Ten, 30 Jan. 1919, Belgian note, n.d. [Feb. 1919], Orts Papers/433; Hymans, *Mémoires*, 1:339–43; Hymans to BMAE, 21 Jan. 1919, BMAE B-348; Curzon to Moncheur, 23 Jan. 1919,

Two weeks later, American experts concluded that, though German East Africa should be divided into three parts, all three should be awarded to Britain. This total disregard of the Belgian claim and her possession of much of the territory almost certainly arose from Beer's prejudices. However, the recommendation received no attention, as the great powers deferred squabbling over the colonial spoils as long as possible. On 20 March, Hymans renewed the Belgian claim to "free disposition" in writing and, acting on rumors, indicated that if a commission were indeed to be established for "liquidation" of German colonies and assignment of mandates, Belgium wished to be represented on it.[25] At the same time he also dealt directly with the British.

As the British knew the real Belgian desires and themselves much wanted part of Ruanda-Urundi for their projected Cape-to-Cairo railway, they also favored direct negotiations. Thus, Orts saw Lord Milner, the British colonial secretary, on 20 March. Because Orts made it clear that Belgium would not evacuate German East Africa unless she obtained satisfaction elsewhere, Milner offered to approach the Portuguese delegation about a three-way exchange of territory whereby Britain would gain most of German East Africa, Belgium would acquire the desired coastal territories from Portugal, and Portugal would be compensated by Britain in southern German East Africa. Milner promised to report back but did not.[26]

There matters rested until, on 30 April, *Le Temps* reported that the colonial clauses of the treaty had been approved, stipulating that Germany would renounce her overseas territories to the five great powers. After obtaining confirmation at the Quai d'Orsay, on 1 May Hymans sent Clemenceau a reminder that Belgium occupied much of German East Africa and asked why she had not been included. This triggered a discussion on 2 May among the Three, reduced from the Big Four during the withdrawal of Italy. Lloyd George termed Hymans's letter "a

BMAE GB/1919/I; Louwers note, n.d., van den Heuvel Papers/30; FRUS PPC, 3: 797–817.

25. Black Book 2, 13 Feb. 1919, Wilson Papers 5B/15; Hymans to Clemenceau, 20 Mar. 1919, no. 309, 184.611/122, ACNP/259.

26. Orts to Milner, 19 Mar. 1919, Orts notes, 20 Mar. 1919, Orts Papers/434. For a more detailed account of the Ruanda-Urundi question at the Paris Peace Conference, based on some of the same sources as this summary, see Louis, *Ruanda-Urundi*, chap. 21.

most impudent claim," adding that when millions of British troops were "fighting for Belgium," "a few black troops" had been sent by Belgium into German East Africa. In fact, the Belgian forces had come to the rescue of British contingents at British request. Wilson tactfully suggested that Hymans be informed that mandates had not yet been allotted and that Belgian interests would be safeguarded by the League Council on which she would be represented.[27] The next day, however, a question arose whether the five great powers might allocate mandates before the League of Nations came into operation. Lloyd George commented, "To inform M. Hymans of this would be an incitement to him of obstruction." Accordingly, Clemenceau sent Hymans an ambiguous letter that did little to soothe the Belgian cabinet, which had been vigorously protesting a number of peace treaty terms to Paris and reporting the excitement of Belgian opinion on a variety of questions, including that of African colonies.[28]

As more could safely be anticipated from Hymans, Lloyd George acted with dispatch and skill. He chose his moment superbly. On 7 May as the Big Four were leaving the Trianon Palace after the formal presentation of the Versailles treaty to the German delegation, Lloyd George drew the other three into a sitting room. From his pocket he pulled out a list allocating the German African colonies. This he read to the others. In the euphoria of the moment, they approved it unanimously without any discussion, presumably not noticing that Lloyd George's list awarded all of German East Africa to Britain.[29]

The next morning, Hymans read the text of the decision in the Paris newspapers. He discovered from the Quai d'Orsay what had occurred, issued an uncharacteristic public protest to the press, and informed Pichon that Belgium categorically refused to recognize the award. As a consequence, he was summoned on 9 May to meet with the Four at Wilson's home. First, he approached Clemenceau, who claimed ignorance and referred him to Wilson. After Hymans explained Belgium's

27. Hymans, *Mémoires*, 1:453–55; Hymans to Clemenceau, 1 May 1919, no. 555, Vin 6B/74; I.C. 179C, 2 May 1919, CAB 29/37.

28. I.C. 181A, 3 May 1919, CAB 29/37; Clemenceau to Hymans, 3 May 1919, BMAE DB/1; Renkin to Delacroix, 2 May 1919, tel. 214, Hymans Papers/150.

29. Hymans, *Mémoires*, 1:457; I.C. 181G, 7 May 1919, CAB 29/37; Hankey to Wilson, 7 May 1919, Wilson Papers 5B/35.

conquest, occupation, and three-year administration of much of German East Africa, Wilson expressed amazement and referred him on to Lloyd George. The British prime minister was amiable but vague, professing little knowledge of the Belgian occupation or of prior Anglo-Belgian negotiations on the subject. However, Lloyd George undoubtedly knew that Belgian troops were in effective occupation of much of German East Africa and showed no signs of departing. In the circumstances, he declared himself unable to discuss the matter without Milner, whom he summoned to Paris forthwith.[30]

Hymans followed his oral protest with another categoric written one and, perhaps as a consequence, Milner arrived in Paris by air on 11 May. Orts found him irritated at having to untangle a snarl created by Lloyd George but determined to drive a hard bargain, utilizing all possible pressure available to a great power. Nonetheless, Belgian possession of territory Britain wanted was an inescapable fact, as was Portuguese intransigence. Milner admitted that he had talked to the Portuguese without success. Through three weeks of meetings, along with exchanges of official and unofficial letters, he and Orts fully agreed that the three-way exchange of territory would be most satisfactory if only Portugal would cooperate. Milner tried initially to cede Ruanda to Belgium while keeping Urundi for Britain, but Orts pointed out that the latter was needed for Belgian communication with the former, and it was clear that Milner really preferred to see Belgium leave German East Africa altogether. He made no objections to the port facilities and frontier rectifications Belgium sought but flatly rejected the proposed financial compensation, which was ostensibly for rebuilding the railway to Tabora and other improvements but primarily designed to placate Belgian opinion over the prospect of ceding an economically valuable territory for one of no known intrinsic worth. The two men agreed to pursue the three-way arrangement, but first Belgium must legally obtain Ruanda-Urundi so that she could later cede it to Portugal. Thus, on 30 and 31 May, Orts and Milner reached agreement on a mandate of Ruanda-Urundi to Belgium (aside from a small strip to Britain for the railway) as a first step. Officially, Belgium renounced the indemnity. Unofficially, Milner was to pursue both a financial arrangement and

30. Lloyd George, *Memoirs*, 1:366; Hymans, *Mémoires*, 1:456–58.

Portuguese cooperation within two months. Because neither materialized, the second step never took place.[31]

The Belgians thought that at least the first phase was settled but discovered that, thanks largely to Beer's objections, they had to defend their ability to administer Ruanda-Urundi before a special Mandates Commission on 17 July. Once that hurdle was past, Beer managed to delay approval by the Four. Nonetheless, the Milner-Orts agreement for Belgium to receive most of Ruanda-Urundi but no financial compensation was laid before the Supreme Council on 7 August. Despite acidulous remarks from Balfour about Belgian colonial administration and some hesitation by the American delegation for the same reason, the agreement was upheld by the Supreme Council on 24 December 1919 and by the League Council on 20 July 1922. As a consequence, Belgium received most of Ruanda and Urundi, one-twentieth of German East Africa, as B mandates.[32] Though this was not what she had hoped to receive and of only moderate interest to her, it was in fact Belgium's largest and most valuable territorial acquisition from the Paris settlement.

ECONOMIC AND EMOTIONAL ISSUES

Although Lloyd George faced facts and gave way on the African mandates, his hostility to Belgium remained constant throughout the peace conference. It seems to have arisen primarily from prejudice, dislike of

31. Notes for Hymans meeting with Milner, n.d., Orts notes, 12, 13, 15, 24, 28 May 1919, Louwers note, 13 May 1919, Orts to Milner, 19 May 1919 (2), 26 May 1919, 30 May 1919 (2), Milner to Orts, 26, 31 May 1919, Louwers note, 18 July 1919, Orts Papers/434; Derby to Curzon, 16 May 1919, Curzon Papers F112/196; Hymans, *Mémoires*, 1:459–60; William R. Louis, "Great Britain and the African Peace Settlement of 1919," pp. 889–90.

32. Louis, "The United States and the African Peace Settlement," p. 430; Maskens to Hymans, 8 July 1919, tel., BMAE GB/1919/II; Louwers note, 18 July 1919, Orts to Milner, 24 Aug. 1919, Orts to Jaspar, 15 Oct. 1921, Rappard to Orts, 3 Sept. 1923, Orts Papers/434; Louis, *Ruanda-Urundi*, p. 253; Hymans, *Mémoires*, 1:460–61; DBFP, 1:365–69, 463, 593–600; Beer to Wilson, 12 May 1919, Wilson 5B/36; Polk to House, 14 Aug. 1919, tel. 325, House to Polk, 16 Aug. 1919, tel. 225, 185.1111/8A, 9, ACNP/297. Texts of the final Anglo-Belgian agreements, whereby Belgium ceded a strip of Ruanda-Urundi to Britain for the railway and Britain ceded the strip back after deciding not to

Hymans, awareness that Belgium was a serious economic competitor of Scotland,[33] and eagerness to preempt Belgium's share of reparations. Lloyd George's attitude was evident not only to Hymans but also to junior members of the Belgian delegation.[34] Almost inevitably, it affected both other members of the British delegation and British policy. There was a particular awareness of the possibility of Belgian economic competition and a corresponding reluctance to contribute to the restoration of Belgian economic life. Britain quickly lent Belgium $45 million in early 1919, not mentioning that the money was borrowed from the United States, but the credits could be used only to buy British manufactured goods, not to restore Belgian production. Thus this loan benefited Britain's trade balance more than Belgium's recovery. Belgian feelings ran high not only about this state of affairs but also about the continuing cumbersome British censorship of mail from Belgium, which caused such delays that simple business inquiries required fifteen days for an answer. As Britain prolonged her policy of flooding the country with manufactured goods while refusing to deliver raw materials and machinery so that Belgium could recommence manufacture herself, those trying to restore the country to productivity became increasingly infuriated. Similarly, both Belgian pride and Belgian pocketbooks were wounded by British requirements that even the most established Belgian firms pay in full for British shipments before their departure from England. As the goods generally did not arrive until two months later, the financial burden on Belgian businesses was considerable.[35]

Although these British practices aroused much indignation in Belgium, other slights and humiliations were hidden from the public view. At the peace conference itself, British aloofness extended to social matters. During the six months in Paris, Hymans received many invita-

construct the railway, may be found in Cmd. 1794 and Cmd. 1974. The retrocession took place partly because the boundary bisected tribal domains, occasioning bitter protest from the tribal chief.

33. I.C. 179C, 2 May 1919, CAB 29/37.

34. Hymans, *Mémoires*, 1:353; Terlinden interview; Terlinden, "Lloyd George," p. 5.

35. Moncheur to Hymans, 30 Dec. 1919, BMAE GB/1918/II; Carl Parrini, *Heir to Empire*, pp. 49–50; Baudhuin, "La Richesse," p. 9; Moncheur to Hymans, 17 July 1919, no. 4567/1476, BMAE GB/1919/II; Jaspar to Theunis, 8 Apr. 1919, Jaspar Papers/199.

tions from leading members of the French and American delegations but none at all from the British. Similarly, whereas the French and Americans accepted his invitations, the British did not, and only John Maynard Keynes came to dine. No letter to Lloyd George was ever answered or even acknowledged, save one.[36] Though these embarrassing facts could be suppressed, others could not. King Albert was honored with a state visit to France in December 1918 and enjoyed an immensely successful tour of the United States in the autumn of 1919, but he was not invited to Britain until July 1921.[37] By the same token, Wilson made a triumphal visit to Brussels in June 1919 and Poincaré came for the Belgian national day in July, but King George V, who did not like the king of the Belgians, and Queen Mary made a reluctant visit only in May 1922.[38]

It was Wilson's visit more than anything else that applied balm to the bruised Belgian national ego. Though the visit was repeatedly postponed, Wilson held to his promise[39] and went to Belgium, the only small country he consented to visit, on 18 and 19 June 1919. Conditions in Brussels remained so poor that Whitlock despaired of finding a respectable wine to serve when Wilson entertained King Albert and Queen Elisabeth at the American Legation until he remembered that he held the keys to the home of a wealthy American who had left in

36. Invitations file, Hymans Papers/150. The offer of the Egmont Palace as the seat of the League of Nations elicited the following reply (in full) from Lloyd George's personal typist (who was also his mistress and close confidante): "I am desired by the Prime Minister to thank you for your letter of the 17th March." F. L. Stevenson to Hymans, 21 Mar. 1919, Hymans Papers/196.

37. Hymans, *Mémoires*, 1:297–99; DDB, 1:33–37; Jaunez to Pichon, 22 Sept. 1919, tel. 637, Vin 6N/128; Cammaerts, *Albert of Belgium*, pp. 382–83; Whitlock diary of Albert's trip, Whitlock Papers (LC); Hoover's papers on Albert's trip, Hoover Papers/271; Stamfordham to Curzon, 6 Jan. 1920, F.O. 800/149; Phipps to Curzon, 5 July 1921, no. 609, F.O. 371/6961; G. Grahame to Curzon, 14 July 1921, no. 640, F.O. 371/6966.

38. Villiers to Curzon, 20 June 1919, no. 224, F.O. 371/3636; Margerie to FMAE, 4 June 1919, tel. 266–67, FMAE Z/Belg./56; G. Grahame to Curzon, 16 Oct. 1920, tel. 116, F.O. 371/5458; G. Grahame to Curzon, 3 Nov. 1920, F.O. 800/152; Stamfordham to Curzon, 6 Jan. 1921, F.O. 800/149; G. Grahame to Curzon, 13 May 1922, no. 355, F.O. 371/8244.

39. Hoover to Wilson, 11 Feb. 1919, Wilson Papers, 5B/15; House to Wilson, 1 Mar. 1919, Wilson Papers 5B/17; Whitlock to House, 13 May 1919, tel. 32, Wilson Papers 5B/36; O'Brien, *Two Peacemakers*, p. 178.

August 1914; he promptly requisitioned his friend's cellar.[40] Wilson was graciousness itself throughout the trip. He visited battlefields and despoiled factories, dined at the palace, greeted Cardinal Mercier and Burgomaster Adolphe Max of Brussels, national heroes both, and, in a poignant ceremony fraught with symbolism, received an honorary doctorate of laws amid the ruins of the shattered library of the University of Leuven. In his address to the Belgian Chamber of Representatives, Wilson paid skillful tribute to the heroism of Belgium and her leaders and announced that the United States Legation would be raised to the rank of embassy in recognition of Belgium's new status as an equal member of the family of nations.[41] Upon his return to Paris, Wilson took care to send charming notes of thanks to all and sundry, however insignificant, whom he had encountered on the Belgian trip and wrote to Whitlock, "The little hurried visit to Belgium will, I think, remain in my mind also as the most vivid impression which I shall carry away from Europe."[42]

Wilson's courteous attentions did much for Belgian amour-propre but nothing for the country's foreign policy or economic revival. The brief visit was long on symbolism but short of substance. Raising the legation to an embassy was a gesture that cost the United States nothing and that, in any event, would soon become inescapable, as other countries were already doing the same. In his speech to the Belgian Chamber of Representatives, Wilson spoke also of the need to restore Belgium's economy, but he was vague, suggesting that this problem, still acute more than seven months after the Armistice, could best be left to the businessmen and bankers. Wilson told the Belgians that "the proof of the pudding is the eating thereof,"[43] but Belgium soon discovered that there was very little American pudding to eat. After Wilson, House, and Hoover left Paris, America remained sympathetic but increasingly at a distance, as American involvement with Europe in general and Belgium in particular rapidly declined.

40. Whitlock to Albert Ruddock, 8 Mar. 1919, Whitlock Papers/39 (LC).
41. *New York Times*, 19 June 1919, p. 4, 20 June 1919, p. 1, 2; Wilson, *War and Peace*, 1:513.
42. Thank you file, Wilson Papers 5B/48; Wilson to Whitlock, 25 June 1919, Whitlock Papers/40 (LC).
43. House to Wilson, 12 June 1919, Wilson Papers 5B/46; *New York Times*, 20 June 1919, p. 2.

Not only had Belgium's best American friends left Europe but a shift in American policy had occurred. In late October 1918, Hoover proposed and Wilson soon approved a plan for full American reconstruction of Belgium designed to restore the country to self-sufficiency within twelve to eighteen months.[44] But the end of the fighting and the election of a Republican Congress in November 1918 generated a "business as usual" mood in the United States, signaling a return to private loans at prevailing commercial interest rates. Even before the new Congress took office in March 1919, discovery that Britain was using American credits for loans to Belgium, thus undercutting the New York bankers in their quest for profit, led to a decision by the outgoing Congress on 15 February 1919 that henceforth European loans should be made by private bankers, not the United States government.[45] By May, Hoover was fighting to preserve previously authorized funds for food shipments to Belgium. As reconstruction credits evaporated, some American firms financed their own exports to Europe because they sorely needed markets to compensate for a cut in domestic consumption. One American locomotive works financed $11.6 million in sales to Belgium in 1919 alone.[46] Although such expedients provided some urgently needed equipment, they did not solve the larger problem of systematic reconstruction or the cash to pay for it. Throughout the peace conference and until Albert's trip to America in September 1919, Belgian leaders of every persuasion pleaded incessantly but with rapidly diminishing success for additional credits toward reconstruction. Because these were not forthcoming, the Delacroix cabinet borrowed heavily on commercial markets, contributing further to Belgium's financial instability.[47]

As time passed, the American government increasingly took the view that even private loans should be discouraged until European war debts

44. Hoover to Wilson, 21 Oct. 1918, Hoover Papers/4; O'Brien, *Wartime Correspondence*, p. 278.

45. Van den Ven to Delacroix, 14 Mar. 1919, de Gaiffier to Hymans, 18 Mar. 1919, no. 2123/837, BMAE B-366/I; Parrini, *Heir to Empire*, pp. 49–50; Baudhuin, *Histoire économique*, 1:106–7; Baudhuin, "La Richesse," p. 9.

46. O'Brien, *Two Peacemakers*, p. 145; Parrini, *Heir to Empire*, pp. 76–77. Belgium and the other debtor governments paid for these purchases in small annual amounts.

47. Vernon Bartlett, *Behind the Scenes at the Paris Peace Conference, 1919*, pp. 88–89; Moncheur to Hymans, 22 Sept. 1919, no. 5827/1887; BMAE GB/1919/II; Margerie to

were funded. This policy became an additional impediment to credits for Belgium because, as a consequence of the struggle over Senate approval of the Versailles treaty, Wilson did not inform the Congress until 22 February 1921, just before he left office, of the 16 June 1919 agreement about the Belgian pre-Armistice debt. As neither this arrangement nor the Versailles treaty was ever approved by the Senate, the American portion of Belgium's war debt reverted from Germany to Belgium, who reached a funding agreement with the United States on 18 August 1925.[48] By that time, Belgium was largely restored to self-sufficiency but chiefly by her own efforts and her own mounting debts, not by any American or Allied reconstruction schemes, as none ever materialized. Partly as a consequence, Belgium never recovered her prominent prewar rank in world trade.[49]

As early as 1921 American interest in Belgium, once so sympathetic, had largely narrowed to concern that the war debt be funded and that post-Armistice loans be promptly repaid out of the first monies received from Germany. When it became clear in the summer of 1921 that Belgium would at last receive some cash from German reparations, the prospect of having to turn all of it over to Britain and America for repayment of post-Armistice governmental loans, in accordance with the agreement on Belgian priority of 24 June 1919, was so alarming to the Belgian government that Georges Theunis, then finance minister, made a trip to London in July. He appears to have enlisted British support in persuading the United States not to press for immediate repayment of post-Armistice governmental loans. Nonetheless, virtually all of the 350 million marks that Belgium ultimately gained from the first milliard gold marks paid by Germany on reparations account in

Pichon, 31 Mar. 1919, tel. 153, Vin 6N/128; Baudhuin, *Histoire économique*, pp. 106–7; Baudhuin, "La Richesse," p. 9.

48. Walworth, *America's Moment*, pp. 245–48; Joan Hoff Wilson, *American Business and Foreign Policy, 1920–1933*, p. 118; de Cartier to Jaspar, 23 Feb. 1921, tel. 43, BMAE B-366/III; FRUS PPC, 13:398. The Belgian war debt to the United States (excluding interest) was $178,780,000. The total pre- and post-Armistice debts, before interest roughly doubled them, amounted to $423,587,630. In principal and interest, Belgium paid $52,191,273. *World Almanac*, 1979, p. 334.

49. In addition to all Belgium's other losses, Belgian business and finance had invested heavily in Russia, Germany, Austria, and Turkey before the war, and few of these holdings were recovered. Baudhuin, "La Balance," p. 45.

the summer of 1921 went towaud repayment of private loans from British and American bankers.[50]

The Belgians, who continued to think primarily in terms of European nations and especially the "faithful guarantor powers," accepted the American withdrawal with a fair degree of equanimity but reacted with alarm to British indifference. Their concern and their persistent illusory hopes of British support arose primarily from fear of France. From the Armistice on, the French made no attempt to hide their intention of displacing British influence in Belgium. When a state of peace officially arrived, the early displays of French military might in Brussels were replaced by other more subtle but equally recognizable techniques. The French were the first to elevate their legation in Brussels to an embassy and they sent an exceptionally aggressive and senior ambassador, Pierre de Margerie, who arrived with pockets filled with money and minor medals, both lavishly distributed in a moderately successful effort to influence the Belgian press. French visitors to Belgian ceremonial occasions were invariably numerous, high ranking, and unmatched by the British. They reiterated the refrain stressed by politicians in Paris and by Margerie in Brussels that France was Belgium's only friend.[51]

France attempted to emphasize Belgian dependence upon French support by drawing attention whenever possible to the inadequacy of British backing for Belgium.[52] The reparations issue and the long nego-

50. BMAE B-366/IV, 24 May–23 Aug. 1921, passim; BMAE B-10.497 passim; Wadsworth to Hughes, 5 Dec. 1921, tel. 58, SD 462.00R29/1296. It appears likely that the price of British assistance was Belgian agreement that Britain receive 450 million of the first milliard marks. However, the main file at the BMAE Archive on U.S. debts has been permanently mislaid, and the telegrams in BMAE B-366/IV and B-10.497 do not present the full story. The Theunis papers remain closed at the time of writing.

51. Villiers to Hardinge, 4, 23 Dec. 1919, Hardinge Papers/39; Whitlock, *Letters*, 2:588, 595; Derby to Balfour, 6 Jan. 1919, tel. 31, F.O. 371/3638; Villiers to Curzon, 31 Jan. 1919, no. 53, F.O. 371/3637; G. Grahame to Curzon, 18 Nov. 1920, no. 824A, F.O. 371/5455; G. Grahame to Curzon, 29 Sept. 1920, no. 696, F.O. 371/5458; Curzon to Balfour, 24 June 1919, F.O. 800/217; Whitlock to Colby, 3 Jan. 1921, no. 1080, SD 751.55/1; documents requested by Poincaré, 19 June 1919, FMAE Z/Belg./56. Margerie arrived in March as minister but was pointedly elevated to ambassador on 28 June 1919, the day the Versailles treaty was signed. Auffray, *Pierre de Margerie*, pp. 356–60.

52. G. Grahame to Curzon, 18 Nov. 1920, no. 824A, F.O. 371/5455.

tiations over revision of the 1839 treaties provided opportunities for invidious comparisons, and other openings were frequently seized or created. France also tried to draw Belgium into the French orbit by insistent offers of a military pact and by emphatic diplomatic support to Belgium except where French and Belgian interests clashed, as they did in Luxemburg, in the Rhineland, and over economic policy. Belgium continued to fear French economic domination, especially because French policy was protectionist and Belgian policy was not. Thus the Belgian government continued to fight steadily against French devices toward economic subjection, notably renewed demands for a customs union and the *surtaxe d'entrepôt* levied upon all goods entering France through Antwerp. Although the surtax arose originally from French domestic considerations concerning the channel ports, which clung vociferously to their privileged position, the price of removing it appeared to be a Belgian economic accord with France. This Belgium resisted and sought instead and in vain entry into the free-trade orbit of Britain.[53]

Belgian efforts to escape French economic pressure by means of an arrangement with Britain began well before the Armistice and continued after peace was established. Belgium initially sought imperial preference but later indicated that a customs union or some lesser arrangement would be equally acceptable. At first, particularly before the Armistice, the Belgian proposals were well received by the Foreign Office and the Board of Trade, chiefly out of sympathy, a sense of moral obligation to aid in the restoration of Belgium, and a fear that, unless

---

53. G. Grahame to Curzon, 9 Feb. 1921, no. 125, F.O. 371/6041; G. Grahame to Curzon, 18, 27 Dec. 1920, no. 906, 918, F.O. 371/5460; Curzon memo, 30 Apr. 1919, F.O. 800/152; Michel Malmain, *Les Relations commerciales franco-belges de 1913 à 1923*, pp. 80–81, 204–5; Whitlock, *Letters*, 2:634. The 1919 Franco-Belgian economic talks failed in October. On goods shipped to Strasbourg, the surtax was partially suppressed on 23 December 1919 at the urgent request of Strasbourg and fully suppressed on 18 April 1921. On 9 April 1921, France declared that she would abolish the surtax completely but, apart from the Alsace-Lorraine traffic, did not. A much more limited commercial treaty than France wanted was concluded on 12 May 1923, but the Belgian Chamber rejected it on 27 February 1924, causing Jaspar's departure from the Foreign Ministry. A limited modus vivendi ensued until a Franco-Belgian commercial treaty was signed on 23 February 1928. Willequet, "Problèmes économiques," pp. 312–13; Soutou, "La Politique économique," pp. 268–71; G. Grahame to Curzon, 10 Apr., 10 Oct. 1921, tel. 66, no. 884, F.O. 371/6957; Suetens, *Politique commerciale*, pp. 195–209.

some special provision were made, Belgium would again come under German economic domination. As time passed and it became evident that German domination was improbable, both the sympathy and the sense of moral obligation evaporated. Despite its concern about mounting French economic pressure on Belgium, the British cabinet rejected the request for imperial preference on 9 May 1919, while leaving open the possibility of some lesser arrangement.[54] Though Belgian diplomatists and cabinet ministers indicated openly that France was then pressing for sweeping economic arrangements that the British recognized would be to their detriment, Britain was more concerned about future Belgian competition and setting a precedent for other small Continental Allies.[55] As it became increasingly clear that an extensive Franco-Belgian economic agreement was unlikely,[56] nothing further was done. Although the Belgians renewed their overtures toward an economic alliance from time to time, particularly after Henri Jaspar became foreign minister late in 1920, British policy was more and more dictated by Lloyd George's hostility to Belgium, which was intensified by the fact that Belgian pig iron was selling on the Glasgow market at half the price of the local product, and by his realization that any Belgian economic revival could only mean competition for Britain's battered trade balance.[57]

Belgium's frequent efforts to flee from France to Britain in large matters and small encountered not only Lloyd George's hostility but also little response, chiefly because British policy toward Belgium was contingent upon British policy toward France, and that was uncertain but, with the passage of time, increasingly antagonistic, as Lloyd George reverted to Britain's traditional preoccupation with the Continental

54. Kearney memos, 10 Aug., 25 Sept. 1918, Wellesley to Cecil, 26 Aug. 1918, Wellesley minute, 31 Oct. 1918, F.O. 371/3165; Steel-Maitland to Cecil, 28 Sept. 1918, Cecil memo, 26 Oct. 1918, Cecil Papers/51094; W.C. 565, 9 May 1919, CAB 23/10; F.O. to Maskens, 26 May, 14 July 1919, F.O. 608/217.

55. Steel-Maitland to War Cabinet, 6 May 1919, G.T. 7206, CAB 24/79.

56. G. Grahame to Curzon, 18, 27 Dec. 1920, nos. 906, 918, F.O. 371/5460.

57. Villiers to Curzon, 1 Apr. 1920, no. 196, F.O. 371/3649; Cabinet 33 (20), 7 June 1920, CAB 23/31; D'Abernon Diary, 22 Dec. 1920, BL D'Abernon Papers/48953; Landsberg to AA, 20 Nov. 1920, GFM 4, Series L, Politik 2, L000725–31, 1:249; Jacques Bardoux, *Lloyd George et la France*, pp. 18, 19, 30; Edgar Vincent, Viscount D'Abernon, *An Ambassador of Peace*, 1:104–5.

balance of power. As he and other British leaders fretted about French military might, yearned to restore prewar patterns of trade (except for Belgium), and demanded drastic dilution of the Versailles treaty, the gulf between Britain and France steadily widened, and British hostility to French policy became pronounced. Because the entire British policy-making establishment assumed Belgium to be an appendage of France, the opprobrium extended also to the Belgians.

The British view of Belgium as a French satellite was rarely accurate and, when it occasionally was, Belgium had usually been pushed into this uncomfortable position by British policy. The British tended to ignore most Belgian overtures and to refuse all requests for rescue from France and then, having driven an isolated and exposed Belgium reluctantly into the eager arms of France, invariably expressed great indignation at finding Belgium just where they had always assumed her to be. Mounting British irritation with France did not generate any gestures toward Belgium or any thought of cultivating the crucial Belgian vote in the Reparation Commission. Even the appointment of the socially ambitious Lord Curzon, whose greatest social achievement was his carefully cultivated friendship with King Albert, as foreign secretary in October 1919 brought no benefit to Belgium, because he was disliked by his colleagues, had very limited control over British foreign policy, and partook of the prevailing view that the Belgians were slavish French lackeys who should obey his commands without question. His complaints were unending and he showed little more inclination than his colleagues to make either symbolic gestures or substantive concessions to Belgium.

RESIDUAL PROBLEMS
AND BELGIAN RESPONSES

All in all, the combination of American withdrawal, French insistence, and British indifference left Belgium with extraordinarily little room for maneuver as she addressed the residue of problems remaining before the peace conference after the Versailles treaty was completed. Important among these in Belgian eyes were a new security arrangement to replace the discredited neutrality guarantee and certain aspects of the treaties with the lesser Central Powers. In regard to the latter, Belgian interest focused primarily on the treaty with Turkey. However, her efforts were circumscribed by the fact, illustrative of the limits upon small-power diplomacy, that although Belgium was a signatory of the Treaty of Sèvres, she was not a party to its negotiation.[58] Under the circumstances, it is not surprising that her efforts to gain her desires met with no success.

Belgian concern with the Treaty of Sèvres focused on two issues, one financial and one emotional. The lesser but more emotive issue, which aroused great indignation in Belgium, concerned Palestine. Even before the end of the war, the Belgian government had hinted at an interest in participating in any future international administration of this area, possibly through the appointment of Albert to the presidency of a future commission. In the summer of 1919, Cardinal Mercier proposed to the former British prime minister, H. H. Asquith, that Albert be made protector of the Holy Places.[59] In view of British plans for Palestine, these feelers came to naught and Belgian concern thereafter focused on one particular holy place in Jerusalem, the Dormition of the Holy Virgin. Before World War I, this establishment, including a basilica and a monastery, had been German property occupied by a congregation of German Benedictine monks. In January 1919, the British authorities expelled the German Benedictines. Through the intercession of a Belgian monk, Pope Benedict XV agreed to their provisional replacement by Belgian Benedictines, although German ownership re-

58. Courtesy of Paul Helmreich (letter of 16 June 1977 to author). See also Hymans to de Gaiffier, 5 Jan. 1920, no. 55, de Gaiffier to Hymans, 4, 6 Mar. 1920, nos. 2827/1660, 2951/1712, BMAE FR/1920/I. During World War I, Belgium had severed diplomatic relations with Turkey. Belgium also signed the Treaty of Neuilly with Bulgaria.

59. Hymans instructions for Belgian mission to Italy, 1918, Hymans Papers/184; Moncheur to Hymans, 26 July 1919, no. 4734/1524, BMAE GB/1919/II. This proposal had been aired from time to time during the war and the peace conference, along with suggestions that Albert or Belgium administer or preside over a commission for Constantinople and the straits. The Belgian government was careful not to make any proposals regarding either Palestine or Constantinople but would have been delighted if another power had done so. Moncheur to Hymans, 7 Feb. 1919, no. 1023/269, BMAE GB/1919/I; de Gaiffier to Hymans, 3 Jan. 1920, no. 49/28, Hymans to de Gaiffier, 5 Jan. 1920, no. 55, BMAE FR/1920/I.

mained unimpaired and the German Benedictines retained the right to reclaim the foundation after the peace settlement. To the joy of Catholic Belgium, the Belgian Benedictines took charge of the Dormition on 11 March 1919.[60]

From June of 1919 on, the Belgian delegation at Paris attempted to render the Belgian possession of the Dormition permanent, resting their case at first on Article 438 of the Versailles treaty, whereby Germany waived her claims to religious missions in territories ceded to the Allies and gave prior consent to their transfer to other agents of the same religious faith, and then on Article 155, which committed Germany to accept in advance the eventual treaty with Turkey. Both the Vatican and the British government, the prospective mandatory power in Palestine, deemed the matter to fall under the Turkish treaty and referred the question to negotiators at the peace conference. Accordingly, Edouard Rolin-Jaequemyns, who remained in Paris for the negotiation of the Treaty of Sèvres and who ultimately signed it on Belgium's behalf, pursued the matter there. But he was unable to gain either admission to the negotiating sessions or the ear of the major powers, and so nothing was done. As a consequence, Britain returned the Dormition to its former occupants, an arrangement that was confirmed on 21 August 1920, and the German Benedictines replaced the Belgian monks in 1921. Although the question was trivial, Belgian opinion viewed it as only one more example of the ill will and indifference of her erstwhile Allies.[61] In response to this public emotion, Hymans expended undue amounts of energy and diplomatic capital in a futile quest over a minor issue where Belgium's legal case had been very weak from the outset.

During the negotiation of the Treaty of Sèvres, Belgian diplomatists pursued another issue with equal futility. They made repeated efforts

60. Vicomte Terlinden, "La Vérité sur l'échec belge à Jérusalem," pp. 3–4; Terlinden interview; *La Nation belge*, 5 Apr. 1919, p. 3; van Zuylen to Hymans, 1 Feb. 1919, no. 20/8, BMAE B-10.806. The Belgian monks were sent from the abbey of Maredsous in Belgium.

61. BMAE B-10.806, passim; Terlinden, "La Vérité," pp. 3–4. Dom Marmion, abbot of Maredsous, had promised at the outset to return the Dormition to German Benedictines later, but then he tried to obtain permanent possession. D'Ursel to Hymans, 22 Aug. 1919, no. 165/87; Marmion to Hymans, 10 Sept. 1919, BMAE B-10.806.

to gain Belgian representation on any bodies to be established to administer Turkish finances, arguing that, after France, Belgium carried the most shares and that the "proportion of the Turkish debt owing to Belgium is greater even than that owing to Great Britain."[62] As with the monastery, Belgian diplomatic efforts were directed primarily at the British, but Curzon explained that only the three great powers would participate in the International Commission of Financial Control. This decision apparently arose from determination to exclude Greece but effectively excluded Belgium as well. The British at first were more forthcoming about representation on the Council for the Ottoman Debt but then began to argue that, as this body was about to expire, there was no point in adding Belgium to it. As a consequence, Belgium did not gain a seat on the temporary Council for the Ottoman Debt established by Article 246 of the Treaty of Sèvres.[63]

In the course of their campaign concerning the Ottoman debt, the Belgians tried to trade abandonment of the Anglo-French interim guarantee for a voice in Turkish finances.[64] This tactic constituted recognition that another long Belgian diplomatic drive had failed and amounted to an offer to relinquish something already lost for another goal where some faint hope lingered. By the time this gambit was tried in late January 1920, it had become clear that Belgium could expect no security guarantees either in conjunction with revision of the 1839 treaties or as a consequence of the Anglo-American guarantee of France of 28

62. Derby to Curzon, 23 Jan. 1920, F.O. 371/3643; Hymans to Moncheur, 9 Mar. 1920, no. 50, Moncheur to Hymans, 16 Mar. 1920, no. 1207/418, BMAE GB/1920.

63. Moncheur to Hymans, 12, 16, 26 Mar. 1920. nos. 1137/393, 1207/418, 1447/502, BMAE GB/1920; Article 246, Treaty of Sèvres, in Fred. L. Israel, ed., *Major Peace Treaties of Modern History*, 3:2141. Belgium was not allowed to sign the Treaty of Lausanne of 24 July 1923, which replaced that of Sèvres. Turkey was determined to limit the Lausanne Conference and treaty to the countries listed in the 23 September 1922 Franco-British-Italian note of invitation to Turkey, partly to exclude a variety of other small powers, partly to force Belgium to a separate commercial treaty. A small Belgian delegation under Moncheur was sent to Lausanne and ultimately gained admission to some meetings of the Economic and Financial Commissions. However, Ismet Inönü threatened to reject the treaty if additional powers signed it. Thus, Belgium was permitted only to sign a special protocol on 24 July 1923, adhering to the economic and financial clauses of the treaty. BMAE B-10.509, B-10.513–14, passim.

64. Derby to Curzon, 23 Jan. 1920, F.O. 371/3643.

June 1919.[65] The Belgians had long hoped that the Anglo-American guarantee could be extended to them but had not pressed the matter as vigorously as the interim guarantee proposed in connection with revision of the 1839 treaties. Their diffidence arose from ignorance of events, fear that additional concessions might be asked of them as the price of extending the Anglo-American guarantee to Belgium, and distrust of France. In addition, Belgian leaders still rarely thought in terms of the United States but rather of the "faithful guarantor powers." Thus they consistently treated as a secondary matter a guarantee that, had it materialized, could have been vital for Belgian security.

When the Anglo-American guarantee of France was initially proposed in connection with the Rhineland negotiations on 14 March 1919 at Paris, the first written French response of 17 March included a postscript, adding, "It goes without saying that by act of aggression against France, the French government understands also any aggression against Belgium." The American delegation was in March proceeding on the same assumption,[66] but the Belgians knew nothing of it until rumors reached them at the beginning of May. Tardieu then confirmed that the guarantee was under consideration and that Clemenceau hoped to be able to surprise Hymans within two or three days with news concerning it. Nothing happened; France did not press the matter; and there was no discussion among the powers about guaranteeing Belgium. When Tardieu read a declaration about the Anglo-American guarantee of France to the closed plenary session of the peace conference on 6 May 1919, Jules Cambon urged Hymans to speak out and demand inclusion of Belgium. Hymans sensibly declined to lay the matter before a plenary session, but he did inquire at the Quai d'Orsay. Tardieu explained that Clemenceau desired the inclusion of Belgium but that the guarantee had been achieved only at the last minute, and so Clemenceau deemed it wise to let a little time elapse before raising the added complication of extending it. The next day, however, Tardieu announced that Clemenceau now wished to discuss such a guarantee within a few days and was willing to visit Brussels in the immediate

65. For texts, see FRUS PPC, 13:757–62.
66. Tardieu, *Truth*, p. 217; Lansing, *Peace Negotiations*, pp. 179–80; Lansing memo, 20 Mar. 1919, Lansing Papers IV/1919.

future to settle the matter with King Albert himself. Hymans concluded that France was less interested in an extension of the Anglo-American guarantee than in a Franco-Belgian military accord. The rest of the Belgian delegation was similarly cautious and Delacroix, when consulted, decided that Belgium should not request the guarantee because the price in concessions, most likely in regard to reparations, would probably be too great.[67]

In late June, the French took the initiative again. Clemenceau gave Hymans the texts of the British and American letters of 6 May 1919 to Clemenceau concerning the Anglo-American guarantee and urged him to consider extension of the guarantee to Belgium, with France joining as third guarantor. Hymans remained wary and the Belgian cabinet in consultation with the king decided to take no initiative.[68] The progress of negotiation for revision of the 1839 treaties, however, led Belgium to fear that her security might be neglected. Thus, because the Versailles treaty was safely signed and Belgium need no longer fear being asked to make additional concessions in respect to its terms, Hymans revived the question during a French ceremonial visit to Liège on 24 July 1919 and proposed to Poincaré and Pichon that an Anglo-American-French guarantee be incorporated in the new treaty to replace those of 1839. Late in August during talks in Paris with Clemenceau and other French officials, Hymans raised the matter once more, only to find the French more interested in a direct Franco-Belgian pact. The French eagerness to extend the joint guarantee had largely disappeared and they made no further effort to do so.[69]

Because an accord with France alone was not a pleasing prospect to Belgium, London was sounded about the possibility of an extended Anglo-American-French guarantee, and when Moncheur reported optimistically, Hymans raised the matter again with Poincaré on 13 September. Although he hinted that the Luxemburg question must be resolved before a French guarantee could be accepted, a week later Hymans

67. Hymans memo, 8 May 1919, Orts memo, 8 May 1919, BMAE Ind/1919/I; Orts to Hymans, 8 May 1919, BMAE DB/13/I.
68. Anglo-American letters to Clemenceau, 6 May 1919, with Pichon notation, 27 June 1919, FMAE A/163; Hymans memo, 28 June 1919, BMAE Ind/1919/I.
69. Hymans memo, 25 July 1919, BMAE Ind/1919/I; Hymans, *Mémoires*, 2:532; DDB, 1:87.

nonetheless formally requested British and French extension of the guarantee to Belgium. Shortly thereafter, King Albert, who was visiting the United States, talked to Lansing, who assured him that if the Senate approved the French treaty, there should be no difficulty about extending the guarantee to Belgium. The Belgian government was briefly optimistic, particularly when Britain ratified its guarantee of France, but by mid-October, Curzon was arguing that British opinion would not accept such a guarantee of Belgium and Villiers was echoing the same sentiment in Brussels.[70] By this time, British leaders recognized that the American guarantee of France might well fail to be approved, and they did not wish to take on any Continental commitment, especially an indefinite one, without the United States at their side. Although the British press was giving full support to Belgium,[71] the British government's reaction to the request for an interim guarantee in connection with the revision of the 1839 treaties was an equally discouraging indicator.

As the year came to a close, Belgian attempts to discuss the tripartite guarantee with the United States came to naught when Lansing replied that the moment was not opportune. With the further passage of time, acceptance of the French treaty by the American Senate became increasingly unlikely,[72] and the issue of the tripartite guarantee gradually subsided. The extended guarantee, which would have been easily obtainable at the peace conference if either Clemenceau or Hymans had pressed for it, had as a result of changing circumstances and policies become an impossibility. Perhaps Hymans should have vigorously sought the Anglo-American guarantee when he finally learned of it in May 1919. However, subsequent events, notably the failure of the

70. Moncheur to Hymans, 10 Sept. 1919, no. 5599/1810, BMAE GB/1919/II; Hymans to Moncheur, 19 Sept. 1919, tel., Hymans to de Gaiffier, 20 Sept. 1919, BMAE Ind/1919/II; DBFP, 5:392–93, 491, 621, 752–53; DDB, 1:33–37; de Cartier to Hymans, 30 Oct. 1919, no. 7742, B Micro/23; British Delegation to Dutasta, 3 Nov. 1919, FMAE A/163.

71. For example, *Times*, 12 Oct. 1920, p. 11.

72. Whitlock to Lansing, 18 Nov. 1919, tel. 395, Lansing to Whitlock, 22 Nov. 1919, tel. 541, Whitlock to Lansing, 8 Jan. 1920, tel. 7, SD 711.55/–, 1; Hymans to de Cartier, 6 Jan. 1920, tel. 3, B Micro/24; Hymans to Albert, 9 Dec. 1919, BMAE Ind/1919/II; DDB, 1:71–76, 87, 90–91, 96. The Versailles treaty was again rejected by the United States Senate on 19 March 1920.

American Senate to vote on the French treaty and the consequent lapse of the British guarantee of France, which was contingent upon the American one, indicate that any victory Belgium might have gained in this respect in 1919 would undoubtedly have turned into nothingness by 1920, no matter how energetically Hymans had pursued the matter.

The Belgian request for the extended guarantee was a secondary effort in pursuit of a primary goal: reinforcement of Belgian security. This goal was pursued through several tactics, none of which succeeded. When the Versailles treaty entered into force on 10 January 1920, Belgian leaders were overwhelmingly conscious that World War I had only destroyed the discredited neutrality guarantee without replacing it. Their bitterness[73] arose in large part from realization that the net effect of four years of suffering was that Belgium now stood alone and exposed against her great neighbors, both Germany and France. They knew that Belgian security had been weakened, not enhanced, by both the war and the peace. Under the circumstances, it is not surprising that Belgian diplomacy for the next five years was constantly preoccupied with the problem of seeking some protection to ensure the future security of the kingdom.

Perhaps fortunately, the failure of all security guarantees still lay in the future when the Belgian Parliament debated the Versailles treaty in May 1919 and voted upon it in August. During the summer of 1919 the lapse of the Anglo-American guarantee to France was not yet predictable and the negotiations to revise the 1839 treaties were just beginning in a spirit of cautious optimism about security guarantees, if not about other matters. Indeed at the time of the parliamentary debates in May, Dutch territorial transfer and international servitudes had not yet been excluded. While the future of Luxemburg remained unsettled, one could still hope for economic union, and members of the Belgian Parliament had every reason to believe that their delegation had won substantial victories on reparations, which most of them assumed Germany would pay promptly and in full.

Still, the debate indicated little pleasure in anything except the reduction in German power. Both Flemish and Walloon leaders demonstrated great concern over the economic future and "hoped" rather

73. Whitlock, *Letters*, 2:583.

doubtfully that the Allies would adhere to their promises. They agreed that Belgium's life or death depended upon the application of the Versailles treaty, particularly its reparation clauses. One Flemish representative, warning that the amounts inscribed in the Belgian budget for German reparation receipts were unrealistic, remarked that it was painful to see Belgium, who had been so great during the war, become so small since the Armistice. A senior Catholic leader said flatly that the treaty was not satisfactory to Belgium: though recriminations against Britain and the United States should be avoided, these powers should be told that the treaty did not provide enough safeguards for Belgian economic restoration and security. The government, he said, should seek improvements by appealing to Anglo-American sympathy and good will.[74]

These appeals were duly made but accomplished nothing beyond formalization of the special arrangements for Belgian reparations and war debts, for Anglo-American sympathy and good will had long since been exhausted. As the parliamentary debate had indicated, Belgium would have to sign in any event. Thus on 28 June 1919 in the Hall of Mirrors at Versailles, all three Belgian plenipotentiaries put their signatures to the peace treaty, along with representatives of twenty-six other Allied nations and Germany. In August both chambers of the Belgian Parliament unanimously approved the Versailles treaty.[75] This unanimity reflected not enthusiasm but lack of choice. Belgium's small size and exposed location did not permit her the luxury of following the course of China and the United States. As Count Charles Woeste, the aged Catholic statesman, sadly noted, "We are under the control of a sort of *force majeure*."[76] That in fact had been Belgium's problem throughout the peace conference.

74. Belgique, Parlement, Chambre des Représentants, *Compte rendu*, 1918–19, pp. 902–4.

75. Margerie to Pichon, 8 Aug. 1919, tel. 561, Vin 6N/128; Joseph Lefèvre, *L'Angleterre et la Belgique à travers les cinq derniers siècles*, p. 291.

76. Belgique, Parlement, Chambre des Représentants, *Compte rendu*, 1918–19, p. 904.

EIGHT

POSTLUDE

UNFINISHED BUSINESS

It is a striking fact that none of the major Belgian claims at the Paris Peace Conference were settled with any degree of permanence. Virtually all of them returned to complicate European diplomacy throughout the next decade. When the senior dignitaries disbanded at the end of June in 1919, it was evident that key Belgian issues such as revision of the 1839 treaties, the Luxemburg question, and the problem of Belgian security remained to be resolved. Other claims, notably in regard to reparations and Eupen-Malmédy, appeared to be settled. Yet because Belgium was so much weaker than her great-power neighbors, even the "permanent" solutions lacked permanence.

Among the items of unfinished business, the two questions of Luxemburg and Belgian security quickly merged, mainly because France insisted that a Franco-Belgian military accord was its price for a Belgian solution to the Luxemburg problem. As the Belgians equally insisted that the status of Luxemburg must be resolved before a military accord could be discussed, the conjunction between the two issues became absolute. In the contest of wills that ensued, the Belgians held firm despite their lack of military security. Their determination arose from Hymans's doggedness, concern over the Luxemburg railways, and deep reluctance to enter a bilateral military arrangement without the counterbalancing protection of Britain. Belgian leaders considered a British tie necessary not only to protect the kingdom against French domination but also to placate the large Flemish population whose traditional hostility to France remained unabated. All overtures to Britain were unavailing, however, and ultimately Belgium accepted the military agreement in return for unfulfilled French promises concerning the Luxemburg railways.

Early in January 1920, when the Versailles treaty was entering into force and the idea of an interim Anglo-French guarantee had just been abandoned, France renewed its long-standing request for immediate negotiations on a military accord. In response, Hymans reiterated the Belgian conditions: British participation and prior solution of the Luxemburg question. When Margerie made a thinly veiled suggestion that France should conduct Belgian foreign affairs, Hymans flared into a sharp statement of Belgian independence. As the Belgian cabinet endorsed his position,[1] the impasse continued. The replacement of Clemenceau by Alexandre Millerand and of Berthelot by Maurice Paléologue improved the tone of Franco-Belgian relations considerably but had no real effect upon the issue, nor did a meeting at Ieper on 28 January of Albert and his ministers with Poincaré and his. France insisted upon majority control of the Guillaume-Luxembourg railway and a military accord, but Belgium held to its stand.[2] The Belgian cabinet again confirmed Hymans's policy, adding that economic problems with France, notably the *surtaxe d'entrepôt*, must also be resolved. France responded by initialing a railway convention with Luxemburg on 7 February.[3] Then Margerie unsuccessfully tried to browbeat Albert into accepting a military pact without French concessions. Though each side continued to present proposals for the other to reject, by mid-March the situation had changed little since mid-January. Only the hostility had increased.[4]

The British were fully aware of the Franco-Belgian tension but made no attempt to capitalize upon it. After the British legation was finally raised to an embassy, Villiers was allowed to stay on as ambassador until the summer of 1920, when he retired. This kindly act meant a continuing

1. Hymans, *Mémoires*, 2:534–35; DDB, 1:320; Margerie to FMAE, 10, 27 Jan. 1920, tels. 42, 72, FMAE Z/Lux/33.

2. DDB, 1:307–13; Hymans, *Mémoires*, 2:536–37. The Belgians were delighted when Deschanel defeated Clemenceau for the presidency of France. Deschanel had been born in Schaerbeek of a Liègeoise mother, had passed his childhood in Brussels, and had always showed himself a warm friend of Belgium, but his health broke before he could be of any help. De Gaiffier to Hymans, 19 Jan. 1920, no. 659/360, BMAE FR/1920/I; de Gaiffier to Hymans, 29 Apr. 1922, no. 5193/2383, BMAE FR/1922.

3. Hymans to de Gaiffier, 31 Jan. 1920, no. 631, BMAE FR/1920/I; Mollard to Millerand, 7 Feb. 1920, FMAE Z/Lux/33.

4. DDB, 1:333–37, 340–46; Hymans memo, 9 Feb. 1920, de Gaiffier to Hymans, 12 Feb., 11 Mar. 1920, nos. 1552/756, 3123/1794, BMAE FR/1920/I; Millerand to de Gaiffier, 19 Feb. 1920, FMAE Z/Lux/33; Margerie to FMAE, 10 Feb. 1920, tel. 88–97, de Gaiffier to Paléologue, 5 Mar. 1920, Millerand to Margerie, 7 Mar. 1920, FMAE Z/Belg./57.

passive British presence in Brussels, because Villiers was no match for the energetic Margerie. The Foreign Office was unconcerned, however. Hymans kept Villiers informed of the impasse with France, stressing Belgium's desire for British participation in any military talks that might result. Although the British army and War Office, which consistently favored ties to France and Belgium, showed some interest, the rest of the British government did not. Both Lloyd George and Curzon declined all overtures and took no advantage of the Belgo-French deadlock, passively observing from the sidelines.[5]

Actually, the French had begun to concede inch by inch. Though mystified by Belgian stubbornness, Millerand and Foch badly wanted the military accord to cover the traditional invasion route from Germany into France.[6] Thus the French conceded first minority Belgian representation in the direction of the Guillaume-Luxembourg network and then equal representation under a French president, which still amounted to a smaller Belgian voice. Similarly, France abandoned its insistence on a military convention without reference to other issues. First it proposed simultaneous discussion of the Luxemburg railways and then, on 13 March, Millerand conceded prior discussion of this question. After some further dispute, on 7 April France accepted Hymans's terms: experts would examine the entirety of the problem of the Guillaume-Luxembourg network and, if negotiations advanced rapidly toward agreement, the military authorities would commence negotiation fifteen days later.[7]

The timing of Millerand's concession owed much to France's need for diplomatic support in a crisis set off by events in Germany. On the heels of the Kapp *putsch* in Berlin on 13 March 1920, first the revolutionary German government and then the restored Weimar regime

5. DDB, 1:304–6, 314–17; Villiers to Curzon, 2, 21 Feb. 1920, nos. 61, 108, F.O. 371/3637; Cambon to Curzon, 2 Feb. 1920, F.O. 371/3648; de Gaiffier to Hymans, 3 Feb. 1920, Hymans Papers/151; Hymans memos, 24 Mar., 1 Apr. 1920, BMAE FR/1920/I.

6. Joostens to de Gaiffier, 15 Feb. 1920, BMAE PB/1920; Millerand to Margerie, 20 Feb. 1920, tel. 394, FMAE Z/Lux/33.

7. Margerie note, 23 Mar. 1920, BMAE FR/1920/I; DDB, 1:344–45; Millerand to Margerie, 7 Mar. 1920, Margerie to Millerand, 29 Mar., 7 Apr. 1920, tel. 191–92, 209–212, FMAE Z/Belg./57.

repeatedly sought Entente permission to send additional troops into
the nominally demilitarized zone to repress disturbances in the Ruhr
valley. In the absence of any agreement among the Entente powers, no
response was made to Germany, who on 20 March and 2 April thus
dispatched additional forces to the Ruhr without Allied consent. On 1
April, Millerand promised the British that he would not act unilaterally,[8]
but on 4 April he set French forces in motion and by 6 April, France
had occupied Frankfurt and four surrounding towns. Although the other
Allied powers had been warned, they had not consented,[9] and France,
in isolation vis-à-vis Germany, sorely needed diplomatic and military
reinforcement.

The British and Belgian cabinets both met on 8 April. In London, the
British decided to protest, to withdraw Lord Derby from the Conference
of Ambassadors, and to seek Belgian and Italian support.[10] Though
underestimating the intensity of British displeasure, the Belgian government assumed that Britain would neither endorse nor participate in
the French action. They merely hoped in vain that Britain would not
publicly disavow France. The deliberations in Brussels were more complicated, for the day before, in the course of seeking Belgian support at
Frankfurt, Margerie had announced French acceptance of Hymans's
latest formula for talks on the Guillaume-Luxembourg network and a
military accord. The connection was clear. Thus, Hymans told the cabinet that, beyond the need to maintain as much Allied unity as possible
toward Germany, to join France to restrain her if possible, and to avoid
French isolation in the face of Germany, it was likely that sending a
token contingent to Frankfurt would end the deadlock with France.
Joining Britain in disapproval would offend France and render a settlement with her impossible without bringing any compensatory concessions from Britain. In brief, nothing could be gained by following
Britain, whereas Luxemburg would be obtained by supporting France.
He therefore recommended that Belgium send troops to Frankfurt on

8. Derby to Curzon, 18 Mar. 1920, tel. 310, F.O. 371/3780; DBFP, 9:158–60, 283–
84; DDB, 1:117–25, 159, 217–18.
9. Hymans, *Mémoires*, 2:543; DBFP, 9:321–23, 326; DDB, 1:224; *La Libre Belgique*,
9 Apr. 1920, p. 1; K. Nelson, *Victors Divided*, p. 167; de Gaiffier to Hymans, 6 Apr.
1920, no. 4025/2218, BMAE FR/1920/I.
10. Cabinet 18 (2), 8 Apr. 1920, CAB 23/21.

condition that the occupation end as soon as the German troops left the Ruhr. At the same time, Belgium should express disapproval of French methods and indicate her expectation of favorable solutions to pending questions, notably Luxemburg. As the cabinet unanimously agreed, a Belgian battalion entered Frankfurt on 14 April and remained until 17 May, when German troops evacuated the Ruhr.[11]

To the dismay of the Luxembourgeois cabinet, which discovered the rush of events from the press, Franco-Belgian negotiations began at once over the Guillaume-Luxembourg railway. Although both Mollard and Hymans promised the Luxembourgeois that they could participate in the final arrangements, they were not included in the Franco-Belgian talks that started in Brussels on 23 April. Though Belgium had suffered the humiliation of exclusion from decision making at the Paris Peace Conference, she was prepared, partly out of distrust of Reuter, to do unto a weaker power what had recently been done to her. At Brussels, agreement was quickly reached on a formula first proposed by Belgium in September 1919, whereby France would retain control of the rail lines south and east of Luxemburg City but the remainder of the net-work would be transferred to Belgian administration.[12] As complications arose over financial aspects of the settlement and Hymans termed mili-tary staff talks premature, on 7 May Millerand sent the long-promised word to Reuter that France would not conclude any economic arrange-ment with Luxemburg and advised the Grand Duchy to pursue an economic union with Belgium, adding that until this was done, France would abstain from all economic talks with Luxemburg, reserving only

11. Hymans, *Mémoires*, 2:544–45; DDB, 1:222–28, 241–44, 301; FRUS 1920, 2:321; Gosling to F.O., 15 Apr. 1920, tel. 19, F.O. 371/3784; Margerie to Millerand, 11 Apr. 1920, tel. 230, FMAE Z/Belg./57; Wertheimer to AA, 12 Apr. 1920, tel. Belgien 188, GFM 4, Series L, Politik 3, L001837–8; Hymans note, n.d., BMAE B-10.430. Vander-velde later claimed (DBFP, 8:805–8, Hankey Diary, 7 Nov. 1920, Hankey Papers 1/5) that this meeting was held in his absence and without his knowledge, but there seems to be no evidence in support of his contention, which in the light of all circumstances, seems improbable. Most likely, he was telling the British what they wanted to hear.

12. Mollard to Millerand, 13 Apr. 1920, tel. 25, Margerie to Millerand, 17 Apr. 1920, tel. 265, minutes 1st and 2d meetings, Belgo-French Commission, 23, 24 Apr. 1920, FMAE Z/Lux/34; DBFP, 12:40–41; Hymans to de Gaiffier, 22 Sept. 1919, BMAE Ind/1919/II; Hymans to d'Ansembourg, 16 Apr. 1920, no. 3516, Hymans to de Gaiffier, 16 Apr. 1920, no. 3553, de Laubespin (Paris) to Hymans, 17 Apr. 1920, no. 4307/2351, BMAE FR/1920/I; Hymans to de Gaiffier, 15 June 1920, no. 1101, BMAE GB/1920.

the right to regulate its economic interests there later in talks *à trois*. In the wake of this decisive French action, Belgian hesitations about concluding the rail negotiations and commencing staff talks promptly evaporated. Thus, on 26 May, with Luxembourgeois representatives in attendance, Franco-Belgian negotiators reached agreement on a definitive railway settlement, the French having given way on the financial questions at issue. Luxemburg not surprisingly disliked the division of its railway and presented a plan of its own but bowed for the moment to the united front of its more powerful neighbors.[13]

As a consequence of Millerand's categoric refusal of economic talks with Luxemburg and a tactfully warm Belgian welcome to Reuter when he visited Brussels immediately thereafter, negotiations began late in June 1920 toward a Belgo-Luxembourgeois economic union. Completion of the convention was long delayed by Luxembourgeois reluctance to divide the Guillaume-Luxembourg railway. Finally, in response to Belgian support of France during Supreme Council meetings, notably that of London in April–May 1921, France secretly renounced its rights on the network, subject to certain economic and military reserves. Thus a formal fifty-year Belgo-Luxembourgeois convention was concluded on 17 May 1921 and went into effect on 1 May 1922. In addition to a full customs union, this convention provided for circulation of Belgian currency in the Grand Duchy, Belgian consular representation of Luxemburg abroad, withdrawal of the French troops, patent reciprocity, and specialized economic measures to ease the adjustment. Further, Article 24 envisaged consolidation of the Luxemburg railways, including the Prince-Henri network, under the Belgian state railway administration, but this article never came into operation. Interminable difficulties developed between Belgium and France over both the economic and the military conditions of the informal agreement reached on 9 May 1921. The chief obstacle to resolution of the problem was the insistence of Foch and successive French governments that Belgium

13. DDB, 1:363–65; Hymans to Moncheur, 15 June 1920, no. 1101, BMAE GB/1920; Millerand to Margerie, 2 May 1920, tel. 1367–68, Margerie to Millerand, 6, 10 May 1920, tels. 291–94, 295–98, 304–5, 21 May 1920, no. 598, 23 May, 12 June 1920, tels. 323, 363, Millerand to Mollard, 7 May 1920, tel. 71, Mollard to Millerand, 10, 12 June 1920, tel. 38, no. 43, FMAE Z/Lux/36; Villiers to Curzon, 12 June 1920, no. 404, F.O. 371/3637.

confirm in writing France's right to use the Luxemburg railways for military purposes in wartime. The Belgian attitude was that no Belgian government could either give formal written permission for wartime violation of the Grand Duchy's neutrality[14] or do anything more effective than protest such violation. As the French were not satisfied, they presumably were seeking a pretext to retain the railways. Although the French regiment finally left Luxemburg on 29 December 1923 in response to repeated Belgian demarches, France did not relinquish any part of the Guillaume-Luxembourg railway and retained control of the entire network until the German invasion in 1940. France's failure to honor the 1920 and 1921 agreements with Belgium received indirect support from a 1933 ruling of the Luxemburg Court of Cassation depriving the grand ducal government of the right to dispose of the railway.[15]

As the French deception was not predictable with certainty in 1920, the Franco-Belgian formula for the railways led directly to military negotiations. The Belgians again sought British participation, stressing that they envisaged no binding commitment, only a prearranged plan to be used when and if Britain decided to aid Belgium in future hostilities. The Foreign Office, still piqued by Belgian support of France at Frankfurt, was unenthusiastic but, at War Office insistence, the question was sent to the Committee of Imperial Defence, which, in response to Lloyd George's intervention, only referred it to the cabinet. On 30 June, the cabinet decided that "the proposed military conversations would be premature at the present time."[16]

14. Luxemburg had not in fact amended her constitution to eliminate neutrality upon her entry into the League of Nations.

15. Mollard to Millerand, 12 May 1920, no. 28, FMAE Z/Lux/35; G. Grahame to Curzon, 19 May 1921, no. 465, F.O. 371/6970; Hymans, *Mémoires*, 2:546–47; *League of Nations Treaty Series*, 11:239–41; Majerus, *Le Luxembourg*, pp. 74–80; Mollard to Poincaré, 3 Jan. 1924, no. 3, FMAE Z/Lux/17; Margerie to Briand, 10 May 1921, no. 586, FMAE note, 14 May 1921, FMAE Z/Lux/37; FMAE note, 13 Nov. 1923, FMAE Z/Lux/14; anon. memo for Jaspar, n.d. [1934], Jaspar Papers/249; Margerie to Briand, 29 Oct. 1921, no. 1170, Foch to Jaspar, 29 Oct. 1921, FMAE Z/Lux/38; Herbette to Poincaré, 10 Apr. 1924, no. 585, FMAE Z/Belg./74. For the railway negotiations, see BMAE B-20 and FMAE Z/Lux/38–48. After World War II, a Société nationale des chemins de fer luxembourgeois was created with all three states participating. Baumont, "La Belgique," p. 178.

16. Hymans to Moncheur, 16 Apr. 1920, no. 656, BMAE GB/1920; DDB, 1:365–67,

While the British were progressing toward this predictable decision, talks had begun in Paris on 10 June between Foch and Gen. Henri Maglinse, the new Belgian chief of staff. The final Belgian decision to accept the French military accord was only reached at the Spa Conference on 16 July after Delacroix had made a last effort on 12 July to persuade Lloyd George that Britain should participate. After Lloyd George refused, fearing that even a limited military agreement might involve Britain in a Continental war, the Belgians signed a carefully restricted, purely technical defensive military accord with France on 19 July. In its final version of 7 September 1920, the Belgians took care to safeguard Belgian freedom of action against embroilment in any future French military adventures.[17]

Nonetheless, the Belgian leaders never gave up hope of the counterbalancing British tie. Particularly after Henri Jaspar became foreign minister in November 1920, Belgian overtures toward a British treaty resumed.[18] They met with no success, however, until an Anglo-Belgian defensive alliance was hastily drafted as a by-product of negotiations toward an Anglo-French alliance during the Cannes Conference of January 1922. Though both cabinets approved the Anglo-Belgian treaty and an agreed text was achieved, it never entered into effect because the British belatedly realized that a treaty with Belgium would effectively guarantee the French frontier and thus render unlikely the French

377–79, 388; DBFP, 9:512–14, 12:37; Villiers to Curzon, 31 May 1920, no. 370, Chamberlain memo, 28 June 1920, CAB 3/7; G. Villiers to Tufton, 28 Apr. 1920, F.O. 371/3637; 133d meeting, C.I.D., 29 June 1920, CAB 2/3; Cabinet 38 (20), 30 June 1920, CAB 23/21; Moncheur to Hymans, 3 June 1920, no. 2681/909, Hymans Papers/177. The War Office was conducting unauthorized staff talks with its French and Belgian counterparts. Moncheur to Hymans, 25 June 1920, no. 3106/1074, BMAE GB/1920.

    17. Landsberg to AA, 17 June 1920, K. no. 64, GFM 4, Series L, Politik 3, L001854–7; Mayer to AA, 16 Sept. 1920, K. no. 232, GFM 4, Series L, Politik 3, L001939; DDB, 1:378–79, 398–401, 408–9; van Zuylen, *Les Mains libres*, p. 119; DBFP, 12:68–69; Whitlock to Colby, 13 Sept. 1920, no. 959, SD 751.5511/5; FMAE memo, 18 Oct. 1920, FMAE Z/Belg./73; Delacroix memo, 12 July 1920, BMAE B-10.926; Moncheur to Hymans, 4 Aug. 1920, no. 3815/1345, BMAE FR/1920/II. On the French-Belgian military agreement, see Jonathan Helmreich, "The Negotiation of the Franco-Belgian Military Accord of 1920," pp. 360–78, and Jean-Marie d'Hoop, "Le Maréchal Foch et la négociation de l'accord militaire franco-belge de 1920," pp. 191–98. For the text of the accord, see DDB, 1:405–8.

    18. Della Faille to Simons, 24 Nov. 1920, no. 8005, GFM 4, Series L, Politik 1, L000732; G. Grahame to Curzon, 27 Sept. 1921, no. 848, F.O. 371/6966.

concessions that Britain was demanding in return for an Anglo-French treaty. As the Anglo-French negotiations gradually lapsed during 1922, so did the Belgian treaty.[19] Thereafter, through the long, tense Ruhr crisis of 1923 and its aftermath, Belgium raised the matter at every opportunity but to no avail.[20] In the end, she had to settle for the inoperative British guarantee embodied in the Locarno treaties of 16 October 1925.[21]

Even the consolation prize of the Locarno guarantee did not come automatically to Belgium. The original proposal put forward by German Foreign Minister Gustav Stresemann on 20 January 1925 offered a perpetual guarantee of the Franco-German frontier but made no mention of Belgium.[22] The omission was deliberate, as Stresemann hoped to trade concessions on another piece of unfinished business remaining from 1919 for a Belgo-German frontier revision. In short, Stresemann, who intended to begin territorial revision of the Versailles treaty in the west at what he deemed to be the weakest point facing him, planned to offer German reassumption of the German marks still remaining in Belgium for retrocession of Eupen and Malmédy to Germany.

The marks question had flickered fitfully ever since 1919 while the Belgian government retained about 6 milliard unwanted occupation marks in its possession. It was typical of Belgium's unresolved issues in that a particularized Belgian problem became entangled in a series of wider questions of general European concern that bore directly upon the permanence of the peace settlement. In succession, Belgium's unredeemed marks became embroiled in the issues of trials of alleged German war criminals, Stresemann's territorial revisionism, and ultimately reparations, as German governments tried to use this matter to maximum advantage.

As the Versailles treaty left Belgium free to negotiate the marks

19. The negotiations may be traced in: DDB, 1; DBFP, 16; Cmd. 2169; France, DD, *Documents relatifs aux négociations concernant les garanties de sécurité contre une agression de l'Allemagne (10 janvier 1919–7 décembre 1923)*; F.O. 371/7000, 8239, 8249–51; FMAE Z/GB/48–49, 69–71, Z/Belg./48; BMAE B-10.926; Hardinge Papers/45.

20. Cmd. 1943, pp. 22, 38, 46; Jaspar to G. Grahame, 27 Aug. 1923, F.O. 371/8651; G. Grahame to MacDonald, 4 June 1924, no. 487, F.O. 371/9818; DDB, 1:526–38, 2:35–38.

21. Cmd. 2525.

22. D'Abernon to Chamberlain, 20 Jan. 1925, no. 49, F.O. 371/10726.

question directly with Germany, Belgian and German experts came to an agreement in Berlin on 25 November 1919. In return for a written German promise to reimburse Belgium for 5.5 milliard marks, Emile Francqui, leader of the Belgian delegation, who was an able financier but without political or diplomatic experience, promised orally to urge the Belgian government to stop fraudulent exports from Belgium to the Belgian Rhineland zone, to end confiscation of German property sequestered in Belgium, and to abandon or moderate demands for extradition of alleged German war criminals for trial under Article 228 of the peace treaty. Although Britain and France both protested the unilateral marks negotiation when they learned of it, Belgium had been fully within her treaty rights and was undeterred. At the end of the year, however, the German government suddenly demanded written confirmation that the Belgian cabinet would fulfill all three proposals. The government was unwilling to make any formal commitment on the second and third recommendations. Nonetheless, it stopped the export, ceased confiscation of sequestered property pending German ratification of the agreement, and cut its list of war criminals from eleven hundred to three hundred. However, the Belgian government also said that it would accept any later Allied decision on war crimes trials.[23] It was this last statement that proved to be the real difficulty.

On 9 February 1920 the *Berliner Zeitung* announced that the German Foreign Ministry had denounced the marks agreement because Belgium was participating in Allied demands for extradition of war criminals. This announcement occurred just before a Supreme Council meeting in London that would decide on application of Article 228 of the treaty. Germany was bitterly resisting extradition in favor of trials at the German Supreme Court at Leipzig and hoping by this means to reduce prosecution to a minimum. Britain and Italy (and also the United States) had become very reluctant to pursue extradition and were largely losing

23. De Gaiffier to Hymans, 3 Dec. 1919, van den Heuvel memo, 18 Dec. 1918, Delacroix to Hymans, 29 Jan. 1920, Kerchove to Hymans, 29 Jan. 1920, tel. 17, Hymans to Kerchove, 2 Feb. 1920, tel. 1, Hymans Papers/150; Kerchove to Hymans, 3, 4 Feb. 1920, tel. 27, nos. 222/92, 239/97, BMAE Alle/1920/I; van der Wee and Tavernier, *La Banque Nationale*, pp. 42–47. The 1919 accord foresaw a special arrangment for the balance of the 6.1 milliard marks, as this balance was judged to have entered Belgium by fraud. DDB, 2:519; van der Wee and Tavernier, *La Banque Nationale*, p. 43.

interest in war crimes trials. Thus, if Belgium, who had the longest list and who was in fact seeking compromise, joined their ranks, France would be isolated on the question and the entire war crimes issue might soon evaporate. However, France realized that she did not have the power to force extradition, Lloyd George was willing to compromise on trial at Leipzig, and the Belgian government, which could hardly abandon trials altogether in view of the intensity of public opinion on the question, accepted the great-power decision with relief. Thus a 17 February Allied note to Germany conceded trials at Leipzig. Immediately thereafter the German Foreign Ministry assured the Belgian chargé that the marks accord had not been denounced but reminded him that it would require Reichstag approval.[24] Obviously the Foreign Ministry was already seeking new ways to exploit the question to German benefit.

As a consequence of talks during the Spa Conference in July 1920, the issue was reopened in the autumn of 1920, but new negotiations in January 1921 were unsuccessful. Finally an agreement for German payment of 4 milliard marks was reached on 1 September 1921 and approved by the German cabinet on 22 September. On 15 October, however, the German government decided not to proceed with the accord pending resolution of the Upper Silesian question, a matter far beyond the power of the Belgian government to arrange.[25] Further negotiations late in 1921, at the start of 1922, and in the summer of 1922 also proved abortive, as Germany escalated her demands and Belgium made new conditions in response.[26] On 15 March 1923, during the Ruhr occupation, the German government (acting through an inter-

24. Van den Heuvel memo, 18 Dec. 1918, Delacroix to Hymans, 29 Jan. 1918, Hymans to Kerchove, 2 Feb. 1920, tel. 1, Hymans Papers/150; Kerchove to Hymans, 3 Feb. 1920, tel. 27, 2, 4, 6, 11 Feb. 1920, nos. 222/92, 239/97, 312/117, 458/180, 8, 9 Feb. 1920, tels. 39, 42, 17, 18, 19 Feb. 1920, tels. 57, 59, 62; Hankey Diary, 15 Feb. 1920, Hankey Papers 1/5. The length of the Belgian list of war criminals arose from the fact that Belgium was almost entirely occupied throughout the war and from Germany's especial contempt for the inhabitants of small nations.

25. Hymans to Jaspar, 21 July 1920, de Wouters to Theunis, 30 Oct. 1920, Theunis to de Wouters, 5 Nov. 1920, no. 4/308, Jaspar Papers/162; Manfred J. Enssle, "Germany and Belgium, 1919–1929," pp. 77, 81.

26. Enssle, "Germany and Belgium," pp. 81–92; DDB, 2:519; della Faille to Jaspar, 30 Oct. 1922, no. 9365/3363, BMAE Alle/1922/IV.

mediary) again raised the marks question to Belgian Reparation Commission delegates, hoping to gain their assent to a German reparations plan of 30 milliard marks to cover all Versailles treaty charges, in exchange for evacuation of the Ruhr, and also to gain their good offices in persuading the French and Belgian governments to accept this offer. Because Belgium declined to be deflected from her chosen path,[27] the mark issue was soon submerged in the larger question of the Ruhr crisis and remained dormant until it reemerged during and after the Locarno negotiations.

During the early stages of the diplomatic maneuvers in 1925 toward the Locarno treaties, energetic action by successive Belgian governments had ensured that Belgium would be a signatory to the Rhineland Pact. Hence the final text of the Treaty of Locarno of 16 October 1925 specified:

> Article 1. The High Contracting Parties collectively and severally guarantee, in the manner provided in the following Articles, the maintenance of the territorial *status quo* resulting from the frontiers between Germany and Belgium and between Germany and France, and the inviolability of the said frontiers as fixed by or in pursuance of the Treaty of Peace signed at Versailles on June 28, 1919. . . .
>
> Article 2. Germany and Belgium, and also Germany and France, mutually undertake that they will in no case attack or invade each other or resort to war against each other. . . .
>
> Article 3. In view of the undertakings entered into in Article 2 of the present Treaty, Germany and Belgium, and Germany and France, undertake to settle by peaceful means and in the manner laid down herein all questions of every kind which may rise between them and which it may not be possible to settle by the normal methods of diplomacy.[28]

In Article 1, the phrase "frontiers as fixed by or in pursuance of the Treaty of Peace" was specifically designed to include Eupen and Malmédy within the guaranteed status quo. However, Friedrich Gaus, who served as Stresemann's legal advisor, had noted that Article 1 also contained the phrase "in the manner provided in the following Articles,"

27. Delacroix to Theunis, 15, 16 Mar. 1923, BMAE B-10.071.
28. Van Zuylen memo, 8 June 1932, Hymans Papers/151; Cmd. 2525.

which in fact provided no guidance except in regard to military breaches. Thus, Stresemann and Gaus unilaterally interpreted Article 1 to mean that only the use of force was ruled out and that peaceful revision of the Belgo-German frontier was authorized by the Treaty of Locarno. No other power accepted this interpretation, but the French foreign minister, Aristide Briand, though disputing it privately, avoided public challenge at Stresemann's request in order not to jeopardize German ratification of the treaty.[29] Meanwhile, five days after the euphoric final ceremony at the Locarno town hall, Stresemann acted on his own interpretation and sought retrocession of Eupen and Malmédy from Belgium in return for a settlement of the mark claim.[30]

These approaches were no more successful than informal overtures in the same vein during the spring of 1925 by Hjalmar Schacht, president of the Reichsbank.[31] However, as the Belgian government went into acute financial crisis in March of 1926 with the franc depreciating alarmingly,[32] Stresemann scented a new opportunity. He proposed to take advantage of Belgian financial desperation to force retrocession of Eupen-Malmédy in return for a mark settlement affording Belgium some much-needed financial relief.[33] Several informal overtures were made by both Schacht and Stresemann, chiefly to Delacroix, then Belgian representative on the Reparation Commission and a close friend of Emile Francqui, who dominated Belgian banking circles and the new government formed in May 1926 to cope with the financial crisis. Because Delacroix showed interest from the start, Stresemann approached the Belgian minister in Berlin on 24 April 1926. The Belgian cabinet

29. BMAE memo, 24 Mar. 1933, Hymans Papers/184; van Zuylen memo, 8 June 1932, Hymans Papers/151; Enssle, "Germany and Belgium," pp. 181, 183; Leger note, 5 Nov. 1925, FMAE Z/GB/86; Briand speech to Chambre, 15 Dec. 1925, FMAE Z/GB/88.

30. Gustav Stresemann, *Vermächtnis*, 2:125–26, 232–33, 467–69; van Zuylen memo, 8 July 1932, Hymans Papers/151; DDB, 2:399, 520.

31. DDB, 2:399–400, 500.

32. On the Belgian financial crisis, see Henry L. Shepherd, *The Monetary Experience of Belgium, 1914–1936*; Richard H. Meyer, *Bankers' Diplomacy*, chap. 2; and van der Wee and Tavernier, *La Banque Nationale*, chaps. 3 and 14.

33. On the 1926 negotiations that followed, see Enssle, "Germany and Belgium," or Manfred J. Enssle, *Stresemann's Territorial Revisionism*, chap. 6. I am grateful to Professor Enssle for providing me with an advance typescript of chap. 6.

flatly refused to link the question of the marks with that of Eupen-Malmédy.[34]

As the Belgian financial crisis continued, further informal German overtures were made, chiefly to Delacroix via Schacht. Negotiations continued in this fashion outside official channels through the summer of 1926. In their concern to salvage Belgian finances, Francqui, Delacroix, and Camille Gutt, another Belgian financier who had long served at the Reparation Commission and as *chef de cabinet* to Theunis at the Finance Ministry, all favored an agreement with Germany. None of them considered the political implications. Hymans, then minister of justice, was vehemently opposed. Jaspar, then prime minister, was unenthusiastic but might have bowed to financial necessity had not a trip to Paris by Francqui and Foreign Minister Vandervelde at the end of July established Poincaré's extreme hostility to any cession of territory. Vandervelde's attitude is less clear. He had earlier reported the German proposal to Briand and to the British foreign secretary, Sir Austen Chamberlain, and found that they both objected to the idea. France feared any territorial revisionism as jeopardizing what remained of the Versailles treaty; Chamberlain disliked the financial implications for German reparations payments and held the Locarno treaties (as he interpreted them) to be sacred.[35]

34. DDB, 2:401–2; van der Wee and Tavernier, *La Banque Nationale*, pp. 178–79; BMAE B-331, B-11.246, B-11.442, passim. The main BMAE file on the marks question is B-11.116A & B.

35. Van der Wee and Tavernier, *La Banque Nationale*, pp. 177–78; de Gaiffier report, 7 Aug. 1926, of Franco-Belgian meeting, 30 July 1926, BMAE B-331; FMAE note, 9 July 1926, Herbette to Briand, 13, 17, 19 Aug. 1926, tels. 181–91, 192–95, 199–202, no. 951, Briand to Herbette, 11 Aug. 1926, tel. 390, Poincaré to Briand, 19 Aug. 1926, FMAE Z/Belg./70; Belga communiqué, 11 Aug. 1926, BMAE B-331. Poincaré took the view that all Locarno signatories must consent to territorial cession and declared that as long as he lived he would not. DDB, 2:403–4; Fleuriau note, 29 July 1926, Lampson minute, 11 Aug. 1926, Chamberlain to Crewe, 20 Aug. 1926, no. 2375, F.O. 371/11823; Enssle, *Stresemann's Territorial Revisionism*, chap. 6. Vandervelde's closest advisor, Henri Rolin, strongly opposed retrocession. Rolin note, 29 July 1926, BMAE B-331. It should be noted that on 21 July 1926, Delacroix, who was always overly optimistic about projects he favored, informed Schacht that the Belgian cabinet had approved the deal with "one small modification." This was apparently a preliminary cabinet discussion in the significant absence of Hymans, and the "modification" proved to be a financial treaty without reference to Eupen-Malmédy, together with a German affirmation of guilt regarding the 1914 attack on Belgium. Enssle, *Stresemann's Territorial Revisionism*, chap. 6;

As German overtures persisted during the summer, encouraged by Delacroix and Francqui, Jaspar finally laid the matter before the Belgian cabinet, even though negotiations had been entirely unofficial. Despite the financial crisis and the obvious support of Francqui, the acute hostility of Hymans and, to a lesser degree, of Jaspar, leaders of two of Belgium's political parties, and the caution of Vandervelde, leader of the third party, sufficed to defeat any further consideration of the German offer. After a two-day debate, the Belgian cabinet decided on 18 August to drop the matter. Because persistent rumors continued in the Belgian press, on 23 August Jaspar publicly and categorically denied any intent to pursue the question, saying, "For once and for all, there have never been any official dealings and I assure you that there will not be any on the subject of Eupen-Malmédy."[36]

Thereafter, Belgium succeeded in stabilizing her currency and by autumn had lost any serious interest in coming to terms over the two cantons.[37] By then, however, France's own financial crisis had become acute, and thus she was inclined to be more flexible. A week after Germany's entrance into the League of Nations, Briand met Stresemann privately at Thoiry in Switzerland on 17 September. Although we shall never know with certainty exactly what occurred at the Thoiry talks, it appears that Stresemann proposed to purchase revision of much of the Versailles treaty and that Briand, out of financial desperation, was prepared to listen. Among other proposals, retrocession of Eupen-Malmédy was discussed without Belgian foreknowledge.[38] However, other aspects of the plan proved impractical and, as France restored her finances, the deal with Germany was quickly dropped.

Hymans, *Mémoires*, 1:467. See also Jacques Bariéty, "Le Projet de rétrocession d'Eupen-Malmédy par la Belgique à l'Allemagne, et la France (1925–1926)," pp. 335, 340.

36. Hymans, *Mémoires*, 1:467–78; Knatchbull-Hugessen to Chamberlain, 23 Aug. 1926, no. 809, F.O. 371/11823.

37. DDB, 2:403–4; G. Grahame to Chamberlain, 26 Nov. 1926, no. 1049, F.O. 371/11810; G. Grahame to Chamberlain, 25 Oct. 1926, tel. 107R, F.O. 371/11820.

38. Compare Georges Suarez, *Briand*, 6:219–27, and Stresemann, *Vermächtnis*, 3:17–23. It has been established that Briand's account is inaccurate (Jacques Bariéty, address at Conference on European Security in the Locarno Era, Mars Hill, N.C., 17 Oct. 1975); see also Bariéty, "Le Projet," p. 346. It does not necessarily follow, however, that Stresemann's version is reliable. Stresemann was attempting to take advantage of Belgian, French, and Polish financial crises to revise the Versailles treaty. His terms included

Nonetheless, Stresemann did not abandon hope of beginning territorial revision of the Versailles treaty on the Belgian frontier. When he
tried again on 28 October 1926, Vandervelde was not forthcoming.
Another effort in September 1927 to link Eupen and Malmédy with
the German marks led Vandervelde to indicate that both issues should
be resolved in conjunction with proposals for an early evacuation of the
Rhineland. After Hymans succeeded him as foreign minister in November 1927, the Belgian government considered the question of Eupen-
Malmédy closed. There were no Belgo-German negotiations on the
subject in 1927 and 1928.[39] Nevertheless, the German government
was careful not to reply to communications from the Conference of
Ambassadors in 1928 and 1929 concerning final delimitation of the
Belgo-German frontier. When the mark claim arose again in 1929 in
conjunction with negotiation of the Young Plan, Germany tried once
again to link it to retrocession of Eupen-Malmédy. As this effort produced only complete Belgo-German stalemate, jeopardizing reparations
revision, the American members of the Young Committee intervened
and obtained on 4 June 1929 a formal written German guarantee that
"no territorial questions will be raised in these negotiations."[40]

With that, the question of Eupen-Malmédy was at last laid to rest.
There remained only settlement of the mark claim. This was accomplished in connection with the "final" settlement of reparations in 1929–
30. As Belgium made it amply clear that she would not sign a new
reparations agreement unless the mark claim was resolved, and, as she
in time gained the support of the other experts, Germany was obliged
to commit herself before the Young Plan was signed to negotiation on
the marks. The plan itself further specified that it would not enter into
effect until Germany and Belgium "come to an internationally binding

purchase of Eupen-Malmédy, immediate return of the Saar, prompt evacuation of the
Rhineland and withdrawal of the Inter-Allied Military Control Commission, and immediate return of the Polish corridor and Upper Silesia in return for financial relief to the
three distressed countries.

39. Enssle, *Stresemann's Territorial Revisionism*, chap. 6; Enssle, "Germany and Belgium," pp. 232, 239–41; G. Grahame to Chamberlain, 15 Mar. 1928, no. 244, F.O.
371/13334.

40. C.A. to von Hoesch, 2 Aug. 1928, no. 77, Technical Geographic Committee to
C.A., 28 Nov. 1928, F.O. 371/12872; Technical Geographic Committee to C.A., 24
Dec. 1929, no. 377, F.O. 371/14345; FRUS PPC, 13:142, Cmd. 3343, p. 58.

agreement on the Mark claim."[41] As a consequence, Belgo-German agreement was promptly reached on a scheme that would enter into force at the same time as the Young Plan. By its terms, Germany was to pay Belgium a total sum of 606 million marks in annual installments of varying amounts over thirty-seven years.[42] In the course of ten years of negotiation, the amount had shrunk from 6.1 milliard marks to 606 million but, as the millions of new Reichmarks had value whereas the milliards of inflated old marks still sitting in the coffers of the Belgian National Bank did not, Belgium was reasonably satisfied. Payments were punctually executed and, thanks to Belgian threats not to sign the agreements reached at the London Conference of July 1931 and the Lausanne Conference of June–July 1932 if mark payments were suspended, they continued after the Hoover Moratorium and the Lausanne Convention accomplished the de facto end of reparations.[43] Further energetic Belgian efforts achieved continuing payment at a reduced rate through 1933 and into 1934, despite a unilateral German moratorium on other payments on 9 July 1933. Nonetheless, on 15 May 1934, Germany defaulted on the mark payments as well.[44]

In its later stages, the history of the mark question became much entangled with the broader problem of German reparations in general. From the first, the intricate reparations issue had been considerably complicated by Belgian questions. At the Paris Peace Conference, Belgium had gained two special concessions concerning German reparations: privilege on her war debts and priority of payment. Neither victory proved to be as substantial as it appeared in 1919. Although Germany did assume the Belgian war debt to Britain and France and although the sums involved, over $750 million, were added to the 132 milliard mark total liability ostensibly established by the Reparation

41. Enssle, "Germany and Belgium," pp. 258, 261–63; Cmd. 3343, pp. 57–59.

42. Cmd. 3484, p. 140; Enssle, "Germany and Belgium," pp. 263–64; Hymans to Moncheur, 10 Mar. 1929, tel. 6, Hymans Papers/159; Ritter-Gutt accord, 13 July 1929, Jaspar Papers/162. Germany finally approved the 1922 Belgo-German agreement on the Eupen-Malmédy railway in 1931.

43. Gutt memo, 3 June 1932, Gutt to Jaspar, 3 June 1932, Jaspar Papers/231; Granville to F.O., 15 July 1931, tel. 25R, F.O. 371/15187; Perowne to O'Malley, 17 June 1932, F.O. 371/15928; Perowne to Sargent, 29 June 1932, no. 16, F.O. 371/15930.

44. Brauer to BMAE, 14 July 1933, Brauer to Hymans, 14 Apr. 1934, Jaspar to Hymans, 14 May 1934, Jaspar Papers/162; FRUS PPC, 13:410.

Commission on 27 April 1921, American failure to ratify the Versailles treaty meant that Belgium was obliged to reassume her war debt to the United States. In recognition that the Belgian situation was unique, the 1925 settlement granted Belgium somewhat more generous terms than those accorded to other countries. Even so, debt payments to the United States absorbed most of what Belgium received under the Dawes Plan. In respect to the 1925 settlement, Belgium paid regularly until the Hoover Moratorium of July 1931 on all intergovernmental debts but, like many other depression-burdened countries, defaulted on the 15 December payment in 1932.[45]

Belgian priority similarly proved to be somewhat less of a victory than it had originally seemed. The overriding difficulty was that the priority of payment accorded to Belgium in 1919 rested upon an Allied assumption that German payments would be large and prompt, thus extinguishing the priority quickly. When German payments, especially in cash, in fact proved to be small and slow, it began to appear that Belgium's priority would absorb what little monies there were for years to come. Not surprisingly, Britain and France, both anxious for some cash on their own accounts, reacted and mounted repeated assaults on Belgium's priority. Though rarely attacking it frontally or demanding its outright termination, they devised one scheme after another to circumvent Belgian priority in order to gain more for themselves.

The 24 June 1919 Allied agreement had provided that Belgium would receive an absolute priority, ranking only after occupation costs and supply of Germany, of 2.5 milliard gold francs (about 2 milliard gold marks or $500 million) on German cash payments and an equal priority after 1 May 1921 on German deliveries in kind. To the displeasure of the victors, occupation and provisioning costs fully absorbed such payments as Germany made before 1 May 1921.[46] Meanwhile, Britain and France, recognizing that the reparations pie was shrinking rapidly, had

45. FRUS PPC, 13:427; G. Grahame to Chamberlain, 26 Jan., 8, 11 Feb. 1926, nos. 111, 133, 150, F.O. 371/11234; G. Grahame to Chamberlain, 18 Feb. 1926, no. 170, F.O. 371/11235; Sargent memo, 13 Dec. 1932, F.O. 371/15916.

46. FRUS PPC, 13:849; RC, *Official Documents*, 4:10, 16. Payments to 1 May 1921 consisted of credits for state properties in territories transferred to victor powers; battle-field salvage; shipments of coal, timber, and dyes; and paper marks requisitioned for the use of the Allied armies in the Rhineland.

begun to nibble away at the Belgian slice of it. At the Brussels and Spa Conferences of July 1920, Belgian representatives successfully defended, against vigorous assault from Lloyd George, an 8 percent share for Belgium of the as yet undetermined total German reparations bill, but, in return, they made a significant concession on priority. Belgium retained the cash priority per se and also the priority on kind after 1 May 1921, but she agreed to take no more than 50 percent of the Allied share of the proceeds from German loans.[47] As it was becoming increasingly clear that the chief source of reparations receipts was almost certainly going to be the proceeds from loans floated by Germany, this was a concession of substance.

Much of the next year was devoted to determining the total German reparations liability and devising a payment scheme. Once this difficult task was completed with the London Schedule of Payments of 5 May 1921,[48] new attempts to circumvent Belgian priority began. First came negotiation on 5 July 1921 of the Wiesbaden Accord between France and Germany, which provided for substantial German reconstruction of French devastated areas. As this arrangement would constitute a de facto unofficial French priority on German reparations payments, which would probably continue even if official payments were defaulted, both Britain and Belgium objected. Although signed on 6 October 1921 and reluctantly accepted by the rest of the Entente in March 1922, the Wiesbaden Accord never went into effect.[49] Curiously, a complementary Belgo-German arrangement, the Bemelmans-Cuntze Accord of 2 June 1922, did go into effect, and Belgium enjoyed some modest benefits from it until the Ruhr occupation put an end to contracts under the accord early in 1923.[50]

In the meantime, however, Germany had made a cash payment, as

47. Hymans memo, 3 July 1920, Hymans Papers/150; DBFP, 8:400–409, 425–30; Curzon to F.O., 3 July 1920, no. 6, F.O. 371/4738; Kerr to Bonar Law, 5 July 1920, Bonar Law Papers 99/3/5; Cmd. 1615, pp. 4–6.

48. RC, *Official Documents*, 1:4–9.

49. Jaspar to de Gaiffier, 16 June 1921, no. 3144, Jaspar Papers/233; McFadyean to Blackett, 5 July 1921, F.O. 371/5972; G. Grahame to Curzon, 14 Sept. 1921, no. 802, Treasury to F.O., 16 Sept. 1921, F.O. to Treasury, 21 Sept. 1921, F.O. 371/6036; Treasury to F.O., 1 Oct. 1921, F.O. 371/5975.

50. Bemelmans-Cuntze Accord, 2 June 1922, Theunis to Jaspar, 8 Nov. 1922, 1 Feb. 1923, BMAE B-366/VI.

required by the London Schedule, of 1 milliard gold marks during the summer of 1921. Under existing agreements, Belgian priority would consume all of it, but neither Britain nor France was prepared to wait for future payments, which might never be made. As a consequence, an Allied financial conference in mid-August 1921 decided that Belgium would receive 550 million marks of the first milliard (the balance going to Britain), priority on deliveries in kind after 1 May 1921, and quarterly cash disbursements after 1 August 1921 to cover one-fourth of the remaining priority.[51] France objected, however, as she gained nothing from this arrangement. In the end, after extended Entente argument, Belgium gained only 350 million marks, as 500 million went to Britain and the remainder of the first milliard was divided between France and Italy. Belgium's share went almost in its entirety for service of postwar reconstruction debts to British and American bankers, although the country's budget remained in substantial deficit as a consequence of emergency expenditures in the first year after the Armistice and continuing reconstruction costs.[52]

In November 1921, Germany fulfilled part of her scheduled payment but soon indicated that she would require a substantial moratorium on payments falling due in January and February 1922. Though there was no Entente agreement on whether to grant a moratorium, it seemed easiest to Britain and France to take the prospective German default out of the share of the smallest nation among Germany's major creditors. At London between 18 and 22 December 1921, Lloyd George and Briand, then French prime minister, secretly agreed to curtail Belgian priority further and to hold a Supreme Council early in January to settle this and other matters officially.[53]

Before the Cannes Conference opened on 6 January 1922, the Belgians discovered what was afoot and vigorously protested further erosion

51. Horne to Cabinet, 16 Aug. 1921, Cabinet Paper C.P. 3228, F.O. 371/6036. Belgium accepted this arrangement without real protest, probably as the price of British assistance in arranging that what monies Belgium did receive not be transferred immediately to the British and American governments toward repayment of post-Armistice loans.

52. Wadsworth to Hughes, 5 Dec. 1921, tel. 58, SD 462.00R29/1296.

53. Furst, *De Versailles*, p. 137; Suarez, *Briand*, 5:346–47; International Conference Paper I.C.P. 209, 19 Dec. 1921, CAB 29/94; D'Abernon, *An Ambassador*, 1:231; DBFP, 15:800–803.

of one of their few solid gains from the peace conference.[54] Because Briand was under intense domestic political pressure, he badly needed Belgian support against British insistence on a German moratorium. Thus he publicly abandoned the attack on Belgian priority, to the fury of Lloyd George. Trapped between Britain and Belgium, Briand then bobbed and wove in an effort to escape his own political crisis.[55] It became obvious that Lloyd George hoped to defer most of the remaining Belgian priority indefinitely. Before this or any other reparations issue could be resolved, however, Briand resigned and the conference collapsed. In its aftermath, the Reparation Commission patched together a partial moratorium until the end of 1922 to avoid formal German default.[56]

In Paris on 11 March 1922, the Entente finance ministers arrived at a new division of the shrinking reparations receipts. On paper, Belgium fared somewhat better than she would have done under the Anglo-French scheme at Cannes, but in fact most of what she salvaged was chimerical. She was obliged to abandon all priority on deliveries in kind, which was the only form of payment likely to be made in the immediate future, especially as the moratorium envisaged only token cash payments. Indeed, France was to receive 65 percent of all payments in kind and Britain 24 percent of the remaining 35 percent. The rest would be allotted according to the Spa percentages. On total German cash payments in 1921 (including the first milliard), Britain would receive 500 million gold marks, France 140 million gold marks, and Italy 172 million lire. Belgium would receive the rest. This was considerably less favorable to Belgium than the 1921 scheme, primarily because German payments had dwindled in the interim. Though Belgium was accorded full priority after occupation costs on all cash payments after 1921,[57] nobody seriously expected that there would be many soon.

54. G. Grahame to Curzon, 24 Dec. 1921, tels. 202, 203, 204, F.O. 371/6039; Moncheur to Curzon, 26 Dec. 1921, Lloyd George Papers F/13/2/62; Jaspar to de Gaiffier, 24 Dec. 1921, Jaspar Papers/214.

55. *L'Etoile belge*, 5 Jan. 1922, p. 3, 7 Jan. 1922, p. 1; Suarez, *Briand*, 5:361–66, 377–78.

56. I.C.P. 225, 7 Jan. 1922, CAB 29/94; Suarez, *Briand*, 5:361–410; C.P. 3916, RC Annex 1352, 21 Mar. 1922, F.O. 371/7476.

57. Cmd. 1616. Occupation costs were held to 220 million gold marks. Total German cash payments in 1922 were about 435 million marks. The 500 million awarded to

On 12 July 1922 the German government declared the existing partial moratorium insufficient and requested a full moratorium on cash payments for the remainder of 1922 and all of 1923 and 1924.[58] As a consequence, the reparations crisis dominated the next twenty-five months. After an inconclusive Entente conference in London in August 1922, Belgium, who was scheduled to receive the remaining cash payments for 1922 on priority account, agreed to accept six-month German treasury bills in lieu of cash. She did so at British behest and over vehement objections from Poincaré, who had succeeded Briand as premier and foreign minister.[59] The treasury bills amounted to a disguised moratorium until 1 January 1923, by which time a new scheme would have to be devised or the London Schedule would revert to full force.

As no scheme was agreed on before the end of the year, Entente representatives met in Paris on 2 January 1923. Every country except Belgium brought a plan and each was published at once, thus inflaming public opinion everywhere. The British refused to discuss any plan except their own, which, while containing many features unacceptable to France and Italy, was particularly offensive to Belgium. British experts had again decided that the small country with the large priority should bear the brunt of the Entente sacrifice. Among its intricate provisions, which included a four-year unguaranteed German moratorium, a virtual prohibition on sanctions against future German default, and a sharp reduction in future reparations payments (if any), the British plan required cancellation of the remainder of Belgian priority, repayment of amounts already received on priority account, and cancellation of the last three of the five installments of the six-month German treasury bills. Although the British plan offered some inducements to France

---

Britain and the 140 million to France were for occupation costs before 1 May 1921. Nothing was allocated for Belgium's occupation costs from the spring of 1919 to 1 May 1921.

58. F.O. memo, 15 July 1922, F.O. 371/7680.

59. Suarez, *Briand*, 5:425–26; Jordan, *Great Britain, France*, pp. 91, 109; RC to German Government, 31 Aug. 1922, F.O. 371/7484; G. Grahame to D'Abernon, 9 Sept. 1922, D'Abernon Papers/48925; G. Grahame to Tyrrell, 12 Sept. 1922, Lloyd George Papers F/49/5/16; Jaspar notes, 3, 15, 16 Sept. 1922, Le Tellier to Jaspar, 19 Sept. 1922, tel. 159, Jaspar Papers/221B; G. Grahame to Curzon, 11 Sept. 1922, tel. 72D, F.O. 371/7485.

and Italy in the form of partial war debt relief and special arrangements for the reconstruction of French devastated areas, there were no inducements for Belgium.[60] Although Belgian protests led on 4 January to withdrawal of the British demand for cancellation of priority, Belgian opinion unanimously condemned the plan as farcical. Not surprisingly, Belgium stood with France and Italy in rejecting the plan, and the conference failed.[61] Two days after the Reparation Commission formally declared German default on coal deliveries on 9 January 1923, France, Italy, and Belgium entered the Ruhr valley in pursuit of both coal and compliance with Reparation Commission requirements.[62]

For France, the larger issue was the survival of the Versailles treaty and of the French victory in the war. Poincaré, caught between British rejection of more moderate sanctions and intense pressure from the French right, reluctantly embarked upon a confrontation he had hoped to avoid. Belgian leaders were even more reluctant. They had hoped never to be forced to choose between Britain and France and for three years had tried to prevent an occupation of the Ruhr. Now the total opposition of British and French policies forced them to the unwanted choice. Driven by financial and economic necessity and influenced to a degree by the political impossibility of the British reparations plan from the Belgian point of view, they unhappily followed France. Once into the Ruhr, the Belgian leaders displayed considerably more nerve than the frightened Poincaré. They wished to act energetically toward a quick and decisive victory in order to terminate the occupation as rapidly as possible. Belgium was a very junior partner, however, and

60. Cmd. 1812, pp. 112–19.

61. Ibid., pp. 101–8, 173, 195; G. Grahame to Curzon, 5 Jan. 1923, tel. 3R, F.O. 371/8626; G. Grahame to Curzon, 7 Jan. 1923, no. 19, F.O. 371/8627. British experts had carefully considered the effect of their plan on every power involved except Belgium. Financial analysis, 1 Jan. 1923, F.O. 371/8625. The assault on Belgian priority was particularly foolish because, under the British plan, it would for four years (at least) be a priority on absolutely nothing, and the unpaid balance, though of crucial importance to Belgium, was too trifling a sum in relation to the whole scheme to warrant alienation of the state holding the decisive vote in the Reparation Commission.

62. Carl Bergmann, *The History of Reparations*, p. 176; FRUS PPC, 13:486–87, 781–82; F.O. memo, 8 May 1923, F.O. 371/9832; Etienne Weill-Raynal, *Les Réparations allemandes et la France*, 2:284. Italy sent no troops to the Ruhr and apparently only two engineers. Charles-Roux to Poincaré, 7 Jan. 1923, tel. 17, FMAE Z/Alle/237.

Poincaré's cautious timidity prevailed. Thus the Franco-German confrontation prolonged itself to the cost of all three powers involved.[63]

One of the side effects of the agonizing Ruhr occupation of 1923–25 and of the accompanying German hyper-inflation was total confusion in the Reparation Commission's accounts. Though the Ruhr occupation was profitable to the three occupying powers, they themselves did not know with certainty exactly what their Ruhr receipts totaled until after the Ruhr accounts were sorted out late in 1925 in what has been called "probably the most complicated translation of values ever attempted internationally."[64] Meanwhile, after the Dawes Plan had replaced all previous reparation schemes late in 1924, the Entente finance ministers met again in Paris in January 1925 to decide on the division of future reparations receipts. Once again Belgian priority became a bone of vigorous contention.

When priority was originally granted in 1919, the great powers had assumed that it would be extinguished by 1 May 1921 or very shortly thereafter. Between German failures of payment and Allied schemes to defer Belgian priority, it still had not been completed. Although no precise figures could be established in the absence of a definitive accounting of the Ruhr receipts, it appeared that about 25 percent of the priority remained to be fulfilled.[65] As German payments under the Dawes Plan were to be sharply reduced in the early years, it was in British and French interest to extinguish this impediment to their own receipts as quickly as possible. Although Austen Chamberlain, the new

---

63. Stephen A. Schuker, *The End of French Predominance in Europe*, pp. 21, 24–25, 117, 220–21; Crowe memo, 27 Dec. 1922, F.O. 371/7491; Ryan to Lampson, 5 Jan. 1923, F.O. 371/8628; Phipps to Tyrrell, 8 Sept. 1923, Phipps to Crowe, 6 Nov. 1923, CC Phipps Papers; Bariéty, *Les Relations franco-allemandes*, pp. 101–9. On the conflict of Franco-Belgian Ruhr policy, see BMAE B-10.071 (especially Rolin-Jaequemyns to Jaspar, 2 Mar. 1923) and FR/1923, passim. De Gaiffier's despatches from Paris are particularly illuminating about Poincaré's approach to the Ruhr occupation.

64. FRUS PPC, 13:785. Net profits after expenses and Rhineland occupation costs to the three occupying powers amounted to nearly 900 million gold marks. Belgium gained over half of this, chiefly on priority account and in the form of such interest as was paid on the six-month Germany treasury bills, which had been substituted for cash in late 1922. Ibid. Because the Bank of England had backed the bills, Germany paid them off during the Ruhr occupation but ceased paying interest. Jaspar to della Faille, 26 Feb. 1923, no. 422, BMAE note, 28 June 1923, BMAE B-366/VIII.

65. Treasury memo, n.d., F.O. 371/9744.

British foreign secretary, forbade any open challenge of Belgian priority, the Foreign Office and the Treasury attempted to undermine it, even though the Treasury privately admitted that at least 20 percent of the priority remained.[66] In conferences of Entente experts, the Treasury argued that Belgian priority had already been extinguished and that Belgium should "repay" it either by immediate reduction of the Belgian share of reparations receipts to 2.25 percent or by creation of annuities whereby Belgium would remit to the Allies sums much in excess of her receipts under the Dawes Plan.[67]

As either scheme would be politically ruinous to Belgian leaders, they defended the remaining priority with energy. Part of the difficulty was that reparations had shrunk so much. Had Germany paid the vast amounts contemplated at the peace conference, the reduction in the Belgian percentage of the receipts to "repay" her priority would have been slight. Now a small reparations pie almost guaranteed a dramatic reduction in Belgian receipts once repayment of priority began. Belgian politicians preferred to postpone the day, preferably until after the 1925 elections. Under the circumstances, they presented a barrage of arguments, some of them specious, in defense of the politically sacrosanct priority, trying every possible device to preserve it or alternatively to increase the Belgian percentage share of reparations so that a future cut would be less painful.[68]

Belgian success at the Paris Conference owed much to Belgian stubbornness, shrewd press relations, and Winston Churchill. The new chancellor of the Exchequer ignored his Treasury experts, who irritated him, and conceded much to the Belgian leaders, whom he liked, particularly Georges Theunis. As a result, the final agreement of 14 January acknowledged that Belgian priority was not extinguished. Until extinc-

66. Chamberlain minute on Lampson memo, 22 Nov. 1924, Phillips to Lampson, 25 Nov. 1924, Niemeyer to Lampson, 26 Nov. 1924, Leith-Ross and Phillips memo, 25 Nov. 1923, F.O. 371/9872.

67. British notes to Committee of Experts, 30, 31 Oct. 1924, NA U.S. Delegation to RC Papers/217.

68. Treasury memo, n.d., F.O. 371/9744; Treasury memo, 31 Oct. 1924, F.O. 371/9871; Belgian note to Committee of Experts, 8 Nov. 1924, Gutt note to Experts, 7 Nov. 1924, U.S. Delegation to RC Papers/217; Expert Report, n.d., compte-rendu, French meeting, 6 Nov. 1924, NA AJ^5/371.

tion sometime between 1 September 1925 and 1 September 1926 (depending upon resolution of the Ruhr accounts), Belgium would continue to receive 8 percent of the Dawes receipts. Thereafter, she would receive 4.5 percent, with the reduction fulfilling in toto her obligation to repay priority.[69] In this settlement, which was more generous than Belgian leaders had expected and considerably more generous than they had any reason to expect, Belgium had won the last battle over priority.

When Churchill returned to London from Paris, he reported a "brooding fear" and overwhelming French anxiety about security. As Chamberlain agreed with his assessment that "nothing could be done with France without some guarantee for security,"[70] the foreign secretary proposed to pursue an Anglo-French-Belgian alliance. In the early months of 1925, however, Stresemann, substantially abetted by the British ambassador in Berlin,[71] deflected him onto the road to Locarno. The intricate negotiations to that end during 1925 soon became further complicated by another piece of unfinished Belgian business from the peace conference: revision of the 1839 treaties. During a lull in the Locarno negotiations at the end of March 1925, the Belgian and Dutch governments together announced that they had reached accord on a new Belgo-Dutch treaty. They asked Britain and France to acknowledge by an exchange of letters the abrogation of Belgian neutrality and the concomitant guarantee of it. The guarantor powers did not accede to this request because they wished to retain their existing jurisdiction, stemming from 1815 and especially 1839, over the status of Belgium and Belgo-Dutch arrangements, particularly concerning the Scheldt. It oc-

69. Phipps to Crowe, 12 Jan., 13 Feb. 1925, Phipps Papers; Crewe to Chamberlain, 14 Jan. 1925, F.O. 800/257; G. Grahame to Chamberlain, 9 Jan. 1925, tel. 4, F.O. 371/10725. The agreement also specified that 5 percent of reparations receipts from Germany each year would be applied to retirement of the Belgian war debt. Though Britain and France would receive the lion's share, 12 percent of the 5 percent would go to Belgium by reason of her war debt to the United States. In the early years of the Dawes Plan, the amount actually gained by Belgium would be minuscule. For text of the 14 January agreement, see FRUS PPC, 13:902–19.

70. Cabinet 2 (25), 15 Jan. 1925, CAB 23/49; Chamberlain to Crowe, 16 Jan. 1925, F.O. 371/10726.

71. On the role of Lord D'Abernon, see Fred G. Stambrook, "'Das Kind'—Lord D'Abernon and the Origins of the Locarno Pact," pp. 233–63.

curred to Headlam-Morley, however, that revision of the 1839 treaties could serve as a convenient pretext for the Rhineland pact, thus obviating the odious implications for the Polish frontier implicit in a voluntary reaffirmation of Germany's western borders. Although Chamberlain remarked, "Each thing takes so much time that nothing should wait on the other thing," the Foreign Office promptly inserted into the preamble of the draft Rhineland pact an additional phrase: "Taking note of the abrogation of the Treaties for the neutralisation of Belgium and conscious of the necessity of stabilising the territorial status quo in the area which has so frequently been the scene of European conflict . . . "[72] So many difficulties arose over the Belgo-Dutch treaty that the idea of linking it to the Rhineland pact was eventually dropped. Nonetheless, the reference to the abrogation of Belgian neutrality remained in the preamble of the Treaty of Locarno.[73] It constituted the only formal recognition ever made by the great powers of the cancellation of this provision of the 1839 treaties.

Both the prior and the subsequent history of Belgo-Dutch negotiations suggest that Chamberlain was wise to divorce revision of the 1839 treaties from the Rhineland pact. After Delacroix's initiatives had failed in October 1920, the matter lapsed briefly until December 1920, when Jaspar, now Belgian foreign minister, asked for new negotiations. In early 1921 the Dutch indicated their willingness through Brand Whitlock. Thus, Jaspar held numerous discussions with the Dutch minister in Brussels and then met privately with van Karnebeek in August 1921, when both men were on holiday at Lucerne, and again repeatedly during the Genoa Conference of April–May 1922. No basis for agreement was found, however.[74] Hymans reopened the question of the 1839 treaties again by secret overtures to van Karnebeek in August 1924.

72. Van Zuylen, *Les Mains libres*, pp. 182–85; Crewe to Chamberlain, 26, 30 Mar. 1925, tels. 114, 118, Moncheur to Chamberlain, 3 Apr. 1925, Marling to Chamberlain, 4 Apr. 1925, Hurst to Chamberlain, 27 Apr. 1925, F.O. 371/11043; Headlam-Morley memo, 16 Apr. 1925, F.O. 371/10730.

73. Cmd. 2525. At German request, the reference to "stabilising the territorial status quo" was relegated to Article 1, being replaced by "ensuring peace." The German purpose was to facilitate retrocession of Eupen-Malmédy.

74. DuD, R.G.P. 162, pp. 264–65, 319–21, 324–25, 391–94, 404–5, 415–16, 492–94, 506, 544; Whitlock to Colby, 31 Jan. 1921, no. 1119, SD 755.56/37; Phillips to Whitlock, 15 Feb. 1921, Whitlock Papers/43 (LC); Capelle memo, 29 Feb. 1924, Jaspar

When he proved receptive, the two men talked privately during the September League meetings in Geneva, where conveniently they both lodged at the same hotel. After further exchanges through normal diplomatic channels, a Belgian delegation quietly journeyed to The Hague in mid-December.[75]

Negotiations went quickly despite certain disagreements. Each side reserved its rights in the Wielingen dispute and Belgium abandoned its request for a joint defense of Limburg. In return, Holland, with some reluctance, maintained its *casus belli* declaration. Both parties accepted the fluvial arrangements of the abortive 1920 treaty. The resultant draft Belgo-Dutch treaty, whose terms were agreed upon at the end of March 1925, merely abrogated Belgian neutrality, canceled the prohibition upon use of Antwerp as a naval base without definitively solving the problem of access to it, resolved technical questions regarding the Scheldt and the Ghent-Terneuzen canal, established a Belgo-Dutch commission to regulate use of the Scheldt, and provided for arbitration of disputes.[76]

As Hymans wished to sign the treaty before the 5 April 1925 Belgian election, the Belgians and the Dutch immediately presented the text to Britain and France, asking them to confirm by an exchange of letters that Belgian neutrality and the accompanying guarantee had been abrogated. Belgium took the view, to which Holland did not at this time object, that both had already lapsed and that only a formal interment was needed. Both Low Countries also maintained that fluvial arrangements between them were matters purely within their own joint jurisdiction. However, Britain and France not only insisted upon formal abrogation of the guarantee by treaty but also considered the 1839 treaties to remain fully in effect. The British declared that Belgium and Holland should seek British and French permission even to revise the

Papers/246; Benoist to Poincaré, 17 May 1922, no. 182, FMAE Z/Belg./75; de Ligne to Hymans, 23 May 1922, no. 771, BMAE PB/1922–26.

75. Bourquin to Hymans, 11 Aug. 1924, Hymans memos, 21 Aug., 7 Sept., 24 Oct., 11 Nov. 1924, de Ruelle to Hymans, 23 Dec. 1924, Hymans Papers/169.

76. De Ruelle memos, 2, 7 Feb. 1925, van Zuylen memo, 12 Feb. 1925, Hymans Papers/169; Phillips to Kellogg, 31 Mar. 1925, tel. 23, SD 755.56/50; van Zuylen, *Les Mains libres*, pp. 167–83.

fluvial arrangements of the old Belgo-Dutch treaty, and France, despite the Franco-Belgian military accord, preposterously claimed that "Belgium is still neutral." With the proviso that formal abrogation of the 1839 treaties would be arranged later on, the British and French did consent to signature of the new Belgo-Dutch treaty, which took place at The Hague on 3 April.[77]

Because the Belgians were eager to lay the 1839 regime to rest, they pressed for an immediate conference, but the British declared the notice too short and objected to some of the fluvial clauses of the new treaty.[78] As the question remained active, Britain and France took the view that they should retain an indefinite veto over both the international status and the maritime arrangements of Belgium. Upon this premise, their legal experts prepared in late April 1925 a draft treaty consenting to the Belgo-Dutch treaty, while rejecting two of its clauses and imposing an important proviso upon any further Belgo-Dutch arrangement for transit of Belgian warships on the Scheldt. In July, this text was presented to the Belgians and the Dutch, who erupted in unheard-of unison, arguing that such a treaty would seriously encroach upon their sovereignty. In reply, Britain and France clung grimly to the Final Act of Vienna of 1815. Britain was determined to maintain veto power for all time over future changes in Belgium's territorial status or in the Scheldt regime, and France responded to the opportunity to reduce Belgian independence. Neither offered any security guarantees in recompense. As a consequence, the issue dragged on interminably. Ultimately, after slight British concessions, a collective treaty was signed in Paris on 27 May 1926 to endorse the 1925 Belgo-Dutch treaty and to abrogate the 1839 treaties, Belgian neutrality, and the special regime for Antwerp. Although Belgium ratified these treaties, Holland did

77. Van Zuylen, *Les Mains libres*, pp. 182–84; F.O. to G. Grahame, 2 Apr. 1925, tel. 22, Fleuriau to Chamberlain, 3 Apr. 1925, Chamberlain to Moncheur, 3 Apr. 1925, Marling to Chamberlain, 4 Apr. 1925, F.O. 371/11043; Moncheur to Hymans, 1 Apr. 1925, tel. 24, de Gaiffier to Hymans, 1 Apr. 1925, tel. 40, Hymans Papers/169; Moncheur to Hymans, 15 Apr. 1925, no. 991/335, BMAE GB/1925; de Gaiffier to Hymans, 7 Apr. 1925, no. 4166/1932, BMAE FR/1925.

78. Moncheur to Chamberlain, 7 Apr. 1925, Campbell to Moncheur, 9 Apr. 1925, F.O. 371/11043; Moncheur to Hymans, 7, 11 Apr. 1925, tels. 26, 27, Hymans Papers/169; Moncheur to Ruzette, 20 May 1925, no. 1446/457, BMAE GB/1925.

not, primarily because of protest from Rotterdam shipping interests. Thus both lapsed.[79]

Belgo-Dutch negotiations resumed in 1928. Despite encouragement from both Briand and Chamberlain, they were brought to an abrupt end by publication in the Dutch press late in February 1929 of a patently forged document purporting to be the text of the Franco-Belgian military accord of 1920, together with another military agreement supposedly drawn up in 1927.[80] Holland thereafter tried to insist that Belgium must still remain legally neutral but ultimately recognized in 1933 via a diplomatic note that Belgian neutrality had in fact lapsed. Aside from the reference in the preamble to the Treaty of Locarno, this constituted the sole formal recognition by any power that any part of the 1839 treaties no longer held effect. Belgian neutrality and the great-power guarantee died a de facto death, and other aspects of the 1839 treaties were never revised.

The Locarno guarantee, such as it was, constituted one of the few Belgian gains from the travail of World War I and the years thereafter of trying to complete a peace settlement. In comparison with many other victors, Belgium did not fare well: Eupen and Malmédy; Ruanda and Urundi; reparations to about 35 percent of her reconstruction costs,[81]

79. Colenbrander, *Nederland en België: Proeve*, p. 157; Moncheur to Vandervelde, 9 July 1925, no. 1905/611, 3, 30 July 1925, tel. 67, 13 Aug. 1925, no. 2227/724, 19 Apr., 11 May 1926, tels. 12, 31, BMAE GB/1925–26; van Zuylen, *Les Mains libres*, pp. 184–86; Hymans, *Mémoires*, 2:493–94; Hurst memo, 28 Apr. 1925, F.O. 371/11043; Fleuriau to Chamberlain, 22 May 1925, Chamberlain to G. Grahame, 7 July 1925, no. 791, Moncheur to Chamberlain, 7 Aug. 1925, van Swinderin to Chamberlain, 7 Aug. 1925, Headlam-Morley memo, 31 Dec. 1925, F.O. 371/11044; van Zuylen to Vandervelde, 15 Aug. 1925, BMAE Ind/1921–1929/I; *Revision*, pp. 24–25; Lalaing to Vandervelde, 11, 20 Nov. 1926, tel. 34, no. 2520/1123, BMAE PB/1922–26; Admiralty, *Netherlands*, p. 627. The collective treaty carried the date of 22 May 1926 but was not in fact signed until 27 May. Crewe to Chamberlain, 27 May 1926, tel. 194, F.O. 371/11814.

80. Granville to Cushendun, 9 Oct. 1928, no. 798, Russell to Cushendun, 22 Oct. 1928, no. 40, F.O. 371/13331; Granville to Chamberlain, 4 Jan. 1929, no. 3, Chamberlain to Beelaerts van Blokland, 15 Jan. 1929, F.O. 371/14047; Stevenson to Chamberlain, 5 Mar. 1929, no. 87, SIS Report, 5 Mar. 1929, C/3915, Hoyar Miller memo, 12 Mar. 1929, F.O. 371/14061; notes for Jaspar, 7, 18 Mar. 1929, Jaspar Papers/248. The documents in question had connotations of offensive arrangements against Germany and Holland and invented a nonexistent British-French-Belgian military convention.

81. Francqui note, Jan. 1932, BMAE Ind/1932–1939/janvier 1932. Because esti-

which in fact went primarily to debt payments; Belgo-Luxembourgeois economic union without the Guillaume-Luxembourg railway; and the ineffectual Locarno guarantee were scant compensation to a small nation for much suffering. To Belgians, World War I proved that their security was inadequate. When the struggle to complete the peace settlement ended, Belgian security was even more inadequate. The protections embodied in the 1839 treaties had to all practical purposes lapsed but had been replaced only by the Locarno treaties, by which Britain guaranteed both sides of the Rhineland frontiers against invasion. The British concluded that they must make military arrangements with all parties or with none, so they made no military arrangements at all. Under the circumstances, in any future attack, Belgium was bound to be inundated before British help could arrive. As Belgian leaders recognized this fact, their enthusiasm for the Locarno treaties was limited but, like the French, they did not dare to decline the long-sought British guarantee even in so unsatisfactory a form.[82]

At the end of World War I, Belgium had argued that she had reached adulthood in the family of nations and thus should enter into the new world order on a footing of equality without humiliating limitations on her sovereignty. Though she also sought new security guarantees,[83] which she never received, and her representatives were often regarded by those of the great powers as children, not adults, otherwise her request was granted. To all practical purposes, Belgium emerged from the war and the postwar on a footing of nominal equality without either servitudes on her sovereignty or special protections provided by the great powers. Given her extremely exposed position, Belgium then had

---

mates, early and late, of Belgium's actual reconstruction costs vary considerably, some would indicate that she received only about 25 percent of her actual reconstruction expenditures.

82. G. Grahame to Curzon, 12 Dec. 1925, no. 927, F.O. 371/10747; *L'Etoile belge*, 16 Oct. 1925, p. 1, 17 Oct. 1925, p. 1; *La Nation belge*, 17 Oct. 1925, p. 3; Phillips to Kellogg, 18 Nov. 1925, no. 350, 26 Jan. 1926, SD 740.0011/245, 298; Belgique, Parlement, Chambre des Représentants, *Compte rendu* (1925–26), p. 12; G. Grahame to Chamberlain, 18 Nov. 1925, no. 858, F.O. 371/10746; FMAE note, 26 Feb. 1925, FMAE draft instructions to London, 12 Mar. 1925, FMAE Z/GB/73; Herriot note, 16 Mar. 1925, FMAE Z/GB/74.

83. Hymans to Moncheur, 18 Sept. 1918, BMAE Ind/1918/II.

no choice but to attempt to keep her three mighty neighbors in precarious balance. For a small nation with no weapons to wield in the harsh world of great-power politics, this was to prove an impossible task.

THE HINGE OF THE ENTENTE

The impossibility of Belgium's solution to this problem, to lean on Britain and France against Germany and to balance between her two protectors to avoid excessive dependency on either, was not evident to Belgian leaders when the Versailles treaty entered into force in January 1920 nor for some time thereafter. Like the great powers at the peace conference, Belgium assumed both that Germany would obey the treaty and that Allied unity, such as it was, would be maintained in the postwar era. Neither occurred, but what happened instead gave Belgium a new diplomatic role to play and new hopes of balancing between Britain and France. As 1920 progressed, it appeared that Belgium's largely unexpected position as a member of the Western Entente would render her chosen course possible. Hymans, and after him Delacroix and Jaspar, adjusted with amazing facility to a dramatic transformation of Belgium's diplomatic status. The little nation that had been so insulated from the main currents of European power politics before 1914 and that in most respects remained isolated throughout the war and at the peace conference became, diplomatically speaking, in the era from 1920 to 1925 one of the most important of the smaller states of Europe. This sudden prominence arose from the emergence of the Western Entente to deal with the unfinished business of the peace settlement and at the same time to enforce or revise this settlement. As America increasingly withdrew from formal participation in Supreme Councils, the Big Four of the peace conference did not become the Big Three. Instead it became the Three and a Half.[84] Three great powers and Belgium took on the job of implementing the peace. Because Italy was not genuinely a great

84. One could equally well maintain that it became a Three composed of the Big Two and two halves. However, Italy was on paper officially a great power and thus had certain privileges, such as an automatic right of participation, which Belgium lacked.

power and lacked much interest in many parts of the German settlement, while Britain and France rarely agreed on what should be done, Belgium's role became both prominent and of considerable importance. Further, on the rare occasions when Britain and France could agree on joint measures against Germany, Belgium could be relied upon to make a substantial contribution, usually far more substantial than that of Britain, whereas Italy could be counted on for nothing at all.

The Belgian role in the Western Entente was in a sense foreshadowed by her prominence in the many commissions of the peace conference. If there was good reason to include Belgium in the key conference commissions, there was also reason to include her in the execution of the peace. However, this logic did not automatically prevail, for the simple reason that many small powers participated in peace conference commissions, which had no power of decision. At the Paris Peace Conference, decision making was reserved to the great powers, and as Supreme Councils began to meet elsewhere late in 1919 to complete the work of the peace conference and to commence execution of the Versailles treaty, the great powers assumed that they would carry on alone as before. At first, Belgian diplomatists assumed the same but, as they realized that matters of direct concern to their security and financial future were being decided without their participation, they began to clamor for admission. France usually supported these appeals on the assumption, which was only occasionally justified, that Belgian support against Britain could be purchased by concessions on unrelated Franco-Belgian issues, such as Luxemburg.

Though Belgium as a small power and indeed the only small power at most Supreme Councils never gained the automatic right of attendance at all sessions that Italy enjoyed, it soon became impossible to exclude her from meetings devoted to most German questions except Upper Silesia. How to exclude from discussion of the Rhineland the country with the second largest military force there and a seat on the Rhineland High Commission? How to bar from consideration of war crimes trials the nation with the longest, best publicized, and most highly emotional list of atrocities? How to discuss punitive expeditions against Germany without consulting the state that, after France, would bear the brunt? How to debate German reparations without the only small power with a Reparation Commission voice on this vital issue, particularly as that state in fact held not only the key vote but also a priority of payment?[85] Just as Belgium's role in the war had been unique, so her role in the peace was also to be, and in due course the great powers had to accept this fact.

It was the reparations question that more than any other issue forced Belgian inclusion in the numerous postwar conferences, and it was this question that led the Belgian government to seek admission to all Supreme Councils, whatever the agenda. As the first five postwar years turned into a continuation of the war by other means, reparations became the terrain upon which most of the key battles were fought. France struggled with mounting desperation to retain the high ground of the Versailles treaty, which represented both her far from unilateral victory in the war and her only hope of escaping from domination by her more populous, economically stronger, and potentially much more powerful eastern neighbor. Germany, which had tried so hard to eliminate Britain from the war on the theory that an isolated France would soon have to surrender,[86] used the same tactic with considerably more success in her continuing war against the peace. It was Weimar Germany's goal to dismantle the Versailles treaty and to rewrite the peace upon the premise of German victory, not German defeat. In time, she succeeded to a considerable extent, thanks to her own persistence, strength, and flat refusal to accept the peace settlement, thanks to the withdrawal of Russia in full and America in part from the diplomatic scene, and thanks above all to the shift of British policy away from France. Seemingly secure on her islands, Britain rarely comprehended France's fear of Germany. Influenced by five hundred years of hostile rivalry and much alarmed by the French air force and submarine-building program, Britain tended to see France as the greater danger. In the very short run, France was indeed stronger than Germany but, as every

85. The fact that the Institut Solvay in Brussels did many of the Reparation Commission's technical studies not only buttressed the Belgian claim but also contributed to the fact that Belgian Foreign and Finance Ministry officials soon became exceptionally proficient at dealing with the thorny reparations problem. It should be remembered that in a country as small as Belgium everybody of consequence knows everybody else, and professors, financiers, and the like invariably double as government consultants.

86. See L. L. Farrar, Jr., *Divide and Conquer*, pp. 86–95.

French premier well recognized, the long run was a different matter. Most of them, Poincaré not excluded, deemed their policy options to be much constrained by the need for British support against Germany. This support was less and less forthcoming as time passed. Although Britain never fully abandoned France in favor of Germany, she did work her way back to the middle position and increasingly chose to balance between the two. It was this British choice that gave Germany so much opportunity for maneuver and that contributed markedly to the growing fragility and instability of the peace. As France found herself more and more isolated against her potentially dominant foe, she tried first confrontation and then accommodation with little success, as time was clearly on Germany's side, and also turned for support to her eastern allies and to Belgium. Of these, only Belgium, the smallest and weakest of all, had any consistent voice in the Western Entente.

Because Belgium was extremely wary of becoming a French satellite, she did not with any regularity play the part for which France had cast her, although identity of interest did sometimes thrust the two countries into the same camp. It was Belgium's role in the Western Entente to bring her two feuding great-power allies together and somehow to cajole them into a semblance of a common policy toward Germany. Belgian leaders fully recognized and gladly accepted this role, as it gave them a voice in matters of direct interest to their country. They maintained that Belgium's shared concerns with France about Germany, together with her identity of economic outlook with Britain, peculiarly fitted them for the role they found themselves in.[87] They tended, especially Jaspar, to take great pride in their delicate and difficult mission, which did indeed cast Belgium into the diplomatic spotlight as the main supporting player until 1926 and which, to a lesser degree, continued her abnormal prominence until 1930.

In Entente debates, Belgian representatives, generally speaking, were willing to accept with relief any proposal that their feuding senior partners could agree on, unless the proposed solution jeopardized their sacrosanct priority. They recognized that if Britain and France could come to any consistent and sustained agreement on policy toward Germany, their role, of which they were so proud, would quickly evaporate.

87. Henri Jaspar, "Belgium and Western Europe since the Peace Treaty," p. 166.

But in the immediate postwar years, there was never any real likelihood of that. As France fought with increasing despair to preserve those portions of the treaty most vital to her financial, economic, and military security, whereas Britain consistently pressed for de facto treaty revision to Germany's benefit, it was Belgium's task to try to bridge the widening gulf. By the time that Belgium became a regular participant in Supreme Council meetings in mid-1920, a bridge was badly needed. One wonders who would have provided it if the Belgians had not been present and willing. Certainly the Italian delegation rarely showed much inclination to mediate.

At first the Belgian team that took on this thankless task consisted primarily of Delacroix and Hymans. It was they who fought for and gained Belgian participation in the London and San Remo Conferences of February and April 1920. They also presided over the long arduous Spa Conference in July, supported the British there in opposition to a Ruhr occupation proposed by France, and then struggled manfully to reconcile the thoroughly opposed British and French views concerning a projected further meeting with German representatives at Geneva. Although Delacroix ultimately succeeded, the conference was never held and Delacroix's government fell before he had to face the next stormy Supreme Council. With the advent of Count Henry Carton de Wiart's government in November 1920, Belgium presented a new diplomatic team consisting of Henri Jaspar and Georges Theunis. These two, who worked together in remarkable harmony, presided over Belgium's foreign policy through several tension-filled years until Jaspar lost office over the Franco-Belgian trade treaty in early 1924. Hymans then replaced him until the Theunis government fell after the April 1925 elections.

Henri Jaspar somehow never achieved Hymans's international eminence but was at least his equal, if not his superior, as a diplomatist. A bouncy, energetic little man with a startling physical resemblance to Lloyd George, he had a larger than life personality of the variety often associated with Winston Churchill or Theodore Roosevelt.[88] He was noted for an explosive temper but, unlike Hymans, largely confined it to domestic politics, although being trapped for two agonizing years

88. The analogy does not extend to the Rough Rider aspect of Roosevelt.

between Poincaré and Curzon did try his patience sorely. It was Jaspar's unhappy lot to have to deal with these two exceptionally unpleasant Allied foreign ministers simultaneously. Both demanded immediate compliance with their conflicting orders, which Jaspar invariably refused, but more diplomatically than Hymans. He was equally dedicated to Belgian independence but less explosively inclined to saying so. Worse yet from Jaspar's point of view, both Poincaré and Curzon would regularly demand that he arrange the full compliance of the other. After Jaspar would laboriously construct a compromise somewhere in the middle, both would erupt with rage. Though Jaspar's task of trying to glue the Entente together was both thankless and painful, he reveled in it. He had considerable ego, which responded to both the news coverage and the niceties (and which was bruised by any omission of the latter), but his primary motivation was intense patriotism and dedication to Belgian independence. Jaspar was reputed to be an Anglophile, in contrast to the supposedly Francophile Hymans, and in fact he deliberately conveyed this impression upon taking office in hopes of improving Anglo-Belgian relations. Jaspar was indeed Anglophile to a considerable degree, but no more so than Hymans. The policy did not change with the new team, but the style altered greatly. Jaspar's ebullient enthusiasm, warmer personality, and ability to joke stood Belgium in good stead, particularly as her role in the Western Entente steadily enlarged. Whether this increased prominence of Belgium arose from the course of events or from Jaspar's ambitions for his country is difficult to say. If any of the postwar directors of Belgian foreign policy aspired to elevate his nation to the status of a real power of the second rank, it was most likely Henri Jaspar, but the evidence is far from conclusive.[89]

Georges Theunis had no such ambitions for Belgium. A quiet, com-

89. Although Jaspar has been widely suspected of such ambitions for Belgium, his voluminous papers shed no light on the subject. The increasing Belgian prominence could easily (aside from Jaspar's insistence on certain attentions both for himself and for his country) have arisen from the course of events. By the time he took charge, Belgian attendance at Supreme Councils was largely established and the recurring crises of the Entente were steadily worsening. Had Hymans presided over the Foreign Ministry from late 1920 to 1924, the policy probably would have been similar. Jaspar certainly was very reluctant to occupy the Ruhr and in later years told a friend that it had been a mistake. Interview with Baron Drion du Chapois (Brussels, 9 Sept. 1967), to whom Jaspar made the comment in 1925 or 1926.

petent man with little inclination for the limelight, he also had a modest ego, both for himself and for his country. He understood his nation's role vis-à-vis the great powers and shrugged off the frequent slights with much more equanimity than either Jaspar or Hymans. With great tact, he also skillfully soothed Jaspar and ministered to the bruises on his ego. Never a politician, Theunis nonetheless had a remarkable political career as the reparations question and his own abilities thrust him into prominence. In foreign policy, he confined himself to reparations, an area in which he was enormously skilled, for he had been involved in the question from the outset. Trained as an engineer, Theunis had a successful prewar career as a financier and then served in the wartime Belgian army, including some middle-level diplomatic missions after he had been invalided out of active duty. He was the key reparations expert in the Belgian delegation to the peace conference and then became the first permanent Belgian member of the Reparation Commission. In the Carton de Wiart ministry, Theunis became finance minister, a post he continued to hold after he became prime minister in December 1921. As long as Jaspar was foreign minister, the two men fully shared the reparations question without policy disagreement, although primary responsibility probably lay in Theunis's hands. After Hymans returned to office in 1924, Theunis took unilateral charge of reparations policy, as Hymans could not possibly master all the intricacies of what had occurred during his four-year absence.

When the new team of Jaspar and Theunis made its diplomatic debut at the Paris Conference in January 1921, what transpired proved to be sharply symbolic of Belgium's role and also an omen of what the future would bring. The clash between Britain and France on both German disarmament and reparations became so acute that more than once both delegations retired to their respective chambers in high dudgeon and Lloyd George threatened to leave altogether. Because the two senior partners were not speaking to each other, Jaspar and Theunis trudged back and forth between them for hours, devising one compromise plan after another and finally concocting one that brought Britain and France back to the conference table and to agreement.[90] Similarly,

90. I.C.P. 155A, 28 Jan. 1921, CAB 29/90; F.O. Summary, 16 Mar. 1921, F.O. 371/6018; Suarez, *Briand*, 5:133–34; Jaspar memo, n.d., Jaspar Papers/244A.

at the London Conference of April–May 1921, Briand indicated that he wished, for domestic political reasons, to march at once on the Ruhr in response to Germany's default on the interim payment of 20 milliard marks due on 1 May 1921; on the other hand, Lloyd George, in an effort to avoid punitive measures altogether, urged waiting until the permanent reparations plan was concocted, transmitted to Germany with a time limit, and rejected. As Briand threatened both unilateral action and his own resignation, the clash again became bitter and once more the Belgian delegation rushed into the breach. It was Jaspar who proposed that sanctions be immediately declared but not imposed at once, thus saving Briand's face and perhaps his government, giving the experts time to devise the Schedule of Payments, and affording Germany time to accept the plan and obviate the need for action.[91]

Belgium's participation in the Western Entente was useful in other ways as well. When the British did not wish to go to Paris and the French declined to visit London, Brussels presented itself as a middle ground. Given the extreme difficulty of achieving enough consensus to hold a meeting at all and the fact that Lloyd George's allergy to every-thing Belgian extended to the climate, food, and central heating there, more conferences were proposed for Brussels than were actually held. Belgium did host and finance the long Spa Conference in July 1920, but the nature of relationships within the Western Entente was such that the Belgian hosts had the greatest difficulty in discovering from their senior partners when it was to be held, whom to invite, and what the agenda would be.[92]

As the reparations question became progressively more technically complex, the presence of Theunis much enhanced the Belgian role. Alone among the prime ministers, he thoroughly understood financial matters, and his talent for translating the fuzzy formulations of others into concrete and workable schemes facilitated progress considerably.

91. I.C.P. 191, 193, 193A, 193C, 194, 195, 30 Apr.–2 May 1921, CAB 29/92; Peace Conference Paper A.J. 286, 1 May 1921, Lloyd George Papers F/25/1/28; Suarez, *Briand*, 5:184.

92. Baron Riddell, *Lord Riddell's Intimate Diary of the Peace Conference and After, 1918–1923*, pp. 220, 214; I.C.P. 220A, 4 Jan. 1922, CAB 29/94; Moncheur to Hymans, 12 May 1920, tel. 94, de Gaiffier to Hymans, 7 June 1920. no. 6005/3181, Jaspar to Delacroix, 8 May 1920, Hymans Papers/155.

Though Jaspar did his share of devising compromise formulas, Theunis's specialized skills were increasingly needed. Further, Theunis would regularly intervene when conferences reached the brink of breakdown, suggesting always that proposals be referred to experts who could examine them in a more dispassionate atmosphere, and thus he saved more than one conference from collapse. Although Belgian compromises almost invariably gave France the form and Britain the substance, there was very rarely any British thanks. Only Briand, who well understood that a few gracious words, especially if uttered to the press, could do much to assuage Belgian disappointment on other issues, ever showed much appreciation of the arduous Belgian role.[93]

In this fashion, Belgium bridged the gap between her senior partners and patched together compromise after compromise. However, as Anglo-French differences concerning the future of Europe and especially Germany's role in it were both fundamental and increasingly profound, the compromises became both more difficult and more awkward as the law of diminishing returns set in. Jaspar and Theunis slogged on, trying to keep the Entente from collapsing altogether. Unfortunately, Lloyd George came to appreciate their utility only just before he left office,[94] and Poincaré never appreciated the Belgian efforts at all, always preferring obedience to mediation. By late 1922 all the ingenuity of Jaspar and Theunis could not paper over the widening gulf and they knew it. Finally, the fatalism and inexperience of the new British prime minister, Andrew Bonar Law, who accepted a reparations plan politically impossible to all three Continental allies, together with the domestic pressures upon Poincaré, forced Belgium, much against her will, to choose and to accompany France into the Ruhr.

Once the Ruhr occupation was launched, the Belgian government first tried to prod Poincaré into more decisive action and then attempted to moderate his flinty stances, both in hopes of ending the occupation

93. I.C.P. 156, 29 Jan. 1921, CAB 29/90; Vicomte Terlinden, "La Belgique aux conférences interalliées de 1920 et de 1921," p. 84; I.C.P. 172, 3 Mar. 1921, CAB 29/91; I.C.P. 200, 200A, 5 May 1921, CAB 29/93; I.C.P. 225, 7 Jan. 1922, CAB 29/94.

94. Conference of Ministers, 9 Aug. 1922, S-58, CAB 23/36 pt 1; Cabinet 44 (22), 10 Aug. 1922, CAB 23/30; Jaspar to his daughter, 11 Aug. 1922, private papers of Mme. Roberte-Jaspar, Brussels.

as quickly as possible. However, the Belgian tail could not wag the French dog, and Belgium soon found herself in the satellite status she had so long sought to avoid. As Poincaré made that fact clear with increasing brutality, Theunis and Jaspar, especially the latter, did all that they could, given the need for a united front in the struggle against Germany, to distance themselves from France. Through a painful spring and summer of ever lengthier diplomatic notes, the Belgian government was consistently more moderate than France but never accommodating enough to satisfy Britain. Further, Jaspar did everything in his limited power to ease Stresemann's surrender in the face of Poincaré's implacability. Once passive resistance had ended, Belgium quickly reverted to the middle ground between Britain and France, taking an independent line on both Rhenish separatism and reparations.

The return to the middle ground and to the mediator's role brought with it a return to the disadvantages thereof. In October 1923, Britain called upon Belgium, France, and Italy to join in an invitation to the United States to pursue one of two forms of reparations inquiry informally suggested by the American government. Knowing that Poincaré would reject the first proposal, which would have bypassed the Reparation Commission altogether, Theunis and Jaspar used every weapon in their diplomatic armory to bring him to accept the second. After a bitter contest of wills, which enraged Poincaré, the Belgian rejection of domination left him diplomatically isolated and with little choice. When the Belgians triumphantly reported Poincaré's acceptance of the second scheme to Britain, Curzon erupted in fury because they had not achieved French acquiescence in the first proposal.[95] Jaspar, who had long since become inured to the misery of existence between Poincaré and Curzon, took these eruptions calmly. In due course the resultant Dawes Committee set to work and eventually drew up a new reparations plan. While its important political aspects were devised by American experts, its technical details rested largely upon Belgian studies prepared in the spring of 1923. Although the British and French had brushed these

95. F.O. to Crewe, 19 Oct. 1923, tel. 356; G. Grahame to Curzon, 25 Oct. 1923, no. 887, F.O. 371/8658; Moncheur to Jaspar, 25 Oct. 1923, tel. 110, 26 Oct. 1923, Jaspar Papers/214B.

aside with disdain, Stresemann had adopted them with considerable enthusiasm,[96] and the Belgian preparatory studies much facilitated progress on technical matters, notably the matter of how Germany would amass the revenues for reparations. Like every other power involved, Belgium accepted the Dawes Plan for lack of any alternative.

Thereafter, Belgian leaders did what lay in their power to nudge France toward putting the Dawes Plan into effect. However, at the London Conference of July–August 1924 they found that their role had diminished, particularly after the German delegation arrived and the great powers began to negotiate alone, often ignoring the one small power with more than a token delegation and certainly more than a token interest in the Ruhr occupation. In the closing days of the conference, the Belgian delegation found itself in the humiliating position of obtaining much of its information from the press corps. Worse yet, Edouard Herriot, who had been refreshingly punctilious about consulting the Belgian government when he had first succeeded Poincaré in June, became so distraught during these final days of the conference that he committed both France and Belgium to substantial evacuations of German territory without either consulting or informing Theunis and Hymans. Though these slights to national pride occasioned a predictable protest from Hymans,[97] the Belgian government was more than satisfied that the long agony of the Ruhr occupation would soon be over.

The 1924 London Conference was something of a watershed in the diplomacy of the 1920s. It brought the long reparations struggle to semipermanent resolution and, in so doing, constituted a substantial revision of the Versailles treaty to Germany's benefit. The decisions taken at London signaled the end, immediate or implied, of so many of the constraints which hitherto France had been able to impose on Germany that the power balance began to shift very perceptibly, and it was obvious that time would bring further shifts, as Britain now clearly

96. The Belgian *Etudes* are most conveniently located in de Gaiffier to Poincaré, 25 May 1923, AJ[5]/387, or Moncheur memo, 11 June 1923, F.O. 371/8639. On Stresemann's attitude, see G. Grahame to Curzon, 8 Oct. 1923, tel. 215, D'Abernon to Curzon, 16 Oct. 1923, tel. 369, F.O. 371/8657.

97. Hymans note, 24 June 1924, Hymans Papers/171; Hymans notes, 15, 16 Aug. 1924, Hymans Papers/157.

positioned herself between France and Germany, and Versailles treaty clauses giving France temporary economic advantages would soon expire.[98] In the course of 1925 the Locarno negotiations brought not only a security pact that formalized Britain's position as the balance in the balance of power but also effective resolution of the disarmament question, again largely to Germany's benefit, and evacuation of the first Rhineland zone in January 1926, a year behind schedule. With disarmament and reparations, the two issues that had occasioned so many Entente conferences, both laid to rest and the Rhineland occupation reduced in size and considerably attenuated in its rigor, the number of questions which in the future Germany would have to ask and the Entente would somehow have to answer in unison was dramatically diminished. As a consequence, Entente diplomacy sharply declined and Belgium's role decreased accordingly.

Even during the long Entente negotiations leading to the Locarno Conference, Belgium was more informed than consulted and not always informed. When the formal invitation was finally presented to Germany on 15 September 1925, Britain and France forgot that Belgium should also participate, forcing her to an embarrassingly belated identic demarche.[99] At Locarno itself, Vandervelde, then foreign minister, was active but not particularly successful. The Belgian delegation participated in the entire conference, unlike the Czechs and the Poles, who were merely summoned for the two final days. But Vandervelde offended Chamberlain both by his open hostility to Benito Mussolini[100] and by his searching questions about the import of the document exempting Germany from participation in League of Nations sanctions. Vandervelde, who showed somewhat more enthusiasm for the League than other Belgian foreign ministers, was concerned because the wording implied that every League member could decide for itself whether to participate in either military or economic sanctions. His reaction was

98. On the entire subject of the London Conference, including the causes and effects of the decisions taken, see Schuker, *End of French Predominance*.

99. DDB, 2:327–28.

100. Van Zuylen, *Les Mains libres*, pp. 215–16; Chamberlain to G. Grahame, 4 Nov. 1925, BUL A. Chamberlain Papers 52/433; Chamberlain to R. Graham, 21 Oct. 1925, tel. 289, F.O. 371/10743. Vandervelde's hostility to Mussolini arose from the murder of Giacomo Matteotti and also from incidents in their mutual socialist past.

a classic example of European small-power diplomacy in the 1920s, as most of the smaller Continental states, far more in fact than Belgium, tried to find some security in the League of Nations. Vandervelde's point about the future viability of any League sanctions was well taken, but Chamberlain and Briand brushed it aside,[101] driven both by their eagerness for agreement with Germany and by their own antipathy to referring anything of consequence to Geneva.

It is a striking fact that there was almost no Entente consultation in advance of the Locarno signing ceremonies at London on 1 December 1925, even though Stresemann had signaled that he wished to negotiate after the formal ceremony. He gained several concessions during the talks, and more were to follow as the Locarno arrangements were put into effect in 1926. Finally, in September 1926, Germany entered the League of Nations. With this dramatic event, European diplomacy altered fundamentally, as Entente conferences were replaced by "Locarno tea parties," informal hotel room gatherings of the great powers in conjunction with quarterly League Council meetings in Geneva. What transpired in the hotel rooms invariably outstripped in importance what occurred in the Council hall, as the great powers quietly arranged European affairs in a manner bearing some relationship to the meetings at Wilson's house in Paris in 1919. Because these discussions ranged over all varieties of European questions and because Belgium had lost her Council seat consequent to the rule of rotation for small-power representation on the Council established in conjunction with German admission, she was not a regular participant in these Locarno tea parties. However, her role was firmly enough established that she was consulted on the infrequent occasions when unfinished business arose between Germany and the fading Western Entente. Thus, Belgium participated fully in the informal gatherings leading to the 16 September 1928 Geneva communiqué calling for a new reparations plan and reconsideration of the Rhineland occupation.[102] Jaspar, then prime minister, presided over the two ensuing Hague Conferences of 1929 and 1930, in which Hymans, again foreign minister, participated actively, but with the entry into force of the Young Plan and the early evacuation of the

101. DDB, 2:346–47; Loc/122/Con, 12 Oct. 1925, F.O. 371/10744.
102. DDB, 2:536–60; DBFP, Series IA, 5:335.

Rhineland, Belgium's decade-long excursion into the diplomacy of the great powers effectively came to an end.

In commenting upon Belgium's decade in the limelight and her role in Entente diplomacy, Jonathan Helmreich has termed her the hyphen of the Entente. His analogy is useful, particularly when he adds that "Belgium, like a hyphen, did not carry enough weight to claim a diplomatic identity of her own."[103] That indeed was always the difficulty, although Belgian leaders consistently attempted to claim and to define an independent diplomatic identity. Perhaps, however, it would be more apt to define the Belgian role, particularly in the early years, as the hinge of the Entente. From 1920 to 1924 it was Belgium's function to make it possible for Britain and France to bend and to move toward each other just enough to make possible a united Entente voice in response to Germany. Theunis's and Jaspar's labors provided lubrication, flexibility, and movement as they sought ways to reconcile opposed French and British positions. As those early years passed, the pressures on the hinge became progressively more severe, for Britain and France tugged with increasingly insistent force in opposite directions. Finally in January 1923 the structure snapped, leaving the Belgian hinge unhappily attached to the French side. Within two months, however, Jaspar and Theunis were trying to revert to their earlier role and, after September 1923, they largely succeeded in regaining their old position until the reparations crisis was resolved by implementation of the Dawes Plan late in 1924.

We shall never know what would have happened to the Western Entente without the Belgian hinge to keep it functioning in creaky fashion or whether an early collapse of the Entente might have been better for Europe's prosperity, security, and peace of mind. It is clear, however, that through those five tension-filled years, the leaders of the small nation with such scant experience in great-power politics toiled mightily and with very little appreciation to provide the flexibility and the awkward compromises that kept the Entente precariously in being. They thought that they were striving to solidify the peace and to enhance their nation's economic and military security; whether their efforts contributed more to Europe's increasing instability is a question historians

103. J. Helmreich, *Belgium and Europe*, pp. 261–62.

will long debate. In all probability, as Belgium's role, while prominent, was distinctly limited, the opposition of British and French policies toward Germany contributed far more to the instability of the peace. As Britain and France embarked on collision courses not long after the Versailles treaty entered into effect, Belgian leaders had a choice between retiring to the sidelines and passively watching the crash or trying to avert it. Not surprisingly, they did all that they could to avert it. Their best efforts succeeded only in postponing it, and when it occurred, their nation suffered as much as any victor. Once the collision had taken place, the Belgian leaders did everything in their limited power to help pick up the pieces and to restore a wounded continent to health. Whether Belgium's Entente diplomacy had always been wise is arguable, but it had always been well intentioned and extremely hard-working. More perhaps could not be expected of such a small and inexperienced power.

EUROPE'S ADOLESCENT

Belgium's decade in the diplomatic limelight was certainly the most unexpected by-product of her role in the war and at the peace conference. After six months of almost total exclusion from great-power decision making at Paris, Belgian leaders had no reason whatever to foresee what lay ahead. The prominent diplomatic role from 1920 on applied considerable balm to a battered national ego, but in 1919 and 1920, as Belgium faced up to her scant gains at the peace conference and in its immediate aftermath, national dissatisfaction was profound. Whether the Belgian chagrin was justified is another question.

In some respects, Belgian expectations of the peace settlement had been unrealistic. Conversely to the situation in many other countries, the government was, relatively speaking, more unrealistic than the citizenry. A certain lack of realism on the part of public and parliamentary opinion was only to be expected everywhere, and the false hopes in this respect in Belgium did not exceed those in other countries. Though annexationist sentiment certainly existed, on the whole Belgian opinion, with some notable exceptions, was fairly moderate on the subjects of Luxemburg and Dutch territory. Because neither of these questions had been fully resolved when the contents of the Versailles treaty became known in May 1919, because daily life remained very difficult, and because the electorate had been given no information on other matters, such as Belgian exclusion from the decision-making process at Paris, public outcry focused almost entirely upon the economic and financial sections of the treaty, notably the reparations clauses. Although the expectations of the Belgian people in this respect had been excessive, they were no more unrealistic than those of ordinary people in other victor countries. Moreover, in Belgium there was more excuse for such large expectations. After all, both the German and the Allied governments had publicly assured them over and over in the most solemn terms that Germany would pay in full for the reconstruction of their country. In the end, of course, Belgium and the other victors paid for the damage done, both in Belgium and elsewhere, and the transfer of this burden from Germany's shoulders to those of her erstwhile enemies only enhanced Germany's potential Continental predominance.

As British officials noted, the Belgian government should have been less trusting to Allied promises, but it was not. The startling failure to give any appreciable thought to the reparations question until after the peace conference began was among the Belgian government's evident mistakes. It arose from unanimity of opinion within the government and naive faith in Allied pledges. Belgian officials did not lack the capacity to study the problem, but they did not anticipate the necessity. Hardheaded analysis probably would have had little effect upon decisions at Paris, as Belgium had so little power and influence there, but at least it would have prepared the cabinet for the disillusionment ahead. However, few Belgian leaders or officials possessed the requisite cynicism to make an effective analysis. While consistently showing a good deal of sensitivity to France's reparations needs, they tended to assume that German resources should be primarily dedicated to the reconstruction of France and Belgium. Anything left over could of course go to other countries. For all its logic in terms of where the war was fought and where the devastation was greatest, this approach was totally unrealistic. With their quaint notions of the fairness and disinterested generosity of great powers, the Belgian leaders never gave a thought to the possibility that Lloyd George would be determined to have a hefty share of the spoils for Britain and would be fully prepared to take it at

Belgium's expense, earlier eloquent British oratory notwithstanding. Similarly, they failed to comprehend that the weakness of Italy's claim upon German reparations was of considerably less significance than her major-power status and her participation in the Big Four.

The reparations concessions that Belgium obtained at the peace conference were largely the work of House and the American experts. Despite their tenacity, Hymans and his delegation deserve only a modest share of the credit, for both priority and privilege were achieved more by American initiatives than by Belgian exertions. In part, Belgium lacked the power, influence, and voice to accomplish much on her own. In addition, Hymans, like his predecessors, failed to see that Belgium should always enlist the most disinterested power in her behalf. Assuming that all Allied great powers were at heart generously disinterested, Belgian foreign ministers usually did the reverse. Thus, during and immediately after the war, they approached France about Luxemburg and Britain about Holland. By the time that Hymans reversed field at the peace conference, it was too late, because Balfour had lost control of the Luxemburg question and France was in pursuit of Dutch loans. It is doubtful whether Hymans recognized that Balfour could support him over Luxemburg just because Britain had no interest in the question or that the United States was the one power that could afford to be generous about reparations. On this latter question, Belgian efforts should have been concentrated upon the American delegation from the outset but, in view of the heavily European orientation of Belgian diplomacy and the overriding belief in the oratorical pledges of the faithful guarantor powers, they were not. Under the circumstances, Belgium was fortunate to gain as much as she did in the reparations settlement.

Because Hymans, with excessive faith and logic, assumed that Belgium's remaining guarantors would be both generous and objective, he failed to see that each issue affected every other and that personal relations affected them all. With considerable naiveté, he thought that decisions would be made on the merits of the question. Not only was he sometimes unrealistic about the merits of Belgium's case, but also he never realized that his outburst to Lloyd George over reparations could deleteriously affect Lloyd George's already doubtful objectivity on both that issue and others. Although Hymans's fierce national pride and flat rejection of all obsequiousness are both entirely understandable and rather moving, they did not constitute wise diplomacy.

Faith in the guarantor powers also caused some failures of adequate preparation, not only on reparations but on other issues as well. In one sense, Clemenceau was justified when he complained that Hymans expected to sit back in an armchair while the great powers arranged matters for him. In another sense, given his lack of effective voice, Hymans could do little else. Nonetheless, more preparatory work should have been done on reparations and, in view of Belgian designs on Dutch territory, serious consideration should have been given before the peace conference began to appropriate German districts for compensation. Hymans apparently assumed that the great powers would arrange such matters. His failure to order any investigation of the question until well after it had been posed directly to him by the Council of Ten probably had no effect upon the course of events, as there was little prospect of Dutch territorial cession from the outset. However, had any real opportunity presented itself early in the peace conference, Hymans would not have been properly prepared to capitalize upon it.

For all the massive dossiers, there were these curious lacunae, most of which arose from faith in the guarantors, Hymans's blind spot in regard to Dutch attitudes, and sheer ignorance of the nature and conduct of power politics. Certainly, once the presence of Loudon and other prominent Dutchmen in Paris had been noted, their activities should have been closely investigated. However, neither Hymans nor anybody else at the Foreign Ministry seems to have realized that the Dutch would react sharply to Belgium's scarcely concealed aspirations or that Holland, a mere neutral, was in fact in an excellent position to counterattack effectively. Just why the Belgian claim to Eupen was not decided before the peace conference opened is not entirely clear. Presumably the tension between the Belgian army's wishes and Hymans's hesitation about incorporating too many Germans had not been resolved. Still, the hasty telegrams between Paris and Brussels at the end of February did not constitute considered decision making. Because Belgium had so few territorial desires that did not involve Allies and neutrals, those few should have been settled in good time and in careful fashion.

The entire embarrassing question of territorial claims upon Holland was ineptly handled, not only by Hymans but also by the cabinet and the Foreign Ministry. By December 1918, Dutch, British, and American hostility to territorial transfer was clear and Clemenceau was complaining about Belgian appetites in Limburg. At this juncture both realism and wisdom would have dictated a clear-cut and forthright abandonment of any thought of annexation. Had the Belgian cabinet taken this step before the peace conference opened, it might have gained more great-power support on other issues concerning the Netherlands and thus emerged with something instead of nothing. As it was, the cabinet recognized the lack of diplomatic support but did not face its implications. Hence the policy of hinting and hoping was adopted. Not only was this approach bound to embitter Belgo-Dutch relations but, in the absence of great-power backing, it was foredoomed to failure. Thus, Belgium suffered severe criticism, lost sympathy, and eroded the moral position that was one of her few assets as a consequence of claims she never actually made but, all too clearly, would have liked to make. However, the Belgian cabinet and Foreign Ministry were both haunted by the need to seize this probably unique opportunity to undo the unfortunate decisions of 1839. Beyond that, it did not occur to Belgian leaders that their Dutch counterparts not only were vastly more experienced horse traders than they but also possessed far superior horses with which to trade. Here, as in other matters, the historic experience of both a privileged and a sheltered status, plus the heady praise of 1914, misled Belgian leaders into a false appreciation of their true position.

It was this traditional isolation from the main currents of European diplomacy that had also led Belgian leaders to unrealistic expectations of a genuine voice at the peace conference. Because Belgium had so little experience of great-power politics, neither Hymans nor other members of the cabinet understood that, one way or another, the great powers generally make the decisions and weak nations do not always have even a real choice of accepting or rejecting these decrees. When the Belgian delegation tried to reject the Big Four's reparations decisions, Lloyd George's threat to cut Belgium out of the treaty altogether and to leave her to settle on her own with Germany was a normal if unusually blatant great-power response, which failed chiefly because of exterior circumstances involving two more powerful nations, not primarily as a result of Belgian resistance. The entire Belgian cabinet failed to understand that, in the eyes of the great powers, it was Belgium's role to obey and to accept whatever they decreed. The wartime experience wherein strenuous Belgian efforts were necessary before Britain and France reluctantly conceded that Belgium would be "permitted" a distinctly partial separate reply to Wilson's December 1916 peace note had not enlightened them about the great-power concept of the proper place and role of small nations. They had all taken the Declaration of Sainte-Adresse as a promise of genuine participation, not of submissive and respectful attendance, and they were astonished by what ensued. Hymans's report from Paris that the Big Four were unapproachable and he did not know what to do speaks volumes of dismay, bewilderment, and despair.

What Hymans in fact did in this unanticipated situation was to pester the second and third echelons of the great-power delegations. Few other courses were open to him, but unfortunately he did so in person. Considering his extreme tactlessness and talent for infuriating, he would have done better to have sent somebody else, preferably de Gaiffier. Even Balfour, whose sympathy for Belgium was both strong and active, termed him intolerable after one of Hymans's lectures. Much of Hymans's prickliness arose from deep national pride, but it impeded his diplomacy, as he failed to appreciate the folly of offending those upon whom his nation's future depended and as he presumed to equality one moment while begging for help the next. Further, his endless complaints of failure to include Belgium in discussion of matters of direct concern to her, while based on a certain logic, were bound only to annoy, not to gain access, for the great powers had no intention of sharing their authority with others.

Although Hymans and the other Belgian leaders made a good many errors, some of their mistakes made little difference just because Belgium's voice at Paris was so small and so many matters lay completely beyond her control. Thus their failure to prepare properly on the reparations question did them no serious harm and had no appreciable effect on the outcome, as American attitudes were decisive. Similarly, although the African question had been poorly handled in 1916 and scarcely considered since, that had no real effect upon decisions at the peace conference. Belgium's desired solution to this question could only be arranged by Britain, and though Milner apparently tried, he failed. For the rest, Belgium handled the question wisely, quietly refusing to evacuate German East Africa, and doing what little could be done to combat irrational prejudices. Although Ruanda-Urundi was not what Belgium wanted, it constituted her largest and most valuable territorial acquisition. She gained it not only because she was in effective occupation but also because she held other territory that Britain much wanted.

Fortunately or unfortunately, Hymans did not learn the lesson. With his illusions about faithful guarantors, he was not prepared to face the fact that unless a small power has the wherewithal and the nerve to hold a great power to ransom, a clash of wills is almost bound to be resolved to the benefit of the great power. Thus, although he knew, he would not accept that Belgium was at France's mercy on the Luxemburg question and that France had no mercy. Though the history of the Luxemburg question well illustrated the fact that great powers often respond with brutality or indifference to the aspirations of the weak, Hymans had another concept of both Britain and France and, even though the facts kept intruding, he could not abandon his concept altogether. Perhaps his dogged persistence in the quest for Luxemburg was not as foolish as it appears at first glance. To begin with, Britain did gain an opportunity to arrange matters and Balfour tried to do so, being defeated only by Lloyd George or Kerr. Later, Hymans stubbornly held out in the face of an apparently hopeless situation on the theory that something would turn up, and something did. As a result, although France found flimsy excuses not to honor either commitment over the railways, he did achieve economic union with the Grand Duchy at the minimal price of a very limited military agreement which by that time Belgium clearly needed and which in any event soon became a dead letter on the Belgian end. Hymans's flat refusal to face facts, together with his intense dedication to Belgian independence, spared Belgium both the sweeping economic and military arrangements and at least in part the satellite status upon which France had planned.

Although economic factors entered into Belgian territorial aspirations in Europe, it is evident that the primary concerns were undoing the decisions of 1815 and 1839 and reinforcing Belgium's inadequate security against Germany. Concerning the latter, one must ask whether acquisition of Eupen enhanced the security or enlarged the danger. Though possession of Eupen did lengthen the distance from Liège to the frontier a little, it was clearly much more Germanic and much less important to Belgian security than Malmédy. Obviously, Belgian acquisition of neutral Moresnet was no issue in Germany, and whether Malmédy would have become one without Eupen is not easy to determine. Undoubtedly, Stresemann's 1925–26 policy would have been much more difficult to pursue without the agitation within the Weimar Republic of emigrés from Eupen. In any event, Stresemann's ploy failed, and the 1940 invasion of both Low Countries suggests that Belgian annexation of Eupen made little if any difference in the long run. Nonetheless, Hitler's grandiose world view was hardly predictable in 1919, and Belgium was perhaps ill-advised to undertake without stronger reason an annexation giving a grievance to the neighbor whom she feared most. Certainly, the decision should have been more carefully weighed.

Though every territorial aim in Europe except neutral Moresnet was in part aimed at increasing Belgian security against Germany, it is evident that, even in the unlikely event that all had been obtained, Belgium could not have been secure against renewed German aggression. Belgian leaders recognized this fact and knew that no territorial solution could possibly make the kingdom strong enough to withstand German attack alone. Their goal was merely to obtain sufficiently defensible frontiers to be able to hold out until help arrived. Although this is a reasonable goal for any country and Belgium's frontiers certainly were not defensible, this modest aspiration clearly was not realizable in the climate of 1919–20. Given British and Dutch reactions to the immediate past, nothing whatever could be done about the Scheldt, Flemish Zeeland, or lower Limburg. Equally, given French reactions to the war, nothing could be done about Luxemburg under French occupation. Like her neighbors, Belgium was reacting to her wartime experience, but her diplomatic assets were the slimmest of them all. Although it is understandable that Belgium's military and civilian leaders wished to obtain a minimal amount of security for their country in hopes of preventing a recurrence of the terrible agony just past, they were very slow to face the cruel realities of their unenviable circumstances. They kept hoping that somehow a way could be found, but because they could change neither geography nor the attitudes of their neighbors, they hoped in vain and at some cost to other Belgian aspirations.

Because Belgian leaders recognized that, even with better boundaries, they must have help to withstand any renewed German attack, they sought commitments of assistance. The consequent quest for guarantees, which focused almost entirely upon Britain and France as the faithful guarantors of 1839, involved fundamental considerations about Belgium's future status that, for all the wartime debate at Le Havre over "this agonizing problem," no Belgian cabinet ever faced squarely. With great consistency until 1923, Belgian leaders tried to avoid making unattractive choices. Whenever what they deemed to be their needs or their rights were at stake, they tended to be inflexible and unrealistic, unwilling to face the unpalatable fact that Belgium's own lack of power together with the lack of great-power support meant that her goals could not all be accomplished. In general, they assumed that what Belgium needed must be obtained—somehow. This attitude was patriotic but impractical. Belgian diplomatists, while very inexperienced in dickering with great powers, were on the whole willing to try, although they did not fully appreciate the handicaps under which they labored. They understood at least in part that in order to get something, one must give something. However, they almost never had anything to give. They were unable to go one step further and accept that in order to gain one vital goal, they must sacrifice something else of importance to them. Because they would not make these hard choices, they gained little of what mattered most to them.

This pattern of reluctance to choose extended to small matters and large. In 1920, Belgium felt entitled as a matter of right to both mark redemption and extradition of alleged war criminals. Because she pursued both against a greater power without weapons, without support, and in the end without much say in the decision on the second issue, which she had declined to sacrifice to the first, she gained neither. The same problem prevailed to a much more serious degree through the wartime debates and immediate postwar negotiations over Belgium's future status. By 1916, Belgium's goals had become full independence, unrestricted freedom of action, and security against renewed German invasion. For all the agonizing, nobody in either the cabinet or the

Foreign Ministry seems ever to have faced up to the fact that, given Belgium's circumstances, these goals were conflicting and incompatible or recognized that a choice would have to be made between independence, possibly without full freedom of action, and security. In the end, Belgium emerged with a certain diplomatic prominence but without much freedom of action or much security.

The choices that Belgian leaders faced were cruel and so, being only human, they did not face them. The alternatives open to them were indeed agonizing. In theory, Belgium could retain her prewar status, but in practice that was politically impossible, especially in regard to the German guarantee. Indeed, the consensus against any form of compulsory neutrality was so overwhelming by the end of the war that it is doubtful whether even a three-party government could have imposed this solution in the improbable event that it had chosen such a course. All Belgium was convinced that the 1839 system had failed and that the deeply craved security must be sought elsewhere.

Voluntary neutrality had been considered during the war. In theory, Belgium could have followed Holland's modest example by retiring into de facto neutrality while joining the League of Nations. In practice, this course would have afforded no security and probably little independence. Both economic and geographic factors rendered this policy less feasible and less attractive to Belgium than to Holland. The flourishing Dutch economy was complementary to that of all three great-power neighbors, whereas the severely damaged Belgian economy competed directly with all three and faced serious problems of both revival and outlets. Moreover, Belgium, unlike Holland, had France on her southern frontier, demanding sweeping military and economic arrangements designed to reduce the kingdom to satellite status. Also, because 1914 had demonstrated that France could be invaded without violation of Dutch territory, Belgium appeared to be more exposed, threatened, and in need of great-power guarantees than Holland. Though such guarantees were obtainable, at least on a temporary basis, formal neutrality proved to be the price and Belgium was not prepared to pay it.

While compulsory neutrality was politically unthinkable in Belgium and voluntary neutrality very unpopular, there were additional drawbacks to following the Dutch example. Any form of neutrality would have meant withdrawal from the Rhineland and from the Supreme

Council. It is easy to argue that Belgium would have been wiser not to participate in the Rhineland occupation, where the presence of a small power's army was so bitterly resented, not to join in punitive expeditions against a great neighbor who could most easily retaliate against her, and not to involve herself in Supreme Councils that constituted a dangerously rarefied setting for the diplomacy of such a small and inexperienced power. Yet, aside from considerations of national amour-propre, there were strong reasons for Belgium to participate in the Western Entente. Her chosen course of balancing between France and Britain against Germany could be pursued only in this fashion. In addition, if the Belgian army were to withdraw from the Rhineland, the French army would undoubtedly replace it. The prospect of French troops on every Belgian frontier except the Dutch one was sufficient reason for Belgium to stay. Also, withdrawal from the Rhineland and from the Supreme Council would have caused Belgium to lose any voice in matters of direct concern to her and almost certainly most of her reparations as well. By her presence and her persistence, Belgium got her priority in the end. In her absence, Britain and France would have had no difficulty and little compunction in arranging matters so that the prior charge of occupation costs consumed all the dwindling reparations receipts. Indeed, they attempted a move in that direction in December 1921 and were frustrated in part only by vigorous Belgian protest at Cannes, where Briand badly needed Belgian support against British policy on other German reparations questions.

Because any form of neutrality was ruled out, there remained the theoretical possibility of seeking security by attachment to a great-power neighbor, but Belgium did not wish to be anybody's satellite. Moreover, the choices were not attractive. Attachment to Germany was unthinkable in view of the immediate past. Close and unilateral attachment to France was equally out of the question because of deep Flemish hostility to any such arrangement. That left Britain, who was not only the least valuable military ally in the short run, which was all that Belgium was likely to have in any effort to prevent occupation, but also the least interested great-power neighbor. Although Britain was in consequence the least likely to interfere in Belgium's internal affairs, its postwar price, to the extent that it was willing to enter into any arrangement at all, was the prohibitive one of formal neutrality, with all that implied. The wartime Belgian cabinet was undoubtedly foolish to reject out of hand the 1916 British offer of a virtual military alliance. Certainly the offer should at least have been explored to the point of discovering the conditions attached, if any. But Belgian cabinet members were still dominated by Belgium's distinctive past, which by definition had never permitted a single alliance, by Albert's distrust of the British and dread of satellite status, and by their own fear, Beyens aside, of interference in decisions concerning the Belgian army. Once politicians finally came to recognize that new guarantees to replace the old were not to be had for the asking and that, in the wake of 1914, the electorate now understood the need for military expenditure, one Belgian foreign minister after another tried in vain to obtain what had been so blithely rejected in 1916.

Because reliance on a single neighbor seemed neither desirable nor really possible, Belgium chose the only other course open to her. She attempted to rest on both Britain and France against Germany and to balance delicately between her two faithful guarantors. This policy, which owed a good deal to the previous course of Belgian history, was designed to afford both security and a substantial degree of independence while placating the Flemish and preventing French domination. In short, Belgium chose to become a satellite to a bloc of powers, hoping to be able to maneuver among them just as Luxemburg had hoped to maneuver between France and Belgium. Because Britain and France were more nearly equivalent in power, the Belgian policy was less unrealistic than that of Luxemburg and, as Belgian leaders noted, their attitudes partook of both British and French viewpoints, for Belgium shared Britain's economic policy and France's reparations and security concerns. As it happened, because the bloc that Belgium joined lacked any coherent policy, the conflicts within the Western Entente not only afforded her a prominent diplomatic role but some limited freedom of action for several years. This state of affairs also obscured the fact that Belgium's chosen course was not viable, owing to circumstances beyond her control.

France reacted to Belgium's policy decision with Gallic logic and realism if not with Gallic finesse. French leaders were much more realistic than their Belgian counterparts about Britain's attitude, at least toward Belgium if not always toward France, and promptly attempted to capitalize upon it. Though French concepts of the structure of post-war Europe varied somewhat from time to time and individual to individual, the Belgian place in the structure never changed in French eyes, and almost every French leader attempted to put Belgium into her appointed place as a French satellite. French needs dictated this role and Belgian needs were irrelevant. As French policy was consistently motivated by fear of another German invasion, it was imperative that the weak little nation astride Germany's invasion route accept French dictation for the sake of France's safety. Although French tactics varied from brutality to cajolery and occasional bribery to duplicity, the goal remained unchanging. Virtually unaided, Belgium fought off this domination with a considerable degree of success until 1923. Though the decision to accompany France into the Ruhr did bring satellite status with it, Belgium never became the docile tool that Poincaré expected and, once the cessation of German passive resistance ended the need for a united front, she quickly reverted to an independent stance, thus inadvertently contributing to France's ultimate defeat at Anglo-American and German hands.

Unfortunately for the success of Belgian diplomacy, the British reaction to Belgium's not very surprising choice of policy was both irrational and unrealistic. The British attitude toward Belgium was compounded out of factors particular to Belgium, Britain's broader view of the European scene, and the oddities of British policy formulation. In regard to the first, although Britain had entered World War I in response to her own national self-interest, she had largely convinced herself that she had been dragged into it by her obligation to defend Belgium. Thus she emerged from the carnage irritated with Belgium, grateful to Holland for her fortuitous neutrality, and at least intermittently determined not to commit herself again to Belgium's defense. Only a few British leaders kept in mind the evident fact that the independence of both Low Countries was a continuing British interest and that Britain would again have to intervene, with or without treaty commitments, against great-power violation of either of them. Such little British thinking as took place about Belgium's role in British security became so muddled that Britain could not bring herself to the largely meaningless step of a five-year interim guarantee to rid herself of the unwanted indefinite commitment without the clearly prohibitive price of formal Belgian neutrality, which in some respects was as unattractive to France as to Belgium. Irritation with Hymans and Lloyd George's prejudices, which Hymans only reinforced, played a role in Britain's growing indifference and antipathy, as did Belgium's economic potential. Lloyd George much wanted to revive prewar trade patterns—except those of Belgium, whose competition he feared. Because Lloyd George was as illogical as the next man, he never feared Germany's potentially far greater competition.

The fact that Lloyd George and many of his colleagues rapidly ceased to fear Germany in any important respect and also became increasingly reluctant to intervene in Continental affairs, especially against Germany, contributed much to the defeat of Belgian diplomacy. Because Belgian policy rested upon a British tie to counterbalance the largely inescapable link to France, it was at the mercy of Britain's view of the European continent. In general, most British leaders did not fear Germany but did fear France, who alone possessed a large air force within striking distance of England. Though British leaders would occasionally acknowledge large-scale German violation of the Versailles treaty, they were rarely willing to take any action. The Weimar Republic was seldom responsive to anything short of Entente unity and a threat of force, but Britain was increasingly opposed to renewed intervention on the Continent and so argued that nothing more should be asked of Germany than she was willing to accept because, if one asked more, Germany would refuse and one would have to occupy the Ruhr. Occasionally, as with disarmament, Britain would consent to firm speech but not to follow-up action, a policy that redounded to German benefit. Under the circumstances, it is not surprising that the peace quickly became unstable or that Britain dodged any renewed guarantee of Belgium.

Both geography and Britain's erroneous view of Belgium as a French satellite contributed considerably to the defeat of Belgian policy and to pushing Belgium toward the very position she wished to avoid. By mid-1920, historic British hostility to France had reemerged at least to the degree of strong antipathy. One major cause of the acute Anglo-French tension was British misreading of French efforts to enforce part of the

Versailles treaty as renewed French imperialism and a new quest for Continental domination. British leaders did half-recognize French fears and periodically considered a guarantee of France in order to induce greater French "reasonableness" about German resurgence, without realizing that what they were proposing to arrange was restoration of Germany's Continental dominance. In any event, Britain was not prepared to guarantee France, as 1922 amply demonstrated, without a stiff price in concessions. Because geography dictated that any guarantee of Belgium constituted a de facto guarantee of France as well and because Belgium was viewed as France's willing helper in vindictiveness and imperialism, Britain was not eager to guarantee Belgium before France was brought to heel. The facts that Holland had become pro-German while Belgium was allegedly pro-French and that a neutral Holland could disarm Antwerp as the pistol pointed at England only contributed further to the defeat of Belgian policy.

Perhaps if the British Foreign Office had made a systematic examination of Britain's underlying security interests, British policy might have pursued another path, but not even a compilation, much less any strategic planning, was undertaken until Ramsay MacDonald took charge in 1924, and by then the course had long been set. One of the architects of post-World War II British foreign policy once characterized it as "an exercise in piecemeal pragmatism."[104] The same was true of British foreign policy in the earlier postwar era. There was the same lack of coherent strategic planning, absence of careful analysis of Britain's fundamental interests, and reliance on tradition, instinct, and intuition. Worse yet, British policy after World War I was a product of a variety of clashing intuitions. In particular, Curzon did not have effective control of foreign policy, as Lloyd George intervened constantly, especially in Franco-German matters. All too often, his moves in foreign policy were dictated by domestic political considerations or his quest for short-term tactical advantage. Moreover, Lloyd George's policies were to a considerable degree derived from nostalgia. In another century when Europe's power structure had been considerably different, Britain had

104. Sir Michael Palliser, permanent under-secretary of state for foreign affairs, address to the Royal Institute of International Relations, Brussels, 12 Apr. 1978.

enjoyed the enviable position of being the pivotal state in the European balance of power. As Lloyd George instinctively set Britain's course to revert to that prized position, neither he nor his successors understood that they were in fact facilitating eventual domination of the Continent by Europe's potentially strongest power, a state of affairs that had never been in Britain's interest.

In view of Belgian illusions about the faithful guarantor powers and particularly about Britain, those who directed Belgian foreign policy were slow to spot Britain's growing inclination to part company from her erstwhile allies. Clearly the weakness of Belgian postwar policy lay in its dependence upon a British commitment that did not materialize, but initially, the Belgian policy decision was neither irrational nor without some apparent hope of realization. Despite Lloyd George's hostility, Balfour and Crowe had done much to try to help Belgium at the peace conference. Austen Chamberlain, the War Office, and the quality press were all known to favor a guarantee of Belgium, which Belgian leaders— more clearly than many British cabinet members—knew to be in British interest. But the support extended no further. For all his cultivation of King Albert, Curzon had little sympathy with Belgian aspirations, and Lloyd George had much less. In due course, even the most optimistic of Belgian leaders saw that Britain showed scant inclination to play the role for which Belgium had cast her. Once this fact was recognized, however, it was not fully faced. Belgium continued to pursue the counterbalancing British tie, partly from lack of any satisfactory alternative policy and partly because British flirtations with a French guarantee gave some basis for hoping that British policy would change and render Belgian policy viable.

Although World War I had destroyed some Belgian illusions, it had reinforced others, and postwar Belgium charted her course largely on the basis of false notions about faithful guarantor powers. Needless to say, no Belgian leader foresaw the nature of postwar Europe. That is hardly surprising: nobody else did, either. After all, the Versailles treaty was not written on the basis of American withdrawal, German refusal to obey, British refusal to enforce, and rapid German resurgence. In the unstable postwar world that actually developed, Belgium became something of an anomaly both in her role within the Western Entente and in her attitudes. Because she had newly emerged from her special protected status, she was often compared to the new nations created by the peace settlement, but Belgium was not in fact a new nation and her eighty years of past national existence deeply affected her attitudes and policies.

Unlike some of the successor states, Belgium was not a convert to what is generally called the new diplomacy. True, she had illusions about a new era based upon justice, but these derived from the victory of the guarantor powers, not from Wilsonian visions. Though grateful for American aid, Belgium made little effort to obtain a guarantee from the United States and accepted the American withdrawal with equanimity, because her interests, aside from the Congo and trade outlets, were exclusively European. However, her hopes never centered on Geneva. After Hymans's successful battle at Paris for small-power representation on the League Council, Belgium recognized that the League could not solve her problems. Although Hymans played a prominent role at Geneva, he did so primarily when out of office, keeping active in foreign affairs and reinforcing his claim to return to the Foreign Ministry. The only other foreign minister of the 1920s who showed much interest in the League was Vandervelde, whose genuine interest may not have been very strong. He was probably placating his Socialist supporters and his principal advisor, Henri Rolin. Certainly at no time in the 1920s did Belgium seek security from Geneva or think that the League could solve her problems. In fact, she knew that it could not and resisted all efforts to shelve her security problem by referring it to the Council, on which she held a seat. What Belgium sought with complete consistency was great-power guarantees.

Yet Belgium was not a convert to the old diplomacy, of which she was so woefully ignorant. For all her participation in the Western Entente, where she was a vital but distinctly junior element, Belgium was never really at home in the ruthless world of power politics. Indeed, her appreciation that international politics rested largely upon power tended to be defective much of the time. Belgium's view of her own role in Europe was shaped above all by her own historic experience and her past tutelary relationship to the great powers. Because World War I had destroyed that relationship to three of the five original guarantors, as

Belgium faced the new postwar world she turned instinctively to the two remaining powers who had been primarily responsible both for her creation and for her deliverance in the war just past.

At the peace conference and in the years that immediately followed, it was profoundly irritating to the middle-aged men who directed Belgian foreign policy to be treated as if they were small children because they represented a small and weak nation. But, in fact, Belgium's relationship to Britain and France did resemble that of a child to its parents. In 1919, Belgium was dependent upon the great powers for food, clothing, money, and safety. Especially at the peace conference, Belgium was incapable, not from lack of ability but from lack of power, of arranging anything for herself. As time passed, Belgium became more able to provide for herself, especially in the daily necessities, but the need for shelter and security remained, perhaps somewhat exacerbated by her sometimes ill-advised territorial ambitions at the peace conference. In this dependence upon others for security, she resembled some of the successor states. Though not the youngest, Belgium was among the smallest, weakest, and most exposed. Unlike Poland and Czechoslovakia, however, she proposed to depend upon two parents, not one. But John Bull and Marianne were a quarrelsome couple, always on the brink of divorce. In addition to trying vainly to flee from a domineering mama to an indifferent papa, Belgium became the anxious child attempting to save the marriage for the sake of its own security.

In arguing for the end of compulsory neutrality, Belgian leaders maintained that the kingdom had reached adulthood in the family of nations and thus was entitled to unrestricted independence. In this assertion they were mistaken. Belgium had in fact progressed only to adolescence, with all the contradictions which that age implies. Like so many adolescents, Belgium wanted unlimited freedom along with support and protection, and did not recognize that she could not have both at once. Adulthood implies taking full responsibility for one's self and one's future. In the circumstances then prevailing, Belgium could not do that and she knew it, but she did not accept that protection meant dependence and restrictions upon her freedom of action. Because Belgium could not face this fact, she kept searching for a solution that did not exist. The course she pursued presented the only hope of avoiding the choices that she was so determined not to make, but the attitudes of both parents and the clash between them, while initially giving her a little freedom of maneuver, ultimately defeated her policy, and she found herself trying with considerable tenacity to resist both domination and dangerous isolation at the same time.

The events of the war and of the peace, together with Belgium's own adolescent urges toward self-assertion, meant that she catapulted with great speed but insufficient thought from the status of a sheltered and, in a sense, handicapped child to that of something resembling a power of the second rank. Although the diplomatic limelight was very satisfying, it did not solve Belgium's essentially insoluble problems. Neither did Locarno. Nor did the 1936 abandonment of what remained of the French military accord and the later reversion to a form of neutrality. Given her weakness, her exposed location, and the attitudes of her great-power neighbors, Belgium could not be both independent and secure in interwar Europe. Only after a second great war and another four years of agonizing occupation had shattered the interwar European power structure beyond recall could Belgium find a reasonable degree of security and some independence of action within a new, larger, and sharply different alignment of powers.

BIBLIOGRAPHY

MANUSCRIPT SOURCES

Government Archives

<small>BELGIUM</small>

Ministère des Affaires Etrangères, archive, Brussels

Classement B

1, 1–1519 (Luxemburg)

20 (Luxemburg railways)

156 (1839 treaties)

216–19 (occupied Belgium)

280–81 (peace)

297 (Armistice)

316 (Armistice Commission, Spa)

318 (Hythe Conference, May 1920)

320 (projected Geneva Conference, 1920)

331 (Eupen-Malmédy)

348–54 (Rhineland)

366 (reparations)

377 (future of Belgium—wartime)

378 (reconstitution of Belgium)

383 (revision of 1839 treaties)

383 bis (Limburg)

10.070 (reparations, 1922)

10.071 (Paris Conference, January 1923)

10.072–74 (reparations, 1923–24)

10.084 (Ruhr)

10.088–90 (Ruhr)

10.097 (reparations, Ruhr)

10.110 (London Conference, February–March 1921)

10.111–12 (Supreme Council, Paris, August 1921)

10.115 (Boulogne Conference, February 1922)

10.121 (French-Belgian relations, 1919–20)

10.430 (occupation of Frankfurt, 1920)

10.440–44 (Rhenish separatism)
10.472 (reparations, 1921–30)
10.479 (reparations 1923–28, Belgian Etudes)
10.506–14 (Lausanne Conference, 1922–23)
10.521 (London Conference, February–March 1921)
10.522 (London Conference, April–May 1921)
10.524 (Cannes Conference, January 1922)
10.525 (London Conference, July–August 1924)
10.792 (Eupen-Malmédy)
10.793 (Montjoie)
10.794 (Moresnet)
10.806 (monastery of the Dormition)
10.926 (projected Anglo-Belgian treaty, 1919–24)
10.997 (Belgian claims, 1915–19)
11.115 (Locarno negotiations)
11.246 (Eupen-Malmédy)
11.442–44 (Eupen-Malmédy)
11.497 (reparations)
Classement Indépendance, Neutralité, Défense militaire de la Belgique, Garantie des Puissances (1914–39)
Correspondance Politique, Légations (1914–26): Allemagne, France, Grande-Bretagne, Pays-Bas
Délégation Belge (to the Paris Peace Conference)
Political Correspondence: The United States, General and Bound (1917–26) (Correspondance Politique, microfilm, Library, National Archives, Washington)

FRANCE
Archives Nationales, Paris
Délégation française à la Commission des Réparations (sous-série AJ⁵)
Haute Commission interalliée des Territoires Rhénans; Haut Commissariat français dans les provinces du Rhin (sous-série AJ⁹)
Ministère des Affaires Etrangères, archive, Paris
Série A, Conférence de la Paix, 1914–31
Série Correspondance politique et commerciale
Guerre, 1914–18
Belgique, Congo belge, Dossier général, Luxembourg
Nouvelle Série
Belgique, 1913–18
Série Y, Internationale, 1918–40

Série Z, Europe, 1918–29

    Allemagne, Belgique, Grande-Bretagne, Luxembourg, Pays-Bas, Rive
    Gauche du Rhin, Ruhr

Service Historique de l'Armée, Château de Vincennes, Vincennes

Série N

    4N, Conseil Supérieur de Guerre

    5N, Cabinet du Ministre

    6N, Fonds Particuliers (Poincaré, Buat, Clemenceau)

    7N, Etat-Major de l'Armée, Deuxième Bureau

Série P

    09P, Fonds des attachés militaires (Brussels and London)

GERMANY

Auswärtiges Amt, Berlin

    GFM 4, Series L (microprint, Foreign Office Library, London)

        Politik 1, Belgien, 1920–24

        Politik 2, Belgien, 1920–23

        Politik 3, Belgien-Frankreich, 1920–27

GREAT BRITAIN

Public Record Office, London

    Cabinet Papers

        CAB 1/, Miscellaneous Records

        CAB 2/, Committee of Imperial Defence, Minutes

        CAB 3/, 4/, 5/, Committee of Imperial Defence, Memoranda

        CAB 16/, Ad Hoc Sub-Committee of Inquiry

        CAB 17/, Committee of Imperial Defence, Correspondence and Mis-
        cellaneous Papers

        CAB 21/, Registered Cabinet Office Files

        CAB 23/, Cabinet, Minutes

        CAB 24/, Cabinet, Memoranda

        CAB 25/, Supreme War Council, 1917–19

        CAB 27/, Cabinet Committees, General Series

        CAB 28/, Cabinet, Allied Conferences, 1915–20

        CAB 29/, Peace Conference and Other International Conferences

        CAB 37/, Cabinet Papers, 1880–1914 [to end 1916]

        CAB 38/, Committee of Imperial Defence Papers to [through] 1914

        CAB 41/, Cabinet Letters in Royal Archives

        CAB 42/, War Council, 1914–16

        CAB 53, Chiefs of Staff Committee, Committee of Imperial Defence

        CAB 63/, Hankey Papers

Foreign Office Papers
    F.O. 371/, General Correspondence, Political
        Belgium, France, Germany, Netherlands, United States
        Central Department: General
        League of Nations
        Peace Conference, Political Intelligence Department
        Rhineland
        Western Department: General
    F.O. 372/, Treaty and Trade
    F.O. 373/, Peace Conference of 1919–20, Handbooks
    F.O. 374/, Peace Conference of 1919–20, Acts
    F.O. 382/, Contraband
    F.O. 608/, Peace Conference of 1919–20, Correspondence
    F.O. 800/, Private Collections (Balfour, Bertie, Cadogan, R. Cecil, A.
        Chamberlain, Crewe, Crowe, Curzon, Cushendun, Drummond, Grey,
        Hardinge, Knatchbull-Hugessen, MacDonald, Mendl, A. Nicolson,
        Oliphant, Sargent, Tyrrell, F. Villiers, Wigram, miscellaneous, League
        of Nations)
    F.O. 801/, Reparation Commission, 1919–31
    F.O. 840/, International Conferences, various
    F.O. 893/, Peace Conference of 1919–20, Conference of Ambassadors,
        Paris, Minutes
    F.O. 894/, Germany, Inter-Allied Rhineland High Commission, Minutes
    F.O. 899/, Cabinet Papers
Records of the Prime Minister's Office
    Premier/1, Correspondence and Papers
UNITED STATES OF AMERICA
National Archives, Washington, D.C.
    Department of State, Decimal File, 1910–29 (Record Group 59)
        Belgium, France, Germany, Great Britain, Netherlands
        Mutual Guarantee (Locarno)
        Reparations
        World War I and Its Termination
    Records of the American Commission to Negotiate Peace (Record Group
        256)
    Records of the Inquiry (Record Group 256)
    Records of the United States Unofficial Delegation to the Reparation Com-
        mission (Record Group 43)

Private Collections and Personal Papers

BIRMINGHAM

   Birmingham University Library

      Sir Joseph Austen Chamberlain Papers

BRUSSELS

   Archives Générales du Royaume

      Pierre Forthomme Papers

      Jules van den Heuvel Papers

      Paul Hymans Papers

      Henri Jaspar Papers

      Pierre Orts Papers

      Vicomte Prosper Poullet Papers

      Baron Edouard Rolin-Jaequemyns Papers

   Collection of Mme. Marcel Roberte-Jaspar

      Henri Jaspar Letters

CAMBRIDGE

   Cambridge University Library

      Stanley Baldwin, 1st Earl Baldwin of Bewdley, Papers

      Charles Hardinge, 1st Baron Hardinge of Penshurst, Papers

   Churchill College Archive

      Maurice Hankey, 1st Baron Hankey of the Chart, Papers

      Sir Hughe Knatchbull-Hugessen Papers

      Sir Eric Phipps Papers (consulted when in possession of Lady Phipps)

CAMBRIDGE, MASS.

   Houghton Library, Harvard University

      Ellis Loring Dresel Papers

EDINBURGH

   Scottish Record Office

      Philip Henry Kerr, 11th Marquess of Lothian, Papers

LONDON

   British Library

      Arthur James Balfour, 1st Earl of Balfour, Papers (Add. MSS 49683–49962)

      Edgar Algernon Robert Gascoyne Cecil, 1st Viscount Cecil of Chelwood, Papers (Add. MSS 51071–51204)

      Edgar Vincent, 1st Viscount D'Abernon (Add. MSS 48922–48962)

   House of Lords Record Office

      Andrew Bonar Law Papers (consulted at Beaverbrook Library)

      David Lloyd George, 1st Earl Lloyd-George of Dwyfor, Papers (consulted at Beaverbrook Library)

India Office Library
George Nathaniel Curzon, 1st Marquess Curzon of Kedleston, Papers
NEW HAVEN, CONN.
Sterling Memorial Library, Yale University
Edward Mandell House Papers
PARIS
Ministère des Affaires Etrangères, archive (Papiers d'Agents)
Philippe Berthelot Papers
Jules Cambon Papers
Paul Cambon Papers
Georges Clemenceau Papers
Aimé de Fleuriau Papers
Jules Jusserand Papers
Charles Laurent Papers
Georges Leygues Papers
Paul Mantoux Papers
Bruno-François-Marie-Pierre Jacquin de Margerie Papers
Alexandre Millerand Papers
Georges Maurice Paléologue Papers
Stephen Pichon Papers
STANFORD, CALIF.
Hoover Institution on War, Revolution, and Peace
Gaston F. Bergery Papers
General Tasker Bliss Papers
Hans-Adam Dorten Papers
Ellis Loring Dresel Papers
Leon Fraser Papers
Hugh Simons Gibson Papers
Herbert C. Hoover Papers
Colonel James A. Logan, Jr., Papers
Louis Loucheur Papers
Ernest Mercier Papers
General Edouard Jean Réquin Papers
Henry M. Robinson Papers
Joseph Brand Whitlock Papers
Arthur N. Young Papers
WASHINGTON, D.C.
Library of Congress
Ray Stannard Baker Papers

Charles Evans Hughes Papers
Robert Lansing Papers
General of the Armies John Pershing Papers
Joseph Brand Whitlock Papers
Thomas Woodrow Wilson Papers
National Archives
Colonel James A. Logan, Jr., Papers (Record Group 43)

PUBLISHED DOCUMENTS

Government Collections and Papers
BELGIUM

Académie Royale de Belgique, Commission Royale d'Histoire.
Documents relatifs au statut international de la Belgique depuis 1830. *Documents diplomatiques belges, 1920–1940.* Edited by Charles de Visscher and Fernand van Langenhove. 5 vols. Brussels, 1964–66.
Encyclopédie Nationale. *La Belgique centenaire, 1830–1930.* Edited by René Lyr. Brussels, 1930.
Etat-Major de l'Armée, Deuxième Bureau. *Traduction du Rapport de la section pour le commerce et l'industrie auprès du Gouvernement-Général de la Belgique pour le Ie semestre de 1918.* Brussels, 1918.
Ministère des Affaires Etrangères. *Correspondance diplomatique relative à la guerre de 1914–1915.* 2 vols. Antwerp, 1914, Paris, 1915.
———. *Documents diplomatiques relatifs à la revision des traités de 1839.* Brussels, 1929.
———. *Documents diplomatiques relatifs aux réparations (du décembre 1922 au 27 août 1923).* Brussels, 1923.
———. *Loi qu'approuve la convention conclue à Bruxelles le 25 juillet 1921, entre la Belgique et le Grand-Duché de Luxembourg et établissant une union économique entre les deux pays.* Brussels, 1922.
Ministère de l'Industrie, du Travail, et du Ravitaillement. *La Situation des industries en Belgique en février 1919 après les dévastations allemandes.* Brussels, 1919.
Ministère de l'Information. *Belgian Handbook.* Edited by Walter Ford. London, 1944.

_____. *The History of Anglo-Belgian Relations*. Edited by H. W. Howes. London, 1943.

Moniteur belge, journal officiel. Brussels.

Parlement, Annales parlementaires de Belgique, Chambre des Représentants. *Compte rendu analytique des discussions des chambres législatives de Belgique: Chambre des Représentants*. Brussels, 1918–26.

Parlement, Annales parlementaires de Belgique, Sénat. *Compte rendu analytique des discussions des chambres législatives de Belgique: Sénat*. Brussels, 1918–26.

_____. *Nos pourparlers avec les Pays-Bas: rapport au Sénat de Belgique par Monsieur Paul Segers, Ministre d'Etat*. Antwerp, 1930.

FRANCE

Assemblée Nationale, Chambre des Députés. *Le Traité de paix: rapport général fait au nom de la commission élue par la Chambre des Députés en vue d'examiner le projet de loi portant approbation du traité de paix*. Edited by Louis Barthou. Paris, 1919.

_____, Sénat. *Le Traité de paix de Versailles: rapport présenté au Sénat le 3 octobre 1919 au nom de la Commission des Affaires Etrangères chargée d'examiner le projet de loi portant approbation du traité de Versailles (28 juin 1919)*. Edited by Léon Bourgeois. Paris, 1919.

Comité d'Etudes, Travaux. Babelon, E. *La Condition politique du Grand-Duché de Luxembourg*. Paris, 1918.

_____. Bourgeois, Emile. *La Frontière orientale du royaume de Belgique*. Paris, 1918.

_____. Demangeon, A. *Le Port d'Anvers*. Paris, 1918.

_____. Gallois, L. *La Frontière franco-belge*. Paris, 1918.

Ministère des Affaires Etrangères, Documents diplomatiques. *Demande de moratorium du gouvernement allemand à la commission des réparations (14 novembre 1922); conférence de Londres (9–11 décembre 1922); conférence de Paris (2–4 janvier 1923)*. Paris, 1924.

_____. *Documents relatifs aux négociations concernant les garanties de sécurité contre une agression de l'Allemagne (10 janvier 1919–7 décembre 1923)*. Paris, 1924.

_____. *Documents relatifs aux réparations*. 2 vols. Paris, 1922–24.

_____. *Pacte de sécurité: documents signés ou paraphés à Locarno le 16 octobre 1925, précédés de six pièces relatives aux négociations préliminaires (20 juillet 1925–16 octobre 1925)*. Paris, 1925.

_____. *Pacte de sécurité: neuf pièces relatives à la proposition faite le 9 février 1925 par le gouvernement allemand et à la réponse du gouvernement français (9 février 1925–16 juin 1925)*. Paris, 1925.

Ministère de la Guerre. *Examen de la responsabilité pénale de l'empereur Guillaume II*. Paris, 1918.

———, Etat-Major de l'Armée, Deuxième Bureau. *Conférences sur l'Europe nouvelle et les traités*. Paris, 1921.

Ministère de la Guerre et des Affaires Etrangères. *Bulletin périodique de la presse belge*. Paris, 1918–25.

GERMANY

Weimarer Republik

Akten der Reichskanzlei. Boppard am Rhein, 1968–.

Auswärtiges Amt. *Bestimmungen betreffend die Grenze zwischen Deutschland und Belgien*. Berlin, 1922.

———. *Documents concernant la consultation populaire dans les cercles d'Eupen et Malmédy*. Berlin, 1920.

———. *Materialen zur Sicherheitsfrage*. Berlin, 1925.

———. *Mémoire concernant le chemin de fer du cercle de Montjoie*. Berlin, 1920.

Peace Delegation. *Comments by the German Delegation on the Conditions of Peace*. Berlin, 1919.

Deutsche Demokratische Republik

Ministerium für Auswärtige Angelegenheiten. *Locarno-Konferenz, 1925: Eine Dokumentensammlung*. Berlin, 1962.

GREAT BRITAIN

Admiralty, Naval Intelligence Division, Geographic Handbook Series. *Belgium*. London, 1944.

———. *Luxemburg*. London, 1944.

———. *A Manual of Belgium and the Adjoining Territories*. London, n.d.

———. *Netherlands*. London, 1944.

Foreign Office. *British and Foreign State Papers*. London, 1841–.

———. *Documents on British Foreign Policy, 1919–1939*. 1st ser., series IA. Edited by Rohan Butler and J. P. T. Bury et al. London, 1958–.

———. *Handbooks Prepared under the Direction of the Historical Section of the Foreign Office*. Nos. 25–29, 149. London, 1920.

Parliament, Command Papers

Cd. 9005: *The War Cabinet: Report for the Year 1917*. London, 1918.

Cd. 9212: *Conditions of an Armistice with Germany, Signed 11 November 1918*. London, 1918.

Cmd. 53: *Terms of the Armistices Concluded between the Allied Governments and the Governments of Germany, Austria-Hungary and Turkey*. London, 1919.

Cmd. 153: *Treaty of Peace between the Allied and Associated Powers and Ger-*

many: Signed at Versailles, June 28th, 1919. London, 1919.

Cmd. 221: *Treaty respecting Assistance to France in the Event of Unprovoked Aggression by Germany, Signed at Versailles, June 29, 1919*. London, 1919.

Cmd. 222: *Agreement between the United States of America, Belgium, the British Empire and France and Germany with Respect to the Military Occupation of the Territories of the Rhine, Signed at Versailles, June 28, 1919*. London, 1919.

Cmd. 240: *Declaration by the Governments of the United States of America, Great Britain and France in Regard to the Occupation of the Rhine Provinces*. London, 1919.

Cmd. 258: *Reply of the Allied and Associated Powers to the Observations of the German Delegation on the Conditions of Peace*. London, 1919.

Cmd. 261: *The Peace Proposals Made by His Holiness the Pope to the Belligerent Powers on August 1, 1917, and Correspondence Relative Thereto*. London, 1919.

Cmd. 1325: *Protocols and Correspondence between the Supreme Council and the Conference of Ambassadors and the German Government and the German Peace Delegation between January 10, 1920, and July 17, 1920, respecting the Execution of the Treaty of Versailles of June 28, 1919*. London, 1921.

Cmd. 1543: *Convention between the United Kingdom and Belgium Relative to Article 296 of the Treaty of Versailles of June 28, 1919 (Enemy Debts), Signed at London, July 20, 1921*. London, 1921.

Cmd. 1547: *Papers Relating to the Agreement between the French and German Governments concerning the Application of Part VIII of the Treaty of Versailles regarding Deliveries in Kind*. London, 1921.

Cmd. 1614: *Memorandum Circulated by the Prime Minister on March 25th, 1919*. London, 1922.

Cmd. 1615: *Agreement between the Allies for the Settlement of Certain Questions as to the Application of the Treaties of Peace and Complementary Agreements with Germany, Austria, Hungary, and Bulgaria, Signed at Spa, July 16, 1920*. London, 1922.

Cmd. 1616: *Financial Agreement between Belgium, France, Great Britain, Italy, and Japan, Together with a Covering Note by the Finance Ministers, Signed at Paris, March 11, 1922*. London, 1922.

Cmd. 1794: *British Mandates for the Cameroons, Togoland, and East Africa*. London, 1923.

Cmd. 1812: *Inter-Allied Conferences on Reparations and Inter-Allied Debts Held in London and Paris, December 1922 and January 1923: Reports and Secretary's Notes of Conversations*. London, 1923.

Cmd. 1943: *Correspondence with the Allied Governments respecting Reparation Payments by Germany.* London, 1923.

Cmd. 1974: *Correspondence regarding the Modification of the Boundary between British Mandated Territories and Belgian Mandated Territories in East Africa.* London, 1923.

Cmd. 2169: *Papers respecting Negotiations for an Anglo-French Pact.* London, 1924.

Cmd. 2258: *Minutes of the London Conference on Reparations, August 1922.* London, 1924.

Cmd. 2339: *Agreement between the Governments of Great Britain, Belgium, France, Italy, Japan, the United States of America, Brazil, Greece, Poland, Portugal, Rumania, the Serbo-Croat-Slovene State and Czechoslovakia, regarding the Distribution of the Dawes Annuities, Signed at Paris, 14 January, 1925.* London, 1925.

Cmd. 2429: *Note Presented to the German Government by the British, French, Italian, Japanese and Belgian Ambassadors at Berlin, 4th June, 1925.* London, 1925.

Cmd. 2435: *Papers respecting the Proposals for a Pact of Security Made by the German Government on February 9, 1925.* London, 1925.

Cmd. 2525: *Final Protocol of the Locarno Conference, 1925 (and Annexes), Together with Treaties between France and Poland and France and Czechoslovakia, Locarno, October 16, 1925.* London, 1925.

Cmd. 3343: *Report of the Committee of Experts on Reparations.* London, 1929.

Cmd. 3392: *Protocol with Annexes Approved at the Plenary Session of the Hague Conference, August 31, 1929.* London, 1929.

Cmd. 3484: *Agreements Concluded at the Hague Conference, January, 1930.* London, 1930.

Cmd. 3947: *Report of the International Committee of Experts respecting Suspension of Certain Inter-Governmental Debts Falling Due during the Year Ending June 30, 1932, Together with Protocols and Declarations signed at London, August 11 and 13, 1931.* London, 1931.

Cmd. 4126: *Final Act of the Lausanne Conference, Lausanne, 9 July 1932.* London, 1932.

Cmd. 4129: *Further Documents Relating to the Settlement Reached at the Lausanne Conference (Lausanne, June 16–July 9, 1932).* London, 1932.

Cmd. 4206: *Protocols respecting Suspension of Certain Inter-Governmental Debts Supplementary to Protocols and Declarations signed at London, August 11 and 13, 1931, and January 21, 1932.* London, 1932.

Parliament, House of Commons. *Parliamentary Debates, House of Commons, Official Reports*. London.

————, House of Lords. *Parliamentary Debates, House of Lords, Official Reports*. London.

LUXEMBURG

Ministère d'État, Direction générale des Affaires Etrangères. *Neutralité du Grand-Duché pendant la guerre de 1914–1918*. Luxemburg, 1919.

————, Grey Book. *Luxembourg and the German Invasion, Before and After*. Edited by Joseph Bech. London, 1943.

Le Luxembourg: Livre du centenaire. Edited by Albert Nothumb. Luxemburg, 1948.

NETHERLANDS

Bescheiden in zake de tussen Nederland en België hangende vraagstukken door de wederzijdsche Regeeringen gewisseld sedert de verwerping van het verdrag van 3 April 1925. The Hague, 1929.

Dutch Orange Books. *Recueil de diverses communications du Ministre des Affaires Etrangères aux Etats-Généraux par rapport à la neutralité des Pays-Bas et au respect du droit de gens*. The Hague, 1916.

————. *Mededeelingen van den Minister van Buitenlandsche Zaken aan de Staten-Generaal: April 1918–Juni 1919, Juni 1919–April 1920, Mei 1920 tot Mei 1921, Mei 1921–October 1922, October 1922–September 1924*. 5 vols. The Hague, 1919–24.

Dutch White Book. *Doorvoer door Nederland uit Duitschland naar België, en in ongekeerde richting (Briefwisseling met de Britsche en Duitsche Regeeringen)*. Vol. 2. The Hague, 1918.

Rijks Geschiedkundige Publicatiën, Grote Serie. *Bescheiden betreffende de buitenlandse politiek van Nederland, 1848–1919: Derde Periode, 1899–1919*. Edited by Joannes Aloysius Woltring and C. Smit. 8 vols. in 10. The Hague, 1957–74.

————. *Documenten betreffende de buitenlandse politiek van Nederland, 1919–1945: Periode A, 1919–1930*. Edited by Joannes Aloysius Woltring. Vols. 1–2. The Hague, 1976–.

UNITED STATES OF AMERICA

Department of State. *Papers Relating to the Foreign Relations of the United States*. Vols. 1910, 1916–25. Washington, D.C., 1915–40.

Department of State. *Papers Relating to the Foreign Relations of the United States. The Lansing Papers, 1914–1920*. 2 vols. Washington, D.C., 1939–40.

Department of State. *Papers Relating to the Foreign Relations of the United States. The Paris Peace Conference, 1919*. 13 vols. Washington, D.C., 1942–47.

National Board for Historical Service. *The Inquiry Handbooks.* 20 vols. Wilmington, Del., 1974.

Senate, Doc. no. 357, 61st Cong. 2d sess. *Treaties, Conventions, International Acts, Protocols and Agreements between the United States of America and Other Powers, 1776–1923.* Edited by William M. Malloy. 3 vols. Washington, D.C., 1910–23.

International Organizations

ARMISTICE COMMISSION

Convention for the Prolongation of the Armistice. Trier, 1919.

Sous-Commission financière réunie à Spa du 23 novembre au 1 décembre 1918. Brussels, 1918.

CONFÉRENCE DES EXPERTS DE BRUXELLES

Rapport aux gouvernements alliés. Paris, 1921.

Deuxième rapport aux gouvernements alliés. Paris, 1921.

LEAGUE OF NATIONS

League of Nations Treaty Series. Geneva, 1920–39.

Official Journal. Geneva, 1920–39.

REPARATION COMMISSION

Official Documents. 33 vols. London, 1922–30.

Individual and Miscellaneous Collections

Bane, Suda Lorena, and Lutz, Ralph Haswell. *The Blockade of Germany After the Armistice, 1918–1919.* Stanford, Calif., 1942.

Beer, George Louis. *African Questions at the Paris Peace Conference.* New York, 1923.

Berber, Fritz. *Locarno, eine Dokumentensammlung.* Berlin, 1936.

Burnett, Philip Mason. *Reparation at the Paris Peace Conference from the Standpoint of the American Delegation.* 2 vols. New York, 1940.

Colliard, Claude-Albert, ed. *Droit international et histoire diplomatique.* Paris, 1950.

Davignon, Henri. *Belgium and Germany.* London, 1915.

Dickinson, G. Lowes, ed. *Documents and Statements Relating to Peace Proposals and War Aims (December 1916–November 1918).* London, 1919.

House, Edward Mandell. *The Intimate Papers of Colonel House.* Edited by Charles Seymour. 4 vols. London, 1926–28.

Israel, Fred L., ed. *Major Peace Treaties of Modern History.* 4 vols. New York, 1967.

Langenhove, Fernand van. *Le Dossier diplomatique de la question belge: recueil des pièces officielles, avec notes*. Paris, 1917.

Lapradelle, A. de, ed. *La Documentation internationale: la paix de Versailles*. 12 vols. Paris, 1929–39.

Lhopital, Commandant René Michel, ed. *Foch, l'armistice et la paix*. Paris, 1938.

Mantoux, Paul. *Les Délibérations du conseil des quatre (24 mars–28 juin 1919)*. 2 vols. Paris, 1955.

Miller, David Hunter. *The Drafting of the Covenant*. 2 vols. New York, 1928.

————. *My Diary at the Conference of Paris with Documents*. 21 vols. Privately printed, n.d.

O'Brien, Francis William, ed. *The Hoover-Wilson Wartime Correspondence: September 24, 1914, to November 11, 1918*. Ames, Iowa, 1974.

————. *Two Peacemakers in Paris: The Hoover-Wilson Post-Armistice Letters, 1918–1920*. College Station, Tex., 1978.

O'Regan, J. R. H. *The German War of 1914*. London, 1915.

Scott, James Brown, ed. *Diplomatic Documents Relating to the Outbreak of the European War*. 2 pts. New York, 1916.

————. *Official Statements of War Aims and Peace Proposals, December 1916 to November 1918*. Washington, D.C. 1921.

Collected Speeches

Baldwin, Stanley. *On England and Other Addresses*. London, 1926.

Balfour, Arthur James, 1st Earl of Balfour. *Opinions and Arguments from the Speeches and Addresses of the Earl of Balfour, K.G., O.M., F.R.S., 1910–1927*. London, 1927.

Briand, Aristide. *Aristide Briand: discours et écrits de politique étrangère*. Edited by Achille Elisha. Paris, 1965.

————. *Dans la voie de la paix*. Paris, 1929.

————. *Paroles de paix*. Paris, 1922.

Chamberlain, Sir Joseph Austen. *Peace in Our Time: Addresses on Europe and the Empire*. London, 1928.

Clemenceau, Georges. *Discours de paix*. Paris, 1938.

Foch, Marshal Ferdinand. *En écoutant le maréchal Foch*. Edited by Charles Bugnet. Paris, 1929.

Lloyd George, David. *Is It Peace?* London, 1923.

————. *Slings and Arrows: Sayings Chosen from the Speeches of the Right Honourable David Lloyd George, O.M., M.P.* Edited by Philip Guedalla. London, 1929.

Poincaré, Raymond. *Messages, discours, allocutions, lettres et télégrammes.* 3 vols. Paris, 1919–21.

Rathenau, Walther. *Cannes und Genua: Vier Reden zum Reparations-problem mit einem Anhang.* Berlin, 1922.

Stresemann, Gustav. *Essays and Speeches.* London, 1930. Reprint. Freeport, N.Y., 1968.

Wilson, Thomas Woodrow. *War and Peace: Presidential Messages, Addresses, and Public Papers (1917–1924).* Edited by Ray Stannard Baker and William E. Dodd. 2 vols. New York, 1927.

DIARIES, JOURNALS, MEMOIRS,
AND PRIVATE LETTERS

Aitken, William Maxwell, Baron Beaverbrook. *The Decline and Fall of Lloyd George, and Great Was the Fall Thereof.* London, 1963.
———. *Men and Power, 1917–1918.* London, 1956.

Albert I of Belgium. *The War Diaries of Albert I, King of the Belgians.* Edited by General Raoul van Overstraeten. London, 1954.

Allen, Major General Henry T. *My Rhineland Journal.* London, 1924.
———. *The Rhineland Occupation.* Indianapolis, 1927.

Bartlett, Vernon. *Behind the Scenes at the Peace Conference, 1919.* London, 1919.

Baruch, Bernard M. *The Making of the Reparations and Economic Sections of the Treaty.* New York, 1920.

Bergmann, Carl. *The History of Reparations.* London, 1927.

Beyens, Baron Napoléon Eugène. *Deux années à Berlin.* 2 vols. Paris, 1931.

Bonsal, Stephen. *Suitors and Suppliants: The Little Nations at Versailles.* New York, 1946.
———. *Unfinished Business.* Garden City, N.Y., 1944.

Callwell, Major-General Sir Charles Edward, ed. *Field Marshal Sir Henry Wilson: His Life and Diaries.* 2 vols. London, 1927.

Cambon, Paul. *Correspondance, 1870–1924.* 3 vols. Paris, 1946.

Carton de Wiart, Comte Henry. *Souvenirs Politiques (1878–1918).* Brussels, 1948.

Chamberlain, Sir Joseph Austen. *Down the Years.* London, 1935.
———. *The Life and Letters of the Right Honourable Sir Austen Chamberlain.*

Edited by Sir Charles Petrie. 2 vols. London, 1940.

Clemenceau, Georges. *Clemenceau: The Events of His Life as Told by Himself to His Former Secretary, Jean Martet.* Translated by Milton Waldman. London, 1930.

———. *The Grandeur and Misery of Victory.* London, 1930.

Colenbrander, H. T. *Nederland en België: Adviezen en opstellen uit de jaren 1919 en 1925–1927.* The Hague, 1927.

Cunliffe-Lister, Philip, Viscount Swinton. *I Remember.* London, 1950.

Curzon of Kedleston, Marchioness Grace. *Reminiscences.* London, 1955.

Davies, Joseph. *The Prime Minister's Secretariat, 1916–1920.* Newport, Monmouthshire, 1951.

Dawes, Charles G. *A Journal of Reparations.* London, 1939.

Escholier, Raymond. *Souvenirs parlés de Briand.* Paris, 1932.

Foch, Marshal Ferdinand. *The Memoirs of Marshal Foch.* Translated by Colonel T. Bentley Mott. London, 1931.

Gibson, Hugh. *A Journal from Our Legation in Belgium.* Garden City, N.Y., 1917.

Hankey, Colonel Maurice P. A., Baron Hankey of the Chart. *The Supreme Control at the Paris Peace Conference, 1919.* London, 1963.

Hardinge, Charles, Baron Hardinge of Penshurst. *Old Diplomacy.* London, 1947.

Headlam-Morley, Sir James W. *A Memoir of the Paris Peace Conference, 1919.* London, 1972.

Hoover, Herbert Clark. *The Memoirs of Herbert Hoover.* 3 vols. New York, 1951–52.

House, Edward M., and Seymour, Charles, eds. *What Really Happened at Paris: The Story of the Peace Conference, 1918–1919.* London, 1921.

Hymans, Paul. *Fragments d'histoire, impressions et souvenirs.* Brussels, 1940.

———. *Mémoires.* Edited by Frans van Kalken and John Bartier. 2 vols. Brussels, 1958.

Jaspar, Marcel-Henri. *Souvenirs sans retouche.* Paris, 1968.

Klotz, Louis Lucien. *De la guerre à la paix: souvenirs et documents.* Paris, 1924.

Knatchbull-Hugessen, Sir Hughe. *Diplomat in Peace and War.* London, 1949.

Lansing, Robert. *The Peace Negotiations: A Personal Narrative.* Boston, 1921.

Laroche, Jules. *Au Quai d'Orsay avec Briand et Poincaré, 1913–1926.* Paris, 1957.

Leith-Ross, Sir Frederick W. *Money Talks: Fifty Years of International Finance.* London, 1968.

Lloyd George, David. *Memoirs of the Peace Conference.* 2 vols. New Haven, 1939.

————. *The Truth about Reparations and War Debts.* London, 1932.

Lloyd George, Frances. *The Years That Are Past.* London, 1967.

[Lloyd George], Frances Stevenson. *Lloyd George: A Diary.* New York, 1971.

Loucher, Louis. *Carnets secrets, 1908–1932.* Brussels, 1962.

McFadyean, Sir Andrew. *Reparation Reviewed.* London, 1930.

Mordacq, Jean Jules Henri. *Clemenceau au soir de sa vie, 1920–1929.* 2 vols. Paris, 1933.

————. *Le Ministère Clemenceau: journal d'un témoin, novembre 1917–janvier 1920.* 4 vols. Paris, 1930–31.

Morgan, Brigadier-General John H. *Assize of Arms: Being the Story of the Disarmament of Germany and Her Rearmament (1919–1939).* London, 1945.

Nicolson, Harold. *Peacemaking, 1919.* London, 1934.

Overstraeten, Général Raoul François Casimir van. *Albert I. Léopold III. Vingt ans de politique militaire belge.* Brussels, n.d.

————. *Au Service de la Belgique.* 2 vols. Paris, 1960–63.

Paléologue, Georges Maurice. *An Ambassador's Memoirs.* 3 vols. New York, n.d.

Pirenne, Henri. *The Journal de guerre of Henri Pirenne.* Edited by Bryce and Mary Lyon. Amsterdam, 1976.

Poincaré, Raymond. *A la recherche de la paix, 1919.* Edited by Pierre Miquel and Jacques Bariéty. Paris, 1974.

————. *Au service de la France.* 10 vols. Paris, 1928–33.

Recouly, Raymond. *Marshal Foch: His Own Words on Many Subjects.* Translated by Joyce Davis. London, 1929.

Ribot, Alexandre. *Journal d'Alexandre Ribot et correspondances inédites, 1914–1922.* Paris, 1936.

Riddell, George Allardice, Baron Riddell. *Lord Riddell's Intimate Diary of the Peace Conference and After, 1918–1923.* London, 1933.

Saint-Aulaire, Auguste-Félix-Charles de Beaupoil, Comte de Saint-Aulaire. *Confession d'un vieux diplomate.* Paris, 1953.

Salter, J. Arthur, Baron Salter. *Memoirs of a Public Servant.* London, 1961.

Schacht, Hjalmar H. G. *Confessions of the "Old Wizard": Autobiography.* Translated by Diana Pyke. Boston, 1956.

Schiff, Victor. *The Germans at Versailles, 1919.* Translated by Geoffrey Dunlop. London, 1930.

Seydoux, Jacques. *De Versailles au plan Young.* Paris, 1932.

Seymour, Charles. *Letters from the Paris Peace Conference.* New Haven, 1965.

Shartle, Samuel G. *Spa, Versailles, Munich: An Account of the Armistice Commission.* Philadelphia, 1941.

Shotwell, James T. *At the Paris Peace Conference*. New York, 1937.

Stresemann, Gustav. *Vermächtnis*. 3 vols. Berlin, 1932–33.

Sylvester, J. A. *The Real Lloyd George*. London, 1948.

Tardieu, André. *The Truth about the Treaty*. Indianapolis, 1921.

Taylor, A. J. P., ed. *My Darling Pussy: The Letters of Lloyd George and Frances Stevenson, 1913–1941*. London, 1975.

Temperley, Major-General A. C. *The Whispering Gallery of Europe*. London, 1938.

Thompson, Charles T. *The Peace Conference Day by Day: A Presidential Pilgrimage Leading to the Discovery of Europe*. New York, 1920.

Tirard, Paul. *La France sur le Rhin: douze années d'occupation rhénane*. Paris, 1930.

Vandervelde, Emile. *Souvenirs d'un militant socialiste*. Paris, 1939.

Vansittart, Robert, Baron Vansittart. *The Mist Procession*. London, 1958.

Vincent, Edgar, Viscount D'Abernon. *An Ambassador of Peace: Lord D'Abernon's Diary*. 3 vols. London, 1929.

Vollenhoven, Maurice W. R. van. *Memoires, beschouwingen, belevenissen, reizen en anecdoten*. Amsterdam, 1946.

Whitlock, Joseph Brand. *The Letters and Journal of Brand Whitlock*. Edited by Allan Nevins. 2 vols. New York, 1936.

Wilson, Thomas Woodrow. *Woodrow Wilson: Life and Letters*. Edited by Ray Stannard Baker. 8 vols. London, 1939.

Woeste, Comte Charles. *Mémoires pour servir à l'histoire contemporaine de la Belgique*. 3 vols. Brussels, 1927–37.

BIOGRAPHIES

Abs, Robert. *Emile Vandervelde*. Brussels, 1973.

Ascherson, Neal. *The King Incorporated: Leopold II in the Age of Trusts*. London, 1963.

Ash, Bernard. *The Lost Dictator: A Biography of Field-Marshal Sir Henry Wilson, Bart., G.C.B., D.S.O., M.P.* London, 1968.

Aston, Major-General Sir George. *The Biography of the Late Marshal Foch*. London, 1929.

Auffray, Bernard. *Pierre de Margerie (1861–1942) et la vie diplomatique de son temps*. Paris, 1976.

Bemis, Samuel Flagg, and Ferrell, Robert, eds. *The American Secretaries of State and Their Diplomacy.* New York, 1927–.

Blake, Robert. *The Unknown Prime Minister: The Life and Times of Andrew Bonar Law, 1858–1923.* London, 1955.

Bosch, Baron Firmin vanden. *Ceux que j'ai connu.* Brussels, 1940.

————. *Sur le forum et dans le bois sacré: portraits politiques et littéraires.* Paris, 1934.

Bréal, Auguste. *Philippe Berthelot.* Paris, 1937.

Bronne, Carlo. *Albert Ier, le roi sans terre.* Paris, 1965.

Brunn, Geoffrey. *Clemenceau.* Cambridge, Mass., 1943.

Butler, J. R. M. *Lord Lothian (Philip Kerr), 1882–1940.* London, 1960.

Cammaerts, Emile. *Albert of Belgium, Defender of Right.* London, 1935.

Carton de Wiart, Comte Henry. *Albert Ier, le roi chevalier.* Paris. 1934.

Chastenet, Jacques. *Clemenceau.* Paris, 1974.

————. *Raymond Poincaré.* Paris, 1948.

Churchill, Randolph. *Lord Derby, "King of Lancashire."* London, 1960.

Churchill, Randolph, and Gilbert, Martin. *Winston S. Churchill.* London, 1966–.

Churchill, Winston S. *Great Contemporaries.* London, 1938.

Craig, Gordon, and Gilbert, Felix, eds. *The Diplomats, 1919–1939.* Princeton, 1953.

Cunliffe-Owen, Sidney. *Elisabeth, Queen of the Belgians.* London, 1954.

Denuit, Désiré. *Albert, roi des belges.* Brussels, 1953.

Dugdale, Blanche. *Arthur James Balfour.* 2 vols. London, 1936.

Dumont-Wilden, Louis. *Albert Ier, roi des belges.* Paris, 1934.

Dundas, Lawrence, J. L., Earl of Ronaldshay. *The Life of Lord Curzon.* 3 vols. London, n.d.

Edwards, J. H. *David Lloyd George.* 2 vols. London, 1930.

Erlanger, Philippe. *Clemenceau.* Paris, 1968.

Eubank, Keith. *Paul Cambon, Master Diplomatist.* Norman, Okla., 1960.

Fenaux, Robert. *Paul Hymans: un homme, un temps, 1865–1941.* Brussels, 1946.

Galet, Lieutenant-Général Emile. *Albert, King of the Belgians, in the Great War.* Boston, 1931.

George, Alexander L., and George, Juliette L. *Woodrow Wilson and Colonel House.* New York, 1956.

Graham, Evelyn. *Albert, King of the Belgians.* London, n.d.

Harrod, Sir Henry R. F. *The Life of John Maynard Keynes.* London, 1951.

Jones, Thomas. *Lloyd George.* London, 1951.

Keynes, John Maynard. *Essays in Biography.* London, 1933.

Lansing, Robert. *The Big Four and Others of the Peace Conference*. London, 1922.

Leclercq, Abbé Jacques. *Albert, roi des belges*. Brussels, 1934.

Liddell Hart, Sir B. H. *Foch: The Man of Orleans*. London, 1931.

Löwenstein, Hubertus, Prinz zu Löwenstein. *Stresemann, das deutsche Schicksal im Spiegel seines Lebens*. Frankfurt am Main, 1952.

Lyon, Bryce. *Henri Pirenne: A Biographical and Intellectual Study*. Ghent, 1971.

Malcom, Sir Ian. *Lord Balfour*. London, 1930.

Marquand, David. *Ramsay MacDonald*. London, 1977.

Martin, William. *Les Hommes d'état pendant la guerre*. Paris, 1929.

Millard, Oscar E., and Vierset, Auguste. *Burgomaster Max*. London, 1936.

Miquel, Pierre. *Raymond Poincaré*. Paris, 1961.

Mosley, Leonard O. *Curzon: The End of an Epoch*. London, 1960.

Nevins, Allan. *Henry White: Thirty Years of American Diplomacy*. New York, 1930.

Nicolson, Harold. *Curzon: The Last Phase, 1919–1925*. London, 1934.

————. *King George the Fifth: His Life and Reign*. London, 1952.

Olden, Rudolf. *Stresemann*. Berlin, 1929.

O'Shaughessy, Edith. *Marie Adelaide: Grand Duchess of Luxemburg, Duchess of Nassau*. New York, 1932.

Owen, Frank. *Tempestuous Journey: Lloyd George, His Life and Times*. London, 1954.

Petrie, Sir Charles. *The Chamberlain Tradition*. New York, 1938.

Robbins, Keith. *Sir Edward Grey: A Biography of Lord Grey of Fallodon*. London, 1971.

Roskill, Stephen. *Hankey, Man of Secrets*. 3 vols. London, 1970–74.

Salter, Sir J. Arthur. *Personality in Politics: Studies of Contemporary Statesmen*. London, 1947.

Sforza, Conte Carlo. *Les Bâtisseurs de l'Europe moderne*. Paris, 1931.

Sion, Georges. *Henri Jaspar: portrait d'un homme d'état*. Brussels, 1964.

Soulie, Michel. *La Vie politique d'Edouard Herriot*. Paris, 1962.

Suarez, Georges. *Briand: sa vie, son oeuvre*. 6 vols. Paris, 1941–52.

————. *La Vie orgueilleuse de Clemenceau*. Paris, 1930.

Tabouis, Geneviève. *The Life of Jules Cambon*. Translated by C. F. Atkinson. London, 1938.

Thomson, Malcolm. *David Lloyd George: The Official Biography*. London, 1949.

Vallentin-Luchaire, Antonia. *Stresemann*. Translated by Eric Sutton. New York, 1931.

Vincent, Edgar, Viscount D'Abernon. *Portraits and Appreciations*. London, 1931.

Walworth, Arthur. *Woodrow Wilson*. Boston, 1958. Rev. ed., Baltimore, 1969.

Watson, David Robin. *Georges Clemenceau: A Political Biography*. London, 1974.

Willequet, Jacques. *Albert Ier, roi des Belges*. Brussels, 1979.

Wilson, Joan Hoff. *Herbert Hoover, Forgotten Progressive*. Boston, 1975.

Wright, Peter E. *Portraits and Criticisms*. London, 1925.

d'Ydewalle, Charles. *D'Albert I à Léopold III: Les Belges de mon temps*. Ostend, 1966.

_____. *Albert, King of the Belgians*. Translated by Phyllis Megros. London, 1935.

Young, Charles Kenneth. *Arthur James Balfour*. London, 1963.

Zévaès, Alexandre. *Clemenceau*. Paris, 1949.

MONOGRAPHS

Adanya, Sima. *Le Régime international de l'Escaut*. Paris, 1929.

Albertini, Luigi. *The Origins of the War of 1914*. Translated by Isabella M. Massey. 3 vols. London, 1952–57.

Aldcroft, Derek H. *From Versailles to Wall Street, 1919–1929*. Berkeley, 1977.

Artaud, Denise. *La Reconstruction de l'Europe, 1919–1929*. Paris, 1973.

Bailey, Thomas A. *Woodrow Wilson and the Lost Peace*. New York, 1944.

Baker, Ray Stannard. *Woodrow Wilson and World Settlement*. 3 vols. New York, 1922.

Banning, Emile. *Considérations politiques sur la défense de la Meuse*. Brussels, 1918.

_____. *Les Origines et les phases de la neutralité belge*. Edited by Alfred de Ridder. Brussels, 1927.

Bardoux, Jacques. *De Paris à Spa*. Paris, 1921.

_____. *Lloyd George et la France*. Paris, 1923.

Bariéty, Jacques. *Les Relations franco-allemandes après la première guerre mondiale*. Paris, 1977.

Barnouw, Adriaan J. *Holland under Queen Wilhelmina*. New York, 1923.

Barrès, Auguste Maurice. *Les Grands Problèmes du Rhin*. Paris, 1930.

————. *La Politique rhénane*. Paris, 1922.

Baudhuin, Fernand. *Histoire économique de la Belgique, 1914–1939*. 2 vols. Brussels, 1944.

————. *L'Industrie wallonne avant et après la guerre*. Charleroi, 1924.

Bernard, Henri. *Guerre totale et guerre révolutionnaire*. 3 vols. Brussels, 1966.

————. *Par la paix armée vers la guerre totale*. Brussels, 1951.

————. *Terre commune: histoire des pays de Benelux*. Brussels, 1961.

Birdsall, Paul. *Versailles Twenty Years After*. London, 1941.

Bovard, Pierre-André. *La Liberté de navigation sur l'Escaut*. Lausanne, 1950.

Bretton, Henry L. *Stresemann and the Revision of Versailles: A Fight for Reason*. Stanford, Calif., 1953.

Briey, Comte Renaud de. *Le Rhin et le problème d'occident*. Brussels, 1922.

Bunselmeyer, Robert E. *The Cost of the War, 1914–1919: British Economic War Aims and the Origins of Reparations*. Hamden, Conn., 1975.

Calmes, Christian. *Au fil de l'histoire*. Luxemburg, 1977.

————. *1914–1919: le Luxembourg au centre de l'annexionnisme belge*. Brussels, 1976.

Carter, Gwendolen. *The British Commonwealth and International Security*. Toronto, 1947.

Chaput, Rolland A. *Disarmament in British Foreign Policy*. London, 1935.

Chastenet, Jacques. *Histoire de la troisième république*. 7 vols. Paris, 1952–53.

Churchill, Winston. *The World Crisis: The Aftermath*. London, 1929.

Clémentel, Etienne. *La France et la politique économique interalliée*. Paris, 1931.

Clercq, Jean de. *Les Petites Souverainetés d'Europe*. Louvain, 1936.

Clough, Shepard B. *History of the Flemish Movement in Belgium*. New York, 1930.

Colenbrander, H. T. *Nederland en België: Proeve tot beter waardeering*. The Hague, 1933.

Connell, John (John Henry Robertson). *The "Office."* London, 1958.

Czernin, Ferdinand. *Versailles, 1919*. New York, 1965.

Devlin, Patrick. *Too Proud to Fight: Woodrow Wilson's Neutrality*. London, 1974.

Dillon, E. J. *The Peace Conference*. London, n.d.

Doepgen, Heinz. *Die Abtretung des Gebietes von Eupen-Malmedy an Belgien im Jahre 1920*. Bonn, 1966.

Dulles, Eleanor L. *The French Franc, 1914–1928*. New York, 1929.

Egerton, George W. *Great Britain and the Creation of the League of Nations: Strategy, Politics, and International Organization, 1914–1919*. Chapel Hill, N.C., 1978.

Elcock, Howard J. *Portrait of a Decision: The Council of Four and the Treaty of Versailles*. London, 1972.

Enssle, Manfred J. "Germany and Belgium, 1919–1929: A Study of German Foreign Policy." Ph.D. dissertation, University of Colorado, 1970.

————. *Stresemann's Territorial Revisionism: Germany, Belgium, and the Eupen-Malmedy Question, 1919–1929*. Wiesbaden, 1979.

Eupen, Malmedy, Monschau. Berlin, 1920.

Eyck, Erich. *A History of the Weimar Republic*. Translated by Robert G. L. Waite. 2 vols. Cambridge, Mass., 1962–63.

Fabre-Luce, Alfred. *La Crise des alliances: essai sur les relations franco-britanniques depuis la signature de la paix, 1919–22*. Paris, 1922.

————. *The Limitations of Victory*. Translated by Constance Vesey. London, 1926.

Farrar, L. L., Jr. *Divide and Conquer: German Efforts to Conclude a Separate Peace, 1914–1918*. Boulder, Colo., 1978.

Favez, Jean-Claude. *Le Reich devant l'occupation franco-belge de la Ruhr en 1923*. Geneva, 1969.

Feis, Herbert. *The Diplomacy of the Dollar: First Era, 1919–1932*. Baltimore, 1950.

Ferro, Marc. *The Great War, 1914–1918*. Translated by Nicole Stone. London, 1973.

Fischer, Fritz. *Griff nach der Weltmacht: Die Kriegszielpolitik des kaiserlichen Deutschland, 1914–1918*. Düsseldorf, 1961.

Flandin, Pierre-Etienne. *Politique française, 1919–1940*. Paris, 1947.

Floto, Inga. *Colonel House in Paris: A Study of American Policy at the Paris Peace Conference, 1919*. Aarhus, 1973.

Fraenkel, Ernst. *Military Occupation and the Rule of Law: Occupation Government in the Rhineland, 1918–1923*. London, 1944.

François-Poncet, André. *De Versailles à Potsdam: la France et le problème allemand contemporaine, 1919–1945*. Paris, 1948.

Furst, Gaston, A. *De Versailles aux experts*. Nancy, 1927.

Garnir, George. *Pendant l'occupation*. Brussels, 1918.

Gatzke, Hans W. *Germany's Drive to the West (Drang nach Westen): A Study of Germany's Western War Aims during the First World War*. Baltimore, 1950.

————. *Stresemann and the Rearmament of Germany*. Baltimore, 1954.

Gavin, Catherine. *Britain and France: A Study of Twentieth-Century Relations*. London, 1941.

Gedye, G. E. R. *The Revolver Republic: France's Bid for the Rhine*. London, 1930.

Gelfand, Laurence E. *The Inquiry: American Preparations for Peace, 1917–1919*. New Haven, 1963.

Goldberg, George. *The Peace to End Peace: The Paris Peace Conference of 1919*. New York, 1969.

Greven, H. B., ed. *The Netherlands and the World War*. 4 vols. New Haven, 1923–28.

Guinn, Paul. *British Strategy and Politics, 1914 to 1918*. London, 1965.

Hankey, Colonel Maurice P. A., Baron Hankey. *Diplomacy by Conference: Studies in Public Affairs, 1920–1946*. London, 1946.

Hanotaux, Gabriel. *Le Traité de Versailles du 28 juin 1919*. Paris, 1919.

Headlam-Morley, Sir James W. *Studies in Diplomatic History*. London, 1920.

Helmreich, Paul C. *From Paris to Sèvres: The Partition of the Ottoman Empire at the Peace Conference of 1919–1920*. Columbus, Ohio, 1974.

Henry, Albert. *Le Ravitaillement de la Belgique pendant l'occupation allemande*. Paris, 1924.

Herchen, Arthur. *Manuel d'histoire nationale*. Luxemburg, 1952.

Hogan, Michael J. *Informal Entente: The Private Structure of Cooperation in Anglo-American Economic Diplomacy, 1917–1928*. Columbia, Mo., 1977.

Höjer, Carl-Henrick. *Le Régime parlementaire belge de 1918 à 1940*. Uppsala, 1946.

Hoover, Herbert C. *The Ordeal of Woodrow Wilson*. New York, 1958.

Howard, John E. *Parliament and Foreign Policy in France*. London, 1948.

Huchmacher, J. Joseph, and Susman, Warren I., eds. *Wilson's Diplomacy: An International Symposium*. Cambridge, Mass., 1973.

Hughes, Judith M. *To the Maginot Line*. Cambridge, Mass., 1971.

Institut de Sociologie Solvay, Université Libre de Bruxelles. "The German Annuities." Unpublished, 1921. Hoover Institution, Stanford, Calif.

Jacobson, Jon. *Locarno Diplomacy: Germany and the West, 1925–1929*. Princeton, 1972.

Jaumin, A., and Jottard, M. *La Question de l'Escaut*. Brussels, 1927.

Jordan, William M. *Great Britain, France, and the German Problem, 1918–1939: A Study of Anglo-French Relations in the Making and Maintenance of the Versailles Settlement*. London, 1943.

———. "The Problems of French Security, 1918–1920." Ph.D. dissertation, University of London, 1940.

Kennedy, A. L. *Old Diplomacy and New: 1876–1922, from Salisbury to Lloyd George*. London, 1922.

Kerchove de Denterghem, Comte Charles de. *L'Industrie belge pendant l'occupation allemande, 1914–1918*. Paris, 1927.

Kernek, Sterling J. *Distractions of Peace during War: The Lloyd George Govern-*

ment's Reactions to Woodrow Wilson, December, 1916–November, 1918. Philadelphia, 1975.

Keynes, John Maynard. *The Economic Consequences of the Peace*. London, 1919.
———. *A Revision of the Treaty*. London, 1922.

King, Jere Clemens. *Foch versus Clemenceau: France and German Dismemberment, 1918–1919*. Cambridge, Mass., 1960.

Kossman, E. H. *The Low Countries, 1780–1940*. London, 1978.

Kuehl, Warren. *Seeking World Order: The United States and International Organization to 1920*. Nashville, Tenn., 1969.

Lamalle, Ulysse. *Histoire des chemins de fer belges*. Brussels, 1943.

Landes, David S. *The Unbound Prometheus: Technological Change and Industrial Development in Western Europe from 1750 to the Present*. Cambridge, 1969.

Langenhove, Fernand van. *L'Action du gouvernement belge en matière économique pendant la guerre*. Paris, 1927.
———. *La Belgique en quête de sécurité, 1920–1940*. Brussels, 1969.

Leffler, Melvin P. *The Elusive Quest: America's Pursuit of European Stability and French Security, 1919–1933*. Chapel Hill, N.C., 1979.

Levin, N. Gordon, Jr. *Woodrow Wilson and World Politics: America's Response to War and Revolution*. New York, 1968.

Ling, Bio. "Parliaments and the Peace Treaty." Ph.D. dissertation, University of London, 1938.

Link, Arthur S. *Wilson the Diplomatist: A Look at his Major Foreign Policies*. Baltimore, 1957.

Louis, William Roger. *Great Britain and Germany's Lost Colonies, 1914–1919*. Oxford, 1967.
———. *Ruanda-Urundi, 1884–1919*. Oxford, 1963.

Luckau, Alma. *The German Delegation at the Paris Peace Conference*. New York, 1941.

MacCallum, R. B. *Public Opinion and the Last Peace*. London, 1944.

McDougall, Walter A. *France's Rhineland Diplomacy, 1914–1924: The Last Bid for a Balance of Power in Europe*. Princeton, 1978.

MacKintosh, John. *The British Cabinet*. London, 1962.

Mahaim, Ernst, ed. *La Belgique restaurée*. Brussels, 1926.
———. *Le Secours de chômage en Belgique pendant l'occupation allemande*. Paris, 1926.

Maier, Charles S. *Recasting Bourgeois Europe: Stabilization in France, Germany, and Italy in the Decade after World War I*. Princeton, 1975.

Majerus, Pierre. *Le Luxembourg indépendant: essai d'histoire politique contemporaine et de droit international public*. Luxemburg, 1946.

Mallinson, Vernon. *Belgium*. London, 1969.

Malmain, Michel. *Les Relations commerciales franco-belges de 1913 à 1923*. Paris, n.d.

Mantoux, Etienne. *The Carthaginian Peace, or the Economic Consequences of Mr. Keynes*. Oxford, 1946.

Marston, F. S., *The Peace Conference of 1919: Organization and Procedure*. London, 1944.

Martin, Laurence W. *Peace without Victory: Woodrow Wilson and the British Liberals*. New Haven, 1958.

Marwick, Arthur. *The Deluge: British Society and the First World War*. Boston, 1965.

Mayer, Arno. *The Politics and Diplomacy of Peacemaking: Containment and Counterrevolution at Versailles, 1918–1919*. New York, 1967.

Mermeil (Gabriel Terrail). *Le Combat des trois: notes et documents sur la conférence de la paix*. Paris, 1922.

―――. *Les Négociations secrètes et les quatres armistices*. Paris, 1921.

Meyer, Richard H. *Bankers' Diplomacy: Monetary Stabilization in the Twenties*. New York, 1970.

Meyers, Joseph. *Deux maisons souveraines, 1890–1955*. Luxemburg, 1955.

Miller, Charles. *Battle for the Bundu: The First World War in East Africa*. New York, 1974.

Miller, Jane Kathryn. *Belgian Foreign Policy between Two Wars, 1919–1940*. New York, 1951.

Miquel, Pierre. *La Paix de Versailles et l'opinion publique française*. Paris, 1972.

Montgelas, Graf Maximilian von. *The Case for the Central Powers*. Translated by Constance Vesey. London, 1925.

Mounier, J. *L'Etat actuel de la question du Luxembourg*. Paris, 1920.

Nelson, Harold I. *Land and Power: British and Allied Policy on Germany's Frontiers, 1916–19*. London, 1963.

Nelson, Keith L. *Victors Divided: America and the Allies in Germany, 1918–1923*. Berkeley, 1975.

Newbigin, Marion I. *Aftermath: A Geographic Study of the Peace Terms*. Edinburgh, 1920.

Newman, William J. *The Balance of Power in the Interwar Years, 1919–1939*. New York, 1968.

Noble, George B. *Policies and Opinions at Paris, 1919*. New York, 1935.

Notter, Harley. *The Origins of the Foreign Policy of Woodrow Wilson*. New York, 1965.

Nowak, Karl Friedrich. *Versailles*. London, 1928.

Ombiaux, Maurice Des. *La Politique belge depuis l'armistice: la grande peur de la victoire*. Paris, 1921.

Orde, Anne. *Great Britain and International Security, 1920–1926*. London, 1978.

Ørvik, Nils. *The Decline of Neutrality, 1914–1941*. London, 1953. Rev. ed., 1971.

Palo, Michael F. "The Diplomacy of Belgian War Aims during the First World War." Ph.D. dissertation, University of Illinois, 1977.

Parrini, Carl. *Heir to Empire: United States Economic Diplomacy, 1916–1923*. Pittsburgh, 1969.

Passelecq, Fernand. *Déportation et travail forcé des ouvriers et de la population civile de la Belgique occupée (1916–1918)*. Paris, 1928.

Perin, François. *La Démocratie enrayée: essai sur le régime parlementaire belge de 1918 à 1958*. Brussels, 1960.

Piérard, Louis. *Belgian Problems since the War*. New Haven, 1929.

Pirenne, Henri. *La Belgique et la guerre mondiale*. Paris, 1928.

Pirenne, Jacques, and Vauthier, Maurice. *La Législation et l'administration allemande en Belgique*. Paris, 1925.

Poincaré, Raymond. *Histoire politique: chronique de la quinzaine*. Paris, 1920–22.

Raeymaeker, Omer de. *België's internationaal belied, 1919–1939*. Brussels, 1945.

Renouvin, Pierre. *War and Aftermath, 1914–1929*. Translated by Rémy Inglis Hall. New York, 1968.

Riddell, George Allardice, Baron Riddell, et al. *The Treaty of Versailles and After*. London, 1935.

Ridder, Alfred de. *La Belgique et la guerre*. 4 vols. Brussels, 1928.

———. *Histoire diplomatique du traité de 1839*. Brussels, 1920.

Rogger, Hans, and Weber, Eugen, eds. *The European Right*. Berkeley, 1965.

Rothstein, Robert L. *Alliances and Small Powers*. New York, 1968.

Roussel de Roy, André. *L'Abrogation de la neutralité de la Belgique: ses causes et ses effets*. Paris, 1923.

Rudin, Harry R. *Armistice, 1918*. New Haven, 1944.

Salewski, Michael. *Entwaffung und Militärkontrolle in Deutschland, 1919–1927*. Munich, 1966.

Sayers, R. S. *The Bank of England, 1891–1944*. 3 vols. Cambridge, 1976.

Schmitt, Royal J. *Versailles and the Ruhr: Seedbed of World War II*. The Hague, 1968.

Schoonhoven, Etienne. *Anvers, son fleuve et son port*. Antwerp, 1958.

Schuker, Stephen A. *The End of French Predominance in Europe: The Financial Crisis of 1924 and the Adoption of the Dawes Plan*. Chapel Hill, N.C., 1976.

Schulz, Gerhard. *Revolutions and Peace Treaties, 1917–1920*. New York, 1972.

Schuman, Frederick L. *War and Diplomacy in the French Republic*. London, 1931.

Schwoebel, Jean. *L'Angleterre et la sécurité collective*. Paris, 1938.

Selsam, J. Paul. *The Attempts to Form an Anglo-French Alliance, 1919–1924*. Philadelphia, 1936.

Sforza, Conte Carlo. *Les Frères ennemies*. Paris, 1933.

Shepherd, Henry L. *The Monetary Experience of Belgium, 1914–1936*. Princeton, 1936.

Simonds, Frank. *How Europe Made Peace without America*. London, 1927.

Smith, Daniel M. *Aftermath of War: Bainbridge Colby and Wilsonian Diplomacy, 1920–21*. Philadelphia, 1970.

Spenz, Jürgen. *Die diplomatische Vorgeschichte des Beitritts Deutschlands zum Völkerbund, 1924–1926*. Göttingen, 1966.

Spethmann, Hans. *Die Rote Armee an Ruhr und Rhein*. Berlin, 1930.

Stampfer, Friedrich. *From Versailles—to Peace!* Berlin, 1920.

Stephens, Waldo. *Revisions of the Treaty of Versailles*. New York, 1939.

Suetens, Max. *Histoire de la politique commerciale de la Belgique depuis 1830 jusqu'à nos jours*. Brussels, 1955.

Tabouis, Geneviève. *Perfidious Albion—Entente Cordiale*. Translated by J. A. D. Dempsey. London, 1938.

Temperley, Harold W. V. *A History of the Peace Conference of Paris*. 6 vols. London, 1920–24.

Tillman, Seth P. *Anglo-American Relations at the Paris Peace Conference of 1919*. Princeton, 1961.

Trask, David F. *The United States in the Supreme War Council: American War Aims and Inter-Allied Strategy, 1917–1918*. Middletown, Conn., 1961.

Vandenbosch, Amry. *Dutch Foreign Policy since 1815*. The Hague, 1959.

———. *The Neutrality of the Netherlands during the World War*. Grand Rapids, Mich., 1927.

Vernon, Maurice. *La Question de l'Escaut*. Castres, 1921.

Visscher, Charles de. *Belgium's Case: A Juridical Enquiry*. London, 1916.

Vos, Henry de, and Bronne, Charles. *Belgians and the Sea*. Brussels, n.d.

Wagner, Camille. *La Sidérurgie luxembourgeoise sous les régimes du Zollverein et de l'union économique belgo-luxembourgeoise*. Luxemburg, 1930.

Walters, Francis P. *A History of the League of Nations*. 2 vols. London, 1952.

Walworth, Arthur. *America's Moment: 1918. American Diplomacy at the End of World War I*. New York, 1977.

Wambaugh, Sarah. *Plebiscites since the World War*. 2 vols. Washington, 1933.

Watson, Charles Albert. "Britain's Dutch Policy, 1914–1918: The View from British Archives." Ph.D. dissertation, Boston University, 1969.

Waxweiler, Emile. *La Belgique neutre et loyale*. Paris, 1915.

Wee, Herman van der, and Tavernier, K. *La Banque Nationale de Belgique et l'histoire monétaire entre les deux guerres mondiales*. Brussels, 1975.

Weill-Raynal, Etienne. *La Politique française des réparations*. Paris, 1945.

———. *Les Réparations allemandes et la France*. 3 vols. Paris, 1947.

Wellesley, Sir Victor. *Diplomacy in Fetters*. London, 1944.

Wheeler-Bennett, John W., and Langermann, F. E. *Information on the Problem of Security, 1917–1926*. London, 1927.

Willert, Sir Arthur. *Aspects of British Foreign Policy*. New Haven, 1928.

Wilson, Joan Hoff. *American Business and Foreign Policy, 1920–1933*. Lexington, Ky., 1971.

Winkler, Henry. *The League of Nations Movement in Great Britain, 1914–1919*. New Brunswick, N.J., 1952.

Wolfers, Arnold. *Britain and France between Two Wars: Conflicting Strategies of Peace since Versailles*. New York, 1940.

Wullus-Rudiger, Jacques. *La Belgique et la crise européenne, 1914–1945*. 2 vols. Paris, 1945.

———. *En Marge de la politique belge (1914–1956)*. Brussels, 1957.

———. *Les Origines internationales du drame belge de 1940*. Brussels, 1950.

Yates, Louis. *The United States and French Security, 1917–1921*. New York, 1957.

Zimmermann, Ludwig. *Deutsche Aussenpolitik in der Ära der Weimarer Republik*. Göttingen, 1958.

———. *Frankreichs Ruhrpolitik: Von Versailles bis zum Dawesplan*. Göttingen, 1971.

Zuylen, Baron Pierre van. *Les Mains libres: politique extérieure de la Belgique, 1914–1940*. Brussels, 1950.

GENERAL WORKS

Albert-Sorel, Jean. *Histoire de France et d'Angleterre: la rivalité, l'entente, l'alliance*. Amsterdam, 1950.

Baumont, Maurice. *La Faillité de la paix, 1918–1939*. 2 vols. Paris, 1951.

Boulter, V. M., ed. *Survey of International Affairs, 1925: Supplement. Chro-*

nology of International Events and Treaties, 1st January, 1920–31st December 1925. London, 1928.

Brogan, Denis. *The Development of Modern France.* London, 1940.

Brugière, Pierre. *La Sécurité collective, 1919–1945.* Paris, 1946.

Cammaerts, Emile. *Belgium from the Roman Invasion to the Present Day.* London, 1921.

————. *The Keystone of Europe: History of the Belgian Dynasty, 1830–1919.* London, 1939.

Carr, E. H. *Britain: A Study in Foreign Policy from the Treaty of Versailles to the Outbreak of the War.* London, 1939.

Chastenet, Jacques. *Vingt ans d'histoire diplomatique, 1919–1939.* Geneva, 1946.

Clio (Marc Naegels). *Pourquoi pas toute l'histoire de Belgique?* 3 vols. Brussels, 1966.

Cooper-Prichard, A. H. *History of the Grand-Duchy of Luxemburg: A Small Country with a Great History.* Luxemburg, 1950.

Dumont, Georges-H. *Histoire de la Belgique.* Paris, 1977.

Duroselle, Jean-Baptiste. *From Wilson to Roosevelt: Foreign Policy of the United States, 1913–1945.* Cambridge, Mass., 1963.

————. *Histoire diplomatique de 1919 à nos jours.* Paris, 1953.

Foot, Michael. *British Foreign Policy since 1898.* London, 1956.

Gathorne-Hardy, G. M. *A Short History of International Affairs, 1920 to 1938.* London, 1938.

Goris, Jan-Albert, ed. *Belgium.* Berkeley, 1945.

Halperin, S. W. *Germany Tried Democracy: A Political History of the Reich from 1918 to 1933.* New York, 1946. Reprint ed., 1965.

Helmreich, Jonathan E. *Belgium and Europe: A Study in Small Power Diplomacy.* The Hague, 1976.

Holt, Stephen. *Six European States: The Countries of the European Community and Their Political Systems.* London, 1970.

Huggett, Frank E. *Modern Belgium.* New York, 1969.

Kalken, Frans van. *La Belgique contemporaine (1780–1930).* Paris, 1930.

————. *Histoire de Belgique des origines à nos jours.* Brussels, 1946.

Landheer, Bartholomew, ed. *The Netherlands.* Berkeley, 1943.

Lapradelle, A. de. *La Paix moderne (1899–1945).* Paris, 1947.

Lefèvre, Joseph. *L'Angleterre et la Belgique à travers les cinq derniers siècles.* Brussels, 1946.

Linden, H. vander. *Belgium: The Making of a Nation.* Oxford, 1920.

Medlicott, William N. *British Foreign Policy since Versailles.* London, 1940. Rev. ed., 1968.

————. *Contemporary England, 1919–1964*. London, 1967.

Meeüs, Adrien de. *History of the Belgians*. Translated by G. Gordon. London, 1962.

Mowat, Charles Loch. *Britain between the Wars, 1918–1940*. London, 1955.

Mowat, R. B. *History of European Diplomacy, 1919–1925*. London, 1927.

Muller, Albert, S. J. *La Seconde Guerre de trente ans, 1914–1945*. Brussels, 1947.

Northedge, F. S. *The Troubled Giant: Britain among the Powers, 1916–1939*. London, 1966.

Omond, G. W. T. *Belgium and Luxemburg*. London, 1923.

Picavet, Camille-Georges. *L'Europe politique de 1919 à 1925*. Paris, 1945.

Pirenne, Henri. *Histoire de Belgique*. 8 vols. Brussels, 1902–32.

Rain, Pierre. *L'Europe de Versailles, 1919–1939*. Paris, 1945.

Reynolds, Philip A. *British Foreign Policy in the Inter-War Years*. London, 1954.

Schreiber, Marc. *Belgium*. Translated by Hilda Becker. London, 1945.

Seton-Watson, Christopher. *Italy from Liberalism to Fascism*. London, 1967.

Siegfried, André. *L'Angleterre d'aujourd'hui*. Paris, 1924.

Smit, C. *Diplomatieke geschiedenis van Nederland*. The Hague, 1950.

Taylor, A. J. P. *English History, 1914–1945*. Oxford, 1965.

Terlinden, Vicomte Charles. *Imperialisme et équilibre: la politique internationale depuis la Renaissance jusqu'à la fin de la seconde guerre mondiale*. Brussels, 1952.

Toscano, Mario. *Storia dei trattati e politica internazionale*. vol. 1. Turin, 1958. Rev. ed., 1963.

Toynbee, Arnold J. *Survey of International Affairs: 1920–1923*. London, 1927.

————. *Survey of International Affairs: 1924*. London, 1928.

————. *Survey of International Affairs: 1925*. London, 1929.

Weber, Paul. *Histoire du Grand-Duché de Luxembourg*. Brussels, 1961.

PAMPHLETS

Alberti, Mario. *L'Aspect actuel du problème des réparations allemandes*. Milan, 1922.

Barclay, Sir Thomas. *M. Poincaré*. London, 1923.

Bas, Lieutenant General F. de. *Les Relations hollando-belges*. The Hague, 1923.

Batavus (pseud.). *Belgian Ports and Dutch Waterways*. London, 1919.

Blondeau, Ange. *L'Escaut, fleuve international et le conflit hollando-belge*. Paris, 1932.

Brenier, Henri. *French Points of View*. Marseilles, 1921.

Brugmans, H. *The Wielingen: Rights and Interests*. The Hague, 1920.

Carnoy, Albert J. *The Past and the Future of Belgium*. New York, 1919.

Cercle des Installations Maritimes de Bruxelles. *Rectification des frontières hollando-belges: l'Escaut et l'enclave de Maestricht*. Brussels, 1918.

Clark, G. N. *Belgium and the War*. Oxford, 1942.

———. *Holland and the War*. Oxford, 1941.

Colson, Lucien. *Malmédy et les territoires rétrocédés*. Liège, 1920.

Crokaert, Jacques. *L'accord belgo-luxembourgeois*. Brussels, 1921.

———. *Les Dispositions générales de l'accord belgo-luxembourgeois*. Brussels, 1922.

Denier, Jean. *Les Relations hollando-belges: le différend des Wielingen*. Paris, 1922.

Destrée, Jules. *La Belgique et le grand-duché de Luxembourg*. Brussels, 1918.

Geyl, Pieter. *Holland and Belgium*. Leiden, 1920.

Henriquet, Maurice. *A quelles conditions pouvons-nous conclure l'union économique avec la France?* Brussels, 1922.

Hervy-Cousin, Ch. *Une Solution de la question hollando-belge*. Brussels, 1923.

Heuvel, Jules van den. *De la Violation de la neutralité belge*. Le Havre, n.d.

Hommel, Luc. *Les Etapes constitutionnelles du grand-duché de Luxembourg*. Brussels, 1920.

Hoon, H. de. *L'Escaut et son embouchure: le différend des Wielingen*. Brussels, 1927.

Hymans, Paul. *La Politique étrangère de Belgique*. Brussels, 1924.

———. *La Politique extérieure de la Belgique*. Brussels, 1924.

———. *La Revision des traités de 1839*. Brussels, 1920.

———. *Le Statut international et la politique extérieure de la Belgique*. Brussels, 1931.

Kalken, Frans van. *Entre deux guerres: esquisse de la vie politique en Belgique de 1918 à 1940*. Brussels, 1945.

Laskine, Edmond. *Luxemburgs wirtschaftliche Vergangenheit und Zukunft*. Diekirch, 1919.

Limburg and the Scheldt Question. Washington, n.d.

Maerterlinck, Maurice; Buysse, Cyriel; and Dumont-Wilden, L. *La Belgique en guerre*. Brussels, 1918.

Mercier, Désiré Joseph. *Courages, mes frères*. Mechelen, 1917.

———. *Au Lendemain de la victoire*. Mechelen, 1919.

———. *Rebâtissons*. Mechelen, 1920.

Nierstrasz, B. *Nederland en België, de gevaren van het verdrag*. The Hague, 1926.

Nothomb, Pierre. *Histoire belge du grand-duché de Luxembourg*. Paris, 1918.

———. *Le Nouveau governement et la question extérieure*. Brussels, 1919.

Nys, Ernest. *L'Escaut et la Belgique*. Brussels, 1920.

Perier, F. de. *La Neutralité de la Belgique*. Paris, 1921.

Pink, Gerhard. *The Conference of Ambassadors*. Geneva, 1942.

Poincaré, Raymond. *Le Roi Albert Ier*. Brussels, 1934.

Prum, Xavier. *The Problem of Luxemburg*. New York, 1919.

Rolin, Henri-A. *La Politique de la Belgique dans la Société des Nations*. Geneva, 1931.

Rolin-Jaequemyns, Baron Edouard. *L'Escaut et le rejet du traité hollando-belge*. Brugge, 1927.

"Ronduit," Kapitein (pseud.) *De Manoeuvre om Limburg: eene studie over de strategische positie van Limburg*. Utrecht, 1919.

Seymour, Charles. *Geography, Justice, and Politics at the Paris Conference of 1919*. New York, 1951.

Société de Propagande Néerlandaise. *Vers l'apaisement hollando-belge*. Paris, 1919.

Struycken, Antonius A. H. *The German White Book on the War in Belgium*. London, 1915.

———. *Holland, Belgium and the Powers*. The Hague, 1919.

Struye, Paul. *La Politique extérieure et le statut international de la Belgique*. Liège, 1937.

Telders, B-M. *La Revision des traités de 1839*. The Hague, 1935.

Texier, Henri. *Principes juridiques de la question des dettes inter-alliées*. Paris, n.d.

Towards a Dutch-Belgian Settlement. The Hague, 1919.

Trevire and Nervien. *Les Traités de 1831 et de 1839*. Brussels, 1918.

Wehrer, Albert. *Le Statut international du Luxemburg et la Société des Nations*. Paris, 1924.

Widung, André. *L'Orientation économique du Luxemburg*. Luxemburg, 1919.

Woeste, Comte Charles. *La Neutralité de la Belgique: doit-elle être maintenue?* Brussels, 1919.

Zwendelaar, A. *La Belgique jusqu'au Rhin*. Brussels, 1919.

ARTICLES

Ambivarte (pseud.). "La Question de Wielingen." *Le Flambeau* 1 (20 June 1920): 758–66.

Artaud, Denise. "Le Gouvernement américain et la question des dettes de guerre au lendemain de l'armistice de Rethondes (1919–1920)." *Revue d'histoire moderne et contemporaine* 20 (April–June 1973): 201–29.

———. "Die Hintergründe der Ruhrbesetzung, 1923: Das Problem der interalliierten Schulden." *Vierteljarhshefte für Zeitgeschichte*, 1979, pp. 241–59.

———. "Aux origines de l'atlantisme: la recherche d'un équilibre européen au lendemain de la première guerre mondiale." *Relations internationales*, Summer 1977, pp. 115–26.

———. "A propos de l'occupation de la Rhur." *Revue d'histoire moderne et contemporaine* 17 (January–March 1970): 1–21.

———. "La Question des dettes interalliées et la reconstruction de l'Europe." *Revue historique* 261 (April–June 1979): 363–82.

Bacon, Ruth. "British Policy and the Regulation of European Rivers of International Concern." *British Yearbook of International Law*, 1929, pp. 158–70.

Bariéty, Jacques. "Le Projet de rétrocession d'Eupen-Malmédy par la Belgique à l'Allemagne, et la France (1925–1926): un cas d'utilisation de l'arme financière en politique internationale." In *Les Relations franco-belges de 1830 à 1934*, pp. 325–48. Metz, 1975.

Bas, Lieutenant General F. de. "Another Version of the Scheldt History." *History* 5 (October 1920): 159–70.

Bastid, Paul. "La Question de l'Escaut et le différend hollando-belge." *La Revue générale de droit international public*, November–December 1928, pp. 689–712.

Baudhuin, Fernand. "La Balance économique de la Belgique avant et après la guerre." *Bulletin d'études et d'information de l'école supérieure de commerce St. Ignace*, November 1924, pp. 3–55.

———. "La Restauration—Deux ans après l'armistice." *Revue catholique sociale et juridique*, December 1920–January 1921, pp. 1–8.

———. "La Richesse de la Belgique dix ans après la déclaration de guerre." *Revue catholique sociale et juridique*, August–September 1924, pp. 3–11.

Baumont, Maurice. "La Belgique, la France, et le Luxembourg en 1919–1920." *Annales d'études internationales*, 1970, pp. 171–79.

———. "Les Relations franco-belges après 1917." In *Les Relations franco-*

belges de 1830 à 1934, pp. 295–301. Metz, 1975.

Bech, Joseph. "Le Grand-Duche de Luxembourg." *Dictionnaire diplomatique* 1 (n.d.): 1268–70.

Bernard, Henri. "La Grande-Bretagne et la Belgique." *Le Phare*, 19 May 1963, pp. 1, 3.

Beyens, Baron Napoléon Eugène. "Albert Ier chez Guillaume II." *Revue des deux mondes*, 15 June 1930, pp. 819–38.

Briey, Comte Reynaud. "La Belgique et le Rhin." *La Revue catholique des idées et des faits* 1 (16 December 1921): 8–10.

――――. "Politique belge et politique rhénane." *La Revue catholique des idées et des faits* 1 (17 March 1922): 12–14.

Burk, Kathleen. "Great Britain in the United States, 1917–1918: The Turning Point." *International History Review* 1 (April 1979): 228–45.

Cammaerts, Emile. "The International Situation of Belgium." *Contemporary Review* 119 (May 1921): 625–32.

――――. "The Passing of Belgian Neutrality." *New Europe* 9 (26 December 1918): 246–52.

――――. "The Present Situation in Belgium." *New Europe* 15 (6 May 1920): 80–85.

Charles, E. M. S. "The Influence of Foreign States on British Strategy." *Army Quarterly* 7 (October 1923): 44–45.

"Les Chemins de fer luxembourgeois." *Le Rail*, January 1967, pp. 14–17.

Colbeck, Archibald. "France, England, and the Rhineland." *Fortnightly Review* 109 (April 1921): 541–48.

Cornebise, Alfred E. "Gustav Stresemann and the Ruhr Occupation: The Making of a Statesman." *European Studies Review* 2 (January 1972): 43–67.

Costigliola, Frank. "The United States and the Reconstruction of Germany in the 1920's." *Business History Review* 50 (Winter 1976): 477–502.

Crokaert, Jacques. "Anvers et l'accord belgo-luxembourgeois." *La Belgique maritime, coloniale, et économique*, 5 February 1922, pp. 109–12.

Davignon, Vicomte Henri. "The Political Situation in Belgium." *New Europe* 15 (27 March 1920): 147–51.

Dendal, Capitaine-Commandant A-E-M. "Le Rattachement d'Eupen et de Malmédy à la Belgique." *Bulletin belge des sciences militaires*, January 1923, pp. 85–100.

Devleeshouwer, Robert. "L'Opinion publique et les revendications territoriales belges à la fin de la première guerre mondiale, 1918–1919." In *Mélanges offerts à G. Jacquemyns*, pp. 207–38. Brussels, 1968.

Duroselle, Jean-Baptiste. "Clemenceau et la Belgique." In *Les Relations franco-*

belges de 1830 à 1934, pp. 245–49, Metz, 1975.

Enssle, Manfred J. "Stresemann's Diplomacy Fifty Years after Locarno." *Historical Journal* 20 (1977): 937–48.

Falkus, M. E. "The German Business Cycle in the 1920's." *Economic History Review.* 2d ser. 28 (1975): 451–65.

———. "United States Economic Policy and the 'Dollar Gap' of the 1920's." *Economic History Review.* 2d ser. 24 (1971): 599–623.

Fitzhardinge, F. L. "Hughes, Borden, and Dominion Representation at the Paris Peace Conference." *Canadian Historical Review* 44 (1968): 160–69.

George, Robert H. "Eupen and Malmédy." *Foreign Affairs* 5 (1927): 332–35.

———. "The Scheldt Dispute." *Foreign Affairs* 6 (1927): 155–57.

Goold, J. Douglas. "Lord Hardinge as Ambassador to France and the Anglo-French Dilemma over Germany and the Near East, 1920–1922." *Historical Journal* 21 (1978): 913–37.

Grathwol, Robert P. "Germany and the Eupen-Malmédy Affair, 1924–26." *Central European History* 8 (1975): 221–50.

———. "Gustav Stresemann: Reflections on His Foreign Policy." *Journal of Modern History* 45 (1973): 52–70.

Grayson, Admiral Cary T. "The Colonel's Folly and the President's Distress." *American Heritage* 15 (1964): 4–7.

Gribble, Francis. "The Luxemburg Railways." *New Europe* 8 (5 September 1918): 177–80.

Grün, George A. "Locarno: Idea and Reality." *International Affairs* 31 (1925): 477–85.

Haag, Henri. "La Belgique en novembre 1918." *Revue d'histoire moderne et contemporaine* 16 (1969): 153–160.

———. "La Démission de Paul Hymans et la fin du second gouvernement Delacroix (juillet–novembre 1920)." In *Mélanges offerts à G. Jacquemyns,* pp. 393–414. Brussels, 1968.

Hall, Hines III. "Lloyd George, Briand and the Failure of the Anglo-French Entente." *Journal of Modern History* 50 (1978): D1121–38.

Hankey, Colonel Sir Maurice P. A. "Diplomacy by Conference." *Round Table* 11 (March 1921): 42, 287–311.

Headlam-Morley, James W. "Plebiscites." *Quarterly Review* 236 (July 1921): 206–24.

Helmreich, Jonathan. "The Negotiation of the Franco-Belgian Military Accord of 1920." *French Historical Studies* 3 (1964): 360–78.

Hommel, Luc. "La France, le Luxembourg et nous." *La Revue générale* 1 (15 March 1930): 157–72.

d'Hoop, Jean Marie. "Le Maréchal Foch et la négociation de l'accord militaire franco-belge de 1920." In *Mélanges Pierre Renouvin: etudes d'histoire des relations internationales*, pp. 191–98. Paris, 1966.

Hymans, Paul. "L'accord économique belgo-luxembourgeois." *La Belgique maritime, coloniale, et économique*, 22 January 1922, pp. 74–76; 29 January 1922, pp. 98–103.

———. "La Belgique depuis les traités de paix de 1919." *Dictionnaire diplomatique* 1 (n.d.): 313–17.

———. "Belgium's Position in Europe." *Foreign Affairs* 9 (October 1930): 54–64.

Jacobson, Jon, and Walker, John T. "The Impulse for a Franco-German Entente: The Origins of the Thoiry Conference, 1926." *Journal of Contemporary History* 10 (1975): 157–81.

Jaspar, Henri. "Belgium and Western Europe since the Peace Treaty." *Journal of the British Institute of International Affairs* 3 (July 1924): 161–89.

———. "Cannes et Locarno." *La Revue générale* 115 (1926): 1–16.

———. "La Conférence de Cannes de 1922." *La Revue générale* 138 (1937): 129–47.

———. "Les Directives de la politique extérieure de la Belgique." *Esprit international* 7 (1933): 3–22.

———. "Encore la sécurité." *La Revue belge* 4 (1924): 512–19.

———. "Etre Belges." *Le Flambeau*, 28 February 1922, pp. 147–67.

———. "Locarno et la Belgique." *La Revue belge* 5 (1925): 154–69.

———. "Locarno, la Sarre, et la sécurité belge." *La Revue générale*, 15 February 1935, pp. 129–40.

———. "Paix et sécurité." *La Revue belge* 4 (1924): 202–15.

———. "Quelques réflexions sur notre politique extérieure." *La Revue belge* 4 (1924): 5–17.

———. "La Sécurité de la Belgique." *Dictionnaire diplomatique* 1 (n.d.): 317–20.

Johnson, D. "Austen Chamberlain and the Locarno Agreements." *University of Birmingham Historical Journal* 8 (1961–62): 62–81.

Jones, K. P. "Stresemann, the Ruhr Crisis, and Rhenish Separatism: A Case Study of *Westpolitik*." *European Studies Review* 7 (1977): 311–40.

Kalken, Frans van. "Les courants politiques dans la Belgique d'après guerre." *Le Flambeau*, June 1930, pp. 209–16.

Knaff-Galot, Louis. "La Question des chemins de fer du Luxembourg." *L'Europe nouvelle*, 22 May 1939, pp. 539–41.

Lannoy, Fl. de. "Où il est reparlé de neutralité belge." *La Revue catholique des idées et des faits* 1 (1922): 5–7.

Laveleye, Victor. "Belgique et Holland." *Le Flambeau*, July 1930, pp. 276–95.

Louis, William R. "Great Britain and the African Peace Settlement of 1919." *American Historical Review* 71 (1966): 875–92.

————. "The United States and the African Peace Settlement of 1919: Pilgrimage of George Louis Beer." *Journal of African History* 4 (1963): 413–33.

McCrum, Robert. "French Rhineland Policy at the Paris Peace Conference, 1919." *Historical Journal* 21 (1978): 623–48.

McDougall, Walter A. "Political Economy versus National Sovereignty: French Structures for German Economic Integration after Versailles." *Journal of Modern History* 51 (1979): 4–23.

Maeterlinck, Albert. "La Liberté de l'Escaut." *Journal de droit international* 46 (1919): 205–22, 705–17.

Maier, Charles S. "The Truth about the Treaties?" *Journal of Modern History* 51 (1979): 56–67.

Miquel, Pierre. "L'Opinion française et la Belgique pendant la conférence de la paix: janvier–juin 1919." In *Les Relations franco-belges de 1830 à 1934*, pp. 251–55. Metz, 1975.

Nothomb, Pierre. "La Declaration de Sainte-Adresse." *Le Flambeau*, 31 January 1922, pp. 10–36.

————. "La Journée de 12 mars 1919." *Le Flambeau*, 28 February 1922, pp. 232–53.

Nouailhat, Yves-Henri. "Français, Anglais et Américains face au problème de la réorganisation du commerce international (1914–1918)." *Relations internationales*, Summer 1977, pp. 95–114.

Omond, G. W. T. "The Scheldt and the Wielingen." *Transactions of the Grotius Society* 6 (1921): 80–88.

Pater, M. "L'Accord économique belgo-luxembourgeois." *La Belgique maritime, coloniale, et économique*, 5 February 1922, pp. 116–22.

Piérard, Louis. "Belgium's Language Question: French vs. Flemish." *Foreign Affairs* 8 (1930): 641–51.

Poulain, Marc. "Querelles d'allemands entre locarnistes: la question d'Eupen-Malmédy." *Revue historique* 258 (1977): 393–439.

Poullet, Vicomte Prosper. "Belgique." *Dictionnaire diplomatique* 1 (n.d.): 307–12.

Rolin-Jaequemyns, Baron Edouard. "L'Entretien de L'Escaut suivant les traités." *La Revue de droit international et de législation comparée*. 3d ser. 9 (1928): 377–99.

Sagnac, Ph. "La Question belge." *Revue du nord* 7 (1921): 1–29.

Satow, Sir Ernest. "Pacta Sunt Servanda or International Guarantees." *Cambridge Historical Journal* 1 (1925): 295–318.

Seymour, Charles. "The End of a Friendship." *American Heritage* 14 (1963): 4–9.

Sibert, Marcel. "La Sécurité internationale et les moyens proposés pour l'assurer de 1919 à 1925." *La Revue générale de droit international public*, 2d ser. 7 (1925): 194–237.

Sieburg, Heinz-Otto. "Les Entretiens de Thoiry (1926)." *Revue d'Allemagne*, July–September 1972, pp. 520–46.

Simon, Paul. "Le Problème ferroviaire luxembourgeois." *Revue économique internationale*, January 1933, pp. 3–23.

Siotto-Pintor, Manfredi N. "Le Régime international de l'Escaut." *Académie de droit international: recueil des cours* 21 (1928): 277–369.

Southern, David W. "The Ordeal of Brand Whitlock, Minister to Belgium, 1914–1922." *Northwest Ohio Quarterly* 41 (1969): 113–26.

Soutou, Georges-Henri. "La Politique économique de la France à l'égard de la Belgique, 1914–1924." In *Les Relations franco-belges de 1830 à 1934*, pp. 257–73. Metz, 1975.

Stambrook, Fred G. "'*Das Kind*'—Lord D'Abernon and the Origins of the Locarno Pact." *Central European History* 1 (1968): 233–63.

————. "'Resourceful in Expedients'—Some Examples of Ambassadorial Policy Making in the Inter-War Period." *Historical Papers*, 1973, pp. 301–20.

Struye, Paul. "Pierre Nothomb, homme politique." *Revue générale belge*, September 1968, pp. 69–78.

Sykes, General F. H. "Air Power and Policy." *Edinburgh Review* 242 (1925): 380–95.

Terlinden, Vicomte Charles. "La Belgique aux conférences interalliées de 1920 et de 1921." *La Revue générale*, 15 January 1922, pp. 107, 69–95.

————. "La Belgique: doit-elle regretter sa neutralité?" *La Revue catholique des idées et des faits* 1 (17 February 1922): 5–6.

————. "Clemenceau au congrès de la paix." *La Revue catholique des idées et des faits* 1 (3 June 1921): 5–6.

————. "The History of the Scheldt." *History* 5 (1920), no. 16: 185–97; no. 17: 1–10.

————. "Lloyd George à la conférence de la paix." *La Revue catholique des idées et des faits* 1 (8 July 1921): 3–4.

————. "La Vérité sur l'échec à Jérusalem." *La Revue catholique des idées et des faits* 1 (2 December 1921): 3–4.

Theunis, Georges. "Belgium Today." *Foreign Affairs* 4 (1926): 264–77.

Thimme, Annelise. "Stresemann and Locarno." In *European Diplomacy between two Wars, 1919–1939*, edited by Hans W. Gatzke, pp. 73–93. Chicago, 1972.

Tobin, Harold J. "Is Belgium Still Neutralized? A Study in the Termination of Treaties." *American Journal of International Law* 26 (1932): 514–32.

Trachtenberg, Marc. "'A New Economic Order': Etienne Clémentel and French Economic Diplomacy during the First World War." *French Historical Studies* 10 (1977): 315–41.

———. "Reparations at the Paris Peace Conference." *Journal of Modern History* 51 (1979): 24–55.

Trausch, Gilbert. "Les Relations franco-belges à propos de la question luxembourgeoise (1914–1922)." In *Les Relations franco-belges de 1830 à 1934*, pp. 275–93. Metz, 1975.

Vandenbosch, Amry. "The Small States in International Politics and Organization." *Journal of Politics* 26 (1964): 293–312.

Visscher, Charles de, and Ganshof, François L. "Le Différend des Wielingen." *La Revue de droit international et de législation comparée* 1 (1920): 293–328.

Visscher, Fernard de. "La Paix de Locarno au point de vue du droit international." *La Revue belge* 5 (1925): 170–79.

———. "Le Problème de notre sécurité et la neutralisation de la rive gauche du Rhin." *La Revue belge* 2 (1924): 336–46.

Wampach, G. "La Situation internationale des chemins de fer du grand-duché de Luxembourg." *Revue générale de droit international et législation comparée* 12 (1905): 416ff.

Wee, Herman van der. "Beschouwingen over de belgische muntsaneringspolitiek ten tijde van Konig Albert." In *Handelingen van het Colloquium Konig Albert*, pp. 35–55. Brussels, 1976.

Wehrer, A. "La Politique de sécurité et d'arbitrage du grand duché de Luxembourg." *La Revue de droit international et de législation comparée* 8 (1932): 326–66, 641–63.

Weinberg, Gerhard L. "The Defeat of Germany in 1918 and the European Balance of Power." *Central European History* 2 (1969): 248–60.

Welderen Rengers, Baron Th. van. "Les Relations néerlando-belges considérées dans le cadre de la position politique internationale de la Belgique." *Bibliotheca Visseriana Dissertationum Ius Internationale Illustrantium* 9 (1931): 149–248.

Welter, Nicholas. "Le Grand-Duché de Luxembourg depuis la guerre." *La Revue de Paris* 33 (1926): 289–324.

Willequet, Jacques. "Gaston Barbanson, promoteur d'une 'Grande Belgique' en 1914–1918." *Revue belge de philologie et d'histoire* 48 (1971): 335–76, 1177–1206.

———. "Guerre et neutralité." In *Actes du colloque Roi Albert*, pp. 69–82. Brussels, 1976.

———. "Problèmes économiques franco-belges en 1919 et 1920." In *Les Relations franco-belges de 1830 à 1934*, pp. 303–13. Metz, 1975.

———. "Sondages de paix en 1918: la dernière mission du Comte Toerring." In *Mélanges offerts à G. Jacquemyns*, pp. 661–75. Brussels, 1968.

Wilson, Trevor. "Lord Bryce's Investigation into Alleged German Atrocities in Belgium, 1914–15." *Journal of Contemporary History* 14 (1979): 369–83.

Witte, Lieutenant General Baron de. "Le Problème militaire belge." *La Revue belge* 5 (1925): 289–308.

NEWSPAPERS

Belgium
  L'Etoile belge (Brussels)
  Gazet van Antwerpen
  L'Indépendance belge (Brussels)
  La Libre Belgique (Brussels)
  La Nation belge (Brussels)
  Le Peuple (Brussels)
  Le Soir (Brussels)
  De Standaard (Brussels)

France
  Le Temps (Paris)

Great Britain
  The Daily Telegraph (London)
  The Manchester Guardian
  The Times (London)
  The Times Belgian Number.
    Supplement (London),
    9 April 1920

United States
  The New York Times

INDEX